THE BURNING BUSH

THE BURNING BUSH

WRITINGS ON JEWS AND JUDAISM

VLADIMIR SOLOVYOV

Edited, translated, and with commentary by
Gregory Yuri Glazov

University of Notre Dame Press

Notre Dame, Indiana

University of Notre Dame Press
Notre Dame, Indiana 46556
www.undpress.nd.edu

Library of Congress Cataloging-in-Publication Data

Names: Solovyov, Vladimir Sergeyevich, 1853–1900, author. |
Glazov, Gregory Yuri, translator, editor, writer of added commentary.
Title: The burning bush : writings on Jews and Judaism / Vladimir Solovyov ;
edited, translated, and with commentary by Gregory Yuri Glazov.
Description: Notre Dame, Indiana : University of Notre Dame Press, 2016. |
Includes bibliographical references and index.
Identifiers: LCCN 2016007508 |
ISBN 9780268029890 (hardcover) |
ISBN 026802989X (hardcover)
Subjects: LCSH: Judaism—Philosophy. | Philosophy, Russian—19th century.
Classification: LCC B4263 .B8715 2016 | DDC 296—dc23
LC record available at http://lccn.loc.gov/2016007508

∞ *This paper meets the requirements of ANSI/NISO Z39.48-1992
(Permanence of Paper).*

To the Sophias of my life: my wife, Regina,

sister, Elena, and mother, Marina

CONTENTS

PART II
COMMENTARY AND PORTRAIT OF SOLOVYOV'S
ENCOUNTERS WITH JEWS AND JUDAISM

SELECTED ABBREVIATIONS

SOLOVYOV'S WORKS

SSVSS   *Sobranie sochinenij Vladimira Sergeevicha Solovyova*
         = Collected Works of Vladimir Sergeevich Solovyov.
         The superscript denotes the edition by its number of
         volumes. For further details, see bibliography.

Letters *The Letters of Vladimir Solovyov.* For further details,
         see bibliography.

THE BIBLE

Unless specified, biblical texts are usually cited from the RSV text.

M.T.   Masoretic Text

OL   Old Latin Text

RST   Russian Synodal Translation (1876)

Slav.   Slavonic: Russian Church Bible text frequently cited
         by Solovyov (probably a reprint of the second, 1757,
         edition of the "Elizabeth" Bible)

Syr   Peshita Version

V   Vulgate Version

RABBINIC WORKS

Mishnaic tractate titles are preceded by "m." The initial "b." or no initial indicates tractates of the Babylonian and the initial "j.," the Jerusalem Talmud. All translations of the Mishnah, Talmud, and Midrash, unless stated otherwise, are taken from the Soncino Talmud and Midrash via Kantrowitz's *Judaic Classics* CD-ROM collection.

TRANSLITERATION

Russian is romanized following the GOST 2002 (B) system; however, *cz* following this system is usually rendered *ts*, and e' is rendered either as *e* or as *è*, while in names, *ya* is frequently rendered *ia* and the terminations *ej, ij, oj* as *ei, y, oy*, respectively. See http://en.wikipedia.org/wiki/Romanization_of_Russian.

EMPHASES AND INTERPOLATIONS

All emphases in citations of Solovyov's works are in the original source, unless indicated otherwise. Interpolations in translated material are denoted by square brackets.

ACKNOWLEDGMENTS

My interest in Solovyov and his Jewish oeuvre was sparked by my father, Yuri Glazov, who inherited it from our godfather, Alexander Men', who was murdered in 1990, shortly after confiding to my mother, Marina Glazov, that he was receiving death threats. The interest was inflamed by a lecture on Solovyov by Pietro Modesto. I perceived wisdom and truth in Modesto's articulations of Solovyov's thought and became eager to study it. This study was energized by Jonathan Sutton when he introduced me to colleagues who were interested in Solovyov at conferences he organized in Leeds and Cambridge on Russian religious philosophy and the issues of civil rights in Russia. At that point, reading Solovyov's Jewish writings, I began translating excerpts for my classes on the Old Testament at Blackfriars in Oxford. Two old friends of the family, Natalya Trauberg and her daughter, Marija Chepaityte, visited me at the time, and we spoke of Solovyov. Marija followed up on these conversations by sending me Sergei Solovyov's biography of his uncle and the volume of memoirs edited by Boris Valentinovich Averin, both of which figure prominently in this study. Subsequently, my friend Stratford Caldecott, codirector with his wife, Leonie, of the Centre for Faith and Culture, introduced me to Paul Valliere and, later, Michael Waldstein. Michael commissioned me to translate the loci classici of Solovyov's Jewish writings and then invited me to present a weeklong seminar on these texts (the first five works in Part III) at the International Theological Institute in Gaming. Thus the translation and commentary were begun. My mother, Marina Glazov, gave this study great impetus; while visiting me in the United Kingdom on her way to and from Russia, she helped me prepare a translation of "Jewry and the Christian Question," brought from

Russia anthologies of Solovyov's writings on Judaism and the books by Getz, and then, at a reunion at the home of my sister Elena and her husband, Kevin Corrigan, again helped me prepare a translation of Solovyov's "Talmud" and "Life of Muhammad" (the latter is not part of this project). Once described by Rachel Polonsky as a "walking encyclopedia," my mother remained always at hand with advice on biographical, topographical, literary, and translational matters, and helped me correct the proofs. My sister Elena brought from Russia the centenary two-volume work edited by Yevgeniya V. Borisova and Anna P. Kozyreva and in the stages of responding to the readers' reviews helped bring my translation of Solovyov's poetry closer to the original. I also owe Elena and Kevin thanks for connecting me with Russian and Ukrainian religious thinkers and figures for whom the issues raised by this book are a matter of lifelong importance. Of these individuals, I became most engaged with Yakov Krotov, not only via his electronic archive, but also through his generous and informed responses to my questions about Solovyov that provided important insights pertaining to Solovyov's relationship with Getz, Baron Gintsburg, and Tolstoy. On a broader level, I would also like to thank Kevin Corrigan and my brother, Jamie Glazov, for providing opportunities to publish and engage with scholars in the fields of patristics and biblical studies and contemporary forms of Jew hatred and Holocaust denial, all of which lent both material and moral inspiration.

Colleagues and friends read and offered important constructive criticism on this work at various stages. These included Judith Kornblatt, who read the initial draft of the translation, and Konstantin Burmistrov, who generously sacrificed his supper at the Society of Biblical Literature and the American Academy of Religion convention in Washington, DC, to discuss how I planned to integrate his ideas about Solovyov's interest in the Kabbalah into my study and understanding of Solovyov's spirituality. Rachel Polonsky read the first completed draft of the translation and commentary. Her interest in the familial story behind the work and its present-day relevance to Jewish-Christian relations, the rise of antisemitism, and the state of civil rights in Russia helped shape the contents and structure of Part I. Thanks to the mediation of Valliere, the entire work was also read by Boris Jakim, who provided detailed professional advice on the translation and content of the work and, as a reflection of his dedication to making Solovyov's writings better known, did so twice, first on the penultimate draft, offering "good news and bad news," and then on the ultimate draft, declaring it ready. In these final cycles of revision, my nephew Yuri Corrigan proofread Part I, and Boris Jakim, Kevin Corrigan, and Tom Guarino helped stabilize my translation of Solovyov's concept of *bogochelovechestvo* (Godmanhood) and commentary on its relationship to *theosis*. A special word of thanks is also owed to Tom for the innumerable occasions on which he inquired into the state of the work, gave strategic advice about dealing with publishers, and reviewed correspondence with the latter.

Grants and awards helped sustain the work. These included the Seton Hall University 2005 Provost's Research Fellowship, thanks to which I was able to spend quality research time in the microfilm rooms of Harvard's Widener Library and thereby assemble an archive of documents that fed the commentary part of the work in succeeding years. Subsequently the Lilly Endowment, secured in large measure by the talents of Joseph Chapel and Dianne Traflet, associate deans of Immaculate Conception Seminary School of Theology (ICSST), to create the new Institute for Christian Spirituality allowed me to design and coordinate the Great Spiritual Books Program, the running of which helped sustain progress on this study, as did Dianne's many other grant-creating ventures. Finally, I am grateful to the former rector dean of ICSST, Msgr. Robert Coleman, for nominating me as ICSST's candidate for Seton Hall's Researcher of the Year award, which provided funds to complete this work.

Many librarians helped. These include Stella Wilkins, at ICSST, who always and speedily orchestrated the acquisition of items that were invaluable to my research, especially the electronic databases and search engines, Bible Works and the Judaic Classics. Similarly, Marta M. Deyrup, Slavic Studies librarian at Seton Hall University, supplied me with many books that facilitated the writing of this one, and often helped me secure obscure articles and pdf's via Interlibrary Loan thanks to her contacts with librarians in other institutions, especially Liladhar Pendse at Berkeley, Urszula Biegaj Lechtenberg at Champaign-Urbana, and Angelina Zaytsev at the HathiTrust.

The book was offered to the University of Notre Dame Press thanks to long-standing interest expressed in it by its acquisitions editor, Charles van Hof. When finally submitted, Chuck and his colleagues Stephen Little, Robyn Karkiewicz, and Rebecca R. DeBoer speedily arranged the review process and provided much subsequent advice on editorial and formatting matters. I am most grateful to the reviewers for their unequivocal recommendation of the book for publication and the thorough, constructive criticism that helped improve the manuscript. I also wish to thank other team members at the University of Notre Dame Press: Susan Berger and Kathryn Pitts, for facilitating the marketing and promotion of the book; Wendy McMillen, for facilitating the acquisition of the front cover; Sheila Berg, who in copyediting the manuscript prompted me to resolve and iron out a host of confusions and hazardous errors that remained; and Elizabeth Sain for correcting the proofs.

As the reader can gauge, the writing of this book took a long time. As I progressed, I enjoyed sharing things that excited me about it with people whose interest and encouragement helped broaden my appreciation of the book's relevance. These include Msgr. Joseph Reilly, rector of ICSST; my colleagues in the Department of Biblical Studies, Chris Ciccarino, Pablo Gadenz, and Anthony Ziccardi; Larry Frizzell, Nathanael Knight, Dermot Quinn, Ines Mursaku, Doug Milewski, Zeni Fox, Jeff Morrow, and Joseph and Monica Rice; Fr. Peter Willi and Sisters Monica, Mirjam, and Birgit of the Spiritual Family "The Work"; and John, Maria, and Sarah Corrigan.

Finally, it is my pleasure to thank my smart and beautiful wife, Regina, for enduring the days and nights, stretching over years, that I spent on this study and for the prayers she directed to it, for all her insights and care thanks to which the labor is completed, the book delivered, a monument built—alongside the greater one that is never finished, in the flames of which our children, Raphael, Augustine, Talitha, and Yuri, were born. For the blessing which their gifts bring to our lives, it is also my joy to give thanks.

PART I

Introduction

CHAPTER 1

Solovyov and the Origins of This Work

Vladimir Solovyov was one of nineteenth-century Russia's greatest Christian religious philosophers, mystics, poets, political theorists, social activists, debaters, and satirists. He taught that there are two absolutes: God and that world which he wills and works in Wisdom to realize. People who encounter Solovyov's writings commend the powerful arguments by which he communicates the sense that this Wisdom (Sophia) informs the world and its history. Those familiar with his poetry, politics, and life also know him as Wisdom's knight who, having a heightened sense of evil, fought this evil energetically, believing that its fragmenting forces would be conquered through the alliance of the human with the divine will.

Solovyov's preoccupation with Wisdom and the alliance between the human and the divine, reflected frequently in his use of the term "Godmanhood," follow on his philosophical and theological reflections. These he grounded in biblical teaching, especially in Old Testament salvation history revolving around divine-human covenants and wisdom teaching and in the New Testament's proclamation of Christ's sanctification and redemption of the world through his incarnation and resurrection. In these he discerned God's calling to humanity to be his steward in the world and transform it through wisdom, hope, labor, and love. Solovyov also disparaged as "abstract" and "medieval" those Christian expressions of commitment to the Gospel that failed to put Christ's teaching to love neighbor and enemy into practice and by this failure devolved into attempts to impose Christian beliefs by force. Conversely, he aspired after an "integral" Christianity, a political ideal that he called theocracy but that may more accurately be called theopraxy. This aspiration impelled him to campaign for freedom of conscience and religious and civil liberties and to call upon church and state to do the same.

As a Russian Christian, he was embarrassed by the lack of religious freedom and civil liberties in tsarist Russia, especially that touching the Jews, since he believed their plight was consequent to and a prime symptom of Christian failure to believe in and practice the Gospel. The problem became more pressing after the assassination of Tsar Alexander II in 1881, when pogroms swept the country and state-sponsored repeals of recently extended Jewish freedoms commenced. Solovyov devoted his lectures, books, pamphlets, letters, protests, political action, and prayers to combating this evil and thereby, as a patriotic Russian Christian, to purging his country's and his church's complicity in it.

Solovyov's contemporaries had difficulty classifying and controlling his allegiances. He was Russian Orthodox but believed that Orthodoxy lost moral strength and succumbed to nationalism by repudiating the primacy of the bishop of Rome. Catholics welcomed his ecumenical efforts but, like most Orthodox Christians, were frequently alienated by his interest in esoteric and seemingly heterodox religious, philosophical, and mystical deliberations on Sophia. He reportedly furnished Dostoevsky with the prototype for the pious brother-hero of *The Brothers Karamazov* (1878–80), Alyosha Karamazov. But his biographers surmise that he was also the model for the God-spurning, Jesuit-educated master dialectician brother, Ivan, introduced in the opening chapters as the author of a book espousing a "theocratic idea" and later presented as the author of the famous Christ-rejecting chapter, "The Grand Inquisitor."[1] Whether or not Dostoevsky, by means of this portrayal, voiced suspicion of Solovyov's Catholic leanings toward social justice, Solovyov explicitly repudiated Dostoevsky's infamous nationalism and antisemitism. In this respect, his politics brought him into closer alignment with the other contemporary giant of Russian literature, Count Leo Tolstoy, who was the first of ninety prominent signatories of Solovyov's petition to the tsar to improve Jewish civil rights. Despite this alignment, Solovyov and Tolstoy engaged in a lifelong debate. A fervent Russian patriot committed to the principles of just war, Solovyov argued that Tolstoy's pacifist ideals were counterfeits of Christianity and sought to persuade him of this through dialogue, letters, and parody, best seen in Solovyov's swan song, *Three Conversations: On War, Progress and the End of History, including the Tale of the Antichrist and Addenda* (1889–1900).

Despite these differences with Dostoevsky and Tolstoy, Solovyov embraced their opposition to capital punishment, but in his case this opposition assumed a much more public form and ended up taking a serious toll on his social status, finances, and health. On March 28, 1881, following the assassination of Tsar Alexander II, Solovyov presented a public lecture appealing to the new tsar to spare the lives of his father's assassins and by means of a heroic Christian act of forgiveness model the way to the healing of Russia's social ills. The tsar, thanks to his chief councillor, the Ober-Procurator of the Orthodox Church, Konstantin Pobedonostsev, who denounced Solovyov as a madman, reportedly found the lecture insulting. In consequence, Solovyov was prohibited from giving further lectures and publishing on ecumenical and Christian-Jewish relations. He responded by continuing to criticize, wherever and whenever possible, policies that subordinated the church to the state, denied freedom of conscience, and repressed religious liberty and civil rights, especially where the Jews were concerned. His campaign on their behalf led him in 1890 to compose a public protest petitioning the tsar to broaden Jewish civil rights and religious freedoms. When publication of the Protest was banned in Russia, he presented another public lecture denouncing as "medieval" the establishment's position on civil rights and religious freedoms but was denounced again to Pobedonostsev, who in turn demonized him to the tsar. Solovyov's poetry on Old Testament and Jewish themes, written at significant watershed moments of this campaign, shows him finding hope and support in typological applications of Old Testament salvation history to Russia and playfully modeling himself and his enemies on the heroes and villains of Israel's salvation history: the patriarchs and prophets and Nebuchadnezzar, respectively.

It was my father, Yuri Glazov, who introduced me to Solovyov. My father was Jewish, a specialist in Oriental languages and Russian literature, history, and culture. A member of the Soviet Academy of Sciences, he was deprived of this membership and blacklisted. He was barred from employment for championing human rights and protesting the Soviet invasion of Czechoslovakia in 1968. This struggle occurred after my father's conversion to Christianity, especially its Roman Catholic form, and the tightening of relations between my parents and well-known human rights activists, or "dissidents," humanist, Jewish, and Christian. Among the latter was Fr. Alexander Men' (1935–1990), the renowned Russian Orthodox theologian of Jewish background who acquainted the Russian intelligentsia with the Gospel and the heritage of Russian religious thought, including that of Solovyov.[2] My father welcomed the intellectual vigor and ecumenism of Men', frequently quoting his belief that the divisions between Catholicism and Orthodoxy do not reach up to heaven. In August 1966, he asked Men' to baptize our family into the Russian Orthodox Church and to be our godfather.[3] By this time, Men' had begun to be harassed by the KGB. The harassment persisted through the 1970s and 1980s. In the late 1980s he received death threats that were tinged with antisemitic sentiments. On September 9, 1990, he was brutally murdered. The failure and passivity of the state security's efforts to solve the case, coupled with bizarre leading questions posed by its interrogators to his friends, such as the insinuation that he may have been ritually murdered by Jews in the context of a broader preoccupation with the extent of his relationships and plots with Jews and Catholics, inclined his friends and family to suspect the KGB, working in tandem with ultranationalists who resented his ecumenical vision in general, evidenced by his friendly relations with Catholics and the welcome his parish offered to Jewish converts.[4] This suspicion was corroborated by the renowned academic Vyacheslav Ivanov, who related that Vadim V. Bakatin, in 1991 the last official chairman of the KGB, personally told him that the KGB killed Men'.[5]

The funeral of Father Men' was conducted by Metropolitan Juvenaly, serving as the representative of Patriarch Alexei II, a fact that testified to the recognition the church accorded Men'. Friends and family members who were present recall that Juvenaly's homily was free of criticism but that when he read a special message from the patriarch, all who had ears to hear were struck by one phrase, which they, not accustomed to hearing theoretical judgments of the departed in settings of mourning, found in bad taste.[6] The dissonance of the phrase, however, harmonizes with the subsequent negative reception given by the church hierarchy to Men', ranging from lack of involvement in conferences dedicated to him to creating conditions that turned his books into underground theological literature to their official burning.[7]

The murder of Alexander Men', the subsequent failure to find those responsible, and the coldness with which the official church in Russia has treated him and his legacy resonate with and amplify the troubles Solovyov had with church and state in his day. What happened to Alexander Men', especially as understood by his friends and family, demonstrates that Solovyov's diagnosis of Russia's national, political, and ecclesial ills retains all of its relevance. To underscore this, I include later in this introduction my translation of an introductory lecture Father Men' gave in 1989 to Solovyov and his writings.

In commending Solovyov to me in my late teens, my father spoke of his brilliance and regarded him as a Russian analogue to St. Thomas Aquinas and a trailblazer for Russian Orthodox Christians seeking unity with the West and Catholicism. Appreciating the might and insight of Solovyov, I returned to reading his works on Judaism and the Bible after completing a DPhil in Jewish and Old Testament studies at Oxford University. In time, while teaching for the Dominicans in Oxford, I developed an introductory course on the Old Testament that was to include lectures on biblical anthropology and Israel's election. Into these lectures I injected Solovyov's insights about the meaning of bodily shame in Genesis and about Israel's soul traits. For the latter, I translated the first portion of Solovyov's "Jewry and the Christian Question." Shortly thereafter, I met Michael Waldstein, rector of the Pontifical University of Gamming in Austria, who told me that Christoph Cardinal Schönborn, then president of the Pontifical Council for

Christian Unity, which oversees Jewish-Christian relations, was seeking a translation of Solovyov's writings on Judaism. Michael asked me for a list and translation of the loci classici. I translated many of the key works and presented, at his invitation, a series of seminars about them at Gamming in 2000. This explains the genesis of this project. Since Catholics engaged in Jewish-Christian dialogue had a role in encouraging the project, I want to explain briefly why these writings hold special interest for them.

Catholic leaders and theologians began to express interest in Solovyov in his own day. The interest goes back to his ecumenical, "theocratic" vision and efforts to build bridges between Orthodox, Catholics, and Jews. As explained above, these efforts alienated him from the tsarist-Orthodox establishment. Tsars Alexander III and Nicholas II, under Pobedonostsev's guidance, demonized him and prohibited the publication in Russia of many of his writings, especially those that commended rapprochement with Rome and greater Jewish civil rights and freedoms. In consequence, he published these works in France and turned for support to Catholic bishops abroad. Bishop Strossmayer of Zagreb introduced him to Pope Leo XIII as an "anima candida, pia ac vere sancta" (pure, pious, and truly saintly soul). Pope Leo, on reviewing Solovyov's *L'Idée russe* (1888), intended as an introduction to *La Russie et l'Église universelle* (1889), called his leading idea "bella . . . ma fuor d'un miraculo, e cosa impossibile" (fine . . . but impossible save by a miracle).[8]

In the decades that followed, Catholic writers described Solovyov as Russia's analogue to Aquinas and John Henry Cardinal Newman. The comparison with Aquinas rests on Solovyov's systematic and comprehensive commitment to faith and reason,[9] which pledge earned him a commendation in John Paul II's encyclical *Fides et ratio* (1998). The comparison with Newman draws on Solovyov's efforts to reconcile the Orthodox East with the Catholic West,[10] efforts that continue to stimulate East-West ecumenical discussions, especially those inspired by John Paul II's encyclical *Ut unum sint* (1995).[11] However, Solovyov's resemblances to both Aquinas and Newman are more extensive. All, for example, were skillful debaters who, in their aspiration to find common ground with their opponents, set great store in the dignity of conscience. Newman is dubbed in Catholic circles a "doctor of conscience," but while Solovyov's commitment to conscience echoes Newman's, Solovyov expressed it more actively in the political sphere, for which he should also be aligned with the other great English cardinal of the day, Henry Edward Cardinal Manning. This latter alignment is remarkably attested by the fact that both of their petitions to Tsar Alexander III to grant Russia's Jews greater civil rights were printed on the same page of the London *Times* on December 10, 1890 (see Pt. III, ch. 12).

Finally, in his writings on Christian-Jewish relations, Solovyov articulated a biblical, familial conception of nationhood and religious affiliation, which resonates with those of modern prelates. Solovyov believed that nations, like people, have callings or vocations, discernible in their cultural and religious institutions, especially those bearing a claim to divine inspiration. For this reason he argued that Jews and Christians must realize their national and religious vocations through fraternal cooperation. His ideas on this subject, developed under the label "theocracy," proved controversial, and assumed, toward the end of his life, as expressed in several works but most clearly in "The Tale of the Antichrist" (1900), included as the last chapter of his *Three Conversations*, an apocalyptic turn. Nonetheless, he did not abandon his belief that nations and religions have world historical vocations but transmuted them, anticipating that the fraternal cooperation between Catholic, Orthodox, and Protestant Christians and Jews necessary to the realization of history would hinge on the steadfastness of their remnant witnesses-martyrs. Resonance with Solovyov's ideas about Christian national vocations is especially evident in the addresses of John Paul II, most strikingly in his words on June 3, 1979, at the cathedral in Gniezno.[12] The most recent papal interest in Solovyov's apocalyptic conception of history is evidenced by the citations of "The Tale of the Antichrist" by Giacomo Cardinal Biffi at the 2007 annual Lenten papal retreat.[13]

Shortly before I finished translating Solovyov's Jewish texts, Vladimir Wozniuk published *Freedom, Faith, and Dogma: Essays by V. S. Soloviev on Christianity and Judaism*.[14] Wozniuk's volume includes many but not all the texts that compose the present volume, which focuses on Solovyov's Jewish writings and seeks to present them as completely as possible. Key texts not found in Wozniuk's volume are Solovyov's correspondence on Jewish issues, which not only provides a running commentary on all the principal texts in question, but contains additional major texts, including the letters to Getz and the Protest to the tsar. These texts and the Protest show most clearly why Solovyov's writings on Judaism were not mere and "abstract" words but works and deeds of courage and solidarity. They also explain why Rabbi Abraham Isaac ha-Cohen Kook (1865–1935), the first Ashkenazi chief rabbi of Israel under the British mandate, like many Jews, read Solovyov's Christian works with respect and gave him a place of honor in Jewish historical writing,[15] following Solovyov's friend Faivel Getz in bestowing on him the honorific title "righteous Gentile."[16] Solovyov's critique of abstract theory and commitment to integrating speculative philosophy and theology with deeds of social activism make it doubly important to present his writings on Judaism in their context, as works that integrate Christian philosophy and practice, as lively expressions of his attempt to respond to the Gospel commandment to love one's neighbor.[17] Given Wozniuk's interest in highlighting Solovyov's commitment to human rights,[18] I trust that my inclusion of further materials that illustrate this commitment will be received as a welcome complement to Wozniuk's volume.

After completing the translations and commentary in 2009, I developed the introductory background section on Jewish history in nineteenth-century Russia and proceeded to show its relevance to the texts and commentary over the next two years. Alas, only at the end of this period, while going over my notes, did I locate earlier scholarly reports about Dmitrij Belkin's work on Solovyov's Jewish writings and discover that he had published a development of his Tübingen thesis focusing on Solovyov's status as "guest" in the thought of German and Jewish intellectuals: *"Gäste, die bleiben": Vladimir Solov'ev, die Juden und die Deutschen.*[19] Although Belkin announced that he did not intend to write a new biography of Solovyov or provide a full analysis of his thought—which were my aims as far as his Jewish writings were concerned, since in developing my commentary I discovered that they were inseparably connected with his biography at many levels so that the commentary became a portrait too—nonetheless, many of his questions mirror mine, and much of his research and narrative develops and answers my questions, especially about the contemporary Jewish reception of Solovyov's writings on Judaism. In the time that remained to me, I introduced into my notes cross-references to his text but did not use his work to alter the contents of any part of this work.

This volume has a dual purpose. It seeks, first, to provide as complete a translation as possible of all Solovyov's writings on Judaism and to annotate these texts by identifying persons, places, and citations, especially of biblical and rabbinic literature; and, second, to synthesize in a commentary the information forthcoming from the translation and annotations with key recollections about Solovyov's attitudes to Jews and Judaism by his immediate family, friends, and early biographers. It should be of particular interest, of course, to scholars specializing in Solovyov, in his relationship to Russian writers, especially Tolstoy and Dostoevsky, and their respective attitudes to Jews. It should also help audiences concerned with Christian-Jewish relations discover Solovyov's historical place therein and ongoing relevance. Solovyov's rebuttals of attempts to defame the Jews by attacking the Talmud, for example, add valuable Christian arguments to those espoused by Jewish groups. Solovyov wrote to challenge Christian and secular antisemitic audiences to rethink and abandon their prejudices. Since his arguments have not lost their relevance, I hope that they may continue to exert their intended effect. Finally, Solovyov integrated Christian patriotism with his tireless use of the media and powerful argument challenging spiritual and secular authorities to respect the dignity of conscience and the principle of religious freedom, which remain pressing issues, both in the East and the West. People interested in the development of these principles, and committed to them in practice, will appreciate knowing that Solovyov espoused them in Russia at the end of the nineteenth century and find in him a model to imitate.

CHAPTER 2

Texts, Annotations, Key Terms, and Translation

This volume collects and translates all the relevant primary texts, including essays, letters, pamphlets, protests, political actions, and prayers, that relate to Solovyov's oeuvre on Jewish matters. Below I explain the key challenges of text selection and translation of key terms.

TEXT SELECTION

One basic criterion and two corollaries were used to identify the primary texts to be included in the translation. The basic criterion defines primary texts as those (a) written by Solovyov himself that (b) bear principally or directly on Judaism and Jewry as indicated by their titles and their explicitly announced aims. The first corollary of this criterion excludes texts written by other people, even if they are about things Solovyov did or said, whether in public (e.g., lectures) or in private (e.g., conversation or prayer). The second corollary excludes texts whose explicitly announced principal aims do not bear directly on Judaism, for example, by having a broader aim. All the texts included on this basis are presented in Part III. Many texts excluded on this basis, however, contain materials that illuminate the primary texts, and as many of such texts as possible are collected in Part II. Part II originated as a commentary on the way one set of the primary texts, Solovyov's correspondence with Jews, illuminated his Jewish writings. It grew, however, by absorbing into itself materials from his other writings and other people's memoirs and thus developed into a full-scale portrait of Solovyov's encounters with Jews and Judaism. This development is reflected in the title given to Part II as well as in the title of the book.[20]

The initial list of primary texts was drawn from the list given by Solovyov's friend and fellow campaigner for Jewish civil rights throughout the 1880s and 1890s, Rabbi Faivel Getz, in the latter's pamphlet on Solovyov's relationship to Judaism,[21] and dependent indexes.[22] This list included the following seven works:

1.   the tractate "Jewry and the Christian Question" (1884);
2.   the essay written in defense of the messianic community of Joseph Rabinovich (Rabinowitz) titled "The Israel of the New Covenant" (1885);
3.   the tractate "The Talmud and Recent Polemics about It in Austria" (1886);
4.   the review of the antisemitic pamphlet by Diminsky, *The Jews, Their Religious and Moral Teachings* (1891);[23]
5.   portions of the review of Ernest Havet's article "La modernité des prophètes" (1891);
6.   the article "Kabbalah, Mystical Philosophy of the Jews" (1896), written for the *Encyclopedic Dictionary*; and
7.   Solovyov's introduction to David Gintsburg's article on the Kabbalah in the journal *Voprosy filosofii i psikhologii* (Questions in Philosophy and Psychology) (1896).

However, this list omits several important textual genres. The most significant are the following:

1.   Solovyov's letters on Jewish matters and to Jews, especially those to Getz (1891–96) and Baron Horace Gintsburg (1896);
2.   Solovyov's poems on Old Testament themes, for example, "Immanu-el" (1896); "To the Promised Land" (1886); "The Burning Bush" (1891); "In the Land of Frosty Blizzards" (1882),

which, composed while writing "Jewry and the Christian Question," closely echoes its themes; "I Was Great" (1892), written on a Mosaic theme; and the poem dedicated to the censor Tertius Philippov (1886) about whom Solovyov wrote to Getz;

3. excerpts from other writings, such as his *Lectures on Godmanhood*; and

4. the Old Testament sections in his giant work, *Theocracy*.

The letters provide a steady stream of commentary on the intentions behind his Jewish writings, on the progress of his and Getz's joint campaign to promote Jewish civil rights in Russia, and on the hopes, frustrations, and outcomes of their respective projects. The letters themselves include additional major independent works. Among these are the essay that Solovyov began writing in 1887 and contributed to Getz's pamphlet-apologia against antisemitism, *The Floor to the Accused*. Its literal title, *A Word to the Accused*, refers to the tradition in imperial Russian courts of giving the accused the last word in his own defense. As the book's publication in Russia in 1891 was censored, Solovyov's essay was only published posthumously as a separate article titled "The Sins of Russia." The letters to Getz reveal the process that led up to the 1890 Protest Letter to the tsar on behalf of Jewish civil rights and a version of the Protest itself. Solovyov penned it and secured ninety signatures by the leading intellectuals of Moscow and St. Petersburg, beginning with Tolstoy. In the course of annotating Getz's letters, I found two additional versions of the 1890 Protest, one in the memoirs of Vladimir Korolenko, a prominent signatory, and another, an English translation in the London *Times*, published anonymously. Part II, "Commentary and Portrait," identifies its translator as Emile Dillon, a correspondent for the *Telegraph* and later a biographer of Tolstoy who served as Solovyov's go-between with Tolstoy in preparing the Protest. Other letters, such as those concerning Baron David Gintsburg's article on the Kabbalah, addressed to the editors of the journals that printed it, Konstantin Konstantinovich Arseniev (1894) and Nikolai Yakovlevich Grot (1896), and to his father, Baron Horace Gintsburg (1896), bear witness to Solovyov's participation in the Society for the Promotion of Jewish Enlightenment, illuminate the contacts he made there with leading Jewish intellectuals, such as the chemist Nikolai I. Bakst, who left tributes to Solovyov in his memoirs, and hint about his charitable deeds in assisting Jewish families to emigrate from Russia.

On the whole, Solovyov's correspondence on Jewish matters depicts not only what Solovyov thought and wrote about Judaism but also what he *did* on behalf of the Jewish people. By revealing the toll these writings and deeds took on Solovyov's career, health, and life, the letters demonstrate that Solovyov's commitment to the Jewish people and Gospel values was much more than merely philosophical or academic. Given Solovyov's commitment to "integral" principles and his critique of "abstract" thought, the letters prove integral to Solovyov's oeuvre on the Jewish question and show that his writings were backed up by his deeds.

The discovery of versions of the Protest, a primary text, in Solovyov's correspondence with friends and colleagues and in their own memoirs and writings, suggests a need to relax the initial criteria for text selection to include the said memoirs and writings. However, as the contents of such materials greatly exceed the initial limits envisioned for this project, the boundaries were broadened to admit only two sets of texts. The first of these includes Solovyov's remaining letters to Tolstoy, in which he attempts to improve Tolstoy's treatment of Dillon and prove the reality of Christ's resurrection to Tolstoy. The issues arising pertain directly to the principles that united and divided them, as I explain at the beginning and end of Part II.

Scholarly literature on Solovyov's works on Judaism reflects a growing interest in his youthful research notes and sketches and the way in which their Kabbalistic or Christian-Kabbalistic and esoteric conceptions anticipate the triadic or trinitarian categories and structures of his more mature thought. Given that these notes and sketches are preserved in the biography by his nephew, Sergei Solovyov, they are dealt with in Part II.

The texts excluded by the criteria above from the list of primary texts contain passages in which Judaism plays a prominent role. The two most important early texts are the 1878 *Lectures on Godmanhood* and his 1883 "Third Speech in Memory of Dostoevsky." The latter

contains a crucial criticism of Dostoevsky's antisemitism and marks
Solovyov's parting of ways with Dostoevsky and the conservative
Slavophile camp of which he was a member in the 1870s. Similarly,
Solovyov's well-known last work, "The Tale of the Antichrist" (1900),
sums up, via the genre of apocalypse, his essential convictions regarding the role of the Jewish people in history. Midway between the 1881
"Anniversary Speech" and "The Tale" of 1900 and immediately following the failed 1891 Protest, stands his 1891 public lecture, "The Fall of
the Medieval Worldview," and the polemics engendered by it in the
reactionary Slavophile paper *Moskovskie vedomosti* (Moscow Register). The lecture does not mention Judaism any more than the essay
"The Sins of Russia," but like the latter it expresses clearly Solovyov's
concern for the civil rights and religious freedom denied to various en-
claves, among which the Jews would have been the most important. To
convey the flavor of these polemics, the primary texts also include
some of the letters to *Moskovskie vedomosti* (1891) in their entirety.
Portions of other letters in this group are included in Part II. The latter
includes, for example, Solovyov's letter to Pobedonostsev asking why
learned societies have been banned from dealing with him and Tolstoy,
and a letter from Pobedonostsev to the tsar complaining about the pair.

The list of texts so drawn up bears close resemblance to that proposed by Jean Halpérin, great-grandson of Baron Horace Gintsburg.
Halpérin rightly emphasized that Judaism constituted "a constant
theme both visibly and behind the scenes, a leitmotiv in the true and
literal sense of the word," in Solovyov's bibliography as a whole.[24] The
list of writings by Solovyov that Halpérin considered particularly relevant to Judaism are (1) *The Spiritual Foundations of Life* (1882–84);
(2) *The History and Future of Theocracy* (1885–87), esp. book 3, "National Theocracy and the Law of Moses"; "Justice and Morality"
(1897); the page on the relationship of *tzedek* and *tzedakah* (justice
and charity) in (3) *The Justification of the Good* (1894–96); (4) "The
Notion of God: In Defense of the Philosophy of Spinoza" (1897);
(5) *Three Conversations* (1899–1900); (6) the letter to Nicholas II on
religious freedom (1896–97); and (7) the poem "Emmanuel" (1896).[25]

Halperin's item (7) is important, but, as noted above, the poetry
on Old Testament and Jewish themes is more extensive. The poems are

markedly autobiographical, interweaving Solovyov's reflections on Jewish history and identity with his reflections on his own life, including his tragic love for Sophia Khitrovo. The poems thus complement the letters by bringing out the dramatic nature of his involvement with Judaism, Jewry, and the Hebrew scriptures, but they do this in a unique fashion, illuminating how he not only interpreted his own and Russia's history by reference to the history of Israel, a level of interpretation clear in his main writings on Judaism, but also playfully or prayerfully identified himself, his friends, and his foes with Israel's traditional biblical heroes, saviors, and foes, applying to himself the calls and vocations of Abraham, Moses, Elijah, and the prophets.

Halperin's item (6), on religious freedom, is omitted here because its scope, while anticipated directly by the Protest of 1890, "The Sins of Russia" (1887), and the "Lecture on the Medieval Worldview" (1891), transcends the Jewish theme.

Halperin's item (4),[26] the essay on Spinoza, raises questions. D. Belkin and Evert van der Zweerde both emphasize that Spinoza was Solovyov's "first love" in philosophy. Having been deeply influenced by Spinoza in his youth, Solovyov, even in his later years, in 1897, "passionately defended him, and indirectly himself, against 'accusations' of atheism and pantheism."[27] After highlighting this indebtedness, van der Zweerde also points out Solovyov's indebtedness to both Philo of Alexandria, whom he called "the last and most significant thinker of Antiquity,"[28] and the Jewish Kabbalah.[29] From this perspective, Spinoza is part of a constellation of Jewish influences. Nonetheless, the work on Spinoza does not mention Judaism at all and is so strictly devoted to Spinoza's philosophical conceptions as to be only tangentially related to the question of Judaism and Jewish-Christian relations. For this reason, it and Solovyov's writings about Philo are omitted.[30]

Items (1), (3), and (5), already available in translation, are excluded because their principal aims do not bear on Judaism directly.

Item (2), Solovyov's massive three-volume *Theocracy* (1885–87), poses a distinct problem. Its first volume deals with Old Testament theology and contains an almost verbatim reprint of the first portion of "Jewry and the Christian Question" (1884). Solovyov himself described *Theocracy* to Getz as being "full of Jewry" (letter to Getz, #14). Nonetheless, *Theocracy* is excluded, first because its focus is larger than Judaism and second because its massive size exceeds the limits set for this work.

The first reason deserves some elaboration. Part 1 of "Jewry and the Christian Question" explains the relationship between Jewish soul traits and virtues and Judaism's repudiation of Jesus as the Christ. Part 2 argues that Jews and Christians must cooperate to fulfill their world historical tasks and that Jewry, situated between Russia and Poland, representatives of the Orthodox East and the Catholic West, had and continues to have a providential role in this task that Christians should recognize and welcome. The correspondence between the title and the second part of this work and the concurrently composed "Russia and the Polish Question" (1884) reflects Solovyov's preoccupation at the time with the problems of Russia's and Orthodoxy's relations to Jewry and Judaism and Poland and Catholicism and therefore with the problems of politics and religion. This points to the fact that the full rationale for the composition of each work is not to be discerned within its respective pages but demands awareness of Solovyov's philosophical and theological interests in politics, religion, and history.[31] *Theocracy* synthesizes these interests. It is indeed "full of Jewry," but the questions it sets out to answer are more global than those that prompt and preoccupy "Jewry and the Christian Question."

"Jewry and the Christian Question" responds to the pressing religious, political, and social crisis affecting the Jewish people in tsarist Russia. Its drafts were presented in public lectures in the wake of the pogroms of 1882–83 that followed the assassination of Alexander II in 1881. The exposition of his theocratic conceptions in part 2 of the work suggests that he understood the crisis as an expression of a deeper problem in Christian culture, a problem that in his view required a political solution grounded on scripture and theology. It is this deeper problem that *Theocracy* seeks to address. It is "full of Jewry" because the solution necessarily involves Israel as a bearer of divine revelation and as God's elect in salvation history. Nonetheless, its scope is more universal than that of "Jewry." This is to say that "Jewry" and *Theocracy* are interrelated as part and whole. It is possible to distinguish their focal points and functions but imperative to understand their complementary relationship.

Implicit in this explanation lies an important point about the rhetorical strategy of Solovyov's "Jewry and the Christian Question." As a response to a pressing crisis affecting the Jews, it would seem to focus on a Jewish problem. Nonetheless, as revealed by the title, the work argues that the solution to the problem lies not in Jewish but in Christian culture. Rhetorically, then, the argument is addressed not to Jews but to Christians. As evidenced by the orientation of the journal in which it was published, the principal target audience was Orthodox and Slavophile.

This point about Solovyov's rhetoric and target audience needs to be borne in mind in considering the reasons for including texts in this volume that on the surface level do not mention Judaism. One such text is the essay "The Sins of Russia," which Solovyov contributed to Getz's apologia for Judaism, *The Floor to the Accused* (1891). While written in defense of the Jews, it barely mentions Judaism by name and focuses on Russia's "sins." But the title, in fact, represents in a subtle but forceful manner a corollary of the title, "Jewry and the Christian Question." For political reasons, it subtly (a) drops the mention of "Jewry," (b) replaces "Christian" with its contextual synonym "Russia(n),"[32] and then replaces "Question/Problem" with "Sins." As the initial paragraph of the essay shows, Solovyov was not pointing the finger at others but, counting himself a member of the targeted audience, writing to castigate, purge, and absolve his Russian Christian conscience and the consciences of his fellow Russian Christian readers. The citation of Ezekiel at the beginning of the essay confirms that this self-castigation expresses a prophetic consciousness, a consciousness that seeks to bear the sin it admonishes and to model the path by which it is to be atoned.

Biblical prophecy supplies one model by which one may understand the relationship between Solovyov's concern with Jewry and Judaism and his Russian and Slavophile patriotism and Christian allegiance. The figure of Wisdom, Sophia, supplies another, as is evident in the first reflections of Jewish interests in his writings, namely, in the Sophiological-Kabbalistic content of his research journals, diaries, and poetry and in the role accorded the Jews in his apocalyptic "Tale of the Antichrist" where their rebellion against the latter ushers in the messianic days and hastens the appearance of Sophia/Wisdom, the Woman adorned with the Sun. But, as attested by his family and friends, his first and last words on Jewish matters were not writings but heartfelt assertions that as Christ and his mother were Jews, Christians must not hate the Jews but identify with them and love them and pray for them. The Hebrew psalms and prayers, including the Shema', which he learned to recite through the 1880s and 1890s, were on his lips in his last days, and he told his friends around him to "not allow him to fall asleep but to compel him to pray for the people of Israel."[33] Because testimonies to these are preserved in memoirs by his friends and family, they are covered in Part II.

Given that Solovyov's Jewish and Christian writings are intimately intertwined, some thought needs to be given to differentiating which belong and do not belong in this volume. If Christian writings are to be excluded, should this apply to writings about Jewish Christianity, or Messianic Judaism? The problem echoes elements of the perennial Israeli debate about who is a Jew and the status of Jewish believers in Jesus. Solovyov deals with the latter in defending the religious liberty of the messianic Jewish community founded by Joseph Rabinovich in 1885. The inclusion of this text prompts in turn the inclusion of the "Obituary of Joseph Rabinovich" (1899), which Solovyov wrote more or less contemporaneously with his "Tale of the Antichrist" (November 1899–spring 1900). This work is missing in all existing lists of Solovyov's Jewish writings, and its existence and significance seem to have gone unnoticed by scholars, apart from Belkin, who are interested in Solovyov's encounters with Judaism. The ethnic factor, concern with antisemitism, and the need to forestall antisemitic pogroms and repression of Jewish religious liberty designate these texts as primary. The themes of both compositions resonate with each other, and the last synthesizes the principal tenets of all the writings mentioned above.

Cognizance of all these factors explains the list of works included in this volume in Parts II and III. Together, the two parts seek to balance what Solovyov wrote directly about Judaism and Jews with what he said, did, and prayed for on their behalf.

Textual Annotations

The aims of the annotations that supplement the translated texts are
(1) to give the biblical and rabbinic sources of Solovyov's citations;
(2) to clarify the extent of his knowledge of Hebrew and rabbinic writings; and (3) to briefly identify the persons and places he mentions. The
biographical notes become especially interesting in his correspondence
with Getz inasmuch as they illuminate the social milieu of Solovyov's
male and female friends, fellow writers, ecclesiastical figures, publishers, financiers, philanthropists, bureaucrats, censors, and enemies. The
places he mentions also shed vital light on the environment in which
these writings were shaped, for example, his favorite apartment in
Moscow's center, soon to be inhabited by Rimksy-Korsakov, the monastic retreat houses of Sergiev Posad, the British Museum, the spas in
Austria and Italy, the summer cottage of his friend and fellow poet Fet
where he took shelter to recover his physical and spiritual strength,
and the house on the property of Sophia Khitrovo. The brief notes on
these people and places prompt further insights and questions into the
sources and multiple legacies of Solovyov and his work.

Key Terms, Translation Technique,
and Transliteration

The key terms include (1) the compound phrase translated as "Jewish question" and "Christian question"; (2) the term underlying Solovyov's religio-philosophical principle of Godmanhood; (3) terms
pertaining to peoplehood, ethnicity, and nationality; and (4) the predominantly nonpejorative Russian cognates for things Jewish, such as
"Jewry," "Judaism," "Jew," and "Hebrew."

Question or Problem?

The title of Solovyov's best-known essay on Judaism is usually translated as "Jewry and the Christian Question." "Question" is the literal
translation of *vopros*. However, the phrase can also be translated as
"Judaism and the Christian Problem."

The phrase "the Jewish question" was popularized if not invented in 1843, first by the title of the book *Die Judenfrage* by the German historian and theologian Bruno Bauer and then by Karl Marx's review of this work (written in 1843, published in 1844).[34] Both the book and the review helped establish a genre of discussion that was usually but not necessarily antisemitic in perspective. On the Gentile side, the "problem" resided in the difficulties of integrating the Jews into post-Enlightenment society founded on the values *liberté, egalité et fraternité*. The difficulty was understood to originate in the nature of Judaism itself because of its own resistance to assimilation. On the Jewish side, following Jewry's emancipation from the Ghetto, the "problem" pertained to the preservation of Jewish identity in this society. The varying solutions to the problem splintered the Jews of the nineteenth century into Orthodox, Conservative, and Reformed congregations, political parties, and nationalist movements such as Zionism. The existence of a "Jewish problem" on the Jewish side may allow the phrase to be used in this context without antisemitic connotations. But in Gentile circles, of course, the phrase retains its largely antisemitic resonance and therefore provided a background, and thereby linguistic impetus, to Nazi attempts to give this "problem" a "final solution" through death camps. The latter phenomena in turn clearly reveal the major "problem" of intolerance and Jew hatred that developed among Gentiles in Europe who claimed to operate by Christian or Enlightenment values. Solovyov, by announcing that he will address the "Christian question/problem" in dealing with Jewry and Judaism, signals two things: his refusal to grant the very presupposition that the problem in question is a problem inherent to Jewry and Judaism, a problem for which Jews are responsible, "their problem"; and, conversely, that the so-called problem posed by Jews for Christians is rather a function of a problem within Christian culture, politics, and perhaps Christianity itself, hence a "Christian problem."

The latter point is foundational to Solovyov's writings on Jewish-Christian relations. As I show in Part II, it was identified as such even by his family and friends. For example, the sister of Solovyov's good friend Lopatin, Katerina M. Lopatina, who wrote under the pseudonym El'tsova, had this to say of Solovyov's relations to the Jews:

Regarding the Jewish *vopros* [question], he used to say that before all else this is a Christian *vopros*, a *vopros* about the extent to which Christian societies in every respect, and, among other things, in their attitudes to the Jews, "are capable of being governed in practice by principles of evangelical teaching, orally confessed by them."[35]

Since the word *vopros* may connote "problem," it is possible to read this statement as highlighting something more than just a "question" about the extent to which Christian societies, in their dealings with "others," especially the Jews, are actually capable of being governed by the evangelical principles that they orally confess. For Solovyov, this characteristic of Christian societies, exemplified by their behavior in "medieval" times, as emphasized in one of his most provocative addresses to church and state, the 1891 lecture, "The Fall of the Medieval Worldview," was not just a question, but a major problem. The phrase "the Christian question" points to this problem and is therefore intentionally highly ironic. Translating this phrase with the term "problem" may help emphasize this irony.

The argument against offering "Christian problem" as the dynamic equivalent of *Khristianskij vopros* is that this translation would transgress the logical limits of Solovyov's actual phrase and implicate him in the idea that the problem in question is intrinsic to the nature or essence of Christianity. But this would contradict his leading concern to draw Christians to attend to their foundational principles by resolving the problem. Consequently, the more neutral term "question" captures better both the irony in his use of the phrase and his call to fellow Christians to resolve it in a properly Christian manner. In this respect, the phrase "the Christian question" comes to connote not the problem with Christianity but the problem or question that Christianity poses to the Christian and non-Christian world. Will Christians follow Christ or not?

In introducing Solovyov's writings on Judaism and the Christian question, it may be of interest to note key similarities and differences between his and Karl Marx's responses to contemporary social discussions of "the Jewish problem." Marx assumed that human relations, desires, social development, and history were fundamentally and primarily determined by economic relations. The major evil that he identified in capitalist society was the dehumanization of human beings orchestrated by the expropriation of human value in work. The pillar of capitalist society was the institution of private property and private control of the means of production, driven by the love of money. Jews were greedy and had great control over means of production in the capitalist world, but this problem was an epiphenomenon of capitalism. In other words, the problems of Jewish nonassimilation into mainstream society and of Jewish capitalist exploitation of that society were rooted not in Jewry or Judaism but in the structures of capitalism, in the institutions that allowed private means of production and consequent expropriation of human beings. This led Marx to argue that as long as the means of production remained private, Jews would exploit the system and come to the fore within it, owing to their talent for making money, which evolved among them in the economic structures of pre-Communist Gentile culture. Marx's solution to the problem was therefore to remove the economic structures that nurtured these interests and talents.

Solovyov, by contrast, assumed that human relations, desires, social development, and history were fundamentally and primarily determined not by economic relations but by "divine-human" ones, that is, by the challenge to unite the material, human, and earthly realm with the divine realm of God's spirit. In his view the root of evil lay in human failure to love God and one's neighbor. Seeing the challenge to unite the divine with the created, the spiritual with the material, as the essence of Jewish and Christian spirituality, Solovyov traced what his contemporaries called "the Jewish problem" to Christian cultural preoccupations exclusively either with spirit or with matter. To the extent to which Gentile culture remained Christian, he also traced this problem to the inability of Christians to tolerate the presence of the "other," to their failure to follow the Gospel of the Incarnate Christ to love one's neighbor as oneself. Furthermore, given his high estimation of creation and matter, he also correlated Jewry's economic talents and interests with its faith, and he saw these talents and interests as an essential resource for the proper functioning of Christian society. Hence, in confronting Jewry and Judaism, Christianity is brought face-to-face with a question that touches its essence and calling to cooperate with God in the divine-human task of transforming the world. This reflection calls for an introduction to Solovyov's concept of *bogochelovechestvo* and its translation.

Bogochelovechestvo: God-Humanhood and Godmanhood

Solovyov's key concept *bogochelovechestvo* is a compound of the words *bog* (God) and *chelovechestvo* (humanity). In 1878–81 Solovyov delivered a series of lectures on this concept, which were serialized in the journal *Pravoslavnoe obozrenie* (Orthodox Review) and published as a book in 1881.[36] The older and traditional rendering of the term is "Godmanhood," as evidenced in Natalie Duddington's translation of part 1 of "Jewry and the Christian Question." The term could be rendered more technically still via Greek cognates, as "theoandry." The latter, however, is too esoteric, even though it preserves the resonance between Solovyov's use of this term and its prehistory in theology, philosophy, and theosophy (i.e., in Origen, Boehme, and Hegel).[37] There is frequent suspicion among Solovyov's Orthodox Christian critics that his concept of *bogochelovechestvo* indicates that he is generally indebted less to the Bible than to heterodox thinkers such as the ones above.

Paul Valliere rendered the title of Solovyov's lectures on the concept as *Lectures on the Humanity of God*. He did so for the sake of euphony and to avoid "encouraging the misconception that *bogochelovechestvo* is a synthesis of commensurate or complementary entities." He noted that the concept is based on the Christian doctrine of the Incarnation, which stresses God's transcendence while implying that humanity "in some sense nestled in the bosom of God from all eternity." The concept allows reference to "the humanity of God" but not to "the divinity of man." Given that humanity's divinization in Christ is denoted in Orthodox theology by the concept of *theosis*, Valliere also chose "the humanity of God" to render *bogochelovechestvo* in order to distinguish it from *theosis* and from its consummation in the world to come.[38]

In translating Solovyov's book on the topic, Boris Jakim also rejected the term "Godmanhood" and opted to render the title as *Lectures on Divine Humanity*. His principal reason for rejecting "Godmanhood" was that when faced with the adjectival *bogochelovecheskij* and the adverbial *bogochelovecheski*, the terms "God-human" and "God-humanly" (or "God-manly") seem too clumsy as compared to "divine-human" and "divine-humanly," respectively. The gender-inclusive nature of the latter, however, threatens the formulation of the Chalcedonian Creed, which (in the English translation) speaks of Christ's Godhead and manhood. Furthermore, in this Christological context the two terms would seem commensurate.[39]

Given these reflections on the issues involved, my contribution is twofold. First, that the term has proved theologically suspect to many furnishes a criterion for rendering it in a way that would preserve its troublesome resonances. This warrants retaining "Godmanhood." Second, Solovyov's invocation of the term resonates with biblical covenantal theology in which the covenants between God and human entities, individual and corporate, convey an I-Thou, divine-human polarity. Philosophically, Solovyov developed this conception by distinguishing between God as the first absolute and the world God created and realized in his Wisdom as the second absolute. It is this relationship that is denoted by the concept of *bogochelovechestvo*. All this warrants using "divine-human" in contexts that deal with the history of divine-human relationships in general and "Godmanhood" when dealing specifically with the hypostatic bond between the divine and human natures in Christ. My solution, then, is to work with a mixture of hyphenated constructs that would register a covenantal relationship between God and humanity. The more gender-inclusive "God-humanhood" will not violate Chalcedonian sensibilities when dealing with God's relationship to Israel and humanity as portrayed in the Old Testament. When the discussion focuses on Christ, I expect audiences to accept "Godmanhood." The adjectival and adverbial forms can be translated as Jakim suggests as "divine-human" and "divine-humanly."

Having explained the translation technique adopted for Solovyov's use of *bogochelovechestvo*, I want to observe how and why this term is important to his writings on Judaism. Jews who deem the Christian doctrine of the Incarnation pagan would likely object to the implication in the previous sentence that Jewish and Christian anthropological conceptions are akin. This objection clarifies some of the issues that should be considered here: (a) the extent to which Christianity in Solovyov's thought is grounded on biblical-Israelite anthropological and theological conceptions and (b) his desire, in using the term *bogochelovechestvo* when writing about Judaism, to remind Christians of the biblical-Israelite foundations of their anthropoloogy, politics, and theology. A few words may be offered here to illuminate where Solovyov stands on these issues.

In explaining Judaism's stance vis-à-vis Hegel, the philosopher Emil Fackenheim explains, "In Judaism, Grace is manifest in the gift of the commandment itself which, bridging the gulf between two incommensurables, makes a human community partner in a divine-human covenant." Because this covenant, a priori, "does not accept the identity of the Divine and the human . . . Hegel's 'absolute' religion, or 'Divine-human identity' is unacceptable."[40] In passing, Fackenheim noted that "Hegel has had no significant Christian theological followers who affirm, and develop philosophically along his lines, his identity of the Divine principle and the human."[41] Does Solovyov's use of *bogochelovechestvo* reflect such a development? The answer is no, because Solovyov explicitly criticized Hegel for this identification and contrasted him negatively on this score to the Neoplatonic philosopher Proclus, whom he praised for speaking of the human *participating* in the divine and *not identifying* the two. Thus, while Solovyov's usage of *bogochelovechestvo* opens him to the suspicion of using a Hegelian category to speak of one substance behind divine and human phenomena, he does not do so. Consequently, in "Jewry and the Christian Question," he consciously sides with the Jewish repudiation of Eastern and Hellenistic pagan visions of human divinization that envision divinization as a process of human dissolution in the divine, and he underscores the absolute distinction of the world and of creatures from God. The ways in which he does this clear him of the charge of pantheism and show his indebtedness to biblical concepts.[42] He uses *bogochelovechestvo* to tease out biblical, Jewish, and Christian covenantal and anthropological conceptions in a variety of senses and at a variety of levels that he believes are acceptable to Jewish readings of the Old Testament and to Christian readings of both the Old and New Testaments. While the levels are interconnected in his thought, he does not confuse them. Judaism and Christianity, he explains, are bound by their morality but divided by their metaphysical orientation to questions about Christ's being (ontology) and the Christian theology of the atonement. He uses the term *bogochelovechestvo* to speak of realities at both levels, the moral and the ontological, redemptive, and eschatological. The grounds of the moral and ontological dimensions are evident in Old Testament creation and salvation history, according to which God created human beings in his own image and then called them to stand in "I-Thou," "face-to-face" relations of friendship, partnership, and covenant. These are developed on the basis of a Chalcedonian reading of the New Testament, according to which the divine and human natures are joined in and through the divine person of Christ so as to elevate their friendship and covenant to a higher and more absolute level. This train of thought is mirrored in Solovyov's concepts of God as the first absolute, of humanity's moral kinship with God as revealed through Old Testament salvation history, and in his conception of the second absolute as Wisdom/Sophia, the *telos* and goal of God's goodwill for the world, real in God, but awaiting realization in history through the imitation of and participation by all in God's goodwill as revealed in and through Christ, the God-man. Consequently, by means of this term Solovyov echoes pantheist philosophers like Hegel but corrects their reasoning via Proclus's Neoplatonic explanation of participation and the Bible's concepts of creation, covenant, and incarnation. For this reason, the term echoes heterodox thought, but it does so in service to the Christian task of integrating reason with Christian faith.

People or Nation?

An interesting translation problem revolves around the term *narod*, which may be translated as either "nation" (also rendered by the Russian word *natsiya*) or "people." In analyzing Solovyov's use of these terms in his writings on the Jewish question, Evert van der Zweerde made the following seven points:

1. *Narod* is an age-old Slavonic word composed of the prefix *na-* (on, at) and the noun *rod* (clan, birth, kind), whereas *natsiya* is derived through Polish from the Latin *natio* during the reign of Peter I (1689–1725).

2. The four basic meanings of *narod* are (i) the population of a state or country; (ii) nation (primarily denoted by the word *natsiya*); (iii) the mass of the population as opposed to an elite; (iv) people, as in "many people" (*mnogo narodu*). The basic meanings of *natsiya* are (i) a stable community of people that has taken shape historically, emerging on the basis of a community of language, territory, economic life, and pyschological mold, expressing itself in a community of culture; and (ii) country or state.

3. The principal problem of understanding and translation pertains not to *natsiya* but to *narod* and its derivative *narodnost'*, whereby *narod* can be linked to the nation, the gentry, or the state. Van der Zweerde illustrates the issue by highlighting that Solovyov believed that Western philosophy begins when the faith of thinking individuals ceases to be *vera naroda*, "the faith of the *narod*," that is, in a split between individual reason and communal faith. In this sense, many of the elite, the *intelligenty*, including Freemasons, agnostics, and atheists, were part of the *natsiya* but not of the *narod*. For this reason van der Zweerde states that Jakim's translation of *vera naroda* as "the faith of the nation" is "to say the least, disputable."[43]

4. Solovyov could describe his relation to the traits or character of the *narod* (conveyed by the derivative term *narodnost'*) without fully sharing in it given his participation in elite intellectual circles.

5. Solovyov sought to distinguish systematically between patriotic and nationalistic expressions of *narodnost'* (national character).

6. While *narod*, not *natsiya*, was the obvious translation of the Greek New Testament terms *laos* and *ethnos*, Solovyov chose to give a modern twist to the ancient term in the French text of his *L'Idée russe* by using "nations" where "peoples" would have been appropriate.

7. However utopian and sympathetic Solovyov's distinction between *narod* and *natsiya*, it remains suspect on account of his notions

of national religion and imperial paternalism, which substantially limit the granting of equal civil rights to national minorities, rights Solovyov claimed for the Jews. Van der Zweerde assumes that the bond between nation and religion would have prompted Solovyov to oppose Jewish participation in government and infers this assumption from Solovyov's comment that Disraeli's becoming prime minister in England testifies not to post-Enlightenment European tolerance of Jews serving in government but to European indifference on this score, and therefore to the decadence of national religion in Europe. This last point, I believe, is based on a serious misreading of Solovyov's argument and rhetoric and his understanding of phenomena such as nationalism, patriotism, and messianism (as succinctly illustrated by his articles on these concepts in the *Encyclopedic Dictionary*, Russia's equivalent of the *Encyclopaedia Britannica*, frequently referred to as "Brockhaus and Efron" after its two main editors). Points 1–6 do not necessarily lead to point 7, but the issue raised by point 7 illustrates important issues bound up with the uses of *narod* and *natsiya* and their derivatives.[44]

To comply with the nuances that van der Zweerde's would like to see, and to allow the reader to identify the underlying Russian terminology, I have decided to ignore the problem of Solovyov using "nation" to render *narod* in his French work (point 6 above), and to render *narod(y)* as "people(s)"; *narodnyi*, as "public" or "of the people" or "ethnic"; and *narodnost'* as "ethnicity,"[45] thereby reserving "nation(s)" for *natsiya* or *natsii*, "national" for *natsional'nyj*, and "nationality" for *natsional'nost'*. The exceptions are restricted to the following expressions: *zhizn' narodov* = "the life of the nations"; *narodnoe bedstvie* = "national woe" or "national disaster"; *ministerstvo narodnogo prosveshheniya* = "Ministry of National Enlightenment."

The process that led to "ethnic" and "ethnicity" being chosen to render *narodnyj* and *narodnost'* may be explained briefly. Van der Zweerde's suggested use of "national character" for *narodnost'* frequently fails, because the term needs to denote both groups (ethnic groups or nationalities) and traits (ethnic or national traits) and furnish a parallel to *natsional'nost'* (nationality). It was tempting to render *narodnost'* as "peoplehood" since the phrase "Jewish peoplehood" (*'amîût*) has some currency in Jewish circles, having been invoked by Mordechai Kaplan to describe the nature of Jewish belonging to the people.[46] However, the plural "peoplehoods" is jarring. In addition to the advantages listed above, "ethnic" works well for adjectives (e.g., *narodnyj kharakter* = ethnic [rather than national] character), compounds (e.g., *narodno-istoricheskoye chuvstvo* = ethnohistorical sensibility), and circumlocutions for such (e.g., *sverkhnarodnaya religiya* = religion that transcends ethnicity [rather than supranational religion]).

Biblical idiom has its own laws, which sometimes calls for literal, sometimes for technical sensitivity; for example, Romans 11:25 requires not "the fullness of the peoples" but "the fullness of the Gentiles." Most important, when Solovyov cites the scriptures, he often does so via Slavonic and Russian versions in ways that have a great impact on his philosophical and political considerations. The most significant example is in the handling of the terms *lᵉ'ōm* (people) and *mišpāâ* (family). Most English versions offer "nation" for the former and "family" for the latter, but the Slavonic and Russian versions render both as *plemya* = "tribe," and I follow suit. I do so because, like "family" but unlike "nation," the term "tribe" underscores that Solovyov had a biblically rooted, familial conception of the relationship of the nations of the earth. This point is vital because, as with his covenantal theology and use of *bogochelovechestvo*, it illustrates how the scriptures influenced his reflections on ethnic relationships and issues of their religious and political freedom.[47] There are two other reasons for adhering to more literal translations of his handling of scripture. First, all such idiosyncrasies contribute to identifying the versions of the Bible that he used. Second, they help identify the specific verses he was citing where a plurality is possible (e.g., the phrase "all the tribes of the earth will bless themselves through you" points to Gen. 28:14 rather than to Gen. 18:18, 22:18, or 26:4).

Iudaism i Evrejstvo: Judaism and Jewry

Solovyov employs the cognates of the roots of "Hebrew," *evrej*, and "Jew/Jewish/Judean," *iudej*. Both terms can be inflected to form adjectives and to connote the essence or "ism" of the respective entities analogous to the English terms "Hebrew," "Hebraic," and "Hebraism," on the one hand, and "Jew," "Judaic," and "Judaism," on the other. Solovyov uses both terms frequently, and the variation in his terminology is of some scholarly interest and may be important. Thus, for example, Judith Kornblatt has argued that Solovyov "moved from an interest in Judaism (*iudejstvo*), including questions of doctrine and the historical significance of the Israelite understanding of God, to an interest in the 'national character' of ancient and contemporary Jewry (*evrejstvo*), ultimately arriving at an understanding of the Jews in terms of the active relationship between Judaism (their 'spirituality') and Jewry (their 'nationhood')."[48] Whether Solovyov differentiated these terms intentionally is debatable.

Having tracked this variation, I am not convinced that it serves to distinguish between ethnic and religious categories.[49] This is obviously not the case where Solovyov quotes other people's uses of these terms and goes on to argue with them using the same terminology (examples of these cases are highlighted in the notes). Extending the principle, it could be that his terminology reflects Russian idiom in general whereby one might propose that he employs cognates of *Evrej* to connote ethnic and religious realities while reserving *Iudej* to convey an ethnic connotation (Judean) and *iudejstvo* a religious one (Judaism). On the other hand, it might be that the variations hold no significant meaning. This possibility is suggested by the fact that virtually the same texts employ alternate teminology. Thus, for example, in his first letter to Getz, Solovyov writes that he hopes to develop his 1881 lectures in defense of the Jews into an article on *iudejstvo* (Judaism), whereas the title of the published work employs *evrejstvo* (Jewry). If Solovyov's disclosure to Getz suggests that he thought he was primarily lecturing about the religious dimension of Judaism, the switch to *evrejstvo* could signal that the published work is intentionally more comprehensive, taking in the ethnic dimensions as well (see Part II below), or, less significantly, could be driven by Russian idiom, which prefers *evrejstvo* for all things Jewish. The former possibility requires preserving the distinction between cognates of *evrei* and *iudei*, between Hebrew and Jew, but the latter does not, suggesting that cognates of "Jew" can freely render cognates of *evrej*.

Failure to preserve the distinction, however, would preclude that Solovyov intended these terminological shifts and obscure the potential peculiarity of his terminology. The shifts may be intentional. For example, antisemites who value the Old Testament are known to argue that modern Jewry and Judaism began after the Babylonian exile and are not continuous with the ancient Hebrews or Israelites and their religion. Such was the position of the founder of Old Testament literary criticism, Julius Wellhausen. Interchanging the terminology could serve to undermine such distinctions and promote as given the view that modern-day Jews are the descendants of Abraham through Jacob/Israel, the chosen people of the Hebrew Bible, and the heirs of its covenants and promises. It is not out of the question that Solovyov, who bore a bias against Wellhausen's assumptions regarding the religious discontinuity between preexilic and exilic Israel/Judah, as evidenced by his review of Havet, may have shifted his terminology for some such reason.

The issue then is interesting enough to warrant the preservation of the terminological variation. The problem, however, is that contemporary English idiom bars the use of cognates of "Hebrew" to connote ethnic categories (e.g., the phrase "Hebrew question" is very grating) and of "Judean" to render cognates of *iudej*.[50] In light of these constraints, I have decided to (1) preserve the cognate of *evrej* (i.e., Hebrew) when dealing with the Hebrew language or texts, including the texts of the Bible, and Hebrew persons mentioned in the Old Testament (e.g., the Hebrew prophets); (2) render *evreistvo* as "Jewry" rather than "Judaism"; and (3) indicate the underlying usage of cognates of *evrej* by cognates of "Jew" with a superscript "E" ([E]). All other instances of cognates of "Jew," "Jewish," and "Judaism" indicate that the underlying text features a cognate of *iudej*. (4) In cases where Solovyov is quoting others, as indicated in the notes, English idiom will render the Russian. This effectively means that, in these cases, cognates of "Jew" will render cognates of *evrej*, so that, for example, *Evrejskij vopros* will be rendered as "the Jewish question" without any font changes.

This technique results in some odd constructions, which in turn explains why I fail to be convinced that Solovyov intended *evrej* and *iudej* to connote ethnic and religious distinctions. No such differentiation is supported, for example, by references to "Orthodox Jewry" and "Talmudic Jewry" rather than to "Orthodox Judaism" and "Talmudic Judaism." The same applies to interchangeable references to the "Jewish people" and the "Hebrew people," or to discourse about Christian conversion to "Jewry" rather than to "Judaism" (Pt. III, ch. 3), or to expectations that criticism of the Talmud should be grounded on a "first-rate knowledge of Jewry" rather than of "Judaism" (Pt. III, ch. 4). All of this seems damaging to the thesis that *evrejstvo* (= Jewry) carries an ethnic rather than a religious connotation. Proponents of the thesis should also be perplexed by "Question 3" of the introduction to Solovyov's "Jewry and the Christian Question" formulated two paragraphs before the beginning of section 1: "Why . . . have the more powerful [religiously speaking] segments of Jewry [*evrejstvo*] settled in Russia and Poland . . . ?" Should he not have spoken of "segments of Judaism" rather than of "Jewry" if he were indeed "speaking religiously"?

From an Orthodox Jewish perspective, however, this entire train of reasoning is based on confusion. It is not nonsense from this perspective to speak of Orthodox Judaism or Orthodox Jewry or of conversion to Judaism or Jewry, or about more religiously powerful segments of the Jewish people. According to this perspective, Jews are a people who stand in covenant with God as a people. This makes them both a corporate ethnic and a religious entity.

This last reflection grounds as sensible all the terminological oddities highlighted above. The text therefore is rendered in such a way as to allow the interested reader to appreciate and be intrigued by the variations. Other terminological issues are highlighted in the notes to the text as they arise.

CHAPTER 3

"The Life and Thought of Vladimir Sergeevich Solovyov" (1989) by Fr. Alexander Men'

Almost ninety years have passed since the death of Solovyov (1853–1900).[51] And seventy years have passed since his works were last published among us. His theoretical works were last published during the First World War. His poetry was published in a scanty edition in 1921 and again later, during the "stagnant" period. Only now has the two-volume edition arrived. I fear that less than 5 percent of those present here could procure a copy of this edition.

Vladimir Solovyov had predecessors who investigated the diverse dimensions of life and mankind's various problems, but he, like Lomonosov,[52] was unique in integrating all these pursuits in himself. He was an outstanding poet and a noteworthy translator; he illuminated the problems of knowledge and wrote about nature, love, and social and political problems. He was a mercilessly incisive literary critic, a commentator on current affairs, a social activist, an ecclesiastical writer. He was a biblical exegete and translated Plato as well as biblical, Old Testament texts. He authored recognized authentic introductions to Christian life. I am particularly thinking of his *Spiritual Foundations of Life*, a laconic, lucid, lapidary, and articulate work presenting the quintessence, as it were, of many tomes dedicated to Christianity's principal foundations. Simultaneously, he was an activist, a precursor of the ecumenical movement, of rapprochement among the churches.

He was a man of unusual gravity simultaneously endowed with the love of a joke and given to composing parodies, puns, and satirical poems. He left twelve sizable volumes of works plus four volumes of correspondence. And still, to this day, various things turn up which were not included in *The Collected Works*. And this man was only forty-seven years old when he died (older than Pushkin by ten years), having begun his activities as a mere youth by throwing down a challenge to a commanding cultural and philosophical tradition.

Vladimir Sergeevich was born into the family of a renowned historian. I hope that you are all familiar with the name of Sergei Solovyov, who is buried in the Novodevichy cemetery and upon whose grave are inscribed the words of the apostle stating that "he has accomplished his *podvig*, run his course, and kept the faith, and hence a crown is now laid up for him."[53] Sergei Solovyov was a man entirely immersed in his work. Strictly speaking, he left nothing behind in life except for his gigantic labor: the university lectures and that comprehensive multifaceted book titled *The History of Russia* (which has been just recently republished).[54] Solovyov's family was very talented and had an interesting ancestry. His mother was part Polish, part Ukrainian, and related thereby to the well-known Ukrainian pilgrim and sage Hryhori Savvitch Skovoroda (eighteenth century). His father was the son of a priest. This means that Solovyov's grandfather, Mikhail, inherited a religious vocation, and, as a priest, served in the liturgy and performed parochial duties. The future philosopher firmly preserved his memory.

Vladimir Solovyov suffered a crisis of atheism, of struggle with God. While still a lad, he threw his icons out the window. One should understand what a time that was!

Born in 1853, his youth coincided with the epoch of the "men of the sixties," the epoch of Chernyshevsky, Dobrolubov, and Pisarev. Once, at dinner, the young Vladimir declared to his father that he had read Feuerbach's *The Essence of Christianity*[55] and cried, "How he thrashes Christianity!" His father, not entering into polemics with his son, simply said, "One should box your ears." Why didn't he argue? He probably guessed that the boy would work everything out by himself. And he guessed correctly, because almost forthwith this thin, lanky youth, whose hair fell down to the shoulders (he let his dark hair grow long as a sign of free and revolutionary thinking), turned to philosophy. And his exceedingly sharp intellect expressed itself very early as he completed his brilliant dissertation at little over twenty.

In his philosophical studies, Vladimir Solovyov focused on Spinoza and Schopenhauer, the weightiest minds of Europe. And he promptly proceeded to form his own conception of the development of philosophy. First of all he repudiated materialism. I said "repudiated," but this is inaccurate. The point is that Vladimir Solovyov from the earliest to the latest years of his life followed a principle which had once been expressed by the philosopher and mathematician Leibniz, who said, "Man always errs when he negates, especially the philosopher, and every doctrine, every teaching is weak at the point at which it negates." This was a leading principle of Solovyov's life and thought.

Whatever he focused on, be it socialism or revolutionary thought, the history of Old Belief or the destiny of Russia, he always found something valuable in it, understanding that there is nothing in the world that is completely fruitless and useless. His thinking bore the stamp of a sign which he himself called "All-Unity." This term has many meanings, but here it can denote Solovyov's magnificent ability to construct and synthesize. Yes, he frequently polemicized, and he often published articles and even whole books against his ideological opponents. But no defeated opponent remained as if dead for him. He always borrowed from the latter something that he found valuable. Thereby, his intellectual syntheses were constructed very quickly. The openness of this manner of thought staggered his university professors.

That period, the period of the 1870s, was dominated by positivism, a near relative of but not identical as a teaching to materialism. It taught that the ultimate truths, the ultimate mystery (the mystery of God, of immortality, of the spirit), are unknowable to man, that man can know nothing but nature, and that as nature, being the only reality, can be known by us, intellectual and philosophical progress ultimately consists in the development of natural science. Positivism regards all preceding thought as obsolete. Initially, Solovyov's natural interests inclined him to the natural sciences in his university studies, but as a maturing thinker, he was drawn to ponder the main mysteries of the

world, and came to regard natural science as but one of the bricks necessary for the construction of his great edifice. And thus, on graduat-
ing from the university, the young Solovyov issued a challenge to his
professors.

He would arrive at the faculty. Imagine the sight: dark blue eyes,
bushy black eyebrows, a thin, drawn face, hair, as I already mentioned,
falling down to the shoulders, a rather iconographic face, a lanky,
slightly awkward youth, thus producing a mysterious, strange impression! While studying during those years, he would come here, to
Sergiev Posad,[56] and freely audit various lectures on theology and philosophy. And even here, where long-haired people were rather common, he still produced a certain mysterious impression! He visited this
city several times and lived in the monastery, liking it. The theologians
and monks also liked him, while the students, at a later period, when
he became a celebrity, would half-reverentially and half-ironically distribute bottles of water in which he had washed his hands, saying,
"This is the water of Vladimir Solovyov."

Well, what did Solovyov declare in his dissertation subtitled
"Against the Positivists"? Its title was "The Crisis of Western Philosophy,"[57] and such was the power of his thought, and one should
add: and such was the fair-mindedness of the philosophers, the university lecturers of the 1870s, most of whom, regardless of the way in
which he criticized their positions and regardless of the fact that they
were his ideological and philosophical opponents, were carried away
by his thought, his methodology, his lucid, crystal clear speech, and
granted him his professorial title.

In the book, he explained why Western philosophy resulted in a
crisis at the end of the nineteenth century. It was because it regarded
the intellect, from the beginning, as a mere tool of reason, increasingly
understanding cognition one-sidedly. Early in the work, Solovyov
demonstrated how, during the Middle Ages, reason was liberated from
theology and from the church and how it became autonomous. He
then described how it expanded its realm until it finally transcended
its own bounds, engendering, at this point, its fragmentation. In this
youthful work, one may already discern a new spiritual synthesis. For
in it he demonstrates how with Schopenhauer and other philoso-

phers, drawn as they were to the sacred books of the East, dry rationalism began to make itself obsolete. So much of all this he predicted!
One can already perceive in this book the presentiment of that synthesis which Solovyov performed and called *(A Critique of) Abstract
Principles.*[58]

To explain this term one needs first to explain the term "All-
Unity." All-Unity is that spirit which binds the elements of nature and
the spiritual worlds, which binds society, ourselves, with the highest
and single Principle. And when people take whichever aspect of All-
Unified being, some finite part of it, and conceive of it separately, the
result is what he called an "abstract principle." On this account, reason,
intellectual cognition, becomes abstract, gets torn away and cut off
from being, and thereby ultimately suffers defeat. Empirical science,
by ceasing to deal with inner, spiritual experience and by failing to engage with abstract metaphysical deductions, ultimately leads to a dead
end. Solovyov demonstrates this by critiquing all the main "abstract
principles," and this critique constituted the main content of his doctoral dissertation.

He was not a simple man. From an early age—he was not yet ten—
he began to experience something uniquely mystical, or if you like, occult. He began to see some kind of feminine being, cosmic in character,
which, following encounters with her, he identified with the World
Soul. Henceforth, Vladimir Solovyov would never believe that creation was a mechanism, an aggregate of things. He saw the Soul of the
World! The first such meeting occurred in childhood, in the church at
the University of Moscow. The second occurred when he began to
consciously search for her, asking for her to appear to him. And this
occurred after his dissertation defense and during his study leave
abroad in Western Europe. He was living in London and working in
the famous British Museum where he was poring over ancient texts
and age-old mystical teachings (of Jacob Boehme and others). There in
the library, during a time of intense labor, he suddenly saw a face, that
same cosmic feminine face which appeared to him in the university
church when he was eight years old. This was a unique experience. He
tried to describe it in his poem "The Three Encounters."[59] The poem
is written with irony and self-parody because he was a sensitive person,

chaste and prone to injury. Despite all his wit, and irrespective of the fact that he appeared to be, as it were, armor-bound, his soul was, in reality, a wanderer and shivered easily in the cold world. And when he spoke about things that were most precious to him, he intentionally invoked irony.

Vladimir Solovyov then traveled to Egypt, the fatherland of mysteries, of great religions, of gnostic theosophy, assuming it would be the place where he would see the constituents of the World Soul. And so, one day, in Cairo, he left his inn and walked out into the bare stony desert. With his top hat, in his European dress, he walked, met up with the Bedouin, and continued to wander. Where he was going, he himself could not say, but finally he fell asleep on the cold ground. Then, with a start, he awoke, and suddenly saw, in the moment of the "phase transition" between sleep and wakefulness, another, completely different world. It was as if a shroud had been removed from the world around him. This is why he wrote in one of his poems, "Dear friend, don't you intuit that whatever we perceive is but a shadow, a reflection, of the things our eyes can't see?" This was a key inner experience of his life.

While residing in Egypt, he was already a committed Christian. Furthermore, during these youthful years, he made a courageous and completely theoretical decision: to construct a system in which the eternal truth of Christianity would be set out in the language of contemporary philosophy and science. Is this possible? He perceived its possibility in his very own method. Thus he commenced work on his book *The Philosophical Principles of Integral Knowledge*. In it, he dispensed neither with science, nor technology, nor economics, nor metaphysics, nor theology—all this was integrated into a colossal synthetic whole. At the elementary level it accords space to the scientific disciplines: to economics and natural science. Then it turns to abstract fields, to metaphysics, and finally to mysticism. Everything is intertwined, as in man himself, in whom the material, the bodily, the biological, lives together with abstract thought, and with something else, something deep and intuitive which engenders a power given the name of faith. And faith is the capacity of man to receive Divine Revelation.

During this time, Solovyov also conceived a plan to write a history of religion, relating the plan to his fiancée and explaining to her that he wished to write a history of religion which would show Christianity's place on the developmental trajectory of world religions. This plan he realized.

What was key in his subsequent labors? He became a freelance writer and philosopher in 1881. How and why must be explained. Endowed with a hereditary scholarly post as the son of the famous Solovyov, first a master and now a doctor, he was due to teach philosophy in the university. But he was also a Christian and a political and social thinker! When Alexander II was killed, Solovyov wrote a letter to Tsar Alexander III and read a public lecture stating that the tsar, as a Christian, must repudiate capital punishment for regicides, for the slayers of Alexander II, precisely as a Christian and without denying that the slaying was a criminal act. For to answer one killing with another is not, he argued, a Christian resolution of the problem. One must explain that this lecture somehow and immediately created around Solovyov an unhealthy aura which constrained him to leave the university. And from that point on, from 1881 to his death in 1900, he led a form of life which, perhaps, resembles that of his distant ancestor Hryhori Savvitch Skovoroda. He lived monstrously! I am only amazed that he did not die earlier. He had no home, he ate whatever was at hand, lived in hotels, roamed from city to city and from country to country. How could he have written so much! This still remains unsolved. He sometimes wrote on various brochures or on strips of paper. He had many friends. In particular he was friendly with the family of the deceased poet Alexei Konstantinovich Tolstoy. In this family he met a woman whom he loved the most in the course of many years. But she was married, and when her husband died, something in their relationship broke, and so he remained alone.

He led an ascetic, spartan life. Yet it contained nothing forced, and nothing pretentious. On the contrary, he loved good company, and liked such company to share some wine. Of course he did not approve of drunkenness but stressed that a bottle of wine can only help intellectual people lift their spirit, citing in support the heroes of Platonic dialogues, especially of Plato's dialogue *Symposium*. This man possessed neither house nor home, distributed whatever money he earned straightaway to whomever happened to be present, and often dressed in secondhand clothes. He could often be taken for a bishop, or for a priest, and once a boy in a hotel exclaimed, "Look, our dear God [*bozhen'ka*] is coming!" Solovyov was approaching in his old fur coat, with long beard, long hair, eyes staring into space on account of nearsightedness. An iconographic face, a mysterious persona!

The poet Andrei Bely, having seen him in childhood, describes him very sharply. His contemporaries also left a mass of recollections about him: about his eyes which changed color, his laughter which some deemed joyfully Homeric, but others somehow demonic, the contradictions of his life, his love of puns.

Then this man, this cryptic, strange, homeless man, proceeds to write "The Great Debate."[60] In it he narrates how the East and the West have already been arguing for a long time! Simplifying: the East holds man to be nothing and God to be everything. In the East, God is inhuman and stern, while in the West, man is godless, and the human "I" is given spiritual emphasis and prioritized. Christianity, the Gospel, according to Solovyov, synthesized the East with the West: "And the light, proceeding from the East, reconciled East with West," he wrote in one of his poems. And then, against a panorama of the church's history, Solovyov brilliantly analyzes its struggle with heresies and formulates the question which he would ponder for the rest of his life: Why, nevertheless, did the antagonism between East and West prevail? Why, when Christianity united them, did they break apart again, despite their being under Christian banners? Why did a Christian East and a Christian West result?

Solovyov's next work was *The Spiritual Foundations of Life*, which I have already mentioned. In it he writes about faith, love, fasting—the three elements. He writes simply, clearly, in a language which was neither especially clerical nor archaic, "ecclesiastical," but in that same language in which he wrote his crystal-clear philosophical books and his social and political journalism. As many of his contemporaries observed, many people became acquainted with the Holy Fathers of the church, with their writings, by means of Vladimir Solovyov's *The Spiritual Foundations of Life*.[61]

Around this time, he also presented a series of lectures in St. Petersburg, *On Bogochelovechestvo*.[62] *Bogochelovechestvo* is another of his dear concepts which should again be explained in the context of the dominant philosophies of the time. On the one hand, materialism and positivism taught that the history of the world and nature were nothing but earthly and secular. On the other hand, those who negated the meaning of the earthly, the spiritualists, or radical spiritualists, considered everything earthly and secular as insignificant. But Christianity does not repudiate matter, flesh, and nature. It sanctifies matter, because matter or nature is a divine creation and because God became incarnate in the world. And because God became incarnate in the world, the entire process of creation must be a *bogochelovecheskij* (God-human) process, a process in which the *bogochelovek* (the God-man) participates.

But Solovyov peers more deeply still, noting that man suffers from his own contradictions and lives an abnormal life. Today we acknowledge all of this. But what is the problem? What has happened to man? He answers: the world fragments. The world fragments! The bonds of love, of mutual understanding, of fraternity break. Bonds break even in a material world. Everything falls apart! The Creator is a Unity, a fullness of harmony. The fullness is the triumph of the design of unity. Unity is the picture created by God outside of time. And what is its contrary? What is it that throws the world into some pit? *Freedom*, he answers.

Solovyov states that nature possesses a single soul. His experience of the World Soul brought him to the idea of the spiritualization of the cosmos, the spiritualization of all creation. He seeks and finds the name of this Principle: Sophia, Greek for Wisdom. The Bible already speaks of divine Wisdom. Divine Wisdom is, in our contemporary language, information which God stores in creation. But for Solovyov, this is a certain spiritual center of the world which seeks freedom. And the world falls away, given the power of this freedom, from its harmonious state, and such it is now. The goal of world history is for us to return to eternal harmony, to eternal divine symphony, which is opposed by the forces of fragmentation and disintegration. Every hatred, every power which divides, which destroys thought, feeling, the body, and nature, is a principle opposed to God. Today, in the epoch of the ecological crisis, of national and geopolitical conflicts, Solovyov's call and idea that the divine unites while all that divides is Satanic remains actual in the highest degree.

Naturally, following this he begins to ponder the problem which I have already highlighted, the problem of *Christian unity*. At first sight, the problem seems simple. For those of you for whom it is unclear, I will explain it using an elementary parable. Suppose some man dies. His children love him dearly and part with him tearfully, asking, "Father, what is your last wish? Whatever you say, we will do." This is natural and completely normal. And he responds, "My children, I have only one request for you, that you should live in unity with each other, without offending each other, without division between yourselves, and that you preserve the family." The father dies, and the children find various objective and perhaps rather serious reasons for discord. So why have they all come to strife? Why do they hate each other? Why do they not wish to reconcile with each other? From time to time, one of them remembers that the father had in fact commanded them to behave otherwise. On such occasions the children perceive that they have offended him and have broken his testament and will. The testament which Christ gave to us, to us Christians, prior to his death, is well known. Everyone can read in the Bible the words which Jesus prayed shortly before his death: "That they may be one, as you, Father are in Me, and I am in you, so let them be one in Us, so that the world should believe that You have sent Me."[63] As the Father and the Son are one, so all are to be one. Here is the thought of Christ. This is his Testament. But the Testament is broken, as is perfectly evident and for objective reasons. All are guilty, each in his own way. Perhaps more blame is to be accorded to some, perhaps to others. Western people say that the East is more to blame on account of its pride. The people of the East say that the West is more to blame on account of its love of power, and so on. But that the Testament is broken, this is clearly evident.

This is how Solovyov reasoned, and he conceived a plan to overcome Christian division. First he confronted us Christians with a relatively important question. He asked, What in fact is our Christian faith? Is this an ideology? Is this an abstract philosophy? Is it some-thing intended for personal use? Under no circumstances! In that case it would not be a part of the all-unified divine design. This touches our life in all of its aspects and manifestations, including the social. People must learn to live on earth in a godly manner, and to submit to the di-vine calling, and so to pave the way for theocracy, the reign of God. But how can they accomplish this if they all remain in enmity and are divided against each other? The questions impelled Solovyov to study the Bible, to learn ancient Hebrew (Greek and Latin he already knew), to read the Old Testament, in Hebrew, and to translate anew its sig-nificant portions. In the process, he emphasized that God intended people to live in a godly way on earth at the very beginning and that the Lord's covenant was not given only to console the heart but be-cause the high divine designs must ultimately become manifest and be realized in society as well.

Of course we must recognize that Solovyov, the young Solovyov of thirty-something, was a bit utopian. He deemed, as is characteristic of impatient youth, that such things are possible, perhaps tomorrow! In particular, he even devised the following scheme. Judging that the strongest power in the East was represented by the Russian tsar and that the center of the greatest spiritual power in the West was repre-sented by the Roman pontiff, Solovyov argued that were these two to join hands and forge a spiritual unity between the kingdom of Moscow (or Petersburg) and the universal ecclesial authority in Rome, Chris-tianity would be unconquerable and thus make theocracy on earth a possibility. Solovyov not only argued this in print, but he even took practical steps in this direction by often traveling to Western countries and befriending advocates of church reunion. He did not wish to leave this idea in an abstract form, as an empty dream, but sought to realize it.

Solovyov's idea—the pope described it, "a beautiful idea, but in need of a miracle to be realized."[64] One should say that Solovyov was absolutely alone in this respect in the East. His Orthodox confreres began to treat him with radical mistrust. His essays and books pertain-ing to theological questions ceased to be published; censorship forbade them, forcing him to publish abroad. And in the West, even though people treated him with love, they considered him a dreamer. They said, "How is it possible to unite two worlds that have been completely split, the Eastern-Orthodox and the Western-Catholic!" But in this regard, Solovyov turned out to be a prophet, for only a few decades after his death there began, completely independently, even if unsurely, but nevertheless steadfastly, a movement toward mutual understanding between Christians and their divided world.

In sociopolitical discussions he was always an advocate of democracy and justice, and his brilliant essays defending liberty of conscience remain fully relevant. He judged that Orthodox Christianity is undermined, undermined amongst us in our country, by being protected by censorship and the state. Solovyov publicly opposed the persecutions of Old Believers and sectarians. He asked, "If the truth is indeed real and genuine, and if those who confess it believe in it, why is it really necessary to invoke censorship, violence, and repression? Censorship, violence, and repression are only a recourse for those who, in the depth of their souls, do not believe in their idea." He, by the way, also spoke of the "truth of socialism"; these are literally his words. "The truth of socialism" is a partial truth. The word "socialism" he understood very broadly, affirming that humans must indeed strive to improve economic conditions. But he was convinced, and advanced proofs, that economic transformations alone are insufficient. For in reality, material security cannot make happy the man who remains spiritually impoverished and deprived. All attempts to solve the question one-sidedly, either/or, either materially or spiritually, prompted him to protest. A radical asceticism, which announced, "We will ascend to the heavens and give up on the earth!," found in his person a harsh opponent. Freedom, labor, love, activism, creativity, active human participation: all these help to define the content he attributes to the idea of *bogochelovechestvo*. God does not alone create the world but engages the participation of man. This engenders a colossal responsibility. Moreover, the word *bogochelovechestvo* is not accidental for him, but it is, in fact, borrowed from canonical usage. Since for us Jesus of Nazareth is the *Bogochelovek* and since *he is the Bogochelovek*, then *by the very fact of his (divine) presence upon the Earth, he sanctifies earthly labor, earthly life, earthly human personality.*

Reflecting on the fate of his fatherland, which Solovyov greatly loved, and polemicizing against the Slavophiles, he desired something more for his own country than might and governmental power. Solovyov described this in his poem "Light from the East."[65] The poem begins by depicting the collision of two worlds: Greece is invaded, in about 500 B.C., by the armies of the conquering Xerxes, a great army. The Greek army, being small, fails to withstand him in open battle, but the Greeks cunningly lure Xerxes' soldiers into the narrow gorge at Thermopylae. The Persians were unable to turn with all their might, and there King Leonidas met them with his soldiers, of which there were only three hundred. Our youth, I think, watched a film about them about ten years ago called *The 300 Spartans*.[66] The Greeks did not allow Xerxes' giant army to pass, and pass they did into that narrow gorge while Xerxes, not knowing how many enemy soldiers remained standing there, was forced to turn back. And so Solovyov identified this historical event, removed as it is by two and a half thousand years from us, as the symbol of the collision of two worlds:

> From East streams light, from East stream forces,
> Xerxes the great, for might prepared.
> To Thermopylae he coerces,
> His flocks of slaves, from Iran led.
>
> But not in vain did Prometheus,
> A heavenly gift to Hellas grant.
> The throngs of slaves run routed, paled,
> Before the free and valiant!

And Solovyov concluded this poem about war between the East and West with an invitation to the fatherland:

> Behold, oh Russia, you are bound,
> to bear a proud and lofty *Geist*,[67]
> What sort of East would you expound,
> the East of Xerxes or of Christ?

Do you wish to be the East of despotism, of violence, of repression, even in the presence of external might, or of a spiritual power first of all? For him, this was a very important question because the spiritual power is always situated at the front.

The events surrounding Solovyov's social-literary life unfolded tragically. He presented a public lecture about the medieval conception of the world. The lecture provoked a stormy reaction. The newspapers bombarded him with dirt. His fellow theologians deemed him practically a traitor to Christianity. Thus commenced a period of loathsome harassment. One might have wondered how a lecture on the medieval worldview might be found so terrible? But here's the rub: for the first time Solovyov clearly stated, Think not that the Middle Ages were a time of Christianity's triumph! The medieval regime was a mongrel of Christian forms and pagan conceptions. Owing to this, when non-Christian thought began to discuss freedom, the dignity of personhood, the evil of human degradation, it, rejecting Christianity, actually served Christianity's ideal. And Solovyov courageously asked, "Who ended torture? Who forbade the Inquisition? Christians or not? No, not Christians!" This was a stern, sharp question, and a difficult one for an honest mind to answer. But I understand why the press and many others went after Solovyov.

When Solovyov lived in the Lavra, in Sergiev Posad, he felt more at peace. He described how much the monks cared for him and desired him to receive the tonsure. "But I am not going to give myself up cheaply," he joked. Indeed, as a scholar he was tempted to remain in the monastery, and all the more so given the ascetical form of his life, so as to engage in scholarship. But this temptation he overcame.

It is impossible to list everything he did and why. He wrote about the ecological crisis, and about the poetry of Tyutchev. Whatever he wrote about always contained a deep and interesting thought. A Greek bishop publishes an ancient Christian tractate belonging to the first or second century. Solovyyov republishes it in his brother's translation and supplies it with commentaries. And these are not simply learned commentaries but in fact a bombshell! For he shows how things were in the original church and what changed later. "And have the changes always been for the better?," he asks. He did not set out to become a church reformer, but he posed the questions.

Toward the end of his life Solovyov understood that his scheme to unite the churches had collapsed and was unrealizable. He turned to theoretical philosophy and wrote a colossal work on Christian ethics. Let each of you not fail to read this book. It is a large volume titled *The Justification of the Good*[68] and contains so much that is important and valuable. Solovyov began by discussing human ideals. What is the good? Is it external happiness, hedonism, power, or something else? He demonstrated that all these ultimately fail. And then he analyzed—scientifically, philosophically, theologically, poetically—the essence of that which we call *the good*.

Several years prior to his death, he received Communion from a Catholic priest. By doing so, he wanted somehow to show that he personally no longer recognized the division of the churches. When he related this to his Orthodox confessor, the latter responded that this should not have been done. They argued sharply. And when Solovyov lay dying, he said, "I was wrong." He wrote that individual conversions, individual transitions from church to church, would not aid Christian unity but would, on the contrary, introduce redundant temptations.

You all know the park behind Belyaevo, formerly the estate Uzkoe. At present it is the site of the sanatorium of the Academy of Sciences. If you happen to be there, stroll down the road leading to the sanatorium, and you will approach a church. It is repaired only externally. Inside there are piles of books, once removed from "Hitler's Chancellery," and lying there since the war itself. Nearby, behind the railing, is a home, a typical estate home. This was the property of Count Trubetskoy, Sergei Nikolaevich Trubetskoy, who was briefly the rector of Moscow University and who died several years after Solovyov, also relatively young, a brilliant philosopher, a sharp polemicist and critic, and the noblest social activist. Trubetskoy took Solovyov in at a critical time, when numerous serious illnesses suddenly crashed upon him. In reality, he was gradually killing himself by his wandering, and suddenly everything surfaced. All too quickly he began to feel so bad that he could no longer leave, and so he died in the care of Sergei Trubetskoy.

Just before his death, Solovyov went to confession and received the Eucharist. He died in possession of his faculties. He was reading and writing in Hebrew, because he always loved to season his prayers with the language of Christ so as to unite their sound with that of ancient Christian tradition. He knew many psalms by heart. Losing and returning to consciousness, he said, "Difficult is the work of the Lord." Indeed, this relatively young man bore a colossal weight. He was simultaneously simple like a child and wise. He was a man who elicited admiration, envy, hatred, abuse, and contempt. He was a man about whom hundreds of books and brochures will be written. Just ten years after his death, the bibliography on him extended to several hundred titles.

And so he died and was buried in Moscow. I would wish that you, if you could spare the time, would go to the Novodevichy Monastery. Directly opposite the entrance, in the first alley, turning slightly to the right, is the tombstone of Sergei Mikhailovich Solovyov, a white marble tombstone with his relief. The cross, obviously, has been struck off. Nearby are the graves of his son and daughter. The tombstones, of course, are destroyed. Over the graves of Vladimir Solovyov and his sister stand the remains of other, crossless, gravestones. But thanks be to God that even such stand. Now, thanks to the funds of our Moscow diocese, of our diocesan administration, we have been assured that the ninetieth anniversary of his death will witness the restoration of the original form of his tombstone.[69]

Very many people have come to visit this grave. Solovyov exerted a tremendous influence on Andrei Bely, on Blok, who called him a "knight-monk." The motif of the Beautiful Lady in Blok's poetry is of course inspired by Solovyov. The entire brilliant pleiad of Russian religious thinkers, Bulgakov, Florensky, Berdyaev, Frank, Eugene Trubetskoy, and many others, would have been impossible—it is difficult to imagine them—without Solovyov. This pilgrim was the founder of an original, distinctive, Russian religious-philosophical school of thought. And so when you come to this grave, remember that *this man lived*. Not in vain did he say, "Death and time prevail on earth. Call them not your lord. Gloom will swallow all that whirls. Love shines undisturbed." This was his deep intuition, this was his deep insight.

This abstract[70] intellectual always lived by faith, always lived by a mystical insight, always lived questing eternity. And this makes Vladimir Solovyov not just a valuable writer, thinker, and poet, but also a unique, peculiar individual whose bright personality would make any culture proud. And it is gratifying that now, after a hundred years of oblivion, he is finally written about, and his works are finally published. Solovyov is returning, however timidly, before our eyes. May this short sketch help you, should you wish, to acquaint yourselves with the thought of such a wonderful man.

CHAPTER 4

Jewish History in Russia up to the End of the Nineteenth Century

Solovyov began to write on the Jewish question in the wake of the pogroms that erupted in the Pale of Settlement during the two years after the assassination of Tsar Alexander II on March 13, 1881. He wrote to combat the tide of Judeophobia in the country's conservative and liberal papers that preceded, accompanied, and followed these pogroms. He also wrote to combat the antisemitic legislation that the tsarist Ignatiev committee passed on May 3 and that the Pahlen Commission, appointed subsequently to investigate the issue of Jewish civil rights, was not permitted to repeal in 1888. He continued to write to prod the tsarist regime to ease Jewish civil rights in Russia, hoping thereby to preserve her Christian mission and dignity and prevent her from sliding into revolutionary violence.

An understanding of Jewish history in nineteenth-century Russia and of Russian history and culture during this period serves to clarify the purpose of Solovyov's writings. His "Jewry and the Christian Question," published in 1884, commenced in a series of lectures delivered in 1882 to address the pogrom crisis. His work "The Talmud and Recent Polemical Literature about It in Austria and Germany," published in 1886, attacked the propaganda directed against the Jews via the Talmud by Jacob Brafman's (1825–79) *Book of the Kahal*, which was reprinted in 1882 and used by tsarist committees working on the Jewish question during the remainder of the decade. Something similar can be said of Solovyov's other Jewish writings.

In these years Solovyov became involved in the Society for the Promotion of Jewish Enlightenment, or OPE, founded and led by the dynasty of Russia's greatest Jewish philanthropists, Evzel Gintsburg (Günzburg) and his son and grandson, Barons Horace and David Gintsburg. As Jewry's principal intercessor with the government, Horace was the leader of the other Jewish members of the Pahlen Commission, including the chemist Nikolai Bakst and the rabbi of St. Petersburg, Abraham Drabkin. Solovyov developed a solid friendship with all these men. He attended a Passover seder hosted by the Gintsburgs and commissioned David Gintsburg, who owned the largest Jewish library in the Pale, to contribute the first scholarly article in Russia on the Kabbalah for the *Encyclopedic Dictionary*. However, finding Gintsburg's work unsuitable for this forum, Solovyov arranged to have it published in the journal *Voprosy filosofii i psikhologii* (1896) and composed his own 1896 article on the Kabbalah for the *Encyclopedic Dictionary* (see Part II, ch. 17).

In December 1890 Solovyov organized a letter to the tsar, signed by more than fifty leading members of Russia's intelligentsia, protesting on behalf of Jewish civil rights. As the tsar banned its publication in Russia, it was published abroad. One version was published in the London *Times*, alongside a letter by Cardinal Manning, as an aid to London's citizenry's attempt, via the Guildhall Conference, to support Jewish civil rights in Russia.

As Solovyov's correspondence with Rabbi Getz reveals, he disagreed with Getz's and the OPE's stance on emigration. The OPE officially opposed Jewish emigration to witness to Jewry's Russian patriotism. This stance, however, given the progressive restrictions imposed on Jewry under Alexander III and then under Nicholas II, was becoming increasingly tortuous, especially for the poor. Solovyov gave material help to poor Jews wishing to emigrate.

After Solovyov died, Rabbi Drabkin commemorated his life in a service in St. Petersburg's synagogue. Bakst contributed a long panegyric explaining his import for Russia's Jewry. In a longer commemoration, Getz declared him a righteous Gentile.

This chapter provides a concise sketch of Russian-Jewish relations in the nineteenth century in order to illuminate the nature and significance of all such declarations, protests, activities, and writings. Methodologically, it seeks to integrate the anti-tsarist Jewish eyewitness perspective on the history that led up to the events of the 1880s and 1890s, classically represented by the work of Simon Dubnov, who entrenched in twentieth-century historiography the view that the pogroms were the result of a tsarist conspiracy, with the historiography of the past three decades, which, by revealing the analogies between Russian tsarist and Eastern and Western European governmental approaches to the Jewish question, rejects the conspiracy theory. I have also taken the opportunity to gloss the discussion with references to Solzhenitsyn's late pro-tsarist explanation of nineteenth-century Jewish-Russian relations.[71] I do this in order to clarify the arguments that may still separate Jews and Russians in interpreting these relations, to highlight where such arguments, particularly Solzhenitsyn's, tend to be selective given what has been written to date, and thereby to put into better perspective what was unique and original about Solovyov's approach to these issues. In addition to shedding light on the persons, events, places, literary and cultural movements, newspapers, and organs of state that figure in Solovyov's writings on the Jewish question, I particularly wish to draw attention to the roles played by Tsar Alexander III and his chief adviser, Konstantin Pobedonostsev.

Given that these two figures, the autocrat and his adviser, dismissed and censured everything Solovyov had to say and argue on behalf of Jewish civil rights in Russia, an examination of their interaction illuminates why tsarist policy was seen to be responsible for Judeophobic measures at the time and the extent to which the tsar and his government were responsible for the Jewish plight at this time. Consequently, the importance of this historical survey exceeds the aim of furnishing a background for understanding Solovyov's oeuvre on the Jewish question. In view of the current historical revisionism that dismisses attributing the pogroms to tsarist state policy, my aim is to highlight its relevance to the debate about what, pertaining to the Jews, the tsars could have done, failed to do, and chose not to do and what they did instead.

1. ORIGINS

Jews began to migrate to Russia, Poland, and Lithuania before the Middle Ages. Their presence is attested by accounts about the conversion of the Khazars to Judaism in 732, by traditions about Prince Vladimir's choosing Christianity over Judaism in Kievan Russia in the tenth century, by testimonies about Jews' mercantile activities up to the Kievan pogrom in 1113, and by legends about a "Jewish tsar."[72] The migration of Jews spiked during the Middle Ages either because they were fleeing persecution or because of the welcome extended to them. Thus, for example, they sought to escape the Crusade-driven pogroms in Bohemia during the eleventh and twelfth centuries and relocated from Germany to Poland when the latter's king and nobility invited them in the thirteenth and fourteenth centuries. On their arrival, however, the Jews quickly experienced restrictions on their residence, often in violent terms, principally for economic or religious reasons. Thus they were expelled from Novgorod in the fifteenth century when many members of the clergy converted to Judaism, while Christian merchants in Polotsk, resenting Jewish competition, persuaded Ivan IV to drive them out when he captured the city in 1563.[73] The eighteenth century saw continued intolerance directed at Jews. Christian fear of Jewish proselytism resulted in the public burning of Borokh Leibov and his convert Aleksandr Voznitsyn in St. Petersburg on July 15, 1738. Peter I's daughter, Elizabeth I, attempted to expel all Jews and Muslims from Russia in 1727, but the edict was loosened in 1728 by Peter II and then by Anne in 1731, 1734, and 1736, until finally Elizabeth II, imitating Western religious intolerance by saying that she desired "no profit from the enemies of Christ," expelled almost all Jews from Russia on December 2, 1742, save for certain key diplomats, scholars, and merchants. The consequent dearth of Jews explains to Klier the absence in Russia of popular sayings or songs about Jews, either in positive or in negative terms.[74]

2. The Jewish Experience in Poland, Lithuania, and the Ukraine, Sixteenth–Eighteenth Centuries

Poland's Jews administered themselves and were taxed as a community (*kehillah*; *kahal* in Polish), an arrangement formalized in 1551. After the Jesuits entered Poland to combat the Reformation in the seventeenth and eighteenth centuries, fears of Jewish proselytism and suspicion of Jews, based on the idea that they carried out ritual murder and

desecrated the sacraments, peaked, resulting in pogroms, the imposi-
tion of distinctive and insulting dress, and the consequent loss of Jewish prestige in native eyes. Legal documents that had described Jews as
providus, *honestus*, and *generosus* now labeled them *infidus*, *perfidus*,
and *incredulus*. The driving force behind this shift may have been economic, given the advances in Jewish marketing techniques during this
period and the concomitant frequency of accusations about "Jewish
exploitation."[75]

2.1. These examples illustrate the many cycles of Jewish immigration,
prosperity, forced ghettoization, and emigration to neighboring lands.
From Poland they fled to Lithuania, and when the cycle resumed
there, they returned to Poland and the Ukraine to serve as stewards to
the Polish Catholic landlords. Invariably, they suffered heavily from
Cossack attacks, especially those led by Bogdan Khmelnitsky (1593–
1657), who massacred one hundred thousand Jews in the Ukraine in
1648 and whose invasion of Poland in 1651, supported by the tsar, resulted in their mass extermination and expulsion. The cycle repeated
itself a century later with Cossack incursions into Poland, in 1734,
1750, and in 1768, when the Zaporozhian Cossack Maksim Zheleznyak
stamped his massacres by hanging a Pole, a Jew, and a dog on a tree
with the inscription, "Lyakh, Zhyd, and hound—by one faith bound."[76]

2.2. The oppression and despair experienced by many Jews during the
seventeenth and eighteenth centuries were reflected in the religious
realm, first by the false messianic movements initiated by self-professed
messiahs such as Sabbatai Zevi, Jacob Frank, and Judah Hasid and then
in the Hasidic mysticism initiated by the sage Israel Baal Shem Tov,
known by the acronym the Besht. He stressed God's immanence in
and providential care over natural phenomena and taught his followers to commune with God through prayer, to seek guidance from the
sages (*tzaddikim*), to esteem faith and immediate religious experience
over knowledge and observance of legal precepts, and to recognize the
power of ethical and loving deeds done in joyful service to God. Hasidism was initially repressed as a heresy by the Rabbinists, or Mitnagdim (Opponents, Protestants), who suspected it of pantheism,
idolatry, and false messianism. The Rabbinists feared that Hasidism
would undermine the traditional Jewish values of studying the Torah,
observing purity laws, and participating in the liturgy. Their strife was

exacerbated by the excommunication of the Hasidim by Elijah ben Solomon Zalman of Vilna, the chief rabbinic authority (the Vilna Gaon) in 1772.[77]

2.3. In spite of all these misfortunes, the Jews remained essential to Poland's economy. At the beginning of the eighteenth century, having reached a population of approximately one million, or one-ninth of the total population of Poland and Lithuania, they constituted 50 percent of the total artisan class and managed 75 percent of the export and 10 percent of the import trade in these kingdoms.[78] As the Christian middle class developed, however, Christians sought to gain an economic edge on the Jews, first by barring Jewish artisans and merchants from mercantile guilds and trade unions, then by limiting Jewish residence in the capital to temporary visits (1768), and finally by expulsion from the capital (1775). To survive, Jews took up land leasing and rural liquor dealing. As a result, Jewish communities, already fractured by the strife between the Hasidim and the Mitnagdim, began to be fractured by economic and social divisions. Having become entwined in Poland's economic organism but remaining strangers to its national and spiritual aspiration, Jews presented Poland, in the years of its three partitions by Prussia, Austria, and Russia (1772, 1776, and 1795, respectively) with its own "Jewish problem." In the period of reform that followed the first two partitions (1788–91), drawing on the French revolutionary policy of integration and the Austrian Joseph II's policy of compulsory enlightenment, Poland's aristocracy sought to make the Jews "useful" to the state and "harmless" to the people by assimilating them through compulsory adoption of Polish language, dress, and education. Despite these measures, Poland's charter of liberty, the Constitution of May 3, 1791, failed to give Jews civil equality and confirmed them as the Cinderella of the realm on the eve of Poland's last partition in 1795.[79]

3. THE CREATION OF THE PALE OF SETTLEMENT UNDER CATHERINE II, PAUL I, AND ALEXANDER I, 1772–1825

The fates of the Russian and Jewish people came together with the partitions of Poland that commenced in 1772. Through the annexation of these territories, as well as those along the shores of the Black Sea won through the Russo-Turkish War of 1768–74, Catherine II (1729–96), wholly unfamiliar with Jews at the start of her reign, came to govern close to a million Jews, concentrated more densely than any other ethnicity in Russia's western regions, and thereby inherited a "Jewish problem." Adopting initially the Polish system of administering Jews separately through the *kahals* and motivated by their commercial potential, she undertook in 1782–84 to make them "useful" and granted them participation in city government on equal terms with Christians. By the standards of her time, the policies were progressive, making this "Semiramis of the North" "the first sovereign in Europe to extend to Jews equality with her Christian subjects."[80] Nonetheless, Belorussian mercantile pressure drove her to circumscribe their residence rights in 1791 to the "vast ghetto that became known as the Pale of Permanent Jewish Settlement."[81] In 1794 she restricted them further by ordering them to vacate district towns and burdening Jewish merchants with double taxation.[82]

3.1. A famine at the start of the reign of Paul I (1796–1801) compounded the complaints of the Pale's landed Polish aristocracy, holders of an ancient alcohol monopoly, that the Jewish tavern keepers were luring its peasants into drunkenness and poverty. In response, Paul issued legislation in 1797 intended to force them into less "harmful," more "useful," occupations, promising acceptance if they became acceptable.[83] In the meantime, the investigation of the complaints proceeded through district governors. The complaints and their proposed solutions, notably those of I. G. Frizel, governor of Lithuania, were finally turned over to the Senate in 1800. The Senate, in turn, committed them to the senator and celebrated poet Gavrila Romanovich Derzhavin (1743–1816), who, following a fact-finding tour in Belorussia, filed the report, "The Opinion of Senator Derzhavin Concerning the Averting of the Want of Foodstuffs in White Russia by Curbing the Avaricious Pursuits of the Jews, also Concerning Their Re-Education, and Other Matters." Despite the differences between Frizel and Derzhavin, the former arguing for integration and the latter for segregation, Klier observes that both reports effectively shifted Russia's framing of the Jewish question from the search to discern where Jews might fit into Russian society to viewing them as an anomaly, a population of exploiters and parasites whose way of life was incompatible with good government and the public weal. Klier's judgment should be qualified by Solzhenitsyn's observation that Derzhavin, while holding that Jews were currently harmful, is on record saying and writing that Providence had preserved them for a socially beneficial reason whose realization he wanted to facilitate.[84]

3.2. The ambivalence toward the Jews, as self-segregating social parasites and *kahal*-controlled exploiters of the peasants with a yet to be realized God-chosen mission, and the question whether to continue to segregate or integrate them into society was debated and then dealt with by a comprehensive effort at "reform and control, inducement and coercion" during the enlightened absolutism of Alexander I (1801–25).[85] In 1804, "in conformity with the example set by other enlightened peoples" (Prussia and Austria),[86] he issued the Statute Concerning the Organization of the Jews, drafted by a committee he appointed to work on materials submitted heretofore on the Jewish problem. The statute aimed at assimilating the Jews through an assortment of restrictive and integrating measures. On the restrictive, stick side, Jews were given four years to withdraw from villages in the hope that this would end their manufacture and sale of liquor to peasants. On the integrating, liberating, carrot side, Jews were given access to higher education, industry, and agriculture, permitted to leave the Pale on business, and given rights to freedom, property, faith, and even self-administration through the *kahal*—an irony given that criticism of the *kahal* was largely the impetus for the statute. The statute, however, was never put into practice. Given the numbers of Jews who stood to be affected, their lack of agricultural experience, and the potential ensuing economic instability in the country on the eve of Napoleon's invasion, during which Jews earned a reputation for remarkable bravery, loyalty, and assistance to Russian forces, enforcement of the statute was postponed. The addition of four hundred thousand Jews in the Pale from the acquisition of central Poland as a result of the war made it ultimately impracticable.[87]

3.3. Alexander's "enlightened" absolutism was manifested in legislation that sought to protect Jews in several significant ways. At the beginning of his reign he intervened to give official protection to the Hasidim, whom the rabbinate denounced as dangerous agitators.[88] In 1816 he forbade Russian courts to accept ritual murder cases without physical proof, even though the blood libel on which these were based continued to surface, most notoriously in the town of Velizh in the Vitebsk province, where cases dragged on in the courts from 1823 to 1835 and ended with the acquittal of all the accused Jews, though some had died in prison.[89]

In 1817 Alexander met with Lewis Way, a preacher in the London Missionary Society who had come to Russia to proclaim the importance of improving Jewish life on the grounds of the honor due to them as God's chosen people who were preserved for a providential historical role. After this meeting Alexander issued two edicts, one to protect baptized Jews and the other to grant baptized Jews land. He then sought to reward Jews who responded to these edicts with civil equality and tax reductions administered through the Society of Israelite Christians, which he founded in March 1817. Few Jews, however, responded to the offer, and since those who did sparked the old Judaizing fear, the project was abandoned.[90]

4. THE REIGN OF NICHOLAS I, 1825–1855

The reign of Nicholas I began with the Decembrist revolt. The leader of the Decembrists, Col. Pavel Pestel, and his colleague Nikita Muravyov mixed republican liberalism with authoritarianism. Pestel's treatise *Russkaya Pravda* (Russian Justice) anticipated future socialist consternation over the Jewish problem by proposing, should the Jews fail to assimilate, to deport them en masse or help them establish their own state in Asia Minor. Unable to meet Pestel's constitutional demand and faced by a mutiny in the regiments, Nicholas crushed the revolt, had Pestel arrested, on December 13, 1825, and hanged him with four colleagues a few months later.[91] Other Decembrists were exiled to Siberia, where they and their wives romanticized their ideals in ways that inspired future generations of revolutionaries.[92]

4.1. Nicholas inherited the committee appointed in 1823 to study the Jewish problem and Alexander's belief that the dangers Jews posed to the nation and the peasantry needed to be tackled through assimilation. These assumptions explain, for example, the application of the 1804 statute's "policy of expulsion" to Jews living (and selling liquor) in the villages of Grodno and Kiev and on the shores of the Baltic and Black Seas in 1827–29, measures that were halted only during the Polish insurrection of 1830–31 for fear of giving Jews cause to support the Poles.[93] What was new in Nicholas's approach was his attempt to accelerate the process of assimilation through military constraints whose shaping can be traced to his own military background and his despotic response to the Decembrist revolt. Nonetheless, as Rogger notes, if this was Nicholas's purpose, "it was defeated by the cruelty of his methods,"[94] whose form took shape in the 1827 conscription statute, which for the first time included Jews in military conscription. Conscription at the time applied to men under the age of twenty-five and lasted twenty-five years. Nicholas, however, made the Jews alone subject to the draft at the age of twelve, even nine or eight, rather than the standard age of twenty.[95] While the older conscripts were quartered in Christian homes, the teenagers (cantonists) were sent for re-education and conversion to camps in Siberia, where they died in large numbers from torture, famine, and cold. To avoid conscription, Jewish youths fled into forests and maimed themselves. The *kahal*, tasked to supply recruits, began taking bribes from those with resources to spare their own children and filled the tsar's quotas by preying on and even kidnapping poor and orphaned children, as young as nine.[96] These activities alienated the poor from the *kahal* and swayed the educated, if not toward revolution, then toward the *maskilim*, advocates of the movement for enlightenment, the Haskalah.[97] The result was a substantial erosion of intermural solidarity and of the authority of traditional Jewish elites.[98] The coercive nature of the conscription laws, together with the exemptions they gave to Jews entering university and agriculture, was evidently having its effect.

4.2. The Civil Code for the Jews, long in preparation by the "Jewish Committee," established in 1823, was finally published in 1835. Reducing in size a gigantic "charter of disabilities," the code effectively forbade everything not explicitly permitted. On the positive side, it ended the policy of expulsion from villages that had devastated Jewish life between 1804 and 1830, welcomed Jews in Russian schools without compelling conversion, expanded provisions for Jewish agriculture, including land allowances in Siberia, and allowed literate Jews to vote in municipal elections and hold offices in town councils and magistracies (with the exception of Vilna). Enforced by imprisonment and fines, it regulated the minimum age for marriage (eighteen for males, sixteen for females), retained forced baptism in the statute of conscription, and forbade the permanent employment by Jews of Christian domestics as well as the building of synagogues near churches. Censorship regulations imposed in 1836 on all Jewish presses and imported Jewish materials subjected all Jewish home libraries to search and resulted in the confiscation of all ancient Hebrew literature printed in the sixteenth through eighteenth centuries and, in 1837, in the burning of tens of thousands of copies of medieval classic works.[99]

4.3. Solzhenitsyn understands the harsh measures of the 1835 Code, like those of the 1827 conscription laws, as sticks to induce Jews to go into agriculture and supplements his argument by pointing to laws enacted in 1839 that also excused Jews who became farmers from conscription, as well as the 1844 law that allowed Jews in the Pale to hire for three years peasants from whom they could learn agricultural techniques, and the establishment of Jewish colonies around Eketerinoslav in the neighborhood of German colonies to learn the same. On the strength of V. N. Nikitin's 1887 study of Jewish agricultural endeavors but ignoring all of Nikitin's testimony about the way in which the regime hampered them, Solzhenitsyn argues that all these measures failed because Jews were by culture poor agriculturalists.[100]

4.4. While highlighting the many improvements of the 1835 Code over that of 1804, especially relating to educational opportunities and openings in various professions, trade, and industry, Solzhenitsyn notes that the *kahal* resisted all of these policies as a form of persecution.[101] This explains why Nicholas I, in 1841, appointed the renowned classicist, statesman, and conservative Count Sergei Semyonovich Uvarov to address the problem as minister of public instruction. Drawing on Prussian and Austrian assumptions that Jewish separatism and obscurantism were fed by the Talmud, Uvarov proposed to the Committee for Defining Measures Looking to the Radical Transformation of Jews in Russia, chaired from 1840 by Count P. D. Kiselyov, that Jewish assimilation be furthered by dismantling the *kahals*, strengthening the *maskilim*'s efforts to counter their "fanaticism" and reform Jewry by compulsory secular education, and dividing Jews into four tolerated classes or estates (merchant, townsman, manufacturer and craftsman, agriculturalist), originally devised under Alexander I, that included the property owning and employed as well as the have-nots. Jews were given five years to improve themselves; if they failed to do so, they would be registered in the "fifth class" of "useless vagrants" marked for conscription in Siberia for ten years. The decree was made law on December 19, 1844. The speed of its adaptation suggests that Kiselyov and the tsar were following familiar European policies aimed at reducing Jewish particularism and peculiarity by removing their autonomy, taxing powers, and executive organs, the *kahals*, and thereby working to produce their rapprochement (*sblizhenie*) and fusion (*sliyanie*) with the original, or root (*korennye*), populations. To counter Orthodox Jewish resistance to the measures, the government established rabbinical schools in 1847 and an institute for Jewish school inspectors in 1850 to educate the next generation of rabbis in Russian and secular subjects.[102]

4.5. In 1846 Moses Montefiore arrived in Russia with a letter for Nicholas I from Queen Victoria, protesting the division of Jews into tolerated categories and the restrictions imposed on their movement in trade, and, conversely, appealing to Nicholas to follow the Western example and grant Jews equal or at least greater rights. The tsar responded that his harsh measures were intended to break up Jewish insularity and stimulate labor and that, depending on the successes achieved, Jewish life would improve gradually.[103]

4.6. Dubnov concluded his account of Nicholas's reign by relating that the stereotype of the Jew as an inhuman fiend was perpetuated among the Russian people by the characters of this period's great writers—the "despised Jew" of Pushkin's "Black Shawl" (1820) and "Beginning of a Novel" (1832) and Zhyd Yankel of Gogol's *Taras Bulba* (1835, 1842)—and resurfaced in the ritual murder charge and trial of 1852 in the city of Saratov in central Russia after the bodies of two Russian boys were found covered with wounds and bearing the traces of circumcision. Suspicion fell on several Jews, including a soldier named Shlieferman and a furrier named Yankel Yushkevicher. A judicial commission appointed by Nicholas in 1854 to investigate Jewish religious fanaticism freed them in 1856 after the baptized professor of Oriental studies Daniel A. Khvolson proved that ritual murder was incompatible with Jewish tradition. The men remained "under strong suspicion," however, and Alexander II's advisers persuaded him to sentence them to penal servitude from 1860 to 1867, from which only Yushkevicher emerged alive thanks to the intercession of Adolphe Crémieux, president of the Alliance Israélite Universelle.[104]

5. THE REIGN OF ALEXANDER II, 1855–1881

The defeat of Russia's serf army by Europe's free and technologically better equipped troops in the Crimean War (October 1853–February 1856) impelled Alexander II to emancipate the serfs in 1861 and address other related problems, including the Jewish and Polish ones. Thus, whereas Nicholas made the gradual removal of administrative limits conditional on Jewish inner reform and progress in the spheres of industry and education, Alexander commenced with rapid removal of external limits without making them conditional on Jewish abandonment of self-segregation. The continuity in their aims, however, is evidenced by the fact that it was Count Kiselyov, chair of the committee established by Nicholas I in 1840 to advise on transforming Jewish life, who identified for Alexander the eleven problems that undermined Nicholas's merger policies and who was appointed by Alexander, one day after his Coronation Manifesto of March 30, 1856, to chair the committee to propose solutions.[105]

5.1. Prodded further by a delegation of influential Jewish merchants, led by the liquor purveyor and banker Baron Joseph Evzel Gintsburg, the committee set out to forge the Jewish equivalent of the peasant emancipation decree, but its work was impeded when Kiselyov was replaced by Count Dmitry Blyudov, who insisted on making the harmonization of Jewish civil rights with the rest of the population dependent on progress in Jewry's openness to enlightenment.[106] Consequently, the decree issued in 1865 harmonized Jewish military conscription with that of other minorities, ending thereby the drafting of juvenile Jews, granted Jewish soldiers who completed their term of service and their descendants the right to settle outside the Pale, and extended civil and economic rights to assimilated ("useful") Jews, ratifying thereby the 1859 permission to Jewish merchants, artisans, craftsmen, builders, mechanics, distillers, doctors, and university students to reside outside the Pale.[107] The decree led to the rapid increase of Jewish interest in pursuing higher education, and by 1881 Jews constituted 9 percent of Russia's university students; in 1887, the number rose to 13.5 percent.[108]

5.2. These reforms allowed Jews to transfer capital from the liquor trade into many industries, especially railroad building, spearheaded by the railway magnate Samuel Solomonovich Poliakov. This involvement contributed to the railway boom of the 1860s and 1870s and together with the burgeoning of shipping and postal services resolved the problem of smuggling on the western border. In 1864 two other significant reforms, the Judicial Regulations and the Zemstvo Organizations Statute, providing for local self-government by elective assemblies, were passed without discrimination against Jews. In his memoirs, the Menshevik leader Leo Deutsch recalls the time as one when he felt no restrictions vis-à-vis freedoms enjoyed by his Christian friends, as compared to those he experienced under the subsequent tsars.[109]

5.3. The early 1860s were also years of Polish insurrection. As Jews joined Polish protests in Warsaw in 1861, Alexander II attempted to win their loyalty by revoking in 1862 numerous restrictions that had been imposed on them since the partition of Poland. The policy succeeded; the Jews did not in the end join the Polish revolt of 1863 and thus escaped the fury with which Russia crushed the revolt but not the long-term russification of the Pale through which Russia sought to punish and weaken the Poles, and in the process the Jews as well, by transferring their lands to Russian peasant communities, the *mir* or *obshhina*. This measure, in turn, robbed individual peasants of legal title to the land and exacerbated their tensions with landowning and upwardly mobile Jews.[110] It is no coincidence then that the tsar decided in 1866 to stop encouraging Jews to go into agriculture and instead pursue crafts and trade, whereby their involvement in the bread and timber export business helped the peasants market their products and led to the creation of a wealthy Jewish bourgeoisie.[111]

5.4. These years witnessed the founding of the Society for the Promotion of Jewish Enlightenment, or OPE, by a group of Jewish merchants, financiers, and intellectuals to advance Jewish political emancipation and cultural assimilation and function as the chief negotiator and intercessor (*shtadlan*) with the government in the cause of russification. Approved in December 1863 in response to the petition by Baron Evzel Gintsburg and Abram Markovich Brodsky, a sugar beet magnate and banker, the organization began operation officially in St. Petersburg in 1866 and in Odessa in 1867.[112] In its first decade, it included Jewish members of the intelligentsia such as Leon M. Rosenthal and Rabbi Abram Isaiah Neuman, prominent officials in the Ministry of Education, and specialists on Jewish life, including the converts Prof. Daniel A. Khvolson and the court physician Joseph V. Berthenson.[113]

6. The Publicists of Alexander's Reign and the Rise of Occult Judeophobia

The advance in Jewish intellectual life, coupled with the easing of press censorship, led to public discussion of the Jewish problem. The issue was first broached in 1858 on the pages of the *Odesskij vestnik* (Odessa Herald) by Osip A. Rabinovich, who called on Jews to enter civic life and defended Judaism's commitment to virtue and love of neighbor. The ensuing discussions led to the creation of the first Jewish Russian paper, *Rassvet* (Dawn), first printed on May 27, 1860, which, renamed *Sion* in 1862 after a new Jewish paper in St. Petersburg adopted the name *Rassvet*, committed itself to clarifying what could and could not be abandoned in Jewish tradition and how Jews could remain sons of Russia while retaining their Jewish identity.[114]

6.1. The Jewish press in the 1860s comprised Hebrew- and Yiddish-language periodicals that promoted the Haskalah, as well as Russian publications that called on the Jewish and Russian intelligentsia to defend Judaism and advocate Jewish civil rights. The Hebrew weeklies included *ha-Karmel* (the Carmel) in Vilna and *ha-Melitz* (the Interpreter) in Odessa, both founded in 1860, as well as *ha-Shahar* (the Dawn), founded by Peretz Smolenskin in 1869. Three Hebrew papers were founded in St. Petersburg, the aforementioned *Rassvet*, founded by Osip (Joseph) Rabinovich with the collaboration of Lev O. Levanda; *Russkij evrej* (Russian Jew); and *Voskhod* (Sunrise). Others included *Sion*, edited by Solovaychik and Leon Pinsker, *Den'* (Day), and the Yiddish pro-Haskalah paper, *Kol Mevaser* (Voice of the Herald [of Good Tidings]).[115]

6.2. On the Russian Christian side, discussion of the Jewish problem had been confined, for the first half of the nineteenth century, to bureaucratic circles. The few books and journals that spoke of Jews' "fanaticism" and "exploitation" were either foreign-language publications originating abroad or specialist publications. Russian publicists began to focus on the issue in 1858 when a St. Petersburg newspaper closely linked to the Russian Orthodox Church began polemicizing against the rise of Jews in British and French politics and objected to the decree of November 27, 1861, offering Jews with advanced academic degrees residence rights and admission to civil service. The debate was largely shaped by the Slavophile publicist Ivan Sergeevich Aksakov (1823–86) in his newspaper, *Den'*. Aksakov argued that Jews, as aliens admitted into the country out of Christian charity, deserved civil rights for their economic talents but not political rights; Christians should retain superior posts in government and politics. His arguments for religious intolerance were answered by the liberal economist Boris Chicherin and Pyotr K. Shhebalsky in the pages of *Nashe vremya* (Our Time) in November 1861 and perhaps pseudonomously by Fyodor Dostoevsky in the same newspaper in February 1862; by Mikhail Katkov, editor of *Moskovskie vedomosti* (Moscow News) in March 1862; and by the editor of *Sion*. The Christian papers objected to Aksakov's claim that Christianity, which hinged on love, could only either tolerate or repress and persecute Jews.[116] Aksakov responded by publishing "[M.] A. Aleksandrov's" article claiming that no Jew who adhered to the Talmud and its antisocial dictates could be a good citizen. This article finally introduced Russia to the 1831 French translation of the Talmud by the Italian professor of Oriental languages and antiquities at the University of Warsaw, Luigi A. Chiarini. Chiarini's translation of the Talmud, commissioned by Nicholas I, as well as his 1830 *Théorie du Judaïsme*, became the basis of Russian anti-Talmudic and anti-Jewish polemics for the remainder of the century.[117]

6.3. In 1867 Aksakov received financial assistance from Moscow's merchants to found *Moskva*, which criticized the government's russification policies in the Pale and printed four significant articles on the Jewish question, two by Aksakov. These popularized the motif of "Jewish privilege," criticized the Jews for constituting a *status in statu*, and argued for the need not to emancipate the Jews from Russia but to emancipate Russians from the Jews. The starting point of the argument was the staging of a demonstration by Jews outside the Staryj Pochaev monastery to prevent the baptism of a young Jewess, echoed by another attack on a Jew seeking baptism, reported by the *Vilenskii vestnik* (Vilna Herald) in 1867. Aksakov's argument, published in July 1867, was reprinted in Kiev's principal paper, the *Kievlyanin* (Kievan). Aksakov went on to claim in 1869 that a local rabbi incited a Jewish crowd to murder a would-be convert.[118]

The editor of the *Kievlyanin*, Vitaly Yakovlevich Shulgin, supported government initiatives to integrate Jews through education but criticized the government for failing to make the granting of external rights dependent on reciprocal inner changes of attitude, the lack of which demanded economic and political discrimination such as not allowing Jews to purchase farmland. Shulgin's positions crystallized in debates with the Jewish Odessan publicist Mikhail (Menashe) Morgulis, then a law student, who argued that, as russification was impeded by the refusal of the emancipated peasants to work for Polish landowners, the problem could be resolved by letting Jews, whose loyalty to Russia had been proven in 1863, purchase or rent land from the Poles, who would then ease the peasants into agriculture. Shulgin responded by declaring the Jews infinitely worse than the brother Poles for their strategic alien and anti-Christian commitment to the ruination of Russians by drink.[119]

6.4. Moscow's and St. Petersburg's principal papers, *Moskovskie vedomosti* and *Sanktpeterburgksie vedomosti* (St. Petersburg News), frequently at odds with each other, both advocated leniency for the Jews.

Before 1863 the editor of *Moskovskie vedomosti*, Mikhail N. Katkov, regularly advocated resistance to Polish separatism through russification and also commented on the Jewish question but connected the two issues first in 1864 when he lamented that Jews, having been denied the right to use Russian in their liturgy, were imitating the Poles by turning to German. The campaign proved successful; on December 25, 1870, all religions were given permission to use Russian in their liturgies. Katkov linked the Jewish problem to that of russification in the Pale again in 1865. Observing that the Pale's emancipated serfs were socially hampered by the concentrated, mutually supportive, and economically advanced Jewish population, he advocated extending the law of November 27, 1861, which permitted educated Jews to live throughout the empire, to all who had the potential to become useful citizens, to accomplish which Russia had to abandon her negative stereotypes of the Jews that had been inherited from Poland. Katkov campaigned against the alleged abuses of the *kahal* and against "Jewish privilege" but, according to Klier, always retained confidence in the good intentions and ultimate success of the Russian Jewish intelligentsia, trusting them to enlighten the Jews and lead them to benefit Russia economically.[120]

6.5. Similarly, the liberal *Sanktpeterburgskie vedomosti*, edited by V. F. Korsh, admitted that Jews could be criticized for isolationism, religious fanaticism, and preoccupation with expanded rights but argued that they had been fundamentally corrupted by Polish domination and, despite stereotypes, were not exploiters but industry-loving people, willing to dirty their hands in trade and, unlike the Polish nobility, conservative and unquestionably loyal to the government. The Jewish problem could be solved, according to Korsh, by equating russification with the abolition of the Pale of Settlement and extending civil rights to the Jews. However, when Lev Levanda invoked this argument in the *Vilenskij vestnik* in 1866, it provoked a torrent of Judeophobic responses that declared Jews were an alien, self-interested race whose domination in the region had to be destroyed.[121]

6.6. Invariably, the period witnessed the emergence of movements that sought to offer solutions to the Jewish problem different from those offered by traditional Jewish authorities, the rabbinate, the Hasidim,

and the *kahals*, thereby seriously fragmenting Jewry. These movements included the emergence of Jewish nationalism and Zionism, as
illustrated by the novels of Peretz Smolenskin (1842–85), and Moses
Leib Lilienblum (1843–1910), the most radical exponent of the Haskalah.[122] As Jewish college youth assimilated Darwin, Buckle, Pisarev,
and Chernyshevsky, some were also drawn to revolutionary, populist,
and Marxist politics, as illustrated by the emergence of the League of
Jewish Socialists in 1876 and by a spate of Jewish socialist magazines
founded abroad but whose issues were initially admitted into Russia:
ha-Emet (the Truth), founded in 1877, and *Asefat Hakamim* (Assembly of Wise Men), founded in 1878 and published as a supplement
to *ha-Kol*.[123]

6.7. Both the tsarist regime and the Slavophile press kept a wary eye
on Jewish progress, interest in assimilation, and revolutionary involve-
ments, as illustrated by their interest in Yakov (Jacob) Aleksandrovich
Brafman's *Book of the Kahal*. Brafman was a Jew who had become embittered against the *kahal* agents in the last years of Nicholas's conscription, deserted Judaism, converted to Christianity, and, in order to
wreak vengeance on the *kahal*, presented himself to Alexander II in
1858 as a detective and a spy. Appointed instructor of Hebrew at a
seminary in Minsk, he moved in 1866 to Vilna to assume the post of
Jewish censor, in which post he contended that the *kahal*, though abolished in 1844, continued to exist as a secret organization, controlling
the world's Jews by Talmudic fanaticism and Hasidic obscurantism
and seeking to exploit the world's economy under the guise of religious organizations and charities, such as Russia's OPE and the Alliance Israélite Universelle, founded in 1860 by Crémieux.[124] In response,
the governor-general of Lithuania convened a commission in 1866 to
investigate the charges that Brafman published serially in *Vilenskij
vestnik* and collected in the *Book of the Kahal* (*Kniga Kahal*), published in 1869. Printed at public expense and sent to all government offices to guide Russian officials in dealing with Jewry, it became the
most successful and influential Judeophobic work in Russian history,
making Brafman the grandfather of all save the occult elements of the
Protocols of the Elders of Zion (1903, 1905).[125] Shulgin's *Kievlyanin* reviewed the book in two lengthy articles and presented it as the key to

understanding Jewry's sins. Stressing that *Rassvet*, *Sion*, and *Den'* must have known about the *kahal*'s abuses, the reviews argued that they failed to report them because they, along with the OPE, were its agents.

6.8. The reports by *Vilenskij vestnik*, *Kievlyanin*, and Aksakov on "Jewish privilege" exerting force to prevent conversion or murder would-be converts in the closing years of the 1860s, coupled with Brafman's "exposure" of the *kahal*, prompted the transference of such charges from obscure individual fanatics to an organized, illegal Jewish community, as illustrated by many press reports in the 1870s about the *kahal* murdering people who resisted its monopoly. This transference helped justify attacks on the Jewish community as a whole, as can be seen in *Kievlyanin*'s justification of the Odessa pogrom of March 1871. The formerly Judeophilic *Sanktpeterburgskie vedomosti*, Russia's oldest newspaper, after a two-month silence on the pogrom, defected to this position when it announced on May 11 the need to reexamine the pogrom and declared that theoretical considerations must yield to the recognition that the Jews are a harmful element that must not be tolerated in the Pale. The liberal press, represented by the journal *Golos*, followed suit by inviting Brafman in 1874 to function as a regular contributor. This process of reflection and reappraisal prefigured the crisis that followed the pogroms of 1881–82.[126]

6.9. The transference of charges of Jewish anti-Christian violence from individuals to the community also paved the way to occult forms of European Judeophobia, which synthesized the idea that Jewish fanaticism was centered on and fed by the Talmud and the idea that its hostility to Christianity was organized and part of a world conspiracy. The forerunner in Russia for this idea, originating in Europe, was the printing in 1872 of a short document titled "The Rabbi's Speech," which was in fact a chapter titled "The Jewish Cemetery in Prague" taken from the novel *Biarritz* by Hermann Goedsche, which was published in Berlin in 1868 under the pseudonym "Sir John Retcliffe." Its hero spies on the centennial meeting of representatives of the Twelve Tribes of Israel held to report their success in undermining Christianity. Its reprinting in 1873 in Polish linked it to Brafman's *Book of the Kahal* by treating the event as factual, at which point Ippolit

Lyutostansky, an unfrocked Catholic priest who joined the Holy Trinity Monastery in Moscow, integrated it into his *Evrei v Rossii* (Jews in Russia). It was regarded as evidence of the Jewish world conspiracy by reviewers for *Sanktpeterburgskie vedomosti* and *Novoe vremya*. Russian reviewers were less impressed, however, with the other foreign Jewish conspiracy text of the time, *The Conquest of the World by the Jews*, by "Major Osman-Bei,"[127] which described the Jewish master plan to dominate the world by unifying its markets and acquiring all of its wealth. The last two pages of the work identified the agency that coordinated this activity with the Alliance Israélite Universelle.[128] Russian reviewers for *Delo*, *Kievlyanin*, and the *Odesskij vestnik* (Odessa Herald) dismissed the premises and the reference to the Alliance. Brafman, however, did not. By citing the Alliance's interventions to help "persecuted Jews" throughout the world, he developed from 1874 on, in the pages of *Golos*, the position that the Alliance was actively working to dominate the Christian Russian state through the OPE. *Golos*'s lead was followed in 1878 by Prince N. N. Golitsyn, former editor of *Varshavskij dnevnik* (Warsaw Diary), and in 1881 by a revised version of *The Book of the Kahal*, with "the protocols."[129] On November 1, 1883, Aksakov's *Rus'* published a purported, world conquest–aspiring manifesto of Adolphe Crémieux, founder of the Universal Israelite Alliance, and issued the call for the Russian government to close the Alliance's "local branch," the OPE.[130] Responding to the Jewish outcry that he had published a forgery, Aksakov inquired why, if the claims were false, Jews had not sued the French newspaper, *L'Antisémitique*, that originally printed it, and ventured the answer that it was because everything in the manifesto, point by point, was true, for example, that Jews were internationally united by religion, considered themselves the "chosen people," and lacked affinity with the Christian ideal of equality and brotherhood in Christ.[131] When Isidore Loeb, secretary of the Alliance, formally appealed to Aksakov's honesty to retract the slander, Aksakov printed Loeb's letter but called the denial of the Manifesto's authenticity irrelevant on the grounds that the document "authentically expressed Jewish views and aspirations."[132] Other prominent newspapers that reprinted the Crémieux Manifesto, *Novoe vremya* and *Sanktpeterburgskie vedomosti*, followed similar lines of defense, thereby implicitly establishing Aksakov as Russia's "leading intellectual Judeophobe."[133]

7. Antisemitic Ultraconservative Trends
of the 1870s

In 1870 the Russian regime signaled its increasing caution regarding Jewish assimilation by restricting Jewish membership in municipal councils and prohibiting Jews from becoming mayors. In 1871 it established the Commission for the Amelioration of the Condition of the Jews to investigate ways of weakening Jewish communal cohesion and separateness.[134] That year also witnessed the outbreak of a pogrom in Odessa, incited by Greek merchants who, seeking to weaken Jewish competition in the grain trade, spread rumors of Jewish violence against a local church. Riots ensued, fed by charges of Jewish separatism and economic exploitation. The commission, guided by Brafman's work, recommended wiping out all vestiges of Jewish self-government, communities, schools, and relief societies. Given the paucity of objections to Brafman's data and arguments on the commission, its recommendations dampened Jewish reform legislation in the last decade of Alexander II's reign. Consequently, the establishment of general military service in 1874, while relieving the Jews, did not harmonize their civil rights with those enjoyed by other ethnic constituencies.[135]

7.1. The antisemitic trend also expressed itself in a new Jewish ritual murder blood libel trial in the Caucasus, eventually resolved in 1879 with the acquittal of the accused. The trial was much publicized from 1875 on by the editor of the Moscow daily *Sovremennye izvestiya* (Contemporary News), N. P. Giliarov-Platonov, a theologically trained censor for the Ministry of Education who was close to Slavophile circles and the Aksakov family. The charge that Jews use the blood of Christian children for ritual purposes was publicized further through Lyutostansky's pamphlet *On the Use of Christian Blood by the Jews* (1876), which originated as a dissertation for Moscow's Ecclesiastical Academy. Rewarded financially for the work by order of the crown prince and future Alexander III, he produced another similarly libelous

work titled *The Talmud and the Jews* (1879–80). The convert Daniel
Khvolson, then professor at the Greek Orthodox Ecclesiastical Seminary of St. Petersburg, refuted the libel but was, in turn, attacked by
many periodicals, including the heretofore liberal paper *Novoe vremya*
(New Time), signaling the paper's turn toward a systematic antisemitic
campaign.[136]

7.2. The rise of revolutionary nihilism in the 1860s and 1870s, interpreted by conservatives as a symptom of the evils of Russian Western-
ism, drove conservatism toward antielitism, nationalism, and xeno-
phobia. Klier credits Solovyov for diagnosing its connection with
chauvinism and Judeophobia: "The worship of one's own people as the
preeminent bearer of universal truth; then the worship of this people
as an elemental force, irrespective of universal truth; finally the worship of those national limitations and anomalies which separate the
people from civilized mankind, that is, the worship of one's own
people with a direct negation of the very idea of universal truth."[137]

7.3. Analysis of these developments inevitably highlights the similarities between Jewish and Russian solidarity and messianism and
raises the question whether rivalry between them would make the
latter Judeophobic on the premise that by denying Christ the Jews denied their own tradition. This premise was put forward by A. S. Kho-
myakov, founder of Slavophilism, but in relatively theoretical form
that did not represent the Jews as a social problem. His ideas may have
been given antisemitic force in the second generation of Slavophile
thought via Aksakov, but Aksakov's antisemitism may also have been
nurtured by the Pan-Slavic phase of his career.[138]

7.4. Pan-Slavism, in contrast to philosophizing Slavophilism, was an
ideology of action and politics, chiefly promulgated by Nikolai Yakovlevich Danilevsky. His *Russia and Europe* (1869) proposed that peoples
had national, historico-cultural peculiarities, capable of organic development, and that the Slavic peoples were in the process of forging history's eleventh civilization thanks to their multifaceted, all-assimilating,
universal humanity that distinguished them from mono-elemental
peoples like the Jews whose genius lay in "vital religious consciousness" but lacked any impulse to join any specific political group. The

work had enormous significance, as attested by Dostoevsky's praise of it as the "future coffee-table book of every Russian."[139] Even though Danilevsky concluded on this count that the Slavs were heirs to the status of chosen people, he was little interested in the Jewish question. Nonetheless, Russian Pan-Slavism peaked during the years of the Eastern Crisis of 1875–79, which, as explained above, witnessed growing conservative Judeophobia, fed by the representation of Jews as exploiters and destroyers of the old agrarian system and by obsession with ritual murder accusations and occult world domination conspiracy theories.

7.5. Klier attributes the integration of these fears to four sets of events. The first was the status of the Balkan Slavs, whom Pan-Slavs such as Katkov and Aksakov wanted Russia to liberate in the Russo-Turkish War of 1877–78. Complaints about Jewish draft evasion at the time led Russia to tighten its recruitment procedures for them, but these complaints were exacerbated by the failure and malfeasance in supply lines that Jewish companies operated. The complaints also coincided with the fact that Britain, Russia's chief European opponent in the war, was deemed by Aksakov and others to have sided with Turkey because its prime minister was Benjamin Disraeli, a Jew who wanted to see the Gospel subjugated to the Koran. The war led to the Congress and then to the Treaty of Berlin that divided Bulgaria into three states, ceding Macedonia back to the Turks and so undoing Russian plans for an independent and Russophile "Greater Bulgaria."[140]

7.6. The three remaining factors contributing to the rise of ultraconservative Judeophobia were the flood of Jews into Russian public education, the emergence of nihilism, and the rise of articulate antisemitism in Europe, especially Germany. Solzhenitsyn observes that the increase of Jews in educational institutions from 1874 on was so rapid as to prompt calls for limits on their admission. The problem was highlighted in 1875 when the OPE indicated to the government that room could no longer be found for Jews without hampering the Russian population. At the same time, Russia's secular universities were also the principal locales where Jews discovered revolutionary ideals and joined revolutionary movements. Three Jews were convicted in 1877 for participation in the revolutionary demonstration at the Church of Our Lady of Kazan on December 6, 1876, and one was executed for terrorism on February 20, 1880. Despite the small number of Jews charged with state crimes (4 percent, compared to 74 percent for Orthodox Russians and 15 percent for Catholics), Dostoevsky attributed their activities to Karl Marx and shared his "discovery" with the editor of the reactionary newspaper *Grazhdanin* (the Citizen). The identification of Jews with nihilism then spread to other conservative newspapers, from minor papers such as *Sovremennye izvestiya* (Contemporary News) and *Russkij mir* (Russian World) in 1879 to one of the most influential, *Novoe vremya* (New Time), the highest-circulation conservative publication in St. Petersburg, in March 1880.[141]

7.7. Dostoevsky's antisemitism had an influence on his friends, including Pobedonostsev, former tutor of the young Alexander III who became chief procurator of the Russian Orthodox Church (1880–95). Pobedonostsev's antisemitism became apparent in 1876 when he recommended that Tsarevich Alexander read Prince N. N. Golitsyn's works on the Jews, explaining that it was "very important" to reform them. Golitsyn's works included a confused, verdict-less study of the blood libel charge based on the works of Lyutostansky.[142] At that time, Pobedonostsev's manner of reference to Jews also became pejorative, shifting from *evrej* to *zhid* (Yid). Significantly, Pobedonostsev regularly followed Dostoevsky's lead in seeing Jews as having pernicious revolutionary influence, as evidenced by his immediate response to Dostoevsky's letter of September 21, 1879:

> What you write about the Yids is quite correct. They fill everything up, they undermine everything, and the spirit of the century is identical to them. They are at the root of the revolutionary-social movement and regicide. They control the periodical press, the financial markets are in their hands, the popular masses fall into financial slavery to them, they guide the principles of present-day science, seeking to place it outside Christianity. And besides this, hardly does any question about them come up when there goes up a chorus of voices for the Jews in the name of some sort of civilization or toleration (that is, indifference to faith).

Given these views, Rogger judges that Pobedonostsev was the most articulate antisemite in the government until his retirement in 1905. Rogger writes that fifteen years before this letter to Dostoevsky, in 1864, he wrote to Ivan Aksakov's wife confessing how disgusted he and his associates were with Alexander II's reforms.[143]

Calling this escalating written Judeophobia a "silent pogrom," Nathans judges that its bombshell came in 1880 with the publication of an anonymous letter to the editor of *Novoe vremya* under the headline, "The Kike Is Coming!" (Zhid idet!). Demonstrating that Jews had achieved a presence in educational institutions far greater than that in the population as a whole, the author postulated that in a decade or so Jews would squeeze out poor Russians from education and come to dominate all professions, both material and intellectual. Becoming the most influential Judeophobic statement between Brafman's *Book of the Kahal* and the *Protocols of the Elders of Zion* (1905), it crystallized concerns about Jewish presence in Russian institutions and unleashed a stream of likeminded articles and letters, especially in the Pale.[144]

8. The Reign of Alexander III and the Pogroms

The assassination of Alexander II on March 13 (March 1, o.s.), 1881, shook the nation. For ultraconservatives, it proved the failure of Alexander II's liberal policies.[145] This is shown by the swing away from these policies directed by Pobedonostsev, procurator of the church and adviser to the new tsar; Vyacheslav Konstantinovich von Plehve (1846–1904), director of police and minister of the interior; and the chief ultraconservative Pan-Slavist and Slavophile papers.

8.1. The social explosion that, as Solzhenitsyn observes, Narodnaya volya (People's Will), the terrorist group that carried out the murder, expected to produce did take place in the form of pogroms. The first pogrom, which occurred on April 15 in Elisavetgrad, was put down by forces shooting at the crowds. According to the most common account, it was sparked when a Christian simpleton was evicted from a Jewish tavern for breaking a glass and a crowd of Christians yelled that Christians were being beaten. A unique, elsewhere unrepeated account, with names attached, holds that tradesmen found glass jars near a market stall that held human anatomical remains (subsequently found to have been marked for medical examination) and, suspecting ritual murder, spread a rumor that resulted in the pogrom.[146] On April 23 the violence spread to Kiev, where it raged unabated for three days before being put down, then reignited on April 26 and spread to as many as fifty neighboring places and farther abroad in the Pale, including the provinces of Kherson, Taurida, Poltava, Chernigove, and Odessa. The violence then spread to other large Jewish communities, including Warsaw, and raged for the next two years.

8.2. A Jewish woman, Gesia (Jesse) Gelfman, was found to be involved in the plot but only indirectly by way of having furnished the regicides with a residence.[147] Nonetheless, the image of the Jewish regicide, popularized by Dostoevsky since 1878, became a reality in the minds of editors of officially influential conservative journals such as *Novoye vremya*, *Vilenskij vestnik*, and *Kievlyanin*, who insinuated that Jews played a role in the assassination. Klier repeatedly exculpates Mikhail Katkov and his *Moskovskie vedomosti* from purveying such Judeophobia, highlighting his interest in seeking socialist-revolutionary involvement in the violence.[148]

8.3. The Pale's papers, such as Odessa's *Novorossijskij telegraf* (Novorossiysk Telegraph), began to publish rumors about proposed organized attacks on the Jews.[149] These rumors, Dubnov asserts, were followed, first, by visits to the Pale's highest police officials by "mysterious emissaries" from St. Petersburg who warned the former not to obstruct any forthcoming "outbursts of popular indignation against the Jews" and, next, by the appearance of tradesmen and laborers at railroad stations issuing a tsar-sanctioned call on the people to punish the Jews at Easter. If the central authorities did not instigate the pogroms, Dubnov argued, they proved, in the short term, indulgent with local officials who were either indolent or criminally negligent; failed, in the intermediate term, to compensate the victims adequately; and, in the end, victimized them further by construing the pogroms as just comeuppance for the Jews' exploitation. Given this constellation of phenomena, Dubnov concluded that the pogroms were organized, instigated, and spread by state agencies; directed by highly placed individuals, Count Nikolai Pavlovich Ignatiev, K. P. Pobedonostsev, and von Plehve, who "welcomed these riots as lessons taught to impudent Jews and radicals"; and carried out by organizations such as the Holy Company and the Union of Russian People and others "lower down the hierarchical ladder who were less than zealous to stop them, the police and other officials." Rogger records the cadet Pavel N. Milyukov telling a New York audience in 1908 his theory that von Plehve disseminated this view "to divert the Russian people's anger against liberal and radical movements directed by Jews and foreigners."[150]

8.4. This analysis helped entrench the conspiracy theory as a century-long scholarly consensus. Recent historians, however, are held to have conclusively disproved this theory as a myth[151] catalyzed by Jewish panic and the belief at the time that the government could turn the pogroms on and off like a faucet,[152] a view that Solzhenitsyn, unaware of this revisionist historiography, attributes to Leo Tolstoy, noting that even he thought it evident at the time that "all is in the hands of the government—if they want, they'll call a pogrom, if they don't there won't be any pogrom."[153] Solzhenitsyn, noting that Dubnov and his colleagues pored over all post-1917 state archives to substantiate his view but only found evidence arguing the opposite, namely, that Alexander III demanded energetic investigation of the pogroms, denounces as slander the unsubstantiated report that the tsar somewhere said to someone that he "personally [was] gladdened to hear that the Jews [were being] beaten." Dismissing the tsarist conspiracy theory, Solzhenitsyn directs his focus to pursuing a number of other theories, including that of Katkov, held temporarily by the government, that the tradesmen and laborers who appeared at railroad stations with pogrom-sanctioning messages from the tsar were in fact members of the revolutionary movements Narodnaya volya and Chernyj peredel (Black Repartition).[154]

8.5. On May 5, 1881, on the recommendation of Pobedonostsev, the tsar replaced the liberal minister of the interior, Loris Melyukov, with the militant Pan-Slavist and renowned master of intrigue, "father of lies," Nicholas Pavlovich Ignatiev. The surprising nature of this recommendation, given Pobedonostsev's documented mistrust of Ignatiev, testifies to the uncertainty and fear that pervaded the government after the assassination of Alexander II. Ignatiev quickly issued circulars, on May 6 and 23, explaining the pogroms as the result of an anti-Jewish campaign engineered by revolutionary agitators who sought to expand the campaign into a movement against the mercantile and capitalist classes.[155] This view was expressed on May 4, 1881, by the tsar's brother, Grand Duke Vladimir Aleksandrovich, and on May 11, by the tsar himself to the first delegation of Russian Jewry led by Baron Horace Gintsburg.[156] The tsar declared that all Russian subjects were equal before him, assured the deputies that the Jews figured only as a pretext in the criminal disorder, and blamed the disorder on anarchists. This pacifying portion of the response was published in the press but not the additional portion in which the tsar told the deputies that the source of the hatred of the Jews lay in their economic "domination" and "exploitation" of Russians. The tsar's invitation to the deputies to challenge this view in a memorandum was promptly complied with in the form of a forty-two-page document penned by M. Morgulis. Rather than accept it, however, Ignatiev adopted the "domination" and "exploitation" theory explaining the pogroms as the result of popular peasant judgment and vengeance against the Jews. He elaborated this theory in his report to the tsar on August 22, stipulating that Jewish fanaticism and quest for domination and exploitation explained the failure of Alexander II's liberal measures to assimilate the Jews. Alternative solutions had to be investigated, he argued, with the help of provincial commissions.[157]

8.6. As the pogroms heated up in the summer of 1881, *Novoye vremya* formulated the Jewish question by paraphrasing Hamlet's *"byt' ili ne byt'"* (to be or not to be) as *"bit' ili ne bit'"* (to beat or not to beat), concluding that "to beat" was the right policy and one to be discharged by the government.[158] The editor of *Rus'*, Ivan Aksakov, contended that the pogroms were the fruit of Russia's righteous indignation and moral protest against Jewish economic domination and exploitation of her people and repeated his frequent contention that the question to pose should be not about the harmonization of Jewish rights with those of Christians but the reverse, which he eventually sought to prove by publishing a version of Brafman's *Book of the Kahal*, thereby directing Russian public opinion toward the theme of Jewish world conspiracy.[159]

8.7. The tsar responded to Ignatiev by authorizing gubernatorial commissions to discover the source of Jewish economic domination and exploitation and the ways in which these could be curbed. Baron Gintsburg visited Ignatiev in September 1881 with another delegation of Jewish notables but was spurned by Ignatiev's denial of the delegation's representative authority. The challenge would have stung, because, despite Gintsburg's constant aid to affected areas and his vigorous commitment to dueling with Ignatiev, many Jewish poor resented the Gintsburg circle for living in pogrom-free cities and judged them ineffective as intercessors. Nonetheless, the delegates secured approval to be represented on future commissions, establishing thereby their intercessory role.[160]

8.8. To assess the reports that would be coming from the commissions, the government appointed D. V. Gotovtsev on October 19 to preside over the new Central Committee for the Revision of the Jewish Question attached to the Ministry of the Interior. Gotovtsev put fourteen points before the commissions to guide their work, the most far-reaching program of its kind to originate in government circles and reach the stage of discussion and containing many disabling measures, including the closure of the OPE. Solzhenitsyn, while listing examples of loaded questions prepared by Gotovtsev to guide the commissions (e.g., "What economic activities of Jews are especially noxious to the root population of given localities?"), fails to note that many followed Aksakov's call to use Brafman's work as a guide. As a result, all commissions alluded in their answers to the *kahal*, and all, save eight, returned verdicts in the spirit of the framed "exploitation" and "domination" indictments. The eight argued that the tensions could be resolved by allowing the Jews to live throughout the empire. In December the pogroms reached Warsaw.[161]

8.9. In January 1882 Ignatiev authorized the Jewish weekly *Rassvet* to report that the government would not hamper Jewish emigration and, while keeping the Pale intact, would also look for thinly populated areas that Jews might colonize. The Jews protested this news on January 18 by holding a day of mourning and fasting in St. Petersburg and many other cities.[162] Supportive protests were soon held abroad, including one by Britain's elite at the Mansion House of London on February 1, on which occasion Cardinal Manning delivered a powerful speech defending the Jews as God's chosen and imperishable people, bound to Christians by their scriptures, and serving them as witness and warning. Gladstone's government, keen to preserve friendly relations with Russia, replied with sympathy to the resolutions but explained that no representations would be made to St. Petersburg so as not to incite further hostility against the Jews. By contrast, the United States lodged direct protests through diplomatic channels in April, May, and July 1882.[163]

8.10. The ineffectiveness of these appeals prompted Jews to think more seriously about the options of immigrating to America or Palestine, both of which were being advocated by intellectuals close to the people. The idea was opposed by the Gintsburg circle, which argued that, in addition to betokening disloyalty and abandonment of the struggle for emancipation, it was impractical since even if hundreds of thousands of Jews left hundreds of thousands would remain. A conference was organized in Balta to debate the issue, but before the delegates arrived, the *Imperial Messenger* announced that it would accurately report all "Jewish disorders," after which Balta was rocked, on the second day of the Russian Easter, March 29, by the biggest pogrom yet, abetted according to Dubnov by leaders of the local police, military, and nobility.[164]

8.11. In response, on April 8–20, 1882, Baron Gintsburg summoned the second assembly of twenty-five Jewish delegates to meet with Ignatiev. Among the delegates were the railroad magnate and financier Samuel Poliakov, Professor Bakst, Dr. Mandelstamm of Kiev, Rabbi Isaac Elhanan Spector of Kovno, and Rabbi Drabkin of St. Petersburg. Mandelstamm and Bakst attacked Ignatiev's proposal to resettle the Jews in Central Asia as deportation and classifying them as criminals. The delegates also refuted Brafman's accusations that Jews retained their autonomous *kahal* organization and were secretly planning to dominate and exploit Russia. They resolved to reject the option of emigration, inform the government about the authorities' passive attitude to the pogroms, petition the government to find means to compensate Jews for their losses, and request that the tsar abolish all discriminatory legislation against the Jews.[165]

9. THE MAY LAWS, COUNT D. A. TOLSTOY, THE PAHLEN COMMISSION, AND THE FORTY CLAUSES

Despite the April 1882 assembly and other efforts by the Gintsburg circle, the Central Committee on Jewish Affairs concluded from the gubernatorial commissions that the Jews must be regarded as aliens and removed from large areas of the Pale. Afraid of enacting the measures by due process through the Council of State, Ignatiev suggested to the Committee of Ministers that they be sanctioned by the tsar as temporary provisional rules. The ministers unanimously objected to the plan, many arguing that it would lead to mass violence against the Jews. The most vehement opposition was offered by the minister of finance, Nikolai Kh. Bunge; the committee's chairman and former minister of finance, Mikhail Kh. Reutern; the state comptroller, Dmitry M. Sol'sky; and the minister of justice, Dmitry N. Nabokov.[166] They dismissed the idea that the government's past conduct was weak or unprincipled, insisting that it was based on the national interest and the significant role played by the Jews in trade and industry. Nonetheless, as it was agreed that it was necessary to assure the Russian peasants of the tsar's desire to rid them of Jewish exploitation, a compromise was reached. The measures were restricted, and diluted, probably thanks to the intervention of the Gintsburg circle, to new Jewish village settlements and sanctioned as temporary laws by the tsar on May 3, 1882, on which day an edict promising prosecution of anti-Jewish violence was also issued. Concurrently, Pobedonostsev, having divined that Ignatiev was toying with the dangerous Slavophile idea of a popular constituent assembly of two thousand delegates—landowners, merchants, clergy, and some thousand peasants—to demonstrate the nation's unity, denounced him to the tsar, who dismissed the latter on May 30 from his post as minister of the interior, perhaps as a diplomatic maneuver to make him the scapegoat for the pogroms. Count Dmitry A. Tolstoy, a champion of autocracy and police power and an enemy of mob

violence, was appointed to replace Ignatiev and immediately issued an edict reiterating the intention to prosecute anti-Jewish violence.[167]
9.1. Tolstoy's edict precipitated a series of legal trials of the rioters and effectively restrained pogroms until the Kishinev massacre of 1903, with isolated exceptions such as Rostov-on-the-Don, May 10, 1882; Yekaterinoslav, July 20–21, 1883; and Nizhnij Novgorod, June 7, 1884.[168] There were also reports of pogroms in Kiev in 1885 and in Odessa in 1886.[169] At the same time, legal prosecutions of Jews on the basis of the newly established May Laws commenced. Solzhenitsyn judges that the harshest of these laws was the limitation on the village liquor trade, which was never carried out; the government had to decide whether to permit the Jewish liquor trade to continue and risk deepening peasant misery or to restrict the trade to just those Jews who were allowed to remain in the villages. The latter course, which entailed restrictions on landownership and industry and the forcible removal of many Jews (Solzhenitsyn disputes that the number was up to one million) from villages and towns to the Pale's cities, was seen to be so punitive as to cause massive disillusionment with the status quo, a prod for emigration, and popular repudiation of the notables who rejected it. Solzhenitsyn disputes that this marked a watershed period for Jewish emigration, arguing that it began with the work of the Alliance in 1869, increased after the pogroms of 1881, and became significant only from the mid-1890s. He fails to observe, however, that it was at this moment that new political visions for emigration arose: auto-emancipation, national liberation, Zionism, and religious reform, including the proposals of Joseph Rabinovich to fuse Judaism with Christianity via the Congregation of New Testament Israelites in Kishinev in 1884–85.[170]
9.2. Dubnov claims that in the summer of 1882 no Russian intellectual, neither Turgenev nor Tolstoy, rose in defense of the Jews, save the satirist Mikhail Saltykov-Shhedrin (1826–89). But he both forgets Solovyov and highlights his significance. Solzhenitsyn also points to Saltykov-Shhedrin's support of the Jews, quoting at length his 1882 essay, "Iyul'skoe veyanie" (The Spirit of July), which castigated the inhumanity and insanity of the stigmatization and scapegoating of the Jewish people as a whole (as deicides and exploiters).[171] In surveying

other modern estimates of the failure of the progressive and liberal or-gans of the time to express solidarity with the Jews, Solzhenitsyn finds one additional figure, the novelist Daniil Lukich Mordovtsev (1830–1905), who wrote the "Letter of a Christian on the Jewish Question" in *Rassvet*, pessimistically calling on Jews to immigrate to America, as if this were the only viable option.[172]

9.3. For Rogger, the "evidence on the government's use, encourage-ment, or toleration of pogroms" remains contradictory largely because the antirevolutionary ends of pogroms and pogrom agitation could be turned against its instigators. The most convincing evidence that Alex-ander III disapproved of them is his surprise on learning of them and his instructions to have them investigated. R. F. Byrnes, Pobedonost-sev's most recent biographer, while highlighting Pobedonostsev's anti-pathy toward Jews, thinks it unlikely that such a conservative figure would have "let racist demagogues instigate riots," especially after he denounced Ignatiev to the tsar in 1882. The proposal that secret orga-nizations such as the Holy Company (Svyashhennaya Druzhina), founded in 1881 to combat nihilism, instigated the pogroms is also dis-missed today, partly because its membership was conservative, op-posed to violence, and at least included Baron Horace Gintsburg, but also because the most detailed Zionist-inspired study of the possibility that the government was involved failed to illuminate a single fact to prove such complicity.[173] Consequently, Rogger draws several conclu-sions: that it is "certain that the pogroms were not arranged [by the government]"; that "they were not put down with requisite dis-patch . . . [while] some local officials encouraged the mobs"; that if von Plehve was involved, "he must have acted on his own"; and that the origin of these "disorders . . . still remains a mystery."[174]

9.4. To advance a more permanent, juridically customary approach to the Jewish problem the tsar formed, on February 4, 1883, the High Commission for the Revision of the Current Laws concerning the Jews, referred to as the Pahlen Commission, after its second chairman, Count Peter Alekseevich Pahlen, minister of justice in 1867–78 and member of the State Council. The commission, composed of fifteen to twenty members, was constituted by representatives of various ministries, including confirmed antisemites such as Princes Golytsin and Kantakuzen-Speransky, who carried Brafman's *Book of the Kahal* to the meetings; other expert advisers; liberal Russians; and seven Jews recommended by Gintsburg, Gintsburg himself, S. S. Poliakov, Jacob M. Halpern, M. Morgulis, N. I. Bakst, Rabbi A. Drabkin, and S. Dubnov. The Pahlen Commission took five years to work through the memoranda supplied by the gubernatorial and other commissions, plus the more than six hundred statutes pertaining to the Jews that had accumulated in Russian jurisprudence by 1885. In addition to discharging this task, the commission, following the tsar's coronation in May 1883, established quotas on admission of Jews to gymnasia and, in January 1884, managed to end the use of the May Laws to evict Jewish families from their homes but not to preserve Jewish rights to rent land.[175]

9.5. On December 5, 1886, the tsar ordered the minister of education, Ivan Davydovich Delianov, to limit Jewish access to secondary and higher education, for fear that it incited Jewish revolutionary ferment. The minister complied with this resolution in July 1887 by limiting Jews to 10 percent of the Christian population in the Pale, 5 percent outside the Pale, and 3 percent in Moscow and St. Petersburg. According to Solzhenitsyn, this process in fact began several years earlier in the Pale. Having thereby effectively closed the avenues to higher education to most Jews, the government laid plans to prevent Jewish soldiers who served outside the Pale from residing there after discharge and to restrict the admission of Jews to civil service and academic careers, limiting Jewish physicians and lawyers to private practice. Ironically, when the Pahlen Commission finally completed the first draft of its report at the beginning of 1888, after reviewing the arguments for discriminating against and repressing the Jews—"exclusiveness," "desire for domination," "revolutionary and anarchist sympathies," and so on—it attributed these behaviors to their miserable conditions and, blaming the latter on previous discriminatory legislation, recommended emancipation and the equalization of laws. At the end of 1888, the commission invited Horace Gintsburg and other Jewish notables to advise on issues such as internal Jewish organization. Nonetheless, the antisemitic minority blocked further progress of the report, perhaps for fear of the unknown, and Alexander III ignored its recommendations and dissolved the commission, leaving the May Laws intact.[176] The OPE, marginalized, was forced to reconsider its mission and turned its energies to the development of schools.[177]

9.6. In the spring of 1890 rumors abounded that Tolstoy and von Plehve had secretly written "forty clauses" to curtail Jewish commercial activity within the Pale and to restrict privileges conferred on others outside the Pale by creating ghettos. The London *Times* protested these antisemitic measures, and the British ambassador followed suit in August, but the Russian government denied their veracity, even though papers such as *Novoe vremya* and *Grazhdanin* continued to publish and recommend them. As tensions mounted, the government issued circulars commanding Jews to show respect to Russian officials and, in June 1890, reduced the area of the urban Pale so as to deprive Jews of the right to vote in the regional post 1864-reform self-government (*zemstvo*) elections. Vladimir Solovyov marshaled the Russian intelligentsia, including Leo Tolstoy and Vladimir Korolenko, to protest these measures in a formal letter. News of the Protest letter, however, was reported by the historian Dmitry I. Ilovajsky to the authorities, and all newspapers were prohibited from publishing it, as well as Solovyov's further attempts to address the matter in a book by his friend, Rabbi Getz. The initiative to defend Russian Jewry then moved abroad. London's aristocracy and two thousand citizens, including the Lord Mayor, Cardinal Manning, the duke of Westminster, and the bishop of Ripon, met in the Guildhall on December 10 to appeal to the tsar on behalf of Jewish civil rights, inciting the tsar to fury. The U.S. Congress, having expressed its solidarity with Russian Jewry on August 20, did so again on December 19, and on February 27, 1891, commissioned the secretary of state's ambassador in St. Petersburg to express its disapprobation and regret on the matter directly to the tsar.[178]

9.7. On March 29, 1891, the Russian government repealed the favorable residency laws of 1865, resulting in pogrom interludes in September and, ultimately, in the deportation of 700,000 Jews to the Pale, including 20,000 Jewish merchants and craftsmen from Moscow and 2,000 inhabitants of St. Petersburg. To prevent Jews from "hiding" in Russia's interior, Jewish use of Christian names was criminalized in

1893, and the establishment by the state of an alcohol monopoly in 1894 finally forbade the sale of liquor by Jews.[179]

9.8. Worsening repression led a group of rabbis in 1893–94 to ask for the assistance of Nikolai Bunge who, as minister of finance, had successfully opposed Ignatiev's schemes in 1882. Bunge's response to this petition is unknown, but he left a memoir in which he ranked the Jewish question as the second most significant for Russia, the most significant being assuring Russia's independence from foreign powers. Tracing the Jewish problem to the aftermath of the Polish partitions, he asked what in Judaism accounted for its evils. The answer he gave was that these evils came from the savage fanaticism and absurd election theology of the Talmud, which fed Jewry's commitment to be a state within a state, resistance to becoming Russians first, and desire for world domination. The cycle could be overcome, he opined, only by guarding the population from them and reforming them gradually, perhaps over centuries. The despair he felt about immediate solutions explains why he had not endorsed the Pahlen Commission's call for full if gradual legal equality.[180]

9.9. Bunge was succeeded as minister of finance in 1888 by I. A. Vyshnegradsky, who, with his colleague I. N. Durnovo, minister of the interior, helped to delay von Plehve's anti-Jewish legislation of 1890 and successfully protested in 1891 obstacles that Durnovo's subordinates were placing in the way of foreign Jews visiting Russia on business. Following the turmoil over the forty clauses and the withdrawal by the Paris Rothschilds in 1891 from a planned consolidation and conversion of Russia's foreign debt, Vyshnegradsky decided to acquaint the tsar with Russia's continued need of Jews and the financial difficulties the current limitations were bound to cause. The petition proved successful; von Plehve's project never reached the State Council. Nonetheless, Vyshnegradsky's victory led to rumors that he was in the pay of the Jews, and he was dismissed in 1892 as punishment for the harvest failure of 1891.[181]

9.10. His successor in 1892–93, Sergei Witte, approached the Jewish question in the spirit of the Pahlen Commission but gave priority to curtailing Jewish liquor traffic by imposing a state monopoly on the sale of alcoholic beverages.[182] Most famously, Witte records that he responded to Alexander III's question whether he was friendly to the Jews by saying that since all the Russian Jews could not be drowned in the Black Sea, there was no other way of dealing with them than to give them the same rights as all Russian subjects but gradually, although how gradually Witte did not specify. In narrating this response to Theodor Herzl in 1903, Witte explained that the principal complication derived from the fact that while the seven million Jews in Russia constituted 5 percent of the population, they accounted for 50 percent of the membership of revolutionary parties, for which he blamed the government for oppressing the Jews too much. His inability or unwillingness to contemplate anything but a piecemeal approach to the Jewish problem is illustrated by the discrepancy between his recollections of the meeting he held with the leaders of American Jewry in 1905 in Portsmouth, New Hampshire, where he stopped on his way to conducting peace negotiations with the Japanese, and the recollections of the Americans. While he reports success in driving a wedge between American Jewish bankers and the Japanese, their letter to him of September 5, 1905, reads in part:

> You have answered that the Russian Jew in general is not sufficiently prepared for the exercise of full civil rights, and that the feeling of the Russian people is such that the Jew cannot be placed on an equal footing with them without causing serious internal disorder. . . . As to this we aver that the million or more of Russian Jews who have come to the United States have become good citizens. . . . While it may be true that a state of envy against the Jews exists among part of the Russian people, for which the Russian government is to some extent responsible, still, in our opinion, placing the Jews at once on a footing of equality with the rest of the population would cause no more friction than each one of the steps leading to the same ultimate end.[183]

9.11. For many Jews, the pogroms of the 1880s proved the hopelessness of remaining in Russia and prompted recourse to radical measures. Tens of thousands emigrated, mainly to the United States, but many, taking the view of Ahad Ha'am (Asher Ginzberg) that the

Russian situation typified Jewish existence in the Diaspora, inferred the need to immigrate to Israel. Those who aspired to preserve Jewish identity by remaining in Russia had to choose between two practical alternatives. The first was to consolidate Jewish workers' societies into the League of Jewish Workingmen of Lithuania, Poland, and Russia (the Bund) and temporarily join the Russian Socialist Democratic Party (SDP). However, the SDP quickly refused to accept the Bund's claim for cultural-national autonomy, echoing, as did more radical groups such as Narodnaya volya, the declaration of the Decembrist leader Pavel Pestel that Jews, being unfit for membership in any social order, should either wholly assimilate or emigrate to form their own commonwealth in Asia Minor. This experience suggested that emigration, especially to Israel, was the only viable way of preserving the Bund's wish to synthesize socialism and national redemption. The second, secular alternative seemed to be that of abandoning Jewish identity altogether and immersing oneself in wider revolutionary activity. The popularity of this alternative explains why the Jewish presence in anarchist and revolutionary societies at the turn of the century exceeded 50 percent.

10. THE REIGN OF NICHOLAS II, 1894–1917

Nicholas II, who acceded to the throne in October 1894, effected no change of status or prospect for the Jews. Rogger notes that in the course of 1896–98, most of the privately owned taverns in the Pale were replaced by state liquor stores, depriving two hundred thousand Jews of their scanty livelihood.[184] The first decade of Nicholas II's reign proved relatively quiet for Jews. Nevertheless an "inner voice" led the new tsar to refuse to repeal earlier discriminatory legislation. In 1906, following the revolution of 1905, the pogroms resumed. The two most infamous manifestations of antisemitism reflective of Nicholas II's policy and the country's nationalist mood were the appearance in Russia of the *Protocols of the Elders of Zion* and the Beilis Affair.

10.1. Fabricated by Russian Judeophobes, the *Protocols of the Elders of Zion* is the most influential and notorious fake "proof" of the Jewish world conspiracy integrating the Judeophobic ideas articulated in Brafman's *Book of the Kahal* with the occult world conspiracy theses of Osman Bey's *The Conquest of the World by the Jews* and *L'Antisémitique*'s Crémieux Manifesto.[185] According to the research of De Michelis, published in 1998,[186] it was concocted in Russia between April 1902 and August 1903 and then edited in 1905 by Sergei Nilus (1862–1929), a devout Orthodox Christian, who published it for the first time as an appendix in his devotional book, *The Great in the Small and the Antichrist as an Imminent Political Possibility: Notes of an Orthodox Believer*.[187] According to the five years of research in previously inaccessible secret Russian archives by Mikhail Lepyohin, published in 1999, the *Protocols* was written by Matvei Golovinsky, a reactionary writer and journalist, in Paris, on the orders of Piotr Rachkovsky, head of the foreign branch of Ochrana, the tsarist secret police.[188] In developing the text, the author plagiarized the work of an opponent of Napoleon III, Maurice Joly, *Dialogue aux enfers entre Machiavel et Montesquieu* (Dialogue in Hell between Machiavelli and Montesquieu), published in Brussels in 1864, and the works cited above. The motive seems to have been to hinder the process of financial modernization initiated by Minister of Finance Witte, who attempted to introduce a gold standard system, thereby opening up the Russian market to international capital, a policy opposed by the aristocracy and landowning classes.[189] The *Protocols* circulated through private channels and was then translated and edited by Nilus in 1903. Its fourth edition was published on the eve of the Russian Revolution in January 1917 by the Holy Trinity Monastery at Sergiev Posad under the title, *"It is Near, Even at the Doors": Concerning That Which We Choose Not to Believe and Which Is So Near*.[190] This title suggests that the catalyst for Nilus's work was the growing expectation of the coming of the Antichrist in Russia and France. The expectation may be noted in the proliferation of late nineteenth-century Judeophobic smear literature produced primarily by the French political and clerical reaction to the belief that an alliance between the forces of Freemasonry and Jewry would bring the Antichrist to power.[191] In Russia, the expectation was fanned by the announcement of the Antichrist's birth by the famous starets Amvrosy (Grenkov) of Optina in 1882. Russian émigrés brought the work to Western Europe and the United States in the 1920s. Reviews in the *Times* and the *Spectator* initially accepted their authenticity.[192] A vast literature documents its role in fanning antisemitism and Judeophobia into the genocidal flame of the twentieth century.[193]

10.2. An early witness to Nilus's relationship with the *Protocols*, Golovinsky, and Rachkovsky was Alexandre du Chayla, an associate of Nilus who worked in 1913 as a journalist supporting the blood libel trial of Mendel Beilis in Kiev and calling on the "secret leaders of the Jewish nation to repent."[194] This trial, known as the Beilis Affair, involved the accusation of a Jewish Kievan factory worker, Mendel Beilis, of ritually murdering a boy, Andrei Yushhinsky. The boy was, in fact, killed by a criminal gang, but until Beilis's acquittal in 1913 the monarchist and nationalist press incessantly accused the Jews of killing Christian children in secret rituals and warned Russia that her existence was threatened by Jewish greed. The case scandalized the world, and many Russian intellectuals voiced positive feelings toward the Jews, contending that Russia stood much to gain, culturally and economically, from their talents. Nonetheless, publicists such as Vasily Rozanov and great theologians such as Pavel Florensky believed in Beilis's guilt.[195]

10.3. Outside the Pale, ignorance of the Jews' way of life prevented intellectuals and writers reputed for goodwill from answering prejudicial charges against them. Thus few Russian intellectuals took the initiative to defend them in the early 1880s. These exceptions were Saltykov-Shhedrin, Mordovtsev, Leskov, arguably Bishop Nikanor, and most famously Solovyov,[196] whose innovative arguments and self-sacrificing efforts on their behalf catalyzed future Russian Christian works in their defense.[197]

1. Sergei M. Solovyov (the younger), *Zhizn' i tvorcheskaya evolyutsiya Vladimira Solovyova* (Brussels: Zhizn' s Bogom, 1922–23). The edition used here was edited by I. G. Vishnevetsky (Moscow: Respublika, 1997), 179–82; see also Konstantin Mochulsky, *Vladimir Solovyov: Zhizn' i uchenie*, 2nd ed. (Paris: YMCA Press, 1951), ch. 5, 79–80. For further details, see Pt. II, ch. 6, below.

2. On his charismatic persona and relevance to the present work, see the firsthand accounts of Michael Aksionov Meerson, "The Life and Work of Father Alexandr Men'," in *Seeking God: The Recovery of Religious Identity in Orthodox Russia, Ukraine, and Georgia*, ed. Stephen K. Batalden (DeKalb: Northern Illinois University Press, 1993); and the memoir of my father, Yuri Glazov, *V krayu otsov: Khronika nedavnego proshlogo* (Moscow: Istina i zhizn', 1998), esp. 67–68, 164–65, 186–87, 194, 224. A rich account of the influence Men' had on Russian Jews is provided by Judith Deutsch Kornblatt, *Doubly Chosen: Jewish Identity, the Soviet Intelligentsia, and the Russian Orthodox Church* (Madison: University of Wisconsin Press, 2004), esp. ch. 3, 69–83; and "Is Father Alexander Men' a Saint? The Jews, the Intelligentsia, and the Russian Orthodox Church," *Toronto Slavic Quarterly* 47 (Winter 2014), www.utoronto.ca/tsq/12/kornblatt12.shtml. See also Wallace L. Daniel, "Father Aleksandr Men and the Struggle to Recover Russia's Heritage," *Demokratizatsiya* 17.1 (2009): 73–92. The 1993 article by Cardinal Lustiger, written as an introduction to the French biography by Yves Hamant, *Alexandre Men: Un témoin pour la Russie de ce temps* (Paris: Editions Mame, 1993), and reprinted as an after word in Elizabeth Roberts and Ann Shukman, *Christianity for the Twenty-First Century: The Life and Work of Alexander Men* (London: SCM, 1996), 192–96, registers the scope of his bridge building with Catholics and increasing reputation abroad.

3. See Glazov, *V krayu otsov*, 186–87.

4. Fr. Yakov Krotov, longtime friend and spiritual child of Men', implicates the KGB (on the basis of his transcript of the 49 questions presented to him during his police interrogation about Men''s murder) in his article "Who Killed Fr. Men'?," http://krotov.info./yakov/varia/engl/engl_01.htm. The questions concern the extent of Men''s "heretical" views, including ecumenical dealings and plots, especially with Jews (qq. 9–18) and Catholics (qq. 19–21), implying that he posed a threat to Russia and Orthodoxy. At the same time,

they also insinuate, by alleging a correspondence between the timing of his murder and the Jewish holidays, that his interests in converting Jews to Christianity may have made him a target for ritual murder by Jews themselves (q. 31). To such insinuations Krotov replied that Jewish Christians felt comfortable in his parish because of its singular lack of antisemitism (q. 15), while his death was publicly celebrated by ultranationalists (q. 28). Regarding the Jewish ritual murder hypothesis, Krotov advised the commissioner to acquaint himself and his directors with the 1913 Beilis Affair in which imperial Russia finally and definitively dismissed as libel the charge that the Talmud sanctions ritual murder (q. 31); "Dopros Po Delu Aleksandra Menya" (Interrogation about the Case of Alexander Men', www.krotov.info/yakov/varia/zlobaday/19921113.html). I thank Father Krotov for this information. See also the Newsru interview with Men''s brother Pavel Men' in which he points the finger at the KGB: Pavel Men', "Aleksandra Men'ya ubili spetssluzhby, schitaet ego brat" (The Security Services Killed Aleksandr Men', According to His Brother), www.newsru.com/religy/17feb2014/pavel_menj.html.

5. See the *Afisha* interview conducted by Yuri Saprykin and produced by Irina Ineshina with Vyacheslav Ivanov: "Sovety Stareishin: Vyacheslav Ivanov, uchenyj, 82 goda" (The Councils of Elders: Vyacheslav Ivanov, Scholar, 82 Years), *Afisha*, Feb. 6, 2012, http://daily.afisha.ru/archive/gorod/archive/wise-advices-ivanov/. The key excerpt is also cited on the homepage of the website www.Alexandrmen.ru hosted by the Aleksandr Men' Foundation.

6. This account is based on information related by Vladimir Yulikov, Men''s son-in-law, to my mother, Marina Glazov, on June 4, 2014, and by Fr. Yakov Krotov to me on the same day. For the phrase in question, Vladimir first cites Krotov's recollection given in a Radio Liberty program celebrating the seventy-fifth anniversary of Men''s birthday. Krotov recalled the phrase as follows: "In his theological challenges, Father Aleksandr occasionally expressed judgments, which, without special consideration, cannot be so characterized as to be unconditionally embraced by the whole church." Assuming that the text would have been composed by Patriarch Alexei's speechwriter of the time, Deacon Andrei Kuraev, Krotov commented on the phrase as follows: "First of all, which theologian ever expressed judgments that all shared? Only the Creed, perhaps, has the status of doctrine that the whole church confesses. Accordingly, no one can speak even about such things as the weather on behalf of the whole church. Second, the setting is wrong, the timing is wrong, and the formulation is completely wrong" (Yakov Krotov, "75-ya godovshhina so dnya rozhdeniya svyashhennika Aleksandra Men'ya" (On the 75th Anniversary of the Birthday of Fr. Aleksandr Men', Radio Svoboda, Jan. 23, 2010, www.svoboda.org/content/transcript/19800645.html). In a follow-up email to my mother on the same day, Vladimir Yulikov recalled the words of

a message by Patriarch Alexei about Father Men' that read: "Father Men' was a talented preacher of the Word of God, a good pastor of the church, who possessed a generous soul and a heart devoted to the Lord. His murderers committed a black deed at a moment when he could still have done much to enlighten spiritually and feed the church's children. Not all of his judgments could be embraced by Orthodox theologians, but none of them contradicted the essence of the Sacred Scriptures. They indeed underscore that 'there must be factions among you in order that those who have withstood temptation among you may be recognized' [1 Cor. 11:19]." This message is now cited at the top of the Men' Foundation website, www.alexandrmen.ru/. Neither Vladimir Yulikov nor Yakov Krotov is sure how this message relates to the one read at the funeral as recalled by Krotov in the Radio Liberty interview and suggest corroborating the issue with Pavel Men', manager of the website.

7. See the testimonies of the participants of the aforementioned Radio Liberty program conducted by Krotov, "75-ya godovshhina." The Holy Synod of the Russian Orthodox Church confirmed on April 4, 1999, that the well-known book-burning incident took place the previous year at the Seminary of Ekaterinburg under the direction of the inspector of the Seminary Aleksei Orlov on the order of Bishop Nikon. As cited to me by Yakov Krotov, the confirmation is reported on the pages of the portal of members of the Russian Orthodox Church, *Pravoslavnaya Beseda*, "O sozhzhenii knig v Ekaterinburge" (On the Burning of Books in Ekaterinburg), June 4, 1999, http://pravbeseda.ru/archive/arc2/1196.html.

8. Ernest L. Radlov, ed., *Pis'ma Vladimira Sergeevicha Solovyova* (Letters of Vladimir Sergeivich Solovyov) (Brussels: Zhizn' s Bogom, Foyer Oriental Chrétien, 1970), 1:191; 4:118–19; S. Solovyov, *Zhizn'*, 234, 258.

9. Frederick Copleston, S.J., *Russian Religious Philosophy: Selected Aspects* (Notre Dame, IN: University of Notre Dame Press, 1988); Hans Urs von Balthasar, "Soloviev," in *The Glory of the Lord*, trans. Andrew Louth et al. (Edinburgh: T & T Clark, 1986), 3:279–352.

10. Michel d'Herbigny, *Vladimir Soloviev: A Russian Newman (1853–1900)*, trans. Anna Maud Buchanan, ed. Fr. Thomas J. Gerrard (London: R. & T. Washbourne, 1918).

11. See, e.g., Vladimir Soloviev, *The Russian Church and the Papacy*, ed. Ray Ryland, foreword by Christoph Cardinal Schönborn (El Cajon, CA: Catholic Answers, 2002); Gregory Glazov, "Vladimir Solovyov and the Idea of the Papacy, *Communio* 24.1 (1997): 128–42; Aidan Nichols, "Solovyov and the Papacy: A Catholic Evaluation," *Communio* 24.1 (1997): 143–49; Jonathan Sutton, "Vladimir Solov'ëv as Reconciler and Polemicist," in *Vladimir Solov'ëv: Reconciler and Polemicist*, ed. Wil van den Bercken, Manon de Courten, and Evert van der Zweerde (Leuven: Peeters, 2000), 1–12. The last

three articles were originally papers presented at the second Kairos Symposium, "Soloviev and the Papacy," org. Stratford Caldecott and Center for Faith and Culture, Nov. 16, 1996, Greyfriars, Oxford.

12. See Pt. III, n. 85, below.

13. Giacomo Cardinal Biffi, "L'Ammonimento profetico di Vladimir S. Soloviev" (Meditation preached on Feb. 27, 2007), *Il Foglio*, Mar. 15, 2007, http://holyqueen.altervista.org/teol_att_anticristo_solovev.htm; and summary "Retreatants Hear of Guises of the Antichrist: Preacher Draws on Work of V. S. Solovyov," Feb. 28, 2007, www.zenit.org/article-19030?1=english.

14. Vladimir Wozniuk, ed., *Freedom, Faith, and Dogma: Essays by V. S. Soloviev on Christianity and Judaism* (Albany: State University of New York Press, 2008).

15. See Hamutal Bar-Yosef, "The Jewish Reception of Vladimir Solov'ëv," in van den Bercken, de Couten, and van der Zweerde, *Vladimir Solov'ëv*, 363–92, esp. 369–74, 376–80. Note especially the citations of Solovyov on pp. 373 and 376 in Simon Markovich Dubnov, *Vsemirnaya istoriya evrejskogo naroda ot drevnejshikh vremyon do nastoyashhego* (World History of the Jewish People) (Riga: Dzīve un Kultura, 1939), 10:136–37; and in Ahad Ha-Am, "'Al-Shtei ha-Se'ipim" (Between Two Opinions), in *Kol Kitvei Ahad Ha-am* (Collected Works of Ahad Ha-am) (Tel Aviv: Dvir, 1947), 375.

16. As documented by Bar-Yosef, "Jewish Reception," notes 24, 48. Getz first bestowed this title on Solovyov in the concluding remarks of his "Nekotorye vospominaniya ob otnoshenii V. S. Solovyova k evreyam," *Voskhod* 63 (Aug. 13, 1900): 30–35; 79 (Sept. 7, 1900): 25. Getz's formulation was repeated by Nahman Syrkin in "V. Solovyov ve-yihusso lishe'elat ha-Yehudim" (Solovyov's Attitude to the Jewish Question), *Sefer-ha-Shana* 3 (1902): 70; and then by Rabbi Abraham Isaac ha-Cohen Kook, "Letter of April 1905," in *Iggrot H.R.A.I.H.* (The Letters of Rabbi Kook), 3 vols. (Jerusalem: Mosad Harav Kook, 1985), 1:18. Kook's honoring of Solovyov was also documented by Jean Halpérin, "Vladimir Soloviev Listens to Israel: The Christian Question," *Immanuel* 26–27 (1994): 204 n. 16, 210.

17. Evert van der Zweerde makes this emphasis in "Vladimir Solov'ëv and the Russian-Christian Jewish Question," *Journal of Eastern Christian Studies* 55.3–4 (2003): 211–44, esp. 214–21. On van der Zweerde's misconstrual of Solovyov's view that Jews are not capable of "abstract thought," see Pt. II, ch. 4, below.

18. See Vladimir Wozniuk, "Vladimir S. Soloviev and the Politics of Human Rights," *Journal of Church and State* 41 (1999): 33–50; Vladimir Wozniuk, "Appendix A: The Jews in Russia," in *Politics, Law, and Morality: Essays by V. S. Soloviev*, ed. Vladimir Wozniuk (New Haven, CT: Yale University Press, 2000), 291–92; Vladimir Wozniuk, trans. and ed., *The Heart of*

Reality: Essays on Beauty, Love, and Ethics by V. S. Soloviev (Notre Dame, IN: University of Notre Dame Press, 2003); Wozniuk, *Freedom, Faith, and Dogma.*

19. Dmitrij Belkin, *"Gäste, die bleiben": Vladimir Solov´ev, die Juden und die Deutschen* ("Guests Who Stay": Vladimir Solov'ev, the Jews, and the Germans) (Hamburg: EVA Europäische Verlagsanstalt, 2008).

20. I thank Paul Valliere for this assessment of the scope of Part II and the recommendation as to the title.

21. Faivel Getz, "Ob otnoshenii Vl. S. Solovyova k evrejskomu voprosu" (Vladimir Solovyov's Attitude to the Jewish Question), *Voprosy Filosofii i Psikhologii* 56 (Jan.–Feb. 1901): 162–63. Reprinted with introduction in Faivel Getz, *Ob otnoshenii Vl. S. Solovyova k evrejskomu voprosu*" (Moscow: I. N. Kushnerev, 1901, 1902), 1–44.

22. V. E. Kel'ner and D. A. Elyashevich, *Literatura o evreyakh na russkom yazyke 1890–1947: Bibliograficheskij ukazatel'* (St. Peterburg: Akademicheskij Proekt, 1995).

23. On the punctuation in the title, see Pt. II, ch. 14; Pt. III, ch. 4 and n. 255.

24. Halpérin, "Vladimir Soloviev Listens to Israel," 198.

25. Ibid., 198 n. 1.

26. Vladimir Solovyov, "Ponyatie o Boge (V zashhitu filosofii Spinozy)" (The Concept of God [In Defense of Spinoza's Philosophy]), *Voprosy filosofii i psikhologii* 3 (1897): 383–414. Reprinted in *SSVSS* 9:3–29. Translation in *The Concept of God: Essays on Spinoza*, ed. and trans. George L. Kline and Boris Jakim (Carlisle, PA: Variable Press, 1999), 25–50.

27. Van der Zweerde, "Vladimir Solov'ëv and the Russian-Christian Jewish Question," 219, citing Nelli V. Motroshilova, "Die philosophischen Grundbegriffe Vladimir Solov'ëvs und die Lehre des Spinoza," *Studia Spinozana* 11 (1995): 319 41. See also Dmitrij Belkin, "'Evrejskij vopros' kak 'Khristianskij vopros': K interpretatsii odnoj formuly V. S. Solovyova," in *Solovyovskij sbornik: Materialy mezhdunarodnoy konferentsii "V. S. Solovyov i ego filosofskoe nasledie"* (A Solovyovian Collection: Materials for the International Conference "V. S. Solovyov and His Philosophical Legacy"), *28–30 August 2000,* ed. I. V. Borisova and A. P. Kozyreva (Moscow: Fenomenologiya-Germenevtika, 2001), 468.

28. Van der Zweerde, "Vladimir Solov'ëv and the Russian-Christian Jewish Question," 219, citing Solovyov's *Opravdanie dobra* (The Justification of the Good), ch. 2, sec. 2, in *Vladimir Solovyov, Sochineniya v dvukh tomakh*, ed. A. F. Losev and A. V. Gulyga (Moscow: Mysl', 1988), 1:271 n.; and Lev Shestov, "Umozrenie i apokalipsis," in *Vladimir Solovyov: Pro et Contra: Lichnost' i tvorchestvo Vladimira Solovyova v otsenke russkikh myslitelej i*

issledovatelej: Antologiya, vol. 2, ed. Viktor Fedorovich Bojkov and Yuri Yur'evich Bulychev et al. (St. Petersburg: Russkij khristianskij gymanitarnyj institut, 2002): 481.

29. Van der Zweerde, "Vladimir Solov'ëv and the Russian-Christian Jewish Question," observing with Judith Kornblatt that this omits the influence on Solovyov of Christian Kabbalah via Jacob Böhme.

30. In his article "Evrejskij vopros" (2000), Belkin announced the intention to treat Spinoza's impact on Solovyov's Jewish writings in a future monograph on Solovyov and Judaism. Perhaps this was the seed of Belkin's Tübingen dissertation on the reception of Solovyov among contemporary German intellectuals, "Die Rezeption V. S. Solov'evs in Deutschland" (Ph.D. diss., Tübingen, 2000), which was published, along with Belkin's analysis of Solovyov's interactions with contemporary Jewish intellectuals in Belkin's *"Gäste."*

31. See M. de Courten, "Two Narratives on History in Vladimir Solov'ëv: The Polish Question," in *Solovyovskij sbornik: Materialy mezhdunarodnoj konferentsii "V. S. Solovyov i ego filosofskoe nasledie"* (A Solovyovian Collection: Materials for the International Conference "V. S. Solovyov and His Philosophical Legacy"), *28–30 August 2000*, ed. Yevgeniya V. Borisova and Anna P. Kozyreva (Moscow: Fenomenologiya-Germeevtika, 2001), 474–502.

32. For a critical assessment of Solovyov's concept of national religion, see van der Zweerde, "Vladimir Solov'ëv," sec. 7, 233–37.

33. Attributed to Countess Praskovya Vladimirovna Trubetskaya, the wife of Solovov's friend and colleague Sergei Nikolaevich Trubetskoy. See S. N. Trubetskoy, "Smert' V. S. Solovyova 31 Iyul'ya 1900 g.," in *Kniga O Vladimire Solovyove*, ed. Boris V. Averin and Dar'ya Bazanova (Moscow: Sovetskij Pisatel', 1991), 294. See also K. Mochulsky, *Vladimir Solovyov: Zhizn' i uchenie* (Paris: YMCA Press, 1951), 268; Savely Dudakov, *Paradoksy i prichudy filosemitizma i antisemitizma v Rossii: Ocherki* (Moscow: Rossijskij gosudarstvennyj gumanitarnyj universitet, 2000), 345 and n. 146; Judith Deutsch Kornblatt, Boris Jakim, and Laury Magnus, eds. and trans., *Divine Sophia: The Wisdom Writings of Vladimir Solovyov* (Ithaca, NY: Cornell University Press, 2009), 25.

34. Karl Marx, "Zur Judenfrage," *Deutsch-Französische Jahrbücher* 1 (Feb. 1844): 377.

35. K. M. El'tsova, "Sny nezdeshnie: K 25-let'iyu konchiny V. S. Solovyova (1926)," in Averin and Bazanova, *Kniga O Vladimire Solovyove*, 141–42.

36. Vladimir Solovyov, "Chteniya o bogochelovechestve" (Lectures on Godmanhood), *Pravoslavnoe obozrenie* (Orthodox Survey), Mar. 1878 (pt. 1:

472–84; Apr. 1878 (pt. 2: 714–26); May–June 1878 (pt. 3: 308–30); July 1878 (pt. 4: 477–79); Sept. 1878 (pts. 5 and 6: 108–13); Oct. 1879 (pts. 7 and 8: 223–51), Nov. 1880 (pt. 9: 441–56); Feb. 1881 (pt. 10: 317–38); Sept. 1881 (pts. 11 and 12: 12–32). Reprinted collectively as *Chteniya o bogochelovechestve*, ed. M. Katkov (Moscow: Universitetskaya tipografiya, 1881); and in *SSVSS*² 3:1–168.

37. Hegel employed the term "godmanhood" in *Vorlesungen über der Religion* (*The Philosophy of Religion*) and regarded Christianity as the realization of the identity of the divine principle and the human. See Georg Wilhelm Friedrich Hegel, "The Godman and Reconciliation," in *Lectures on the Philosophy of Religion*, trans. Peter C. Hodgson et al. (Berkeley: University of California Press, 1998), sec. 3.4, pp. 101–22.

38. Paul Valliere, "Sophiology as the Dialogue of Orthodoxy with Modern Civilization," in *Russian Religious Thought*, ed. Judith Deutsch Kornblatt and Richard F. Gustafson (Madison: University of Wisconsin Press, 1996), 176–91 passim. All quotes from Valliere in this paragraph are from 191 n. 1.

39. Boris Jakim, pers. comm., Nov. 14, 2011; May 21, 2013.

40. Emile Fackenheim, "Demythologizing and Remythologizing in Jewish Experience: Reflections Inspired by Hegel's Philosophy," in *Myth and Philosophy*, ed. George F. McLean, OMI, Proceedings of the American Catholic Philosophical Association, vol. 45 (Washington, DC: Catholic University of America, 1971), 20, 22, 23.

41. Ibid., 20.

42. Peter Aelen, O.I., "Ideya bogochelovechestva v filosofii Vladimira Solovyova," in Borisova and Kozyreva, *Solovyovskij sbornik*, 304–6.

43. Van der Zweerde, "Vladimir Solov'ëv, 228, citing pp. 12 f. and 162 of Boris Jakim, trans. and ed., *The Crisis of Western Philosophy: Against the Positivists* (Hudson, NY: Lindisfarne, 1996).

44. Van der Zweerde, "Vladimir Solov'ëv," 227. On Solovyov's understanding and critique of nationalism and its relationship to patriotism and national messianism, see Pt. 1, ch. 4, §7.2, and n. 137 below. The entries on nationalism and messianism do not appear in the early editions of *SSVSS*, and I owe my discovery of them to Belkin, "*Gäste*," 50–51.

45. Examples where "of the people" is used as the adjectival form are *narodnaya tolpa* = "a crowd of the people," *narodnaya zhizn'* as "the life of the people," and *Narodnyye massy* as "masses of its peoples." Examples of the use of "public" occur in the phrase *politika i narodnoye upravlenie* = "politics and public administration" and in the epigraph at the beginning of "The Sins of Russia": *delo ne politicheskikh soobrazhenij, a narodnoj i gosudarstvennoj sovesti* = "a matter not of political reasoning but of public and state conscience."

46. On Mordechai Kaplan's seminal ideas about Jewish peoplehood, see Ezra Kopelwitz and Ari Engelberg, "A Framework for Strategic Thinking about Jewish Peoplehood" (Nadav Fund, Tel Aviv, 2007), 3–4, available at www.nadavfund.org.il/Peoplehood_Position_Paper.pdf.

47. See Solovyov's essay "Sem'ya Narodov" (The Family of Nations), in *Voskresnyya Pis'ma, 1897–1898, SSVSS*[9] 8:75–77.

48. Judith Deutsch Kornblatt, "Vladimir Solov'ev on Spiritual Nationhood, Russia and the Jews," *Russian Review* 56.2 (1997): 159–77. Cf. Belkin's observation in *"Gäste,"* 54, that until 1881 Jews in Russia were denoted predominantly by the religious *iudei* over and above the ethnic term *evrei*.

49. It should be pointed out that from an Orthodox Jewish perspective, the belief that ethnic and religious dimensions are easily separable in Judaism rests on a misunderstanding that may ground or presuppose antisemitism. A clear explanation of this was provided by Melanie Phillips in her critique of the misunderstanding of the problem issued by the (Jewish) judge of the U.K. Supreme Court on Dec. 16, 2009; see M. Phillips, "An Illiberal and Ignorant Judgment," posted on Dec. 16, 2009, http://images.spectator.co.uk/melanie phillips/5641976/an-illiberal-and-ignorant-judgment.thtml.

50. No such difficulty would have presented itself in the nineteenth century, as shown by the Dec. 8, 1890, London *Times* containing Solovyov's protest letter to the tsar, which frequently uses the terms "Hebrew" and "Hebrews" to connote ethnicity.

51. Fr. Alexander Men' was the principal intellectual architect of Christian renewal in the late Soviet period. Father Men' gave this lecture in 1989 as part of a cycle of lectures on Russian religious philosophy. See www.alexandr men.ru/lectures/index.html; and Aleksandr Men', "Vladimir Sergeevich Solovyov," in *Mirovaya dukhovnaya kultura, Khristianstvo, Tserkov': Lektsii i besedy,* ed. Anastasiya Andreeva et al., 2nd ed. (Moscow: Fond imeni Aleksandra Menya, 1997), 425–26, www.vehi.net/men/soloviev.html.

52. Mikhail Vasilyevich Lomonosov (1711–65), a polymath, scientist, poet, and writer.

53. See 2 Tim. 4:7–8: "I have fought the good fight, I have finished the race, I have kept the faith. Henceforth there is laid up for me the crown of righteousness which the Lord, the righteous judge, will award to me on that Day, and not only to me but also to all who have loved his appearing."

54. Published in St. Petersburg, 1851–79, in 29 volumes.

55. Ludwig Feuerbach, *Das Wesen des Christenthums* (Leipzig: Otto Wigand, 1841, 2nd ed. 1843, 3rd ed. 1849).

56. The Soviet-era town of Zagorsk, situated about 45 miles north of Moscow, the site of the Holy Trinity Monastery, founded by St. Sergius of Radonezh (d. 1392), and of the famous icon of the Trinity by Andrei Rublev.

57. Published as *Krizis zapadnoj filosofii: protiv pozitivistov* (Moscow: V Universitetskoj tipografii, 1874).

58. Published as *Kritika otvlechennykh nachal* (Moscow: V universitetskoj tipografii, 1880).

59. Composed in September 1898, as recounted by S. Solovyov, *Zhizn'*, 339, and dated by the poem to Sept. 26–29. See *SSVSS*[12] 12:82–86. For the English translation, see Boris Jakim, Sergius Bulgakov, and Laury Magnus, *The Religious Poetry of Vladimir Solovyov* (Kettering, OH: Semantron, 2008), 99–107.

60. As described by S. Solovyov, *Zhizn'*, 195–207, the chapters of *Velikij spor i khristianskaya politika* (The Great Debate and Christian Politics) were published separately as installments in Moscow in 1883 in Aksakov's journal *Rus'*: 1 (Jan. 3); 2 (Jan. 17); 3 (Feb. 1), 14 (July 15); 15 (Aug. 1); 18 (Sept. 15); 23 (Dec. 1). Solovyov's wish to expand and publish the work in Russia failed on account of tsarist censorship, and the alternative plan to publish the work abroad eventually resulted in the publication of *La Russie et l'Église universelle* five years later (see S. Soloviev, *Zhizn'*, 206–7).

61. Published in installments in *Pravoslavnoe obozrenie* beginning in January 1884 and as a volume in 1884 under the title *Religioznye osnovy zhizni* (Religious Foundations of Life) and revised in a second (1885) and third edition (1887) under the new title *Dukhovnye osnovy zhizni* (Spiritual Foundations of Life), as described by S. Solovyov, *Zhizn'*, 210–13.

62. The lectures were serialized in 1878–81 and published in one volume in 1881; see Pt. II, ch. 6, below.

63. John 17:21.

64. "Bella idea, ma fuor d'un miràculo è cosa impossibile," as cited in S. Solovyov, *Zhizn'*, 289. See Paul Valliere, *Modern Russian Theology: Bukharev, Soloviev, Bulgakov: Orthodox Theology in a New Key* (Edinburgh: T & T Clark, 2000), 178.

65. "Ex oriente lux." The poem was written in 1890. See *SSVSS*[12] 12:27–28. For the text, see http://solovev.ouc.ru/ex-oriente-lux.html.

66. A 1962 Cinemascope film about the Battle of Thermopylae made with the cooperation of the Greek government; see http://en.wikipedia.org/wiki/The_300_Spartans (Ed.).

67. Lit., "thought."

68. Published as *Opravdanie dobra: nravstvennaya filosofiya* (St. Petersburg: Tipografiya M. Stasyulevicha, 1897). For an electronic version, see http://babel.hathitrust.org/cgi/pt?id=inu.320000009170657;view=1up;seq=3.

69. The current tombstone simply bears the inscription "Solovyov, Vladimir Sergeevich, 1853–1900, publitsist filosof." See www.openmoscow.ru /kladbnovodevichy/27big.html.

70. Men' is probably intentionally applying to Solovyov the term *otvle-chennyj*, "abstract," which Solovyov used pejoratively to criticize Western philosophy for being not concrete, impractical, and therefore non-Jewish. Is Men' here criticizing Solovyov for failing to live up to his ideal of *bogochelove-chestvo*? Men' did criticize Solovyov's theocratic ideas and ecumenical efforts as youthful and utopian, but he also stressed that these ideas and efforts sprang from faithfulness to Christ and his striving to integrate thought and deed, which made his lifestyle more Christian at root than the less utopian and apparently more practical lifestyles of most Christians. For this reason, using this term to describe Solovyov seems too harsh. Perhaps it should be rendered more softly by something like "theoretical" or "preoccupied" so as to refer principally to his attitudes toward money, food, and clothing rather than to his intellectual and spiritual deficiencies.

71. The most influential anti-tsarist work published before World War I was that of Simon Markovich Dubnov (1860–1941). This chapter uses his *History of the Jews in Russia and Poland: From the Earliest Times until the Present*, trans. I. Friedlander (Philadelphia: Jewish Publication Society of America: 1916; repr. KTAV, 1975), 2 vols. Modern revisionist views are largely based on the following: Richard Pipes, "Catherine II and the Jews: The Origins of the Pale of Settlement," *Soviet Jewish Affairs* 5 (1975): 3–20; Hans Rogger, "Government, Jews, Peasants and Land in Post-Emancipation Russia," *Cahiers du Monde Russe et Sovietique* 17.2–3 (1976): 5–21, 171–211; Hans Rogger, *Jewish Policies and Right-Wing Politics in Imperial Russia* (Berkeley: University of California Press, 1986), henceforth *JPRWP*; Jonathan Frankel, "The Crisis of 1881–1882 as a Turning Point in Modern Jewish History," in *The Legacy of Jewish Migration: 1881 and Its Impact*, ed. David Berger (New York: Brooklyn College Press, 1983), 9–22; Jonathan Frankel, *Prophecy and Politics* (Cambridge: Cambridge University Press, 1981); Michael Aronson, *Troubled Waters: The Origins of the 1881 Anti-Jewish Pogroms in Russia* (Pittsburgh: University of Pittsburgh Press,1990); Benjamin Nathans, *Beyond the Pale: The Jewish Encounter with Late Imperial Russia* (Berkeley: University of California Press, 2002); A. I. Solzhenitsyn, *Dvesti let vmeste* (Two Hundred Years Together) *(1795–1995)* (Moscow: Russkij put', 2001), vol. 1.; John Doyle Klier, *Russia Gathers Her Jews: The Origins of the "Jewish Question" in Russia, 1772–1825* (DeKalb: Northern Illinois University Press, 1986), henceforth *RGHJ*; John Doyle Klier, *Imperial Russia's Jewish Question, 1855–1881* (Cambridge: Cambridge University Press, 1995), henceforth *IRJQ*; John Doyle Klier, "Evrejskij vopros v slavyanofil'skoj presse 1862–1886 gg.," *Vestnik evrejskogo universiteta v Moskve* 1.17 (1998): 41–60; John Doyle Klier, *Russians, Jews, and the Pogroms of 1881–1882* (Cambridge: Cambridge University Press, 2011), henceforth *RJP*; Brian Horowitz, *Jewish Philanthropy*

and Enlightenment in Late-Tsarist Russia (Seattle: University of Washington Press, 2009) (henceforth *JPELTR*).

72. Solzhenitsyn, *Dvesti let vmeste*, 13–17.

73. Dubnov, *History*, 1:chs. 1–3; Klier, *RGHJ*, 4, 21–25; Solzhenitsyn, *Dvesti let vmeste*, 17–18.

74. Dubnov, *History*, 1:36–38; Rogger, *JPRWP*, 5; Klier, *RGHJ*, 25–30, 33; Solzhenitsyn, *Dvesti let vmeste*, 18–29.

75. Klier, *RGHJ*, 7–14; Cf. Solzhenitsyn, *Dvesti let vmeste*, 33–34; Dubnov, *History*, 1:ch. 3, 79–91, 95–97, and ch. 5, esp. 172–80, regarding Clement III's 1763 confirmation of the declaration of Cardinal Ganganelli and the Holy Inquisition and of Innocent IV in 1247, that the prejudice that Jews need human blood to prepare their unleavened bread lacks all foundation.

76. Dubnov, *History*, 1:ch. 4, 144–58, 180–87, esp. 184 (translation mine); Klier, *RGHJ*, 13; Martin Gilbert, *The Routledge Atlas of Russian History*, 3rd ed. (London: Routledge, [1972] 2002), maps 31, 69.

77. Dubnov, *History*, 1:ch. 6, esp. 198–240; Klier, *RGHJ*, 17, 20; Solzhenitsyn, *Dvesti let vmeste*, 35–36.

78. Dubnov, *History*, 1:261–66.

79. Ibid., 1:270–97; Rogger, *JPRWP*, 3–4; 115–16; Klier, *RGHJ*, 15–19, 38–52, 270–97, esp. 289.

80. Rogger, *JPRWP*, 6, citing: Pipes, "Catherine II," 4; and John Doyle Klier, "The Ambitious Legal Status of Russian Jewry in the Reign of Catherine II," *Slavic Review* 35.3 (1976): 504–17.

81. Rogger, *JPRWP*, 6.

82. Dubnov, *History*, 1:ch. 9, 310–22; Rogger, *JPRWP*, 6–7, 116–17. For recent revisionism on Catherine's reign, see Klier, *RGHJ*, 19–20, 32–37, 55–82, esp. 75–82; and Solzhenitsyn, *Dvesti let vmeste*, 30–44. On the notoriously unreliable demographic data, cf. Rogger, *JPRWP*, 234 n. 16. Klier, *IRJQ*, 9, estimates that the Jewish population in the Pale reached 1,041,000, of a total of 16,697,000, or 2.5 percent of the total population of 68 million in 1849.

83. Dubnov, *History*, 1:ch. 9, 321–27; Rogger, *JPRWP*, 8; Klier, *RGHJ*, 82–95; Solzhenitsyn, *Dvesti let vmeste*, 44–45.

84. Cf. Klier, *RGHJ*, 113; and Solzhenitsyn, *Dvesti let vmeste*, 45–60, esp. 52, 60; Dubnov, *History*, 1:ch. 10, 327–33.

85. Rogger, *JPRWP*, 8.

86. Ibid., citing Arnold Springer, "Gavriil Derzhavin's Jewish Reform Project of 1800," *Canadian-American Slavic Studies*, 10.1 (1976): 5.

87. Dubnov, *History*, 1:ch. 10, 335–65; Klier, *RGHJ*, 116–66; Solzhenitsyn, *Dvesti let vmeste*, 60–71, 77–83.

88. Dubnov, *History*, 1:ch. 11, 371–89; Klier, *RGHJ*, 142–43.

89. Klier, *IRJQ*, 418.

90. Dubnov, *History*, 1:ch. 12, esp. 396–403; Rogger, *JPRWP*, 8–10; Klier, *RGHJ*, 164–66; Solzhenitsyn, *Dvesti let vmeste*, 83–84.

91. Pestel's treatise *Russkaya Pravda* (Russian Justice) anticipated future socialist consternation about the Jewish problem by proposing, in the event of their failure to assimilate, to either deport them en masse or help them establish their own state in Asia Minor; cf. Solzhenitsyn, *Dvesti let vmeste*, 85.

92. On the romanticization of the Decembrists in Russian nineteenth-century literature, see Nekrasov's poem "Russian Women" (1872–73) as analyzed by Anna Biel, "Nikolai Nekrasov's Representation of the Decembrist Wives," *Australian Slavonic and East European Studies* 25.1–2 (2011): 39–59; available at http://miskinhill.com.au/journals/asees/25:1-3/nekrasovs-decembrist-wives.pdf.

93. Dubnov, *History*, 2:ch. 13, 30–33.

94. Rogger, *JPRWP*, 118.

95. Rogger gives nine as the youngest figure in *JPRWP*, 11, 12. Nathans, *Beyond the Pale*, 27–28 and n. 13, gives eight, also citing eyewitness accounts of self-mutilation.

96. Dubnov, *History*, 2:ch. 13, 13–30; Klier, *IRJQ*, 2–3. Solzhenitsyn, *Dvesti let vmeste*, 97–103, admits these hardships but disputes that children as young as twelve were drafted by government policy, blaming the delivery of poor and orphaned youngsters on the *kahal*. But if conscription of such youngsters was not the norm, those alienated from the *kahal* would have reported such abuses to the government. That such reports are not discussed suggests that this was in fact the norm. The draft of children was stopped by law in 1856. A few pages later, to argue that Jews failed in the sphere of agriculture because they found it too labor intensive, Solzhenitsyn invokes the testimony of V. N. Nikitin (1839–1908), who became a cantonist at the age of nine, was forcibly converted, and, on completing his military service, published an important work in 1869 (see below) on Jewish cantonists and Jewish agricultural endeavors. Such failures on Solzhenitsyn's part to acknowledge that the government drafted children at such early ages illustrates that his pro-tsarist apologetic rests on rather selective and shallow use of evidence, which in turn corroborates the impression of antisemitic bias suggested by his reviewers, e.g., Richard Pipes, "Solzhenitsyn and the Jews, Revisited," *New Republic* (Nov. 2002): 26–28.

97. The *Haskalah* was largely initiated by Moses Mendelsohn (1726–89) and Solomon ben Joshua Maimon (1754–1800) who, doubting that Jewry's problems could be solved through traditional legal observance, mysticism, or miraculous messianism, encouraged Jews to study secular subjects, learn European languages, and assimilate into European society. Recognition of the

maskilim as an internal threat to Judaism by both the rabbinate and the Hasidim helped the latter two reconcile by the mid-nineteenth century; cf. Dubnov, *History*, 2:ch. 16, 125–38.

98. For further details, see Michael Stanislawski, *Tsar Nicholas I and the Jews: The Transformation of Jewish Society in Russia, 1825-1855* (Philadelphia, PA: Jewish Publication Society, 1983), 15, 32–33, 127–33. Cited via Nathans, *Beyond the Pale*, 28.

99. Dubnov, *History*, 2:ch. 13, 34–46; ch. 17, 145–50. Rogger, *JPRWP*, 10–11, also notes that a small group of *maskilim*, guided by European experience, welcomed the educational initiative, 117–19. See also Klier, *IRJQ*, 3–4.

100. Viktor N. Nikitin, *Evrei zemledel'tsy: Istoricheskoe, zakonodatel'noe, administrativnoe i bytovoe polozhenie kolonij so vremeni ikh voznikoveniya do nashikh dnej. 1807–1887* (St. Petersburg: Tipografiya Gazety "Novosti," 1887).

101. Cf. Solzhenitsyn, *Dvesti let vmeste*, 106 15, 115–25; Nathans, *Beyond the Pale*, 34, notes the officially sanctioned and *maskilim*-supported device to integrate Jews into the Russian social order by means of settlement in agricultural colonies and observes, but without explanation, that only the exemption from military service boosted Jewish temporary enrollment in the colonies beyond the several hundred families involved.

102. Dubnov, *History*, 2:ch. 14, 46–66; ch. 17, 140–43; Rogger, *JPRWP*, 8–12; Klier, *IRJQ*, 1, 5–6; Solzenitsyn, *Dvesti let vmeste*, 126–31.

103. Solzhenitsyn, *Dvesti let vmeste*, 128–29. See David Sorkin, "Montefiore and the Politics of Emancipation (Review of Abigail Greene, *Moses Montefiore: Jewish Liberator, Imperial Hero* [HUP, 2010])," *Jewish Review of Books* 2 (2010), www.jewishreviewofbooks.com/publications/detail/monte fiore-and-the-politics-of-emancipation.

104. On antisemitic types in Pushkin and Gogol, see Dubnov, *History*, 2:ch. 17, 138–39; on the ritual murder trial in Saratov, see Dubnov, *History*, 2:ch. 17, 150–53; Klier, *IRJQ* 418–19.

105. Rogger, *JPRWP*, 120–21.

106. Ibid., 122; Solzhenitsyn, *Dvesti let vmeste*, 136–38.

107. Dubnov, *History*, 2:ch. 18, 154–72; Rogger, *JPRWP*, 123–25; Klier, *IRJQ*, 13–31; Solzhenitsyn, *Dvesti let vmeste*, 141–45.

108. Solzhenitsyn, *Dvesti let vmeste*, 164, citing the memoirs of Mark Aldanov/Landau.

109. Dubnov, *History*, 2:ch. 18, 173–74, 184–86; Solzhenitsyn, *Dvesti let vmeste*, 138–39, 175.

110. Dubnov, *History*, 2:ch. 18, 177–83; Rogger, *JPRWP*, 125–26; Klier, *IRJQ*, ch. 13, 145–58; 300–303; ch. 14, 332–49; Solzhenitsyn, *Dvesti let vmeste*, 150–52; Horowitz, *JPELTR*, 30.

111. Failing completely to discuss the Polish uprising and the issue of rus-sification, Solzhenitsyn, *Dvesti let vmeste*, 156–61, concludes that this shift of tsarist policy resulted from the judgment that Jews could neither succeed in agriculture nor be induced to be interested in it.

112. On the Gintsburg dynasty, see Horowitz, *JPELTR*, 42–51; Nathans, *Beyond the Pale*, 40–47, 50–60, 126–30; Solzhenitsyn, *Dvesti let vmeste*, 160, 168–75.

113. Klier, *IRJQ*, 245–62; Horowitz, *JPELTR*, 29–41. Dubnov, *History*, 2:ch. 20, 214–16, wrongly dates the establishment of the society to 1867.

114. Klier, *IRJQ*, 84–101, 102–22.

115. Dubnov, *History*, 2:ch. 20, 216–21; Klier, *IRJQ*, see esp. ch. 4, 84–101, on *Rassvet*; ch. 5 on *Sion*; and *ha-Melitz*, 102–22; ch. 11, 251–54 on *Kol Meva-ser*; pt. 3, 295–98, 348–49, on *Voskhod* and *Russkij evrej*; 350–58 on *Den'*. On the "New Jews" of St. Petersburg, including Levanda, Landau, Levin, Man-delshtam, Orshansky, and Sliozberg, see Nathans, *Beyond the Pale*, 127–64, 208–14, 313–39; and Solzhenitsyn, *Dvesti let vmeste*, 174–78.

116. Klier, *IRJQ*, 123–32, 288; cf. Solzhenitsyn, *Dvesti let vmeste*, 197.

117. Klier, *RGHJ*, 176–77; *IRJQ*, 132–43. Belkin discusses Aksakov and Katkov in *"Gäste,"* 64–67.

118. Klier, *IRJQ*, 436–37.

119. Ibid., 186–95, esp. 191–92, 306–31, 409–10; Solzhenitsyn, *Dvesti let vmeste*, 197.

120. Klier, *IRJQ*, 153–58, 194; Horowitz, *JPELTR*, 30. Solzhenitsyn, *Dvesti let vmeste*, 168, again fails to connect the issue of language to the Pol-ish question.

121. Klier, *IRJQ*, 157–58, 166–68, 231.

122. Dubnov, *History*, 2:ch. 20, 233–42.

123. Ibid., 221–24.

124. The first edition of Jacob Brafman's *Book of the Kahal* (*Kniga Ka-gala*) appeared in 1869 in Vilna, the second in 1875 in St. Petersburg, with a supplementary second volume. The third edition, also published in St. Peters-burg, was edited by Brafman's son, Alexander, in 1882. Cf. Byakster Betankur, "Brafman, Yakov Aleksandrovich," in *Russkij biograficheskij slovar'*, ed. A. A. Polovtsev (St. Petersburg: Tip. Glavnogo Upr. Udelov, 1908), 3:336–37; Dub-nov, *History*, 2:ch. 19, 187–90. Horowitz, *JPELTR*, 43, 56, 58–59; Solzheni-tsyn, *Dvesti let vmeste*, 166, 178–80. Belkin covers Brafman in *"Gäste,"* 58–60.

125. See Pt. II, ch. 17.

126. Klier, *IRJQ*, 361–63, 368, 374–83, 436–38.

127. Major Osman Bey (Frederick Millingen), *Die Eroberung der Welt durch die Juden* (The Conquest of the World by the Jews) (Basel: Krüsi, 1873; 7th ed., Wiesbaden: Bechtold, 1875). For an electronic version of the 1878 English translation by F. W. Mathias, see https://archive.org/details/Conquest OfTheWorldByTheJews and http://www.scribd.com/doc/25983863/Bey -Osman-the-Conquest-of-the-World-by-the-Jews-Trans-1878-by-F-W -Mathias-Zionism-Jewish-Lob. For further details on Lyutostansky and his relationship to Brafman, see Belkin, "*Gäste*," 59–60.

128. Klier, *IRJQ*, 197–98, 263–83, 440–41; Horowitz, *JPELTR*, 58–59.

129. Klier, *IRJQ*, 440–44.

130. I. Aksakov, "Evrejskaya Internatsionalka i bor'ba s Evrejstvom v Evrope" (The Jewish International and the War with Jewry in Europe), *Rus'* 21 (Nov. 1 o.s./13 n.s., 1883): 20–26.

131. I. Aksakov, "Razbor tsirkulyarnogo vozzvaniya 'Evrejskogo Vsemirnogo Soyuza'" (Analysis of the Manifesto of the International Jewish Alliance), *Rus'* 23 (Dec. 1/13, 1883): 2–12.

132. See Isidore Loeb, "Pis'mo v redaktsiyu Tsentral'nogo Komiteta Izrailskogo Vsemirnogo Soyuza" (Letter to the Editor from the Central Committee of the Universal Israelite Alliance), *Rus'* 24 (Dec. 15/27, 1883): 56–57; I. Aksakov, "Eshhyo o vozzvanii 'Vsemirnogo Izrail'skogo Soyuza" (More on the Manifesto of the Universal Israelite Alliance), *Rus'* Dec. 15/27, 1883): 57.

133. Klier, *IRJQ*, 440–46.

134. Dubnov, *History*, 2:ch. 19, 187–90; cf. Klier, *IRJQ*, 169–72, 179–81, 196–97.

135. Dubnov, *History*, 2:ch. 19, 190–201.

136. Ibid., 202–205, 244; Klier, *IRJQ*, 419, 423–32.

137. Klier, *IRJQ*, 384–85, following Richard Pipes, "Russian Conservatism in the Second Half of the Nineteenth Century," *Slavic Review* 30.1 (1971): 120. The citation of Solovyov is from "Slavyanofil'stvo i ego vyrozhdenie, 1889" (Slavophilism and Its Degradation), *SSVSS*[9] 5:228, via Nicholas V. Riasanovsky, *Russia and the West in the Teaching of the Slavophiles: A Study in Romantic Ideology* (Cambridge, MA: Harvard University Press, 1952), 197. The same ideas, however, are advanced succinctly in Solovyov's article on nationalism (ÈSBE 20a: 110 = http://ru.wikisource.org/wiki/Natsionalizm), complemented by the articles on messianism (ÈSBE 19: 150 = http://ru.wiki source.org/wiki/Messianizm) and patriotism (ÈSBE 23: 36–38 = http://ru .wikisource.org/Patriotizm; *SSVSS*[10] 10:252–53).

138. Klier, *IRJQ*, 386–87, surveying Nicholas Berdyaev, *Christianity and Anti-Semitism* (New York: Philosophical Library, 1954), 5; Stephen Lukashevich, *Ivan Aksakov, 1823–1886: A Study in Russian Thought and Politics*

(Cambridge, MA: Harvard University Press, 1965), 167–68; and Aleksey Stepanovich Khomiakov, *Notes on Universal History*, via Riasanovsky, *Russia
and the West*, 115; Andrzej Walicki, *The Slavophile Controversy: History of a
Conservative Utopia in Nineteenth-Century Russian Thought*, trans. Hilda
Andrews-Rusiecka (Notre Dame, IN: University of Notre Dame Press, 1975),
212, 502 n. 2; and Shmuel Ettinger, "Ha-reka ha-idiologi le-hofa'ata shel ha-
sifrut ha-antishemit he-hadashah be-Rusia," *Zion* 35.1–4 (1970): 194–95. Cf.
the discussion of Khomiakov in Belkin, *"Gäste,"* 57–58.

139. F. Dostoevsky, "Letter to N. N. Strakhov from Florence, 18 (30)
March 1869," in F. M. Dostoevsky, *Sobranie sochinenij v 15 tomakh*, vol. 15:
Pis'ma [Letters], *1834–1881* (Leningrad: Nauka, 1991), 659 n. 359, available at
www.e-reading-lib.org/chapter.php/1005943/140/Dostoevskiy_-_Tom_15
._Pisma_1834-1881.html.

140. Klier, *IRJQ*, 389–95. Horowitz, *JPELTR*, 64, also adduces A. Kaufman's view that the Pan-Slavist struggle for liberation in the Russo-Turkish
War years instructed the Jews in how nationhood could provide a practical
and unifying ideology against oppression. Further, on p. 64 n. 48, Horowitz
cites Kaufman's report of a writer opining that the Odessa pogrom in 1871 was
orchestrated to heat up Russian hatred for local non-Russians and non-
Christians so as to motivate simple Russians to risk their lives for distant Slavs.
Solzhenitsyn, *Dvesti let vmeste*, 180–81, notes that Crémieux specifically declined to help Russian Jews dodge military service and that the Alliance was
committed to combating religious persecution. On the Treaty of Berlin, see
Barbara Jelavich, *Russia and the Formation of the Romanian National State,
1821–1878* (Cambridge: Cambridge University Press, 2004), 286.

141. Cf. Klier, *IRJQ*, 396–416; Solzhenitsyn, *Dvesti let vmeste*, 181–84.
On Dostoevsky's antisemitism, see Belkin, *"Gäste,"* 61–64.

142. Klier, *IRJQ*, 427.

143. Ibid., 414–15, citing Leonid Petrovich Grossman, "Dostoevskii i
pravitel'stvennye krugi 1870-kh godov," *Literaturnoe nasledstvo* 15 (1934):
142; Rogger, *JPRWP*, 66–67.

144. Nathans, *Beyond the Pale*, 258–59.

145. Klier, *RJP*, 17.

146. Klier, *IRJQ*, 433.

147. On the identity of the revolutionary group that carried out the assassination, Narodnaya volya (People's Will), and other revolutionary groups
of the time, see Klier, *RJP*, 155–77, esp. 166.

148. Klier, *IRJQ* 403; Klier, *RJP*, ch. 4, 128–50; and on Katkov, see *RJP*
133–35.

149. Cf. Klier, *RJP*, 131–32, 135–41.

150. Dubnov, *History*, 2:ch. 21: 247–58, esp. 248; cf. Klier, *RJP*, ch. 3, 91–127; Klier, *IRJQ*, 433. The quotation is from Rogger, *JPRWP*, 28, who notes, 239 nn. 10 and 11, three of many advocates of this conspiracy theory other than Dubnov (G. Ia. Goldhagen, Joseph Krasnyj-Admoni, and J. J. Leschinsky).

151. Klier, *RJP*. As noted above, the point of departure for the revisionist view is the works of Rogger, Aronson, and Frankel.

152. Horowitz, *JPELTR*, 71 n. 2, citing Simon Markovich Dubnov, *History of the Jews: From the Congress of Vienna to the Emergence of Hitler*, trans. Moshe Spiegel (New York: A. S. Barnes, 1973), 2:255.

153. Solzhenitsyn, *Dvesti let vmeste*, 190, citing *Mezhdunarodnaya Evrejskaya gazeta* 70.6 (Mar. 1992): 7.

154. Sozlshenitsyn, *Dvesti let vmeste*, 188–97. The attribution of this remark to Alexander III is taken for granted by Rogger, *JPRWP*, 29, who provides an extensive list of witnesses to his and his son Nicholas II's antisemitism, 57, 243, nn. 2, 3.

155. See Rogger, *JPRWP*, 58; Klier, *RJP*, ch. 5, esp. 178–83 where Ignatiev's nickname "Father of Lies" is explained.

156. On the substance of this view, see Klier, *RJP*, 15–177.

157. Dubnov, 2:ch. 21, 260–61; Rogger, *JPRWP*, 59, 136; Klier, *RJP*, 331–33; Horowitz, *JPELTR*, 73–74.

158. The cartoon may be seen in Klier, *RJP*, 140.

159. Dubnov, *History*, 2:ch. 22, 276–78; Klier, *RJP*, 146–47; Solzhenitsyn, *Dvesti let vmeste*, 197, significantly states nothing of Aksakov's use of Brafman.

160. Horowitz, *JPELTR*, 71–73; Klier, *RJP*, 338–40.

161. Cf. Solzhenitsyn, *Dvesti let vmeste*, 200–201; Dubnov, *History*, 2:ch. 21, 270–75; Rogger, *JPRWP*, 59–61; Klier, *RJP*, 183–206, esp. 201, which modifies Dubnov's "five" proponents for the relaxation of the Pale to "eight."

162. Klier, *RJP*, 343–47.

163. Dubnov, *History*, 2:ch. 23, 287–97; regarding Manning, see 290 n. 1, citing the *Jewish Chronicle* of Feb. 3, 1882; Klier, *RJP*, ch. 7, 236–45.

164. Dubnov, *History*, 2:ch. 23, 297–304.

165. Ibid., 304–8; Klier, *RJP*, 351–62; the date for the duration of the second assembly follows Horowitz, *JPELTR*, 74–75.

166. On Bunge's, Reutern's, and Sol'sky's opposition, see Rogger, "Russian Ministers and the Jewish Question, 1881–1917," in *California Slavic Studies*, ed. N. Riasanovsky, G. Struve, and T. Eekman (Berkeley: University of California Press, 1975), 8:21. Nabokov's intervention is cited by Solzhenitsyn, *Dvesti let vmeste*, 8:202.

167. Dubnov, *History*, 2:ch. 24, 310–17; Rogger, *JPRWP*, 60–62, 143–44; Klier, *RJP*, ch. 6, 207–33; Horowitz, *JPELTR*, 75; Solzhenitsyn, *Dvesti let vmeste*, 202–3. On Pobedonostsev's role in dismissing Ignatiev and the theory of J. H. Billington (*Mikhailovsky and Russian Populism* [Oxford: Oxford University Press, 1958], 142) that this was part of Pobedonostsev's plot to destroy all opposition, see Rogger, *JPRWP*, 29.

168. Dubnov, *History*, 2:ch. 27, 356–62; Klier, *RJP*, 84.

169. Ami Iseroff, "Pogrom," *Zionism and Israel–Encyclopedic Dictionary*, Apr. 6, 2009, www.zionism-israel.com/dic/pogrom.htm, citing Robert Weinberg, "Visualizing Pogroms in Russian History," *Jewish History* 12.2 (1998): 71–92.

170. Dubnov, *History*, 2:ch. 24, 318–35; Klier, *RJP*, 264–323; Solzhenitsyn, *Dvesti let vmeste*, 204–7.

171. Mikhail E. Saltykov-Shhedrin, "Iyul'skoe Veyanie," *Otechestvennye zapiski* (Homeland Notes) 8 (1882): 248–58.

172. Dubnov, *History*, 2:ch. 25, 325 n. 1; Solzhenitsyn, *Dvesti let vmeste*, 197–98.

173. Rogger, *JPRWP*, 30, n. 19, here cites *Die Juden-pogrome in Russland* (Cologne: Herausgegeben in Auftrage des Zionistischen Hilfsfonds in London, 1910), 1: 26 ff.; S. Dubnov and G. Ya. Krasnyi-Admoni, eds., *Materialy dlya istorii anti-evrejskikh pogromov v Rossii* (Petrograd: Gosudarstvennoe Izdatel'stvo, 1919–23), 1:xvi. According to Klier, *RJP*, xv, Rogger's dismissal of the "pogrom policy" thesis has been made definitive by Michael Aronson's *Troubled Waters* (1990).

174. Rogger, *JPRWP*, 28–31, 57, and 67–68, on Pobedonostsev's power during the reigns of the last two tsars.

175. Horowitz, *JPELTR*, 78–79; Rogger, *JPRWP*, 63; Solzhenitsyn, *Dvesti let vmeste*, 208–9.

176. Dubnov, *History*, 2:ch. 27, 348–80; Rogger, *JPRWP*, 63–65, 68–69; 144–50; Horowitz, *JPELTR*, 83–93, esp. 78, which states that Dubnov wrote the first report; Solzhenitsyn, *Dvesti let vmeste*, 209–11.

177. Horowitz, *JPELTR*, 80–143.

178. Dubnov, *History*, 2:ch. 28, 378–98; Rogger, *JPRWP*, 69, 154.

179. Dubnov, *History*, 2:ch. 29, 399–429; Gilbert, *Routledge Atlas of Russian History*, map 69.

180. Rogger, *JPRWP*, 70–74.

181. Ibid., 74–75.

182. Ibid., 155–56.

183. Ibid., 86–90, 186–87. The cited passage is found on pp. 87–88.

184. Rogger, *JPRWP*, 156.

185. Klier, *RJP*, 440.

186. Cf. C. G. de Michelis, *Il Manoscritto inesistente: I 'Protocolli dei savi di Sion'—un apocrifo del XX secolo* (Venice: Marsilio, 1998). De Michelis established that the *Protocols* were authored in Russia between 1902 and 1903 and only in later editions crudely Frenchified to make them look more authentic as a foreign document. See Michael Hagemeister, "Vladimir Solov'ëv and Sergej Nilus: Apocalypticism and Judeophobia," *Eastern Christian Studies* (2000): 288, 293, nn. 6, 21.

187. Sergei Nilus, ed., "Protocols of the Elders of Zion," in Nilus, *Velikoe v malom i antikhrist, kak blizkaya politicheskaya vozmozhnost': Zapiski pravoslavnogo* (The Great in the Small and the Antichrist as an Imminent Political Possibility: Notes of an Orthodox Believer) (Tsarskoe Selo: Tip. Tsarskoselskago komiteta Krasnago Kresta, 1905), appendix.

188. Michael Hagemeister, "The 'Protocols of the Elders of Zion': Between History and Fiction," *New German Critique* 35.1 (2008): 83–95; Chiara Voplato, "Empowering the 'Jewish Threat': *The Protocols of the Elders of Zion*," *Journal of US-China Public Adminstration* 6.1 [#44] (2009): 23–36.

189. Voplato, "Empowering the 'Jewish Threat,'" 24.

190. Sergei Nilus, ed., "Protocols of the Elders of Zion," 4th ed., in *'Bliz est', pri dverekh.' O tom, chemu ne zhelayut verit' i chto tak blizko* ("It is Near, Even at the Doors": Concerning That Which We Choose Not to Believe and Which Is so Near), published by the Holy Trinity Monastery at Sergiev Posad, Jan. 1917. Cf. Hagemeister, "Vladimir Solov'ëv and Sergej Nilus," 288.

191. Following Hagemeister, "Vladimir Solov'ëv and Sergej Nilus," 293, nn. 21 and 22, see, e.g., Henri-Roger Gougenot des Mousseaux's *Le juif, le judaïsme et la judaïsation des peuples chrétiens* (Paris: H. Plon, 1869), which predicts the appearance of a Jewish magician depicted as a "genius of deception."

192. Hagemeister, "'The Protocols.'"

193. Cf. Hagemeister, "Vladimir Solov'ëv and Sergej Nilus," 287–96; Norman Cohn, *Warrant for Genocide: The Myth of the Jewish-World-Conspiracy and the Protocols of the Elders of Zion* (New York: Harper & Row, 1967).

194. Hagemeister, "'The Protocols,'" 90–91.

195. Cf. Emanuel Glouberman, "Fyodor Dostoyevsky, Vladimir Soloviev, Vasilii Rozanov, and Lev Shestov on Jewish and Old Testament Themes" (PhD diss., University of Michigan, 1974), 442–77; Rogger, *JPRWP*, 40–55; Michael Hagemeister, "Pavel Florenskij und der Ritualmordvorwurft'", in *Appendix 2: Materialien zu Pavel Florenskij* (Anhang zu Pawel Florenski,

Werke in zehn Lieferungen), ed. Michael Hagemeister and Torsten Metelka (Berlin u. Zepernick: Kontext, 2001), 59–74.

196. Bar-Yosef, "The Jewish Reception," 364–65, citing Syrkin, "V. Solov'ëv ve-yihusso lishe'elat ha-Yehudim," 77.

197. See Walter Moss, "Vladimir Soloviev and the Jews in Russia," *Russian Review* 29.2 (1970): 181–91 n. 11, citing Louis Greenberg, *The Jews in Russia: The Struggle for Emancipation* (New Haven, CT: Yale University Press, 1965), 2:57–58. Taking note of Saltykov-Shhedrin, Moss also allows, on Solovyov's testimony in "Jewry and the Christian Question," that Bishop Nikanor delivered and printed a speech pleading for tolerance for the Jews. See, however, my note on this passage in Pt. II, ch. 8.

PART II

Commentary and Portrait of Solovyov's
Encounters with Jews and Judaism

CHAPTER 1

Solovyov's Writings on Judaism in Light of His Notes, Letters, and Other Testimonies

The drama lying behind Vladimir Sergeevich Solovyov's writings on Judaism is intertwined with his maturation as a Christian philosopher and his great life crises. Little brings out this drama as poignantly as his letters on the Jewish question, and further salience may be drawn from his poems on Jewish themes.[1] The letters reveal his reasons for composing these works and their cost to his personal welfare. The poems illuminate the extent to which he interpreted not just Russia's history but also his own life by reference to the history of Israel, for they show how playfully he identified himself and his foes with Israel's traditional biblical saviors and foes. The letters are translated into English here for the first time. Many of the poems have recently been translated, but little has been written about their relevance to his Jewish writings. The poems that are clearly relevant to this work have been newly translated for this volume.

The earliest detailed study of Solovyov's life and the evolution of his thought is that of his nephew Sergei Mikhailovich Solovyov "the younger," to differentiate him from his grandfather, Solovyov's father, Sergei Mikhailovich Solovyov, the distinguished nineteenth-century Russian historian. As evident from the patronymic middle names, the father of the younger Sergei was Solovyov's brother Mikhail. Solovyov's letters to Mikhail illuminate his writings on the Jewish question in important ways, as the younger Sergei shows. Despite the richness of Sergei's study, however, the space he devotes to Solovyov's writings on the Jewish question is minimal, and he fails to mention the Protest of 1890 and all the efforts that Solovyov undertook to organize it. These efforts and the events surrounding them, to which historians of Jewish life in Russia have devoted a page or two (Dubnov, for example; see Pt. I, ch. 4, §9.6), are revealed best in Solovyov's letters.

The most important of Solovyov's letters on the Jewish question are the thirty-five he wrote to Rabbi Faivel Meir Bentsilovitch Getz. Solovyov befriended him in 1879 at the University of St. Petersburg and thereafter employed him as a tutor in Hebrew and biblical and rabbinic literature, and with whom inevitably after the pogroms of 1881–82 and the state-sponsored restraint of Jewish civil rights he began to campaign on behalf of the Jews. Written between 1881 and 1896, these letters cover the period of Solovyov's principal writings on Jewish matters and help to explain and reveal, in addition to the purposes of the latter, the persons who subsidized them, the officials whose favor Solovyov sought to secure to ensure their publication, the disappointments he suffered when his or Getz's writings were censored or destroyed, and the toll they took on his health.

Equally important letters to other persons pertaining to Judaism and Jewish-Christian relations fall into three categories. The first category comprises the letters associated with his 1890 Protest to the tsar on behalf of Jewish civil rights, which include letters to Leo Tolstoy, a version of the Protest preserved by the humanitarian writer Vladimir Korolenko, and another version translated and printed in the London *Times* by the British journalist Emile Dillon, whom Solovyov introduced to Tolstoy and who would become one of Tolstoy's earliest English biographers. The second category comprises letters addressed to the reactionary editors of *Moskovskie vedomosti* defending his 1891 "Lecture on the Medieval Worldview." The letters in the third category relate to the article by Baron David Gintsburg on the Kabbalah, which Solovyov initially commissioned for the *Encyclopedic Dictionary* of Brockhaus and Efron. Having decided to replace this article with one of his own, Solovyov arranged to publish it instead in the journal *Questions of Philosophy and Psychology*, edited by N. Y. Grot. After doing so, he took care to explain the matter in a friendly and diplomatic letter to the author's father, Baron Horace de Gintsburg. The letters to the Gintsburgs, the highest-ranking intercessors for Jewry with the Russian government, illustrate the degree of friendship and respect that Solovyov attained among them.

The latter-day works on the Kabbalah echo Solovyov's youthful interests in philosophy, mysticism, and Sophiology. This is clear from the journals he kept during his 1875–76 doctoral research trip to England, Egypt, Italy, and France. His nephew, Sergei Solovyov, explains that Solovyov was seeking to recover for Christianity the "spoils of Egypt," that is, the wisdom and truth of pre-Christian and non-Christian pagan tradition. By means of this trip he sought to retrace, as it were, the "journey with the Magi." In presenting and analyzing the Jewish, Kabbalah-themed contents of the journal notes, Sergei explains their relationship to Solovyov's 1874 master's thesis, "The Crisis of Western Philosophy (Against the Positivists)," the 1877–81 *Lectures on Godmanhood*, and the 1880 doctoral dissertation, "A Critique of Abstract Principles." Recent studies of these early writings, especially those by Konstantin Burmistrov and Judith Kornblatt, have helped to demonstrate these relationships.[2] They demonstrate that the Jewish motifs in the youthful journal notes relate to Solovyov's graduate works in ways that foreshadow the relationship of his principal Jewish writings to the rest of his corpus. A summary of the Jewish-themed contents of the journal notes, therefore, is also in order.

To explain the personal and faith-based roots of his Jewish interests, testimonies from close friends and family members are also helpful, especially those that shed light on his first and last thoughts, words and prayers about Jews, Judaism, and Jewish-Christian relations.

The poems translated here are those whose titles have explicit bearings on Jewish biblical motifs. The first four are Old Testament–Jewish and the fifth is New Testament–Judeo-Christian: "In the Land of Frosty Blizzards" (1882), "To the Promised Land" (1886), "The Burning Bush" (1891), "I Was Then Great" (1892), and "Immanu-el" (1894). Many other poems less directly related to Old Testament–Jewish themes exist, however. Examples are the unpublished verses about Terty Filippov written on July 30, 1889 (see commentary below on letter to Getz, #22), probably on the occasion of the latter's promotion to the position of chancellor of the Russian Empire (from July 1889). The letter marks the critical time when Solovyov was still hoping that history would occasion the liquidation of the pseudotheocracy propped up in Russia by the "malicious triumvirate": the false high priest Pobedonostsev, the false statesman D. A. Tolstoy, and the false prophet Katkov.[3] Additional poems that would be fitting to include here but are not included are those dedicated to Pobedonostsev, one comparing him to Nebuchadnezzar, the destroyer of the first Temple of Solomon and thus one of Judaism's greatest ancient enemies. While serving to illuminate Solovyov's understanding of present Jewish history in light of biblical typology, the poems are also markedly autobiographical and therefore semantically multilayered.

This mosaic of sources, fitted together, constitutes the following commentary and introduction to Solovyov's Jewish writings and the drama associated with them. That this narrative is chronologically coherent and approaches the shape of a biography testifies to the fact that his interests in Judaism were never marginal, never just a phase or a series of phases, but foundational and organically integral to his Christian thought and life.

CHAPTER 2

Solovyov's Unique Respect for Judaism and His Philosophy of History

---

Why Solovyov emerged in the early 1880s as the leading one of only five Russian spokesmen for the Jewish cause requires explanation.[4] In considering this question, Walter G. Moss answered that Solovyov, the son of Russia's most prominent historian, inherited "a universal outlook which freed him from the exclusive Great National nationalism of many of his contemporaries."[5] Savely Dudakov ventured that Solovyov "must have sooner or later stopped to consider the mystery of Israel's four-thousand-year history and that," as observed by N. O. Lossky, "the wondrous image of Israel's triumphant spirit, prevailing over all the sufferings of its flesh, exerted a charming effect upon his poetic soul."[6] These are important points. Solovyov did articulate a conception of history that, by its universalism, was consciously opposed to the Pan-Slavist chauvinism of Danilevsky and to the particularly Judeophobic Pan-Slavism of Aksakov (see Pt. I, ch. 4, §§7.3–7.6, esp. §7.2 citing Klier's reference to Solovyov's 1889 work "Slavophilism and its Degradation"). Danilevsky's *Russia and Europe* (1869), it will be recalled, theorized that nations had historico-cultural peculiarities whereby Russia, constituting the world's eleventh civilization, would take on the mantle of the Jewish people, which Jews, because of their self-segregation, could not bear. In contrast to Dostoevsky's praise of the work to Strakhov, the chief exponent of Danilevsky's nationalist ideas at that time, as the "future coffee-table book of every

Russian" (see Pt. I, ch. 4, §7.4), Solovyov, in a heated letter of August 23, 1890, to the same Strakhov, declared it "the Koran of all scoundrels and fools," of which, he said, Dostoevsky was an unfortunate victim.[7] Charging that Danilevsky used the semblance of scholarly apparatus to buttress what is ultimately romantic Russian nationalism, he went on to criticize Strakhov for believing in "the pathetic stupidities of Descartes and Leibniz . . . [that God is] immovable and passive . . . [and can only be] the object, in part, of abstract thought, and undefined affects, dissociated from any practical imperatives or concrete goals."[8] In short, faulting Strakhov for representing the synthesis of Western decadent mechanistic philosophy with Buddhist passivism, he asked him:

> You regard history as a Chinese Buddhist, and for you there is no sense in my Jewish[E]-Christian question: is the present intellectual climate beneficial or harmful for the divine-human *task* on earth, in the *present historical moment*? And by the way, how can Danilevsky's theory explain that the pure Russian (since it is Orthodox) national culture which we share does not prevent you from being Chinese, and me a Jew[E]?[9]

The first sentence of the quoted passage above (Solovyov's emphasis) is somewhat mysterious because it points to a conception of history that presupposes every moment is an opportunity for human beings to respond to a divine call and declares that this conception, being neither Western-mechanistic nor Buddhist-impersonal/passive, is specifically Hebrew-Christian. The sentence, written in 1890, in fact holds a precious clue to a crisis in Solovyov's understanding of history at that time and to the evolution of his reflections on Judeo-Christian relations, illustrating that his conception of these relations is not static but in the process of development. The commentary on the texts written at the time returns to these words.

In the meantime, this quotation serves to underscore that Moss was right to suspect that Solovyov's conception of history had a lot to do with his approach to Jewish-Christian relations and that the universalism of this conception was inherited by him from his father. Like

Moss, Solovyov's nephew credits Solovyov's father for preserving Solovyov from nationalism, but he goes beyond Moss in specificity. Not only does he contrast Solovyov with Danilevsky, which as the excerpt from Solovyov's argument with Strakhov shows is crucial, and not only does he explain that Danilevsky failed to captivate Solovyov as he did so many others, but he specifies the work that proved particularly influential in this regard, Sergei Solovyov the elder's "Observations on the Historical Life of Nations," published in the liberal journal *Vestnik Evropy* (European Herald) over the period 1868–76.[10]

The linkage of Solovyov's universalism to his father's philosophy lessens the degree of abstraction that can be found in both Dudakov's and Lossky's explanations of the origins of Solovyov's ability to transcend nationalism on account of "universalism" or fascination about Israel's "four-thousand-year existence." The motif of this long history does interest him as it did Dostoevsky. The latter, in his 1877 March installment of *The Diary of a Writer,* frequently alluded to Israel's four-thousand-year history in his treatment of the Jewish question, but given the Judeophobic tenor of his writing, he never did so appreciatively, never as a pointer to a mysterious historical vocation, a divine calling.[11] In contrast, Solovyov did so explicitly and graciously, freely underscoring thereby the messianic role that Russians, as illustrated by the policies of Derzhavin and Tsar Alexander I, recognized but begrudged and so wished but feared to facilitate.[12] The reason for this fear was, arguably, their Christianity, but here one needs to be careful, for the point that Solovyov wishes repeatedly to underscore is that it is Christianity that requires transcendence and repudiation of Judeophobia. Thus, as explained by Solovyov's friend, the chemist, rabbi, and member of the Pahlen Commission, Nikolai Bakst, Solovyov's wonder about Israel's perennial cultural receptivity was in fact rooted in his "active and living, rather than abstract and formal, Christian faith which did not permit him to fail to respect other confessions which grew on the same foundations."[13] Solovyov's friend Rabbi Faivel Getz also confirms this evaluation in recalling that Solovyov often characterized Jewish history as one of unprecedented moral heroism, suffering, and martyrdom (*podvig*) for its faith, believed this history was axial for the world, and confessed its people were "God-bearing" or "God-begetting" (*bogorozhdayushhij*). For this reason, in reflecting the threat that the pogroms posed to Jewry, he judged that given its greatness, given its ability to prevail over so many threats to its existence in the past, the present Israel had less to fear from Russian antisemites than Russia herself since her support for these pathetic anti-Christian voices within her threatened to undermine her own messianic task.[14] These points are strongly expressed at the end of the article "The Sins of Russia" (Pt. III, ch. 10 [#37]), which Solovyov began to compose in 1887, and at the end of his letter to Getz of March 5, 1891 (Pt. III, ch. 9, #25).

> I completely understand and share your pity for the present personal sufferings of your coreligionist, but I am sure, dear friend, that you do not attach to this feeling any fear for the future fate of your people. You also know its history. Is it really possible even for a moment to imagine that after all these glories and wonders, after so many triumphs of the spirit and endured sufferings, after all these astonishing forty centuries in the life of Israel, that he should fear some antisemites?! Were this malicious and filthy campaign to provoke within me any fear, then of course it would not be for the Jews but for Russia.

The same sentiment is expressed in the second stanza of his poem "In the Land of Frosty Blizzards" (V strane moroznykh vyug), written contemporaneously with the composition of the lectures on Jewry and the Christian question (1882). The first two stanzas read as follows:

> In the land of frosty blizzards, 'midst winters wild,
>   You came, girl, to this earth.
> And twixt two warring camps, abandoned child,
>   You had no sheltered berth.
>
> But hostile cries will not confound you
>   Nor din of arms, nor swords,
> In thought you stand and hear the mighty
>   Old Testamental words . . .

In supplementing Moss's and Dudakov's insights with these faith-related nuances, it should also be noted that Solovyov's conception of the nations and their histories was rooted in the biblical concept of the peoples of the world as a family of nations for each of whom, he said, adapting Genesis 2:18 to this corporate conception, "it is not good to be alone." Guided further by his Christian trinitarian understanding of God as Love, Solovyov was therefore convinced that this vocation necessitates fraternal cooperation, that is, love of the other, who, being a brother, is necessarily a rival and potentially difficult to be with. Just as the prophet Isaiah envisioned the divine task of blessing the earth as fulfilled through cooperation between Israel and its traditional enemies, Egypt and Assyria (Isa. 19:24), so he argued Russia, as a Gentile Orthodox nation, must develop its messianic vocation by cooperating with Israel, God's chosen people, and with her Western Catholic brothers, represented by Poland. Only such cooperation, he said, would enable each of these to fulfill their messianic mission to heal the schism between East and West, between spirit and flesh, the universal and the particular.[15] What is delightful here is Solovyov's application of scripture and doctrine to political theory and debate on Jewish-Christian relations. The scriptures are frequently cited in strategic places. Isaiah 19:24, for example, serves as an epigraph to "Jewry and the Christian Question," but it appears again in other writings and proves significant in answering questions about the evolution of his own reflections, and specifically about positions he retracted or developed. Such observations are facilitated by the work that has been done in the notes in the translation on his citations of biblical and post-biblical Jewish writings.

We see then that Solovyov's advocacy of the Jewish cause has not only philosophical and historical but also theological and scriptural grounds. Consequently, Lossky's, Dudakov's, and Moss's tracing of Solovyov's Jewish-Christian standpoint to a universal historical outlook inherited from his father is a good start but one that points to the need to press the question of Solovyov's commitment to the Jews further in the direction of the family's Christian faith.

CHAPTER 3

Judaism and Christ: The Testimony of Family and Friends

The earliest testimonies about Solovyov's attitudes to Jews come from Solovyov's family and friends. These are the memoirs of his sister Maria Bezobrazova; his good friend's sister, Katerina Mikhailovna Lopatina, who wrote under the name El'tsova; and his nephew Sergei Solovyov. These memoirs are discussed here. Those of Getz and Korolenko, which add the theme of conscience to that of Christ, are discussed in the next chapter.

The following excerpt from the memoir of Maria Sergeevna Bezobrazova (neé Solovyova; 1863–1918) explains that while affection for the Jews prevailed in their family, Solovyov's was exceptional and inspiring.[16]

> Returning in memory to what has long ago passed, I also remember equally that special feeling for Jews which I had to a large extent thanks to my brother's exceptional attitude to them. Of course, a part of it existed in me independently of my brother, presumably congenitally, as with other members of our family, but when still in childhood I used to think how much goodness Jews must possess if Volodya loves them so — that was already indubitably the influence, the charm of my brother. And when I was still a child and, on account of my exceptional passion for music and several other physical and moral traits, was called a Yid, I was

rather flattered, and when once some grown-up, having become angry at me (this time completely groundlessly), cried, "Well, truly, a real Yid," I did not utter a word to justify myself but simply thought, "Well and splendid, Jews have always been persecuted and still are persecuted unjustly, without any clear understanding of the reason, and so am I, and so be it! But a person such as Volodya loves Jews and understands them."

As time passed, alongside my love for Jews, there grew also my incomprehension and disgust over the attitude to them held by so-called and self-confessing Christians, and on such occasions I always drew a mental picture of my brother, of Christ, and of my brother's attitude to Christ. . . .

Two years after the birth of my third daughter we were forced to leave Moscow and spend several years in the southwest.[17] Here, observing how poor Jews lived, and becoming acquainted with some of them, I constantly thought of my brother and strengthened my resolve regarding Jews and Christian attitudes to them, and so much so that I rejoice to share that in my small experience I have never had any occasion to be disillusioned by them. Were this to happen, however, my personal and actual experience would not allow individual people and facts to alter my feeling and attitude to God's chosen people.[18]

Maria's recollections underscore several essential points about Solovyov's attitudes to Jews. The first is that his affection for them was grounded on his familial, Christian understanding of Jesus as a Jew. She further stresses that this affection was nurtured both by his own contemplation of Christ as a Jew and by his disgust for Jew hatred as un-Christian.

She also clarifies that, despite occasional reports to the contrary, the Solovyov family did not have Jewish ancestry.[19] In explaining her pride about being called a Yid and being mistaken for a Jew, she relates that those who knew and later wrote about Solovyov recall that he himself sought to emulate the qualities he ascribed to the Jews. The chief of these, she judges, consisted in his "passionate desire not only theoretically to discover divine truth but also to contribute to its incarnation on earth." This is why he was wont to call himself a Jew,[20] she explains, citing his oft-cited statement to Strakhov as to how Danilevsky's theory of national types could account for Strakhov being a Chinese Buddhist and Solovyov a Jew. Maria's last paragraph, by highlighting Solovyov's intuition that Christian antisemitism intrinsically manifested the failure of Christians to love Christ and to partake of his spirit of love, also underscores that Solovyov made it a principle to check discussions of the "Jewish problem" by speaking of the "Christian problem" instead.

This same core principle is underscored in the memoir of Katerina Mikhailovna Lopatina (El'tsova; 1865–1935), the younger sister of Solovyov's friend Lev Lopatin, whom Solovyov befriended in 1878 in Moscow during his doctoral studies. In those days, Solovyov and Lopatin became involved with the Shakespeareans, a group that hosted comedies, dances, and plays and drew its inspiration from the writings of Koz'ma Prutkov, the joint pseudonymous creation of Alexei Konstaninovich Tolstoy and his cousins.[21] Solovyov gave a role to Lopatin in his own play titled *Koz'ma Prutkov*. The young Solovyov's sense of humor and talent as a playwright, and the value he placed on humor and dramatic dialogue, will resurface in his later interest in Plato's dialogues and in his swan song, *Three Conversations* (1899–1900), in which he criticizes Tolstoy's pacifism and satirizes antisemites.

In recollecting Solovyov's views of Judaism and love of Jews, Katerina also traced the latter to his love of Christ.

> From his faith in Christ and love for Christ stemmed his defense of the Jews. The life, which surrounded him, however enlightened and given to lofty interests, was nevertheless far removed from such love. From this stemmed not only all the difficulties of his way but also all the misunderstandings erected upon it. Solovyov was neither a monarchist, although he called a Christian monarchy the "autocracy of conscience," nor a revolutionary, although succumbing to persecution he unwillingly shared their lot, nor a Catholic, nor an Orthodox, inasmuch as these words are understood. He was a Christian in the true meaning of the word, and thus it is necessary to say that he was not apolitical but transpolitical.

Regarding the Jewish question, he used to say that before all else this is a Christian problem, a question about the extent to which Christian societies in every respect, and, among other things, in their attitudes to the Jews, "are capable of being governed in practice by principles of evangelical teaching, orally confessed by them." It is curious that in this question he found support in M. N. Katkov and cited his articles in the *Moskovskie vedomosti* [Moscow News]. In saying such things, his position was just as far removed from the norm, and his struggle was [just as much] lacking [external] incentive as when he was dismissed from Petersburg for saying what he said about the Gospel of Christ. . . .

. . . From the diagnosis of the doctors, an opinion has been formed that Solovyov died "from old age" in the forty-seventh year of his unusual, high and pure life. All the time he retained his memory. On the morning of the day that he lost consciousness, he received communion from the local priest. . . . On that same day, Solovyov lost consciousness and did not regain it until the very end.

Before death he began to rave, during which, among other things, he prayed for the unfortunate Jewish people. He died quietly, surrounded by family. . . .

Vladimir Sergeevich Solovyov was buried beside his father. For a long time, upon his wooden cross, there hung an Orthodox icon, a mother-of-pearl image from Jerusalem, and a Catholic silk-woven image of the Mother of God of Częstochowa, which he especially revered, bearing a Latin inscription. Upon his tombstone, erected by Nadia, and following the insistence of his sister Poliksena, were inscribed the words "Come O Lord.". . .[22]

There are people for whom one fears not when accompanying them to their grave. Such were they . . . the Solovyovs. This lack of fear is especially strange and touching in the case of people who passionately loved life, the earth, and its loveliness. Their hearts burned with a flaming love, with the spirit of Christ, and with an unconquerable faith in eternity. Perhaps then, it would be appropriate to inscribe, on each of their crosses, the great words written upon the cross of Vladimir Solovyov: "Come, O Lord."[23]

The testimonies of Maria and Katerina highlight that for Solovyov the Jewish problem was an epiphenomenon: when Christians speak of the Jewish problem, they register the Christian problem, the problem of actually and concretely believing in Jesus as the Christ and following his commandment to love one's brother, neighbor, and enemy. Maria and Katerina further stress that this position of Solovyov was not grounded in abstract philosophical principles but on his love of Jesus Christ and on his contemplation of Jesus Christ's earthly, human nature. This needs to be kept in mind, for critiques of Solovyov typically attribute his views to abstract philosophical, otherworldly, dualistic, gnostic, esoteric, and, ultimately, heretical principles. That Solovyov engaged with philosophy and esoteric spirituality is a fact. The charge that this engagement preceded his commitment to Christ, and did not flow out of the latter, is, as shown by the testimonies above, a debatable inference.

Sensitivity to this issue is a theme throughout Sergei Solovyov's study of Solovyov. Sergei points out that Solovyov wrote "Jewry and the Christian Question" (1884) immediately after his *Spiritual Foundations of Life* (1884). This is important because, according to Sergei, the *Spiritual Foundations* marks Solovyov's maturation as a Christian thinker and furnishes the key to understanding the spiritual state in which he composed works produced at this time.

> The book closes with a short conclusion of two pages: "The Image of Christ as an Examination of Conscience." Here Solovyov counsels his readers, "prior to doing something personally and socially important, to evoke in one's psyche a moral image of Christ, to concentrate on it, and then ask oneself: 'Could he do this? In other words: would he sanction this action? Would he or wouldn't he bless me in its accomplishment?' I propose this examination to all—it will not prove deceptive. In any doubtful case, if the possibility arises of recollecting oneself and thinking, remember Christ, imagine him to yourselves alive, as he indeed is, and hand over to him all your burdensome doubts" (C.W. III. 146).[24]

This 180-page book furnishes the key to understanding the spiritual state which arose in Solovyov during his stay abroad in 1882–83 and corroborates the words of Bishop Strossmayer: "Soloviof anima candida, pia ac vere sancta est" (Solovyov, a pure, pious, and truly holy soul). Following the brilliant and dire storms of his youth, Solovyov heard the "still small voice":[25]

> The still small voice flutters, and in its secret breathing
> He discerned God.

What Strossmayer took as proof [of] *castitatis, pietatis et sanctitatis* appeared to the Olympian Katkov as "childish prattle," while the most noble I. S. Aksakov even declined to publish the "edifying essays" in his *Rus'*.

Silence, humility, crystal clarity of thought, and simplicity of language—this is what distinguishes *The Spiritual Foundations of Life* from Solovyov's various other works. We remark that this book was composed simultaneously with *The Great Debate*.

The Spiritual Foundations of Life sufficiently repudiates many accusations aimed against Solovyov: V. V. Rozanov's judgment that Solovyov could not shake off his pride, M. M. Tareyev's judgment that Solovyov never spoke about the historical Christ, E. N. Trubetskoy's judgment that the 1880s were for Solovyov a period of "theocratic *temptation*," and so on.

Reviewing *The Spiritual Foundations of Life* three years prior to his death in 1897, Solovyov found that "the book, in its humble measure, attains its objective and requires no substantial modification. . . . Reappearing now after my large work on moral philosophy, the present booklet can serve as its supplement for some of my readers and as its replacement for others."[26]

The Spiritual Foundations of Life, as it were, provides a glimpse of Solovyov's entire worldview, and also constitutes the first book which introduces us to the entire sphere of his ideas, excelling over *The Justification of the Good* by the youthful freshness of feeling and the absence of schematization and heaviness. *The Spiritual Foundations* was composed at a time of joyful hopes, while *The Justification of the Good* was composed at a time of bitter disillusionment. These "edifying essays" are also free from the Schelling-echoing romanticism which sometimes spoils Solovyov's youthful works. And its outstanding insight into the theology of the Fourth

Gospel can be attributed to the sufferings he experienced while wrestling with typhoid fever in the spring of 1883, as related by Maria Sergeevna in her account of how Solovyov, in feverish delirium, begged her to read the account of the marriage feast at Cana to him.

As already noted, Solovyov spent the summer of 1883 in Krasnyi Rog, with the Khitrovo family. In June, Solovyov wrote to his brother Mikhail:

> I think that I have more or less recovered, but I was really sick with typhoid fever, and even my hair started to fall out, forcing me to shave my head. This so improved my looks, that the youngest lad present, Ryurik, anxiously started inquiring of all the members of the household, "But Solovyov's a deformed freak, right, a deformed freak?"[27]

Highlighting that "Jewry and the Christian Question" was composed in the same spirit as *The Spiritual Foundations of Life*, Sergei Solovyov corroborates Maria's and Katerina's testimonies that Solovyov's thoughts on Judaism and opposition to antisemitism were Christian in foundation and spirituality. Sergei Solovyov repeatedly stresses this point to confute the frequent criticism that Solovyov's thought was ultimately grounded in personal mystical, visionary experiences, and synthetic philosophical insights rather than on an ecclesially established rule of faith and Christian spirituality.

CHAPTER 4

Judaism, Christ, and Conscience:
The Testimony of Colleagues

———

If the content and spirituality of Solovyov's *Spiritual Foundations of Life* are relevant to understanding "Jewry and the Christian Question," it is salient to note the title of its last chapter: "The Image of Christ as an Examination of Conscience." Conscience and Christ both played key roles in prompting Solovyov to defend the Jews because by doing so he sought to atone for Christianity's historical mistreatment of Jews. He explains this point by citing Ezekiel 3:18–19 or 33:8. He does so, for example, in his petition to Tolstoy to sign his and Getz's Protest to the tsar in defense of Jewish civil rights (Pt. III, ch. 11, letter to Tolstoy, #2, February 1890; see below). He does so again in his preface to Getz's book *The Floor to the Accused*:

> My dear friend, you wish me to express myself once more on the Jewish[E] problem on account of your book. I do so eagerly not only for your sake but also for mine: for the purification of my conscience touching our preachers of antisemitism. For as is stated by the prophet Ezekiel: "If you do not warn the wicked that he should turn from his way and live . . . his blood I will require at your hand. But if you warn him and he does not turn from his wickedness, or from his wicked way, he shall die in his iniquity, but you will have saved your life."

131

Getz himself finds in these sentiments the key to Solovyov's view on the Jewish question, explaining that Solovyov regarded the defense of the Jews as his personal task, as the task of his own conscience and of his conscience as a Russian patriot.[28] The passage that Getz goes on to quote at this point is frequently cited, though I cannot find its source in any surviving text. I presume that Getz either derived it from conversation with Solovyov or pieced it together from things that Solovyov wrote on different occasions or both (hence the word *approximating* in the first sentence below).

V. Solovyov himself explained his attitude to the Jewish question in words approximating the following: "Some people represent me as a Judeophile, while others accuse me of being blindly partial to Jewry. Fortunately, they do not suspect me of being in the pay of Jewish[E] gold. But in what, I would like to know, is my Judeophilia or partiality to Jewry expressed? Do I not acknowledge the weak aspects of Judaism, or do I in fact justify the latter? Have I ever manifested the least inclination to idealizing Jewry? In reality, I am just as far from Judeophilia as from Judeophobia. But I cannot curry up and turn a blind eye to bad taste or morals so as not to see obvious facts. I do not want and cannot twist my soul and, following the example of the antisemites, make the Jews solely responsible for all the sins and misfortunes that have befallen us. I do not conceal that I am vitally interested in the fortunes of the Jewish[E] nation, but this is because it is itself, in the highest degree, interesting and instructive in many respects. But now and then do I defend the Jews[E]? Yes, only regretfully not as often as I would have liked and ought to have done as a Christian and a Slav. (As a Christian I acknowledge that I owe Judaism the greatest gratitude, for my Savior was a Jew according to the flesh, and the prophets and the apostles were Jews, and the cornerstone of the universal church was chosen in the house of Israel; as a Slav, I feel a great guilt regarding Jewry, and would like to expiate it in whatever way I can.) The Jewish[E] question is in essence a question of truth and justice. In the face of the Jew[E], justice is trampled, because the persecutions to which the Jews[E] are subjected have not the slightest justification, for the accusations leveled against them by the anti-semites cannot bear the most contemptible critique, for they are in the main a malicious lie."[29]

The terms "Christ," "expiation," "Christian," "Slavic," and "conscience" and the emphasis on defending Jews by concrete "deeds" and not abstractions also appear in the recollections of Vladimir Korolenko about Solovyov's role in organizing the public Protest on behalf of the Jews in 1890 that Korolenko signed. Toward the end of his memoir about Solovyov's role in organizing this Protest, Korolenko wrote:

> My signature was far from the last. Solovyov very heatedly, passionately even, approached this literary undertaking, trying to unite under the declaration distinguished names in literature and science independently of their various different viewpoints on other questions. Those who should have first of all responded to his short formula were people for whom religious and national tolerance constitutes an organic part of the common order of convictions. But to persons with whom he closely shared the other side of his very complex intellectual constitution, he appealed with arguments based on purely Christian morality, in which there was much strength and winsome charm. In *his* Christianity he did not go for compromise. For him, Christianity was a fount of absolute morality. From this font he drew also a formula on the Jewish question, distinguished by an unusual lightness and simplicity. He said: "If the Jews are our enemies, then deal with them according to the Gospel: love your enemies. If they are not enemies [and he verily thought that they were not enemies] then there is no need to persecute them." Many of Solovyov's dogmatic views are swathed in thick, often almost impenetrable metaphysical mists. But when he would descend from these misty heights, so as to apply these or those foundational formulas of Christianity to passing life, he was sometimes magnificent on account of his precise clarity of thought and for his skill in finding for it a simple and condensed formula. Such was his argumentation on the Jewish question. Listening to it, people who would profess to possess a

true Christian faith had to either agree with his conclusion or acknowledge that Christianity is only an abstract doctrine, inapplicable to broad phenomena of contemporary life, which must yield
before anti-Christian invocations to hatred and vengeance. But
this, from the point of view of a man of sincere faith, is blasphemy.
In this manner, to the formula of a pure liberalism on a given question, Solovyov especially was able to involve a wide circle of
people, far, perhaps, from being liberal in the exact meaning of this
word but sensitive to the logic of a sincere faith, which could be
heard in Solovyov's liberal formulation.[30]

Korolenko's observations regarding Solovyov's foundational Christian commitment and rhetorical genius for finding common ground
with people of alternate and opposing viewpoints are also crucial to
understanding Solovyov's strategies in debating with people of other
faiths and philosophies, and will be commented on in due course
below.

CHAPTER 5

1875–1877: Judaism and Sophia in Solovyov's "Journey with the Magi"

Despite the testimony to Christ's centrality in Solovyov's thought, there is much in his writings that Christians, especially the Orthodox but Catholics as well, find heterodox. The principal problem turns on the suspicion that the true center of his thought is not Christ but Wisdom/Sophia and that, lacking method and discipline to control his thought by reference to Christian Orthodox dogma, he was constantly fitting Christian dogma to personal "Sophia-logical" intuitions and thereby lapsing into syncretism with heterodox esoteric thought and practice.[31] Solovyov's own testimony to understanding himself as laying the foundation of a new ecumenical church furthers these suspicions. As Kabbalistic mysticism comprises one of these suspicious interests on his part, and from a very early period, it would be well to examine the reasons for his interest in it.[32]

Solovyov's interest in Wisdom/Sophia is famously correlated with his three visions of her, as described in his autobiographical poem, *The Three Encounters*, written in the last days of September 1898, less than two years before his death. Although narrated in a somewhat self-parodying style, he composed it to fulfill a calling conceived on the evening of September 26, in the deep, quiet forest recesses of Pustyn'ka, the domain of Sophia P. Khitrovo (see below), "to compose in joking verses *the most significant experiences of his life*," whereby "on the third day after two days of recollection and harmonization, he wrote this short autobiography," which, although disliked by Sophia Khitrovo, he deemed his best and most significant poetic composition.[33]

According to the poem, he first saw the heavenly Sophia at the age of nine. This vision came on the heels of his first infatuation with a young girl, Yulia Sveshnikova, and after a "duel" with a rival for her affection. He saw her in church, on the feast of the Assumption, at the sound of the divine liturgy, when she appeared to him with a "radiant smile," holding in her extended hand a flower from "some unearthly land." The second and third visions occurred during his doctoral study trip abroad in 1875–76, the former in, as Judith Kornblatt remarks, the churchlike reading room of the British Museum, the latter in the desert outside the city of Cairo, where he sought out hermit-ascetics and claimed to have experienced the "light of Tabor."[34]

Discussion of Solovyov's interest in Sophia may be prefaced with the observation that interest in and devotion to both Wisdom-Sophia and Christ are not logically incompatible for Christians. The Septuagint version of the Christian Bible personifies Wisdom/Sophia as female in Proverbs, Sirach, Wisdom of Solomon, and Baruch, and all of these encourage the reader to seek and love her. In light of the identification in Proverbs 8:22 of Wisdom as "the Beginning," Jewish Targumim (Aramaic translations of the Bible used in synagogal liturgy and study) and rabbinic midrashim (exegetical commentaries) frequently see Wisdom as the agent, "the Beginning" in and with whom God created the world according to Genesis 1:1, and Solovyov in fact follows this tradition in his own commentary on Genesis in his *Theocracy*. Judging by the Logos doctrine of the prologue to St. John's Gospel and by St. Paul's identification of Christ with the wisdom of God (1 Cor. 1:24, 30), this personification of Wisdom seems also to have interested the authors of the New Testament.[35] Continuing interest in Wisdom in Christian philosophy is evidenced in Boethius's *Consolation of Philosophy*, which depicts a dialogue with Lady Wisdom to illustrate the consoling power of dialogue between Christian faith and (Platonic philosophical) reason. Orthodox Christianity, Greek and Russian, developed further grounds for referencing heavenly Wisdom in medieval churches dedicated to Hagia Sophia, Holy Wisdom, and while the Greeks, according to Solovyov's *La Russie et l'Eglise universelle*, published in Paris in 1889, identified Sophia with the Logos, the Russians distinguished her from the Theotokos (Virgin Mary) and Christ, believing her to be "a heavenly reality, hidden behind the veil of the lower world, the effulgent spirit of revived humanity, the guardian angel of the earth, the future and ultimate Theophany."[36] The speculative interest in Wisdom that surfaced in Solovyov's *Lectures on Godmanhood* (1877–81) and subsequent mature works such as *La Russie et l'Eglise universelle* was sustained and developed in Russian Orthodox theology by Pavel Florensky and Sergius Bulgakov, and since this interest is unmatched elsewhere, it is usual to look for its sources at an earlier point in his life.[37]

Solovyov embarked on his research trip after completing his master's thesis at Moscow University in 1874. The thesis constituted a critique of the shortcomings of Western philosophy under the title, "The Crisis of Western Philosophy (Against the Positivists)" (Krizis zapadnoj filosofii [protiv pozitivistov]). His request to the university to undertake the trip stated that he intended to study "Indian, gnostic, and medieval philosophy" so as to prepare for his PhD dissertation whose anticipated title was "The Principles of Integral Knowledge." Published in 1880 as *A Critique of Abstract Principles*, this work sought to ascertain to what extent the fruit of "partial" and "abstract" "truths" of Western liberal philosophical knowledge could be "integrated" with the fruit of various Eastern and esoteric sapiential traditions and with that of Christian theology. The titles of these works suggest what their final contents confirm—that he was committed to "wholeness" or "integral principles" and opposed to "abstract" or "partial" truths. The rationale he supplied for this research to Moscow University sheds light on his preoccupation in the course of his travels with Eastern thought, ancient religion, the Kabbalah, spiritualism, and the occult. It allows us to see that his preoccupation need not be interpreted as a rebellion against dogma but as an expression of his quest for a "whole" or "integral" worldview that would justify Orthodox Christianity in the language of contemporary and perennial philosophy, mysticism, and religious traditions. He was, in short, imitating the early Christian apologists who sought to justify Christianity to their Hellenistic intellectual and gnostic contemporaries by finding common ground in their thinking.[38]

Solovyov's interest in reconciling Eastern and Western mystical, philosophical, and theological tradition is evidenced by his journal notes at the time.[39] Were one to peruse these notes unaware of Solovyov's research aims, they would likely appear ridiculous, and not only to people of opposing philosophies. They certainly seemed so to I. I. Yanzhul, a self-confessed positivist and Westernist, who was himself doing research in London at the time and took Solovyov into his lodgings after Solovyov's father asked him to watch over the boy, prone as he was to financial exploitation and mismanagement. In his memoirs, Yanzhul admitted a priori resentment against Solovyov for critiquing positivism in his master's thesis and for associating with the editor of the reactionary journal *Moskovskie vedomosti*, N. N. Strakhov, and its contributors, for example, Konstantin Leontiev[40] and Nikolai Lyubimov,[41] all of whom Yanzhul detested. Yanzhul found Solovyov's behavior in the British Museum quite bizarre.

> For whole hours . . . he would sit beside me, with some book on the Kabbalah, poring over curious, wild sketches and signs, completely immersed and oblivious to everything around him. A concentrated and sad expression of some internal struggle was reflected almost constantly on his face. He sat so close to me that I was able to observe this scene many times. When I would turn to him and ask, "Well, Vladimir Sergeevich, what are you pondering now?" or "This book must be very interesting to you since you are reading it for so long. Why don't you change it?," and so on, I would receive answers such as the following: "I'm fine. . . It is extremely interesting. One line of this book holds more knowledge than all of European science. I am delighted and gratified to have found this publication."[42]

Sergei Solovyov introduces the things recorded in Solovyov's notebook as dictated by Sophia and other spirits, heavenly and demonic. He called this notebook Album #1 and appended it to the sixth and seventh editions of Solovyov's poetry. Noteworthy among the contents is the "Prayer for Revelation of a Great Mystery," which reads as follows:

> In the Name of the Father and of the Son and of the Holy Spirit
> Ain-Soph, Jah, Soph-Jah.

Kornblatt has followed S. M. Lukianov, an early biographer of Solovyov, in rendering the Kabbalistic terms "Ain-Soph" (Without End, Infinite, First Principle), "Jah" (the Tetragrammaton, the Name of God) and "Soph-Jah," which is etymologically related to both terms and interpreted as "Completion of the One Who Is" but also a homophone of Sophia.[43]

Yanzhul's impressions of Solovyov as a braggart and his references to the "curious and wild signs" presumably refer to notes and sketches such as the following.

Excerpt 1

In his latter system, Schelling, by means of a logical understanding of the process, offers a relatively incomplete and rather confused conception of spiritual principles; and it is for this reason that the goal of the process assumes in his thought a rather satisfactory determination; on this account he recognizes a concrete spiritual world, with Boehme and Swedenborg, but not demons or hell, which is why Schelling is the true forerunner of universal religion. The teachings of Boehme and Swedenborg are the full and ultimate theosophical expression of ancient Christianity. Schelling's positive philosophy is but the first conception, weak and incomplete, of the new Christianity or of the universal religion of the Eternal Testament.

Kabbala and Neoplatonism
Boehme and Swedenborg
Schelling and Myself

The Law
Neoplatonism—Kabbala—The Old Testament
The Gospel
Boehme—Swedenborg—The New Testament

Freedom
Schelling—Myself—The Eternal Testament[44]

Judging from his correspondence, Solovyov also devoted much of his time in London to investigating spiritualism and its principal representatives or mediums.[45] His letter from this period to Dmitry Tsertelev, nephew of Alexei Tolstoy, shows that he already judged spiritualism to be full of charlatans: "Local spiritualism (and thus spiritualism in general, since London is its center) is in an absolutely pitiful state. I have seen famous mediums as well as famous spiritists, and don't know which of them are worse."[46] The letters to people around Alexei Tolstoy evidence that Solovyov's interests in occult spiritualism and esotericism reflected contemporary preoccupations, which were shared by other members of his family, principally by his eldest brother, Vsevolod (1849–1903), whose interests in the occult led him to study Madame Blavatskaya in Paris in 1884.[47] Thus, even though Solovyov's own estimation of spiritualism, as also reflected in his reviews of Blavatskaya, shows him to have judged much of it fraudulent,[48] he did not dismiss it wholly. Probably the most important reason for this was his own experience with such phenomena, including demonic visions and hallucinations, from this point to the end of his life.[49]

Having devoted the first phase of his trip to Gnosticism, esotericism, and spiritualism, Solovyov departed for Egypt to seek out its ascetics. Reaching Cairo on November 12, 1876, he commenced writing his "Principes de la religion universelle," also called "Sophie," never published in his lifetime, whose contents he outlined in London, as follows:

Introduction
Chap. 1. On the Three Types of Philosophy in General
Chap. 2. Man's Metaphysical Character and the General Possibility of Metaphysics
Chap. 3. On Positive Metaphysics in Particular. Its formal principles. Its relationship to two other types of philosophy, to religion, the positive sciences, art and life.

Exposition of principles.
Chap. 4. Anthropological Foundations of Positive Metaphysics
Chap. 5. Theological Principles
Chap. 6. Cosmogonic and Soteriological Principles
Chap. 7. Eschatological Principles

At this point the following schema appears:

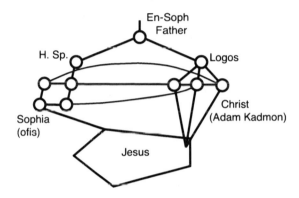

The first three chapters of *Sophie* are dialogues. The second contains this schema in the margins:

En-Soph	Logos	Sophia
Spirit	Will	Good
Mind	Knowledge	Truth
Soul	Sensation	Beauty

According to Sergei Solovyov, this schema matches, almost verbatim, the one found in the *Philosophical Principles of Integral Knowledge*:[50]

Being as Such (God)	Substance (Content or Idea)	Being (Potential or Mode of Being Nature)
1. Spirit	Good	Will
2. Mind	Truth	Cognition
3. Soul	Beauty	Sensation

Sergei Solovyov observes that *Sophie*, while being "a mix of brilliant insight and helpless childish illusion . . . which would have convinced many of Solovyov's madness," "contained *in nuce* all of [the] future Solovyov." He goes on to say that it already evinces positions that Solovyov retained for the rest of his life, such as the quest to reconcile mystical teaching of ancient religions and Christianity with the conclusions of modern philosophy and science, in ways that increasingly show his efforts to purify and reconcile his positions and ideas with Christian and Catholic orthodoxy and, as far as his preoccupation with the relationship between chaos, matter, and evil is concerned, seek to explain it not just as privation, not as the absence of good, but as the expression of active, spiritual power.[51]

The relationship of Solovyov's youthful visions, temptations, and writings to his Jewish interests and wider corpus has received detailed commentary from Judith Kornblatt[52] and Konstantin Burmistrov.[53] The latter identifies Solovyov's sources in the British Museum as the works of Boehme, Swedenborg, John Pordage, and perhaps Theophrastus Paracelsus, Georg Gichtel, and Gottfried Arnold, who are mentioned in Solovyov's letter of April 27, 1877, to Countess C. A. Tolstaya. Burmistrov doubts that Solovyov actually studied books by Jewish authors in the British Museum and suspects them to have been the schema-filled compositions of Christian kabbalists and mystic-occultists (Gnostics) such as Boehme's *Amphitheatrum Sapientiae Aeternae* (1608), Henryk Kunrat's *Opus Mago-Cabbalisticum* (1719), Georg Von Welling's *Oedipus Aegyptiacus* (1652–55), and especially Baron H. Knorr von Rozenrot's *Kabbala Denudata* (Sulzbach-Frankfurt, 1677–84). Burmistrov traces the sources of *Sophie*, some of whose schemas are reproduced above, to Louis Claude de Saint-Martin, Faibre D'Olivier, Eliphaz Levi, and E. P. Blavatskaya.[54]

Sergei Solovyov completes his account of this period by relating that Album #1 contained poems that evidence Solovyov's ultimate renunciation of his youthful chimerical visions and hubristic supernatural temptations and signal a humble "conversion" to the objectivity of ecclesial Christianity or, more precisely, a maturation in already established Christian allegiance.[55] Noting that the purpose of Solovyov's activities in Egypt, such as his visits to the ascetics at Thebes, lay in retracing the spiritual journeys toward wisdom made by Moses, St. Paul, and St. Anthony, Sergei reiterates what can be inferred from the rationale supplied for the trip and the titles of the lectures and dissertations that followed. The entire trip conformed to a simple but strikingly meaningful schema: the British phase focused on Neoplatonic, Jewish, and Eastern esotericism, gnosticism, and English spiritualism (i.e., the Wisdom of the Magi); the Egyptian phase, on the journey toward wisdom made by Hebrew prophets and Christian ascetics. This framework provides a key to understanding Solovyov's intentions in composing the comparative esoteric schemas found in his British Museum album and "Journey with the Magi" journals. This, in turn, facilitates understanding the relationship of these schemas to his writings on Judaism and on Jewish-Christian relations in the following decade, bridged as they are by the *Lectures on Godmanhood* (1878–81) and *A Critique of Abstract Principles* (1880).

In reflecting on this early phase of Solovyov's life and work, Sergei Solovyov offers five explanations as to why Solovyov did not publish "Principes de la religion universelle," "Sophie"), which he intended to use in his PhD dissertation, originally titled "The Philosophical Principles of Integral Knowledge" (1877) (left unpublished at ch. 5). The first explanation is that he simply had the good sense to recognize its chimerical follies. The second was his growing political interest, as indicated by letters to his father from Egypt in 1876 about the looming Eastern Crisis (see Pt. I, ch. 4, §§7.4–7.5) and his perspicacious observation that in the coming Russo-Turkish War Russia would lose.[56] The third explanation is simply that the work was interrupted when he fell off a horse when riding on Mount Vesuvius on April 20, 1876, and had to recuperate in Naples for a week.[57] The fourth is that he fell in love with a real Sophia when he returned to Moscow after a short stay in Paris.[58] The fifth is the death of his father in January 1879, which taught him that life presents misfortune and that ideals fail.[59] All of these caused an Aristotelian shift from idealism toward realism in Solovyov's life and thought.

It would be interesting to speculate whether the "journey with the Magi" phase of his study ended and this Aristotelian turn began at Naples accidentally, with his fall from a horse, or whether the latter was a coincidence and he meant to turn in the Aristotelian direction in Italy and Naples, given the latter's symbolic association with the secular university built by Frederick II and chosen by St. Thomas Aquinas to pursue empirical sciences and Aristotle and so synthesize commitment to these along with his Dominican commitment to the Gospel.[60] As Solovyov himself simulated this same synthesis by supplementing his undergraduate studies of philosophy and science with the study of theology in a seminary and with writing the first two chapters of his master's thesis, "Against Positivism," in a monastic setting, and as his travels to England and Egypt represented a retracing of the journey with the Magi and then with Moses and the desert fathers, he may have come to Italy to retrace the Thomistic, medieval Catholic synthesis.[61] Nothing in his correspondence, however, corroborates this proposal. S. Solovyov reports that nothing in Italy gained his interest, not even its architecture or its landscape, which disinterest the nephew interprets as a witness to Solovyov's ultimate indifference to objective beauty. Longing for Russia, Solovyov hurried to return, pausing for six weeks in Paris and a few days in London to recover his books. Paris also disappointed him, and he visited no one famous there save Renan. Having listened to the latter declare admiration for ideas while being surrounded by a bevy of admiring women, Solovyov described him as a "vapid and ill-mannered loudmouth."[62] His mood on his return was caught in Strakhov's letter to Leo Tolstoy of September 12, 1876.

> Vladimir Solovyov cheered me up. He is much stronger health-wise, doesn't eat meat and doesn't drink wine. Perhaps he'll recover. I very much hope so. "Whom did you meet? Whom did you hear?" "No one and nobody." "What did you do?" "I worked on my book, *The Principles of Positive Metaphysics,* and even in Paris I didn't visit a single theater. By the way, I did meet Renan, whom I very much disliked as a person, and Wallace, whom I found rather limited. The spiritualists are such trash, simply unendurable. I have completely recovered [i.e., from spiritualism]. For all that, I can give you something to chuckle over: Wallace said that Darwin, little by little, is turning to spiritualism: his wife turned out to be a medium (as was the case with Butlerov)." Vladimir

Solovyov's book is ready. It will consist of 400 pages, which he is ready to publish, and he will be coming to St. Petersburg at Christmas to receive his doctoral degree.[63]

From this point on, Solovyov's Aristotelian turn toward seeking Platonic ideals in incarnate form is signaled by the accompaniment of his Platonic love of the heavenly Sophia with love for flesh-and-blood Sophias, one lifelong, in the person of Sophia Khitrovo, a possible prototype for Leo Tolstoy's *Anna Karenina* (1873–77). This is attested by his first poem to her during the summer of 1878 and by his self-satirizing description of his devotion to her as verging on idolatry by comparing it to Christian veneration of icons. Subsequent poetry to her parodies his former theosophical interests so intensely as to suggest displacement of his former love of the heavenly *Sophia* by the earthly.[64]

Sophia Khitrovo was the niece of another Sophia, Countess Sophia Andreevna Tolstaya, the cultured widow of the recently deceased romantic and pantheist poet Count Alexei Konstantinovich Tolstoy (1817–75), with whom Solovyov also developed an intimate, but not erotically charged, friendship on his return from abroad. The countess owned two beautiful estates, Pustyn'ka (Little Desert), near St. Petersburg, and Krasny Rog (Red Horn), comprising 60,000 acres, about 250 miles southeast of Moscow, and frequently invited Solovyov and others to stay there with her extended family, which included the family of Sophia Khitrovo. Many of Russia's writers and thinkers developed their friendships during these visits, and so she also fostered Solovyov's friendship with Dostoevsky (although they met independently in 1873), as illustrated by her arranging for Solovyov to deliver from Dresden a large reproduction of Raphael's *Sistine Madonna*, Dostoevsky's favorite painting, for his birthday in 1879.[65]

Solovyov's love for Sophia Khitrovo was doomed to tragic futility. She was the wife of Mikhail Aleksandrovich Khitrovo, who was serving in those years as a diplomat in Constantinople, then from 1880 in Bulgaria, and later, until his death in 1896, in Japan. In describing their marriage to Lukianov, Count Ukhtomsky recalled it as unhappy, explaining that Sophia married less for love than on account of family influence and that Mikhail, despite his brilliance and talent for poetry and diplomacy, had the reputation of a Don Juan. Lukianov also records the great jurist A. F. Koni (1844–1927) describing her as a woman capable of inflaming passion, whose attitude to Solovyov could at times be disrespectful, and who, after Solovyov's death, struck him by her appearance and ungrounded judgments, as instanced by an attempt to persuade Koni that Solovyov's attitudes to Jews were very hostile. When Koni sought to rebut these charges, recalling Solovyov's deathbed prayers for the Jews, she became more agitated, contending that because of their closeness he expressed himself to her more openly. Nonetheless, she confessed to Koni the next day that she said many things that were excessive, and Koni got the impression that she was prone to occasional mood swings, especially in the evenings, and not without the influence of external agents.[66]

There is no indication that Solovyov's love for her was anything but chaste and courtly and that he gave much thought to marrying her should she divorce. Nonetheless, in 1887 he understood that this would not happen. Consequently, as illustrated by his poetry, plays, and diary entries, his love for her imbued him with agonizing despair.

Given the hopelessness of this relationship, Solovyov experienced a fiery infatuation, peaking in the spring of 1892, with another Sophia, Sophia Mikhailovna Martynova, but it was short-lived. When Sophia Khitrovo's husband died in 1896, he proposed to her, but by then, as Sergei Solovyov notes, "he could only love lakes."[67] Nonetheless, their friendship resumed, and in 1897, when she was grieving over the death of her eldest son, Andrei, Solovyov returned to live at Pustyn'ka, where he had not been since 1887,[68] and rented a cottage from her second son, Ryurik, with whom he was very close, and lived there up to the last month of his life. He loved to walk on the property, always pausing before a favorite stone, saying, "Here is my grave." When he died in the home of his friend Count Sergei Trubetskoy, Sophia explained that he wished to be buried at Pustyn'ka, but this wish was not granted, as Sophia was treated coldly by Solovyov's sisters. Solovyov was buried by his family next to his father.[69]

Solovyov's love for both of these flesh-and-blood Sophias has some bearing on his Jewish interests and writings. First, as explained above, for him love was an incarnational reality crucially connected with what he posited to be the Judeo-Christian understanding of matter and the Judeo-Christian commitment to the spiritualization of bodily existence. Love, consequently, was a force that enabled active participation in the realization of the purpose and meaning of creation as intended by divine Wisdom. Useful here is his very brief definition, in a letter of June 10, 1892, to Sophia Martynova, of the meaning of the heavenly Sophia. The meaning of Sophia, he explains, is, "'We are with God' as Christ is God with us. Do you understand the difference? 'God is with us' means that he is active and we are passive; 'We are with God' is the reverse, here God is passive, he is body, matter, and we are will, spirit."[70]

Crucially, in his thought, the experience of love is associated with freedom and so serves to explain his expectation of a new, "free" stage of Christianity. This expectation necessarily involves criticism of the forms of historically attested Christian forms of life. He explained this criticism laconically three months after breaking off contact with Sophia Khitrovo in a letter of April 28 to Aksakov's widow, Anna Fedorovna Aksakova. The context of this letter deserves brief explanation. Solovyov shared theosophical interests with Anna Fedorovna, but the strains in his relationship with her husband also had a negative impact on theirs. On this occasion, Solovyov speaks of a poem that he recently sent her that spoke about their past loves and featured wordplay on the dying and resurrecting Adonis. The pagan allusions apparently incensed Anna Fedorovna. Writing to dispel her anger, Solovyov explained that he was speaking not of the Greek Adonis but of the Jewish[E] Adonai, the Lord, the prototype of Christ, who had nothing to do with Venus and Mars, and then added: "About the Church Fathers, I must say that their limited capacity to value beauty (whether in mythological representations or in the forms of interesting women) is a singularity that I do not envy. Christianity exists among them in a repressed[71] and exclusive condition, it is not free—this is not the highest stage of Christianity. . . . At night, instead of French romances, I read Swedenborg in Latin. My own Russian romance has reached freezing point. It is three months already that I have no news."[72]

Second, the fact that he lived at Pustyn'ka from 1880 to 1887 (and finally from 1897 to 1900) also bears on his Jewish writings in the

1880s, since most of these would have been composed there. In a letter to his brother Mikhail in January 1886, Solovyov writes that he spent the month alone, in the large, cold house, writing about Old Testament theocracy with a Bible under one elbow and white paper under the other.[73] Sergei Solovyov surmises that it was in that atmosphere that Solovyov heard the call to journey abroad to Bishop Strossmayer of Croatia in the spring and connects this calling with the poem "To the Promised Land" (1886).[74] Consequently, the Old Testament and Jewish themes and contents of the poem are also intimately autobiographical, illustrating a sense of identification with Abraham and his call. At the same time, the vocational crises and illnesses that Solovyov frequently reports to Getz during the correspondence of this period, especially the monastic crisis and the neuralgia of 1887, would seem to be related to the crises in his relationship with Sophia Khitrovo.

Sergei Solovyov's attempt to relate the Old Testament themes of "To the Promised Land" to Solovyov's life encourages the drawing of such relationships with his other poems on Old Testament, Hebrew, and Jewish subjects. Hence, the poem "The Burning Bush," written on September 4, 1891, seems, on the one hand, to apply to the Jewish situation in Russia, but Sergei Solovyov observes that both it and the 1892 poem about Moses sound very autobiographical, as indeed they do.[75] Interestingly, Sergei Solovyov has little to say about their literal bearing on the Jewish question, and this omission or lack of interest fits his failure to comment in any way on Solovyov's engagements in Jewish affairs in 1890 and 1891, for example, in the Protest (1880) and in the relationship to the Jewish question of the lecture "The Fall of the Medieval Worldview" (1881). The point to be made here is not that Sergei Solovyov fails to understand the poem's historical, Jewish, reference points and therefore wrongly reads them autobiographically. Rather, the poems are multilayered and their reading in certain respects corresponds to the ways in which Jews and Christians often read scripture by referring the drama of its protagonists, such as Abraham and Moses, to the drama faced by their Jewish and Christian readers in their present circumstances. Accordingly, at one level the poem speaks to the experience of the Jewish people in Russia, at another it is about Solovyov himself.

A good illustration if not proof of this multilayered meaning of his poetry on Jewish themes is the 1882 poem "In the Land of Frosty Blizzards," which applies perfectly to his 1882 lectures, published in 1884 as "Jewry and the Christian Question," but for the fact that the gender of "you" in its second line, designating the poem's addressee, is feminine. This suggests that the addressee is Sophia Khitrovo, while the Elijah-like prophet, who has begun to hear the "still small voice of God" is Solovyov. Indeed, Sergei Solovyov, again deaf to the poem's biblical and Jewish resonances, refers the poem to the spiritual maturation of those years that yielded *The Spiritual Foundations of Life.* In short, his Jewish poetry, being multivalent, testifies to Solovyov's multivalent approach to scripture, and to his reading it in the traditional ecclesial manner, which is to say, not killing its letter by historicizing the text but keeping the text alive by allowing it to apply to history, current events, and his own life drama.

To return to the history of 1877, these were the years of the Eastern Crisis of the Russo-Turkish War and witnessed the first expression of the militarist streak in Solovyov that is so pronounced in *Three Conversations* (1899–1900). Thus, having returned to Russia as a committed Slavophile, he found it difficult to remain reading mystical literature in libraries while Slavs were shedding their blood in the Balkans. By April 1877 he informed his old and new friends, including Sophia Andreevna Tolstaya, of his desire to go to Central Asia and started on his journey in June. Passing through Kishinev on June 18 and Bucharest on June 28, and even obtaining a revolver, he suddenly understood that he could neither shoot nor serve as a good war correspondent and returned to St. Petersburg, shaken with shame over his incapacity to participate in "history's grand events." Immersing himself again in academic work, he published the first ethical portion of his work *Philosophical Principles of Integral Knowledge* (1877) and then, out of a desire to contribute to the war effort, declared in January 1878 his intention to deliver twelve lectures on Godmanhood for the partial benefit of the Red Cross and of the restoration of the Hagia Sophia Basilica in Constantinople.[76]

CHAPTER 6

1878–1881: *Lectures on Godmanhood* and *A Critique of Abstract Principles*

The promised lectures on Godmanhood were delivered between January 26 and March 1878 under the auspices of the Society of Friends for Spiritual Enlightenment at Solyanyj Gorodok, a museum lecture hall in St. Petersburg and published serially in *Pravoslavnoe obozrenie* (Orthodox Review).[77] In these lectures and the doctoral work published as *A Critique of Abstract Principles* (1880), Solovyov was aspiring to provide a Christian resolution to the tension between positivism and idealism, matter and spirit, sensual experience and transcendent truth. Identifying the tension between the absolute dogmatism of (medieval Christian) metaphysics, rich in abstractions, and the absolute skepticism of (Enlightenment) empiricism, rich in facts deprived of meaning, Solovyov argued that rich dialogue between Christianity and humanism could yield "a new level of insight into the mysteries of faith and the course of world history"[78] so as to build a "world not only *freer, but also richer in its spiritual forces.*"[79] This aspiration advanced the theses developed in his travel notebooks, as reflected by Excerpt 1 above, concerning his expectation that the Old and New Testaments would be succeeded by a final "Eternal Testament of Freedom." Given the strength of current positivist philosophies, the lectures were unprecedented for their religio-philosophical vigor and evangelizing force and, as all of St. Petersburg came out to hear him, the audience often exceeding a thousand, marked the apogee of his fame.[80] The lec-

150

tures were attended by Sophia Andreevna Tolstaya and Sophia Khitrovo and Fyodor and Anna Dostoevsky, who, according to Anna's memoirs, came to hear him several times and at the March 10 lecture saw Strakhov in attendance with Tolstoy.[81]

The *Lectures* frequently engage with Old Testament and postbiblical Hebraic and Jewish phenomena in ways that clearly anticipate the conceptions advanced in "Jewry and the Christian Question," *Theocracy*, and later works. The strongest antecedents of those conceptions can be found in Lecture 5, where Solovyov draws comparisons and contrasts between the Indian Buddhist and Greek idealist conceptions of the divine and the idea of the individual, personal, *living God* that appears for the first time in the Hebrew Bible in the narrative where God reveals himself to Moses as the "I am." The Hebrew expression *ehyeh asher ehyeh*—"I will be who I will be"—receives philological commentary in a modest footnote that, by clarifying the inadequacy of translations that use the future tense, reflects the need to understand Hebrew (64–66). The lecture concludes with the explanation that in the Old Testament the Law of Moses is understood, and stated explicitly by the prophets, as a necessary transition to the affirmation of all, the good of all, without envy, that is, absolute love, as *consciously chosen good* (68–72).

Recapitulating this point, Lecture 6 explains how the personal Yahwism of Old Testament prophecy, "preeminently revealed to the genius of the Jewish nation," was synthesized with the absolute idea of Divinity especially perceived by Hellenism through the intellectual labor begun among Hellenistic Jews in Alexandria (74–75) and proceeds to articulate the essential truth of this doctrine as appearing in Greco-Judaic and Christian speculations on the subject (in Philo, Plotinus, Origen, Gregory the Theologian). Lecture 7 explores Christian trinitarian thought and in the process explains the relation of the Word or Logos "as the principle that expresses the unity of that which absolutely is" to "the second kind of unity, the produced unity" called Sophia, in Christian theosophy and how pre-Christian conceptions of it in the Old Testament need not be seen as an introduction of new gods (107–8). In its reflections on how unity is produced by the divine will, Lecture 9 also develops a conception of evil, explaining it ultimately as having a metaphysical origin by originating in a free product of individual entities endowed with will (125–26) and resulting in the falling away of the produced unity, the ideal humanity (Sophia) and world soul, and consequently in the chaos and discord of the natural world, that, as argued in Lecture 10, is to be reversed by God through his incarnation and deification (*theosis*) of all that exists (136–37), which happens slowly and gradually because of *freedom* that allows rebellion (138–47). At this point, Solovyov turns to a consideration of how the human soul was understood to be liberated from cosmic forces by the "great peoples of antiquity." In doing so, he compares Hindus, Greeks, and Jews, as he did in Lectures 3 through 5, but this time to advance the idea that it "was preeminently in the Jewish nation" that God was revealed as a living personal force capable of penetrating the soul and overcoming evil in the human will (150–51). The paragraph that follows, penultimate in the chapter, anticipates the introductory pages of "Jewry and the Christian Question" and is noteworthy for its non-romanticized content.

> The divine principle was revealed to the Hindu spirit as nirvana and to the Greeks as idea and ideal cosmos. To the Jews, it had to appear as a person, as a living subject, as an "I," because their national character consists precisely in the predominance of the personal, subjective principle. *This character is manifested in the entire historical life of the Jews, in all that this nation has created and is creating.*[82] Thus, we see that in poetry the Jews have created something peculiarly their own only in the form which constitutes the subjective, personal element of poetry. They created the lyricism of genius of the Psalms and the lyrical idyll of the Song of Songs. But they could create a real epic or drama, such as we find in Hindu and Greek literature, neither during their independent historical existence nor afterward. We can point to Heine, a Jewish lyrical writer of genius, but we cannot find among them a single outstanding dramatist, precisely because drama is an objective kind of poetry. It is also remarkable that the Jews have distinguished themselves in music, the art that best expresses the inner, subjective motions of the soul, but they have not produced any-

thing significant in the plastic arts. In the domain of philosophy, during their flourishing epoch, the Jews never went farther than moral didactics, the domain in which the practical interests of the moral individual outweigh objective contemplation and thought. Correspondingly, in religion, too, the Jews were the first to know God fully as a person, as a subject, as an existent "I." They could not remain satisfied with the representation of Divinity as an impersonal force and an impersonal idea.

This character of the assertion of the subjective element in everything can be the bearer of the greatest evil as well as of the greatest good. The force of the human individual, when it asserts itself in its own separateness, is evil and the root of evil. But when it subordinates itself to the supreme principle—the same flame but permeated with the divine light—it is a force of cosmic, all-embracing love. . . .

The whole Old Testament is the history of the personal relations of the self-revealing God (Logos or Jehovah) with the representatives of the Jewish nation, its patriarchs, leaders, and prophets. . . . The last[,] . . . the prophets[,] . . . have a presentiment of and proclaim the inner unification of Divinity with the human soul in the person of the Messiah, the son of David and the Son of God. They have a presentiment of and proclaim this Messiah not only as the highest representative of Judaism but also as "an ensign for the nations" [Isa. 11:12], as the representative and the head of all regenerated humanity.[83]

Having arrived at the figure of the Messiah, Lectures 11 and 12 move on to Christ, including his resurrected body and his body understood as the church, which "is growing little by little and at the end of time will encompass all humankind and all nature" because, citing Paul, the rest of nature is awaiting with hope the manifestation of the "glorious liberty of the children of God . . . for which creation groans and travails . . . until now" (Rom. 8:19–22).

This *manifestation*, this glorious liberty of the children of God, which all creation awaits with hope, is the complete realization of the free, divine-human union in humankind as a whole, in all the spheres of human life and activity. All these spheres must be brought into harmonious divine-human unity, entering into that free theocracy in which the Universal Church will reach the full measure of Christ's stature.[84]

The *Lectures* concludes by discoursing on the strengths and weaknesses of the realization of this theocratic ideal[85] in historic Christian cultures and on the false avenues taken in Catholicism and Protestantism, as well as in post-Enlightenment rationalism, and how these succumbed to the "Three Temptations" from which the Orthodox East was preserved.

Solovyov's estimation of the weaknesses of Jewish talent in the spheres of drama, plastic arts, and nonmoral philosophy is debatable. The ancient Books of Genesis, Samuel, Job, and Ruth evince drama and ground contemporary drama that gives transcendent value to common people, precisely for reasons that Solovyov's philosophy of creation (see below) articulates.[86] Jews' supposed lack of talent in the plastic arts is contingent on Judaism's compliance with Mosaic proscriptions against images and so should at least be attributed to channeling of Jewish creativity into other areas. The charge that Jews have contributed little to nondidactic philosophy during the time of their "flourishing" requires consideration of what epochs this "flourishing" contains, especially since Solovyov underscores that they continue to be creative. He at least mentions Philo. Spinoza's contributions are questionable because of his excommunicate status, but figures such as Sa'adya Gaon, Ibn Gabirol, and Maimonides may have been noted, as might also Solovyov's contemporary Kantian philosopher, Herman Cohen (1842–1918). These omissions may also be contingent on Western philosophy's dependence on subconscious Christian supercessionist attitudes to Judaism and hence lack of interest in Jewish philosophers of note.[87] Nonetheless, Solovyov's near-contemporary, the Jewish philosopher Samuel David Luzzatto (1800–1865), also contended that Judaism differs from and surpasses Atticism by espousing the personal over the abstract, heart over head, and blamed Maimonides for poisoning Judaism with Aristotle. The important point is that the supposed lack of Jewish cultural contributions to world civilization, the most negative observation made of Judaism in the *Lectures*, and in fact not a criticism, brings into relief the otherwise recurrent affirmation of Judaism as a bearer of revelation about and ongoing witness to the personal living God, which revelation emphasizes that God not only seeks justice for the world and creatures he created, but loves them, a philosophy of Godmanhood that prepared for the Gospel historically and continues to be an essential partner with it. The extended citation taken from the end of Lecture 9 is thus remarkable for its recognition, as underscored by the third italicized sentence, of Judaism's *ongoing* creativity and genius in the spheres of its religio-cultural distinctiveness, those committed to personal and subjective entities and phenomena. How different all this is from the treatment of the Jews by the Russian publicists of Alexander II's reign (see Pt. I, ch. 4, §§6.2–6.7), especially those of Slavophile and Pan-Slavist affiliations, such as Aksakov, Danilevsky, and Dostoevsky (see Pt. I, ch. 4, §§7.2–7.5, 7.7). Anti-Jewish sentiment peaked in these years of the Eastern Crisis given the concern with Jewish draft evasion (see Pt. I, ch. 4, §7.4) and the other three factors that strengthened conservative Judeophobia in these years: the increased number of Jews in educational institutions, the emergence of nihilism, and the rise of articulate European antisemitism, resulting in Dostoevsky's discovery of their nihilistic revolutionary threat (see Pt. I, ch. 4, §7.6) and polemical treatment of the "the Jewish question" in chapter 2, sections 1–4, of his March 1877 installments of *The Diary of a Writer*, which portrayed the Jews overwhelmingly, over the course of their entire four-thousand-year history, as religiously motivated nationalists bent on economic and political exploitation of the world, with which polemic Solovyov would soon engage but not before a mutually constructive relationship with Dostoevsky (see ch. 7 below).[88]

In *A Critique of Abstract Principles*, Solovyov takes up the issue of duality and tension characterizing human life and consciousness, the tension between inner freedom and external necessity. Seeking criteria to evaluate this tension, he surveys "positive," traditional and mystical, as well as "abstract," empirical and rationalistic, streams of thought. Reviewing how the latter give expression to ethics and subjectivity (hedonism, utilitarianism), he finds their highest but necessarily limited and inadequate expression in Schopenhauer.[89] Surveying then the relation of rationalist attempts to ground ethics via Kant, he explores their various understandings of the freedom of the will and argues for the possibility of integrating the consciousness of phenomenal necessity with transcendent freedom.[90] Moving on to rationalist attempts to establish objective ethics in individualist, socialist, and capitalist politics, economics, and law, he finds the inadequacy of grounding these on the concept of rights.[91] He thus considers how religious and ecclesial principles give form to society, first in abstract, clericalist, and false theocratic ways, and next in ways suggestive of positive, true, and free theocracy and its actual possibility. He then argues the relevance of this possibility to all ethics, and, given the inadequacy of materialist and rationalist philosophies to explain knowledge, matter, and nature, the need to ground ethics and epistemology in metaphysics and religion.[92] At this point he considers the meaning of the True and its relationship to Absolute and Contingent Being, to Absolute Being and Absolute Becoming, to man as the Second Absolute,[93] and to faith, imagination, and creativity as foundational elements for objective knowledge, and the elements of the knowledge of all in abstract dogmatic theology and free theosophy.[94]

In the last chapters of this work, Solovyov may be seen following through on the conception reflected in his graduate study sketches and adopting the language of the idealist philosophers Schelling and Hegel to argue that Schelling rightly stressed the realities of the spirit but failed to give due recognition to the spiritual realities traditionally affirmed in Christian doctrine, such as hell and demons, which recognition marked latter-day Protestant mystics and Christian visionaries such as Boehme and Swedenborg. As for Hegel, Solovyov judges him to have correctly given primacy to Spirit as the first and absolute principle but to have erred in identifying the substance of the Absolute Spirit with the spirit of rational creatures and the world, whereby he mistakenly envisioned history as a dialectics and phenomenology of spirit. Solovyov's solution was to build on the great Greek Neoplatonist Proclus, who, like Hegel, taught that the world derives from the One divine spiritual absolute, but rather than identify the One with reason and the created world, Proclus taught that these latter would participate in and exist through him/it. It is this espousal of Proclus that distances Solovyov, on the one hand, from Hegel and from Gnostics and Manichaeans who disparage the created world and matter and, on the other, enables him to reconcile elements of their teaching with Judeo-Christian scripture and doctrine, which hold the world to be created by God's Word and through his Wisdom. By making this synthesis, he argued that being created and willed into existence by God, the Divine Absolute, the intended world merits being called a Second Absolute. Perceived as the object, the Thou of his Love, in its divinely intended beauty, goodness, and truth, this intended world is Wisdom/Sophia in eternity and the soul by which it is realized in time, and through which it is organically united and integrated in itself and with God. Since, from the point of view of creatures, this integration connotes spiritual union between them and God, it transpires through moral action, through intentional acts, free acts and exploits of will (*podvig*), that realize God's will to the extent that they are inspired and permeated by and united to his Holy Spirit.[95] This synthesis echoes the content of the "Prayer for Revelation of a Great Mystery," composed in his research notebooks as noted above, which read: "In the Name of the Father and of the Son and of the Holy Spirit // Ain-Soph, Jah, Soph-Jah." As implied by the structure of this prayer, Sophia is Soph-Jah, the third reconciling and synthesizing principle, corresponding to the Holy Spirit in the Trinity. As Solovyov will later pithily explain to Sophia Martynova, Sophia relates to the "being with God" by which creatures respond to God's being with his creatures.[96]

The relevance of these ideas to his writings on Judaism is evident on many levels and at least via five interrelated themes and terminology that this commentary highlights. The first pertains to the importance of the will, to intentional moral acts, to acting in accord with conscience and the Holy Spirit. The culmination of this theme emphasizing that people are measured by their will and their intentions may be glimpsed (1) in Solovyov's letter to Filippov in 1889 (see commentary on letter to Getz, #22, below) and (2) at the end of his obituary for Joseph Rabinovich, especially in the way this obituary synthesizes the same motifs enunciated in Solovyov's polemic with *Moskovskie vedomosti* about his 1881 lecture "The Fall of the Medieval Worldview."

The second theme relates the preceding theme of acting intentionally in accord with conscience and the Holy Spirit to the notion that human beings and peoples have tasks, missions, and vocations (through which God's intent for the world [= Sophia in creation] is realized in time). This theme relates to the italicized portion in his famous letter of August 23, 1890, to Strakhov, cited above, in which Solovyov differentiates Strakhov's Western-mechanistic / Buddhist-passive / pacifist standpoint from his question, which he identifies as Hebrew-Christian, about how "the present intellectual climate [can be] beneficial or harmful for the divine-human *task* on earth, in the *present historical moment.*" Among the most profound expressions of this theme is one found in the last stanza of the poem "Immanuel," written in Imatra during Christmas 1894 (along with the poem "Night, at Christmas" and according to Sergei Solovyov after abandoning expectations to see the theocratic ideal realized any time soon in history).[97]

> In depths of time that night is now nested,
> On which, fatigued from anger and much fuss,
> The earth, embraced in love by heaven, rested,
> And gave birth in the quiet to God-with-us.
>
> And much indeed impossible is now.
> Our kings no longer look up at the sky.
> And shepherds do not listen in the desert,
> How angels about God to humans cry.
>
> But the eternal, which this night did open,
> Time has no power to vanquish and consume,
> And in your soul the new-born Word is spoken,
> That was begotten in the manger's gloom.
>
> Yes! God is with us, not in tents enchanting,
> Not in the sky's immeasurable deeps,
> Not in the evil fire, nor in wild panting,
> And not in memory of yore that sleeps.

He's now here, in vanities accidental,
In the chaotic streams of daily strife
You hold the joyous mystery fundamental:
God is with us, ends evil, revives life.

The third theme relates to Solovyov's insistence that conscientious fulfillment of this calling must be organic, unconstrained, free, and moved by love. The *Lectures* and *Critique* advance the belief that historical Christianity has failed in many ways to realize this mission and that an Eternal Testament of Freedom is yet to be established, whether in history, as Solovyov seemed to think throughout his theocratic phase in the 1880s, or following his disillusionment with current history in the 1890s, and the postponement of the realization of the theocratic ideal to the eschaton, whether to a far distant apocalyptic future or to a world to come. One illuminating comment on the meaning of this freedom, already cited above, is that which Solovyov will give to Anna Fedorovna Aksakova about the church fathers lacking full Christian appreciation for the beauty of the world in its bodily existence. A fuller and more esoteric explanation was supplied by him in a letter to Anna Schmidt, a woman who professed interest in Solovyov's Sophiology, in the last year of his life but clearly applicable to his thoughts in the *Lectures* and *Critique* and later. The last line of the quote shows that if he did postpone his theocratic ideal to the eschaton, he did not give up on it.

I am happy to see how close you came to the truth in a matter of the greatest importance, embedded in the very essence of Christianity, but not yet clearly formulated, neither in the ecclesial nor in the common-philosophical consciousness, even though individual theosophists speak about this dimension of Christianity (especially Jacob Boehme and his followers: Gichtel, Pordage, Saint Martin, Baader). From 1877, I frequently had to touch upon this subject in public lectures, articles, and books, preserving due care. I think, on the basis of many givens, that broad revelations of this truth in the consciousness and life of Christianity and all humanity are expected in the nearest future.[98]

Solovyov regretted writing these words so openly to Anna because he soon discovered that she was a disturbed woman who professed to be the incarnation of Sophia and Solovyov's divine partner. Solovyov then sought to distance himself from her gently, informed her that he had burned her *Profession* to him, expressly out of caution and to affirm that "it is all ashes," and asked her not to discuss him with anyone and to pray to God in all her spare time. Nonetheless, the contents of the letter are clearly an important gloss on the *Lectures* because of their testimony that in 1899 Solovyov still believed what he advocated from 1877 on about truths essential to Christianity that individual theosophist mystics like Boehme and Baader expressed and that Christian magisterial tradition had yet to articulate, notions he clearly believed to be essential to Christianity and orthodoxy.[99] According to Evgeny Trubetskoy, the notion in question is one that Solovyov first developed on his own and then recognized in the thought of the European mystics mentioned. The notion, constituting the root and essence of his philosophical and religious conception of Godmanhood, is the teaching on "holy corporeality," for which he found innumerable parallels in the foundational "spiritual materialism" of Boehme and Baader.[100] This positive attitude to matter is evident, for example, in the last stanza of the poem "Immanu-el," which celebrates the fact that the great mystery of Godmanhood is to be perceived in things seemingly "vain and accidental," in the "chaotic streams of daily life." It is also evident in Solovyov's emphasis, in his letter to Strakhov, on the importance of making decisions in the present moment, in the midst of history's contingencies.

The promise of a new level of insight integrating the mysteries of faith with the course of world history, implicit in Solovyov's youthful thought, as represented in Excerpt 1, is further unpacked in another letter written shortly before his death, this time in January 1898 to the French journalist and essayist Eugène Tavernier (1854–1928), who translated his *Three Conversations and the Tale of the Antichrist* into French. The letter of January 1898 conveys the desire to integrate his persistent preoccupations with scripture, historical philosophy, and eschatology.

I have published the first chapter of my metaphysics in a review and I hope to complete the book in fifteen months. Otherwise I am preoccupied with Plato of whom I am attempting a complete translation. After completing the metaphysics, Plato, one [work] on aesthetics (half completed), a book on Russian poetry (3/4 completed), and a history of philosophy (for which I will take advantage of my articles in the *Encyclopedia*). I will be concentrating completely on the Bible, which, from Genesis to Revelation, provides the most wonderful frame for all that can interest me henceforth. I still do not know whether my final labor will assume the form of a new translation with long commentaries or whether it will be a systematization of historical philosophy, grounded on the data and spirit of the Bible.

This is what I plan to accomplish with God's help in the future; with you, my wonderful friend, my frankness is unlimited and I will tell you that I am convinced that the unification of the Churches first among themselves, and then with the Synagogue, and the coming of the Antichrist must be preceded by the publication of my biblical labor.[101]

The letter retrospectively illuminates the intensity with which Solovyov engaged in and the importance he accorded to his work on the Hebrew and Christian Bibles, engaging directly with their original respective languages, as evidenced in his Jewish writings of the 1880s, including his *Theocracy*. The point of departure for serious engagement with Hebrew can be noted in the *Lectures*, for example, in his notes on the syntax of the Hebrew terms for the Divine Name or for Wisdom, *Hokhmah*.[102] This interest, indicative of a desire to engage with Hebrew and Jewish tradition at a deeper level, will impel Solovyov to ask Rabbi Faivel Getz for instruction in Hebrew and rabbinic literature.

The fourth important, interrelated theme, as stated in the *Lectures* excerpt above on Judaism, pertains to the explanation that the use of the individual will to assert its own separateness is evil and the root of evil. This theme relates to that of the Antichrist already mentioned in the *Lectures*, anticipating the discussions on this theme with Dostoevsky (see below) and Solovyov's own apocalyptic composition "The Tale of the Antichrist" (1900) in the dramatic *Three Conversations* (1899–1900), which Tavernier was to translate. The theme relates to the vitally important Solovyovian teaching that evil exists in the world as an active and personal spiritual force that cannot be redeemed (on which point Solovyov is clearly distinguishable from Origen) and must be resisted actively (for which militancy he is to be distinguished from Tolstoy, and indeed *Three Conversations* may be read as a polemic on Tolstoyan spirituality; see below) but successfully only through the harmonization of the created will with the good and saving will of God (a teaching that will be elegantly clarified in Solovyov's commentary on the Lord's Prayer in his *Spiritual Foundations of Life* [1884]).

Ultimately, the theme of evil and the Antichrist, like "The Tale of the Antichrist," brings the discussion full circle—to the center and ground of his teaching, which is Christ, the Word made flesh, through whose incarnation and resurrection reason is unified with matter, meaning with experience, in a concrete "holy corporeality." This holy corporeality is that which, or rather Who allows human beings to understand organically the integral meaning of things and gives them the courage and power to open themselves up to reality, freely, in all its wholeness and perfection, for eternity. As clarified by the chapter headings of Solovyov's *Spiritual Foundations of Life,*[103] Solovyov's Sophiology and conception of the Eternal Testament of Freedom are focused and grounded on Christ.[104] This explains why he presents Christianity in the *Lectures* as original and not an aggregate of preceding religious and philosophical systems.

If Christianity only synthesized these elements, then it would not represent any new world power, but would be only an eclectic system, such as are often encountered in the schools, but which never become active in life, they do not bring about any world historical revolutions, and do not destroy one world and do not create another. Christianity has its unique content, independent from all these elements, which it takes up, and this unique content is singularly and exclusively Christ—this truth is much proclaimed but hardly assimilated. . . . If we investigate all the theoretical and moral content of Christ's teaching, which we find in the Gospel, then the only new teaching, specifically distinct from all other religions, will here be Christ's about himself, his pointing at himself as at a living incarnate truth: "I am the Way, the Truth and the Life: he who believes in me has eternal life." In this way, if we are to search for the characteristic content of Christianity in the teaching of Christ, then here too we must acknowledge, that this content resolves into Christ himself.[105]

Because of passages such as this, the *Lectures* signal Solovyov's maturation as a Christian thinker, making explicit his commitment to the centrality of Christ and so to the biblical and orthodox Chalcedonian doctrine that, in fact, informed and underpinned his early religious-philosophical travels, his dabbling with esoteric thought, his experiments with heavenly and infernal spirits, and his interest in Wisdom/Sophia.[106] Failure to grasp this point will make these interests appear either heretical and demonic, as illustrated by the frequent reaction of Orthodox Christians and by Solovyov's own self-satirizing representations of the Antichrist in "The Tale," or mad and ridiculous, as illustrated by the reaction of the secular-liberal Yanzhul, or childish and unworthy of being taken seriously, as illustrated by the reaction of Tolstoy, who came to hear Solovyov only once, on March 10, as reported by Anna Dostoevsky.[107]

At the time, as shown by Tolstoy's correspondence with Strakhov over the preceding months, he was engrossed with contemporary attempts to demythologize religion (Max Müller), ethics (Kant and Mill), and Christ (David Friedrich Straus and Ernest Renan). As part of this preoccupation, he was reading Solovyov's just published *Critique of Abstract Principles*[108] and puzzling over his insistence that ethical principles can be abstract or integral and that the latter must be grounded theologically.[109] In a letter of April 17–18, largely devoted to Renan's repudiation of the miraculous in the life of Christ and to similar questions about the church's teaching on the Eucharist, which Tolstoy confessed in the same letter to have received for the first time in many years, he evidently faults Strakhov for siding seriously with Solovyov's metaphysical approach to the issues: "I am hurt on your behalf by the fact that you have demeaned yourself to such an extent as to take keen interest in this debate. Is it not immediately evident to you that all this is childish prattle? How could you even consider it?"[110] In the 1890s, Solovyov will return to "childish arguments" to attempt to persuade Tolstoy of the doctrine of Christ's resurrection (see below).

By contrast, Dostoevsky, the other giant of Russian literary thought, found much of value in Solovyov, and came to hear him several times. They became good friends, thanks to the nurturing of their relationship by Sophia Andreyevna Tolstaya's salon.

CHAPTER 7

1878–1881: Dostoevsky, Tolstoy, and Getz

The earliest firsthand witness to Dostoevsky's relationship with Solovyov is provided by Anna Dostoevsky's reminiscences of their friendship during this period, for which she expresses gratitude that Solovyov, when they were both in grief over the death of their son, accompanied Dostoevsky for a summer retreat to Optina Pustyn' to see the Elder Father Amvrosy (Aleksandr Mikhailovich Grenkov, 1812–91), the model for Father Zosima in *The Brothers Karamazov* (1879–80). Sergei Solovyov follows Anna Dostoevsky in positing that Dostoevsky drew on Solovyov as a model for the good-hearted and religious Alyosha. An important point of contact is Solovyov's poetic connections between the "white lily and red rose" and "the earthly soul and unearthly light" and Christ's first miracle at Cana where he graced human joy and relations and the chapter "Cana of Galilee" where Alyosha experiences a spiritual moment after falling asleep listening to the chapter on the marriage at Cana.[111] But Sergei also proposes the theory, developed by Mochulsky, that Solovyov additionally furnished the model for the brilliant dialectician, the Jesuit-trained and God-spurning Ivan. As attested by the *Lectures,* Solovyov was already developing his "theocratic" ideals and clearly believed at this stage, as he did already in *Sophie,* that the church needed to and would use the state to transform the world, ideas espoused by Ivan in the opening chapters of *The Brothers Karamazov.* Sergei reports that Father Amvrosy took a colder view of Solovyov because of these ideas than did Father Zosima of Ivan. The last, twelfth chapter of the *Lectures* also articulates a philosophy of Christ's "Three Temptations," anticipating the same theme in "The Grand Inquisitor" chapter placed on the lips of Ivan and echoed again by Solovyov in a possibly self-parodying vein in his "Tale of the Antichrist" (see below). Thus, despite the negative attitude expressed in chapters 11 and 12 of the *Lectures* to Roman Catholicism—sections the nephew in fact attributes to Dostoevsky's influence—Dostoevsky already prognosticated in the young Solovyov the author of future pro-Catholic works who would hear from his friends in 1888, during the composition of *La Russie et l'Église universelle*, the words Alyosha said to Ivan: "You are going to join them [the Jesuits]."[112] On the other hand, Solovyov, the student who had spent many hours in the British Library poring over Jewish esoteric texts and had just delivered a series of remarkable Judaism-affirming passages in his *Lectures on Godmanhood*, was himself not slow in repudiating the nationalism and antisemitism with which he held Dostoevsky to have been poisoned by Danilevsky's Pan-Slavism.

But before this repudiation would be made, Dostoevsky, unconsciously, served to occasion the meeting and lifelong bond between Solovyov and Rabbi Faivel Getz (1853–1932). Getz worked in the 1870s as a reporter for various Hebrew, Russian, and Hungarian Jewish periodicals and toward the end of the decade, thanks to Alexander II's lifting of restrictions on Jewish access to higher education (see Pt. I, ch. 4, §5.1), entered the University of St. Petersburg to pursue a doctorate in the Faculty of Oriental Languages. They met in 1879, in the home of a fellow student. Solovyov, noticing that Getz was observing Jewish dietary restrictions, entered into an erudite "Talmudic" conversation with him and asked whether he could offer him instruction in Hebrew. Getz, knowing that Solovyov was close to Dostoevsky, was in awe of him and quickly accepted. According to Getz, Solovyov worked assiduously, visiting him from 10 P.M. to 2 A.M. As reported in their correspondence, he progressed over the years not only through much of the Bible but, thanks to Getz's tutoring, through many Talmudic tractates.[113]

CHAPTER 8

1881–1883: The Break with the Slavophiles and Critique of Dostoevsky

On March 1 (o.s.), 1881, two years after Solovyov met Getz and one year after he defended his dissertation, the tsar was assassinated, and pogroms broke out in the Pale of Settlement, first in Elisavetgrad on April 15 and then more widely, spreading to fifty towns and reaching Kiev and Odessa over the next two years (see Pt. I, ch. 4, §8.1).

The causes of the pogroms remain mysterious (see Pt. I, ch. 4, §§8–8.6, 9.3). They may have resulted from the socioeconomic tensions that had precipitated a pogrom in Odessa a decade earlier (Pt. I, ch. 4, §§6.8, 7, n. 140). They may have been fed by the silent pogrom developed in much of the ultranationalist conservative press in preceding years, fueled by writers and publicists such as Dostoevsky and Aksakov; the most influential tsarist adviser, the director general of the Orthodox Church, Konstantin Pobedonostsev; and influential newspapers such as *Novoe vremya*. All promoted the view that, thanks to the liberal policies of Alexander II, the Jews were coming not just to exploit society but also to promote regicidal revolution (Pt. I, ch. 4, §7.6). The appearance, shortly after the assassination, of populist figures at provincial train stations inciting the people to answer the tsar's call to wreak vengeance on the Jews, and of mysterious individuals who visited governors and police officials who then failed to quash pogrom violence over the next two years, has made many suspect that the pogroms were orchestrated through some kind of state-sponsored conspiracy. The leading Jewish view, entrenched in scholarship as a near-consensus for almost a century, was that the tsarist regime either (a) orchestrated the pogroms or (b) allowed them to rage for a time so as to vent the socioeconomic frustrations of Russian peasants in the Pale of Settlement who, still landless, drunken, and impoverished after the Emancipation reform of 1861, blamed their misery on Jewish tavern keepers and merchants. The first, active government conspiracy theory has been impossible to prove. The second theory, according to which the government played a role but a passive one, runs against the fact that influential councilors such as Pobedonostsev and Ignatiev's replacement as minister of the interior, Count Dmitry Tolstoy, were terrified of social chaos (see Pt. I, ch. 4, §§8–8.5, 9–9.1). Consequently, a third theory arose as a result of suspicions, voiced for example early on by members of the royal family, by the tsar and his brother, by Ignatiev (before he was replaced by Tolstoy), by Katkov, editor of the most influential conservative but not Judeophobic *Moskovskie vedomosti*, and in recent times by Solzhenitsyn, that the pogroms were orchestrated by terrorist revolutionaries, somehow ideologically allied with Narodnaya volya, the group that carried out the assassination, to exacerbate class warfare and lead the country to the brink of revolution.

On March 13, after the tsar's assassination, Solovyov delivered a speech at the Institute of Women's Higher Education (where he was giving very popular lectures as an adjunct faculty member), condemning the Russian revolutionary movement by arguing that violence betrayed faith in truth and reason. On March 26 and 28 he delivered two supplementary lectures in the Grand Hall of the St. Petersburg Credit Society, the second of which played a decisive role in his life. Declaring in his concluding words that the perpetrators had been caught and awaited death, the tsar, being the anointed of the Lord, the agent and model of Christian principles, could and should forgive them. Chaos ensued. Some charged him with treason and screamed for him to be hanged; others, especially the students, acclaimed him as their leader. The next day the mayor of St. Petersburg, Nikolai Mikhailovich Baranov, advised him to explain his views in writing and, returning a day later, was shocked to see Solovyov, clearly suffering, composing a letter to the tsar. The letter expounded his Free Theocratic principles, explaining the incompatibility of capital punishment with Christianity, explaining the value of his teaching about forgiveness of one's enemy, and reiterating his faith that the tsar, being a disciple of Christ, by following his example through such a heroic act, would inspire a spirit of reconciliation in Russia that would heal its body politic.

Baranov delivered the letter to Loris Melikov, who delivered it to the tsar. Judging from their later correspondence with Pobedonostsev, both judged Solovyov insane and conceived a deep distrust of him. Orders were issued forbidding Solovyov from giving public lectures, and Solovyov, sensing the royal disapproval, without apologizing, offered to resign his academic post in November 1881.[114] As highlighted in the one-page resume that he sent to Getz in May 1887 (Pt. III, ch. 9, #36), the event divided his life in two, sealing his break with the establishment and with many erstwhile Slavophile friends and colleagues. At the same time it stamped him as a man of principle, for whom the spirit of Christ connoted tolerant engagement with brotherly differences and heroic forgiveness of enemies rather than their exclusion and execution. However, the lecture again failed to make any positive impression on Tolstoy, even though the latter shared Dostoevsky's and Solovyov's fiery opposition to capital punishment. Tolstoy's diary entry for October 5, 1881, reads: "Poor Solovyov, having failed to understand Christianity, he has judged it and wants to invent something better. Talk, interminable talk."[115]

Solovyov's views, of course, flowed out of his belief, developed in his *Lectures on Godmanhood* and *A Critique of Abstract Principles*, that each nation was called to function as an organ in a divine-human organism whose flourishing and unification was the task of Christianity and so the challenge of every Christian person and nation, including Russia. In time, Solovyov's repudiation of nationalism, espousal of the freedom of conscience and the rights of ethnic minorities in Russia, and criticism of the survival of medieval perspectives in the church would bring him into a closer alignment or even make him a "fellow traveler"[116] with Tolstoy and result in their cooperation in protesting on behalf of Jewish civil rights.

In the meantime, Solovyov turned to applying his views to contemporary events and issues in a concluding series of academic and public lectures and in writing. Those that touched on Jewry directly included the series of lectures titled "Jewry and the Christian Question" and delivered at the University of St. Petersburg on February 11, 12, and 13 and February 18, 1882, at the Institute, as well as parts of the lectures delivered to commemorate Dostoevsky, delivered in February 1881, 1882, and 1883, respectively (see below).

The former have the honor of being perhaps the first defense of Judaism, or *Apologia Judaeis,* in the Russian language,[117] and, as such, received immediate and broad coverage in the Russian Jewish press.[118] The first lecture was reviewed briefly on February 18 in *Russkij evrej* (Russian Jew) and on February 19 in *Nedel'naya khronika voskhoda* (Weekly Chronicle of the Dawn), and then in detail on February 26 in *Nedel'naya khronika voskhoda, Rassvet,* and *Russkij evrej.* The anonymous writer(s) emphasized Solovyov's praise of the Jews for their moral character and way of life and his explanation that this was the reason for their being in the past and forever the chosen and Christ-begetting people. Scholars have found it noteworthy that the reviewer in *Nedel'naya khronika voskhoda* puzzled over Solovyov's opinion that Jews, contrary to Christians, were incapable of "abstract thought."[119] Sympathizing with this observation, Van der Zweerde picks up on the irony by noting that Solovyov's views would hardly explain why Jews would come to hear him. This reading, however, takes Solovyov's usage of "abstract" out of context and fails to take account of the value he placed on its opposite, integral thinking, as explained in his *Lectures on Godmanhood* and *Critique of Abstract Principles.* Accordingly, as understood by his sister in her recollections of his thoughts on the Jewish question, abstract thought for Solovyov was synonymous with Hellenic disembodied thought and antonymous to embodied, pragmatic, integral thought. He therefore did not use the term in a racist way to deny Jews the capacity for academic, scientific, mathematical discourse and thought but to emphasize, as did Samuel David Luzzatto a generation before, that Judaism is distinct from Atticism in favoring personalism over abstractions. The reviewer reported that in the discussion that followed the lecture Solovyov attributed the pogroms not to the Russian people but to the scum of society (*podonki obshhestva*) and advocated giving equal civil rights to Jews as the best way to integrate them with Russians.

On February 26 two summaries of the February 13 lecture on the historical role of Judaism were published in the journal *Rassvet* by nineteen-year-old Akim Volynsky (Flekser), who was to become, in 1891, editor of *Severnyj vestnik* (Northern Herald). Covering Solovyov's ideas on Jewish and Russian theocratic vocations and the providence that brought Jews and Russians together at this point in history, Flekser demurred about Solovyov's understanding of Judaism's mission, citing the pogroms as proof that Jews and Russians could not be integrated, but celebrated Solovyov's expression of sympathy for Jewish victims of the unbridled passions of the Russian people and the loud applause given him by the audience. Flekser also reviewed (under the signature "Q") Solovyov's February 18 lecture at the Grand Hall of St. Petersburg University in the journal *Russkij evrej;* the editor, Lev Kantor, added a footnote to point out that Solovyov's lecture was intended to explain to the reader an enlightened and true Christian view of the problem that reflected his interest in fostering a Jewish enlightened identity in Russia. This review also reported that the discussion following the lecture focused on the pogroms, which Solovyov described as the outburst of the people's Stygian impulses, and on queries about what is to be done, with Solovyov standing for the granting of full civil rights and the development of unconditional humane relations between Russians and Jews.[120] Consequently, Solovyov came by himself, in 1882, to the conclusion that the Pahlen Commission articulated and for which it was dissolved by the tsar in 1888 (Pt. I, ch. 4, §9.4) and that the otherwise progressive Witte could still not stomach by 1905 when the point was articulated to him on the basis of Jewish life in America by a committee of Jewish bankers in New Hampshire (Pt. I, ch. 4, §9.10). The poet Nikolai Minsky also left a recollection of the impact of this lecture.

> I remember . . . when in my youth I attended in the assembly hall of the University one of Solovyov's lectures on Judaism. Before the astonished crowd of a thousand, there stood a pale ascetic, of endearing beauty. With a deep voice, with frequent and tense pauses, he did not speak, but as one having authority proclaimed the duty of the Russian God-bearing people to spiritually merge

with the eternally God-begetting people of Israel. Frankly, Solovyov's deeply worrying words then seemed paradoxical to me. Only later did I grasp their sacred content.[121]

In these lectures Solovyov was also responding to the silent pogrom that was being stoked by conservative, nationalist papers such as *Novoe vremya* (New Time[s]) and *Rus'* (Russia). The latter was edited between 1881 and 1883 by Ivan Sergeevich Aksakov and from 1885 by a figure with whom Solovyov will engage in the 1890s, Konstantin Evst. Istomin, a member of the Kharkov Theological Seminary administration and frequent contributor (under the pseudonyms T. Stoyanov; I; I–n; I–n, K; K; and K. I.) to its journal, *Vera i razum* (Faith and Reason). Both Aksakov and Istomin followed Dostoevsky's line that it was Christians and not Jews who suffered most when they came into contact with each other because, according to them, Jews were cosmopolitan nationalists marked by egoism, pride, and materialism, and the essence of Judaism, as explained by Jacob Brafman, lay in subduing the earth and its peoples (see Pt. I, ch. 4, §§6.7–8.8, esp. 8.7).

Assuming that "Jewry and the Christian Question" is the published form of the lectures given on the same topic in 1882, one may here note the strong terminological and thematic contacts between this work and Dostoevsky's treatment of the Jewish question in chapter 2, sections 1–4, of his March 1877 installments of *The Diary of a Writer*,[122] where Dostoevsky focused on the Jewish successes in European circles of government (citing Disraeli as an example), finance, and media to assert that while the fall of Christianity in Europe was the fault of Europeans, the consequent rise of materialism and economic exploitation of the masses, elevated to the status of the highest virtues, could not be purely coincidental with the social elevation of the Jews but must be the result of Jewish influence. How terrible it would be for Europe, Dostoevsky proclaimed, if its peoples and institutions lacked the strength to resist Jewish domination in all these spheres![123] Following this line, Aksakov, the leading intellectual antisemite in Russia, put out a steady stream of articles in 1881–83 defending the pogroms as a natural response to Jewish oppression and economic exploitation of Christians in the Pale (see Pt. I, ch. 4, §6.9).

As a friend of Aksakov and regular contributor to his *Rus'*, Solo-vyov was familiar with these views but judged them to be forms of paranoia gravely detrimental to Russia's Christian soul and conscience and expressed this view clearly by engaging with the Slavophiles in lecture and in print. Solovyov picks up the argument in his "Jewry." Thus, in the seventh paragraph, he speaks to the point of Jewish, for example, Disraeli's, prominence in Europe and echoes Dostoevsky in affirming that this phenomenon is the result of Europe's decadence and Christianity's demise.

> The fact that England is governed by the Jew[E] Disraeli does not constitute a unique case, for in other countries as well, the financial sectors and considerable portions of the periodical press are managed by Jews[E], directly or indirectly. But this Jewish[E] dominance, rather than undermining, actually confirms my proposition that the Christian world has never treated the Jews in a Christian manner. Could it be that the present tolerance, concession to, and even subservience to Jews[E] derive from Christian conviction and feeling? Quite the contrary: all this flows not from the largesse of our religious views but from their total *absence*, from a complete indifference to matters of faith. It is not a Christian Europe that tolerates Jews[E] but a faithless Europe, a Europe deprived of its living roots, a decaying Europe. Jews thrive not via our moral strength but via our moral or rather amoral weakness.

This passage and those that follow have been noted to mark "Jewry and the Christian Question" as one of Solovyov's most anti-Enlightenment writings. The observation constitutes a plank in van der Zweerde's argument that Solovyov's theocratic conception could not allow civil society. This is, however, to misunderstand the passage and its rhetorical context. First, that the passage is singular for its anti-Enlightenment disposition must be referred to the anti-Enlightenment disposition of his target audience and thus to Solovyov's rhetorical strategy of establishing common ground with his opponents.[124] Second, he is not advocating that Christians should not show largesse to Jews, as van der Zweerde posits, but is simply stressing the fact that

Jews have come to occupy such positions in Europe on the basis of Enlightenment values, values that are indifferent to religion (which values van der Zweerde seems to advocate as the basis for civil society), and not on the basis of Christian tolerance. To stress, in clear opposition to Dostoevsky, that it is not Jews who are ruining Europe and that Christians would fare better under them, Solovyov quips, a few pages into the argument, "Better Spinoza than Voltaire: better Joseph Salvador than Mr. Ernest Renan."[125] More saliently, he will go on to argue in the latter, theocratic part of the work that it is vital for Christian Slavic nations, Russia and Poland, to show their largesse by engaging Jewish entrepreneurial, financial, talent. In respect to the financial sector at least, it should be clear that van der Zweerde is taking Solovyov's words out of context and misrepresents the largesse or civility that Solovyov's Christian theocratic vision supports.[126]

Other notable works representing Solovyov's attacks on Slavophile and Pan-Slav nationalism during this period include "The Great Debate and Christian Politics," published in 1883 in Aksakov's *Rus'*, which appealed for Orthodox-Catholic unity on the basis of their commonly held authentic apostolic succession and full sacramental life. The work, dealing with ecumenical issues in pro-Catholic ways prohibited in Russia, prompted Aksakov to close the pages of *Rus'* to Solovyov henceforth. Their rift was sealed by an open letter by Solovyov to Aksakov in 1884 in issue 4 of the literary review *Pravoslavnoe obozrenie,* edited by the priest Pyotr Alekseevich Preobrazhensky (1828–93). The latter was one of several ecclesiastics who continued to support Solovyov's work through the years.[127] In this letter Solovyov declared himself still a Slavophile but one who, in distinction from Aksakov and others, insisted that Russia, to be holy, must perform a holy deed, a *podvig,* the chief of which was the renunciation of the sin of schism as expressed by the first Slavophile, Yuri Krizhanich, the seventeenth-century Croat champion of Orthodox-Catholic rapprochement whom Solovyov will recall in his epigraph to "The Sins of Russia" (see Pt. III, ch. 10 [letter to Getz, #37]). Solovyov's "Great Debate" received recognition abroad, especially from the Croat Catholic bishop Josip Jurai Strossmayer (1815–1905) of Bosnia, who in coming years would spur Solovyov to resolve the problem of censorship of his ecumenical writings in Russia by publishing them in France, an effort that would yield the publication of his most mature work on church unity, *La Russie et L'Église universelle*,[128] which, however, owing to its sophiological content, alienated the Jesuits and undermined Catholic support for his views.

The series of public lectures in which Solovyov engaged Dostoevsky's antisemitism directly were the "Three Speeches in Memory of Dostoevsky" marking the anniversary of the latter's death on February 9, 1881, and delivered on February 18, 1881 (and thus two weeks before the assassination of the tsar), February 1, 1882, and February 19, 1883, respectively. In these lectures he did not so much explain his agreement with Dostoevsky about Russia's messianic mission as take the opportunity to correct him for his xenophobic outbursts against the Yids, Poles, French, Germans— the whole of Europe—and foreign confessions. It was the third speech, however, probably thanks to his preceding lectures on "Jewry and the Christian Question," that addressed Jewish-Christian relations most directly. Its conclusion is key to understanding his subsequent writings on Jewish Russians and on Christians and reads as follows:

> If Christianity is a religion of salvation, if the Christian idea consists in healing, in an inner unification of those principles whose separation means death, then the essence of the true Christian act will be what in logic is called *synthesis*, and in ethics *forgiveness*. . . . With this common character did Dostoevsky mark out Russia's vocation in his Pushkin speech. This was his last word and testament. . . . The real problem consists not in *imitating* but in *understanding* foreign ways, to consider and comprehend the positive essence of another spirit and to morally unite with it in the name of the highest universal truth. Reconciliation is necessary *in essence*, the essence of reconciliation is God, and true reconciliation consists in relating to an enemy not in a human way but in a godly way. This is all the more pressing for us, given that both of our principal opponents are now not outside of us but in our midst. Latinism, in the guise of the Poles and the Infidel, that is, the un-Christian East, in the guise of the Jews[E], has entered the

body of Russia, and if they are our enemies, then they are already internal enemies, and if we must have war with them, then this will be an internal war. For this reason, not only Christian conscience, but human wisdom also urges reconciliation. And conciliatory feelings to opponents as to people *in general* are here insufficient, since these enemies are not just people *in general*, but people who are completely *unique*, possessed of their own distinct character, so that real reconciliation requires especially a deep understanding of their distinct character—it requires us to turn to their spiritual substance and to relate to it in a godly way. (Footnote: From what has been said, I think, it is clear, that the matter pertains *not to allowances or compromises* in the external war [the ecclesial-political and national] but to the removal of the inner *cause* of this war through a spiritual reconciliation on a purely religious basis. As long as inner religious unity is not established, so long will political and nationalist strife retain their rights.) The spiritual essence of the Poles is Catholicism, the spiritual essence of the Jews[E] is the Jewish religion. To truly reconcile with Catholicism and Judaism means first of all to distinguish within them that which is from God and that which is from man. . . . If for us all that is humanly bad, all that is petty and dirty, throws itself into our eyes, if we so clearly and distinctly see all this dust of the earth, while all that is divine and holy for us is, on the contrary, unnoticeable, dark and incredible, then this only means that there is little of God within us ourselves.[129] Let us give Him more space within ourselves and we shall see Him more clearly in the other. Then we shall see His power not only in the Catholic church but also in the Jewish synagogue. Then we shall understand and accept the word of the Apostle about the Israelites: "to them belong the sonship, the glory, the covenants, the giving of the law, the worship, and the promises; to them belong the patriarchs, and of their race, according to the flesh, is the Christ. God who is overall . . . [Or] has God rejected his people? By no means! I myself am an Israelite, a descendant of Abraham, a member of the tribe of Benjamin. God has not rejected his people whom he foreknew. . . . [But] lest you be wise in your own conceits, I want you to understand this mystery, brethren: a hardening has come upon part of Israel, until the full number of the Gentiles come in, and so all Israel will be saved. . . . For God has consigned all men to disobedience, that he may have mercy upon all."[130]

In truth, if God's word is more true that all human conceptions and the work of His Kingdom is dearer than all earthly interests, then the way to reconciliation without historical enemies lies open before us. And let us not say: but will our opponents choose peace with us, [and] how will they deal with this, and how will they respond? Another's conscience is unknown to us, and another's deeds are not in our power. It is not in our power that others should treat us well, but it is in our power to be worthy of such treatment. And it behooves us to think not about what others will say to us but about what we shall say to the world.

In one conversation Dostoevsky applied to Russia the vision of John the Evangelist about the woman adorned with the sun and in labor desiring to give birth to a human child:[131] the woman is Russia, and her offspring is the new Word, which Russia must speak to the world. Be this interpretation of the great sign right or not, but the new Word of Russia, Dostoevsky guessed correctly.

This is the word of reconciliation for East and West in an eternal alliance with God's truth and human freedom. This is the highest challenge and duty of Russia, and such is the social ideal of Dostoevsky. Its foundation is the moral renaissance and the spiritual exploit, no longer of a separate, isolated individual, but of an entire society and nation. As of old, this ideal is unclear to the teachers of Israel, but it contains truth and it will conquer the world.[132]

The speech clearly builds on Solovyov's foundational ideals of God-manhood, his understanding of Sophia as the telos of humanity, and as the medium for the realization of the Eternal Testament of Freedom. It also invokes the biblical representation of the peoples of the world as a family of nations (Gen. 2:18), articulated in his work "The Family of Nations" (1897),[133] to argue on the basis of the Old Testament and the Christian doctrine of the Trinity, whereby the otherness of persons makes God Love, that familial otherness, such as that of Christians (Catholics and Orthodox) and Jews, is intended by God as a historical necessary good as a schooling for love. By emphasizing the Christian teaching that reconciliation touches on what is divine, a teaching that Dostoevsky should have embraced, he concludes that Christians must practice tolerant dialogue, grounded not on religious indifference or relativism but on consciously held religious convictions. The conclusion is reinforced by drawing out the corollary that Orthodox Russia would implode in a self-destructive vortex should religious nationalism and secular socialism prevent her from channeling the energies of her authentic messianic consciousness into building a supranational theocracy in partnership with Catholic Europe and Jewry.

Pobedonostsev was scandalized by this speech as well and forbade both its publication and its discussion. Katkov also declared the lecture childish prattle. Sergei Solovyov observes, with irony, that Katkov respected and esteemed Solovyov's thought until it turned to the Jewish and Polish question, whereupon it became dismissible.[134] Katkov, it may be remembered, first linked the Jewish and Polish questions in 1864, sought to win the Jews over to Russia to curb Polish power in the Pale, and, on the whole, consistently averted Judeophobia (see Pt. I, ch. 4, §6.4).

As will be seen, Solovyov esteems Katkov for this effort but fails to find in it sufficient common ground to judge Katkov a friend in his campaign on behalf of Jewish and minority civil rights. He parts ways with Katkov definitively by representing him as the Goliath and pillar of Russian governmental statehood in 1885 in the article "State Philosophy" in the program of the Ministry of National Enlightenment because his support for bureaucratic autocracy turned the church into one of its agencies and the people into undifferentiated material for its jurisprudential experiments. The publication of this article in Aksakov's journal *Rus'*, shows that Aksakov, for all his differences about the great (ecclesial) debate with Solovyov, on this occasion found deep sympathies within himself for Solovyov's position and could not but brave tsarist displeasure by publishing the article, demonstrating thereby the complexities of the Slavophile camp.[135]

As with the reception of his appeal to the tsar to forgive his father's assassins, these pressures took a heavy toll on Solovyov's finances, nerves, and health. But they also helped him to conform to the two models by which he judged authentic Christian religiosity: (1) the Old Testament prophets who, not being in the pay of the monarch, were free to seek his and the people's welfare through admonition (see Amos 7:12–14); and (2) pre-Constantinian Christians who risked persecution and martyrdom to profess their religion.

Solovyov took advantage of his newfound freedom from regular academic duties to develop his positions, wherever and whenever possible, in print and to foster friendships and alliances where these were offered. As concern to help Jews pragmatically and concretely figured centrally in these engagements, his relationship with Faivel Getz developed from a collegial, student-tutor relationship to a lifelong alliance on behalf of Russian Jewry. In the meantime, as evidenced by the 1882 poem "In the Land of Frosty Blizzards," his love for Sophia Khitrovo persisted, and if she is the reference for the female presence signified by the second feminine singular form of "you appeared [*ty yavilas,'*]," then her unfortunate condition between two rival camps (perhaps between her husband and Solovyov, or more generally between the forces of earthly chaos, Death and Time, on the one hand, and eternal, divinely willed peace, the sun of love, on the other)[136] somehow became autobiographically intertwined in Solovyov's thinking with the position of Jewry between Poland and Russia and, judging from the conclusion of the poem, did so in a way that allowed him personally to identify with Elijah, the prophet of zeal, and so to experience the "still small voice," which Elijah heard at Mount Horeb, and to express hope in Jewry's chosen and unconquerable vocation:[137]

In the land of frosty blizzards, 'midst winters wild,
    You came, girl, to this earth.
And twixt two warring camps, abandoned child,
    You had no sheltered berth.

But hostile cries would not confound you
    Nor din of arms, nor swords,
In thought you stand and hear the mighty
    Old Testament words.

As God Most High to Hebrews chosen
    Himself swore to reveal
This God, with ardent prayers spoken
    The prophet sought with zeal.

The depths then roared, the ground rumbled
    And the sun's light did fade
The earth rocked deep, but Prophet, humbled,
    Saw no God while afraid.

Then tempest came and whirlwind weather
    And thunder in the sky,
And mighty flame with lightning blazing
    Yet no God did he spy.

Then all grew still, the storms had ended
    The Prophet, not in vain,
Discerned a voice of quiet stillness
    In which God spoke again.

CHAPTER 9

1884: "Jewry and the Christian Question"

Solovyov compiled and edited the lectures on Jewry and the Christian question and sent them to Fr. Pyotr Preobrazhensky for publication in issues 8 and 9 of *Pravoslavnoe obozrenie*. They were later republished together in a separate book(let).[138] The work begins by setting out Solovyov's premise that Jews are repelled by Christians' failure to act on their principles and that this failure points to an endemic problem in Christianity that Christians are called to resolve, namely, whether they have the will and ability to apply Christ's precept to love, not just one's neighbor, but also one's enemy, to their relationships with Jews, and if not, whether this failure betokens an absence of practical faith in Christ or an absence of faith in the practicability of Christ's teaching.

Solovyov then proceeds to explain why the Jews originally rejected Christ. This explanation begins with Solovyov's characterization of the Jews as a God-begetting people on account of their ability to harmonize three principles that many peoples and religions have deemed contradictory: (1) a deep sense of religiosity and reverence for a transcendent God; (2) a strong sense of a personal, familial, and national self; and (3) a broad materialism arising from their conception of nature and matter as divinely created. These qualities influence behavior and attitudes. Jews are (a) devoted to God unto martyrdom, (b) chiefly because of their historical experience of his personal saving power, their mutual covenant with him, and their faith in his ongoing

181

saving and resurrecting power, and (c) are hence preoccupied with preparing for him not just holy souls, but holy bodies. These qualities and virtues explain Israel's elect status: the value that Israel set on its self allowed it to recognize God's self in history. Its quest for holiness and its desire to see the divine practically realized on earth therefore enabled it to become the milieu and matrix for God's historical revelation and incarnation. All this, in turn, provides a foundation for understanding why the Jews rejected Christ, the Suffering Messiah. The rejection turned, Solovyov explains, on their failure to preserve a proper hierarchy among these values. The latter two, the affirmation of the self and materialism, ought to be subordinated to the first, to the spirit and God. Failure to do so necessarily leads to nationalism, contempt for the rest of humanity, and unscrupulous profiteering. Nonetheless, it must be understood that the Jewish messianic conception was not only political, as widely believed, but also spiritual-political, and not only sensible but also spiritually sensible, and this understanding should also have an impact on Christian messianism. Christians should not conceive of Christ's kingdom as exclusively spiritual, which is a gnostic heresy, but as entailing a sensible and social element. Consequently, Jews and Christians possess a common goal: the incarnation of the heavenly in the earthly. Their difference lies in the means by which they believe the goal must be attained. Jews aspire to it by means of a straight, unmediated manifestation of divine power and glory. Christians believe it to consist in following Christ by embracing the Cross, that is, by seeking the resurrection with Christ through death and the transfiguration of the flesh with him through its mortification. This double exploit, which on the corporate level demands the rejection of national egoism and worldly ambition, proved incomprehensible to the majority of Jews, since they, desiring to realize the Kingdom by practical steps and as soon as possible, deemed the Christian notion that all must be united and saved through one to be incredible, unrealizable, and therefore false. However, since this practical thinking can be confuted only on the basis of practice or fact, nothing will confute it save the realization of the Christian idea, the introduction of the Gospel commandment into the personal life of individuals and into the social life of the human race.

At the conclusion of his fifteen-page critique of Solovyov's "Jewry and the Christian Question," Solovyov's friend and fellow philosopher Count Evgeny Nikolaevich Trubetskoy reports that his brother, Count Sergei N. Trubetskoy, also a close friend of Solovyov and in whose home Solovyov died,[139] related to him that at some period in his life Solovyov, having become disenchanted with the work, attempted to remove it from circulation and to destroy its remaining copies. Evgeny Trubetskoy does not remember when this actually happened but notes that when Solovyov published *The History and the Future of Theocracy* in 1887, he republished in it part 1 of "Jewry," containing his "wonderful characterization of the Jewish national character given earlier in the brochure" (i.e., *Theocracy*, 126–34, 392–400), but not the second part pertaining to the relationships of Israel, Russia, and Poland. On this basis he concludes that 1887 must have been the *terminus ante quem* for Solovyov's admission that part 1 was the work's kernel and part 2 its husk, unworthy of reprinting. As Evgeny Trubetskoy surmises that Solovyov must have himself grasped the weaknesses that he, Evgeny, identified in the work, his criticism may be briefly summarized.[140]

Trubetskoy praises Solovyov's opening premise and "brilliant" threefold characterization of Jewry and Judaism and judges that the entire first part reflects and expresses Solovyov's pure, deep, Christian understanding of life. However, he deems the "golden brilliance" of this explanation spoiled by the alloy of romantic national dreams that drive the second, theocratic part of the work on the relationship of Jewry's and Russia's messianic roles. Trubetskoy charged Solovyov with falling prey in this part of the argument to the very temptations he exposed in explaining the Jewish rejection of Christ.

The problem, Trubetskoy explains, is felt right from the posing of the three questions pertaining to (a) the meaning of the history of the Jewish nation, (b) why Christ was born a Jew and why the majority of Israel rejected him, and (c) why most Jews came to be situated in Russia and Poland and on the borders of the Greco-Slavonic worlds. According to Solovyov, the three questions correlate with Israel's past, present, and future, but Trubetskoy suggests that the reader feels, in this observation, a violation of perspective arising from the juxtaposition of the central global and world historical mystery of the incarnation with the mundane and contingent facts of Israel's sojourn on Russian territory. The answer given to the last question also violates, Trubetskoy affirms, the proper proportion between Christianity and patriotism, for the answer itself succumbs to the temptations of nationalism and materialism.

The argument begins with Solovyov reiterating his thesis that Judaism and Christianity are called jointly to build a righteous divine-human society in which people willingly submit to God, live harmoniously with each other, and have total power over nature and material reality. As this thesis clearly refers to the biblical new heaven and new earth, Trubetskoy deems it theologically sound. What Trubetskoy finds problematic is how Solovyov mixes the features of the "new earth" with the features of Russia. For example, in arguing that Judaism, Orthodoxy, and Catholicism must cooperate in their theocratic task, Solovyov thinks that history has providentially situated the Jews between the Orthodox and Catholic Slavs in Russia and Poland, seeing here an expression of the prophecy of Isaiah 19:24, quoted at the start of the essay, regarding the day when "Israel will be the third with Egypt and Assyria, a blessing in the midst of the earth." Next, to explain the nations' need for cooperation, Solovyov reviews history to show how each people's virtues, strengths, and talents proved complementary to the others. Russia possesses autocratic power in its Orthodox tsar but lacks the guidance of an independent spiritual priestly authority, possessed by Catholic Poles, and an intelligent entrepreneurial class, possessed by the Jews, which could guide that power and help transform her earth. The union of churches and the realization of theocracy by joint Slav effort would reveal Christianity practicable in deed and power and so remove the obstacle to Jewish acceptance of Christ and union with Christians in their calling to establish Godmanhood.

In Trubetskoy's eyes, the achievement of world theocracy hinges here not on the performance of that same double exploit that Solovyov said was demanded for Jewish recognition of the Christ—the repudiation of national egoism and detachment from earthly welfare—but rather on the promise of worldly blessing. True, Russia is called to self-renunciation by ceding spiritual authority to the pope, political privilege to the Poles, and economic governance to Jews, but this, for Trubetskoy, does not so much affirm the Cross as replace it, since it rewards this recognition with the lion's share of political power and economic welfare. The Jews, too, join this Christian theocracy not by way of the Cross but because the theocracy makes the Russian and Polish kingdom a promised land flowing with milk and honey. In essence, Trubetskoy concluded, Solovyov simply forgot to announce to Russia that same moral demand whose violation he judged to be the root sin of the Jewish nation. What he dreamed of for Russia, on account of his love for her, was an unsuffered-for beatitude, and because he wanted this beatitude to be realized directly and "as soon as possible," his Slavophilic messianism was revealed as essentially Jewish, and "Jewish" became a synonym for the merely and representatively human.

The criticism is worth bearing in mind in evaluating how Solovyov's thinking on Jewish-Christian relations developed and how "Jewry and the Christian Question" relates to Solovyov's final statement on these relations in his apocalyptic "Tale of the Antichrist." In anticipating this evaluation, it may be instructive to point out that Trubetskoy's criticism fails to do justice to Solovyov's position in several ways. First, there is some inconsistency between Trubetskoy's commending Solovyov for repudiating the widespread Christian misconception of Jewish messianism for being purely political and nonspiritual and his accusing Solovyov of modeling his Slavophile Christian messianic vision on Old Testament–Jewish messianic models and therefore on purely human or *secular* models. Trubetskoy accepted Solovyov's correction that deeming the Old Testament and Jewish messianic model *purely* secular and nonspiritual is a Christian misconception. The argument entailed, therefore, that to think of messianism in *purely* spiritual and nonpolitical terms is equally not Christian but gnostic. Consequently, to emphasize the importance of secular realities and talents in the secular sphere should not be regarded a priori as capitulation to false, anti-Christian messianism.

Second, it is not at all clear that Solovyov's appeal to Russian Orthodoxy to recognize Rome, and thereby to liberate itself from the nationalist forces that threaten to sap its moral and spiritual energy, necessarily bypasses the Cross. This implies that the Cross must entail some grand act of asceticism verging on literal crucifixion or physical martyrdom and not on a humble act of moral self-renunciation or even fraternal cooperation with the other, which Solovyov's theocratic vision entails for each of the three parties. Trubetskoy accuses Solovyov of compromising Christianity and the Cross by offering to Catholics ecclesiastical power and to Orthodox empire and to Jews economic power, but in Solovyov's scheme these offers do not promise absolute hegemony and are not, in each case, devoid of the element of self-sacrifice. They involve the sacrifice of triumphalist hubris and the yoking of national virtues or historical patrimonies to a common good. As Solovyov argued in "The Great Debate" (1883), to be saved from nationalism and orthodoxism, Russia and Orthodoxy must recognize Rome. Similarly, as he argues in "Jewry," Rome and Catholicism, to be saved from Caesaropapism, must surrender political power and recognize the tsar. Both, to be saved from economic sluggishness, must embrace the Jews. Jewry, to be saved from nationalism and materialism, must subordinate its entrepreneurial skill and prowess to the service of the universal destination of created goods. These are ascetic moments. That Solovyov continued to think of it as a key ascetic moment, beyond 1887, is attested by his citing of Yuri Krizhanich, whom he identifies as the first Slavophile, to Aksakov when he parted ways with him in 1884 and again in the epigraph to his essay "The Sins of Russia," stipulating that the ultimate sin that Russia and Orthodoxy need to overcome is that of schism (see Pt. III, ch. 10 [letter to Getz, #37]).

At issue in this discussion are in fact two separate points. The first pertains to the question of the integrity of Solovyov's position from a Christian theological, salvation-mediated-through-suffering perspective. The second pertains to the question of whether Solovyov repudiated his theocratic ideal of insisting that it is to be achieved through the messianic cooperation of three agents: Catholicism, Orthodoxy, and Judaism, represented by Poland, Russia, and Jewry. As noted above, Evgeny Trubetskoy recollects that his brother S. Trubetskoy reported that Solovyov retracted this vision around 1887, in the years when he hoped to publish his *Theocracy*. Some clinching arguments against this latter assumption might include the reuse by Solovyov of the epigraph of Isaiah 19:24, 25, which introduces this present 1882 (lecture stage) / 1884 (published) work, "Jewry and the Christian Question," in section 3 of his 1896 (!) review essay, "When Lived the Hebrew Prophets?," where Solovyov again celebrates these verses, emphasizing that the prophet's main point of interest here concerns not politics or military matters but "the spiritual union of Egypt, Assyria, and Israel in the service of one God, who blesses all three of them." Even if Solovyov is thinking of the literal, original, historically contextual sense that Isaiah would have attributed to Egypt, Assyria, and Israel, the fact that he recalls this significant verse to speak of the "spiritual union" of these three nations in God's messianic task argues that he has not given up the idea that God continues to achieve his end of the spiritual union of Israel and its contemporary brother nations/enclaves, in the present case, Russia and Poland. That Solovyov continued to apply this prophecy to Russia, Poland, and Jewry into the 1890s is further attested by the conclusion of Solovyov's foreword to Getz's book (Pt. III, ch. 9, letter #25), dated March 5, 1891, which ends:

> But I confess that I don't feel such fear either. Infatuation for imaginary "social opinion" is a rather transient phenomenon, and in the final end we have a government, which stands above all passions and all intrigues; and the Russian people itself, is not an enemy unto itself; it knows enough to not kick against the goads[141] and to not argue with divine destinies. And it is not for nothing that providence has settled the greatest and strongest portion of Jewry in our native land.

The initial sentiments of this paragraph could be the result of a rhetorical attempt to coax the government with a show of patriotism and piety, but the last two lines about "kicking against the goads," "divine destinies," and "providence" argue that despite not reprinting part 2 of "Jewry" in *Theocracy*, he was still willing to express its thesis in print in 1891. In this case, the poem "Immanu-el" (1894), like "Panmongolism" (1894),[142] may highlight the point in his life at which he, noting that "Our kings no longer look much at the sky," abandoned the expectation of fulfillment of his theocratic ideal any time soon in history and postponed his hopes into apocalyptic mode. But such a shift is not necessarily an abandonment of the *theocratic* ideal, not the admission that the vision of the need for the three powers to cooperate is tantamount to a capitulation to the "Three Temptations" of the Grand Inquisitor, but principally the expression of the realization of the persistence and strength of the power of evil to frustrate divine wisdom and a falling in line with scriptural apocalyptic visions about the process through which God, as "God with us," will finally defeat it (see ch. 18, commentary on "The Tale of the Antichrist," below).

All this would suggest that there is something amiss in Trubetskoy's contention that Solovyov repudiated part 2 of "Jewry" and sought to destroy its exemplars and withdraw it from republication. Since the contention is based partly on the observation that this part of "Jewry," the theocratic part, was not reprinted in volume 1 of *Theocracy*, that omission must be explained. This is relatively easy to do, for volume 1 was published in Zagreb in April 1887 and dealt principally with theocracy in the Old Testament. As such, part 1 of "Jewry" was chronologically directly relevant to it and was reprinted, whereas part 2, relating to materials that would have belonged to the unfinished (and never finished) part 2, would have been postponed for integration.

Second, the idea of "destroying" manuscripts and seeking to withdraw them from publication must have arisen from something Solovyov shared with S. Trubetskoy sometime around 1887. If one searches for this theme in Solovyov's biography, one will find Sergei Solovyov relating that Solovyov attempted to secure the influence of Alexander Alekseevich Kireev, a prolific Slavophile polemicist, closely connected to the royal court and official ecclesiastical circles, in publishing the first volume of *Theocracy* in Russia but was informed by him on May 25, 1887, that the book would be subjected to ecclesiastical censorship, a fate that Solovyov feared like the "lion's den."[143] Then, shortly before discovering that the book would be "unconditionally banned," Solovyov appealed to Kireev again, only to receive the book back from Kireev on July 20, with the following explanation: "You tell me that you attempted to remove everything that could justify forbidding its publication; but in *practice* you did not excise anything."[144]

Thus arises the theme of Solovyov "removing" things from *Theocracy* which he initially reported to Fr. Paul Pierling, S.J., while corresponding with him about his progress on publishing *La Russie et l'Église universelle* (1889) in France. Admitting the need to remove portions that would fail to win approval from the Catholic Church, he declared on June 17 (Pt. III, ch. 9, letter #29) his intention to "destroy conjectural passages, that is, the entire first part[,] . . . and to change the title of the work to *La theocratie dans l'histoire et la réunion des églises.*" He finally wrote about this plan to his brother Mikhail on September 18, saying that he "threw out everything theosophical and called the composition *La Russie et l'Église universelle.*"[145] Here then, in 1887, is the theme of anxiety over and confession to throwing out entire sections of works dealing with theocratic issues for the sake of securing their publication. It could be proposed that either S. Trubetskoy himself, in relating the matter to E. Trubetskoy, confused the identity of the work that Solovyov sought to prune because of this anxiety or E. Trubetskoy himself, perhaps out of his own wish to have Solovyov admit his criticisms of his theocractic "three powers" conception, confused the work with the second part of "Jewry."

One of the reasons the first volume of *Theocracy,* completed by 1886, was condemned by Russian censors relates to Solovyov's engagement with Hebrew throughout the 1880s and the fruit of this engagement in his writings. The initial books take on the form of a commentary on theocracy in the Bible. Books 1 and 2 cite the scriptures from Slavonic versions, but book 3, on Exodus, titled "National Theocracy, and the Law of Moses," and book 4, on Judges, Kings, and Prophets, titled "The Culmination of National Theocracy by the Development of the Three Powers: The Priestly, Royal, and Prophetic, and the Shift to Universal Theocracy," cite directly from the Hebrew and present names and terms in Hebraic forms, for example, YHWH rather than Yehova, Shimshon rather than Samson. Solovyov wrote to his friend Mikhail Matveevich Stasyulevich in 1886 to report that the censors were prohibiting the publication of the "innocent" volume 1 of his *Theocracy* for this reason.[146] The shift to citing the scriptures from Slavonic to citing them from the Hebrew will also be evidenced in the citations differentiating "Jewry," published in 1884, and "The Talmud," published in 1886, as the textual annotations show.

The last remaining level on which Trubetskoy's criticism fails to do justice to Solovyov's "Jewry" relates to his failure to recognize its rhetorical strategies. Solovyov was committed to engaging conservative, Orthodox, Slavophile public opinion distrustful of Jews. The target audience needs to be borne in mind in order to understand the work's rhetoric. Above it was noted that this may explain why this work contains sentiments that have the sharpest anti-Enlightenment slant in all of Solovyov's oeuvre. The same may be said about the observation that the chapter contains and the argument seems to be grounded on certain antisemitic-sounding assumptions. Such may be said, for example, about the "fact" that Jews are characterized as having a pronounced sense of self, individual and tribal, or about the stipulation that the Jewish character combines "fleshly materialism" with "lofty monotheism." Taken on their own, such characterizations may verge on the antisemitic, and do in fact echo stereotypical charges in Judeophobic tracts of the time, as in Dostoevsky's treatment of the Jewish question in his *The Diary of a Writer* or in the pages of Aksakov's *Rus'*. What Solovyov achieves in part 1 of the essay is to apply the insights expressed in his *Lectures on Godmanhood* about the Old Testament revelation of the living God and Jewish[E] personalism to these stereotypes and thereby demonstrate that these are the indispensable virtues and media by which God was revealed first to the human race through the patriarchs as a personal self and second as God who became incarnate and thereby sanctified matter and the body in the most intimate manner. It would be impossible to remain hostile to these character traits and values without betraying the fundamentals of Christian doctrine.

Evidence that Solovyov seeks to ground his polemics on the premises of his opponents may be taken from his explanation of his rhetorical strategy to Getz in a letter of March 5, 1891 (Pt. III, ch. 9, #25). It is also noteworthy that on this occasion he introduces "Jewry" by reporting that he was encouraged to include in this present work the contents of the lectures presented back in 1882 by the "splendid pronouncement" on Jewish-Christian relations given in Odessa in April 1884 by Bishop Nikanor of Kherson and Odessa. This "pronouncement" was printed, he points out, in the earlier (May–June) issue of *Pravoslavnoe obozrenie*, the same journal that carried "Jewry." Claim-

ing that he is simply unpacking the bishop's ideas, he quotes them
at length. To appreciate the significance of this citation it is helpful
to delve briefly into Bishop Nikanor's views on Jewish-Christian
relations.

Nikanor Brovkovich (1827–90), a distinguished clergyman and
philosopher, taught at the St. Petersburg Academy and served as rector of several seminaries, including the Academy of Kazan', prior to
becoming archbishop of Kherson and Odessa. He is known for several
polemics against Tolstoy and for his philosophical work, grounded on
Plato and Leibniz.[147] Trotsky read him in prison and remarked scorn-
fully on his references to Balaam's talking ass and to parakeets as proof
against the Darwinian theory of evolution.[148] Nikanor's popularity
with conservative, nationalist elements is attested by the familiar tone
of his report of December 4, 1884, to Pobedonostsev on the proceedings of the Council of Kiev in 1884 in which he lists Jewry (specifically,
the inclusion of Jews in Russian classrooms) as being one of the sixteen
questions discussed and, after summarizing the debate, concludes by
saying that he "doesn't remember what decision the Council finally
adopted."[149] This failure of memory reflects either the archbishop's
evasive and canny defensive maneuver on behalf of the Jews or little
more than a lack of personal interest in Jewish welfare. If the latter, the
attitude would have disappointed Solovyov, who, for example, on
learning that the Ministry of National Enlightenment issued a circular
limiting Jewish access to educational institutions, wrote to Getz that
"this circular in particular adds to my nervous pains," adding that the
need to counteract such politics impelled him to prepare a French
article on Russia's *obligation* to grant Jews equal rights.[150]

That Nikanor did care about Jewish rights is corroborated in a letter from Strakhov to Tolstoy, sent from St. Petersburg and dated January 3, 1891, in which he refers to an obituary in the right-wing paper
Grazhdanin on December 30, reporting Nikanor's death on December 27. In the postscript, Strakhov adds, "People relate that Nikanor
was wont to defend the Jews and that while he was ill prayers for his
recovery were conducted in the Synagogue. There is a hint of this in
his farewell discourse." V. Zhdanov, editor of Strakhov's correspondence with Tolstoy, explains that during the commemoration of the

centenary Jubilee of the city of Odessa, "Archbishop Nikanor delivered a speech, published in September 1890 in *Novoe vremya,* castigating drunkenness, sloth, and licentiousness in the Russian populace, and in doing so cited the moral example of nonnative populations (German, Jewish, and others)."[151]

Strakhov's note and Zhdanov's citation of Nikanor's discourse in *Novoe vremya* (New Time) also record the following report:

> In 1887, after the Jewish pogroms in Odessa, Archbishop Nikanor of Kherson and Odessa delivered a sermon titled "Poucheniya v sredu svetlyya sedmitsy po sluchayu buistvennyh beshinstv" [Homily on Holy Wednesday concerning the Rabid Riots]. It was a direct and unqualified condemnation of the pogroms, which he called "rabid riots." . . . [He asked,] "What do we name a man who beats, tortures, and beggars people of another belief?" Then he answered: "This is not a student and servant of Jesus Christ, but one who fosters the Antichrist's spirit, a servant and follower of anarchy." Nikanor's sermon was a passionate appeal to his congregation to understand that "the highest level of Christian perfection is to care and pray not only for fellow Christians but also for people of other beliefs." [152]

The principal pogroms in Odessa took place in 1881 (see Pt. I, ch. 4, §8.1), and a minor one occurred in 1886. In light of this, it is possible that Nikanor indeed made this speech in 1887, but if so, this would have been his second noteworthy speech on the Odessa pogroms after the one printed in 1884 in *Pravoslavnoe obozrenie* and commented on by Solovyov a little later in that same journal. As Nikanor would have been better known for the former speech, it is more likely that the present report is also based on it.

In addition to the ambiguous report Nikanor made to Pobedonostsev about Jewish quotas in education and his unambiguous criticism of the pogrom in Odessa, he is on record for saying the following about Jews.

Religion is the basis that gives strength to the Jewish spirit. [Theirs is] a more or less secret religious organization [*kahal*]—a mighty multipotent machine which drives Jewry's millions to secretly marked aims. Only a blind man can fail to see how frightening, how dreadful is this power! It seeks neither more nor less the enslavement of the world! And knowing this, consider that in the last century it made appalling accomplishments, finding support in European liberalism, in equality before the law, etc. It increasingly and ever more tightly entangles the adherents of other faiths while steering its own like a machine. All Jews are substantially like one man. We liberally discuss whether it is beneficent or detrimental to ban markets on feast days. But the secret Jewish power tells its own: "Do not dare! Observe the Sabbath! Observe the law of the fathers! The law gives life and strength to Jewry." And behold, not a single Jew dares to ride out on the Sabbath from Nikolaev into Kherson or into Odessa. The trains are empty and shipping between these great towns stops completely. It's strange and hurtful for a Christian nation and for such a Great Kingdom such as ours! But how great is the foreign power! And how brave and daring! This is a religious power, rooted in the religious organization of the Kahal.[153]

Pronouncements of this sort, grounded in Brafman's *Book of the Kahal*, would not fail to uphold Nikanor's popularity among ultranationalist elements, as is evident from his 1890 obituaries in *Novoe vremya*.[154] His authority with such conservative, ultranationalist audiences would constitute an important reason for Solovyov's citation of his defense of the Jews on this occasion.

CHAPTER 10

1885–1886: Joseph Rabinovich
and "The Talmud"

———

Solovyov soon supplemented "Jewry and the Christian Question" with two other works, the first published in 1885 in defense of Joseph Rabinovich (Rabinovitch), founder of the messianic Jewish community, "The Israel of the New Covenant," and the second, "The Talmud and Recent Polemical Literature about It in Austria and Germany," published in 1886 in defense of the Talmud.

Joseph Davidovich Rabinovich (1837–99) commenced his public career as a Hasidic scholar, writer, and rabbi in Kishinev, Bessarabia, Ukraine. He became the first person in modern times to call himself a messianic Jew, which he defined as a Jew who recognizes Jesus as the Messiah, retains faith in Judaism, and does not convert to Christianity, ecclesially or culturally, withholding allegiance from its mainstream churches because of their painful historical legacy for Jewish memory. As such, he has become a subject of increasing research interest in the past two decades. In Solovyov's day, the tsarist government wanted to undermine Rabinovich's community by labeling it a Protestant sect. Rabinovich's biography evidences that he did eventually affiliate his movement with Protestantism.[155]

Solovyov took issue with the government's classification of and attack on Rabinovich's community and explained his views to his brother Mikhail.

The State Councillor Leskov has seemingly led you into confusion regarding the New Israel. I have read the documents, their symbol [Credo], liturgy, etc. This is the contrary of Protestantism, even though very similar to it. The point is that Protestantism, if one looks at its root, is the negation of Law, whereas the New Israel holds to the Law with both hands. It is before all else the original Jewish form of Christianity, from which emerged, not Protestantism, but the Church.[156]

In his essay on Rabinovich, "The Israel of the New Covenant," Solovyov rises to Rabinovich's defense by taking up the simile of two trains standing side by side at a station but going in opposite directions. He argues that while Rabinovich's creed looks Protestant, the two differ fundamentally: Protestantism proceeds by protest against and elimination of core traditional Catholic and Orthodox dogmas, whereas Rabinovich proceeds by simply supplementing his Old Testament Jewish faith with belief in Jesus in a way reminiscent of Jews who converted to Christianity in the days of the early church, resembling the trajectory of primitive apostolic Christianity. It would be unjust, Solovyov argues, to expect Rabinovich's community to adopt the dogmatic positions of all the ecumenical councils without experiencing the historical debates that prompted their formulations. To support the argument, Solovyov invokes its precedent in St. Gregory the Theologian's reconciliatory approach to Christians of his day who had difficulty accepting the divinity of the Holy Spirit. Solovyov will supplement these reflections on Rabinovich's significance in his obituary for the man (see below, ch. 18).

Solovyov's correspondence with Getz also shows him working energetically through 1885 on a defense of the Talmud against the animosity stirred up against it in Austria on account of the Rohling affair but also dealing with the ongoing attack exerted on the Talmud in Russia by Brafman's *Book of the Kahal*, especially in its uses under Ignatiev by the provincial governors comprising Gotovtsev's commissions and by members of the Pahlen Commission, which operated from 1883 to 1888 (see Pt. I, ch. 4, §§4.8.7–8.9; §§9.4–9.5).

Dr. August Rohling was a Prague academic whose work *Der Talmudjude* (1871) attempted to defame Judaism by attacking the Talmud. Sued for perjury by the rabbi Joseph Samuel Bloch, Rohling countersued and, in preparing his case, employed Robert Pattai, M.P., and Ahron Briman, an apostate Jew who wrote under the pseudonym Dr. Justus a commentary on one hundred alleged passages pertaining to Talmudic ordinances against Christianity in the Jewish code *Shulchan Aruch*. Briman's work, titled the *Judenspiegel,* asserted that the whole Talmud consists of such passages and was cited by an antisemitic paper in Münster.[157] In the trial that followed in 1883, Rohling and Briman were accused of inciting racism. Briman ended up in prison; while Rohling, advised by the Christian scholar Franz Delitzsch that he could not win, withdrew his complaint.

Solovyov devotes the first part of his article "The Talmud" to describing the three Jewish sects of Jesus's time: Sadducees, Pharisees, and Essenes. He describes the Sadducees as the party that turned Moses's law, the Torah, into a nonliving Word of the past; the Pharisees as the party that turned the Torah, by means of their oral law, into a Word to live by in the present; and the Essenes the sect that discerned within it the revelation of the goal of the future. He then explains that Christianity and Judaism differ not in their ethics, for example, not in what they have to say about the importance of altruism but in their metaphysics, in the question of the divine-human significance and redemptive sacrifice of Christ. He then takes up his polemic against the two antisemitic works by Rohling and Justus to show, first, how they misinterpreted many anti-Christian Talmudic injunctions and, second, by repeating the key point of his "Jewry and the Christian Question," namely, that Christian civilization, with its confessional division and the tension between its life and ideals, is in no position to accuse Jews, who retain their religious national unity and follow their own injunctions. Among the many examples he gives to support his argument, one concerns the evil of slavery. The palliatives of early church canons were so weak, as compared to Moses's injunctions against it, that slavery was abolished only in the eighteenth and nineteenth centuries, during the epoch of religious decline and rising unbelief. In view of such circumstances, Jews could justifiably tell Christians, "Learn first how to fulfill your New Testament as we fulfill our Old Testament and then we will come and join you."[158]

Publishing "The Talmud" proved difficult for Solovyov because of Pobedonostsev's censorship. He complains to Getz that Pobedonostsev had informed one of his friends that *"every* activity of [Solovyov] is harmful to Russia and Orthodoxy and, consequently, cannot be tolerated" (see Pt. III, ch. 9, letter #9, 1886). Mochulsky states that Pobedonostsev, having already prohibited the publication of the first volume of Solovyov's *Theocracy,* also made an official declaration against "The Talmud."[159] In sharing his worries with Getz, Solovyov then explains that rather than become depressed, he cheers himself up with the proverb that roughly translated reads, "Whom God will sustain [lit., "not betray"], the swine won't retain [lit., "eat"]." In context, the "swine" refers to Pobedonostsev and, judging from a parallel letter to his friend Tsertelev, as well as to D. A. Tolstoy and Katkov (Pt. III, ch. 9, letter #9). In a similar vein, he regretted at this time that Russia, instead of giving birth to the theocratic ideal, had realized within itself a pseudotheocracy headed by the "malicious triumvirate of the false priest Pobedonostsev, the false statesman D. A. Tolstoy, and the false prophet Katkov."[160]

In June 1886, after failing to publish the work in the progressive *Vestnik Evropy,* edited by Solovyov's friend Mikhail Stasyulevich (see Pt. III, ch. 9, letter #4, 1885), Solovyov departed for his second trip abroad, to Austria and Croatia. Sergei Solovyov connects his poem "To the Promised Land" (1886) about the call of Abraham with a personal call to go to Archbishop Strossmayer in Austria. The poem is dedicated to A. P. Salomon/Solomon.[161]

> "Forsake with haste your native borders,
> And all your race, and father's home.
> And as the arrow heeds the archer,
> My mouth's words heed as you roam.
> Go forth, for former things not caring
> Go forth, what's past, do not recall

Until I tell you keep on going,
To reach the place of my love's call."

He left his couch, confused and shaking
Unable to decide, was it truth or dream . . .
When suddenly he feels above a flutter
An alien gust—from which he hears *the theme*:

"From your native Mesopotamian plain
From Aram's grassy hillsides and earth,
From Haran, where grey hairs your own head did arraign,
And from Ur, where flowed quickly the years of your birth,

> Not just only one year,
> Not just numerous ages,
> But forever I bid thee to fare."

So gathering again his band of nomads
Directed by the rising sun's new light
He hastened for the misty-blue horizons
Sustained by the call's mysterious might

"Warm and salty the sea breeze will buffet your face,
'gainst this wind, without stopping, go.
And when heaven's horizon recedes beyond trace,
And the waters stretch broadly below,

> See that leftwards you turn
> And proceed at a run,
> The straight way do not spurn,
> And seek rest from the sun,

And at noon when you feel the sun burn—,
Then a village you'll see or a city,

Walk on then, pass it by,
And go on, don't sojourn,

Until I myself say, 'It's here, see!'

I'm forever with you,
For my covenant yearn,
Pure in heart and of firm spirit be!

Remain faithful to me in mishap and fine days,

Walk before me,
Look not to past ways,
What ahead awaits always
By faith you will see.
For I swear verily,
And I promised in love,

That from you, I will raise up my home for the world,
That the ends of the earth will in fame your name hold,
That the seed of your race to each nation,
Will bring peace and their longed-for salvation."

On leaving, Solovyov granted Getz power of attorney to present the manuscript to *Russkaya mysl'* (Russian Thought), the most widely read literary-political monthly, dedicated to the principles of constitutional democracy, freedom of conscience, and speech (Pt. III, ch. 9, letter #6). He was surprised and pleased by the speed with which the manuscript was accepted for publication (Pt. III, ch. 9, letters #6, #8).[162]

The letters to Getz from this period show Solovyov recuperating at the famous spa in Styria, Austria, and progressing, systematically, through the Hebrew Bible, reaching now the Book of Kings. He also reports his pleasure at having personally witnessed during his travels solicitude by a Jew to not commit Hillul ha-Shem, meaning "the profanation of the Name [of God])," the principle, amply explained by

Solovyov in his "Talmud," refers to a scandalous act by which a Jew might provoke people, especially Gentiles, to think and speak badly of God, Judaism, and Jewry. At this time he also expresses his distress over the news, received from Getz, that Russian Jews had suffered more pogroms (see Pt. III, ch. 9, letter #5, 1886). While pogroms became relatively rare after 1884, they were not unknown between 1884 and 1903 and are reported to have occurred in Kiev in 1885 and Odessa in 1886. One of these, probably the latter, should have been the subject of the news reported in Getz's letter (see Pt. I, ch. 4, §9.1).

CHAPTER 11

1887–1890: Getz's Journal and the Gestation of the Protest

On returning to Russia in autumn 1886, Solovyov encountered the mounting pressure of censorship of his writings, from both state and church. He learned that the first volume of *Theocracy* would not be published because of the citations from the Hebrew Bible and that his article "The Sins of Russia," despite friendly letters from Evgeny Mikhailovich Theoktistov (or Feoktistoff), director of the Ministry for Affairs of the Press, would also not be published in *Novosti* (see below). As a result he turned to seeking new allies, finding them in Stasyulevich, editor of the liberal *Vestnik Evropy*, and Russian Jesuits in France, for example, Fr. Ivan Matveevich Martynov, companion of Father Pirling. *Vestnik Evropy* would publish a number of his poems in 1887, as well as his critique of Danilevsky's *Russia and Europe* (1869), with which he would commence a more concerted campaign against Slavophiles and especially Strakhov. Toward the end of 1886, something also went awry in his personal relations with Sophia Khitrovo, prompting him to spend the three weeks of Advent on a retreat at his beloved Holy Trinity Monastery at Sergiev Posad, where due to his difficult state and loneliness, as reported in his letter of January 11, 1887, to Strakhov and others, he gave some thought to the idea, proposed to him by the monks, to join them. Upon his return, he fell ill again and, seeking rest and peace, departed to spend some time with his friend, the poet Afanasy Afanasievich Fet, and the two entertained each other by reciting Catullus and jointly translating Virgil's *Aeneid*.[163] The illness, which he attributed to the pressures of censorship rather than his personal life, is reported in his next letters to Getz (Pt. III, ch. 9, letters #11 and #12, the latter dated to April 1887).[164] Having read through all the historical books and the prophets of the Bible in Hebrew, he was pleased to report that he had reached the Psalms and would soon be able to add Hebrew phrases to his daily prayers. The passages he chose to apply to his present situation are rather bitter laments from Psalm 41:8–10 — "All who hate me whisper together about me; they imagine the worst for me. They say, 'A deadly thing has fastened upon him; he will not rise again from where he lies.' Even my bosom friend in whom I trusted, who ate of my bread, has lifted his heel against me" — and Psalm 25:16–17 — "Turn thou to me, and be gracious to me; for I am lonely and afflicted. Relieve the troubles of my heart, and bring me out of my distresses."

After informing Getz of his three-week monastic retreat in April 1887, he announced the publication of volume 1 of his *Theocracy* abroad (letter #12). In August, he reported that it had been definitively banned in Russia and that his neuralgia had consequently worsened. He then reviewed the quotas imposed in July 1887 by the tsar and Pobedonostsev through Minister of Education Ivan Delianov on Jewish students (see Pt. I, ch. 4, §9.5). Asking "what is to be done against these stupid and criminal politics," he proposed two courses of action, both involving public activism (letter #13; see also letter #34 and ch. 16 below).

The first was to work behind the scenes to ensure that the editorship of *Moskovskie vedomosti* would be acquired by one of his friends rather than by the colleagues of Katkov, its longtime editor, who kept it uninfected by Judeophobia. The designation of Katkov as a Judeophile resonates with what Solovyov says of him elsewhere (letters #14, #16, #25) and with Klier's judgment about him (see Pt. I, ch. 4, §6.4, §8.2). The friend that Solovyov is thinking of is probably Dmitry Tsertelev, who in 1896 would be considered for but fail to win this post a second time. Three letters later, Solovyov reported his loss of hope about *Moskovskie vedomosti* not capitulating to Judeophobia (letter #16).

The second course of action was to press on with the publication of his French work "pertaining to Russia's principal political problems or *obligations*." This refers to Solovyov's chief accomplishment in 1887: the publication of *La Russie et L'Église universelle* in France. As the principal obligations that Solovyov envisioned for Russia included the bestowal of full civil rights on Russian Jews, Solovyov asked Getz to help him think of some practical measures to promote this goal. Getz suggested two concrete measures, which became the subjects of the next two letters.

Getz's first proposal, implicit in the correspondence, was the creation of a Jewish newspaper with an editorial board that could advocate for the expansion of Jewish civil rights in a publicly effective manner. To advance this, Getz petitioned Solovyov for letters of introduction to influential people who could help him establish such a paper. In response (letter #14), Solovyov attached two letters, the first to Theoktistov, head of the state agency for press affairs, the second to the renowned Slavophile poet Apolon Nikolaevich Maikov (1821–97). The letter to Maikov, never delivered, was preserved by Getz in his collection of Solovyov's letters and is included in the collection of Solovyov's letters to him between letters #20 and #21. Getz also evidently asked Solovyov for a letter to Countess Elizaveta Grigorievna Volkonskaya (1838–97), the niece of a minister of the court of Alexander I and Nicholas I, a widely read, highly cultured, profoundly Russian woman, and, as attested by her composition on the church, a strong proponent of Catholicism to which she secretly converted in the 1890s. Solovyov valued her especially for her strength of will and thought and, implicitly, social connections, such as her friendship with Bishop Strossmayer. [165] As evident from letter #20, and probably from letter #28, if the abbreviation "V" there refers to her, Getz hoped that she would help subsidize his newspaper. Solovyov regretfully responded that he was not able to contact her because she had left Russia to care for a son who was dying abroad. However, if she is the person to whom the "V" in letter #28 refers, we may infer that Solovyov managed to orchestrate their meeting and that she provided Getz with the principal subsidy for printing his book, *The Floor to the Accused.*

In letter #14, obviously pertaining to the issue of founding a journal, Solovyov expresses regret over his inability to write to Katkov on account of having finally severed their relationship. The regret is poignant since, as in the previous letter where he credited Katkov for preserving *Moskovskie vedomosti* from Judeophobia while serving as its editor, Solovyov again acquits Katkov of harboring prejudices against Jews, implying that Katkov would have proved a powerful ally in the battle for Jewish civil rights. Indeed, in the essay Solovyov contributed to Getz's book (see letter #25, March 5, 1891), he grounded his argument with Judeophobes on Katkov's fact-based exculpation of the Jews against the widespread prejudice that "tavern Yids" were responsible for Russian drunkenness and impoverishment in the Pale of Settlement. Solovyov's mention of Katkov testifies to his respect for Katkov's capacity to ground argument in evidence and follow it to its logical conclusion. This in turn explains the hope Solovyov invested in polemics with conservative Slavophiles who shared Katkov's values and modes of argument.

At the same time, as attested by letter #16, written in or after May 1887 (the date of letter #15), which relates Solovyov's expectation that Katkov's journal would most likely be taken over by colleagues who, "imitating only his bad qualities," would "join the Judeophobes," Solovyov clearly saw the limits of what argument could achieve on the pages of journals controlled by Judeophobes. He ends despondently, citing a poem by Pushkin that contains the very word for "despondency" to which he earlier said he would not, with God's help, succumb on account of "swine" such as Pobedonostsev.

Getz's second proposal was to collect weighty signatures for a public protest in defense of the Jews. Getz suggested doing so in the liberal daily newspaper *Novosti*, edited by Osip Konstantinovich Notovich, a Jewish journalist, playwright, and convert to Russian Orthodoxy. Biographical entries about Notovich explain that his *Novosti* received two major official warnings, one in 1883 for an article in defense of the journal *Golos* (the Voice), the second in 1891, for Judeophilic articles on the Jewish problem. A second major warning usually proved fatal for a daily, as a third warning spelled its confiscation by the state. Notovich learned this by bitter experience with an earlier paper, in the 1870s. The 1883 warning came from Theoktistov and was followed by a temporary interdiction on the sale of *Golos* in 1884. Solovyov's letters to Getz suggest that the 1891 Judeophilic articles in question were none other than those that Solovyov delivered to him (see letter #24, March 21, 1891). *Novosti* was finally seized by the state in 1905 after it issued an appeal for a trade union. Notovich, to escape imprisonment, emigrated in 1906 (see letter #18 and notes).[166]

Solovyov accepted Getz's second proposal immediately, stating, "My quill is always ready for the defense of Israel in distress," and announcing that he had already begun penning the article for *Novosti*, which was to be titled "The Sins of Russia." Solovyov listed Russia's sins as pertaining to the condition of Jewry, the russification of Poland, and the absence of religious freedom. The article is eventually presented in letter #37 (see Pt. III, ch. 10). It begins with an epigraph by Yuri Krizhanich: "So long as your national and unacknowledged sins remain upon you, you will never wage a decisive victory, you will never restore your good name."

Krizhanich (1617–93) was a Croatian polymath dedicated to Slavic unity, one of whose greatest accomplishments was the unification of Slavic languages. Receiving his doctorate in 1642 in Rome at the Greek College of St. Anastasia, devoted to Catholicizing the Greek Orthodox, he was an ardent proponent of church unity. Setting out to defend the authority of the papacy against all who contested it, he became acquainted with Russian and took a post in Moscow to serve Tsar Alexei Mikhailovich (1659), only to be exiled by the latter to Tobolsk for sixteen years for espousing the ideal of a church independent of worldly disputes. In Tobolsk he wrote his principal works. Being pardoned by the next monarch, he left for Poland (1676), entered the Jesuit order, and died on September 12, 1683, in Vienna during Jan III Sobieski's campaign against the Ottoman Turks. Sergei Solovyov states that Solovyov identified Krizhanich as the first Slavophile and subscribed to his belief that Russia's woes and sufferings were the consequence of the great and unacknowledged sin of schism. The importance of Krizhanich's significance for Solovyov is evidenced by Solovyov's earlier allusion to his conviction in the 1884 letter to Aksakov in which Solovyov underscored the differences in their understanding of Slavophilism and which sealed the end of their friendship (see Pt. I, ch. 4, §7).

The article then summarizes Solovyov's critique of the Russian Pan-Slavist Nikolai Danilevsky (1822–85; see Pt. I, ch. 4, §7.4), whose classic *Russia and Europe* was referred to by Dostoevsky as the coffee-table book of every Russian. Taking up Danilevsky's point that only a hard lesson could inspire Russians to stop fighting with each other and develop social solidarity, Solovyov points to the Crimean War as being just such a lesson. The terrible defeat at Sevastopol revealed that the militarism and serfdom of Nicholas I's regime was demoralizing for Russia's army and so gave way, on his death, to the epoch of emancipation, civil reforms, and imperial expansion under Alexander II. However, Russia failed to educate the people it liberated to live freely and thus lost in 1878, at the treaty of the Congress of Berlin, the territories it had recently acquired (see Pt. 1, ch. 4, §5, §7.5). For Solovyov, these failures and losses constitute a new moral lesson that Russia refused to acknowledge and take to heart. How can it, he asked, "resolve the Eastern Question when it cannot with a clean conscience raise a banner to national, civil, and religious independence and free development for all the peoples of the Christian East?" "Tsarism must remain in Russia as an *unchangeable* fact," he argued, "but Russia cannot live tranquilly and flourish while infringing the *moral* demands of national, civil, and religious freedom which its official patriots laid claim to before Turkey and Austria." He concludes the article with perennially resonant words.

> As long as false political reasoning will preserve in Russia a system of forced russification at the frontiers, as long as, on the other hand, millions of Russian citizens will be forcibly separated from all other people and subjected to a new form of serfdom, as long as the system of criminal punishment will tower over religious convictions and the system of compulsory censorship over religious thought, so long will Russia, in all her dealings, remain morally bound, spiritually paralyzed, and incapable of seeing anything but failure.[167]

In this argument one may find Solovyov's response to the reactionaries who blamed Alexander II's assassination on his civil reforms, arguing that the latter only served to encourage radicalism. This, Solovyov states, is false political reasoning. The problem lies not in the reforms but in moral failure, in infringing the demands of national, civil, and religious freedom, and in Russia's failure to inculcate these freedoms among its peoples.

As to collecting signatures for a public protest, Solovyov expressed disappointment and shock over Getz's report that some of his friends, to whom Getz appealed for help, either expounded "humane" views but proved too afraid to write a single word in defense of the Jews or advocated a savage solution (exile and castration) for the Jewish problem. Solovyov agreed with Getz that collecting important signatures for such a public document would be an important counterweight to such savagery but regretted his personal inability to offer nothing else but his own words. This letter was sent before September 20, 1887. The next letter (#17), dated October 5, 1887, expresses consternation over not having received the proofs of his article for *Novosti*, inferring that even this simple measure proved troublesome for the censors. In letter #18, dated November 10, 1887, Solovyov reports that the article has been suppressed and adds that he must keep his indignation private given the troubles already encountered by Notovich for printing things of this nature.

Letter #18 is also of note because in it Solovyov explains his reluctance to agree with something positive that one of Getz's friends said about Ernest Renan, the French philosopher whose influential *Vie de Jésus* (*Life of Jesus*, 1863), like David Strauss's *Life of Jesus* (1835–36),[168] claimed to treat Jesus's life and the Bible with the same scientific methodology applied to any historical subject or ancient work of literature. The genre of Renan's writing, Solovyov states, is closer to that of a feuilleton, serialized light fiction, than to history proper. How, he asks, can Jews sympathize with an author who presents the heroes of biblical narrative as myths and rascals? Understanding that Jews may admire Renan and Strauss because of their mutual enmity for Christianity, Solovyov compares this admiration to the practice of Japanese feudal servants who would commit ritual suicide to protest some decision of their masters. Solovyov does not wish to ignore the reason for the Jewish animus against Christianity but states that in such forms it is clearly suicidal. He ends the letter on a note of firm hope.

Letter #36 constitutes a one-page summary of Solovyov's career, written, according to Getz, in 1887. Solovyov probably sent it to Getz to accompany one of his works that Getz was translating into German. Its significance here lies in showing that Solovyov singled out his chief interests after 1881 as revolving around "religious questions, chiefly the problem of the unification of the churches and the reconciliation of Christianity with Judaism." He also explains in this letter that the three volumes of his present magnum opus, *The History and the Future of Theocracy*, are to relate to the philosophy of biblical history, the philosophy of church history, and the challenges of theocracy, respectively. The first volume was completed that year and included the first part of "Jewry and the Christian Question" almost verbatim. The theme of the third volume clearly relates to the latter part of "Jewry." This correlation suggests that despite Solovyov's purported embarrassment with that *theocratic* part of "Jewry," he did not give up on the central thesis but planned to correct, develop, and deepen it in the third volume of *Theocracy*. The correlation between the second part of "Jewry" and the third part of *Theocracy* underscores that the two works are intimately related and that, ultimately, for Solovyov, the significance of Judaism is intertwined with that of Christianity and theocracy. The elect status of Judaism necessarily highlights the "Christian question," the question of how Christians will relate to Jews, but Judaism must also confront and relate to Christianity and Christ. Consequently, the rationale for excluding the subject of theocracy from this volume on the grounds that it deals with issues that transcend Judaism is not wholly sound; the two are organically interrelated.

Letter #19, dated January 18, 1888, reports the completion of *La Russie et L'Église universelle*, the preparation of the second volume of *Theocracy*, and the coming publication, with no trouble from the censors, of his anti-Slavophile essay "Russia and Europe," aimed against Danilevsky and Strakhov, and published the same year in Stasyulevich's *Vestnik Evropy*.[169] Letter #20, dated February 23, 1888, reports a two-week retreat at the Holy Trinity Monastery of Sergiev Posad and expresses excitement about Getz's communications regarding his intention to persevere with acquiring permission to found a Jewish newspaper. In reply, Solovyov authorizes Getz to use the earlier letter to Theoktistov but not the letter to Maikov, now labeling the latter a "radical Judeophobe" and anticipating that he would have been annoyed by Solovyov's article in *Vestnik Evropy*. The contrast drawn implicitly credits Theoktistov, as will be confirmed first by letter #27. Theoktistov will also receive commendation in Emile Dillon's article "The Jews in Russia" in the London *Times* on December 10, 1890, which explains that "the very same literary gentleman, M. Theoktistov, now head of the Censor Committee[,] . . . put his name to a precisely similar protest some years ago." From letter #20 we learn that Getz again asked for a letter of introduction to Countess Volkonskaya. This time Solovyov assures him that while he will contact her, Getz should know that she and her husband have fallen into political disfavor.

In letter #21, written from Paris between July 16 and 28, 1888, Solovyov encourages Getz to remain hopeful but excuses himself from writing a substantial contribution for a volume of essays that Getz is planning to edit. In this same letter, he also lets Getz know that he has written to thank Vladimir Pavlovich Bezobrazov (1828–89), the economist, publicist, and new father-in-law of Solovyov's sister (via her marriage to his son Pavel Vladimirovich Bezobrazov, a Byzantine historian and early promoter of women's and animal rights [1859–1918]) for hosting Getz and Simeon Grigorievich (Shimon Shmuel) Frug (1860–1916). Frug was a popular Russian Jewish poet and publicist who wrote in Russian, Yiddish, and Hebrew and who, from the 1880s, played an active role in proto-Zionist movements, consoling and supporting Jews with national songs and ballads. By 1887 he had published two well-reviewed books of poetry, richly imbued with biblical and prophetic motifs, and was contributing energetically to leading progressive Russian and Jewish[E] papers. In spite of this, he had pariah status in St. Petersburg, from which he was banned by the legislation of 1891 but to which he was allowed to return in 1892. His funeral in Odessa was attended by one hundred thousand people. We hereby glimpse the broadening of Solovyov's acquaintance with the Jewish intelligentsia and of his active collaboration with them in promoting Jewish civil rights by all the means and contacts at his disposal.

Letter #22, dated 1889, features a major coup on Solovyov's part: securing for Getz an audience with Terty Ivanovich Filippov (1825–89), Russian government activist, senator (from 1883), acting secret counselor (from April 1889), and chancellor of the Russian Empire (from July 1889). Filippov was also famous as a conservative-nationalist publicist, Orthodox theologian, and specialist in questions of ecclesial division, as well as a music lover who collected Russian sung folklore and assisted troubled composers and musicians. Solovyov's letter to him of July 30, 1889, congratulates him on his new appointment and thanks him for his long-standing assurances of goodwill. Then, while expressing doubt as to whether Filippov's new position would allow him to help Solovyov in his present straits by "removing the burden of theological censorship thanks to which my literary activity was forced to take a completely wrong and for me most undesirable and uncomfortable character," Solovyov states that his new position is bound to influence and provoke changes in government circles responsible for theological censorship. "The change in views," Solovyov writes, "which I allude to . . . is important and necessary not just for me, but for the whole of Russia, and not just for her, but for the whole universal church." He then adds:

> Always and everywhere, the important thing is the *will*: intellectual convictions, thoughts, and theories only clear and lighten the ways which lead to the goal, established not by theoretical but by practical reason. We are united not so much by common thoughts as by a *common will*. You *will* deeply and fervently a spiritual liberation, a strengthening and an enlivening of the Russian, and via her, of the universal church. This I will as well. We have one and the same goal: *ignem fovere in gremio sponsae Christi* [to nurture a fire in the bosom of the spouse of Christ].

Solovyov's emphasis on the will deserves some comment as it is integral to Solovyov's Sophiology, as explained above in chapter 6, commentary on his *Lectures on Godmanhood* and *Critique of Abstract Principles*. It will be met again in his lecture "The Fall of the Medieval Worldview" and in his obituary of Joseph Rabinovich. Solovyov's letter to Filippov dated September 27, 1890, concludes:

> I continue to grieve over the absence in our midst of conditions for determining any possible sort of confusion in the religious and

ecclesial realm, and I also continue to think that a change of these conditions is your vocation, deeply respectable Terty Ivanovich, and that your elevation has its foundation not just in the past, in your labors and merits, but also in the future, in that great work of liberating the Church, which you will accomplish when the hour comes.

Solovyov's tone here is very respectful but is revealed as groveling by the history of Solovyov's dealings with Filippov[170] and the rather caustic private poem he wrote about him. (The poem is dated to 1886, but as Filippov did not receive a promotion that year and as his principal promotion was to the position of chancellor in July 1889, it makes more sense to posit that 1886 is a typographical error.) Perhaps the point of the poem is to emphasize that, as an agent of the triumvirate of the pseudotheocracy built by Pobedonostsev, Tolstoy, and Katkov, he is more on the side of Sodom than of the Lord, and has, as a result, lost the salt of his apostolate (see Matt. 5:13, Mark 9:50, Luke 14:34).[171]

To T. I. Filippov (October 1886)

When Palestine my Tertius you did visit,
And even the Dead Sea construed to find,
The doom which rained down on the illicit,
foul ancient towns piqued not your devious mind.

And now you wish the Sodomite idea,
To buttress on our Neva's shores instead,
Run and begone, o madman, run more quickly.
And turn not back your criminal old head,

By fire and brimstone singed all-round and thickly,
To Sheol's shades you, Prince of Sodom, fled.
In God's sight, Bishop, fear I, not a salty,
But an insipid pillar you'll form, dead.

CHAPTER 12

1890: Tolstoy, Ezekiel 3:18 and 33:8, and the Launch of the Protest

In the spring of 1890, rumor spread that on March 28, 1890, D. A. Tolstoy and von Plehve established a special commission to prepare legislation (the "forty clauses"; see Pt. I, ch. 4, §§9.6–9.9) to curtail Jewish commercial activity within and outside the Pale by, for example, prohibiting Jews from participating in land organizations, depriving Jewish artisans from settling in Moscow and its provinces, creating ghettos, and retroactively canceling earlier allowances to do all these things. Jews who, like Frug, were already living in Moscow were therefore facing the prospect of relocating to the Pale.[172]

At the end of February 1890, having been assured that the rumor regarding the establishment of this commission was true, Solovyov wrote to Leo Tolstoy (Pt. III, ch. 11, letter #2) to petition him to "raise his voice against this outrage." Solovyov recommended that Tolstoy do this alone because (a) his voice would prove resounding and, as we later learn, (b) his reputation would make him immune to the reprisals bound to fall on anyone else. A significant feature in Solovyov's letter to Tolstoy is the citation from Ezekiel: "If you do not warn the wicked man about his wickedness, I will require his soul at your hand." As explained in the editorial footnote to the translated letter, Solovyov is citing Ezekiel 3:18 or 33:8 in Slavonic and from memory (the citation does not exactly correspond to either verse). As the letter-essay that Solovyov contributed to Getz's book *The Floor to the Accused* (Pt. III, ch. 9, letter #25, March 5, 1891) also begins with this same citation, to underscore that he is writing "eagerly not only for [Getz's] sake but also for [his] own: for the purification of [his] conscience touching [Russia's] preachers of antisemitism," one may identify this sentiment as a touchstone of Solovyov's attitude to the Jews and the Jewish-Christian problem. Indeed, as pointed out above, in his book on Solovyov's attitude to the Jews, after describing Solovyov's unparalleled humanitarian efforts to aid the plight of the Jews, Getz identifies this clause concerning the duties of personal conscience as the key to understanding the sources of Solovyov's exceptional attitude to Jews (see note to letter #25). The concern for the welfare of his own conscience regarding the Jews is of course the same concern that informs Solovyov's argument in "The Sins of Russia" that Russia's future welfare requires similar corporate and collective moral action.

Solovyov's letter to Tolstoy is also signed by Emile (Mikhailovich) J. Dillon (1854–1933), an English journalist and correspondent for the *Daily Telegraph* (1887–1914) who lived for a long time in Russia and wrote prolifically on Russia and Russian literature under the pseudonym Lanin. The letter served to introduce Dillon to Tolstoy, and Dillon went on to become an early English translator and biographer of Tolstoy. The texts in this volume contain translations of the correspondence between Solovyov and Tolstoy relevant to Jewish-Christian relations.[173]

Tolstoy answered Solovyov and Dillon on March 15, 1890. According to the version of Tolstoy's letter preserved in Getz's *The Floor to the Accused*, Tolstoy entrusted Solovyov with penning the text and volunteered to be the first to sign it. He wrote:

> I know in advance that if you, Vladimir Sergeevich, express that which you think about this subject, then you will express also my thought and feelings, because the foundation of our disgust from the measures taken in persecution of the Hebrew nationality is one and the same: the consciousness of fraternal ties with all peoples and especially with the Jews[E], among whom the Christ was born and who have suffered so much and continue to suffer from the pagan ignorance of so-called Christians. Your admirer, L. Tolstoy.

This version of Tolstoy's words to Solovyov, however, should be fleshed out by reference to Tolstoy's actual letter, reprinted by V. Popov in 1939 (Pt. III, ch. 11, letter #3), where, between the reference to "so-called Christians" and his signature, as cited by Getz, one finds the following paragraph.

> It is natural for you to write, because you know what precisely threatens the Jews and what people say about this. I cannot enjoin myself to write on the assigned theme, and lack the impulse.

Popov glosses this paragraph by a reference to what Tolstoy wrote to Getz on May 22, 1890.

> I regret the persecutions which the Jews suffer, considering them not only unjust and cruel but mad. But this subject does not command me exclusively or predominantly over and above other feelings and thoughts. There are many matters which worry me more than this one, for which reason I cannot write about this matter in a way that would touch people.[174]

Solovyov thus proceeded to compose the "The Text of the Protest against Antisemitism in the Press," reprinted by Radlov, between letters #23 and #24 (Pt. III, ch. 9). The Protest expounds three "elementary truths" exposing the immorality of antisemitism and the radical danger it presents to Russia's future and soul.

In May 1890, Solovyov wrote to Getz (letter #23) to celebrate a successful visit to Sergei Andreevich Muromtsev (1850–1910). Muromtsev was a jurist, publicist, political activist, and professor of law at Moscow University between 1878 and 1884, specializing in civil and Roman law. He was dismissed from his post as assistant rector of the university in 1881 and finally, in 1884, as professor for his conciliatory approach to progressive causes. He also served as editor, in 1879–92, of the *Yuridicheskij vestnik* (Juridical Herald). In 1906 he would attain distinction by being elected president of the state Duma. In the context of Solovyov's letter to Getz, Solovyov clearly sought him out as a potential signatory from the list of people provided by Getz. Muromtsev would thus have been one of "several" people on the list.

That Solovyov asked to see the list himself suggests that the other people on the list were approached by other colleagues. According to Korolenko, Muromtsev signed the Protest. The testimony to Solovyov's contact with him demonstrates also that Solovyov was seeking the advice of leading progressive strategists and specialists in civil law when preparing the Protest. Solovyov concludes the May letter by adding, "If you wish to receive immediately a dozen new signatures, then come to collect them on Sunday morning, for on Saturday I am counting on a great harvest." Getz explains the phrase as a reference "to the collective signatures under the Protest against antisemitism in the press in which Solovyov took lively interest."

Vladimir Galaktionovich Korolenko (1853–1921) was a renowned populist writer who had spent much of his life in exile from Moscow, including three years in Siberia for refusing to sign an oath of allegiance to Alexander III in 1881. At this time he was serving as a correspondent for *Russkie vedomosti* (Russian News). In his memoirs of the Protest, he records receiving it in October 1890 and preserves a version that already bears the signatures of L. N. Tolstoy and others but traces Russian antisemitism to Germany, a nuance to which Korolenko objected.[175] Solovyov was extremely grateful to Korolenko for his support, thanking him in a letter in January 1891.

> That letter of yours truly gladdened me and it would be very beneficial to publish it. It produced the best impression on all to whom I read it. By the way, the observation which you disliked regarding the German origin of antisemitism was inserted by me according to the demand of one of the signatories, and I am in complete agreement with you that it is redundant. It would seem that it has been omitted in the English and German translations which have been published in London and Vienna.

Korolenko reports that Solovyov, earlier, preserved the nuance (apparently inserted by Getz) because he did not wish to lose time on redactional arguments but that he ensured its omission from the versions published in London and Vienna. With regard to the London version, this assurance is not quite correct, as the transcript of the version published in the *Times* shows.[176]

Popov relates that the fate of the Protest was described in an unpublished letter of Getz to Tolstoy on November 15, 1890 (see Pt. III, ch. 11, letter #2 n. 4). It read:

> Your noble initiative attained brilliant success. The most leading Russian scholars and literary activists followed your encouraging example. More than fifty signatures were already collected by V. S. Solovyov, and he could have collected at least as many more signatures, but for the false denunciations by the antisemitic press that the protest was directed against the government, which elicited a powerful circular by the Ministry of Internal Affairs from the eighth of this month prohibiting the publication of any sort of collective declaration pertaining to the Jews, under threat of the most severe punishment.

In his memoir about the Protest, Korolenko recalls that reactionaries quickly caught wind of Solovyov's efforts and that one of them, the publicist "P. D." Ilovajsky, took pains to denounce it, not for its arguments, but for its "seditious" intentions, and thus sought to have the Ministry for the Affairs of the Press issue an edict to stop its publication. Observing that the "sedition" was thus published only abroad, in Paris and Vienna, Korolenko draws two lessons from the episode: (1) for Europeans, the declaration by Russian writers of axioms recognized by the cultured world was probably significant only as a curious illustration of the conventions of Russian censorship; and (2) for the Russian writers in question, what was significant was the degree of fear and respect implicit in the efforts expended by the antisemites of that time on stifling Solovyov's Protest in its conception. He took this as a "fact that a categorical declaration by the leading ranks of Russian writers can deliver a palpable blow to government-supported antisemitism."[177]

The Protest was thus printed abroad in a number of European papers, including the London *Times* on December 10, 1890. The letter is printed anonymously and must have been translated by Dillon. The date is significant because it complements the letters issuing on the same day from the famous meeting in the Guildhall of eighty-three prominent persons, led by the archbishop of Canterbury and Cardinal Manning, who, on behalf of London's citizens, petitioned the tsar to grant Russian Jewry political and social equality with the rest of his subjects. The letter was not officially received but returned via the foreign office. Solovyov's Protest is translated in its entirety, with slight modifications, and is followed by a letter from Cardinal Henry Edward Manning (see Pt. I, ch. 4, §9.6; and Pt. III, ch. 19).

In introducing Solovyov's letter, Dillon adds many interesting details. First, he reports that sixty rather than fifty of Russia's leading intellectuals signed the Protest. Second, according to Dillon, only one of the signatories, Tolstoy, enjoyed special immunity, on account of his literary reputation. Third, the prohibition on publishing the Protest in Russia was signed by Theoktistov. Given that Theoktistov had authored a similar protest earlier and sought to help Solovyov, his present "betrayal" illustrates the weight of the pressure imposed on him by the regime.

The nonreception of the Guildhall letter by the tsarist regime reflects the contempt in which the government held Solovyov's campaign. This is confirmed by Pobedonostsev's letter to Alexander III of December 6 (o.s.), 1890.

> Your Majesty knows the devious and ridiculous agitation, raised in London, in defense of the Jews from imaginary persecution as if such came from the Russian government. . . . And even in Moscow the crazy Solovyov has taken it into his head to assemble something in the way of a meeting to protest the measures taken with regard to the Jews. They began to compose an address, which they signed, first Leo Tolstoy and after him, unfortunately, several weak-willed professors of the University. This action in Moscow has been stopped, but we can expect these gentlemen to not calm down, and so already in the newspaper the *Times,* on December 10, there appeared a letter from Moscow where the text of this Protest has been published.[178]

The margins of this letter bear a gloss from Alexander III: "I have already heard about this. A pure psychopath."

CHAPTER 13

1891: The Foreword to Getz's
The Floor to the Accused

As the Protest was quashed, Getz endeavored to publish a volume in defense of the Jews consisting of an apologetic piece by him and supporting articles from leading scholars and men of letters.[179] To obtain the latter, he again enlisted Solovyov's help. Solovyov thus wrote again to Tolstoy on January 29, 1891 (Pt. III, ch. 11, letter #4), to secure Tolstoy's earlier letters to him on the Jewish question for this volume. Tolstoy agreed. By March 21, 1891 (Pt. III, ch. 9, letter #24), Solovyov reworked his introduction to Getz's book and received many responses, including several antisemitic ones. The most significant contributions that he proposed to include in the volume were those by Boris Nikolayevich Chicherin and Korolenko. Chicherin (1828–1904) was a large-scale estate owner from Tambov Province, a professional jurist, Hegelian philosopher, economist, historian, and honorary member of the Petersburg Academy of Sciences. He was a firm believer in authority, which turned him against revolutionary ideology and endeared him to conservatives during the reign of Alexander II. At the same time, he actively campaigned for the expansion of civil rights to all social classes, which endeared him to liberals.

Solovyov announced to Getz that he would be coming to St. Petersburg on the morrow or the day after to deliver to Notovich the proofs of his article and the two unpublished letters by Chicherin and Korolenko. He then suggested a title and a subtitle for the volume. The

title, he said, should refer to the Russian jurisprudential custom of giving the floor (i.e., a last word) to the accused, and the subtitle should
announce that the work includes unpublished letters of Count L. N.
Tolstoy, B. N. Chicherin, V. S. Solovyov, and V. G. Korolenko. As the
booklet was published by Notovich's *Novosti* in 1891, this must be the
work on the Jewish question for which Notovich received his second
official warning of 1891.

Solovyov's own article, running to just over four thousand words,
takes the form of letter #25 and must thus, along with the Protest and
the unpublished "Sins of Russia," be listed as one of his most significant compositions on Jewry and Judaism. Four points may be highlighted. (1) Both the beginning, via the citation of Ezekiel 3:18–19, and
the end of the essay underscore that for Solovyov defending Jews is
bound up with his personal integrity, Russian patriotism, and Christian conscience. As explained in chapter 4 above, Getz identified this
principle as the core of Solovyov's attitude to the Jewish(-Christian)
problem. (2) The essay then proceeds, in the second paragraph, to trace
the lies sown about the Jews in Russian society, over the past ten
years, to the "father of lies." Getz explains the phrase as a reference to
"Shtekmer," a garbled reference, seemingly to Bismarck's court pastor
Adolf Stoecker (1835–1909), who stirred up conflicts with the Jews in
1880/81, but it is more likely, given the Russian context, that Solovyov
is referring to Ignatiev, who was known by this nickname and who, on
his appointment as minister of the interior in 1881, began to promote
the theory that the pogroms resulted from popular peasant resentment
against Jewish "domination" and "exploitation."[180] (3) Toward the end
of the letter Solovyov excuses himself to Getz for helping individual
Jews emigrate from Russia. Evidently they argued about this. Solovyov explains that he did so because it seemed to him to be the practical, life-preserving necessity for individual Jewish families. He did not
wish to oppose Getz in his belief that Jews should not abandon Russia
but press its authorities to grant them civil equality and allow them to
integrate into and contribute to Russia's civil society. (4) He concludes
on a note of hope and trust that Russia, thanks to her Christian roots
and the Christian nature of her people, will eventually do the right
thing and not permit nationalist Jew-hating policies to triumph in the

end. To a twenty-first-century reader, mindful of the pogroms of 1905 and of subsequent attacks on Jews in the Soviet era, including Stalin's planned contribution to the "final solution" of the Jewish question by mass deportation of Jews to Siberia,[181] this final sentiment sounds rather naive. Did Solovyov fail to understand the depth of antisemitic feeling in the nation? Some evidence for thinking that he did not comes from his disagreement with Getz about the need to help Jews emigrate.

There are at least two ways to understand this rather optimistic conclusion. First, many of Solovyov's letters to Getz evince a battle within him as to hope or despair about the outcome of their campaign and the pressures on his person. As bouts of despair forced him to cite psalms of lament and pray to God for delivery from evil, he frequently ended his letters on positive, hope-affirming sentiments. This is one of those attempts. Second, the style and content of the conclusion relate to his style of argumentation. Since the letter is written to persuade his Slavophile antisemitic opponents, the sentiment returns to the theme with which the letter opens, highlighting the common ground he shares with them. It appeals to their Russian patriotism and Christian beliefs and uses these as a lever by which to shift them away from antisemitism. Consequently, the conclusion synthesizes genuine personal theological commitment to hope, grounded in prayer, and his sense of personal responsibility to work to change history, in his case through constructive and respectful dialogue and argument with his "enemies." The structure and political ends of Solovyov's composition are therefore carefully coordinated. It would be fruitful to unpack them in further detail.

Solovyov's ends are clearly and explicitly announced: the cessation of state-sponsored repression of Jews, the elimination of Judeophobia, the promotion of political and juridical processes by which Jews would be integrated into the body politic and granted civic equality, and the stimulation of Russian public respect for the Jewish character and social virtue. He believes these goals to be not just fully compatible with Russia's Christian polity, but, as fully explained in his "Jewry and the Christian Question," its necessary concomitant and precondition. Consequently, by articulating the biblical and Christian motivations for composing this letter-essay and by concluding it on an expression of faith in Russia's Christian soul and conscience, Solovyov hearkens back to the foundational principle of his "Jewry" and the Protest letter, namely, the conviction that Russia's future and fate are intimately bound up with and dependent on the purity of her soul and conscience.

By sandwiching the contents of this letter-essay with appeals to Russia's Christianity and conscience, its structure and rhetoric underscore that these constitute the common ground of Solovyov's argument with his audience. They at once evince and ground his hope that honest argument, that is, appeal to conscience, can and must play a role in effecting political change. But while this optimistic appeal to Christianity and conscience constitutes the sandwich's "bread," its "meat" highlights his very realistic awareness of the need to reckon, in the course of the argument, not with Christians but with reactionary nationalists, and thus not via godly and spiritual appeals to conscience but via human and secular, rationalist and empiricist arguments. This is made manifest midway through the letter-essay where Solovyov states that Christian principles and conscience cannot be presupposed to work in dealing with nationalist reactionary secular attitudes to Jews. These, he says, will only heed plain economic data and arguments from reactionary authorities. To satisfy the first requirement, he cites the data furnished by Chicherin. To satisfy the second, he cites the pronouncements of Katkov. Both serve to demonstrate that the widely disseminated belief that the Jewish control of taverns in the Pale of Settlement impoverishes Russians is a lie. Russian peasants, in fact, turn out to be relatively more prosperous in areas where taverns are run by Jews than in those run by fellow Russians. While the appeal to economic data raises the argument above the level of anecdotal and subjective pronouncements, the irony with which he speaks about abandoning the principles of conscience to stoop down to this level of argumentation is significant for at least three reasons. First, it reveals his own desire to integrate the empirical and the spiritual, the "human" and the "godly" levels of the argument, and so to stay faithful to the principle of Godmanhood. Second, the employment of irony to achieve this result is brilliant and profoundly Solovyovian, illustrating his skill as a debater and his penchant for humor. Third, by speaking disparagingly of the secular nationalists, he is employing a rhetorical device that shows, on the one hand, that he is not addressing them directly but rather audiences who give their views some weight but who should know better and who may yet, therefore, be wrenched away from doing so by being shown that such arguments are rationally unconscientious. The name Katkov identifies the audience as Christian reactionaries presided over by Pobedonostsev.

Solovyov had little hope in fact that the publication of Getz's book would have a speedy and successful outcome and warned Getz of this in the next letter, that of March 28, 1891 (Pt. III, ch. 9, letter #26). In line with his expectations, the book was published but its sale prohibited. Solovyov then advised Getz to petition for copies of the book to be delivered to a committee of ministers. He counseled him to not lose heart, for happiness is not, in any case, to be found on earth. He fleshed out the point by citing a few lines of poetry written by his friend Fet with whom he was at the time engaged in translating the *Aeneid*. Solovyov then vowed to do what he could to promote the book. He reported a month later that he had renewed contacts with Theoktistov and that Theoktistov had generously visited Solovyov twice to discuss the matter, an obviously good sign (Pt. III, ch. 9, letter #27, May 1, 1891).

CHAPTER 14

1891: The Central Committee for the Organization of Jewish Emigration, Diminsky, Bakst, and the *Encyclopedic Dictionary*

Letter #28 illuminates two further courses of action or inaction contemplated by Getz and Solovyov.[182] The first is evident in Solovyov's report that he had, over the previous month, declined an invitation to join the Central Committee for the Organization of Jewish Emigration. As the conclusions of letter-essay #25 and letter #29 show, Getz believed that Jewish emigration would weaken Jewish commitment to pressure Russia to broaden their civil rights and was therefore unhappy with Solovyov for helping Jews emigrate. Clearly Getz was representing the official, 1882 position of Horace Gintsburg and the Society for the Promotion of Jewish Enlightenment, the principal intercessory and representative Jewish body since the 1860s (see Pt. I, ch. 4, §§5.4, 8.11) but one that, in view of the pressures being imposed on Jewry, was becoming increasingly difficult for individual Jews to support (see Pt. I, ch. 4, §§8.10, 8.11; §§9.1–9.2, 9.12). Solovyov's letter therefore symbolizes his decision to side with Getz on this issue. Solovyov concludes the letter by stating that he had come around not just morally but also psychologically to Getz's position, and expresses gladness over the fact that their friendship has withstood this trial and been strengthened accordingly. At the same time, Solovyov expresses hope that Getz would also recognize his, Solovyov's, "moral duty."

Getz's letter of July 21, 1891 (#29), reveals that he remained upset with Solovyov over the issue. In the context of the problem of Jews staying or leaving, Solovyov was presumably referring to the moral duty of helping individuals and families to emigrate. A possible way to understand the resolution of their differences is to posit a compromise whereby Getz came around to Solovyov's position that Jewish emigration is a practical necessity for the survival of individual Jews and Jewish families while Solovyov granted that the organization of an official central committee for Jewish emigration would weaken Jewish determination to remain in Russia and help it develop as a civil society, tolerant of ethnic and religious differences.[183]

The second issue raised in letter #28 concerns Solovyov's review of the antisemitic booklet on the Jews and the Talmud by Stepan Iakovlevich Diminsky, titled *The Jews*[E](*,) *Their Religious and Moral Teaching(.) The Study of S. Ia. Diminsky*. The work, first published in St. Petersburg in 1891, was based on a master's thesis that Diminsky submitted to and printed at the Kiev Theological Seminary, in 1868 and 1869 respectively, under the title *A Study of the Talmud*. It was republished in 1893, with the comma and period in the title. Solovyov's review supplied and thereby sarcastically highlighted their ungrammatical omission in the first edition. Letter #28 reveals that Solovyov's review of the work was published in the *Severnyj vestnik*, a monthly literary journal, which had been sold the previous year by its founder, Anna M. Evrejnova, and passed, via its shareholders, to the editorship of the literary critic and philosopher A. L. Volynsky. The letter also reveals that Solovyov's work on the review was assisted by "N.I.B." Subsequent letters reveal that this individual is the rabbinically trained and eminent chemist N. I. Bakst, who, from 1882, played a leading role, including that of being a member of the Pahlen Commission, in assisting Gintsburg to represent Jewish interests to the regime (see Pt. I, ch. 4, §§8.11, 9.4).

Diminsky's thesis and booklet, running along the same tracks as the Austrian Rohling's, Briman's, and Pattai's *Judenspiegel*, was obviously a matter of great concern for Russian Jewry, and thus for Getz and Solovyov. Getz evidently proposed to write a detailed response to its charges and petitioned Solovyov once again to put him in touch with an unnamed philanthropist who could subsidize the rebuttal's publication. Solovyov responded by saying that he was not in a position to do this, first because the party in question had gone abroad to a location unknown to him and second because if this party, whom Solovyov now refers to as "it," wanted to burn "its" money twice a year, "it" could do so directly in "its" own chimney and not engage the services of the internal affairs department.

The party in question can probably be identified. First, "it" has already funded one book that year which was published and burned. Second, Getz was reaching out to this party "again." The party is evidently then the same as the one who helped him publish *The Floor to the Accused*. Solovyov's words about "burning" graphically clarify what happened to Getz's book at the start of that year. Third, Solovyov's care to hide this party's identity highlights that "its" involvement in subsidizing Getz's publication was a risky and courageous act. Fourth, "it" is not Notovich, since Getz had direct ties with him. And fifth, because Solovyov refers to this party by the neuter "it," it is likely a woman, since a truthful reference to her as "she" would have given her identity away more readily than a generic but untruthful "he." The party therefore must be Countess Elizaveta Grigorievna Volkonskaya, whom Getz had sought to contact through Solovyov several times before (see letters #14 n. 32, #20). Were this confirmed, it would explain what Getz hoped to gain from her on earlier occasions and flesh out for history this woman's political interests and accomplishments.

Letter #29 (July 1891) marks the summer of 1891 as another watershed in Solovyov's career. The confession regarding his financial difficulties explains simply the "cares and straits" to which he referred in Letter #27 and described as "matters of which it was uncomfortable to write." We see here that these cares and straits are not just political difficulties but also financial ones. Finding himself incapable of declining Getz's offer to lend him money and being pressed to find remunerative work, Solovyov asks Getz to send the money directly to his new address, the apartment of Vladimir Kuz'min Karavayev, a member of the editorial board of the *Encyclopedic Dictionary*. Solovyov was seeking a paying position as editor of one of the dictionary's departments. In advancing these plans, he mentions N. I. Bakst, which finally identifies the N.I.B. who gave him advice on his review of Diminsky's article. By telling Getz that he has not yet heard from Bakst about his chances of an appointment to the editorial board of the *Encyclopedic Dictionary*, Solovyov's letter reveals that Bakst is both a member of this board and a person interested in promoting Jewish welfare.

Solovyov's appointment to an editorial position at the *Encyclopedic Dictionary*—he was appointed to supervise its philosophical content—is registered in the conclusion of letter #30 of August 22, 1891. This letter begins with a humorous ditty that sheds further light on N.I.B, revealing he is a rabbi in St. Petersburg who was responsible for an error in Solovyov's review of Diminsky's article. The error in question is Solovyov's translation of the Hebrew word "Rab" as "rabbi" in a citation from a particular Talmudic tractate. However, "Rab" in that passage was a nickname, meaning "the Master," for a renowned rabbi. Solovyov is aware that N.I.B. will be embarrassed about failing to catch this error and petitions Getz to keep quiet about it.[184]

All of these implications are corroborated by the biographical details of N. I. Bakst, who was born Noah Isaacson Bakst (1843–1904). In addition to majoring in physiology at the University of St. Petersburg, he received rabbinical training in Zhitomir. Significantly, after being sent abroad by the Ministry of Enlightenment to study under G. Helmholtz and then becoming a teacher at the St. Petersburg I. P. Pavlov Medical University, he became a member of the Committee of the Ministry of National Enlightenment in 1886. In that year he also published a volume commemorating the centenary anniversary of the death of Moses Mendelsohn, father of the Jewish Enlightenment. He was well known in his faculty for standing up to antisemitic harassment, including that of D. I. Mendeleev.[185] Most crucially, he was a member of a Gintsburg-founded intercessory commission in 1880 associated with the OPE,[186] from which, in turn, Gintsburg selected the seven expert Jews for the Pahlen Commission in 1884. Bakst was so influential in this committee that he persuaded its Russian Gentile majority to recommend resolving the Jewish question by expanding Jewish civil rights, a resolution that backfired by prodding the antisemites on the commission to recommend its dissolution to the tsar, which was realized in 1888. Throughout the 1890s, Bakst continued to work on behalf of Russian Jewry, by public activism and philanthropy and distributing funds to needy Jews and helping them to relocate. The present testimony to Solovyov's contacts with Bakst develop the picture of the breadth of his contacts with Russia's leading liberal-Enlightened Jewish public activists at this time.[187] Bakst may well have been the inspiration for Solovyov's disagreement with Getz over the need to help individual Jews to emigrate.

CHAPTER 15

October 1891: The Lecture "The Fall of the Medieval Worldview"

The political, financial, and health-related "cares and straits" of which Solovyov complained to Getz in his letters of 1891 prompted him to confront them at their source. Once secure financially by his appointment to an editorial post at the *Encyclopedic Dictionary*, he delivered, in October 1891, a lecture titled "The Fall of the Medieval Worldview," hosted by the Moscow Psychological Society, whose president was his friend Nikolai Yakovlevich Grot (1852–99). In this lecture Solovyov applied the principles of his philosophy of Godmanhood to criticize "ecclesial dogmatism, false spiritualism, and individualism" as hallmarks and vestiges of a medieval pagan aberration of true Christianity and as a betrayal of Christ. Given the light this lecture and its aftermath in the press shed on Solovyov's final reflections on Jewish-Christian relations, a summary of both must be presented here.

Solovyov charged that the medieval worldview recognized Christ as true but that medieval society, committed to a pagan lifestyle, treated the kingdom of God as something outside of and external to the world and so reduced it to a fruitless decoration of secular rule. Consequently, rather than heroically embrace Christianity as something newly born, a matter of life, the norm of reality, this society identified faith with external deeds, constraining dogmas, and obedience to spiritual powers. Furthermore, by unlawfully unifying church dogmatism with the idea of salvation, it begot the monstrous teaching that the only path to salvation is faith in dogma. The subsequent transformation of Christianity into a religion of individual salvation, which treated material nature as evil, necessarily exposed it to evil spirits, whereby its representatives, behaving like demons in their dogmatism and false spiritualism, failed to follow Christ and the apostles and, by negating the working power of the spirit, came to serve its contrary. To heal the possessed, Christ and the apostles exorcized demons. But their "medieval followers," in order to exorcize demons, started killing the possessed. Asking, "Where has the spirit of Christ gone?," Solovyov answered by invoking Christ's parable of the Brothers in the Vineyard. On the one hand, he compared nominal Christians to the elder brother who said that he would do the work of the Father but did not; on the other, he compared non-Christians to the younger brother who said he would not do the work but chose to serve him in the end. Solovyov saw this service in the Christian forms of social progress achieved over the last centuries by complete unbelievers. In conclusion, he counseled nominal Christians, proud of their demonic faith, to remember the history of two apostles, Judas Iscariot and Thomas, and, instead of persecuting the work of unbelieving progressives, outdo them by achieving something better, by working toward a living, social, world-embracing, and transforming Christianity.

The lecture was an event in Moscow's life that year. The assistant secretary of the Psychological Society, Yakov Nikolaevich Kolubovsky, recorded his surprise on arriving fifteen minutes early and not being able to enter the hall because of the crowds filling the staircase. Among the attendees were the notables of Moscow, including the conservative representatives of church and state, who realized that they would be the lecture's target. After Grot moved the audience to a larger hall, Solovyov began to lecture, in a fairly disorganized manner. Solovyov frequently stopped to locate and translate Greek scriptures and texts while the conservatives repeatedly rose to protest. As this was unsuitable to the lecture's format, Grot, chair of the event, declared that a debate would follow in a different location behind closed doors. Those who immediately enlisted and paid the ten-ruble entrance fee included Vladimir Andreevich Gringmut, secretary of *Moskovskie vedomosti*, and Yu. P. Govorukha-Otrok, the fueilletonist for the same paper who published under the name "Nikolaev." Kolubovsky wrote that on returning from the session to his home that evening and commencing to write his report about it, he was summoned to the editorial board of *Moskovskie vedomosti* and thus witnessed the beginning of a stormy two-month-long attack by the journal on Solovyov, led by Gringmut and Nikolaev, during which its pages were filled with articles and letters dedicated to the subject. The reactionary press reviewed Solovyov's lecture as a "popular and total mockery of the Orthodox church." Excerpts from Solovyov's four letters to the editor, contesting that he did not attack the church but rather the anti-Christian spirit of Christian culture, are provided in Part III of this volume. When Solovyov, in order to prove that his lecture did not attack the church, finally decided not to develop it into an article but offered his notes as they were publicly read to *Moskovskie vedomosti*, the censors forbade their publication, whereby the lecture was published only posthumously, in *Vestnik Evropy*. In the course of these events, Solovyov was informed that Pobedonostsev, learning that Solovyov played an operational role in Grot's journal *Questions of Philosophy and Psychology*, threatened to prohibit its publication and asked its editors, "Why do you need this wild bull?"[188]

The storm began to subside after the warden of the district, Count P. A. Kapnist, and Archimandrite Antony (Khrapovitsky) (1863–1936) came to Solovyov's defense. The latter had frequented Solovyov's and Dostoevsky's lectures as a youth and was, after the revolution, when he became head of the Russian Orthodox Church Abroad, falsely rumored, because he was not acquainted with Dostoevsky, to have been a model for Alyosha Karamazov.[189] Nonetheless, as a result of this battle, Solovyov stood condemned in many quarters as an "ill-intentioned man."[190] Mochulsky describes this period as a moment when, for official circles of Russian tsardom, the names Tolstoy and Solovyov became equally detestable and their literary and social activities, from the viewpoint of governmental bureaucracy, were restricted to protect society from their harmful influence. In writing to Pobedonostsev to defend himself, Solovyov asked, "Over the past few days, several learned societies (including, by the way, those to which neither Tolstoy nor I have ever belonged) received an order to exclude us unconditionally from their dealings. What is the meaning of such a personal proscription?"[191] All this trouble took a heavy toll on his health. In a letter to his brother Mikhail, he writes, "In the latter time, a considerable part of my existence consists in empirical commentary to the poem by Lermontov: 'For the vengeance of enemies and slander of friends.'" He became ill with diphtheria. During the illness, he went to confession and communion.[192]

Mochulsky commends Solovyov for being the first Russian preacher of an active social Christianity who, had he spoken less stridently, would not have found any objection to his basic line of reasoning: namely, that Christianity is not a religion of individual salvation but of the salvation of the world, that it has a still-unfulfilled social goal, and that Christian history is represented by many Christians who proved to be unworthy of their high calling.[193] This seemingly simple critique, however, risks dealing too abstractly with the issues, because it takes them out of the context of the concrete issues about which Solovyov was passionately concerned: the Jews. Is one really to believe that had he spoken a little less stridently about the relationship between Christian norms and Christian-Jewish relations in tsarist Russia, he would have found ready accord with the editors of *Moskovskie vedomosti* and with Pobedonostsev and so should have spared himself from critiquing them for not treating the Jews in a Christian manner because he would then have said everything in a different tone, while they, for their part, would have readily agreed with his propositions? The commentary eschews facing concrete questions as to whether capital punishment, execution of heretics, or pogroms against the Jews are Christian or pseudo-Christian actions.

CHAPTER 16

1892–1894: Final Correspondence with Tolstoy

At the start of 1892, on January 26–27 to be precise, Solovyov sent Tolstoy a letter via Emile Dillon (Pt. III, ch. 11, letter #4), petitioning him to correct a storm brewed up by *Moskovskie vedomosti* touching on Dillon's printing in England of his translations of Tolstoy's articles and letters to him. After *Moskovskie vedomosti* published translations of these letters, Tolstoy denied sending them to the English papers, which implied that Dillon had forged them. This stood to deprive Dillon of his post and put him, a family man, in financial jeopardy. Solovyov appealed to Tolstoy to resolve the matter in England "in such a way that the responsibility for the unacceptable and inaccurate promulgation of [his] views [in Russia] would shift from Mr. Dillon upon those who are really to blame, that is, upon *Moskovskie vedomosti*." The letter survives in English translation in Dillon's 1934 book on Tolstoy and is retranslated into Russian by Popov. Tolstoy in response corroborated that Dillon translated his original letters on famine. One import of the letter to this correspondence, in addition to illustrating Solovyov's ready and instinctive solicitude for the welfare of his colleague and Tolstoy's need to be reminded to express solicitude for the translator of his own works, is that it corroborates that Dillon was the anonymous Russian correspondent for the *Times* who wrote the article "The Jews in Russia" of December 10, 1890.

The last letter from the Solovyov-Tolstoy correspondence pertaining to Jewish motifs is Tolstoy's letter to Solovyov of August 7, 1894

(Pt. III, ch. 11, letter #7), in which Tolstoy tells of his meeting with Rabbi Joseph Krauskopf (1858–1923), who came to Russia in 1894 to investigate the condition of Jewish colonies, visited Tolstoy, and then went on to found an agricultural school in America, considering Tolstoy his ideological inspiration. "Dr. Krauskopf," Tolstoy writes,

> turned out to be a man of very un-Christian spirit . . . [on account of his] brochure . . . on the theme of "An Eye for an Eye," and non-resistance[,] . . . [stating] that "an eye for an eye" is right,[194] while turning the cheek is wrong, and that when it comes to being struck on the cheek and having one's cloak taken, one should neither turn the other cheek nor yield the shirt but show a fist and a whip.

Apparently Tolstoy gave this report to Solovyov because Solovyov (in addition to A. Waite, a U.S. diplomat in St. Petersburg) would have helped Krauskopf secure this meeting either directly, with a letter of introduction, or indirectly, by writing complimentary things about him. While evidencing their outward solidarity, this correspondence continues to hint at some of their divisions. Despite Tolstoy's reputation as a Christian moralist, he seemed oblivious to his later biographer's personal straits and only helped Dillon after Solovyov, who readily grasped the problem, wrote to him. The criticism of the rabbi's nonpacifism as anti-Christian is a point that Solovyov will pick up in part 1 of the *Three Conversations*. Sergei Solovyov records that Solovyov repudiated Tolstoy both as a thinker and as an artist and judged the main point of contention between them to lie in the latter's denial of Christ's resurrection. Solovyov alluded to this in the first line of a letter to Tolstoy dated October–November 1, 1894, while explaining that he had written a long letter on the subject in July but chose to hold on to it so as to read it personally to Tolstoy later in January.[195] In this July letter, published posthumously, Solovyov attempted to prove the resurrection to Tolstoy on the basis of the latter's own philosophy.[196] The letter never reached Tolstoy, but its contents were related to him by Count Aleksei D. Obolensky in 1901, on which occasion Tolstoy expressed irritation over "how educated and intelligent people can seriously speak about such a manifest and obvious absurdity as the resurrection or the assumption of some kind of human being who is, together with that, deemed to be 'God.'"[197]

From this period on, the correspondence with Getz subsides. The two letters of August and September 1892 (Pt. III, ch. 9, letters #31, #32) report Solovyov's preparation and publication of the second, significantly corrected edition of his *Critique of Abstract Principles* and his decision to let Getz translate it into German. There are no surviving letters from 1893 and only one from 1894 (Pt. III, ch. 9, letter #33). In the latter Solovyov thanks Getz for his gift of a bottle of Jewish wine and reports on a series of amiable reciprocal visits and dinners between himself and Lazar Solomonovich Poliakov (1842–1914), the Jewish banker, social activist, and philanthropist who was the assumed father of the ballerina Anna Pavlova and brother of the railroad magnate, co-founder with Gintsburg of the OPE, and therefore second most "important" Jewish *shtadlan* (intercessor) of the past thirty years, Samuel Solomonovich Poliakov (see Pt. I, ch. 4, §§8.2, 8.11, 9.4). The letter raises the issue of a German translation of another article by Solovyov, evidently dealing with the Jewish problem, and Solovyov reflects that ideally it should be included alongside a collection of articles on the Jewish problem by prominent figures and so "take advantage of the burning of the two perished manuscripts of our friends: F. G. and N. B." Solovyov here obviously refers to the burning of Getz's *Floor to the Accused* and to Bakst's "Russkie lyudi o evreyakh" (Russian People on the Jews), which represented a collection of painstakingly obtained positive testimonies of Russian people from diverse sectors of society, published under the pseudonym N. Borisov and Ph. Nezhdanov. Solovyov concludes the letter by telling Getz that he will notify him of his decision to reprint the articles that have perished in these fires after further thought and deliberation with Bakst.

CHAPTER 17

1894–1896: Gintsburg, Arseniev, Leskov, and the Articles on the Kabbalah

The year 1894 witnessed Solovyov's developing friendship with the Orientalist and Jewish philanthropist and community leader Baron David Goratsiyevich Gintsburg (1857–1910), whose many accomplishments included membership in the OPE (see Pt. I, ch. 4, §§4, 5.4; on its marginalization after the closure of the Pahlen Commission, §9.5) and in the Central Committee of the Jewish Colonization Association on the board of which Solovyov declined to serve, as he explained in his letter of June 1891 to Getz (Pt. III, ch. 9, letter #28). Given the invitation to serve on this committee, Solovyov's and Gintsburg's acquaintance probably went back to 1891 (see letter #28 n. 22). Their friendship is attested by three letters. The first of these is the letter dated September 30, 1894, to Konstantin Konstantinovich Arseniev, editor of the *Encyclopedic Dictionary*, explaining why the dictionary could not use the article on the Kabbalah that Solovyov commissioned from Gintsburg. The second and third letters are addressed to David Gintsburg himself on the same subject, one dated to 1896 and the other undated. Given the time that Solovyov must have taken to write this article after receiving Gintsburg's version, presumably at least six months, and the time Gintsburg took to compose it, presumably at least three months, the date of letter #24 to Arseniev, September 30, 1894 (Pt. III, ch. 14), attests that the article was commissioned in 1893 or earlier.

As the editor responsible for the philosophical content of the *Encyclopedic Dictionary*, Solovyov reputedly contributed about two hundred articles, forwarding them to Arseniev in alphabetical order. In the present letter, #24, written from Imatra, Finland, he has arrived at "K" and is sending an article on the Italian philosopher and writer Tommaso Campanella, baptized Giovanni Domenico (1568–1639), one of the earliest representatives of utopian socialism. He then announces his resolution of the problem pertaining to the article on the Kabbalah that he commissioned from Gintsburg but that was too scholarly and not written for the general public, as demanded by editorial policy. This compelled Solovyov to compose the article himself and, to avoid upsetting Gintsburg, arrange the publication of his article in a philosophical journal. He therefore shares this difficulty and plan with Arseniev and enlists his help in assuaging Gintsburg's feelings on the subject via his father with whom Arseniev will be meeting shortly "on a green field," presumably a reference to a croquet pitch.[198] The concluding paragraphs of this letter reveal that there is more than scholarship precluding the publication of Gintsburg's article; Solovyov fears that its contents would easily give occasion to all kinds of mockery and faultfinding by "*Novoe vremya* and K," a reference to one of the most antisemitic journals of the time (which Solovyov cited repeatedly in his polemical letter to Getz, #25, of March 5, 1891 [Pt. III, ch. 9]).

Letter #34 to Getz, begun on February 21, 1895, was sent a few days after March 5 of that year (see Pt. III, ch. 9). In this letter Solovyov petitions Getz to help an unfortunate Jewish author, the Hebraist Chaim Naumovich De-Glin, obtain a subsidy from the Ministry of National Enlightenment and specifically from Ivan Davydovich Delianov, with whom Getz apparently had friendly relations, to publish a Russian translation of his Hebrew book. This is the same Delianov whom the tsar ordered to prepare the quotas restricting Jewish education in 1887 that so upset Solovyov and Getz (see Pt. III, ch. 9, letter #13; ch. 13 above; and Pt. I, ch. 4, §9.5). This datum suggests that the Judeophilic leanings that Delianov expressed to Getz privately could not be espoused by him publicly and that he felt constrained to toe the government line, just like Theoktistov and Witte (on the latter, see Pt. I., ch. 4, §9.10).

Solovyov also tells Getz that he has relocated to Finland to improve his health and finances, and that he has prepared for publication, instead of the second edition of the *Critique of Abstract Principles*, three mature monographs on ethics, metaphysics, and aesthetics and "a little article for a Hebrew collection of essays against the insolent Have[t] who insists that *all* prophets wrote after the Maccabees." A portion of this article-review is translated in this volume. Letter #35, sent in 1896, accompanies a manuscript of Solovyov's book on Muhammad and is the last of Solovyov's surviving letters to Getz. The remaining two items in that collection, letters #36 and #37, are, respectively, Solovyov's career summary, penned in 1887, and the unpublished article "The Sins of Russia" (see Pt. III, chs. 9 and 10).

The postscript to this letter informs Getz that Solovyov is on his way to the funeral of the celebrated Russian storyteller, novelist, and journalist Nikolai Semyonovich Leskov (1831–March 5, 1895), whom Maxim Gorky rated alongside Tolstoy, Gogol, and Turgenev for verbal wizardry in describing the Russian soul and whom Tolstoy valued for his powers of critiquing nihilism by explicating the connection between Christian spirituality and Russian communal and fraternal life, describing him as a "writer of the future."[199] Given the paucity of Russian writers who defended Jews in the 1880s (apart from Saltykov-Shhedrin and Mordovtsev, see Pt. I, ch. 4, §10.3), Solovyov's depiction of him as "one of Jewry's friends" is noteworthy, for after the establishment of the Pahlen Commission in 1882 the Jewish community of St. Petersburg commissioned Leskov to write a defense of them for the commission, which he spent the whole of 1883 composing. The resulting work, titled *Jews in Russia: Several Observations on the Jewish Question,* was thus published as a brochure of fifty copies for the Pahlen Commission in 1884. As it concluded that Jews should be granted full civil rights it would have greatly influenced the commission's final recommendation to do the same (see Pt. I, ch. 4, §9.5). Nonetheless, with the dissolution of the commission it was forgotten and lost, until 1916 when it was found by the Jewish historian Yuly Gessen. Republished by him in 1919, it was suppressed again for the next seventy-one years. Despite the resultant widespread ignorance of his work, he must be added to the list of Russian friends of the Jews in the 1880s, bringing the number to four. Further inquiry into Solovyov's description of him as such to Getz reveals that Solovyov had himself read the work and returned it to Leskov in 1890 with a letter (not preserved in heretofore published collected works of Solovyov) stating, "With gratitude I return your books, which I read with great pleasure. *Jews in Russia*, by its vitality, fullness, and strength of argument, is the best tractate that I know on this subject."[200]

In 1896 Solovyov finally wrote to David Gintsburg explaining why his article on the Kabbalah could not be published in the *Encyclopedic Dictionary* and proposing to facilitate its publication in a philosophical journal. This letter must have been written before the end of February 1896, at which point Solovyov, having evidently received Gintsburg's approval of the plan, sent the article to his good friend Grot, editor of *Voprosy filosofii i psikhologii,* with a letter introducing Gintsburg as the son of the famous banker and as the favorite student of Baron Victor R. Rozen, a competent Orientalist and expert in Jewish mysticism and philosophy. He petitioned Grot to include it in the March issue, vouching to edit its Russian at the proof stage (Pt. III, ch. 15, letter #30). The postscript of letter #30 issues an ultimatum to publish the article in the May issue. Solovyov's urgency requires some explanation.

Undoubtedly he was embarrassed about commissioning the article from David Gintsburg and allowing two years to pass without a formal response about its fate. The Gintsburgs had become good friends of his. Jean Halpérin, Baron Horace Gintsburg's great-grandson, recalls his mother's clear memory of Solovyov's fervent participation in a Passover meal at their home, during which he followed the Hebrew text of the Exodus story. Lukianov's last recorded details from the conversation with A. F. Koni are of Koni recalling that he liked Solovyov's habit of crossing himself before and after a meal and that he did this even when he and Koni were invited to supper at the Gintsburgs.[201] The urgency regarding the publication of the baron's article must have increased because the "K" contents of the *Encyclopedic Dictionary,* containing Solovyov's own article on the Kabbalah, written using Gintsburg's as a blueprint, were quickly approaching publication (vol. 10, 339–43). Gintsburg's article was finally published with Solovyov's introduction in issue 22 of *Voprosy filosofii i psikhologii* (1896): 277–300, constituting thereby the first academic article on the Kabbalah to be printed in Russia.

Solovyov's qualms that including Gintsburg's article in the *Encyclopedic Dictionary* would occasion public mockery and fault finding with the Kabbalah goes some way toward explaining what many have observed to be his own article's distinctive treatment of the subject. It did not confuse Kabbalistic with theosophical and occult teaching but concentrated on comparing and contrasting it with Greek philosophy and Neoplatonism, in ways favorable to the former, and underscoring its correspondences with biblical and Christian doctrine.

1898–1899: The *Protocols of the Elders of Zion* and "The Tale of the Antichrist"

———————

The most infamous and influential document that identifies the Kabbalah, Judaism, and Jewry with theosophy, Freemasonry, and the occult and is linked to a purported "proof" of a worldwide Jewish conspiracy to dominate the world and destroy Christianity is the *Protocols of the Elders of Zion,* concocted in Paris by members of the tsarist secret police, the Ochrana, and then translated, edited, and published in Russia between 1903 and 1905 by Sergei Nilus (1862–1929) as an appendix in his devotional book, *The Great in the Small and the Antichrist as an Imminent Political Possibility: Notes of an Orthodox Believer.* Its fourth edition was published on the eve of the 1917 Revolution by the Holy Trinity Monastery at Sergiev Posad under the title, *"'It Is Near, Even at the Doors': Concerning That Which We Choose Not to Believe and Which Is So Near."* The title indicates that Nilus was reflecting the growing belief in Russia and France that an alliance between the forces of Freemasonry and Jewry would bring the Antichrist to power. In Russia, the expectation was fanned by the announcement of the Antichrist's birth by the famous starets Amvrosy (Grenkov) of Optina Pustyn' in 1882 (for details, see Pt. I, ch. 4, §10.1).

E. Trubetskoy reported that already in the early 1890s Solovyov had expressed his conviction that the Freemasons would be involved in organizing the coming empire of the Antichrist[202] and that the end of the world was approaching.[203] This belief is expressed in Solovyov's

"Tale of the Antichrist," which presents the Antichrist as a charismatic political genius who forges world peace with the help of the "mighty brotherhood of the Freemasons." The work was composed between November 1899 and spring 1900, as the fourth chapter and apocalyptic conclusion to his final and most famous composition, *Three Conversations*. As with the first three chapters, Solovyov read it out loud to his friends and family and once in a public reading in spring 1900, which incited protest and ridicule.[204]

Three Conversations is a deceptively simple but mysterious work owing to how it integrates the genres of biblical apocalypticism (he had been engaged with the Bible for the past twenty years), Platonic dialogue (he had just completed a work on the life of Plato [1898]), and Shakespearean comedy (he developed his satirical skills in the late 1870s and early 1880s as a "Shakespearean" in the circle of Alexei Tolstoy). Solovyov commenced work on it in spring 1899, during his last trip abroad, in Cannes on the French Riviera. The work synthesizes Solovyov's principal positions and arguments with liberals and naturalists such as L. Tolstoy and Slavophile conservatives or reactionaries representative of the regime such as Dostoevsky and *Moskovskie vedomosti*. It will be seen that the role accorded to the Jews in this chapter serves to clarify Solovyov's main and final position vis-à-vis his life work and differences from all of his interlocutors.

The work as a whole is preoccupied with the problem of evil and with the elucidation of a proper Christian response to it. The foreword, written on Easter 1890, explicitly states that the work is written against Tolstoy and his followers, who represent Tolstoyan naturalism as Christian but who, nonetheless, lack Christ and his resurrection. The first chapter contests that this naturalism, by its pacifism in the face of evil, is an anti-Christian lie.[205]

In this chapter, then, Solovyov concludes his lifelong debate with Tolstoy, who ridiculed his belief in Christ's divinity and resurrection. Solovyov sought to persuade Tolstoy of the truth of these beliefs. He did so in the letter of July 28–August 2, 1894 (Pt. III, ch. 11, letter #6). One may find Solovyov's arguments in this letter puzzling and childish for not attempting to prove Christ's resurrection on the basis of apostolic testimonies presented by the Gospels but, in the case of the first two of three proofs, on natural phenomena. However, it should be understood that Solovyov was attempting to argue chiefly on the basis of assumptions that he believed Tolstoy would accept. The argument illustrates and corroborates this commentary's observation that Solovyov was wont to ground his arguments on assumptions granted by his opponents. This principle is key to understanding some of the problematic assumptions underlying works such as "Jewry and the Christian Question" and "The Sins of Russia." The assumptions reflect less Solovyov's perspective than the assumptions he attributes to his opponents.

While the first chapter of *Three Conversations* parodies Tolstoy, the fourth and last chapter, "The Tale of the Antichrist," resonates strongly with Dostoevsky's chapter "The Grand Inquisitor" in *The Brothers Karamazov*. It clarifies what unites Solovyov and Dostoevsky and what divides them and, in the process, responds to the charges implicit in Dostoevsky's using Solovyov as a model not just for Alyosha Karamazov but also for Ivan. At issue here is whether Solovyov's representation of the Antichrist involves self-parody. This suspicion is warranted by phrases and positions attributed to the Antichrist that echo positions Solovyov either espoused or was perceived to espouse in earlier days. One such echo is the metallic voice of the Antichrist at the moment he turns away from Christ: it evokes Solovyov's own and others' testimonies that he was haunted by demonic manifestations and auditions. The depiction of the Antichrist not as a horned devil but as a charismatic, learned, beneficent political genius who forges world peace may also represent a self-parody of Solovyov in his "theocratic phase," given that in the course of asking humanity to choose between himself and Jesus as the Christ, the Antichrist bribes Christians and Jews with goods associated with their value systems: ecclesiastical power to Catholics, empire to the Orthodox, scripture study to Protestants, and economic power to the Jews. Almost everyone, save for a few adherents of the pope, the patriarch, and the Protestant professor, follows the Freemasons in betraying Christ. It will be recalled that Trubetskoy faulted Solovyov's theocratic conceptions precisely along these lines, charging that by means of these conceptions (with the addition of scripture study for Protestants), Solovyov, in part 2 of

"Jewry," replaced Christ's cross with earthly goods and thereby capitulated to the very temptation that he faulted in the original Jewish rejection of Jesus in part 1 of that work. If Dostoevsky modeled Ivan on Solovyov, he anticipated this same criticism and anxiety by according ultramontane "theocratic" views to that character. To what extent, then, does Solovyov's "Tale" respond to these charges?

Solovyov's account of the battle between the Christ and the Antichrist certainly echoes the theocratic expositions of Ivan at the beginning of Dostoevsky's *Brothers Karamazov*, as well as the "poem-stories" placed on the lips of Ivan Karamazov in the chapters "Rebellion" and "The Grand Inquisitor." Ivan's position is that Christ's refusal to trade piety and the freedom to do evil for militarily enforced state security that banishes hunger, sickness, and subjugation by foreign powers is too high a price to pay for living in this world and for gaining a ticket to the next. He would "return the ticket." He illustrates his views by means of a "poem" in which Christ returns to Seville, ruled by the Grand Inquisitor, and is told to leave because his repudiation of the primacy of bread, power, and temporal life vis-à-vis the primacy of spiritual freedom and allegiance to God undermines the regime of socialized and political security that the Grand Inquisitor has established.

The utopian vision of the Grand Inquisitor corresponds with the "messianic model" repudiated by Christ in his Three Temptations and with the utopian program presented by Solovyov's Antichrist. Solovyov thereby follows Dostoevsky in defending the Judeo-Christian understanding of creation and the kingdom of God as founded on freedom and condemns as false and satanic the utopian visions that sacrifice spiritual freedom through allegiance to God for secondary goods, however great. Solovyov's principle of Godmanhood, however, was designed to negate a dualistic opposition between the secular and the temporal, the human and the divine. Temporal goods, while subordinate to the divine absolute, are not rejected or repudiated in his Christian universe. By being created and divinely willed by God, the first absolute, they are meant to flourish and express his wisdom and will, the second absolute. Emphasizing that Judaism and Christianity are religions of love that demand the giving of the self, Solovyov insists that betrayal of Christ consists not only in the failure to subordinate nature and the self to the will of God but also in the failure to love God's nature and other selves and to will their flourishing and development. Consequently, when Christianity becomes so spiritual as to give up on created goods, on nature, society, fraternal charity, it too betrays Christ, creating thereby a vacuum for the scourges of Christianity, whose main historical forms are Islam and inquisitorial Eastern states that compromise freedom to ensure justice. This point helps to pinpoint the difference between Solovyov and Dostoevsky. In his "Third Speech in Memory of Dostoevsky," it may be recalled, Solovyov criticized Dostoevsky for debasing his Slavophile Christian messianism into nationalism by demonizing other nations and their messianic callings. Solovyov precluded such demonization and turned the argument around with the help of his philosophy of Godmanhood. Accordingly, he argued that it is the failure to recognize and establish fraternal relationships between East and West, Catholicism, Orthodoxy, and Judaism, that betrays Christ and serves the Antichrist. This was his point in 1883 and also the point in 1891 as articulated in his public lecture "The Fall of the Medieval Worldview" and consequent polemic about it with *Moskovskie vedomosti* that defended secular liberals by saying that, like the younger son in Christ's parable of the two sons in the vineyard, they proved truer to Christ's cause on earth than Christians and Christian institutions. The conclusion of his October 26, 1891, letter to that journal read, "As for my point of view, it is necessary to struggle not against this or that confession or church but solely against the anti-Christian spirit, wherever and however it may be expressed" (Pt. III, ch. 17, letter #2).

The issue at hand concerns the extent to which "The Tale" synthesizes these views and/or corrects them. Is the Antichrist espousing Solovyovian theocratic ideas criticized by Trubetskoy? Is the Antichrist's alliance with the Freemasons an admission by Solovyov of naïveté concerning the seductive nature of evil residing in secular liberalism and an admission that by means of their defense he has contributed to the impetus for betraying Christ, truth, and freedom inherent in secular romantic liberalism and progressivism, including that evidenced in radicalized Jewry? There are passages in "The Tale" that permit this reading. To return to Sergei Nilus, he was apparently so deeply impressed with the work that he understood the Comité Permanent Universel as the Alliance Israélite Universelle. If he thought Solovyov's work a visionary revelation of the satanic "Judeo-Masonic world conspiracy," he may have found in *The Protocols* the proof of this vision.

> Whereas, when he [the Antichrist] moved to Jerusalem, secretly maintaining rumors among Jewish circles that his main task was to establish Israel's global powers, the Jews recognized him as the Messiah, and their enthusiastic loyalty to him was boundless.

This passage from "The Tale of the Antichrist" raises the issue of Solovyov's position in "The Tale" to a more serious level. If it contributed to Nilus's editing of the *Protocols*, it would ironically have become a material accessory to the harm that they were to bring to the Jews. This would prove a cruel mockery of Solovyov's formal intention and commitment to defend the Jews from Judeophobia.

"The Tale" does not easily lend itself to such a reading. True, it depicts the Jews as committing themselves to the Antichrist initially, when he moves his base to Jerusalem, but their alliance is short-lived for, thanks to a comic revelation "from below," highlighted by Solovyov's use of italics, the passage just quoted continues as follows:

> [But then] the Jews, who considered the Emperor a genuine and absolute Israelite, accidentally discovered that he was *not* even *circumcised*.

The Antichrist is thus exposed as a non-Jew. On discovering this, the Jews rise against him, march on Jerusalem, and are followed by the pope, the patriarch, the Protestant professor, and their adherents. Since the Jews rise against the Antichrist on account of their rootedness in their religious tradition and identity and since their active insurrection is the catalyst that inspires the Christians to march against him also, it is clear that "The Tale" represents in the form of a simple and popular story Solovyov's perennial admiration of the Jews for their ability to act with heroic initiative and for their willingness to subordinate their personal secular interests and desires to the God of Abraham, as symbolized by the covenant and rite of circumcision.

The enemies [of Jewry] saw with astonishment that the soul of Israel in her depth lives not by calculation and the desire for Mammon, but by the power of the heart's feeling and by the confidence and the fury of her eternal messianic faith.[206]

The similarities between Solovyov's "Tale" and the *Protocols* are many, but the comical exposure of the Antichrist as uncircumcised and not a Jew, as well as the leading and active role given to the Jews as the vanguard that leads the remaining true Christian alliance of Catholics, Orthodox, and Protestants against the Antichrist, shows that Solovyov is engaging the period's apocalyptic mood, secularist messianism, and religious phobias and working to correct their chief errors. These include the subordination of spiritual good to temporal values, the denial of grace and the Cross, but also Judeophobia. The value given to human initiative, enterprise, and exploit and to the subordination of the human to the divine, so central to Solovyov's religious philosophy of Godmanhood, and embedded in his characterization of Judaism and Jewry, is here preserved. Consequently, in light of the leading role given to Judaism and Jewry in exposing the Antichrist as non-Jewish and in leading the Christian world to combat him, the contacts between "The Tale" and "The Grand Inquisitor" chapter, on the one hand, and the *Protocols,* on the other, are best explained as evidencing, first, Solovyov's mature articulation of where his messianism or eschatology stands vis-à-vis that of Dostoevsky and, second, his consciousness of the urgent need to engage with and polemicize against Judeophobic antecedents of the *Protocols* through a combination of Shakespearean satire, Platonic dialogue, and biblical apocalypticism.

The depiction of the Antichrist as holding a doctorate in theology from Tübingen recalls Solovyov's criticism of liberal scripture scholars such as Havet and Renan, as illustrated by his letter #17 to Getz, in which he expressed his consternation with the sympathy accorded to Renan's *Life of Jesus* by progressive Jews. Noting that he understood this favor to be rooted in their hostility to and alienation from Christianity, he nonetheless denounced this sympathy as suicidal for Jews given Renan's soap-operatic approach to biblical history and Jewish values. The interpretation of the Antichrist of "The Tale" as a Solovyovian self-parody is therefore exaggerated. The portrait lines up better with the originators of the gap that modern liberal theology introduces between faith and history, as evidenced in Havet's attempt to show the prophets of faith as unhistorical or Renan's differentiation of the historical Jesus from the Christ of faith. As Solovyov's letters evidence, he was never seduced by such thinking and always considered it counterfeit.

CHAPTER 19

1899–1900: The Obituary of Joseph Rabinovich and "The Tale"

Solovyov's mature understanding of the boundaries between his position on Christian-Jewish relations and those of the Slavophile establishment is also made explicit in his obituary of Joseph Rabinovich, written on May 5, 1899, that is, concurrently with the commencement of his work on *Three Conversations*.

The obituary begins with the argument that the present age poses more inward difficulties for Christians than did the age of the early church, when Christians were subjected to outward persecution. The greater present difficulties result from the heaps of falsehood and evil that have accumulated in the Christian world because these impede souls from uniting inwardly with God, the spirit of truth. The argument reiterates, almost verbatim, the opening paragraph of Solovyov's letter to *Moskovskie vedomosti* of October 30, 1891 (Pt. III, ch. 17, letter #3), in defense of his lecture "The Fall of the Medieval Worldview."

Solovyov then observes that the opposite situation applies to modern-day Jews. They are outwardly persecuted in Christian domains and do not witness Christians applying to them the commandment to love neighbor and enemy. This, of course, is the perennial "problem" or "question" that Solovyov highlights in all his writings and pronouncements on Christian-Jewish relations, as illustrated in all the commentaries above.

Solovyov next infers that because of this persecution of Jews by Christians, and so because of the Christian culture's failure to put Christianity into practice where Jews are concerned, Jewish conversion to Christianity, whether en masse or in significant minorities, is for most Jews a moral and psychological impossibility and therefore something that Christians have no right to demand or expect. This point also is implicit in Solovyov's writings in defense of the Jews and other minorities. It is implicit, for example, in the concluding paragraph of his article "The Sins of Russia" (see Pt. III, chs. 9 and 10: letters to Getz, #16 and #37), which begins with the sentence: "How can we resolve the Eastern Question when we cannot with a clean conscience raise our banner bearing the inscription, 'national, civil and religious independence and free development for all the peoples of the Christian East'?" Nevertheless, the starkness with which this inference is drawn is unprecedented in Solovyov's writings.

Solovyov then brings the argument to bear on Rabinovich by saying that the latter's accomplishment of founding a Jewish community of believers in Jesus, and sustaining it for twenty years independently of Christian confessions, is rather amazing. In light of the unfolding argument, the reason for the amazement must be twofold. Christian persecution did not deter Rabinovich and his community from embracing Christ. Their belief in Christ evolved organically and soundly on the basis of the New Testament and independently of Christian confessions and churches. The genesis of this community, he argues, therefore represents a modern Jewish reconnection with the flow of Jewish believers in Jesus and the Gospel at the point at which this flow stopped after the death of Stephen. This last point recaps Solovyov's defense of Rabinovich in the essay "The Israel of the New Covenant," which argued that it would be unjust to label and repress this community as Protestant because it has not negated traditional conciliar Christian dogma as Protestantism has but, on the contrary, followed the trajectory of Jews who turned to Christianity in the earliest centuries.

In conclusion, Solovyov states that while Rabinovich's demand for Jews to embrace Christianity and behave like Christians was based on a mistaken notion of the historical situation, the worth of his life, as that of any man, is to be gauged not by reference to this error but by reference to "the direction and the measure of the effort exerted by his will" in living out the principles to which he was committed, by reference to the harmony of his deeds, words, and thoughts. This, of course, is again a corollary of his understanding of the "Christian problem," the problem of Christians' failure to practice what they preach. The point is also foundational to Solovyov's writings on non-Christian religions, as evidenced, for example, in his essay on Islam. There he states that while the faith of Muslims (taking "faith" to denote *what* Muslims believe, i.e., the content of their doctrine) contains falsehood and is inferior to the truths of Christian revelation, this same faith (now taking "faith" to denote *how* they believe, i.e., the pattern of their lifestyle) manifests a harmony of belief and practice superior to that witnessed in Christian culture. The point also resonates with the principle reiterated in Solovyov's letters to *Moskovskie vedomosti* in 1891 in his explanation that what he sought to criticize in "The Fall of the Medieval Worldview" was neither Christianity nor Christian asceticism but Christians, especially lay Christians, who hypocritically espouse the ideal of personal holiness and piety so as to free themselves, by means of this pretext, from any kind of public work for the common good (Pt. III, ch. 17, letter #2, pars. 1 and 9, October 26, 1891). He criticized this position because he believed that Christian piety and spirituality unaccompanied and unattested by good deeds, that is, by an active will to do good, is a form of pseudo-Christianity.

The words about the worth of a man being gauged by his will echo a phrase in Solovyov's letter to Filippov of July 20, 1889 (see Pt. III, ch. 9, letter #22 n. 48):

Always and everywhere, the important thing is the *will:* intellectual convictions, thoughts, and theories only clear and lighten the ways which lead to the goal, established not by theoretical but by practical reason. We are united not so much by common thoughts as by a *common will.* You *will* deeply and fervently a spiritual liberation, a strengthening and an enlivening of the Russian, and via this, of the universal church. This I will as well.

This emphasis on will involves more than Solovyov's insistence on the importance of harmonizing beliefs, principles, and deeds. Beyond this it relates to Solovyov's understanding of creation and the world as being "willed" by God, and attaining its realization and completion by conforming to his "will." As he comments in explaining the Lord's Prayer in *The Spiritual Foundations of Life*, the realization of God's will and delivery from evil temptation in the future entails concrete prerequisites: material and spiritual conditions and sustenance in the present, denoted by the requests for "daily bread" and "supersubstantial bread" in the Lucan and Matthean versions of the Lord's Prayer; and liberation from the evils of the past through the granting and receiving of forgiveness.

The obituary helps to definitively resolve issues relating to Solovyov's *Three Conversations and the Tale of the Antichrist*. Christ is crucial in "The Tale." It aims to clarify the nature of the lie by which humanity is seduced to betray him. Where did Solovyov understand his theocratic position vis-à-vis Tolstoy, Dostoevsky, the regime, and so on, to stand in this battle? The obituary helps resolve the issue because of the way in which it touches on the identities of those who side with Christ and against him in "The Tale." The majority of Christians fall away and betray Christ for the Antichrist, while only a small "remnant," centered around the leaders of the church—the pope, the patriarch, and the Protestant professor—stands firm to witness to Christ by martyrdom. In this, the remaining faithful are like the Christians of the early centuries as described in the first paragraph of Solovyov's third letter, of October 20, 1981, to *Moskovskie vedomosti* (Pt. III, ch. 17). By this emphasis "The Tale" gives voice to the traditional biblical image of "the remnant" and the dogma of the indefectability of the church. In the obituary Solovyov identifies this remnant as consisting of "elect individuals, distinct groups of select religiously attuned people," through whom "the spirit, truth, blows where it will" and who therefore "spiritually break though these historical barriers." But the obituary also echoes the phraseology of "The Fall of the Medieval Worldview" and the letters to *Moskovskie vedomosti*, by emphasizing that over and against this remnant of the elect, the church contains within itself "heaps of falsehood and evil" that have accumulated "in the Christian world historically" and that stand to "separate a believing soul from the Christian God" in ways more effective and tragic than effected by "the beasts of the circus and the iron of the Roman warrior." "The Tale," after depicting many Jews and Christians following and entering into alliance with the Antichrist, depicts an active contingent of Jews rising against him and catalyzing the Christians to do so. Similarly, the obituary, after depicting Christians who have become separated from God by the heaps of lies that have accumulated in their world, states that "those who feel these heaps most are the Jews," because what the Christians "make visible to them by their deeds" and by "the noise of the pogroms against the Jews[E]" gives a palpable lie to the claim that Christianity is a religion of love and exposes where and in what it has betrayed the spirit of Christ for that of the Antichrist.

The close parallels in thought and phraseology between the letters to *Moskovskie vedomosti* in defense of his lecture of October 19, 1891, and the obituary for Rabinovich of May 5, 1899, prove how firmly Solovyov maintained at the latter date the views espoused in the former. However, the lecture of 1891 and the polemic with *Moskovskie vedomosti* that follows amplify and deepen the views that Solovyov espoused in "The Sins of Russia," written in defense of the Jews, and in the Protest that he published abroad in December 1890. The deepening is pneumatological inasmuch as Solovyov's concern in "The Fall," in the letters to *Moskovskie vedomosti* and in the obituary is with the exposure of the difference between the *spirit* of lies and falsehood in the Christian world and the spirit of Christ. The spirit of Christ in these letters is closely identified with *a good will*, with the firm will to do the good. The will to do the good as understood is a medieval Christian definition of love, especially in Dante with whose *Divine Comedy* Solovyov was preoccupied in the last decade of his life, but the emphasis on the will he found in and credited early to Schelling while working on *A Critique of Abstract Principles*. Since the converse of willing the good is the failure to intend and do what one understands and believes to be the good and since this is the content of what Solovyov originally envisioned to be the Christian question exposed by Christian-Jewish relations, we may see that Solovyov's writings on Judaism progressively move in the direction of redefining and exposing the content of the Christian question as turning on the betrayal of the Creator and of Christ and on capitulation to the Antichrist. "The Tale of the Antichrist" declares Judaism's faith in God and His Messiah to be furious and ultimate. In doing so, it gives it an instrumental role in the church's and humanity's battle with the Antichrist. Consequently, "The Tale," far from retracting Solovyov's perennial thoughts, words, and deeds about Judaism and Christian-Jewish relations, recapitulates, synthesizes, and sharpens the principal tenets he held over the previous two decades.

CHAPTER 20

July 1900: Last Days and Burial

Solovyov spent his last weeks vacationing in the house of his friend Count Sergei Nikolaevich Trubetskoy. There he fell ill and understood that the illness was terminal and that he would not fulfill two key remaining desires of his life, to produce an annotated translation of the Hebrew Bible, which he had been studying for the past two decades, and to journey to the land of Israel.

Witnesses relate that on the day he died, August 13 (July 31 [o.s.]), 1900, he received the sacraments of confession and communion from an Orthodox priest and then began to lose consciousness. As he fell in and out of consciousness, surrounded by his family and friends, he began praying fervently and did so to the end. In the course of his prayers he asked those around him, "Don't let me fall asleep. Let me pray for the Jewish people . . . I have to pray for them," and proceeded to recite aloud the Psalms, in Hebrew, as well as the Jewish profession of faith, Shema' Yisrael ("Hear, O Israel, the Lord our God, the Lord is One").[207]

He was buried near his father. The wooden cross placed on his grave bore, for a long time, an Orthodox icon with a mother-of-pearl image from Jerusalem and a silk-woven Catholic image of Our Lady of Częstochowa, whom he especially revered. The inscription on his tombstone, placed by his sister Nadya, read, "Come Lord Jesus," a citation from Revelation 22:20. One may observe that these objects and inscription elegantly symbolize the realities that he desired and strove to integrate throughout the last three decades of his life: Russian Orthodoxy, Catholicism, Judaism, Divine Wisdom, Mary and Christ.

NOTES TO PART II

1. See principally the memoirs and studies of Solovyov's life and thought by his nephew Sergei M. Solovyov, *Zhizn'*; the memoir and collection by Getz, "Nekotorye vospominaniya"; and *Ob otnoshenii Vl. Solovyova k evrejskomu voprosu: Talmud i novejshaya polemicheskaya literatura o nyom; Evrei - ikh verouchenie i nravouchenie; Ob otnoshenii Vl. Solovyova k evrejskomu voprosu*, ed. Faivel Getz (Berlin: Zarya, 1925); Nikolai Ignat'evich Bakst, "Pamyati Vladimira Sergeevicha Solovyova" (In Commemoration of Vladimir Sergeevich Solovyov), *Voskhod* 11 (1900): 84–89; Syrkin, "V. Solov'ëv ve-yihusso"; Vladimir Galaktionovich Korolenko, "'Deklaratsiya' V. S. Solovyova: k istorii evrejskogo voprosa v russkoj pechati," *Polnoe sobranie sochinenij* 9 (1914); repr. *Rasskazy* 3 (1903–15), http://ruslit.traumlibrary.net/book/korolenko-ss05-03/korolenko-ss05-03.html#work002003\ and http://vehi.net/soloviev/korolenko.html; and *Vospominaniya* (Paris: Knigoizdatel'stvo E. Siial'skoy, 1927); the two-volume critique of his thought by his friend Evgeny N. Trubetskoy, *Mirosozertsanie Vl. S. Solovyova* (Moscow: Izdanie avtora, 1913); the biographical materials assembled by Sergei Mikhailovich Lukianov, *Materialy k biografii Vl. S. Solovyova (Iz arkhiva S. M. Lukianova)*, ed. with introd. A. N. Shakhanov (Moscow: Studiya TRITÆ, 1992); the memoirs edited by Averin and Bazanova, *Kniga O Vladimire Solovyove*; the biography by Mochulsky, *Vladimir Solov'ëv*; Ernst Müller, "Solowjeffs Gedanken über Judentum," *Der Jude* 1 (1916–17): 815–22; David Flusser, "Vladimir Soloviev und unsere Lage," *Freiburger Rundbrief* 21 (1969): 8–11; Moss, "Vladimir Soloviev and the Jews" (1970); Glouberman, "Fyodor Dostoevsky, Vladimir Soloviev . . . on Jewish and Old Testament Themes" (1974); Jonathan Sutton, *The Religious Philosophy of Vladimir Solovyov: Towards a Reassessment* (Basingstoke: Macmillan, 1988); Halpérin, "Vladimir Soloviev Listens to Israel" (1994); Judith Deutsch Kornblatt, "Solov'ev's Androgynous Sophia and the Jewish Kabbalah," *Slavic Review* 50.3 (1991): 487–96; Judith Deutsch Kornblatt, "Russian Religious Thought and the Jewish Kabbala," in *The Occult in Russian and Soviet Culture*, ed. Bernice Glatzer Rosenthal (Ithaca, NY: Cornell University Press, 1997), 75–95; Kornblatt, "Vladimir Solov'ev on Spiritual Nationhood, Russia and the Jews" (1997); Kornblatt, *Doubly Chosen*, 2004; Judith Deutsch Kornblatt, "Visions of Icons and Reading Rooms in the Poetry and Prose of Vladimir Solov'ev," in *Aesthetics as a Religious Factor in Eastern and Western Christianity*, ed. Wil van den Bercken and Jonathan Sutton, Eastern Christian Studies 6 (Leuven: Peeters, 2005),

125–41; Kornblatt, Jakim, and Magnus, *Divine Sophia*; Judith Deutsch Kornblatt and Gary Rosenshield, "Vladimir Solovyov: Confronting Dostoevsky on the Jewish and Christian Questions," *Journal of the American Academy of Religion* 68 (2000): 69–98; Konstantin Yur'evich Burmistrov, "Vladimir Solov'ev i Kabbala: K postanovke problemy" (Vladimir Solovyov and the Kabbalah: Towards a Formulation of the Problem), *Issledovaniya po istorii Russkoj mysli* (1998): 7–104; the centenary volumes edited by Wil van den Bercken, Manon de Courten, and Evert van der Zweerde, *Vladimir Solov'ëv: Reconciler and Polemicist: Selected Papers of the International Solov'ëv Conference Held in Nijmegen, September 1998* (Leuven: Peeters, 2000); and Borisova and Kozyreva, *Solovyovskij sbornik*; Hagemeister, "Vladimir Solov'ëv and Sergej Nilus"; Bar-Yosef, "The Jewish Reception of Vladimir Solov'ëv"; van der Zweerde, "Vladimir Solov'ëv and the Russian-Christian Jewish Question"; Savely Yur'evich Dudakov, "Vladimir Solov'ëv I Sergei Nilus," in *Russian Literature and History: In Honour of Professor I. Serman*, ed. Wolf Moskovich et al. (Jerusalem: Hebrew University of Jerusalem, Department of Russian and Slavic Studies, 1989), 163–69; Savely Yur'evich Dudakov, *Paradoksy i prichudy filosemitizma i antisemitizma* (Moscow: Rossijskij gosudarstvennyj gumanitarnyj universitet, 2000), http://book.e-reading-lib.org/book.php?book=94034; Manon de Courten, "Two Narratives on History in Vladimir Solov'ëv: The Polish Question," in Borisova and Kozyreva, *Solovyovskij sbornik*, 475–502; Manon de Courten, *History, Sophia and the Russian Nation: A Reassessment of Solov'ëv's View of History and His Social Commitment* (Bern: Peter Lang, 2004); Valliere, "Sophiology"; Paul Valliere, "Solov'ëv and Schelling's Philosophy of Revelation," in van den Bercken et al., *Vladimir Solov'ëv: Reconciler and Polemicist*, 119–29; Valliere, *Modern Russian Theology*; Wozniuk, "Vladimir S. Soloviev and the Politics of Human Rights"; Vladimir Wozniuk, *Politics, Law, and Morality: Essays by V. S. Soloviev* (New Haven, CT: Yale University Press, 2000); Wozniuk, *Freedom, Faith, and Dogma*; Belkin, "Evrejskij vopros"; Belkin, *"Gäste."*

2. For details, see previous note.

3. S. Solovyov, *Zhizn'*, 266.

4. As explained in Pt. I, ch. 4, §§9.2, 9.6, 10.3, Dubnov mentioned only Saltykov-Shhedrin and Solovyov. Moss, taking a cue from Solovyov, proposed Bishop Nikanor, while Solzhenitsyn added Mordovtsev. The commentary below explains why Nikanor's mention is problematic. All these, however, fail to take stock of Leskov, whom Solovyov, on the way to the latter's funeral, described to Getz as "a friend of the Jews." The commentary also highlights that Leskov, whom Gorky rated alongside Tolstoy, Gogol, and Turgenev, wrote in 1883 a major work on the Jewish question, reputed to have greatly influenced the proceedings of the Pahlen Commission. The work was banned

in Soviet Russia after its initial reprinting by the Jewish historian Gessen. This brings to four and, with Nikanor, possibly five, the number of Russian intellectuals who wrote on behalf of the Jews in the 1880s prior to Solovyov's Protest letter. Tolstoy signed the letter but did not campaign himself on behalf of the Jews, for, as he explained to Solovyov (see below), "he had other things to worry about."

5. Moss, "Vladimir Soloviev and the Jews," 184. On the indebtedness of Solovyov's philosophy to his father's work as a historian and to the way in which the father and the philosopher son model the ideal of philosophical history, see Belkin, "*Gäste,*" 67–70, 78.

6. Dudakov, *Paradoksy i prichudy,* 332, citing Lossky, "V zashhitu Vl. Solov'ëva," *Novyj zhurnal* 33 (1953): 234.

7. Solovyov, "Letter to Strakhov, 23 August 1890," *Letters,* 1:59. See S. Solovyov, *Zhizn',* 270–71.

8. Solovyov, *Letters,* 1:56, 57.

9. Solovyov, "Letter to Strakhov, 23 August 1890," *Letters,* 1:60. See also S. Solovyov, *Zhizn',* 272; Kornblatt, "Vladimir Solov'ev on Spiritual Nationhood," 157.

10. S. Solovyov, *Zhizn',* 270, citing S. M. Solovyov (the elder), "Nablyudenie nad istoricheskoj zhizn'yu narodov," *Vestnik Evropy,* 1868–76; available at http://dugward.ru/library/solovyev_s_m/solovyev_s_m_nabludeniya_nad_istorich.html.

11. Fyodor Mikhailovich Dostoevsky, "I. Evrejskij vopros," "II. Pro I contra," "III. Status in statu. Sorok vekov bytiya," "IV. No da zdrastvuyet bratstvo!," in "*Dnevnik Pisatelya* za 1877 god," in *Polnoe Sobranie Sochinenij 1888 goda,* 11:81–85, 85–89, 90–95, 95–98.

12. See Pt. I, ch. 4, §3.1 n. 84, following Solzhenitsyn; and §3.3 on Lewis Way's influence on Alexander I and the latter's founding in 1817 of the Society of Israelite Christians.

13. Bakst, "Speech on 12 Nov. 1900," esp. 86.

14. Getz, "Ob otnoshenii Vl. S. Solovyova k evrejskomu voprosu" (Vladimir Solovyov's Attitude to the Jewish Question), repr. Getz, *Ob otnoshenii Vl. S. Solovyoa k evrejskomu voprosu,* 15–16, 25 (on Solovyov's "Jewry and the Christian Question," 29, 40 (on Solovyov's Protest letter of Mar. 5, 1891).

15. M. Klimenko, "Vladimir Solovyov o meste Rosii v mire," in Borisova and Kozyreva, *Solovyovskij sbornik,* 426–33. More broadly, see de Courten, "Two Narratives," 475–502; and even more broadly, de Courten, *History, Sophia, and the Russian Nation.*

16. Maria / Marie Bez(s)obraz(s)ov(f)a, one of Solovyov's sisters, a distinguished writer who went under the pseudonym "Allegro" (see Eugène Tavernier's introduction to *Three Conversations,* n. 3), recently has been hailed as

Russia's "first woman philosopher of the silver age"; see Elena Petrovna Borzova and A. I. Novikov, "Mariya Bezobrazova—pervaya zhenshhina-filosof 'serebryanogo veka'," in *O blagorodstve i preimushhestve zhenskogo pola: iz istorii zhenskogo voprosa v Rossii* (Sbornik nauchnykh trudov), ed. R. Sh. Ganelin (St. Petersburg: Peterburgskaya gos. akademiya kul'tury, Nevsky institut yazyka i kul'tury, Zhenskaya gumanitarnaya kollegiya, 1997), 153–58.

17. I.e., in the Pale of Settlement.

18. Maria S. Bezobrazova, "Vospominaniya o brate Vladimire Solovyove (Recollections about [My] Brother Vladimir Solovyov" (1908), in Averin and Bazanova, *Kniga O Vladimire Solovyove*, 77–112.

19. Unlike his closest friends, the Trubetskoy brothers, who were eighth-generation descendants of Baron P. P. Shafirov and his wife, A. S. Kopyova. See Dudakov, *Paradoksy*, 603 n. 146.

20. Lossky, *History of Russian Philosophy* (New York: International Universities Press, 1951), 121, cited by Kornblatt, "Vladimir Solov'ev on Spiritual Nationhood," 157.

21. See Barbara Heldt Monter, *Koz'ma Prutkov: The Art of Parody* (Paris: Mouton, 1972).

22. Rev. 22:20.

23. El'tsova, "Sny nezdeshnie: K 25-let'iyu konchiny V. S. Solovyova" (1926), in Averin and Bazanova, *Kniga O Vladimire Solovyove*, 141–42, 153, 155. The title of El'tsova's memoir, which may be translated as "Dreams of Elsewhere," refers to the line "zdes' vy nezdeshnie" (here you-are as-of-elsewhere) in Solovyov's (possibly last) poem, written on June 8, 1900 (he died on July 31), "Vnov' belye kolokol'chiki" (Again the white bluebells) (*SSVSS*[12] 97, 98). The poem, roughly translated, reads: In the dire heat / of summer, —/ white and stately / they remain. // Vernal ghosts / Consumèd maybe, —/ Here of elsewhere / You're true dreams. // Evil suffered / In blood drowns, —/ But love's sun / Washed clean ascends. // Brave designs / In heart that's ailing, —/ Pure-white angels / 'round me stand // Stately - airy / they remain —/ In stifling, heavy / dire days.

24. Sergei Solovyov is here referring to p. 146 of vol. 3 of Solovyov's *Collected Works*. However, vol. 3 of the first edition (*SSVSS*[9]) contains this passage on pp. 381–82, while vol. 3 of the second edition (*SSVSS*[10]) contains it on pp. 415–16. Given that he is clearly able to state the length of the work, he is most likely referring to one of the separately published editions (1884, 1885, or 1887), most probably the last, given that the earlier editions bore the title *Religious Foundations of Life*. On the editions of the work, see Pt. I, n. 61.

25. 1 Kings 19:12.

26. S. Solovyov, *Zhizn'*, 213–14, cites here the third edition of the work, p. 6.

27. Ibid.

28. Faivel Getz, *Ob otnoshenii Vl. S. Solovyoa k evrejskomu voprosu* (Vladimir Solovyov's Attitude to the Jewish Question) (Moscow: I. N. Kushnerev, 1901; 2d ed. 1902), 6, 7, 17.

29. Ibid., 19–20.

30. Vladimir Korolenko, *Polnoe sobranie sochinenij* (Collected Works), 9 (1914): 259. For more detail, see Pt. III, ch. 13.

31. Catholic discomfort with Solovyov's Sophiology is evidenced in his correspondence with Fr. Paul Pierling, the Russian Jesuit who, commenting on the progress of Solovyov's *La Russie et l'Église universelle*, advised him in 1877 to excise everything theosophical (*Letters*, 3:153; 4:38, 113) and, anticipating the book's condemnation by his brother Jesuits in Paris, ultimately decided not to help with the publication of the book (S. Solovyov, *Zhizn'*, 256–57). For a summation of the Orthodox position, see Sergei Khoruzhy, "Nasledie Vladimira Solovyova sto let spustya" (The Legacy of Vladimir Solovyov a Hundred Years Later), in Borisova and Kozyreva, *Solovyovskij sbornik*, esp. 13–19.

32. For detailed analysis, see the works of Kornblatt and Burmistrov cited in note 1 above; and Valliere, "Sophiology," 176–91.

33. Composed on Sept. 26–29, 1898. The source of the quote is S. Solovyov, *Zhizn'*, 339. See Pt. I, n. 59.

34. See S. Solovyov, *Zhizn'*, 32–33, 339. On the links, ecclesial and iconic, between the second and the first vision, see Kornblatt, "Visions." On the relationship of his interest in the light of Tabor to the rest of his mysticism, see Khoruzhy, "Nasledie," 7.

35. Thomas H. Tobin, "The Prologue of John and Hellenistic Jewish Speculation," *Catholic Biblical Quarterly* 52 (1990): 255–62; Thomas H. Tobin, "Logos," in *Anchor Bible Dictionary*, ed. David Noel Friedman et al. (New Haven, CT: Yale University Press, 1992), 4:348–56; Peter Schäfer, *The Jewish Jesus: How Judaism and Christianity Shaped Each Other* (Princeton, NJ: Princeton University Press, 2012).

36. S. Solovyov, *Zhizn'*, 264–65, citing Solovyov's *La Russie et l'Église universelle*, 371.

37. Oliver Smith, "The Sophianic Task in the Work of Vladimir Solov'ëv," *Journal of Eastern Christian Studies* 59.3–4 (2007): 167–83; Brandon Gallaher, "The Christological Focus of Vladimir Solov'ev's Sophiology," *Modern Theology* 25.4 (2009): 617–46.

38. Following Kornblatt, "Russian Religious Thought," 77.

39. Labeled Album #1 by S. Solovyov, *Zhizn'*, and attached to the sixth and seventh editions of Solovyov's poetry.

40. Konstantin Nikolaevich Leontiev (1831–91) was a monarchist Slavo-phile philosopher and the author of *The East, Russia, and Slavdom* (1885–86). He advocated closer ties between Russia and the East and predicted a socialist revolution led by the Antichrist. Being cured of cholera in 1871 after praying to the Virgin Mary, he became a secret adherent of the Optina monastery in 1887 and ultimately died a monk at the Troitse-Sergieva Lavra (Holy Trinity Monastery of St. Sergius). For V. Solovyov's article on Leontiev in the Brockhaus-Efron dictionary, see Solovyov, *SSVSS*[12] 10:507–11; and http://krotov.info/library/18_s/solovyov/10_506.html.

41. Nikolai Alekseyevich Lyubimov (1830–97) was a physicist and ener-getic opponent of Western liberalism. He contributed to *Moskovskie vedo-mosti* under the pseudonym Varfalomei Kochnev and wrote the editorial "Against the Stream," which highlighted the correspondence between Alexan-der II's Russia and prerevolutionary France. Finding justification for his views in Alexander II's assassination, he played a leading role, along with Katkov, in the same paper, in encouraging counterrevolutionary measures to support Al-exander III's regime. See "Lyubimov Nikolai Alekseevich," www.hrono.info/biograf/bio_l/ljubimov_na.html.

42. S. Solovyov, *Zhizn'*, 96, citing Lukianov, *O Vladimire Solov'ëve v ego molodye gody*, 3:126.

43. S. Solovyov, *Zhizn'*, 97, citing Lukianov, *O Vladimire Solov'ëve v ego molodye gody*, 3:146–48.

44. S. Solovyov, *Zhizn'*, 97–99.

45. Kornblatt, "Russian Religious Thought," 76, citing Lukianov, *O Vla-dimire Solov'ëve v ego molodye gody*, 3:64.

46. Kornblatt, "Russian Religious Thought," 76, citing Solov'ëv, *Letters*, 2:229.

47. Vsevolod Sergeevich (front cover erroneously gives first name of au-thor as Vladimir), *A Modern Priestess of Isis*, ed. and trans. Leaf [2011]; Engl. trans. published in 1895).

48. See Solovyov's critical review of Madame Elena Blavatskaya's book *The Key to Theosophy* in *Russian Review* (1890): 881–86 (*SSVSS* 6:291–92); and his article about her, "E. P. Blavatskaya," in S. A. Vengerov, *Kritiko-bibliograficheskij slovar' russkikh pisatelej i uchyonykh* (St. Petersburg: I. Efron, 1892), 36:316–18. Blavatskaya's response to Solovyov, "Answer to a Russian Philosopher," was published in Boris de Zirkof, ed, *H. P. Blavatsky: Collected Writings* (Wheaton, IL: Theosophical Press, 1980), 12:334–49, www.theosophyonline.com/ler.php?id=223#.URAWF_JO-So.

49. See the testimony of his friend and fellow philosopher Prince Sergei Nikolaevich Trubetskoy: "Solovyov believed in the reality, actuality . . . of

communication with the dead, and experienced not only frightening visions in sleep but also when awake, becoming thereby an unwilling medium, and a victim for the most diverse 'spiritual influences' in the course of his entire life" (E. Trubetskoy, *O Vladimire Solovyove*, 1: 61; also discussed by Burmistrov, "Vladimir Solov'ev i Kabbala," 21). There are numerous citations to this effect in S. Solovyov's *Zhizn'*, e.g., 139, 330, where he notes that Solovyov omitted writing about the devil in his initial metaphysical works despite his personal experiences with demons, especially in 1896–97. The jurist A. F. Koni narrated to Lukianov a series of stories about Solovyov's visionary experiences, including claims to have seen the devil, once in Koni's presence, in "Zapis' besed s. A. F. Koni (8-go oktyabrya 1914)," in Lukianov, *Materialy k biografii,* www.rodon.org/svs/_mkbvssiasml.htm and www.runivers.ru/new_htmlreader/?book=5600&chapter=83883.

50. The work, *Filosofskie nachala tsel'nogo znaniya,* was first published in installments in the *Zhurnal ministerstva narodnogo prosveshheniya* (Journal of the Ministry for National Enlightenment) between March and November 1877. Its first chapter, "On the Law of Historical Development," served to introduce Solovyov's dissertation, published as *A Critique of Abstract Principles.* See S. Solovyov, *Zhizn',* 108–21.

51. S. Solovyov, *Zhizn',* 125.

52. Kornblatt, "Vladimir Solov'ev on Spiritual Nationhood," 159–60; Kornblatt, "Solov'ev's Androgynous Sophia," 487–96.

53. Burmistrov, "Vladimir Solov'ev i Kabbala," 11–20 (re London) and 21–39 (re Egypt and *Sophia*).

54. Ibid., 12–14, 38–39, and nn. 19, 21.

55. S. Solovyov, *Zhizn',* 132, 161.

56. Ibid., 126, citing *Letters,* 2:20, 132.

57. S. Solovyov, *Zhizn',* 127.

58. Ibid., 161, 184, 191, 192.

59. Ibid., 162–65.

60. Joseph Pieper, *The Silence of St. Thomas: Three Essays,* trans. Daniel O'Connor (London: Faber and Faber, 1957), 12–13.

61. Cf. Kornblatt, "Russian Religious Thought," 77.

62. *Letters,* 4:147; S. Solovyov, *Zhizn',* 128–30.

63. Lukianov, *O Vladimire Solov'ëve v ego molodye gody,* 3:358; S. Solovyov, *Zhizn',* 129–30. On Solovyov's attitude to Renan, see Belkin, *"Gäste,"* 72–74.

64. Mochulsky, *Vladimir Solovyov,* 7:107–9, on Solovyov's first poem dedicated to S. P. Khitrovo, *Gazeli pustyn' ty stroynee i krashe* ("You are more gracile and fair than a stag of the deserts").

65. Walter G. Moss, *Russia in the Age of Alexander II, Tolstoy and Dostoyevsky* (London: Anthem Press, 2002), 214–16; Anna Dostoyevsky, *Dostoyevsky: Reminiscences*, trans. Beatrice Stillman (New York: Liveright, 1977), 378; Mochulsky, *Vladimir Solovyov*, 79–80.

66. For Lukianov's description of Sophia Khitrovo's relationship to her husband and her outburst about Solovyov's hostility to Judaism to Koni, see S. M. Lukianov, "Zapis' besed s. E. E. Ukhtomskim," "Iz razgovora 30-go maya 1920 g.," and "Zapis' besed s. A. F. Koni" (8-go oktyabrya 1914), in *Materialy k biografii Vl. S. Solovyova iz arkhiva S. M. Lukianova.*

67. S. Solovyov, *Zhizn'*, 325.

68. Except, it seems, at least once in 1890 (*Letters*, 2:259). Cf. S. Solovyov, *Zhizn'*, 276.

69. S. Solovyov, *Zhizn'*, 186, 192, 214, 325, 375, 379.

70. Ibid., 284.

71. The term is "stressed," but "repressed" fits the context and need not be read as a Freudianism.

72. S. Solovyov, *Zhizn'*, 241–42.

73. *Letters*, 4:94.

74. S. Solovyov, *Zhizn'*, 224.

75. Ibid., 281–82; and *Letters*, 4:159.

76. *Letters*, 4:145; and Mochulsky, *Vladimir Solovyov*, 84, 91, 145, correcting S. Solovyov's error of dating this declaration via *Letters*, 2:242, to January 1876.

77. For indications of dates of delivery, see Pt. I, n. 36.

78. Valliere, "Sophiology," 178. On the 1878–81 phase of Solovyov's writings on Judaism, which he takes as the first half of the first, pre-1884 phase, which assumed a dialectic of Law and Grace and a coordination of Judaism and Christianity leading to the synthesis of a universal Christian religion, see Belkin, "*Gäste*," 74–78.

79. Solovyov, "Lecture 2," in Peter Zouboff, trans. and ed., *Lectures on Divine Humanity*, rev. Boris Jakim (Hudson, NY: Lindisfarne, 1995), 13. The emphasis is Solovyov's.

80. S. Solovyov, *Zhizn'*, 145–51; Mochulski, *Vladimir Solovyov*, 91–103.

81. Anna Dostoevsky also relates that when they approached Strakhov to ask him to introduce them to Tolstoy, Strakhov explained that Tolstoy didn't wish to meet anyone that day. When Tolstoy heard this story from her lips in 1885, that is, after Dostoevsky's death, he voiced shock to learn that he was, on that day and only once in his life, in the same hall with Dostoevsky, implying that he never instructed Strakhov to keep the Dostoevskys away.

Beatrice Stillman, translator and editor of Anna's *Reminiscences*, suggests that Strakhov lied to Anna and Dostoevsky about Tolstoy's directive, perhaps because of jealousy (over Tolstoy's friendship) and growing secret dislike of Dostoevsky; see A. Dostoyevsky, *Dostoyevsky: Reminiscences*, 290–91, 364, 403 nn. 1 and 2, 411–12 n. 2.

82. Emphasis mine.

83. Jakim, *Lectures on Divine Humanity*, 151–53.

84. Ibid., 164.

85. Jakim, *Lectures on Divine Humanity*, 164, here invokes George Kline's suggestion that as Solovyov's term "theocracy" does not designate a form of political authority but rather forms of social institution, "theopraxis" may be more appropriate. See George L. Kline, "Russian Religious Thought," in *Nineteenth Century Religious Thought in the West*, ed. Ninian Smart et al. (Cambridge: Cambridge University Press, 1985), 2:210.

86. Cf. Murphy, *The Comedy of Revelation*, 2001.

87. Cf. Fackenheim, "Introduction," *Jewish Philosophers.*

88. Dostoevsky, "1: Evrejskij vopros," "2. Pro I contra," "3: Status in statu. Sorok vekov bytiya," "4: No da zdrastvuyet bratstvo!," in *Dnevnik pisatelya za 1877 god*, 81–85, 85–89, 90–95, 95–98.

89. V. Solovyov, *Kritika otvlechennykh nachal, SSVSS*[9], 2:chs. 1–5, 3–44.

90. Ibid., chs. 6–10, 44–89.

91. Ibid., chs. 11–20, 110–58.

92. Ibid., chs. 21–41, 158–289.

93. Ibid., chs. 42–44, 290–324.

94. Ibid., chs. 45–46, 324–53.

95. See therefore Gallaher's citation ("The Christological Focus," 617) of Milbank's "at first rather startling and puzzling claim that Sophiology, of which the Russian philosopher, theologian, poet, and mystic Vladimir Solov'ev (1853–1900) is the founder, is the most important theological movement of the last two hundred years: 'At the dawn of the twenty-first century, it increasingly appears that perhaps the most significant theology of the two preceding centuries has been that of the Russian sophiological tradition.'" See John Milbank, "Sophiology and Theurgy: The New Theological Horizon," in *An Encounter between Eastern Orthodoxy and Radical Orthodoxy: Transfiguring the World through the Word*, ed. Adrian Pabst and Christoph Schneider (Aldershot: Ashgate, 2009), 45.

96. Michael Aksionov Meerson, "The Retrieval of Neoplatonism in Solov'ëv's Trinitarian Synthesis," in *Vladimir Solov'ëv: Reconciler and Polemicist*, eds. van den Bercken et al., 233–50; Gallaher, "The Christological Focus," 617–46.

97. S. Solovyov, *Zhizn'*, 304.

98. *Letters*, 4:8. Johann Georg Gichtel (1638–1710) was a German mystic and a disciple of Jacob Boehme. John Pordage (1607–1681) was an Anglican priest, astrologer, alchemist, and Christian mystic, founder of the seventeenth-century English Boehmenist group. Louis Claude de Saint-Martin (1743–1803) was a French Roman Catholic philosopher who, on being inspired by Catholic mystical tradition and Jewish Kabbalistic thought, became a preacher of mysticism and the first translator into French of Jacob Boehme. His ideal society was a spiritual theocracy of a pure, church-free spiritual Christianity. His first work, *Of Errors and Truth,* was placed on the Index. Franz Xaver von Baader (1765–1841) was a German Roman Catholic philosopher and theologian, friend of Schelling, and follower of Meister Eckhart, Saint-Martin, and Boehme.

99. See Solovyov, *Letters,* 4:8–11; Anna Schmidt, "Iz rukopisei: S pis'mami k nei Vl. Solovyova," *Russkie Zapiski* 9 (1916): 324–27; and Samuel Cioran, *Vladimir Solov'ev and the Knighthood of the Divine Sophia* (Waterloo, ON: Wilfrid Laurier University Press, 1977), 71. See also S. Solovyov, *Zhizn',* 372–74; Bernice Glatzer Rosenthal and Martha Bohachevsky-Chomiak, *A Revolution of the Spirit: Crisis of Value in Russia, 1890–1924* (New York: Fordham University Press, 1990), 37 n. 6.

100. Trubetskoy, *Mirosozertsanie,* 1:56; also cited by Burmistrov, *Vladimir Solovyov i Kabbala,* 51.

101. Translated from the French original in Solovyov, *Letters,* 4:204 (following the 1970 Bruxelles edition and the 1911 supplement volume of the Letters edited by Radlov), in which the last two words of the passage cited are "oeuvre publique" (public work), via S. Solovyov translation of the passage (*Zhizn',* 326–27), which reads the words as "biblical work" (presupposing "oeuvre biblique"). Given that the immediate preceding context is biblical and the immediate following context relates to the reunification of the Churches with the Synagogue, S. Solovyov's reading makes good sense, whereby "publique" would have resulted from an editor's or typesetter's error. However, given that the wider context includes Solovyov's preoccupation with metaphysics, Plato, aesthetics, poetry, and the history of philosophy, "publique," however difficult (is it, for example, to be contrasted with his esoteric and unpublishable interests) is not impossible. In the latter case, the phrase would denote the hopes that Solovyov attached to his entire, public oeuvre. More data concerning the original are needed to determine Solovyov's meaning.

102. Zouboff and Jakim, trans., *Lectures,* 108.

103. The chapter headings according to SSVSS[9], 270–382 are: "Part I. Introduction. On Nature, Death, Sin, Law and Grace; Chapter II, i. On Prayer,

ii. On Sacrifice and Almsgiving, ii. On Fasting; Part II, i. On Christianity, ii. On the Church, iii. On Christian government and society. Conclusion: The Image of Christ as an Examination of Conscience."

104. Gallaher, "The Christological Focus," 639 passim.

105. Solovyov, "Chteniya o bogochelovechestve" (Lectures on Godman-hood), *SSVSS*⁹ 3:103–4 (trans. mine).

106. A. Dell Acta, "Realizm V. S. Solovyova" (The Realism of V. S. Solovyov), in Borisova and Kozyreva, *Solovyovskij sbornik*, 272–94; and Gallaher, "The Christological Focus."

107. See note 81 above.

108. As noted above, the work was published in November of that year in *Russkij vestnik*, 5–50.

109. Letter to Strakhov of Dec. 18, 1877. Lev Nikolaevich Tolstoy and Sofia Andreevna Tolstaya, *Perepiska L. N. Tolstogo s N. N. Strakhovym*, ed. V. V. Zhdanov, Literaturnoe nasledstvo (Moscow: Akademiya Nauk [Institut Russkoj Literatury (Pushkinskij Dom)], 1939), 37:181, http://feb-web.ru/feb/litnas/texts/137/t37-181-.htm.

110. See Tolstoy's letter to Strakhov of Apr. 18, 1878, http://feb-web.ru/feb/tolstoy/texts/selectpe/ts6/ts62429-.htm.

111. S. Solovyov, *Zhizn'*, 181, citing *SSVSS*⁹ 3:270.

112. S. Solovyov, *Zhizn'*, 179–182; Mochulsky, *Vladimir Solovyov*, 5, 79–80, also citing Sergius Hessen's "Der Kampf." It should also be noted, however, that S. Solovyov also proposed, *Zhizn'*, 18–24, that Ivan may have been based more fittingly on Solovyov's brother Vsevolod, whom Dostoevsky also knew well and whose tragic life and rivalry with Vladimir, and their stories about their third brother, Mikhail, he observed and probably drew on in delineating the characters of Alyosha, Ivan, and Dmitry.

113. In 1881 Getz became a teacher in the Vilensky educational district and in 1884 a minister of national (Jewish) enlightenment. He went on to write several books on Jewish education, ethics, the status of women, and, in 1891, the Jewish question, to which Solovyov's letter #25 served as the foreword. Getz wrote an obituary eulogizing Solovyov as well as a booklet on Solovyov's attitude to the Jewish question. See Getz, "Nekotorye vospominaniya ob otnoshenii V. S. Solovyova k evreyam"; and his *Ob otnoshenii Vl. S. Solovyova k evrejskomu voprosu* (Moscow: I. N. Kushnerev, 1901; 2nd ed. 1902). On Getz, see I.Ch. (name unknown), "Gets, Fajvel' Meer Bentselovich," *Evrejskaya èntsiklopediya* (Jewish Encyclopedia) (St. Petersburg: Obshhestvo dlya nauchnykh Evrejskikh izdanij i izdatel'stvo Brokgauz-Efron, 1910), 6:467. On his relationship with Solovyov, see Burmistrov, "Vladimir Solovyov i Kabbala," 35; Bar-Yosef, "The Jewish Reception," 363–92; S. Dudakov, *Paradoksy i prichudy*, 333, 602, nn. 112–14. Solovyov's letters to him are

reprinted in *Letters*, 2:142–91. In this volume, the spelling of Getz's second middle name Bentisolovich follows that found in Solovyov's letters to him.

114. For testimonies of the lectures' contents and subsequent events, see Mochulsky, *Vladimir Solovyov*, ch. 8, 122–30.

115. Mochulsky dates their first meeting to 1875; Mochulsky, *Vladimir Solovyov*, 268.

116. Velichko, *Vladimir Solovyov: Zhizn' i tvoreniya* (St. Petersburg: Knizhnyj magazin A. F. Tsinzerlinga, 1904), 128.

117. See Dudakov, *Paradoksy i prichudy filosemitizma*, 334.

118. Cf. description by Bar-Yosef, "The Jewish Reception," 365–68; Anonymous, "Nam pishut," *Russkij evrej* 8 (Feb. 2, 1882): 301; Anonymous "Peterburgskaya letopis'," *Nedel'naya khronika voskhoda* 8 (Feb. 19, 1882): 184; Anonymous (Akim Volynsky [= A. Flekser]), "Peterburgskaya letopis'," *Nedel'naya khronika voskhoda* 9 (Feb. 26, 1882): 212–13; Anonymous, "V. S. Solovyov," *Voskhod* 60 (Aug. 3, 1900): 18–19; Anonymous, "Pamyat'i Vl. S. Solovyova," *Voskhod* 69 (Sept. 3, 1900): 6–7; ["Q"], "Lektsiya prof. V.S. Solovyova," *Russkij evrej* 9 (1882): 344; Anonymous, "Otgoloski pechati," *Nedel'naya khronika voskhoda* 6 (Feb. 5, 1895): 133–35; A. Flekser, "Istoricheskaya rol' evrejstva: Lektsiya prof. Vl. Solovyova," *Rassvet* 9 (Feb. 26, 1882): 335–37; Adolph [Aharon] Landau, "Otgoloski pechat'i," *Nedel'naya khronika voskhoda* 36 (Sept. 7, 1886): 955–60; 47 (Sept. 14, 1886): 980–84; 38 (Sept. 21, 1886): 1005.

119. Bar-Yosef, "The Jewish Reception," 366 n. 23, citing Anonymous, "Peterburgskaya letopis'," 184. Cf. van der Zweerde, "Vladimir Solov'ëv," 243 n. 23.

120. Bar-Yosef, "The Jewish Reception," 367–68. On Flekser and other Jewish journalists, see Belkin, *"Gäste,"* 114–17.

121. Dudakov, citing Pavel A. Berlin, "Russkie mysliteli i evrei: Vl. Solovyov, S. Bulgakov, P. Struve, V. Rozanov" (Russian Thinkers and the Jews: V. Solovyov . . . "), *Novyj zhurnal* 70 (1962): 232.

122. Dostoevsky "I. Evrejskij vopros, II. Pro i contra, III. Status in statu. Sorok vekov bytiya, IV. No da zdrastvuyet bratstvo!," available at http://imwerden.de/pdf/dostoevsky_pss_1888_dnevnik_1877.pdf.

123. Ibid., 90–95.

124. Belkin, "'Evrejskij vopros," 470.

125. See Pt. III, ch 1.

126. Analyzing Solovyov's commitment to the concept of national religion, van der Zweerde maintains that Solovyov's "divine scenario" would be undermined by the empirical realities of intermarriage and migration.

127. Another cleric who continued to express friendly support for Solovyov was Antony Vadkovsky, future bishop (metropolitan) of St. Petersburg.

See S. Solovyov, *Zhizn'*, 219–20, 225. Vl. Solovyov remembered Preobrazhensky fondly as a beekeper in the obituary he composed about him in 1890 (*SSVSS*[9] 9:428–29). Cf. S. Solovyov, *Zhizn'*, 228, 364.

128. *La Russie et l'Église universelle* (Paris, 1889). For an online facsimile, see http://babel.hathitrust.org/cgi/pt?id=njp.32101068979747;view=lup; seq=15.

129. Cf. Matt. 7:3–5 // Luke 6:41–42.

130. Rom. 9:3–5; 11:1–2, 25–26, 32.

131. Solovyov cites Rev. 12:1–2 in Slavonic.

132. Translated from *SSVSS*[9] 3:197–200.

133. The essay is the first of ten constituting the collection titled *Voskresnye Pis'ma* (Sunday Letters). It is reprinted in *SSVSS*[10] 10:3–6.

134. S. Solovyov, *Zhizn'*, 195–98.

135. See Vl. Solovyov, *Letters*, 4:92; S. Solovyov, *Zhizn'*, 220. For further discussion of Solovyov's relationship to Dostoevsky on the Jewish question, see Kornblatt and Rosenshield, "Vladimir Solovyov: Confronting Dostoyevsky," 69–98; Belkin, "*Gäste*," 88–91.

136. Cf. S. Solovyov, *Zhizn'*, 190–91, 249, for commentary on other poems written in 1882 alongside *Bednyj Drug*, "Poor/Pitiable Friend," written in 1887 (*Letters*, 4:114), which speak of his compassion for Sophia Khitrovo.

137. See Poems, *V strane moroznykh vyug*, 1882. Note that in the third stanza, the Jew[:] whom God chose and to whom he promised/swore to reveal himself could be an allusion to the Hebrew Abram (Gen. 12; 22:16; 14:13), as well as to Israel, standing corporately before God at Sinai (Exod. 19), or to Moses (Exod. 33:18–23). The allusions, namely, the references to "zeal" in stanza 3 and to the "gentle breeze" and "secret breathing" in the last stanza, the shift to God's self-revelation on Mt. Horeb/Sinai to the prophet Elijah, renowned for his zeal (1 Kings 19:10, 14) and experience of God there in the "still small voice," or as Jewish tradition, following the Hebrew text would have it, in "the voice of quiet stillness" (1 Kings 19:12). On S. Solovyov's reading of the poem as autobiographical and relating it to Solovyov's own experience of being caught between two rival camps and attainment of serenity in the years 1882–83, see *Zhizn'*, 207, 213.

138. Writing in 1922–23, S. Solovyov, *Zhizn'*, 218–20, may have been referring to at least two editions of the contents of this work in book form, one as *Evrejskij vopros—Khristianskij vopros: Sobranie statei* (The Jewish Question—a Christian Question: A Collection of Essays) (St. Petersburg: Pravda, 1906), and the other as *Evrejstvo i Khristianskij vopros* (Kniga dlya vsekh, no. 59; Berlin: Mysl', 1921). Since these were published posthumously, the work is here considered an essay. Its reprint in *SSVSS*[10] 4 is followed by

Solovyov's essay "Reply to N. Ya. Danilevsky," defending his expressed criticisms of Orthodoxy and sympathies for Catholicism. Belkin, *"Gäste,"* 75, 77–79, sees 1884 as marking the beginning of a second phase in Solovyov's writings on Judaism, this time to defend the Jews' commitment to the Law, which lasts until 1890. As shown by my discussion, the writings of 1884 and later are already rooted in lectures delivered and projects conceived at least two years earlier. For Belkin's coverage of Solovyov's discussion of the "Jewish question" as a "Christian question," see *"Gäste,"* 80–81; and for its Jewish reception, 83–88. My longtime suspicion that Solovyov's main point in the opening of this work—that Jews have always treated Christians in a Jewish way whereas Christians have failed to treat Jews in a Christian way owes something to Shakespeare's depiction of this contrast in *The Merchant of Venice*—resonates with Belkin's discovery and report (82) that Solovyov made this precise comment about the play when a theatrical group from Munich performed it in Moscow in 1886.

139. On Solovyov's relationship to the Trubetskoy brothers and on their philosophical and religious differences, see S. Solovyov, *Zhizn'*, 296–97.

140. E. Trubetskoy, *Mirosozertsanie*, 1:493–506, esp. 506 n. 3.

141. Acts 26:14 (RST).

142. Cf. Sutton, *The Religious Philosophy of Vladimir Solovyov*, Appendix 2, 194.

143. See S. Solovyov, *Zhizn'*, 237, for Kireev's notice to Solovyov and Solovyov's letter #20 to Kireev, dated only 1887 (*Letters* 2: 126–27). Solovyov's discovery that the book was to be unconditionally banned in Russia may be dated by his report of the same in his letter of June 20/July2, 1887, to his friend Fr. Paul Pierling, S.J. (*Letters*, 3:126–27).

144. S. Solovyov, *Zhizn'*, 246, citing A. Kireev's letter to Solovyov, A. Kireev, "Iz Perepiski Vladimira Solovyova s A. A. Kireevym" (From the Correspondence of Vladimir Solovyov with A. A. Kireev), *Russkaya mysl'* (Russian Thought) 7–8 (1917): 137–38.

145. Quotations from *Letters*, 3:152–53, 156; 4:113. And see S. Solovyov, *Zhizn'*, 244–46.

146. *Letters*, 4:128–29; S. Solovyov, *Zhizn'*, 223–24, 237.

147. On Archbishop Nikanor (Alexandr Ivanovich) Brovkovich (b. Nov. 20, 1826; d. Dec. 27, 1890), see the reproduction of articles on him in the *Russian Biographical Dictionary*, the *Encyclopedic Dictionary*, and the *Russian Philosophical Encyclopedia* at www.runivers.ru/philosophy/lib/authors/author64261/. On his work, *Pozitivnaya filosofiya i sverkhchuvstvennoe bytie*, see Georges Florovsky, *Ways of Russian Theology* (Belmont, MA: Nordland, 1979), 5 n. 143.

148. Leon Trotsky, *My Life: An Attempt at an Autobiography* (New York: Charles Scribner's Sons, 1930), ch. 8, "My First Prisons," www.marxists .org/archive/trotsky/works/1930-lif/ch08.htm.

149. Nikanor Brovkovich, *Vospominaniya Archiepiskopa Nikanora* (Moscow: Synodal Typography, 1908), 82, 87–89.

150. See in Pt. III Solovyov's letter to Getz, titled "The Sins of Russia" (ch. 10); Getz, *Ob Otnosheni*, 4.

151. Strakhov, "Letter No. 386, Jan. 2, 1891, to Tolstoy," in Tolstoy and Tolstaya, *Perepiska*, ed. Zhdanov, 849–51, n. 6, http://feb-web.ru/feb/tolstoy/texts/selectpe/ts6/ts72849-.htm.

152. The report cited is that of Leonid Lvov, director of the Union of Councils for Soviet Jews (UCSJ) in the former Soviet Union's Human Rights Bureau in St. Petersburg, published on May, 27, 1998, and titled "Fascist and Antisemitic Activity Poisons Inter-Ethnic Relations in St. Petersburg" (*News from Union of Councils for Soviet Jews*), www.fsumonitor.com/stories/052798rnws.shtml. Lvov's dating of Nikanor's speech to 1887 is odd because reference in scholarly literature to pogroms in Odessa that year is hard to find. Isseroff (www.zionism-israel.com/dic/pogrom.htm) notes a minor pogrom there in 1886.

153. Nikanor Brovkovich, "Pouchenie," *Strannik* (October 1890): 236–37. The paragraph is frequently cited in current (antisemitic) sources; see, e.g., Sergei Vladimirovich Fomin, ed., *Rossiya pered vtorym prishestviyem* (Russia before the Second Coming) (Moscow: Rodnik, 1994), 92, www.pravoslavie .ws.html/ru/6.htm.

154. Anonymous, "[Obituary for] Nikanor, Arkhiepiskop Khersonskij i Odesskij" (Nikanor, Archbishop of Kherson and Odessa), *Novoe vremya* 5327 (Dec. 28, 1890/Jan. 9, 1891): 1.

155. One of the earliest testimonies devoted to his activities is in Samuel H. Wilkinson, *The Life of John Wilkinson: The Jewish Missionary* (London: Morgan & Scott, 1908), 207–21. Interest in Rabinovich has grown after Kai Kjaer-Hansen, *Josef Rabinowitsch og den messianske bevægelse: Jødekristendommens Herzl* (Århus Forlaget: Okay-Bog, 1988; Engl. trans. *Joseph Rabinowitz and the Messianic Movement: The Herzl of Jewish Christianity*, trans. Birger Petterson [Grand Rapids, MI: Wm. B. Eerdmans, 1995]). For an assessment of Rabinovich's role and his twelve articles of the faith, see Dan Cohn-Sherbok, *Messianic Judaism* (New York: Continuum International, 2000), 18–24. For Belkin's coverage, see *"Gäste,"* 95–108.

156. *Letters* 4:90; S. Solovyov, *Zhizn'*, 218. The interpolation explaining "symbol" as the Credo is mine.

157. Briman (Dr. Justus), *Judenspiegel*.

158. Since the passages Rohling cited are the fodder of antisemitic tracts to this day, Solovyov's arguments, by their originality, logic, Christian grounding, and eloquence, complement well standard Jewish rebuttals of such propaganda; e.g., the ADL's "The Talmud in Anti-Semitic Polemics" (February 2003), www.adl.org/presrele/asus_12/the_talmud.pdf.

159. Mochulsky, *Vladimir Solovyov*, 177–78.

160. *Letters*, 4:30, 44; S. Solovyov, *Zhizn'*, 266.

161. Sergei M. Solovyov, ed., *Vladimir Solovyov: Stikhotvoreniya*, 7th ed. (Moscow: Russkij knizhnik, 1921), 51–53; cf. Jakim, Bulgakov, and Magnus, *The Religious Poetry of Vladimir Solovyov*, 28–32.

Aleksandr Petrovich Salomon (Solomon; 1855–1908) was a graduate of the Alexandrov Lyceum, a participant in the Russian-Turkish War of 1877–78, secretary of the prison council for the Ministry of Internal Affairs, director of the chief Prison Bureau, an Arabist, and director of the Alexandrov Lyceum. He became acquainted with Solovyov in 1877. Their relationship was described by Ukhtomsky to Lukianov, especially in the interview on May 30, 1920. Accordingly, Salomon reprimanded Solovyov for his speech of March 1881 but supported him morally nonetheless. Ukhtomsky also recalled that Solovyov once assumed that Salomon had Jewish roots and confessed that he would give anything to have some Jewish blood. Ukhtomsky and Salomon were also among the few friends of Solovyov who knew about Countess Volkonskaya's conversion to Catholicism. Cf. S. M. Lukianov, "Zapis' besed s. E. E. Ukhtomskim," "Iz razgovora 30-go maya 1920 g.," 2–3:393–402.

162. For Belkin's coverage of "The Talmud" and its Jewish reception, see *"Gäste,"* 93–95.

163. S. Solovyov, *Zhizn'*, 237–39, 244; *Letters*, 1:25, 171; 3:191.

164. Unless indicated otherwise, see Pt. III, ch. 9, for all Getz letters referred to in this chapter.

165. Cf. Lukianov, "Zapis' besed s. E. E. Ukhtomskim," "Iz razgovora 30-go maya 1920 g.," 2–3:393–402. The first edition of Countess Elisaveta Grigor'evna Volkonskaya's book on the Church, *O tserkvi*, was published in Berlin, in 1888.

166. See www.jewishvirtuallibrary.org/jsource/judaica/ejud_0002_0015 _0_14929.html; and E. S. Sonina, "Vzlety i padeniya peterburgskogo isdatelya: O. K. Notovich i gazeta 'Novosti,'" *Izvestiya (Ural'skogo Gosudarstvennogo Universiteta)* 4.68 (2009), 85–94; http://proceedings.usu.ru/?base=mag/0068 %2803_$04-2009&xsln=showArticle.xslt&id=a13&doc=../content.jsp. For Belkin's coverage of Notovich, see *"Gäste,"* 117–19; on Solovyov's relationship with Getz and the gestation of the Protest, see 120–27.

167. See Pt. III, ch. 10, for this and preceding quotes from the article.

168. Ernest Renan, *Vie de Jésus*, 5th ed. (Paris: Michel Lévy Frères, 1863); David Friedrich Strauss, *Das leben Jesu, kritisch bearbeitet* (Tübingen: C. F. Auslander, 1835–36).

169. For commentary on how Solovyov's critique of Danilevsky developed into polemics with Strakhov, see S. Solovyov, *Zhizn'*, 270–72.

170. See the commentary by the literary critic and religious philosopher Dmitry Merezhkovsky (1865–1941) on the history of Solovyov's painful relationship with Filippov and the degree to which Solovyov stooped to write this letter, given that three years prior, in 1886, Solovyov filed away the "rarity" of having his term *bogochelovek* (Godman) removed by the censor (he knew that Filippov was ultimately responsible) from the second edition of his *Dogmatic Development of the Church* (*Letters*, 2:142). See also Merezhkovsky, *Bol'naya Rossiya*, part 3 of the essay "Zemlya vo rtu" (Earth in the Mouth), www .e-reading.ws/chapter.php/97223/40/Merezhkovskiii_-_Bol%27naya _Rossiya .html.

171. This is the context in which S. Solovyov, *Zhizn'*, 266, cites the first stanza of the poem. The source for the poem and epigram is *Letters*, 4:28.

172. For Belkin's coverage of the Protest, see *"Gäste,"* 127–35.

173. For the letters and details about their sources, see Pt. III, ch. 11, and n. 395 there.

174. For corroboration of Tolstoy's indifference to the Jewish problem, see the account of his correspondence with Ilya Ginzburg reported in Musya Glants, *Where Is My Home? The Art and Life of the Russian-Jewish Sculptor Mark Antokolsky, 1843–1902* (Plymouth, MA: Lexington Books, 2010), 330–31.

175. Professors Gerie, Vinogradov, Timiryazev, Yanzhul, A. N. Veselovsky, V. A. Gol'tsev, Bezobrazov, F. Fortunatov, S. Fortunatov, V. S. Solovyov, Vsev. Miller, A. I. Chuprov, N. N. Milyukov, Sizov, Gambarov, Shhepkin, G. A. Dzhanshiev, P. P. Minilov, S. A. Muromtsev, Professor Stoletov, Count Komarovsky, and Professor Grot. The memoir first appeared in *Russkie vedomosti* 20 (1909) and was reprinted in Korolenko's *Collected Works* (1914), 9:257–60. For further details, see Pt. III, ch. 13, n. 418.

176. Occasional Correspondent (E. J. Dillon), "The Jews in Russia," *The (London) Times*, 33191 (Wednesday, Dec. 10, 1890): 3; col. B. For the text, see Pt. III, ch. 12.

177. See the penultimate paragraph in Korolenko's memoir in Pt. III, ch. 13. Ilovajsky's correct initials are "D. I."

178. Cf. Konstantin Petrovich Pobedonostsev, *Konstantin P. Pobedonostsev i ego korrespondenty: Pis'ma i zapiski*, foreword M. P. Pokrovsky, 2 vols. (Moscow: Gosizdat, 1923), 2:938. See also Pobedonostsev's letter to

Alexander III of June 22, 1891 (letter #87) warning him of the danger that Tolstoy posed to the social and religious order of Russia and describing Solovyov as a crazed self-proclaimed prophet and, on account of his public lectures, a dangerous demagogue: ibid., available at www.krotov.info/acts/19/1880/pobed.html#_Toc464028741.

179. See Belkin's coverage of work on *A Word to the Accused, "Gäste,"* 136–41.

180. On Getz's interpretation of the "father of lies," see Pt. III, n. 341. On Ignatiev's contribution to Russian-Jewish tensions and his reputation as "father of lies," see Pt I., ch. 4, §8.5 and n. 155.

181. See "Pogromy," Elektronnaya evrejskaya èntsiklopediya, www.eleven.co.il/article/13251; Asya Pereltsvaig, "Birobidzhan: Frustrated Dreams of a Jewish Homeland," http://geocurrents.info/place/russia-ukraine-and-caucasus/siberia/birobidzhan-frustrated-dreams-of-a-jewish-homeland; Alexander Rashin, *Why Didn't Stalin Murder All the Jews? The 50th Anniversary of the Doctor's Plot and Stalin's Death* (New York: Liberty, 2003); Jonathan Brent and Vladimir Naumov, *Stalin's Last Crime: The Plot against the Jewish Doctors, 1948–1953* (New York: HarperCollins, 2003); and Antonella Salomoni, "State-Sponsored Anti-Semitism in Postwar USSR: Studies and Research Perspectives," *Questions in Contemporary Jewish History* 1 (Apr. 2010), www.quest-cdecjournal.it/focus.php?id=212. Note that Salomoni's relegation to mythical status of the memory that Stalin was preparing a final solution to the Jewish problem follows the revisionist position of Kostyrchenko. The latter is charged with supporting the rehabilitation of Stalin's reputation under Putin by Fedor Lyass, "O Statie Gennadiya Kostyrchenko, 'Deportatsiya-Mistifikatsiya,' opublikovannoj v zhurnale, 'Lechaim,'" *Zametki po evrejskoj istorii* 22 (Nov. 2002), http://berkovich-zametki.com/Nomer22/Lyass1.htm.

182. Unless indicated otherwise, see Pt. III, ch. 9, for all Getz letters referred to in this chapter.

183. Cf. Belkin, *"Gäste,"* 142–44.

184. See Pt. III, nn. 272, 365, 371.

185. On Bakst, see *Encyclopedic Dictionary,* 1891, 1a: 756; Yu. G., "Bakst, Nikolai Ignatievich (Isaakovich)," *Evrejskaya èntsiklopediya* of Brokhaus and Efron. ru.wikisource.org/wiki/ЕЭБЕ/Бакст,_Николай_Игнатьевич; Dudakov, *Ètyudy lyubvi i nenavisti.* http://lib.rus.ec/b/136492/read.

186. The commision was composed of Baron Horace Gintsburg (senior member), Samuel Poliakov (chair), A. I. Zak (treasurer), N. I. Bakst, A. B. Bank, A. M. Varshavsky, Y. M. Halpern, Rabbi A. N. Drabkin, I. I. Kaufman, L. M. Rosenthal, and M. P. Friedland. I. Trotsky, *Kniga o russkom evrejstve:*

Ot 1860-kh godov do revolyutsii 1917g. (Jerusalem: Gesharim, 2002), http://old.ort.spb.ru/history/ort_statia.htm.

187. Trotsky, *Kniga o russkom evrejstve.*

188. Mochulsky, *Vladimir Solovyov*, 196, citing the memoirs of Ya. N. Kolubovksy, "Iz literaturnykh vospominanij," *Istoricheskij vestnik* 4 (Apr. 1914): 134–49.

189. Mikhail Emmanuilovich Posnov, "Mitropolit Antony, kak pravoslavnyj bogoslov-dogmatist," *Tserkovnye vedomosti (Archiereevskogo sinoda)* 11–12 (1930): 7.

190. Mochulsky, *Vladimir Solovyov*, 196.

191. Pobedonostsev, *Pobedonostsev i ego korrespondenty*, 969–70.

192. S. Solovyov, *Zhizn'*, 278–79, citing letter #42 (*Letters*, 4:124–25) to his brother Mikhail.

193. Mochulsky, *Vladimir Solovyov*, ch. 12.

194. Joseph Krauskopf, "'Eye for an Eye' or 'Turning the Other Cheek,'" in *A Sunday Lecture before the Reform Congregation Keneseth Israel*, Ser. VII, no. 29 (Philadelphia: S. W. Goodman, 1894).

195. For Solovyov's letter of "October–November 1, 1894," see Pavel Sergeevich Popov, ed., "Perepiska L. Tolstogo s V. S. Solovyovym" (L. Tolstoy's Correspondence with V. S. Solovyov), in *L. N. Tolstoy. II*, ed. Vladimir V. Zhdanov, Literaturnoe nasledstvo (Literary Inheritance), vols. 37–38 (Moscow: Akademiya Nauk, 1939), 274–76.

196. For these letters of July 4 and July 28–Aug. 2, 1894, see Pt. III, ch. 11, #5, #6.

197. For Obolensky's memoir on Tolstoy's reaction, see Aleksei D. Obolensky, "Dve vstrechi s L. N. Tolstym," in L. N. Tolstoy, *Pamyatniki tvorchestva i zhizni*, ed. Vyacheslav Izmail Sreznevsky (St. Petersburg: Ogni, 1923), 3:34–35, cited in P. V. Popov, "Perepiska L. Tolstogo s V. S. Solovyovym," 274 n. 1. http://feb-web.ru/feb/litnas/texts/l37/t37-2742.htm.

198. Thanks to Yakov Krotov for this interpretation of the phrase.

199. On Gorky, see Maxim Gorky, "N. S. Leskov," in N. S. Leskov, *Izbrannye sochineniya v 3 tomakh* (N. S. Leskov: Selected Works in 3 Volumes), ed. Aleksandr Amfiteatrov (St. Petersburg: I Grzhebin, 1923), 1:5–13. On Tolstoy, see Anatoly Faresov, "Umstvennye perelomy v deyatel'nosti N. S. Leskova" (Intellectual Fractures in the Oeuvre of N. S. Leskov) *Istoricheskij vestnik* 3 (1916): 786. Both works are cited in Andrei N. Leskov, *Zhizn' Nikolaya Leskova po ego lichnym, semejnym i nesemeynym zapisyam i pamyatyam v dvukh tomakh* (The Life of Nikolai Leskov According to His Personal, Familial, and Extrafamilial Writings and Recollections in Two Volumes) (Moscow: Khudozhestvennaya literatura, 1984), 1:33, 421 n. 6; 255, 463 n. 83.

200. Nikolai Leskov, *Evrei v Rossii: Neskol'ko zamechanij po evrejskomu voprosu* (1883), ed. Valerly G. Kadzhaya (Moscow: Mosty Kultury, 2003). For the text, see www.vehi.net/asion/leskov/html. On the impact of Leskov's work on the Pahlen Commission, on the explanation of Russian-Jewish relations, and on the contrast between it and Solzhenitsyn's work, see Oleg Schuster, "Kak Nikolai Leskov o evreyakh pisal," *Secret*, June 6, 2011, available at www.jewish.ru/history/press/2011/12/news994302543.php. On Solovyov's letter to Leskov, see Dudakov, *Paradoksy*, 163–64 and n. 153. On Solovyov's relationships with Leskov, see Belkin, *"Gäste,"* 70–72.

201. Halpérin, "Vladimir Soloviev Listens to Israel," 200; Lukianov, "Zapis' besed s. A. F. Koni" (8-go oktyabrya 1914), in *Materialy k biografii Vl. S. Solovyova*. For Belkin's coverage of their relationship, see *"Gäste,"* 150–54.

202. E. Trubetskoy, *Mirosozertsanie*, 294–96, cited by Hagemeister, "Vladimir Solov'ëv and Sergej Nilus," 294.

203. Letter to Tavernier (July 21, 1888), in *Letters*, 4:184; letter to Velichko (June 3, 1897), in *Letters*, 1:232. See also Hagemeister, "Vladimir Solov'ëv and Sergej Nilus," 290 n. 14.

204. The first two chapters were penned in 1899, and the foreword was completed on July 31, 1900. Cf. S. Solovyov, *Zhizn'*, 361–62, 365, 369. Cf. also Solovyov's letter to Rozanov, *Letters*, 4:143; and Mochulsky, *Vladimir Solovyov*, 254, 260.

205. Cf. Mochulsky, *Vladimir Solovyov*, ch. 17 (245–61); on the dating of the writing of the foreword to 1900, see 250.

206. Solovyov, *Sobranie sochinenij, SSVSS*[10], 219.

207. Sliosberg, *Baron Horace de Gunzburg*, 57, cited by Halpérin, "Vladimir Soloviev Listens to Israel," 200 n. 5. For citations and discussion of Solovyov's friendship with Sliosberg and the reactions of some Jews, e.g., Ilya Ginzburg, to Solovyov's death, and photos of the deceased Solovyov at his wake, see Belkin, *"Gäste,"* 16–18.

PART III

Primary Texts

CHAPTER 1

"Jewry and the Christian Question" (1884)

In that day Israel will be the third with Egypt and Assyria, a
blessing to the whole earth, by which the Lord Sabaoth will
bless it, saying, "Blessed be my people: Egypt, and the work
of my hands: Assyria, and my inheritance Israel."

Isaiah 19:24, 25

The mutual relations between Judaism and Christianity, in the course
of their centuries-long coexistence, are characterized by one remarkable circumstance.[1] The Jews have always and everywhere regarded
and treated Christians in accordance with the precepts of their own *religion*, in conformity to their own *faith*, and in accord with their own
law. The Jews have always treated us in a Jewish way. We Christians,
however, have still not learned to treat Judaism in a Christian way. In
dealing with us, they have never broken their religious law, but we,
on the other hand, in dealing with them, have constantly broken, and
continue to break, the precepts of the Christian religion. If the Jewish law is flawed, then their stubborn adherence to this flawed law, is
of course, regrettable. But if it is bad to be faithful to a flawed law, it
is much worse to be unfaithful to a good law, to a commandment that
is unconditionally perfect. Now such a commandment we have in the
Gospel.[2] It is a perfect commandment, but is, as such, relatively difficult. But special aids have been revealed to us: the assistance of grace,
which does not destroy the law but gives us the strength to fulfill it.[3]

277

Consequently, we are without excuse[4] if we first reject this grace and then refuse to fulfill the Gospel precept, under the pretext that it is too difficult. The issue, in fact, is not whether the Gospel precept is difficult or not but whether it can be fulfilled at all. But if it can not be fulfilled, why would it have been given? On this score, those Jews would be justified who criticize Christianity for introducing into the world fantastic principles and ideas incapable of any practical application. But if the Gospel precept can be fulfilled, if we are capable of treating everyone, including the Jews, in a Christian manner, we should be roundly condemned whenever we fail to do so.

Instead of sincerely repenting of this failure, however, we seek a scapegoat for our guilt. It's not we who are to blame, it's the Middle Ages, with all their fanaticism, or the Catholic Church. But pogroms against the Jews have now commenced in our own days and in countries that are not Catholic. And the blame this time falls not upon us but upon the victims themselves.[5] The Jews who dwell in our midst treat us in a Jewish way; we, clearly, must treat them in a *pagan* manner. They do not want to love us; we, clearly, must hate them. They stand for segregation, eschew assimilation, repudiate recognition of mutual solidarity with us, and generally strive to exploit our weaknesses; we, clearly, must exterminate them.

It is true that neither the persecution of the Jews nor the overt justification of such persecution constitute a *general* trend in Europe today. On the contrary, and in general, Judaism has not only taken advantage of the tolerant atmosphere existing in the most progressive nations, but has even succeeded in securing a dominant status among them. The fact that England is governed by the Jew Disraeli does not constitute a unique case, for in other countries as well, the financial sectors and considerable portions of the periodical press are managed by Jews, directly or indirectly. But this Jewish dominance, rather than undermining, actually confirms my proposition that the Christian world has never treated the Jews in a Christian manner. Could it be that the present tolerance, concession to, and even subservience to Jews derives from Christian conviction and feeling? Quite the contrary: all this flows not from the largesse of our religious views but from their total *absence,* from a complete indifference to matters of faith. It is not a Christian Europe that tolerates Jews but a faithless Europe, a Europe deprived of its living roots, a decaying Europe. Jews thrive not via our moral strength but via our moral or rather amoral weakness.

People talk of the Jewish question, but essentially the entire matter boils down to one fact, evoking a question not about Jewry but about Christendom. This fact can be expressed and explained briefly. What modern Europe is principally interested in is money; as the Jews are masters of monetary affairs, they are naturally sovereign in modern Europe. And so it is that after centuries of antagonism, Christendom and Judaism have finally found reconciliation through one common interest, in one common passion for money. But here too a vital difference emerges between them, to the credit of Judaism, but to the shame of pseudo Christian Europe, the difference thanks to which money liberates and magnifies the Jews but binds and debases us. The point is that Jews are not bound to money solely on account of its material benefits but because they regard money as the main weapon for securing the triumph and glory of Israel, that is, for the triumph, in their understanding, of God's cause on earth. For besides a passion for money, Jews have another distinction: a firm mutual unity in the name of a common faith and a common law. Only thanks to this does money benefit them, for when wealth and greatness come to this or that Jew, it enriches and exalts all of Judaism, the whole house of Israel. In the meantime, Enlightenment Europe espouses money not as a means to attaining some high *common* goal but solely for the sake of those material blessings which money brings to each of its *separate* owners. And so we can see that Enlightenment Europe *serves* money, while Judaism *subordinates to itself* both money and money-serving Europe. Consequently, progressive European attitudes to Judaism have turned into a parody, as it were, of the prophetic biblical image: ten heathens grasp the hem of one Jew and beg him to lead them into the Temple,[6] not however of YHWH, but of Mammon; for they have as little interest in YHWH as in Christ.

Consequently, Enlightenment Europe has neither any grounds for reproaching the darkness of the Middle Ages, with their religious fanaticism, nor for boasting of its own tolerance.[7] Religious tolerance is commendable in believers when it derives from the fullness of faith and the consciousness of a supreme moral strength. But in unbelievers, religious tolerance only expresses their unbelief. If Christianity, Judaism, or idolatry are all one to me, how could I contrive to be intolerant in matters of faith, and what would be so virtuous about my tolerance? However remote religious fanaticism might be from Christian perfection, it remains a moral force, albeit undeveloped and coarse, and, being wild, prone to abuse. It remains, in any case, a positive quantity, while religious indifferentism[8] reflects the absence of heartfelt warmth and spirit, registering, as it were, the moral freezing point, the coldness of spiritual death. And when societal indifference to the highest ideals attends extreme partiality for the basest interests and material benefits, it is clear that we are facing a social *degradation*.

And so, in dealing with Judaism, Christendom has hitherto discovered *within itself* either an irrational jealousy[9] or a decrepit and impotent indifferentism. Both of these attitudes are alien to the authentic Christian spirit and have no place at the summit of the Christian ideal. But as early as the thirteenth century, we may witness, through the singular efforts of leading Christian activists and thinkers, the existence of a different, truly Christian attitude to Judaism.[10] And albeit these efforts have not yet borne any actual results, they still constitute the beginning of that true resolution of the Jewish question of which Paul the apostle prophesied in his Letter to the Romans (ch. 11).

Acknowledging only a religious resolution of the "Jewish question," and believing in the coming unification of the house of Israel with Orthodox and Catholic Christianity on a mutual, theocratic base, I had the opportunity to express my conviction on this score from the podium.[11] I now venture to present my views on Judaism in more detail and give them greater publicity. I am encouraged to do so, by the way, by the authoritative voice of one of our archbishops, since I can follow it without fear of being led astray by some temptation.

In April of this year, the Reverend Nikanor, bishop of Kherson and Odessa (and the author of a notable and still undervalued work on religious philosophy), issued in Odessa an inspired and truly Christian pronouncement affirming the most intimate kinship between the religions of the Old and New Covenants. The main idea of this splendid pronouncement[12] is that Judaism and Christianity are to be united, not on the basis of indifferentism, nor on the basis of sundry abstract principles, but on the basis of their natural and spiritual kinship and positive religious interests. Without renouncing and negating Christianity, we must unite with Jews in the name of, and on account of that which is vital to, Christianity, while Jews must unite with us, without negating Judaism, in the name of, and on account of, that which is vital to true Judaism. We are separated from the Jews because we are *incomplete as Christians*, while they are separated from us because they are *incomplete as Jews*. For the completion of Christianity requires it to embrace even Judaism, while the completion of Judaism is Christianity.

My thoughts on Judaism, which follow, directly supplement those uttered by the reverend Nikanor. His words appear to me to be the best encouragement and prompt for expounding these thoughts in print.

The fortunes of the Jewish people, in my view, are chiefly connected with three facts of its history. The first fact is that Christ, by his mother, was a Jew, and that Christianity emerged from Judaism. The second fact is that a large part of the Jewish people rejected Christ and assumed a decidedly hostile attitude in relation to Christianity. The third fact is that the chief mass of the Jewish people and the religious core of contemporary Judaism are found not in western Europe but in two Slavic countries: Russia and Poland. The first of these facts: Christ's incarnation in Judea, defines Israel's *past*, its original designation as God's chosen people. The second fact: the nonrecognition of Christ by the Jews and their rejection of Christianity, defines Judaism's *present* lot in the world, its temporary alienation. Finally, the third fact: Israel's settling in Slavic lands, amid peoples who have not yet spoken their word to the world, presages the *future* destinies[13] of Judaism, the final reestablishment of its religious significance. The former Judaism lived by faith and hope in the *promise* of Godmanhood;[14] present Judaism lives by protest and hostility to its unrecognized Messiah, the God-man,[15] the *first fruits* of Godmanhood on earth;[16] the Judaism to come will live a full life when it will find and recognize in renewed Christianity the image of *perfect* Godmanhood.

This hope possesses the firmest of foundations in the word of God. YHWH predestined Israel for election, made a covenant with him, and gave him promises. "YHWH is not a man so as to deceive, nor a son of man so as to repent of His promises."[17] A part of the people of Israel rejected the Messiah on his first coming and suffers heavily for this, but only temporarily, for the word of God cannot be broken,[18] and this word of the Old Testament is decisively confirmed in the New by the mouth of the Apostle to the Gentiles who clearly and indisputably proclaims: *all Israel will be saved.*[19]

Jews, demanding the execution of Christ, cried: "His blood be upon us and upon our children."[20] But this blood is *the blood of redemption.*[21] And the cry of human malice is surely incapable of drowning out the word of divine forgiveness: "Father, forgive them, for they do not know what they do."[22] The bloodthirsty crowd which gathered at Golgotha consisted of Jews, but Jews also comprised the three thousand, and later the five thousand, who, hearing the apostle Peter's preaching, were baptized and formed the first and foundational Christian Church. Annas and Caiphas were Jews, but so were Joseph and Nicodemus. To one and the same people belong both Judas, who handed Christ over to crucifixion, and Peter and Andrew, who were themselves crucified for Christ. Thomas who disbelieved in the resurrection was a Jew and a Jew Thomas remained on coming to believe in the Resurrected one, declaring before Him: "My Lord and My God."[23] Saul, the cruelest persecutor of the Christians, was a Jew, and a Jew of Jews he remained as Paul, persecuted for Christianity, *"the one who worked harder than all"* for Him.[24] And what is greater and most important of all is that He Himself, betrayed and killed by the Jews, the God-man Christ, He Himself, was, by his flesh and human soul, the purest Jew.

In view of this striking fact, is it not strange that we, *in the name of Christ*, should condemn all of Judaism, to which Christ himself indissolubly belongs? Is this not strange especially on the part of those among us who, while never having renounced Christ directly, have, in any case, nothing by which to show our ties to Him?

If Christ is not God, then the guilt of the Jews is not greater than that of the Greeks who killed Socrates. If, though, we acknowledge

Christ as God, then we must also acknowledge the Jews to be a *God-bearing* people. Blame for Jesus's death belongs not only to the Jews but also to the Romans, but His birth belongs only to God and to Israel.[25] The Jews, people say, are Christianity's inveterate enemies; but the leaders of the anti-Christian movement of the past few centuries are not Semites but cradle Christians of the Arian race. The rejection of Christianity and the struggle against it by some thinkers of Jewish origin possess a more honest and religious character than the rejection and struggle against it by writers who have abandoned the Christian sphere. Better Spinoza than Voltaire; better Joseph Salvador than Mr. Ernest Renan.

To despise Judaism is madness. To argue with Jews is pointless. It is better to understand Judaism, even if this is more difficult. It is difficult to understand Judaism because those three great facts, with which its fates are linked, do not constitute anything simple, natural, and intrinsically understandable. They require a special and a complex explanation. These three facts are at the same time three questions, or three riddles, in need of a solution. They are

1) Why was Christ a Jew? Why was the cornerstone of the universal church taken from the house of Israel?

2) Why did a large portion of Israel not recognize its Messiah? Why did the church of the Old Testament not dissolve in the church of the New Testament? Why do most Jews prefer living without any temple to entering a Christian temple?

3) Why, finally, and for the sake of what have the more powerful (religiously speaking) segments of Jewry settled in Russia and Poland, on the boundary of the Greco-Slavic and Latino-Slavic worlds?

Let the significance of this last fact be denied or minimized. And, as touching the second point, let the haters of Jews deem it natural that such an unworthy and unscrupulous a people should have rejected and killed Christ. But then let them explain why Christ belonged especially to this people. Conversely, if one readily grasps the reasons for the first fact, that Christ belongs to the people of Israel because it was originally chosen and foreordained for this purpose, then how, in this case, is one to explain that this chosen people became unworthy of election *precisely to that task for which* it was chosen? In this or that instance, the matter nonetheless presents itself as puzzling and demands an explanation. Let us begin with the first fact and the first question.

I. WHY WAS JUDAISM PREDESTINED TO GIVE BIRTH TO THE GOD-MAN MESSIAH OR CHRIST?

Since election derives from God, it is a work of unconditional freedom.[26] But divine freedom in no wise resembles human whim or partiality. True freedom does not exclude reason, and in keeping with reason, this election or choice, being God's *relationship* to a familiar object, is determined not only by the character of the chooser but also by the quality of the one chosen. The national character of the Jews must contain the *conditions* of their election. In the course of four thousand years, this character has sufficiently defined itself, and it is not difficult to find and indicate its distinctive features. But this is insufficient: it is also necessary to understand their integral unity and mutual bonds. No one is going to deny that the national character of the Jews possesses wholeness and inner unity. However, we also find in it three main peculiarities which, seemingly, are not just difficult to harmonize, but directly contradict each other.

Jews, first of all, are distinguished by a deep religiosity, and by faithfulness to their God to the point of total self-sacrifice. It is a people of the law and of the prophets, of martyrs and apostles, "who through faith subdued kingdoms, wrought righteousness, and obtained promises" (Heb. 11:33).

Second, Jews are distinguished by a supremely developed sense of self, self-consciousness, and personal initiative. As all Israel, so every family in it and every member of this family, to the depths of their soul and marrow, are permeated by a feeling and consciousness of their national, familial, and personal *I*, and seek in every possible way to express this sense of self and self-consciousness, persistently and indefatigably working for themselves, for their family, and for all Israel.

The third and final feature distinguishing the Jews is their radical materialism (in the broad sense of this term). The sensual nature of the Jewish *worldview* is symbolically expressed even in their letters (in the limitation of the alphabet to consonants, the body of words, while either completely dropping the vowels, the spirit of words, or demarcating them by mere points and small lines). As for the worldly materialism of the Jews, that is, the prevalence of utilitarian and mercenary considerations in their activity, ranging from their dealings in Egyptian wares to playing the contemporary European stock markets, this, presumably, needs no elaboration.

Thus, the character of this remarkable people reveals with equal force: the strength of the divine principle in the religion of Israel, the strength of human self-assertion in national, familial, and personal Jewish life, and, finally, the strength of the material element that colors all their thoughts and actions. But how do these mutually contending elements coexist in one and the same living individuality? What unites the religious idea of Israel with Judaism's human capacity for personal initiative and both with *yid*[27] materialism? It would seem that complete fidelity to the one God must either abolish or at least weaken both the energy of the human *I* and the attachment to material goods. Thus we see, for example, how in Indian Brahmanism the predominant sense of divine unity brought religious people to completely negate both human individuality and material nature. In its own turn, the dominant development of the human principle, humanism, in this or that form, must, it would seem, both squeeze out the transcendent power of religion and raise the human spirit above coarse materialism, as we may witness in the best representatives of ancient Greece, Rome, and Renaissance Europe.[28]

It is equally clear that the preponderance of materialistic conceptions and strivings is incompatible with either religious or humanitarian ideals. In Judaism, however, all this coexists without any harm to the integrity of ethnic character. In order to find the key to the solution of this riddle, it is not necessary to ponder abstractly on the principles of religion, idealism, or materialism *in general* but to examine more attentively the special characteristics of *Jewish* religion, of *Jewish* humanism, and of *Jewish* materialism.

Believing in the unity of God, the Jew never posited that mankind's religious goal is to fuse with the deity and disappear in His all-embracing unity. And indeed he did not acknowledge God to have such a negating and abstract all-embracing unity or indifference. Regardless of certain mystical conceptions of the latest Kabbalists,[29] regardless of the pantheistic philosophy of the Jew Spinoza, generally speaking, Judaism always saw in God, not the infinite emptiness of the universal substratum, but the infinite fullness of being, having life in itself and giving life to another. Being free from all external limitations and determinations but not dissolving in general indifference, the God Who Is[30] defines Himself and manifests Himself as a complete personality, an absolute *I*. Religion, accordingly, must also involve not the destruction of man in universal divinity but a personal cooperation between the divine and the human *I*. It is precisely because the Jewish people was capable of *such* an understanding of God and religion that it could become God's chosen people.

The God Who Is made Israel His own people because Israel too made the God Who Is its own God. The forefather Abraham, dwelling amid pagans, was, even before receiving a direct revelation of the true God, dissatisfied and wearied by idolatrous cults, so alluring to all people. The worship of nature's elemental and demonic powers repelled the Jewish soul. The progenitor of Israel could not believe in what was lower than man and sought for a personal and a moral God in whom it would not be humiliating for man to believe, and this God came, and called him, and gave promises to his seed: "By faith Abraham obeyed when he was called to go out to a place which he was to receive as an inheritance; and he went out, not knowing where he was to go" (Heb. 11:8).[31] That which led Abraham out of the land of the Chaldees also led Moses out of Egypt. Regardless of all the temptations of Egyptian theosophy and theurgy, "being great by his faith,[32] Moses refused to be called the son of Pharaoh's daughter . . . and by faith he left Egypt, not being afraid of the anger of the king" (Heb. 11:24–27).

Having separated themselves from paganism and having surpassed, by their faith, Chaldean magic and Egyptian wisdom, the progenitors of the race and the leaders of the Jews became worthy of divine election. God chose them, revealed Himself to them, and forged a pact with them. The pact or covenant between God and Israel constitutes the core of the Jewish religion. It is a unique phenomenon in world history since in no other people did religion assume this form of union or covenant between God and man—two entities, unequal in power, yet morally of one kin.[33]

This high conception of man in no way impairs the greatness of God, but on the contrary, allows Him to reveal Himself in all His power. In man's independent moral existence, God obtains for Himself a noble object for action, for otherwise He would have *nothing upon which* to act. If man did not have a free personality, how could God reveal His own *personal* being in the world? As far as the self-existent and self-determining God, ruler of the world, surpasses the impersonal nature of cosmic phenomena, thus far the holy religion of the Jews surpasses all the naturalistic and pantheistic religions of the ancient world. In these religions neither God nor man preserved any independence: for they enslaved man to unknown and alien laws, and in the end (in the artistic mythology of the Greeks) made the Deity the plaything of human fantasy. In the Jewish religion, on the contrary, from the very beginning, both sides, the divine and the human, are equally preserved. Our religion begins with a *personal relationship* between God and man in the ancient covenants of Abraham and Moses, and it is confirmed by the most concrete *personal unification* between God and man in the new covenant of Jesus Christ, in whom both natures exist inseparably but distinctly. These two covenants are not two separate religions but only two stages of one and the same *religion of Godmanhood* or, to speak in the language of the German school, two moments of one and the same process of Godmanhood. This one true Hebrew-Christian religion of Godmanhood follows a straight and royal road between the two extreme errors of paganism in which the deity either swallows up mankind (as in India) or becomes man's shadow (as in Greece and Rome).

The true God who chose Israel and was chosen by Israel is a strong God, a self-subsisting God, and a holy God. Being strong, God chooses for Himself a strong person who can struggle with Him; as self-subsisting, God reveals himself only to a self-conscious personality; as holy, God unites Himself only with a person who seeks holiness and is capable of a practical moral *podvig*.[34] Human weakness seeks divine strength, but only a strong person possesses such weakness, for a naturally weak person is incapable of strong religiosity. Likewise, a person with no character, identity, or any developed self-consciousness could hardly understand aright the truth of God's self-subsistent being.

Finally, a person whose freedom to shape himself by moral choices is paralyzed, who is incapable of initiating action, performing a *podvig*, and attaining holiness—for such a person, God's holiness will always remain somewhat external and alien—he will never become a "friend of God."[35] From this it is clear that the true religion which we find in the Jewish people demands rather than excludes the development of a free human personality, along with self-consciousness, self-knowledge, and personal initiative. Israel was great in faith, but to have great faith, one requires great inner spiritual strengths. It is specifically faith that best expresses the energy of man's free spirit. There is a general prejudice that faith suppresses the freedom of the human spirit and that positive knowledge expands it. But, in fact, it is the other way around. By faith, the human spirit transcends the frontiers of the given, apparent reality and affirms the existence of objects which *do not compel* man's recognition—he recognizes them freely. Faith is the *podvig* of the spirit which evidences things unseen.[36] The believer does not passively await the effects of external objects but goes out bravely to meet them. He does not slavishly follow phenomena but anticipates them; he is free and acts independently. As a free *podvig* of the spirit, faith possesses moral dignity and merit: "blessed are those who have not seen and yet believe."[37] The contrary is the case with empirical cognition where our spirit passively and slavishly follows external facts. Here there is no *podvig*, no moral merit. It stands to reason that this opposition between faith and knowledge is not unconditional, for the believer somehow always knows the object of his faith, while positive knowledge always relies on faith concerning matters that cannot be empirically proven, namely, the objective reality of the physical world, the constancy and universality of the laws of nature, the truthfulness of our cognitive methods of research, and so on. Nevertheless, one cannot contest that the realm of faith is predominantly characterized by spiritual activity and freedom, while passivity and dependence characterize the realm of empirical knowledge. In order to recognize and know the externally given fact, no human spiritual independence and energy is required, but such independence and energy are required to believe in that which has not yet crossed over into visible fact.[38] The apparent and the real both *insist* on recognition; but the power of the spirit lies in its capacity to guess the future, and to recognize and proclaim the mysterious and the holy. That is why the highest form of human spiritual energy reveals itself in the Israelite prophets, not as a detriment to religious faith, but as its mainstay.[39]

This union between a most profound faith in God and a most lofty concentration of human spiritual energy was also preserved in late Judaism. How strikingly it is expressed, for example, in the concluding prayer of the Paschal prayer for the coming of the Messiah:

> Almighty God, now, soon and speedily build your temple; speedily, in our days, as soon as possible, now build, now build, now build, now soon build your Temple.
> Merciful God, great God, meek God, most high God, blessed God, sweetest God, immeasurable God, God of Israel, soon build your Temple, speedily, speedily in our days, now build, now build, now build, now build, now speedily build your Temple!
> Powerful God, living God, mighty God, glorious God, merciful God, eternal God, fearsome God, splendid God, reigning God, rich God, wonderful God, faithful God, now, without delay, rebuild your Temple, speedily, speedily, in our days, speedily without delay, now build, now build, now build, now build, now speedily build your Temple.[40]

In this characteristic prayer, in addition to the sincere faith in Israel's God, and the persistency of the human will, directed in petition to Him, one may note another distinctive feature: the supplicants do not wish their God to remain in the transcendent sphere. Seeing in Him the ideal of all perfection, they invariably demand that this ideal should become incarnate on earth, so that the Deity should give itself an external visible expression, *build Itself a Temple,* a material habitation for Its power and glory, and do so *now and as speedily as possible.* In this impatient striving to incarnate the divine on earth we may identify the guiding thread for understanding both Jewish materialism and the Israelite people's current position.

Speaking of materialism, three forms of it should be distinguished: the practical, the scientific-philosophical, and the religious. The first form of materialism depends directly upon the dominance exerted over the people in question by the lower aspects of their human nature, upon the prevalence of animal impulses over reason, and of sensual interests over spiritual ones. In order to justify in himself such a predominance of lower nature, the practical materialist begins to deny the very existence of all that does not fit into this lower natural realm, all that cannot be seen or sensed, weighed or measured. On raising this denial to a general principle, practical materialism passes into the theoretical or scientific-philosophical form. The latter, by means of rational analysis, reduces all that exists to elementary facts of the material order, systematically denying all truths of the divine and spiritual order. As practical materialism always existed among morally coarse people, so theoretical materialism persists through the whole history of philosophy, adopting alternate aspects, but usually espousing atomism in metaphysics, sensualism as a theory of knowledge, and, for ethics, appealing to the doctrine of pleasure as the highest good (hedonism), all the while embracing determinism and asserting thereby the unfree character of all our actions.

Neither of these forms of materialism belongs in any special way to Judaism. Practical materialism in its pure form is rather rarely found among real Jews; as has already been noted, even their universal love of silver is illuminated by a higher goal: the enrichment and glorification of all Israel. In the same way, scientific-philosophical materialism sprang up not out of Semitic but out of Greco-Roman soil, and then out of Romano-Germanic culture; only through the structures of this culture can the Jews assimilate to themselves a materialistic philosophy so completely alien to their own national spirit. But at least this national spirit had been characterized from antiquity by a third, distinct form of materialism which differs radically from the first two and which I, for brevity's sake, designate by the somewhat inexact name of *religious* materialism.

The Jews, recognizing full well, in faithfulness to their religion, the spirituality of the Deity and the divine nature of the human spirit, neither knew how nor wished to separate these two high principles from their material expression, from their embodied form and veil, and from their radical and final realization. For every idea and every ideal, the Jew demands a visible and a palpable incarnation, as well as beneficial results. The Jew does not wish to recognize an ideal which is incapable of subduing reality and incarnating itself in it. The Jew is able and ready to recognize the highest spiritual truth but only if he can see and feel its real activity. He believes in the invisible, since all faith is faith in the invisible, but he desires this invisible to become visible, and to manifest its power. He believes in spirit but only in spirit which permeates all that is material, and which uses matter as its veil and arms.

By not separating spirit from its material expression, Jewish thought also does not separate matter from its spiritual and divine origin. Thus, it never recognized "matter in itself," or gave significance to material being *as such*. The Jews never served or worshipped matter. On the other hand, being unfamiliar with abstract spiritualism, the Jews could not be indifferent to matter or regard it as alien, let alone treat it with the enmity which Eastern dualism reserves for it. In material nature, they saw neither the devil nor the deity but simply the *yet-to-be-completed dwelling for the God-human spirit*. And thus, while practical and theoretical materialism submit to physical fact as if it were law, and whereas the dualist revolts from matter, deeming it evil, the religious materialism of the Jews enjoins them to pay the greatest attention to material nature, not in order to serve her,[41] but that in her and through her they may serve the Highest God. Thus they were driven to separate in material nature the pure from the impure and the holy from the sinful, so as to make her into a worthy temple for the Most High. The idea of a *holy corporeality* and the concern given to its realization occupy an incomparably more important place in the life of Israel than in that of any other people. Here belong a significant part of Moses's legislation regarding the separation of the pure from the impure, as well as the rules governing the processes of purification. One could say that the whole religious history of the Jews was directed to one end: to prepare for the God of Israel not just holy souls but also holy bodies.

If we now relate this desire of the Jews for the divine to be materialized with their concern that our bodily nature should be purified and sanctified,[42] then we can easily understand why Judaism itself provided an especially appropriate material domain for the incarnation of the divine word. For both reason and piety demand the acknowledgment that the incarnation of the divine, in addition to a holy and virginal soul, demands the service of a holy and pure body.

It is clear now that this sacred Jewish materialism in no way contradicts but rather directly complements this people's first two characteristics, its strong religiosity and the energy deriving from its human self-awareness and capacity for independent activity. The believing Israelite desires that the object of his faith should be fully actual and completely realized. Taken by itself, the human spirit, with its energy and dynamism, cannot be satisfied with abstract ideas and ideals; it demands their real incarnation, it demands that the spiritual principle should completely dominate material reality, and this presupposes in matter itself a capacity for such a spiritualization—it presupposes, in other words, *a spiritual and holy corporeality*. The religious materialism of the Jews derives not from their unbelief but from the superabundance of a faith which desires its fulfillment, not from weakness of human spirit, but from its strength and energy, not from the fear of being defiled by matter, but from the desire to purify her[43] and use her for one's own ends.

Thus, the three main characteristics of the Jewish people, seen as an integral whole in all of its doings, directly correspond to this people's high destiny and enable God's work to be accomplished in it. Firmly believing in the God Who Is, Israel attracted to itself the manifestation of God and His revelation; believing also in itself, Israel became capable of entering into a personal relationship with Yahweh, of standing face to face with Him, of completing a covenant with Him, and serving Him not as a passive instrument but as an active ally; and, finally, striving, in virtue of this active faith, for the ultimate realization of its spiritual principle. By purifying material nature, Israel prepared in its midst a pure and holy dwelling for the incarnation of God the Word.

This is why the Jews are God's chosen people; this is why Christ was born in Judea.[44]

II. Why Did the Jewish People Reject Christ and Now Shun Christianity?

All that is good in man and humanity can be preserved from distortion and perversion only by being joined to the divine. Directly the divine-human bond is broken, man's inner moral equilibrium also breaks, however imperceptibly at first.

We have discerned three main qualities of the Jewish character:[45] a firm faith in the living God, a most powerful sense of their own human and ethnic self, and an unrestrainable and limitless drive to realize and materialize their faith and passion, to endow them speedily with flesh and blood. These three qualities, in their right relationship, with the requisite dependence of the last two upon the first, constituted Israel's great advantage and glory; they made it the chosen people, the friend of God, and the helpmate of divine incarnation. But these same three qualities, when their right relationship is lost and the last two come to outweigh the first, become the source of great sins and misfortunes.

When unconditional faith in the living God and His providence takes first place, the Jewish sense of self and Jewish materialism both serve the work of God and provide the foundations for a true *theocracy*.

But as soon as these purely human and natural peculiarities of the Jewish character outweigh the religious element and subordinate it to themselves, then inevitably that great and universally unique national character manifests itself in those distorted forms which do explain the general antipathy toward Jewry (but which do not thereby justify hostility toward it). In this distorted form, national self-consciousness becomes a mix of national egoism, boundless self-idolization, and contemptuous hostility for the rest of humanity, while the realism of the Jewish spirit degenerates into that exclusively utilitarian, miserly, and totally unscrupulous character which almost completely obscures from external observers, especially the prejudiced ones, the best features of authentic Judaism.

Without this profound deformation of the national character in a significant part of the Jewish people, many events in Jewish history, especially the foundational event of Christianity, would remain inexplicable. True, in Jesus Christ's *immediate* opponents we see typically human rather than specifically Jewish vices and failings: the embittered vanity of the "teachers," exposed by their own pettiness, as well as the false patriotism and spurious political wisdom of ethnic rulers, a relatively infamous and universally attested phenomenon before and after Christ. The personal enmity and anger, aroused by Christ, are also fully understandable. His immediate opponents hold nothing mysterious within themselves; they are the most typical models of spoiled human nature. It is likewise evident that these people were not to be convinced by Jesus Christ's miracles. Those miracles were works of mercy for the suffering, not signs for the unbelieving. People who only heard about those miracles could have easily denied their reality, while those enemies of Christ who actually witnessed His miraculous works found no difficulty denying their *divine* character and ascribing them to demonic powers.

But how are we to explain the fact that a crowd of the people, formerly captivated by the divine character of Christ's teachings and deeds, suddenly repudiated Him and handed Him over, their Messiah, to His enemies? I find it difficult to adopt the following commonly accepted explanation: the Jewish people indeed awaited the Messiah but, owing to their crudely sensuous character, conceived of the messianic kingdom *exclusively* in the form of Israel's political triumph and domination over all the peoples, which expectation had nothing in common with the Gospel proclamation of the kingdom of God in purely spiritual terms, whence, presumably, the Jews could not recognize in Jesus their Messiah-King. It seems to me that this explanation limps on both sides and, to be sustained, requires a double adjustment. It is indubitable that the Jews expected the Messiah to bring, among other things, Judaism's political victory. It is likewise incontrovertible that Christ proclaimed, before all else, the kingdom of God in spirit and in truth. But as the mission of the Messiah was not to be exhausted, in Jewish expectations, by his political triumph, so on the Christian side, the kingdom of God as announced by Christ is not to be exhausted solely by the worship of God in spirit and truth. As for the Jews, their messianic expectations were founded, first of all, upon prophetic writings, writings which portray the coming messianic kingdom as being, primarily, the fullest revelation and triumph of true religion, involving the spiritualization of the Sinaitic covenant, the confirmation of divine law in human hearts, the dissemination of the true knowledge of God, and, finally, as the outpouring of God's Holy Spirit upon every creature:

By myself I swear, says YHWH, from My mouth issues righteousness, a Word irrevocable; To them[46] shall every knee bow before Me, by Me shall every tongue swear. Only with the Lord, they will say of Me, are righteousness and might; all those who warred against Him shall come before Him and be ashamed. (Isa. 45:23, 24)

Hear Me, My people, and incline your ear to Me, my tribe. For a law will go forth from me, and my justice I will establish as a light for the peoples. . . . Lift up your eyes to the heavens and look down upon the earth, for the heavens will vanish like smoke and the earth will wear out like an old garment and all that live in it, but my salvation will endure for eternity and my truth will not cease. (Isa. 51:4, 6)

Behold, I gave him [the Messiah] as a witness to the peoples, a leader and commander for the [peoples speaking different] tongues.[47] Behold, you shall call a tribe that you did not know, and the nations that knew you not shall run to you for the sake of the LORD your God, and for the sake of the Holy One of Israel, for he will glorify you. (Isa. 55:4–5)

Let the wicked man forsake his way, and the lawless his thoughts; and let him turn to the Lord, and he will have mercy on him, and to our God, for he is abundantly merciful. (Isa. 55:7)

For My thoughts are not your thoughts, and your ways are not My ways, says the Lord. But as the heavens are higher than the earth, so are My ways higher than your ways and My thoughts are higher than your thoughts. (Isa. 55:8–9)

For, behold, I create a new heaven and a new earth: and the former things shall not be remembered, nor arise in the heart. (Isa. 65:17)

If you wish to return, O Israel, says the Lord, return to me: and if you would put away your abominations out of my sight, then you shall not wander. And you shall swear: The Lord lives in truth, in judgment, and in righteousness; and the peoples shall bless themselves in Him, and shall glory in Him. For thus says the Lord to the men of Judah and Jerusalem, plow for yourselves fallow ground, and sow not among thorns. Circumcise yourselves to the Lord, and take away the foreskins of your heart, men of Judah and inhabitants of Jerusalem. (Jer. 4:1–4)

Behold the days are coming, says the Lord, when I will make a new covenant with the house of Israel, and with the house of Judah, not such a covenant as I made with their fathers in the day when I took them by the hand to bring them out of the land of Egypt; that covenant of mine they broke, although I remained in union with them, says the Lord. But here is the covenant that I will make with the house of Israel after those days, says the LORD: I will insert my law into their inward parts, and write it upon their hearts; and I will be their God, and they shall be My people. And no longer shall they teach each other, every man his neighbour, and every man his brother, saying, "Know the Lord," for they shall all know me, from the least of them unto the greatest of them, says the Lord, for I will forgive their lawlessness, and their sins I will remember no more. (Jer. 31:31–34)

And I will give them one heart, and I will put a new spirit within them, and I will take the stony heart out of their breast and will give them a heart of flesh, so that they would walk in my statutes, and keep mine ordinances, and fulfill them: and they shall be my people, and I will be their God. (Ezek. 11:19–20)

Neither will I hide my face any more from them, for I will pour out My spirit upon the house of Israel, says the Lord God. (Ezek. 39:29)

And I will betroth you unto me for ever; and I will betroth you unto me in righteousness, and in judgment, and in lovingkindness, and in mercies. And I will betroth you unto me in faithfulness: and you shall know the Lord. And it shall come to pass in that day, that I will hear, says the Lord, I will hear the heaven, and it shall hear the earth; and the earth shall hear the bread, and the wine, and the oil; and they shall hear Jezreel. And I will sow her unto me in the earth; and I will have mercy upon her that had not obtained mercy; and I will say to them which were not my people: you are My people; and they shall say, You are our God. (Hos. 2:19–23)

For I desire mercy, and not sacrifice, and knowledge of God, rather than burnt offerings. (Hos. 6:6)

These are the things that you must do: speak the truth to one another, in truth and with love for peace render judgments in your gates. Let no one among you devise evil in his heart against their neighbour and love no false oath, for all these things I hate, says the Lord. (Zech. 8:16, 17)

For from the rising of the sun to its setting, My name shall be great among the nations, and in every place incense will be offered to My name, a pure offering; great will be My name among the nations, says the Lord of Hosts. (Mal. 1:11)

"They shall be Mine," says the Lord Sabaoth, "My special possession, on the day which I shall make, and I will pity them as a man pities his son who serves him. And then you shall see the difference between the righteous and the wicked, between one who serves God and one who does not serve Him." (Mal. 3:17–18)

And you, offspring of Zion, be glad and rejoice in the Lord your God; for He will give you rain in measure and he will send down rain to you, the early rain and the latter, as before. . . . And it shall come to pass afterward, that I will pour out from My Spirit, on all flesh, and your sons and your daughters shall prophesy, your old men shall dream dreams, and your young men shall see visions. And likewise, upon the menservants and maidservants in those days, I will pour out My Spirit. . . . And it shall come to pass that anyone who will call upon the name of the Lord shall be saved; for on Mount Zion and in Jerusalem there shall be salvation, as the Lord has said, and among others whom the Lord shall call. (Joel 2:23, 28, 29, 32)

That part of the Jewish people which did not recognize the prophetic writings (the Sadducees) did not expect *any* Messiah; while those who expected him *on the basis of the prophets* could not exclude from their expectations that religious element which the prophets stressed. The kingdom of the Messiah, for Jews who expected him, was to possess not an exclusively political but a *religiously* political character; it must have been envisaged by them not in exclusively sensible but in *spiritually* sensible images. On the other hand, Christian teaching never entailed preaching abstract spirituality. The basic truth of Christianity, the incarnation of the divine Word, is a spiritually *sensible* fact. When Christ said, *"he who has seen me, has seen the Father also,"* He, of course, was not distancing but bringing God closer to the perception of man who apprehends with the senses. In addition, Christ by His word and example hallowed the practical foundations of religious life—prayer, almsgiving, and fasting. And as far as the juridical and politico-economic decrees of Mosaic legislation are concerned, it is not surprising that the Gospel keeps silent about them on the eve of the great changes that were about to take place. The most radical partisans of contemporary Judaism hardly could have thought that the civil laws given by Moses before the conquest of the land of Canaan could remain unchanged in the kingdom of the Messiah when the people of God would rule over the whole earth. Christ spoke of the destruction of the Temple of Jerusalem not, of course, from disdain for its holiness, for which, on the contrary, he was greatly zealous (see the Gospel narratives about the expulsion of the moneychangers from the Temple), but only because he foresaw the destruction which indeed occurred soon afterward. Moreover this prediction of the destruction of the Second Temple could not by then have been so excessively injurious to the sensibilities of the Jewish people, which had already suffered the destruction of the First Temple, immeasurably surpassing the Second in greatness and glory.

In general, the teaching of Christ did not negate the sensible forms of religious life but spiritualized them; nor did it deny that the kingdom of the true God must subdue the whole world to itself. If Christ's kingdom was of this world, then it would not have the right to rule over the world, but it is precisely because it is not of the world and is alien to the world's malice that it receives the whole world as its *rightful* inheritance: "blessed are the meek, for they shall inherit the earth."[48] The Christians, like the Jews (who recognize the prophets), strive not only for the renewal of the human spirit but also ardently hope, in accordance with His promise, for a new heaven and a new *earth*, for it is there that righteousness lives. The kingdom of God is not only inward, in the spirit, but also outward, in power; it is real *theocracy*. The Christian religion, in raising the human spirit to God, brings God down to human flesh: in this manifested sacrament lies all its superiority, its fullness, and its perfection. Christianity differs from pagan wisdom by its very *goal*, but from Judaism it differs only by a different *relation* to this goal.

The final goal for Christians and for Jews is one and the same: universal theocracy, the realization of the divine law in the human world, the incarnation of the heavenly in the earthly. This union of heaven and earth, this new covenant between God and creation, this completed cycle and crown of the universal task is identically recognized by both Christianity and Judaism. But in Christianity we also receive the revelation of the *way* to this crown, and that way is the *cross*.[49] And this way of the cross is what the Judaism of that time proved unable to understand. Judaism then was seeking a sign, that is, a direct and unmediated manifestation of divine *power*. Jews then strove directly toward the final conclusion, the final judgments. They wanted to acquire from without, by a *conditionally* formal way, that which must be acquired through suffering and achieved by a complex and heavy process, by the way of inner division and moral combat. Confining themselves by a formal fidelity to an ancient *treaty*,[50] so as to receive the kingdom of God *by its conditions*, they did not wish to understand and accept that way of the cross by which the kingdom is not attained directly from without but *is first* appropriated from within, so as to manifest itself outwardly *later*. Unwilling to understand and accept Christ's cross, of Christ, for the last eighteen centuries they have now been bearing, against their will, their own heavy cross.

The cross of Christ, by which the kingdom of God is appropriated, demanded from the Jewish people a double *podvig:* first, a renunciation of their own national egoism, and second, a temporary renunciation of worldly strivings and attachment to earthly welfare. While preserving the *positive* peculiarities of its character, Judaism should have simultaneously widened and deepened its religion, endowing it with a completely universal meaning, and most important, imparting to it that ascetical spirit which it always lacked. The Jews should have temporarily assumed the same position before the hostility of the world as was assumed by the persecuted Christian Church: they ought to have risen against the pagan empire not as rebels but as martyrs; they would then have defeated it and united with Christianity in a common triumph.[51]

In order to incarnate the kingdom of God on earth, it is necessary *first to withdraw* from earth; in order to realize a spiritual idea in material reality, it is necessary to be free, to be detached from that reality. The slave of the earth cannot rule her and consequently cannot make her a foundation for God's kingdom.[52] In order to make natural life the instrument and *means* of the higher spiritual life, one must renounce natural life as the *goal*. One must sever the senseless union between spirit and matter in order to establish a true and holy bond between them.

The *highest* goal of Christianity lies not in ascetic detachment from natural life but in the purification and hallowing of this life.[53] But in order to purify her, it is first necessary to be pure from her. Christianity's challenge lies not in destroying earthly life but in *raising* her toward God who descends to meet her. And as the lifting of a great weight in the physical world requires a lever, to apply the active force at a certain distance from the point of resistance, so also in the moral world, the ideal-bearing force must withdraw to a certain extent from the life of immediacy in order to act on her all the more powerfully, and in order to turn and raise her all the more quickly. Only he who is free from the world can act to its advantage. A captive spirit cannot rebuild its prison into a luminous temple; he must first of all liberate himself from it.

Christian asceticism seeks not to weaken the flesh but to *strengthen the spirit for the transfiguration of the flesh.* Analogously, Christian universalism aims not at destroying the natural peculiarities of each nation but rather at strengthening the national spirit by purifying it from all egotistical leaven. These goals were not foreign to the Jewish people. They cared not only about the purity and holiness of their own bodily nature but also about *justifying* their national spirit. But the actual process of this justification was envisaged by Jewish lawgivers more as a matter of form than of substance. They sought union with God by means of an external conditional agreement, and not by an inward divinization through the experience of the cross, through a moral *podvig*, through personal and national self-renunciation.[54] But this wondrous way of attaining the goal by receding from it was totally incomprehensible to the majority of Jews, who strove to reach the final goal as directly and speedily as possible. Their intense sense of self rose against Christian self-renunciation, their attachment to material life left no room for Christian asceticism, their practical mind could not reconcile the apparent contradiction between the end and the means; they could not understand how voluntary suffering can yield beatitude, how mortification of the body can serve to restore it, and how renunciation of personal and ethnic interests can yield the fullness of personal and national life.

If the idea of the cross, and of man bearing it, greatly scandalized[55] the Jews, then the cross, taken up by God Himself, became for them a scandal of scandals. Consequently, that very same Jewish people which by means of its best elements prepared the milieu and the matter for the incarnation of God-the-Word,[56] turned out, in its mass, to be the least receptive to the mystery of this incarnation.

The *God-man*, that is, the unification of the deity with human nature in one individual person is *the first fruits*, the necessary foundation
and core, while the end and completion is Godmanhood (or, more precisely, divinized humanity), that is, the union of God, by the mediation
of the God-man, with the whole human race,[57] and through it also with
the whole creation.[58] The Jews, in any case, seeking a final practical result, gave thought only to collective unification with God and failed to
understand the necessity of attaining this common goal via an individual starting point and mediation. Even those Jews who were ready
to concede the possibility of the incarnation of a divine person (e.g.,
the Kabbalists)[59] rejected the way of Christ as impractical and purpose-
less. By the same token, by rejecting the God-man as the sole and universally common starting point of salvation, as the ensign[60] to the
peoples speaking different tongues, the Jews also distorted the meaning of Godmanhood, making it the exclusive privilege of the people of
Israel. This was wholly in keeping with the realistic character of the
Jewish standpoint. For although a people is a collective entity, it remains a real, palpable entity, whereas humanity, ever since the collapse
of the tower of Babel, is an abstract notion and simply does not exist
as a real and integrally concrete whole. This is why the Jew who did
not subordinate carnal reason to the knowledge of truth when imagin-
ing the form that the kingdom of God would assume, would naturally
stop at the boundaries of his ethnicity, rejecting all humanity as an abstract fantasy that deprives the kingdom of God of its real foundation.
Accordingly, when regarding Christianity as the proclamation of universal human brotherhood, the Jew sees it as something excessively
broad, abstract, and unreal, while, in noting how Christianity links the
work of universal salvation to the one Person of Jesus, the Jew per-
ceives it as something narrow, arbitrary, and insufficient. And so from
this and that side, Christianity, which seeks to gather *all* around *one*
and through *one* to join each to all, appears to the Jew—pragmatist
and realist that he is—as an idea that is unrealizable and, for that single
reason, false. To prove to the Jews that they are mistaken can only be
done *factually*—by realizing the Christian idea in practice and by consistently introducing it into actual life. The more fully the Christian
world would express the Christian idea of spiritual and universal

theocracy, the more powerfully would Christian principles have an impact upon the private lives of Christians, upon the social life of Christian peoples, and upon the political relations within Christendom. The more obviously, then, would the Jewish view of Christianity be overturned, and the nearer and more possible would the conversion of the Jews be. Accordingly, *the Jewish question is a Christian question.*

III. The Fortunes of Jewish and Christian Theocracy: Russia, Poland, and Israel

Christianity and Jewry have a common theocratic task: the establishment of a righteous society.[61] And since God is the source of all righteousness, the righteous society is a divine-human society. In it, the whole man serves God willingly, and all people live in mutual unanimity and possess full mastery over material nature. According to Jewish conceptions, such an ideal society must become incarnate in the people of Israel (in the kingdom of the Messiah).[62] According to Christian conceptions, all peoples are equally called to it. This Christian universalism should not be understood to imply that all ethnicities provide undifferentiated material for the universal theocracy. All peoples are equal at least before the law of the Gospel in the same sense as, for example, all the citizens of a kingdom are equal before the law of the land. This in no way prevents the different constituencies and categories of citizens from having their own special rights, rights deriving from the particular responsibilities of their service (thus in the most egalitarian country, the doctor possesses particular rights which the farmer does not have, while in the most democratic republic the minister possesses privileges not granted to the night guard, and so on, even though they are all equal before the law, which determines both the common rights of all and the particular rights of each). Likewise, in God's commonwealth (*in civitate Dei*) different peoples can have different privileges depending on their particular historical position and national calling, provided that no harm would be done to mutual love and solidarity. Consequently, no inevitable contradiction obtains between the Christian and Hebraic theocratic ideas. If the Jews hold a claim to a special status and role in the universal theocracy, we have no a priori need to reject this claim, especially if we recall what the apostle Paul said about this subject: "to them belong the sonship, and the glory, and the covenants, and the giving of the law, and the worship, and the promises; to them belong the patriarchs, and from them, according to the flesh, is the Christ, the God who is over all. . . . Or has God rejected His people? By no means! . . . God has not rejected his people whom he foreknew. . . . But lest you not pride yourselves, I do not wish to leave you, brethren, in ignorance about the mystery, that a blindness has come upon Israel, in part, until the full number of the Gentiles come in. . . . And then all Israel will be saved."[63] But *how* shall he be saved, how will he enter the city of God?

In order to understand the theocratic status of a given people, it is necessary to determine more closely the essential content of theocracy.

Until God shall be all in all (Eph. 11:23), until every human being becomes a receptacle for the deity, so long will divine government over humanity necessarily require specific organs or mediators to act within humanity.

Furthermore, divine government must extend over all human life and cannot be confined to some one particular sphere of this present life. For this reason, the organs of divine government must also be present not only in specifically religious but also in the political and social spheres. The specifically religious sphere has its theocratic organ in the *priest* (or rather archpriest, since a *priest* presupposes a *consecrator*);[64] the political sphere has its own theocratic organ in the *tsar*, as God's anointed; while finally, the social life of the people has its own theocratic organ in the person of the *prophet*, that is, in the free preacher and teacher. Each of these three representatives of theocracy has his own sphere of operation but exists, in virtue of the nature of these spheres, in distinct reciprocal relations with the others. *The priest directs, the tsar governs, the prophet redirects.*[65] In the economy of divine government, the priesthood possesses authority, founded on *tradition*, the tsar possesses *power*, grounded on *law*, and the prophet exercises the *freedom of personal initiative.*

The fullness of the theocratic ideal demands a consistent and con-cordant development of these three instruments of divine government.

If we now look at the Judaic (Old Testament) theocracy, we will easily notice that although it possessed both priesthood (from the time of Aaron) and kingship (from the time of Saul), both of these minis-tries, the priestly and the royal, were shielded by and eclipsed by the prophetic ministry. The greatest representative of the Jewish people was not the high priest Aaron but the prophet Moses, and if David subsequently acquired such a prominent position in the fortunes of Jewish theocracy, this happened not only because he was a king but also a prophet. In any event, it is to be noted that Moses as a prophet establishes the priesthood, while the prophet Samuel establishes the kingdom and anoints the first kings. It is thus apparent that among the Jews, the prophetic service contained in itself the sources of both the royal and the priestly power. Of the three kings of the undivided Jewish state, the first, Saul, despite his courage, and the third, Solomon, despite his wisdom, turned out to be unworthy representatives of the theocratic kingdom. Solomon's reign reveals the moral collapse of this kingdom (idolatry), while its division in the reign of Solomon's son marks the depletion of its external splendor and might; the division of the kingdom means that enslavement to foreigners is simply a question of time. On this count, the view of the prophet Samuel, who agreed so unwillingly to the establishment of the monarchy in Israel, was justi-fied. He was proved right not because royal rule was superfluous for the Jewish people (on the contrary, there was too great a need for it) but because this man of God, knowing his people well, foresaw that the royal principle would not graft itself into Israel and that its hapless actualizations would only multiply the people's woes.

Just as the fragility of governmental power turned out to be ruin-ous for Jewish political life, so the defective development of the pon-tifical principle inflicted an injury upon Jewish religious life. The priesthood, established to function with one tribe and bound by for-mal duties of sacrificial service, could not exert a life-giving religious effect upon the people. By means of its negative qualities it rather ac-celerated that pharisaic-Talmudic crystallization of Judaism, which, albeit retaining within itself a grain of the truth, becomes enclosed in too tough and impenetrable a shell. By the way, this crystallization was finally realized only when, following the disappearance of the last traces of the kingdom and consequent on the destruction of the Second Temple, the priesthood also disappeared, while inspired prophecy underwent total rebirth into a deductive and precise doctrinal system—rabbinism—which set its whole soul upon the implementation of the paternal bequest *to put a hedge around the law*[66] and erected this hedge with such dedication and diligence that the hedge soon gave rise to a veritable labyrinth in which it became difficult for Jews themselves to find the way of true life.

From our point of view, the fortunes of Judaic theocracy provide, before all else, an educational lesson, which is that for all the great grace that God bestowed on the Jewish people through their prophets, the prophetic ministry could not by itself compensate for the lack of either a strong and united governmental power or an authoritative and active priesthood. The first of these shortcomings deprived the Jews of political self-sufficiency; the second arrested their religious development.

Christianity represented the broadening and fulfillment of Jewish theocracy not only by endowing it with new national elements but also and especially by elevating and strengthening the formative principles of theocracy itself. First of all, it gave the world an authentic priesthood based upon direct divine right independent of any human office or institution. In Judaism, as we know, priesthood was originally established through human mediation, through the mediation of God's prophet Moses. The Jewish priesthood was thereby genetically dependent upon another ministry, the prophetic, which stood alone, among the Jews, in immediate connection with the deity. In Christianity, on the contrary, the original priesthood is represented by the divine person of Jesus Christ. From him, *without mediation*, the apostles received and transmitted to their successors through the laying on of hands the sacramental gift of the priesthood. Strictly speaking, Christ was and still is the sole true high priest; but while the visible church has separate existence on earth, there must necessarily exist visible bearers of Christ's priesthood who derive their ministry and perform their sacred work neither from themselves nor from any human name but only as the stand-ins of Christ, by His might and grace. To this corresponds the fact that in the temporal order, the ecclesial hierarchy is linked to Christ Himself by a direct and unbroken chain of succession without any external mediation.

The inner unity of the ecclesial hierarchy depends upon its divine origin, but the visible expression of this unity in ecclesial life was effected by the ecumenical councils and by the pope.

Alongside this hierarchical element, Christianity also elevated the royal element of theocracy. The development of this element became the lot of Byzantium, the representative of the hellenized East which had drawn the center of the Roman Empire over to itself. In the Orthodox tsar of this new Rome, Christianity purified the royal idea of all its pagan elements and gave them new birth. The East brought its image of the ruler as supreme lord and unrestrained autocrat; Greece contributed its idea of the king as wise ruler, shepherd of the people; Rome provided its conception of the emperor as incarnate state law; Christianity bound all this together with the highest designation of the Orthodox tsar as the privileged servant of the true religion, as the defender and guardian of its interests on earth. Recognizing in Christ a special royal dignity, our religion bestows supreme consecration to state authority and makes the Christian tsar an entirely self-sufficient and effectively supreme ruler. As God's anointed, reigning by the grace of God, the Christian sovereign is independent of the people's self-will. But although the power of the Christian monarch is not restrained from below, it is restrained from above: being the father and the lord of the people, the Christian tsar must be a son of the church. Furthermore, in the temporal order, the tsar, lacking connection to Christ himself by any actual succession, must receive his consecration from direct representatives of Christ's authority, from the high priests of the church, which is what occurs in the holy process of the tsar's anointing and coronation. This does not give the ecclesial hierarchy any ruling rights in the state sphere, but it does oblige the tsar to be a dedicated son of the church and a faithful servant of God's work. Only on this condition can he have the significance of a Christian tsar and function as one of the formative organs of true theocracy. Those Byzantine emperors who evinced this ideal of Christian tsardom most clearly, by always remaining loyal to it in principle, however much they fell short of it in the actual usage of power, were highly revered and glorified by the church during their lifetimes and posthumously. Such were Constantine the Great, Theodosius the Greek, and Justinian. The reverence which these great representatives of Caesarism received from the church clearly shows that the church values the principle of the Christian tsar and is not at all indifferent to the issue of the form of government, as some affirm.

But Christian tsardom, significant as it is, is only a part of the theocratic idea. Its one-sided development would impair the other theocratic elements; its prevalence over them could imperil God's work on earth. Thus it happened in Byzantium. Most of its rulers thought that the supreme lordship over the Christian people, which they received from Christ through the church, also extends over the Christian faith itself as well as over the church's most fundamental institutions, permitting them to exercise full authority in the sanctuary itself, and allowing them to force the church to serve their lordship instead of putting their lordship at the service of the church. From this arose great woes for the Christian world. These woes include the heresies which were patronized by emperors and sometimes even invented by them (such as monothelitism[67] and iconoclasm); from this stem the constant persecutions and depositions of Orthodox bishops and the unlawful appointments in their place of heretics and sycophants; from this too stem many other abuses of power.

But the abuses of Byzantine Caesarism bore still more profound consequences, for they distorted the very life of Christian society in the East. Given that the spiritual authority in Byzantium lacked sufficient independence, strength, and capacity to restrain royal authority, the latter bore down with all its weight upon social life and suppressed in it every energetic personal initiative and any independent activity. Everything potent withdrew to the monasteries, everything frail became enslaved to rude whim. Despotism was thereby nurtured by moral impotence and spawned social depravity. The salvation of the soul was left to the monasteries, while the main task of secular life consisted in pleasing the emperor and his servants. In Byzantium, the theocratic task of Christianity, the establishment of a just society, was decisively destroyed. It is true that, thanks to the positive aspects of the Byzantine character—piety and loyalty to ecclesial tradition—Orthodox faith was preserved in the East, but these qualities failed to provide a basis for the establishment of a Christian society as well as for the defense of the Orthodox world from the victorious intrusion of the Muslim faith.[68] The victory of Islam, which had almost eradicated Christianity in Asia and Africa, was, first of all, the work of brute force, even though it carried some moral justification. The Muslim, believing in his simple and not too lofty religious-moral law, conscientiously fulfills it in his personal and social life. Thus he *judges* both the civil and criminal affairs according to the Qur'an, *fights* according to the direct commands of the Qur'an, and treats the infidel and the conquered in accord with the prescriptions of the Qur'an, and so on. In the meantime, the Gospel never took on that significance in the social life of the Christian world which the Qur'an acquired in the Muslim state and society. For this reason, if the Muslim gives himself over to sensuality, then he is able to live so without hypocrisy, for such is his law, for they all live like this; but a believing Christian is bound, willy-nilly, to constantly transgress his faith, for the society that he inhabits is minimally governed by Christian law. As for Byzantium, in its latter days, in consequence of its exclusively ascetical religiosity, this division between faith and life, between the personal salvation of the soul and social action, became, it could be said, a constant rule. Consequently, the victory of Islam was a just punishment upon the Christian East.

As far as the West is concerned, then, while it never forgot or abandoned the theocratic task, it nonetheless proved unsuccessful in realizing it practically, albeit for rather different and partially contrary causes.

For if in Byzantium the principal cause of all evils consisted in the excessive predominance of imperial autocracy, then the root obstacle facing the theocratic task in the West lay in the weakness and fragmentation of state authority. Charles the Great was the first and the *last* real, that is, autocratic, emperor in the West (where his name was amalgamated with the cognomen "the Great": into Charlemagne; while among the neighboring Slavs, it became synonymous with "the Sovereign": *Carolus-Korol*). After this typical representative of Western theocratic monarchy, only the *idea* of the "Holy Roman Empire of the German nation" remained, because in actuality there disappeared not only the unity of the Roman Empire but the unity of the German nation as well. With the annihilation of imperial autocracy, the Western church lost its main instrument for implementing its theocratic task. This church, united by and concentrated in the Roman altar, did not fear the *strong* empire of Charles the Great but utilized its might. The ensuing weak and fragmented empire turned out to be hazardous and dangerous for the papacy, for remaining in the midst of feudal chaos as the solitary agents and representatives of order and of the common good, the popes themselves became confronted with leaderless, chaotic crowds of semibarbarian criminals, relative to whom the papal authority had to acquire, against its own will, the character of a coercive power. As the sole authority commonly recognized in the whole of the European world, the Roman bishop was constrained to assume the functions of imperial authority which belonged only nominally to the German kings. By this very fact the popes not only aroused the hostility of those semibarbarian rulers, whom they had to bridle, but even and signally induced rivalry among the German kings. For these latter, not knowing how to cope with their own direct vassals, strove to realize their own imperial claims at the expense of both the pope and the Italian cities, seeing in the defenseless Italy a reward for their own powerlessness in Germany and remaining Europe. Thus was inflamed that tragic struggle between the papacy and the empire, which until its epilogue in France continued for three centuries and dealt a decisive blow to the work of Christian theocracy. In the first place, the spectacle of this struggle between two supreme powers exerted a deeply demoralizing effect upon the Christian peoples, undermining in their eyes both the authority of the church and the authority of the imperial government, preparing thereby the ground for Protestantism. Second, this struggle totally exhausted the already deficient powers of the German empire, so that with the passing of the Middle Ages under the emperors Friedrich III and Maximilian imperial power became a total nonentity. Third, and what is most important, this ill-starred struggle constrained the papacy to don "the rotten weight of earthly armor" which caused, directly or indirectly, many ecclesiastical abuses and many erroneous uses of spiritual authority. And these abuses and errors provided, in turn, the pretexts and justifications for anticlerical movements. In the meantime, imperial power, having been totally degraded, could no longer, in spite of its late concordat with the papacy, stop this revolutionary movement or limit the egoism of subsidiary rulers who patronized the coup, finding in it a double profit for themselves. For Protestantism first placed all church and monastic possessions at their complete disposal and then granted them supreme rights in the religious sphere itself, following the principle of *cujus regio, ejus religio*. Consequently, as is well known, many German knights *forcefully* introduced Protestantism into their own domains. As far as the essence of Protestantism is concerned, it consists in the abuse of the third principle of Christian theocracy: the principle of prophecy or of personal spiritual freedom in religious affairs.[69] The *abuse* in the present case consisted first of all in the fact that the principle of prophecy, that is, the freedom of personal inspiration, is not recognized as belonging to the third place, that is, the condition of faithfulness to the other two principles of theocracy, which possess the privilege of positive divine institution, but is recognized as the first and, essentially, as the only principle of the kingdom of God. For that excessive power in religious affairs, which Luther granted to the rulers who pledged him loyalty, bears the character of a practical and temporary concession; for wherever Protestantism freely and consequentially developed its principles, in Switzerland, among the English and Scottish Puritans, and among American sects, it is deeply hostile to the monarchic idea. And as regards the apostolic priestly authority, its total negation, both in theory and in practice, constitutes an indisputably distinctive character of Protestantism, according to which every believer is, by definition, already a priest. Priesthood here blends into prophecy, and this latter is recognized not as a special service or *responsibility of some* people called to this task by God but as the natural *right of all*. But according to the true Christian notion, as is the case with the Hebrew, the prophetic vocation requires a high degree of righteousness and of particular moral heroic acts (Elijah, John the Baptist);[70] but Protestantism denies the significance of human righteousness and of heroic activity and reduces all religion to the sole state of faith, thereby granting to every believer an unconditional right to act as a self-appointed and self-assured executor of religious affairs.

Verily, all true believers will become prophets of God at the end of time, with the manifestation of the church triumphant, when everyone will become both king and priest. But that point is still a long way off, and to transform the end into the beginning is not a measure that guarantees success.

The true Jewish and Christian prophet does not *rise up* against sacerdotal and royal authority but *adheres* to them and helps them by his admonitions and exhortations. The true prophet is conscious of his vocation not as a natural right common to him and all and, likewise, not as his own private privilege but as a special divine gift, which demands moral cultivation on his part. By rejecting these two necessary conditions of true prophecy—submission to lawful authorities and the striving to be worthy of the highest vocation—Protestantism essentially distorted the third theocratic principle, and by separating prophecy from priesthood, it even failed to give the world any true prophets.

Protestantism's great success depended in no small measure upon the preceding row between the two supreme authorities in the Christian world. Had there obtained, instead of this row, that desired equilibrium and proper reciprocal action between the ecclesial and imperial powers, there could have been found neither such seemingly plausible pretexts for the launching of anti-ecclesiastical movements nor such favorable conditions for their proliferation. The strength of Protestantism rose upon the ruins of the Western theocratic edifice. The fragility of this edifice hinged on the faulty relationship of two principle theocratic authorities, and this faulty relationship, in turn, was directly conditioned by the division and antagonism between the tsarist East and the high priestly West. Among the willful and self-assured peoples of the West, universal imperial authority—the main instrument for the achievement of theocracy—could have no power. For the papacy, this shaky empire turned out to be the reed-staff spoken of by the ancient prophet: wishing to lean upon this reed, the spiritual Lord of the West broke it and also pierced his hand.[71] It would have been a different matter if he could have leaned upon an unshakable Eastern Caesarism,

which, moving from one country to another, and thanks to the patriarchal character of the Eastern peoples, never lost its fullness of sover-
eignty and might. In that case, one power would have balanced and
complemented the other. The Eastern tsars, loyal to the traditions of
Constantine and Theodosius, would have then become the main servants and guardians of the church, and her external higher clerics.
Then, with the church undivided, the hierarchy of the Eastern church
would, as at present, enjoy the protection of the Orthodox tsar but,
above that, would also be able to confirm its authority with all the concentrated strength of its Western fellow servants. Analogously, the
support of the entire pious East would have allowed the Western hierarchy to resolve its arduous struggle with anticlerical and antireligious
elements by delegating its external aspects to the supporting power of
the Orthodox Caesar, thereby delivering itself from any pressure to
contaminate the high image of its spiritual authority with the detailed
features of administrative government politics. Such conditions would
neither have yielded those private abuses which are advanced, with
greater or lesser justice, as rebukes for Catholicism's historical activity
nor provided sufficient grounds for Western anti-Christian movements. And were these movements still to arise ("for even heresies are
due"), then they could neither have claimed for themselves any lofty
principles or ideals nor obtained and attained those broad measures
and those firm successes which they now enjoy.

The division of the churches, having upset the balance between the
first two formative principles of Christian theocracy—priesthood and
kingship—facilitated, by the same token, an unlawful manifestation of
the third theocratic principle: prophecy. But Protestantism was not
only an unlawful manifestation of the prophetic principle; it was also
a reaction of the German national element against the Latin. And in
this regard also, the real, albeit remote, cause of Protestantism, the
division of the churches, undermined the universal character of Christianity and gave the upper hand to national and tribal conflicts.

The German world also, in its turn, displayed its own *specific* theocratic idea and adversely set it over and against the theocratic idea of
Catholicism. Taking its stand under the banner of free prophetic ministry, Protestantism represented, to a well-known degree, a return to

Hebraic principles. But concomitantly there remained between them an immense difference favoring Jewry. For first of all, the Hebrew prophets, as we know, did not revolt against the lawful priesthood as Protestants did; and second, the Hebrew prophets preached justification by faith and by *works*, and not by faith alone. When, following the dispersion of Israel, the prophetic ministry was replaced by that of the teachers (rabbinism), the rabbis, as Israel's new representatives, set themselves the task of "putting a hedge around the Law," that is, of supporting the keeping of the law in life from every angle. This practical task remained prevalent in all Talmudic literature. As in Judaism so in Protestantism, but even more speedily, prophecy was replaced by teaching. (Were Luther and Zwingli to be called the prophets of the new confession, Melanchthon, Luther's learned friend, would much more readily resemble the rabbi than the prophet.) The point of departure for Hebraic and Protestant teaching was one and the same: the Bible. Both were rooted in scribalism, but each treated their book in a completely different way. The Jewish rabbis regarded the book first of all as the Law, that is, as *the norm of life*, and directed all their efforts to the strengthening of this law of life by an impenetrable hedge of traditions and interpretations. Such was the attitude to the sacred book which issued from the *Jewish* national character; rather different was the attitude assumed by the national German genius. In the eyes of the German Protestant school, the Bible became not so much a norm of life as a *subject of theoretical research*. Caring least of all about the practical hedge of traditions, it forcefully strove to exclude every traditional element from the understanding of the word of God. Protestant biblical studies turned into criticism and criticism became negation. In our days, the progressive teachers of Protestantism have ceased to treat the Bible as the basis of faith and basically regard it as the subject of negative (= higher) criticism. If they still continue to grant it any exclusive meaning and exclusively preoccupy themselves with it, this is only a matter of habit. Initially, the leaders of the Protestant world moved from being prophets to being teachers; now, in turn, the religious academy concedes its place to scholastic erudition with a predominantly anti-Christian tendency. And here there remains not even an imprint of that distinctive though false theocratic idea which inspired the first Protestant leaders. The contemporary wreckers of biblical texts have *nothing* to say to the world and lead it *nowhere*.[72] And already from its inception, Protestantism, in its struggle against the papacy and the empire, surrendered itself to the power of local states in order to have a direct influence upon folk life. But now when its religious representatives devote themselves to destructive pedantry, the life of the nations remains wholly in the hands of secular politics, in the power of private interests, wavering between military despotism and the dominion of plutocracy.

This collapse of the Christian idea was not confined solely to the Germanic countries in which Protestantism triumphed. Although the religious cause of the Reformation did not succeed in Latin or Romance Europe, its practical result—universal secularization, that is, the separation of all spheres of human activity—of politics and public administration, of science and schools, of art and social life—from religion and from the church, this universal secularization also spread itself over Latin Europe. As represented by their ruling classes, the Romance countries also followed the example of the German in repudiating the theocratic idea. One could have despaired over the fortunes of Christianity had the store of world history not preserved fresh strengths—the strengths of the Slavic peoples.[73]

Both nations, representing in themselves the two opposite poles of the Slavic domain—Russia and Poland—have not yet disavowed the principles of Christian theocracy. Poland's aristocracy and the entire mass of Polish common people remain zealous Catholics and diligently support Rome's theocratic idea. Russia's aristocracy and mass of people remain faithful to Eastern Orthodoxy and adhere to the theocractic tradition of Byzantium. Into the midst of these two religious nations, each possessing its own distinctive theocratic idea, history inserted a third religious people, also possessing a distinctive theocratic conception: the people of Israel. Whether this is an accidental fact or whether it is the outward joining of the three theocratic peoples in preparation for their spiritual unification in one all-encompassing theocratic idea, regardless of the enmity which still divides them, the resolution of this question depends on how these theocratic ideas, born by these three peoples, relate to each other *in actual practical terms*; do these ideas exclude each other, or are they, on the contrary, mutually compatible?

In general, theocracy aims at the actualization of religion (i.e., the union of God with man) in the whole of life of the nations. The successful fulfillment of this task necessitates three conditions: (1) *the complete independence of the religious principle* in society, for this principle constitutes the essence and goal of the whole task, and if the religious element should occupy in common life a subordinate and a dependent status, then theocracy would be robbed of all its meaning; (2) *a correct subdivision of the social body and a firm order* in its government, since without this, religion would lack the permanent and purposeful *means* to influence life and guide it theocratically; and (3) the *free and energetic activity of personal forces*, since without such activity the best social organization in the world would remain an empty form.

Let us now turn to the present structures of life in Russia, Poland, and contemporary Jewry, which is now concentrated in these two countries, in order to examine how well these nations satisfy the aforementioned conditions of true theocracy, each of which is summoned to realize by its own respective national genius and historical fortunes.

Let us begin with Russia and the structures of life in her church, state, and social spheres. The historically shaped structure of Russian life is expressed in the following clear features: the church, represented by an archpriestly *council*, and dependent on the *monasteries*; the government, concentrated in the autocratic *tsar*; and the people, who live by agriculture in *village communes*. The monastery, the palace, and the village—these are our social foundations, which will not be shaken as long as Russia exists. These elements of our existential order encompass great advantages but cannot for all that make up for several vital shortcomings. Thus, the *monastery* attracts, protects, and instructs believing souls, but it cannot arouse, support, and protect faith where it is weak; this requires a constant activity in the world which is uncharacteristic to a monk. Eastern asceticism, although partially altered by the Russian national character, still remains primarily *contemplative* and is, consequently, not called at all to prepare the church's activists and rulers. For religious life in general, asceticism is essential, but the special duties of ecclesial government will require additional particular moral and practical qualities besides that of ascetic holiness. An unwavering firmness and an indefatigable activism are required in the struggle with secular powers that are hostile to the church and which arm themselves more and more against religion. The entire matter consists in the fact that the church on earth must not only *safeguard* the sacredness of faith but also unceasingly *fight* for it with external enemies; it must fortify, protect, and strengthen religious life. But the proper conditions required for such an active struggle are not provided for either by the monastic character of ecclesial administration or its synodic image. Struggle requires a sufficiently independent, concentrated, and energetic church power. The dependence of the spiritual power upon the secular and the lack of an inner core paralyze the church's external activity and undermine her ability to influence national and social life. The Russian church, thanks be to God, enjoys the protection of the Orthodox tsar, who is autocratic and consequently independent of contemporary godless social elements. But besides this negative condition, which we face directly, that is, in addition to the political boundlessness of tsarist power, its capacity to successfully serve God also requires a positive condition: the powers of a Christian government must be guided by the instructions of an independent spiritual authority, by a manifest representative of Christ's church on earth, and this requires the spiritual authority, which personifies society's religious element, to have full independence. A church which is deprived of a sufficiently independent representative cannot exert any real influence either upon government or upon society. And so we see that, in spite of the piety of the Russian people, in spite of our sovereigns' loyalty to Orthodoxy, in spite of the many beautiful qualities of our clergy, our church lacks its proper status and fails to direct Russia's life. Our people sets divine righteousness above all else, it is theocratic to its soul's core, but it lacks the first real condition needed for the realization of theocracy, thanks to the deep-rooted shortcomings of our ecclesial order.

As regards Russia's *political* system, its great strength lies in its tsarist monarchy and in the people's unanimous attachment to the tsar.

But the present weakness of this system consists in the fact that nothing fills the space between the tsar and the people, no well organized and disciplined society, no ruling class. From olden times, especially from Peter the Great to Alexander II, Russia's civil order depended upon two specific adjacent or partially overlapping but never completely coinciding groups: the gentry and the civil service. The latter directly served the state, while the former stayed closer to the people and represented, to some degree, Russia's land. Without their help, Russia could not have developed into that homogeneous and sturdy body which it still is in spite of all her faults. The main shortcoming of this double arrangement consisted in the fact that being a reliable instrument of state authority, it was not also a loyal conductor of folk needs, from the land to the tsar. The *alteration* of our civil order became a necessity. But this order was *wrecked* by the reforms of the sixties. The gentry, deprived of independent status and become coldly indifferent to the land, as well as significantly bankrupt (partly through its own fault), formed the main contingent of that contemporary intelligentsia which is unable to have any governmental or civil status, for given its routine opposition to the government, and its alienation from the people, it can in no wise serve as an intermediary link between the tsar and the land. Along with the gentry, a decisive blow was also dealt to the old civil bureaucracy, which had to share its domain with new qualitatively different institutions. In addition to this, the sturdy state spirit and the civic discipline of the old civil bureaucracy were uprooted by the influence of the new intelligentsia, armed by the liberalism of a slavish press. As for the new institutions, on the one hand, they turn out to be totally impotent on account of the economic bankruptcy of that social element which predominantly constitutes them (the remnants of the "dispersed" gentry in the rural establishments), and, on the other hand, some of these institutions are accused, not without foundation, of partaking in that *false* tendency which makes them serve not so much the tsar and Russia as the "liberal" intelligentsia and its public opinion, a service which is all the more fruitless because there cannot be any real intelligentsia or any real public opinion in Russia for the absence of society itself, for the lack of definite social groups, organized for corporate action.[74] Those public elements which

normally constitute the active segment of society are among us decisively weak and economically insolvent. The former class of civil servants, consisting of gentry and bureaucrats, has lost its distinctiveness
and status. Next, besides the professional scholars and literati, which
in no case constitute society, and do not, in Russia, even represent a
major social force—besides these we have a certain number of educated and thinking people, but given the absence of a unifying principle and a clear goal for action, their social significance is absolutely
null. There remains, then, a considerably large and constantly growing
semieducated crowd, capable at times of good impulses and movements but in large measure given over to crude and petty instincts.
This milieu also fails to provide any real elements of social organization. We possess an organized activity but only that whose tenden-
cies are destructive, turning the best people in the crowd into unwary
sacrifices of deception.

Given this state of affairs, even if the supreme government were
inspired by the highest and holiest ideal, it would fail to find in Russian society appropriate instruments for its realization. Self-sacrificing
leaders and rank-and-file heroes will always be found amidst our
people for every endeavor, but from what, in our society, could we
establish a ruling class capable of and accustomed to acting with solidarity? Thanks be to God that we still retain sufficient social forces,
though barely, to support the day-to-day functioning of the state
mechanism.

In the meantime, such social insolvency is not only regrettable in
the civil sense, but is reflected in the most hazardous manner in Russia's economic conditions. As Russia lives by agriculture, its whole
economic structure must in reality be determined by agricultural factors. The impoverishment of the soil signifies Russia's demise, and
everything now leads to this impoverishment. In contemporary Russia, with its population of a hundred million, agriculture continues to
be conducted by the same methods as three hundred years ago when
the population was ten times smaller. But if then the only possible economics were predatory ones, they now, with every passing year, become ever more dangerous. The earth's natural productive forces are
not unlimited—the people, sooner or later, *consume the earth*. To

prevent such an outcome or at least to forestall it necessitates a transition from primeval or predatory economics to an artificial or a rational system. But it is impossible even to conceive the people changing the economic system by themselves. Their fathers and forefathers taught them the old methods, who would teach them the new? An entire class of educated and skilled people devoted to this task is indispensable. But we have no such class. On the other hand, rational agricultural economics, just considering the material aspect of things, is a matter of considerable complexity. It demands active industrial support and requires technical innovation and discovery. Under such conditions the *village* cannot survive without the *city*. Country life, left to itself, falls into routine and stagnation. Invigorating activity belongs to the city. To the city belong enterprise, initiative, and innovation. The city must help the village. It must be in solidarity with it for the common good. And this too we do not have. We do not have an enterprising and active industrial class, which, utilizing the country's natural resources, would by its industry help agriculture. Our city element is not organically linked to the life of the land; it does not participate in it in any positive manner but is exclusively occupied with its own *private* profits. Yet it is precisely because Russia is predominantly an agricultural country that it most greatly requires the help of the city with its concentrated economic and spiritual forces. But our city class turns out to be too weak, fragmented, and disorganized to execute its commission successfully. The growth of our cities, especially in the past thirty years, only engendered a distinct bourgeois civilization with its artificial needs, more complex but not any more elevated than those of simple country folk. Meanwhile, a large portion of our industry exists only to satisfy those artificial, and sometimes also revolting, needs of urban civilization. Industry thus serves not the land but the city, and this would not become a tragedy if the city itself were to serve some good purpose. But in all reality our cities, instead of functioning as the principal ligaments of the social organism, are more akin to hazardous parasites which exhaust the national body. Our urban civilization takes everything from the land and gives nothing in return. More harm than good is also brought to the land by the most important inventions and discoveries, of which our century is so proud, for example, the railroads and steamships. The profit which they apparently provide for the whole country, the alleviated distribution of agricultural products, is decisively outweighed by the harm which they bring to agriculture itself; by saying *harm*, I am using too weak an expression, for it will soon become clear to all that the proliferation of such comfortable means of communication is the *demise* of our agriculture. Railroads mercilessly devour forests, and without forests our huge continental plain will sooner or later, and rather sooner than later, turn into a barren wilderness. And as for the striking rate by which our rivers become ever more shallow and the draughts more frequent, this is no longer a prophecy but a fact. In other countries irrigation is provided either by proximity to the sea or by high snowy mountains. But we maintain ourselves only by forests and marshes, from which flow and by which are fed all of our great rivers. And now we, not confining ourselves to the destruction of the forests, have begun diligently to dry up the marshes.

In this manner, agriculture, the foundation of our economic life, perishes on account of a false civilization, that is, on account of a civilization which transforms means into ends, which turns tools into idols, and for the comfort of some sacrifices that which is necessary for all. Conquered by this civilization, the city, instead of helping the village, threatens it with ruin, a ruin from which the village cannot save itself. The economic activity of our country commune is determined by ancient routine and is absolutely defenseless against the new and complex disasters that threaten agriculture. These disasters could only be prevented by that which we precisely lack: the energetic and friendship-inspired activity of personal forces, animated by the apprehension of the common good, and directed toward a common *creative* goal. But our society, or the so-called intelligentsia, has decisively proved its incapacity for such friendly and solidarity-based activity for the common good, while the individual element in the general populace is too weak and passive.

In summary, we come to the following conclusion. All the historical advantages of our existential order, which illuminate Russia's specific and great vocation, are decisively paralyzed by such substantive shortcomings as considerably hamper the fulfillment of this vocation. First of all, we possess God's most important gift, the Orthodox and Holy Church, *but the church does not possess us*. The ecclesiastical sphere, represented by the spiritual authorities, is deprived among us of practical independence and cannot freely direct and influence social and national life: we are members of the holy and blessed body, the church, but the first condition for *growth* of this body within us is absent.

Furthermore, and second, we have another great advantage: a sacred and autocratic tsarist power, but this blessing we also poorly utilize. Given the civil insolvency of our society, the extreme disorganization of social forces, the absence of a real ruling class, the supreme authority is deprived of the instruments necessary for forging Russia's destiny. Finally, our third treasure: the people, deeply pious, possessing a clear governmental sense, and dedicated to the most real and healthy of enterprises: agriculture; a people that is patient, calm, and self-sacrificing—and this blessing also brings us no benefit. Without the friendly labor of personal enterprising forces in the socioeconomic sector, the national masses, with all of their virtues, are not only incapable of transforming the land into a docile instrument of the human spirit, but are even incapable of providing for themselves the means necessary for existence, they can hardly manage to survive on the land. The power of the village, lacking the help of urban reason, remains a force that is blind and defenseless against all possible disasters. But where is our urban, that is, civilized, reason, capable of really helping the village, and of teaching and directing the people toward a common task?[75]

Given such conditions, or, better, given the absence of the necessary conditions for genuine progress, the great advantages of our national-historical order are only good *inclinations* or possibilities whose fruitful actualization awaits other conditions and new elements. Russia, left to her own devices, *solitary* Russia, is powerless. It is not good for man to be alone.[76] This divine word is applicable also to collective man, to the people as a whole. Only in unity with what Russia lacks can Russia utilize that which she has, and utilize it in full measure both for herself and for the whole world. Then will our faith be justified in Russia and in those positive forces by which she lives: in the

Orthodox Church, founded on tradition and crowned by the ideal of ascetic holiness; in the sacred and autocratic power of the Orthodox tsar; and in the strength of the Orthodox people attached to the land but not forgetting God, a people that prefers the righteousness on high to mundane goods, a people that does not make an idol out of itself, a people that is not democratic but theocratic. Here are our great positive forces whose creative actualization and manifestation must await the practical principles which they themselves lack.

Moving on from Russia to the historical order of Poland, we encounter here traits of a directly opposite character. If the main defect in the order of our civic affairs consists in a weak public community, in the absence of a self-sufficient and active upper class, then in Poland, on the contrary, the higher class was and continues to be everything. Poland and *szlachta* (the Polish gentry) are one and the same thing. (If the word *Pole* evokes in our mind a definite and specific image, then it is invariably an image of the *szlachtich*—Polish aristocrat—but never a peasant or a merchant.) Given the absence in Poland of a national urban class and due to the suppression of the rural class (half of which, moreover, was of non-Polish origin), *szlachta* by itself represented the whole nation. And given the nullity of royal power, *szlachta* comprehended the whole *state*. The exclusive development and prevalence of *szlachta* gave Poland her original public community and her distinctive and considerably elevated culture. Thanks to the same circumstance, the Poles, more than any other Slavic nation, are capable, if not of *friendly*[77] activity, then at least of *cooperative* activity.[78] But these social and cultural advantages did not prevent the *pani* (Polish landowners) from godlessly and inhumanely oppressing the common people and giving themselves over to unbridled self-will instead of governing the state. Poland's *entire* strength was contained in *szlachta,* and Poland perished.[79] It did not perish because it possessed a strong gentry, for that was its advantage, but because her gentry, instead of being a public communal class, organized to serve the state and to govern the people, turned into an unboundedly dominating class, containing the whole state within itself. It would be a great mistake if, basing oneself on the nullity of royal power and on the absence of common national rights, one was to see in Poland an aristocratic republic. The distinctive character of such a republic is well known (e.g., Venice) and contrasts directly with Poland's political system since the latter is not much more than a legalized anarchy. For it is well known that the Polish *szlachta* represents the sole historical example of a ruling class in which each member *separately* possesses full state authority. This absolute independence of each single person made the independent existence of the whole Polish state impossible.

Nevertheless, in spite of losing her political independence, Poland has not yet (completely) perished: she lives by her national idea, which carries, although in a frequently distorted manner, a specific theocratic character. And even though most Poles have been incorporated into Russia's tsarist territory, they do not want to and cannot merge and disappear in the Russian sea; for they not only constitute a specific national force but also represent a specific spiritual idea—the idea of Catholicism. We know that Catholicism contains one of the essential elements of Christian theocracy, since therein the high priestly principle has reached its extreme stage of development.[80] Avoiding here a theological analysis of the issue, we cannot deny the fact that only Catholicism exhibits an *unconditional* independence of church authority vis-à-vis state and society. With us in the East, the one universal church increasingly hides itself behind the many national churches, whose union becomes progressively weaker. The exclusively or at least predominantly *national* church unavoidably becomes a *state* church. Political national independence devours the independence of its church. To restore an independent church within itself, our tsarist East must find a point of support outside of itself, as Eastern Orthodoxy formerly did find for itself a firm fulcrum in the Western archpriest. But the Western archpriest in his turn needs the protection and defense of the Eastern tsar, and of the patriarchal piety of the tsarist people. The reunification between Orthodoxy and Catholicism must liberate and strengthen the church in the East and restore Christian statehood in the West. And since the state power of the East belongs to Russia in her tsar and the spiritual power of the West belongs to the Roman archpriest, then might not our Poles, being both the subjects of the Russian tsar and fantastical spiritual children of the Roman pope,

and being, as Slavs, close to Russians by blood, but in spirit and culture to the Romano-Germanic West, be natural mediators for this
unification?

In the present time, the Poles think least about playing such a role;
all their efforts are directed not to the universal-religious but to the
national-political task: the restoration of the great Polish state. For
everyone else, however, the fantastical nature of this goal and the fruitlessness of their efforts are quite obvious. It is true that following the
collapse of the Polish kingdom, the Poles both forgot and learned
something. They forgot the limitlessness of their personal self-will
and their "we will not allow,"[81] and learned to act in a cooperative
and organized manner; currently, the active part of the Polish nation,
the *szlachta*,[82] represents a relatively cohesive and disciplined collective
force. Nevertheless, for their political restoration, the Poles lack the
most primary and necessary conditions. For lacking any foundations
for a strong state power, and possessing an exclusively passive rural
class, and lacking an urban class, the whole of Poland is solely represented by the *szlachta*. Given favorable circumstances, *szlachta* could
constitute a useful and important organ for the body of the state and
nation, but it could in no way constitute this body. The Poles must understand (and the best among them have begun to understand) that this
endeavor of an individual organ to become *in its separateness* the whole
organism is a mindless and an immoral endeavor. They wish to liberate and extol the Polish nation and regard everything else as a means
and an instrument for achieving this goal. But what if the Polish nation
itself is only a means and an instrument? What if the true essence and
significance of this nation lies not in itself, and not in that by which it
seems to be represented, that is, not in *szlachta*, but in *that* which it
represents, that is, Roman Catholicism? Verily this is how it is. Verily
the entire significance and the entire strength of the Polish people lies
in the fact that in the midst of the Slavs, facing the East, they bear and
represent the great spiritual principle of the Western world. The Polish
state has perished, and Polish nationalism will also perish, and all the
plans and endeavors of the Poles will turn to nothing.[83] But Poland,
called to sacred service, has not perished and will not perish. To serve
Catholicism—this is the highest vocation of the Polish nation. And the

primary and greatest service—the reunification of Catholicism with Orthodoxy, the mediation of a reconciliation between the pope and the tsar—is the starting point of a new Christian theocracy.

If Christianity is not destined to inaction, then it must show the world its moral might, and justify itself as a religion of peace and of love. I am not speaking about love for all and everything, regardless of who it is; nor am I talking about peace-making with everybody and everything. I know that the church on earth is a militant church, but let fratricidal war be accursed! Let the old deception which nurtures and is nurtured by lawless enmity be exposed and dispelled. Let a new fire be inflamed in the cooled heart of the bride of Christ! And let all the barriers dividing that which has been created to unify the world[84] collapse and turn to dust!

A day will come when Poland, healed from prolonged madness, will become a living bridge between the holiness of the East and of the West.[85] The mighty tsar will then extend his helping hand to the persecuted pontiff. Then will true prophets also arise from the midst of all the peoples and serve as witnesses for the tsar and the priest. Then will the faith of Christ be glorified, and then will the people of Israel be converted. It will be converted because it will clearly perceive and know the kingdom of the Messiah in power and in action. And Israel will not then be superfluous among Egypt and Assyria, amidst Poland and Russia.[86]

And is it really even true that Jewry now constitutes a completely superfluous and exclusively harmful, parasitic element in the place where it predominantly multiplies: in the Russian-Polish region? This region, especially the White- and Red-soiled Rus' represents a wonderful phenomenon: the social elements are here sharply distributed among different ethnic groups.[87] Russians constitute the village agricultural class, the upper class is constituted by Poles, and the urban industrial class by Jews. If the Jews managed, not only under favorable but also, and predominantly, under considerably unfavorable conditions, to take such firm and complete control of Western-Russian cities, this obviously demonstrates that they surpass the Russian people and the Polish *szlachta* in the ability to form an urban industrial class. If the industrial class, instead of helping the agricultural class, lives *everywhere* at the latter's expense and exploits it, it is not surprising that in those places where Jews constitute the whole industrial class, that they also exploit the people. But it is not they who created this situation. They had spent too long in the school of the Polish *pans* who equally oppressed both the yid and the serf. And besides the *pans*, is it not the case that the self-interested oppression of one class by another constitutes the general rule of social life in Europe as a whole? If our peasants need the Jews and tolerate their oppressiveness, this occurs only because of these peasants' helpless socioeconomic conditions, and these conditions are not brought about by the Jews. The needy peasant goes to the Jews because *his own will not help him.* And if the Jews, in helping a peasant, exploit him, then they are doing this not because they are Jews but because they are masters of monetary affairs which are founded in their entirety upon mutual exploitation.

The tragedy lies not in the Jews and not in money but in the dominion, in the *almightiness of money,* which in itself is not created by the Jews. It is not the Jews who make profit and enrichment the aim of all economic activity, and it is not the Jews who have separated the economic domain from the religious and the moral. It was Enlightenment Europe that first established godless and inhumane principles in the social economy, and now it blames the Jews for following these principles.

The deeds of the Jews are not worse than our deeds, and it is not for us to blame them. If they are to be blamed for anything, it is that they remain being Jews and preserve their segregation. But show them then a visible and a *tangible* Christianity, so that they would have something to attach themselves to. As they are a people of action, show them Christian action: unite the church, unify it righteously with the state, create a Christian state and a Christian society. The Jews will not, of course, accept Christianity when Christians themselves reject it; they would doubtfully unite with something which is itself divided. Do not object that the Jews showed no interest in the Christian world when it had the benefit of unity. For that was an involuntary, semiconscious, untried, and untested unity. For when the trial and the temptation came, this unity did not endure, to the shame of the Christian world, and to the justification and vindication of Jewry. And it will continue to be justified in its victory as long as we do not reestablish a Christian unity, freely and consciously. This is the first duty that lies upon us, Russians and Poles, for it is in us that the Christian East and West have come face-to-face, with all the untruth of their enmity, with all the necessity of their reconciliation.

The unification of Christianity will occasion a great division in Judaism. But if the division of Christianity was, for it, a tragedy, then the division of Israel will be, for the latter, a great blessing. The best part of Jewry will enter the Christian theocracy, while the worst will remain outside of it, and only be saved in the last times, after receiving its retribution according to God's righteousness, by His mercy, for firm is the word of the apostle, that *all Israel will be saved.*

And when the Jews enter Christian theocracy, they will bring to it their strengths. At some point in the distant past, the best strengths of Jewry were represented by the prophets. Prophecy was the first expression of a free and active personality. The prophets were later replaced by the *teachers of the law*, whereby prophecy passed over into rabbinism—a new manifestation of that still same personal and active principle. Now, finally, the main strengths of Jewry are predominantly directed toward economic activity—the last extreme expression and the materialization of the personal principle. The Jewish personality first affirmed itself in the divine sphere, then in the ratio-human sphere, and is now concentrating in the material and human sphere. This last sphere is the forum of the final expression of Jewish strength, and it will persist in Christian theocracy and remain indebted to Jews. But here the Jewish spirit will have a different character, a different aim, and a different relationship to the object of activity. For in the present godless and inhuman existential order, the goal of economic activity, for Jews and non-Hebrews alike, is mere profit (material advantage); in this setting, the objects of material nature, even living ones, are merely *instruments* for satisfying blind self-profiting desires. In theocracy, the goal of economic activity is the *humanization* of material life and of nature, its ordering by human reason, its animation with human feeling. In this way, this nature, the earth and that which is on it, animals and plants, already enter into that very aim of human activity and are not used as its mere instruments, for such use is abuse. When self-interest ceases to reign in social relations between people, it will also cease to rule in man's relationship with nature. And in theocracy, material nature will serve man, and much more so than it does now, for this service will be founded upon reciprocal love. Nature will lovingly subordinate itself to man and man will lovingly become its steward. And what people is preeminently capable of and called to this stewardship over material nature, if not the Jewish, which, from the beginning, recognized her right to exist and, not surrendering to her blind power, saw in her transfigured form the pure and holy veil of the divine essence? And just as the flower of Jewry formerly served to provide the receptive milieu for the incarnation of the Deity, so the future Israel will serve as an active mediator for the humanization of material life and nature and for the creation of a new earth where righteousness dwells.

CHAPTER 2

"The Israel of the New Covenant" (1885)

———

This coming Christmas, the prayer hall[88] Bethlehem in Kishenev will celebrate the first anniversary of its founding. Had someone said several years ago that a Jewish chapel would appear in southern Russia, dedicated to Jesus Christ the Son of God, and allow hundreds of Jews to hearken to the preaching of the Gospel every week, no one would have believed it. The man who accomplished all this, Joseph Rabinovich,[89] stirred up bitter hatred and persecution against himself from among his kinsmen. Initially, people said he was a deceiver, then that he was mad. But whoever listened to him dispassionately recognized in him a *true Israelite in whom there is no guile*.[90] In this lies the whole story of his conversion. By way of the Law and the Prophets, he came to Christ, and saw and said: "Rabbi, You are the Son of God, you are the King of Israel."[91]

Need it be said that someone who is born a Jew and reared on the promises of the Old Testament gives the phrase "the King of Israel" a completely different sense from the one it bears for us? Were someone born a Jew to recognize Christ as the true King of Israel, he would find in Him not just the fulfillment of his religion but also the complete satisfaction of his ethnohistorical sensibilities. And it is not just this one expression "King of Israel" but also the more general title "Savior" that sounds different to a Jewish convert than it does to us. We think of a Savior from common sins and troubles affecting human nature, but the Jew who comes to Christ also finds in Him a Savior from the particular historical illnesses affecting his people.

The following shows how Joseph Rabinovich expounded this subject in one private conversation:[92]

> My people's suffering has always weighed upon my heart, and I tried to help them with all sorts of remedies, but all were in vain. When a doctor visits a sick man, he must examine and inspect him before prescribing a treatment for his illness. He takes the pulse, then presses this, then that part of the body, asking each time, "Does this hurt? Is that sore?" But only when the doctor reaches the sore spot does the patient really cry out, provoked by the feeling of pain: "Don't press, it hurts!" So it was with me when I busied myself with the sufferings of my people. I probed carefully in different places. As long as I did not touch the sore spot, the response was hardly audible. When I said: "The Talmud and all the rabbinic additions in no way derive from Sinai, as is claimed, but are mere human labor, half sense and half nonsense," my people were hardly troubled. Were I to continue and add that "both the Torah (the Law) and the whole Tanach (The Old Testament) contain only human injunctions, untrustworthy histories, and improbable miracles," here too I would remain a *reverend Rabinovich*, for these words of mine would bring my people no pain. My people would even remain calm when I would set Moses on par with contemporary magicians and label him a deceiver. I could have even denied God himself, and my people would have still not cried out in pain. But now, when I returned from the Holy Land with the joyful news that *"Jesus is our brother,"*[93] I finally struck the sore spot, and from everywhere a cry of pain resounded: "Don't press, don't touch, it hurts!"
>
> Of course it hurts, but know nonetheless, my people, that this is indeed your illness, for only on His account do you suffer—on account of your brother Jesus. Your ailment consists only in the fact that you do not have Him. Receive Him and you will be healed from all your sufferings.

In a sermon uttered on the third of August this year, the founder of the Israel of the New Covenant[94] developed this same personal thought in detail. Since this sermon was printed only in Hebrew, I will present it here with some omissions and abridgements, using a hand-written Russian translation, sent to me by its preacher.[95]

Having read the law of the king's appointment in the Old Testament (Deut. 17:4–20)[96] and the corresponding New Testament passage from the Gospel of Luke (22:24–29), the preacher began to speak, addressing the people as follows:

> Dear brethren, People of Israel! Your name and memory excite all my senses. Israel! This noble and meaning-laden name contains and conceals weighty thoughts and enthralling memories! But who is *now* this people? Who bears this name? Is Israel really your name? *Yid*, they call you, and despised and detested are you in the eyes of the whole world. Are you that same people whom God chose before all others as His own possession?[97] Are you that same people to whom were granted the writings and the prophecies that constitute the source of life for all the world's active nations.[98] Are you that same Israel upon whom, already three thousand years ago, its faithful lawgiver, Moses, bestowed its foundational laws and institutions, comparable to the best legislation produced by today's enlightened nations? What has now happened to you, my people? Why have you changed so much that no one can recognize you? Truly you are ill. Alas, how long your illness lasts! To what may one compare you, my people?, and to what may you be likened?[99] You are like a wrecked ship, which had long ago sunk in the water with all its goods and cargo, with only the mast showing, swaying to and fro, above the surface of the sea. Scores of ships pass it by on their courses, some successfully, others suffering shipwreck and sinking completely to the bottom of the sea, but this ship alone continues to sway just below the waves, unable either to surface or to sink completely. Such are you too, my people Israel! For a long time you have been totally wrecked. There is not a sound spot in your body, your brain is paralyzed, and all your affective organs are atrophied. Only in one portion of your heart can one still, at times, discern a pulse. Yet your limbs quiver and your facial lines show that you are not yet to be listed among the nations who have perished. Yes, you still live, and the name Israel

still hovers above you. You sway, this way and that, in the midst of the gulf of mundane life, standing between life and death, unable to live, unable to die.

The preacher then recalls the various remedies which have been proposed to heal the Jewish people of their ages-long illness. Thus the Talmudists thought that the best remedy would consist in *imitating* health and in replacing the actual fulfillment of the Law by various artificial signs (e.g., the so-called tefillin, the ribbons worn on arms and forehead and inscribed with the words of the Law). But when, with the passage of time, it turned out that such methods, instead of healing, only intensified the pain and, moreover, delivered the Jews to universal ridicule, the people of Israel began to tear off these Talmudic bandages in the hope that the *spirit* of the *new age*, by its mere blowing, would heal all its illnesses. Then it was that Moses Mendelsohn, the bearer of enlightenment for modern Jewry, came and revealed a new therapy. All the sufferings of the Jews, according to his teaching, stem from the fact that they consider themselves a *special*, separate *nation*. Were they simply to repudiate this; were the Jews living in Germany simply to declare themselves to be German observers of the Mosaic Law, and the Polish Jews to declare themselves Polish observers of the Mosaic Law, and so on, then straightaway all the Jews would become assimilated with other enlightened peoples and thereby be delivered, once and for all, from all their national woes, which means, in other words, that the ship of Israel would sink completely, mast and all, into the depths of the sea. But now one century has passed and the spirit of the new age, in whose reviving breath the enlightened Jews had placed so much hope, has suddenly turned into the menacing gust of an antisemitic gale, which has begun to rage over all Europe, shattering houses into splinters and scattering to the wind the acquisitions of all these German, Polish, and Russian observers of the Mosaic Law. During this miserable period, new saviors of the Jewish people have appeared: publicists declaring, contra Mendelsohn, that the Jews possess nationality, and that their nation is still capable of living separately, without assimilating to other peoples, and that its renaissance only requires a change of climate and migration to Palestine.

Here before you is a dangerous patient, who can hardly breathe and who lacks the strength to stir, but around whom three doctors gather for a consultation. The first begins broadly to review those movements and exercises which it would profit the patient to perform; the second preoccupies himself with the patient's real name, positing that unless his name were clearly presented on a prescription at a pharmacy, one could not proceed to treat him; the third, finally, begins to contend that the patient needs a change of scenery and should depart to distant lands. Such are your doctors, O Israel! But when will you finally discern their lack of discernment? You have apparently completely forgotten the words, addressed to you and written in your Torah, in that same Torah which you read weekly, twice in the original and once in translation: *I am God, your Healer* (Exod. 15:26).[100] Know then, O Israel, that as long as you will expect help and healing to come from mortal hands, and not from your God, you will remain perpetually unhealed. "*He sent forth his word and healed them,*" says the Spirit of God through the mouth of the psalmist (Ps. 107:20).

The prophet Isaiah, seeing in his prophetic vision that the God of Hosts[101] would accomplish a predetermined extermination upon the whole earth, and that the branches that were great in height would be hewn down, and the lofty brought low,[102] consoled himself and said: "*And a shoot will arise* from the hewn tree of *Jesse* . . . and the Spirit of the Lord shall rest upon Him."[103] Brothers! these words do not require various interpretations, but demand simply an attentive ear, a pure heart, and an upright understanding. These words, "shoot of the stump of Jesse," permit us to understand the counsel of God at the time that He founded His heavenly kingdom upon the earth. The godly husbandman Isaiah, when God's Spirit rested upon him and lofty prophetic thoughts seized his soul, and divine portents presented to him from times that transpired ages before, fell into rapture and indescribable joy on seeing in the events that occurred in the life of the first true Israelite King David, the *youngest* of the sons of Jesse, *the shepherd of sheep,*[104] the whole history of the Christ of the God of Jacob, the hope and glory of the people of Israel,[105] in whom all the promises given to this people are fulfilled, and through whose action, in the end of times, the wolf will dwell with the lamb, and the leopard with the goat, and a *little child*,[106] Christ, by his flesh a son of the youngest of the children of Jesse, the shepherd from Bethlehem, will lead them like a good shepherd. The sixteenth chapter of the first Book of Kings[107] illuminates and explains to us these two prophetic words: *a little child.*

Having retold the biblical story of how the prophet Samuel, against his personal sensibilities, and despite all outward appearances and all human conceptions, anointed as king the little shepherd David, whom God Himself had chosen, the preacher continues:

> The Lord's aim in such a choice, as evident from the following chapter (17:41–47), was that through this shepherd's combat with the Philistine Goliath, *the whole earth should come to know that there is a God in Israel,* and that it is not by sword or by spear that the Lord delivers. This fearsome Philistine, relying on his fleshly strength and on his gigantic armaments, so elaborately described in the sacred book, reviled the Israelite army, saying, "Give me a *man* to battle with me in a duel."[108] Having highlighted the fright and confusion of Saul and all the Israelites, scripture goes on to tell us that Jesse's elder sons followed Saul to war, while David, the youngest, continued to shepherd his father's flocks in Bethlehem. Only *by chance* did he come to be in the military ranks, for the simple reason that his father Jesse sent food by him to his elder sons. Brothers! one only needs to notice this circumstance: that the elevation of David, king of Israel, on whose reign are founded the most cherished and resplendent hopes of the entire Jewish people, which even now, in the time of its exile, never ceases to remember in its prayers that *David the King of Israel lives and is eternal,*[109] as it is said: "the scepter shall not depart from Judah"[110] — one only needs to notice, I repeat, that this greatest event of Jewish history occurred, as it were, in an *indirect and accidental* manner. This is so because, as it is said, "truly, you are a God who hides yourself, O God, Savior of Israel,"[111] and this allows man freedom to ascribe this or that happening either to divine providence or to simple coincidence, and thereby tests the believing

heart. Thus, unforeseeably finding himself in the military ranks and hearing the insulting challenge of the Philistine, David invested himself with zeal for the God of Hosts and exclaimed: "Who is this uncircumcised [Philistine], that he should so revile the army of the living God?"[112] And when they presented him before King Saul, and the latter said to him, "You cannot go against this Philistine, for you are still a child, while he is a man, a warrior from his youth,"[113] David objected in simplicity of heart: "As your servant would beat down a lion or a bear, so shall it be with this foreigner. I will go and smite him, and remove the reproach from Israel, for who is this uncircumcised [Philistine], that he should so revile the army of *the living God*?"[114] By these words, the future king of Israel wanted to say that only the Spirit of God enlivens and strengthens man, and that without it, by one's own personal strength, man is comparable to a wild beast. For this reason he added with full confidence: "The Lord, who has delivered me from the claws of the lion and from the claws of the bear, will also deliver me from the hand of this uncircumcised [Philistine]."[115] Following this, when David was endowed with Saul's military gear, with helmet and sword, he doffed all these, took his shepherd's staff, put into his pouch five smooth stones ("for it was the stone which the builders rejected"),[116] and approached the Philistine, saying, "You come against me, with spear and shield, while I come against you in the name of the Lord of Hosts, the God of the host of Israel, whom you have reviled, and now the Lord will deliver you into my hand—*and the whole earth will know that there is a God in Israel* and all this horde will understand *that not by sword, nor by spear does the Lord deliver*."[117] And now this desire, the desire to demonstrate not his own power but the *power of the living God*, so that the whole earth should know that there is a God in Israel, this wondrous desire, which God saw earlier in the heart of the little shepherd from Bethlehem, was what made this shepherd God's elect.

Such was the calling of the first founder of the kingdom of God on earth, the first king from the house of Jesse, and such also is the calling of the last king of Israel, from the stock of Jesse, the

eternally existing Son of God, Jesus Christ, namely: to show the
world *that there is a God*, and to give eternal life to all who believe
in Him, as the same Christ said, "This is eternal life, that they
know You the only true God and Jesus Christ whom you have
sent" (John 17:19).[118] And as David, the shepherd of sheep and the
smallest among his brothers, was chosen despite all human outward appearance, so also the Son of David, our good shepherd,
who humbled Himself and took on the form of a slave,[119] teaches
us not to judge according to our fleshly eyes. He indeed told his
disciples, "Whoever is greatest among you, let him be like the
smallest, and the one who commands like the one who serves: only
such will inherit the kingdom" (Luke 22:24–26).

Such is the king that God commends to Israel, saying: "Set
over yourself a king whom the Lord your God will choose, so that
this king would neither multiply horses, nor multiply wives, nor
set his hope on gold or silver, but only on God and on the teaching of the Lord, so that his heart would not become haughty,
then *he and his sons* will continue in his kingdom in the midst of
Israel."[120]

Thus God said, and thus He accomplished. He found for himself such a king according to His own heart: David, and in order
that he and his sons should always endure in the kingdom in Israel,
God gave to Jesus our Messiah or Christ (i.e., the anointed, the
King), the son of David and the Son of God, the throne of David,
His father, and He assumed reign over the house of Jacob forever,
and to His kingdom there will be no end (Luke 1:32, 33). Yes,
brothers! He is that shoot from the hewn tree of Jesse, and *that
little child*, who jointly leads the wolves, the sheep, the lambs, the
leopards, the goats, the cows and the bears (i.e., folk and people of
every sort, humble and wild), as Isaiah the prophet foresaw. And
if we, with full heartfelt repentance, follow and enter the kingdom
of this descendant of Jesse according to the flesh, then *He*, following the prophecy of Isaiah, *will judge the poor* (i.e., us) *in righteousness and will smite the earth* (arising against us) *with the rod
of His mouth*[121] — the holy Gospel, for our Heavenly Father promised Him His kingdom as an inheritance, and only those who believe in Him will inherit with Him.

Lay all these words to heart, brothers, remove all love of false-hood from your midst, approach and draw near to your Messiah, to your King Jesus. He will heal you from that blindness, which the prophet additionally noted, saying in our regard, "who is as blind as my servant?" (Isa. 42:19). Yes! you, Israel, are that same blind man about whom the disciples of the Lord Jesus asked, "Who has sinned, he or his parents?"—and Jesus answered them, "Neither he sinned, nor his parents, but that the works of God would become manifest upon him" (John 9:2–4).[122] Yes, Israel! you are blind, the light of the world is dark for you, and stumbling stones lie on all your paths. Some (the socialists) say, that *you* have sinned, others (the antisemites) say that it was your *parents*; but the only truth is that which the Lord Savior said: "*this has been purposed so that the works of God would become manifest upon him.*" For this you became blind; for this you are broken and per-secuted, and for this you *nevertheless* live, that the works of God become manifest upon you. As soon as you turn to *Yehovah*,[123] your *God*, you will love Him and will believe in His Son Jesus Christ, the redeemer of all human sins, and you will become see-ing, like that blind man of Jerusalem. Through this faith in Jesus there will also be revealed to you the *light of life* under which all the enlightened peoples walk, and you will again mount up unto the platform of this world's renowned nations.

This Messiah Jesus, who descended into the depths and as-cended to heaven, will descend also to you, so as to submerge all your sins into the depths of the sea, and he will draw the drowned ship of Israel up from the sea of sorrows, and you will again be-come a people of God. The Prince of life and of peace,[124] may He make peace between Israel and the Gentiles.[125] Let the words of the prophet be speedily fulfilled: "and the wolf shall dwell with the lamb and the leopard will lie down together with the kid, and *a little child*—our Lord Jesus Christ—will lead them. Hallowed be that Name for ever and ever, Amen."[126]

Behold the spirit in which the founder of the new Israel preaches: "Every spirit, which confesses that Jesus Christ has come in the flesh, is of God."[127] That our preacher has the faith of Christ is clear. One may only ask, "By what *way* has he reached it?" Christ himself is the way, the truth and the life. And although Christ is like a way, or alternatively, although the way of Christ is one in its moral essence, which is meekness and obedience to the highest will, still in its visible manifestation this way differs significantly when one considers *who (is it that) comes (and) from where.* If we who are born into the church understand Christ's way in terms of a free subordination to this church in all her judgments, then for a Jew, born outside the church, the lawful way of Christ, indicated by Christ himself and His apostles, involves an attentive and pure-hearted pursuit of the prophetic meaning of the Old Testament.

There is a great difference and even a direct antithesis between the Christian sects which have separated from a *definite* church and departed, to varying degrees, into the indefinite desert of rationalism and this Israel of the New Covenant, which proceeds from ancient promises to attain Him Who is the measure and fulfillment of all truth. And if in the consciousness of this newborn commune, the fullness of Christian truth has not yet received all of its definitions, if the outline of many matters here, including some that are rather substantial, appears infirm and unclear, then exactly the same applies to the whole Christian Church at the beginning of her history. The whole truth was given in Christ, but not all of it was immediately revealed to Christian consciousness. Only by total indifference to history could one affirm that all the Orthodox dogmas which we now hold were confessed clearly and definitively by the whole church from her very beginning, from the time of Christ and the apostles. In reality, the original Christian catechesis was not at all a mechanical aggregate of separate dogmas but rather a living seed of truth, from which a complex and extensive system of Orthodox dogma only gradually grew and branched out. The Israel of the New Covenant also presents us with this living seed of Christian truth in its Credo, which is essentially identical with the ancient Apostolic Symbol. Here is this Credo:[128]

1. I verily believe that our heavenly Father is the living, true and eternal God, who created heaven and earth, all that is visible and

invisible by His Word and Holy Spirit. He is one, all is from Him, all is in Him, and all is to Him.

2. I verily believe that Our Heavenly Father, in accord with his promises to our fathers, the prophets and our king David, the son of Jesse, has raised a redeemer for Israel: Jesus, born from the Virgin Mary in Bethlehem, the city of Judah, who suffered, was crucified, died, and was buried for the sake of our salvation, who rose from the dead, who lives and sits at the right hand of the Father in the heavens, and will come thence to judge on earth the living and the dead. He indeed is the eternal King over the house of Jacob and his Kingdom will have no end.

3. I verily believe that by just verdict and divine foreknowledge our fathers were stricken with hard-heartedness and impiously resisted their Messiah, the Lord Jesus, so as to provoke a great jealousy among the other peoples of the earth[129] and reconcile them all by faith in Christ,[130] by the word of His evangelists, so that the earth would be filled with the knowledge of the Lord[131] and the Lord would be enthroned upon the whole earth.[132]

4. I verily believe that every person is justified without works of the law, by faith alone[133] in Jesus the Messiah, for he is the Word of the Heavenly Father, eternally begotten from the Father,[134] and that the one and same God justifies Jews, circumcised on account of faith, and Gentiles, uncircumcised through faith,[135] and that there is no distinction between Jew and Greek, slave and freeman, husband and wife, but that all together are one in Christ. [136]

5. I verily believe in one holy and apostolic church.

6. I confess a single baptism for the forgiveness of sins.

7. I hope for the resurrection of the dead and life everlasting. Amen.

In this confession only the truth of the promised Messiah stands out clearly and distinctly. Everything else is either shaded or in conception. But it is precisely the truth of Jesus as Messiah that constituted the entire contents of the original apostolic proclamation, as we see this in the Book of Acts. And as then, so now, it is precisely with this messianic truth that a believing Jew must begin, so as to consciously receive Christianity onto his own religio-historical soil. All other approaches to Christ from the side of Judaism would have been pointless and fruitless. And did the promises hold decisive significance only for Old Testament Jews? Did not the church also predominantly cite these messianic promises in her catechetical formulations? It is true that for us, now, these church formulations have an independent significance and an unconditional authority. But to demand that a religious and conscientious Jew should immediately adopt all the dogmatic decrees of the Ecumenical Councils would be extremely unwarranted and unjust. We know that the decisions of the universal church were evoked by well-known historically prompted demands and requirements. Each of these dogmatic positions was a distinct response to a *distinct question*. But if I do not pose a well-known question, if this question is alien and unintelligible to me, then what meaning can its answer hold for me, even if this answer were itself unconditionally correct and true (as are indubitably all the dogmatic definitions of the universal church)? If I *myself* do not ask, then the answer to alien questions would also pass me by like an empty sound. If I, for example, never occupy myself with metaphysical questions about the powers and operations of divine and human nature, if I mark no distinctions between the natural will (*thelesis*) and that which is willed (*gnome*),[137] then what spiritual harm would I suffer if the dogma of the Sixth Ecumenical Council about the two natural wills and operations in Christ remains for me, for the time being, mute talk?

The Symbol of the Israel of the New Covenant declares the divine significance of Christ as *Word* eternally begotten by the Father. It also expresses the Trinity in the Deity (the Father, His Word, and the Holy Spirit). It is true that this Symbol lacks a formal definition of the *three hypostases* that are one in being, but we will also fail to find it in our Apostolic, Nicene, and Constantinopolitan Symbols. But if the whole church managed to exist for several centuries without this formula, then why can a small community of Jewish Christians not exist without it for several years? And what if the Jewish mind finds the distinction between substance (or being or nature) and hypostasis obscure? Such a distinction was not immediately elucidated even in Christianity itself. How greatly was the church scandalized at the end of the fourth century when Meletius of Antioch first invoked the expression "three hypostases"! Since the Greek word *hypostasis* was literally translated into the Latin by the word *substantia*, the Western Christians began to accuse the Eastern of manifest tritheism. Only thanks to the learned Jerome, equally expert in the Greek and the Latin tongues, was the misunderstanding resolved and ruinous ecclesial discord prevented. And so some will say, "Let not these Jews of the New Covenant invoke Greek terms which they find incomprehensible; it is enough for them to simply recognize the absolute divinity of the Word and of the Spirit." Rather than offer any of our own personal responses to this proposal, we will adduce what St. Gregory the Theologian[138] said about a similar case, namely, with regard to Christians who denied the divinity of the Holy Spirit:

> You are constrained by words, and arrested by mere speech, and it becomes for you a stumbling block and a scandal, which Christ became for some as well. This is a human weakness. Let us meet one another spiritually and let us express filial rather than self-love. Grant us the power of God, and we will offer to you concession in speech. Confess the nature through other names, whichever you most respect, and we will heal you as if you were infirm, and *even conceal some things for your pleasure.* For it is shameful, truly shameful and quite irrational, to be healthy in soul and make too much ado about sounds, to conceal treasures as if envying (them to) others, or fearing lest one sanctify one's own tongue. *But it is even more shameful for us to fall prey to the same thing of which we accuse others, so that by condemning (your) disputes about sounds, to find ourselves disputing over a letter.* Confess in the Trinity, a single Deity, or, if you will, a single nature, and I will pray the Spirit to give you the word God. For I know well that the one who grants you to confess the former will also grant you to confess the latter, especially if the cause of the dispute is some kind of spiritual timidity and not a diabolical stubbornness. I will say it even more clearly and briefly: accuse us not of employing lofty speech (for one should not envy loftiness), and we will not condemn you for that speech *which is within your present capacity, until you should reach, even if by some other way,* the same harbor

which we also seek. We are striving not for victory but for the
return of brothers, separation from whom torments us.[139]

Let us follow the exhortation of the great prelate. As the Jews of
the New Covenant do not condemn us for our lofty pronouncements
(in respect to the dogma of the Holy Trinity), so also let us not condemn them for that true, albeit partial, understanding of this subject,
which is currently beyond their capacity, until they too should reach,
even if by some other way, our common harbor. For to depart from a
complete definition of the truth is one thing; to fail to attain this definition is quite another. Protestant rationalism seeks an artificial sim-
plification of Christianity; the Israel of the New Covenant proceeds
from the natural simplicity of a primary messianic fact, and is able to
attain, given favorable conditions, the mature stature of the fullness of
Christ.[140] What developed from the apostolic community's original
simplicity was not Protestantism but the universal church. In the
meantime, there are some in our midst who, influenced by one superficial external resemblance, wish to forcefully classify the Jews of the
New Covenant as Protestants. Two trains going in opposite directions
can meet and stand side by side for some time at one and the same station; should one infer from this, however, that they should both be
perpetually linked together? Protestants, seeing that the train of the
Israel of the New Covenant presently stands next to their own, cry,
"You must ride along with us!" This is perhaps understandable from
their side, but on what grounds and interest does our government remove independence from the Jewish commune which attained Christ
by its own lawful path, receiving its Messiah on its and His own personal native soil, the soil of a historical, three-thousand-year-long tradition? What grounds, and what interest, are there to subordinate such
a commune to a foreign, groundless confession of a negating tendency?
Is there any sense in taking people who confess a positive *religion*,
founded by God Himself, and sacrifice them to people who confess
only subjective human opinions? In the confession of the Israel of the
New Covenant, it is impossible to specify a single position which
would express any personal opinion of Joseph Rabinovich. Is this
Protestantism?

Remaining wholly a Jew, the founder of the Israel of the New Covenant acknowledges his tightly knit bond with Russia and speaks quite sympathetically about the Orthodox Church. This is what he writes, by the way, in one private letter:

> I see that the Guardian of Israel neither slumbers nor sleeps.[141] For in the hearts of my Russian brothers in Christ, He has begun to work, mercifully and actively, for the sake of the unfortunate and nearly dead Israel. As a matter of fact, it is high time for Russian Christianity, possessing an incalculable reserve of faith in Christ, to recognize that this faith is not her private possession, belonging only to herself. The Lord has said: "He who believes in Me, from his heart, as is written in the Scriptures, will flow rivers of living water."[142] . . . Every *Christian* government must know that the dismal Jewish question consists not in the question, what is to be done with the Jews? how are their rights to the acquisition of worldly goods amidst the Christian population to be broadened or limited? The question is: how are they to be made into true and not guileful Israelites; that is, how are they to be brought to those rivers of living water which flow from the hearts of those who believe in Jesus Christ? For only then will they cease being faithful subjects of the *prince of this world*[143] and the sons of the *father of lies*,[144] that is, of the Talmud . . . Yes! Tell all the brethren in Christ who grieve over the blindness of Israel that its return to his own true Messiah is inevitable, for God has consigned all to disobedience, so as to have mercy on all. Oh, the depth of the wealth and wisdom and knowledge of God.[145] The finger of God, the intensification of the Jewish question over the whole of Europe, shows us that now is the moment to work for these heretofore obstinate Jews, and especially in Russia, where divine providence has gathered them up into such a huge mass. Western Christianity gave the Jews an opportunity to become acquainted with the Gospel, it is there translated expertly into the ancient Hebrew tongue, and Eastern Christianity, over which Russia stands as custodian, is destined, I believe, to give them the opportunity to construct a church.[146]

Let us not be embarrassed over this wish to construct a church instead of simply joining an already constructed church. The Israel of the New Covenant, like a small but living branch, wishes to be grafted onto the trunk of Christianity.[147] Many branches have already withered and broken off, but the trunk is firm and indestructible. It is empowered to give even to this small branch all the sap of life to help it grow into its own fullness. It is clear that the Israel of the New Covenant is an embryonic phenomenon. It is, at any rate, set on the way to its true goal. Why should we then set stumbling blocks for it on this way? Would it not be better to show that "we are striving not for victory but for the return of brothers, separation from whom torments us"?

CHAPTER 3

"The Talmud and Recent Polemical Literature about It in Austria and Germany" (1886)

On more than one occasion have we read and heard the following view: "The Jewish question could be simply resolved, and reconciliation with the Jews achieved, and full civic and social rights granted to them, if they would only renounce the Talmud, which nurtures their fanaticism and segregation, and return to the pure religiosity of the Mosaic Law, as it is confessed, for example, by the Karaites."[148]

Imagine for yourselves, though, that in some sundry country, where the Orthodox Church has neither the support of the government nor of the majority of the population, in Austria let's say, that the following views would be expressed in public and in the press: "We will eagerly reconcile ourselves with the Orthodox and will not limit their rights, if they would only and decisively renounce their church statutes and customs, derived from such old scholastic rubbish as *The Teaching of the Church Fathers* or from such monuments of superstition and fanaticism as *The Lives of the Saints*, and return, instead, to the pure teaching of the Gospel, as it is confessed, for example, by the Hernhutters[149] or the Molokani."[150] To justify such a demand, the opponents of our church would say that its traditions rest on the same foundations as those which Judaism's opponents see in the Talmud. Whoever has, for example, perused the so-called Kormchaya,[151] by which our church has governed itself these many centuries, knows what absurd and ignorant fabrications have nurtured former

Orthodox hostility toward other confessions. And if the Russian government, responding to the need to regulate our church, has recently found it necessary to issue the so-called *Law Book* which excludes all the wild tales of the old "Kormchaya," then the same, it may be argued, may be done for Orthodox Jewry whereby the antiquated parts of its Talmud would lose their authority and necessity.[152] It is, however, considerably easier to free oneself from antiquated traditions and laws than from the old bad habit of using double standards to judge oneself lightly but others harshly. Consequently, in this present estimation of the Talmud and of Talmudic Jewry, we have attempted, first and foremost, to observe the highest norm of Judeo-Christian morality, to treat the other as one would wish the other to treat oneself.[153]

The Talmud is the literary expression of that organic form of life which the Jewish people developed over the course of many centuries after losing its political independence. Once the kingdom fell and prophecy ceased, the only foundation of ethnic life that remained was priestly teaching, that is, the Torah given by Moses on God's mountain.[154] But this common holy deposit was variously regarded and the differences in attitude, by their inner logic, directed religio-ethnic life into three different directions, and became incarnate in three well-known Jewish parties, often but erroneously labeled as sects, namely, the Sadducees, the Pharisees, and the Essenes. The peculiarities of these parties are all well known, but their common deep significance and relationship to Christianity are very often imagined or represented in too one-sided a light. For the Sadducees, the Torah was a foundation upon which they did not wish to build anything. Regarding religion principally in terms of its ritual, priestly aspects, they viewed it as a factual testimony to the past which one needs to recognize and invariably preserve but which does not compel any kind of further action. The established ancient teaching was for them something that had been finalized once and for all, as an immutable holiness, immovable and inviolable. But whenever religion is so reduced to archaic customs and sacrifices, to the memory of the past only, then real life is sacrificed to base passions and interests which have nothing in common with religion. And indeed, the Sadducees, the guardians of the foundations and the zealous custodians of ancient piety, turned out, in fact, to be the party of selfish oligarchs who abused religion and deceived the people. Depending on the circumstances, they either excited ethnic fanaticism or slavishly served and pandered to the Romans, lest they should forfeit their ruling position in the Temple and in the Sanhedrin.[155]

But besides the Sadducees' obvious selfishness and dubious patriotism, the very core principle of this party contained an inner, self-undermining contradiction. Taking a stand under the banner of preserving the Torah free from any addition, the Sadducees must have concomitantly acknowledged a significant part of the Torah to be a dead letter, not admitting of any adaptation to reality. But in point of fact, a great part of the juridical-social and economic injunctions of the Mosaic Law demanded social arrangements that differed completely from those which became entrenched during the Second Temple period, under the ruling influence of just that priestly caste from which the Sadducees arose. The latter, thereby, began to crack and break up on account of their very own custodial principle: religious conservatism demanded the pious keeping of the ancient revelation of the Torah, while social conservatism demanded the support and defense of customs decisively opposed both to the spirit and to the letter of Mosaic legislation. Either radical inconsistency or extreme lack of scruple was required to defend, simultaneously and identically, the inviolability of the law of Moses and of that social structure which became entrenched under the Idumeans. And this is why the more consistent or the more honest Sadducees abandoned the faith of their fathers and openly took their stand under the flag of a foreign power and of pagan ideas. Such were the Herodians mentioned in the Gospel,[156] and such were those Apikorosim, that is, the Epicureans, who are not infrequently mentioned in the Talmud.[157]

As for the people who retained a heartfelt faithfulness to their national religion, then these had to seek for another way out and they found it in Pharisaism. Like their Saducean opponents, the Pharisees regarded the Torah as a true, unfalsifiable foundation for religion, but for them, this Torah was not only a fact of the past, which one had to revere, but also the Law of real life which one had to fulfill. The Pharisees would not allow the demands of religion to contradict real life; for them, all life had to conform to religious law; the divine commandments had to be realized in all human affairs. Thus, while the Sadducees only *mechanically* linked the divine law to the social reality that remained extraneous to it, and honored it only as an external safeguard for Judaism, as a kind of Palladium for Jerusalem,[158] the Pharisees, on the contrary, regarded religion *organically* and saw in the law of Moses a real and inseparable form of ethnic life. However, to realize this idea was no easy matter. Many of the Torah's injunctions, in their simple, literary meaning, turned out to be unrealizable under changed historical circumstances, while, on the other hand, many newly arisen living complications were not anticipated in Mosaic legislation. Moreover, to leave one or another divine law without fulfillment, or in some cases, to ground a decision upon some marginal principle entailed, in either case, the destruction of the law. Thus, in order to positively safeguard the law from destruction, and preserve it, neither as a dead nor as an unneeded letter, but as a principle of real life, one had to develop it by means of a complex system of explanations, interpretations, and casuistic distinctions. This preserved the supreme authority of the ancient Law and, in making it adaptable to altered living conditions, prevented it from dying out, and endowed it with the strength of a stable life for all time.

Pharisaism espoused as its motto the famous formulation of the Great Sanhedrin: *One needs to build a hedge around the Law.*[159]

Thus, if for the Sadducees, as noted above, the Law was a foundation upon which they did not want to build anything, then for the Pharisees, on the contrary, it was the point of departure for a whole row of exegetical, casuistic, legendary constructions—peculiar and disconnected in appearance, like life itself. But these constructions, growing over the course of six or seven centuries, were finally assembled, by the labors of the latest gatherers, into the one huge labyrinth of the Talmud.

But alongside these two Judaic parties, which we have just surveyed, there must have also appeared, among the religious Jews, a third. For if, for the Sadducee, the Word of God was only the completed *fact of the past*, and if, for the Pharisee, it was the *law of current life*, then there must have existed people who discerned in it the *ideal of the future*. These people, who received the name Essenes,[160] sought in religion not a support for their selfish inclinations, or a source of practical guidance for temporal life, but the highest fulfillment and be-atitude. If the Sadducees, in their worldly wisdom, valued only the force of fact, and the Pharisees, in their labor and longing for formal justification, traced all fact to its moral-legal foundations and subordi-nated life to law, then the Essenes worried neither about the force of facts nor about the formal foundations for action but only about that highest *goal* for which both fact and action exist. If the first Judaic party treated religion mechanically and the second organically, then the third preserved a *purely spiritual* understanding of religion. This, nevertheless, in no way ascribes any unconditional advantage to this religious party over the others. Exclusive spirituality and one-sided idealism can exceed in fruitlessness both the practical wisdom of the Sadducees and the moral juridical formalism of the Pharisees. The place for the highest ideals is the kingdom of heaven, but such is not attained freely but taken by force.[161] For this reason, those who find themselves walking the earthly path are forced, willy-nilly, to consider the practical measures and the formal foundations by which one may reach the goal more surely. Here one may readily apply the axiom, "He who would attain a goal must obtain the means,"[162] and these are right and power, law and authority. And if it is blameworthy to pursue these proximate means while forgetting the highest goal, it is more pitiful still to dream about ideal perfection but take no practical step to ap-proach it.

The origin and fates of the Essene party are a question which his-torical research is yet to resolve. In any case, it is indubitable that while the Sadducees were busying themselves with Temple rituals and po-litical intrigues and the Pharisees were, with ardent zeal and passionate industry, constructing and building their innumerable hedges around the law, a good number of Israelites, having withdrawn to desert places and established communal lifestyles, dedicated themselves to studies of a different kind. They prayed, they fasted, they sang hymns, and they waited for the kingdom of God. This last trait makes the Essenes undoubtedly the forerunners of Christianity. In other respects, Christianity preserves or reflects its historical rootedness not in Essenism but in Pharisaic Rabbinism. It cannot be doubted that the principle genre of evangelical preaching (the Parables) contains nothing specifically Christian but assumes the typical form of the Talmudic Haggadah.[163] Below, the reader will see that the similarity here is sometimes limited only to the mode of exposition. In general, the construction of the temple that is the New Testament did not require the invention of any new materials. Christ and His apostles used, in their labor, those bricks which were at hand. Even the very plan of the edifice was not novel in its parts but in its interconnections, in the integral *whole* of its religious ideal. The Gospel idea most directly united in itself that which was positive and true in the three Jewish parties. The principle of religious power and pragmatic wisdom which the Sadducees preserved and abused was not rejected by Christ but received from Him the highest sanctification and confirmation: "All *power* is given to me . . . ,"[164] "Be ye *wise* as serpents . . . ,"[165] and so on. In the same way, the Pharisaic espousal of the law and of justification by works was also decisively confirmed in the teaching of Christ who came not to destroy the law but to fulfill it[166] and who demanded from his disciples the practical fruits of true faith.[167] In this manner, what was truthful in the paths of the Sadducees and the Pharisees was brought together in the path of the Gospel, while the goal of the path proclaimed that which the Essenes dreamed of: the kingdom of God and His righteousness.

But in this very synthesis of these different religious ideas and principles, their negative aspects, everything in them that was false, was also destroyed. In this regard, we find, in the Gospel, a merciless censure of all three Jewish parties. Censured here is the materialism of the Sadducees who, basing themselves upon earthly powers, lost all sensitivity to the powers of a higher order ("you are wrong, because you know neither the scriptures nor the power of God,"[168] etc.). Censured too is the formalism of the Pharisees, constraining them, in their pursuit of legal rectitude in action, to occasionally forget both the spirit and the goal of the Law itself. And as for the Essenes, the one-sidedness of their contemplative and ascetic idealism is condemned not by words but by the actual character of the earthly life of Christ, by his struggle and by his heroism.[169]

The fact that the Gospel is especially concerned with the Pharisees in particular, and that entire chapters are filled with vigorous polemic against them, does not at all prove that Christianity arose as some kind of antithesis to Pharisaism as people usually suppose. The point is that because the Pharisees were the main leaders and teachers of the people, it was first with them that any new religious teaching clashed as soon as it turned to address the people. Neither the Sadducees nor the Essenes, generally speaking, went out as preachers and teachers in the synagogues and on the streets. In order to dispute with the Essenes, one had to go to the desert, and in order to censure the priestly aristocracy (except for certain exceptional circumstances), one had to slip into their temples. If today someone wanted to introduce into Christian society some kind of religious or social idea, he would, in principle, need to debate not with the high-ranking representatives of the spiritual or secular order and not, for that matter, with the monks of Mount Athos but with the journalists, the literati, and the professors; in one word, with the representatives of the so-called intelligentsia, which indeed the Pharisaic teachers were in the time of Christ. Only when the matter comes to bloodshed do the Sadducees, the experts in bloody sacrifices, enter the foreground and, conjoining the sacred mystery of the High Priest with the manifest wisdom of mundane politics, pregnantly declare: *it is expedient for us, that one man should die.*[170]

As regards the Pharisees, then, it is altogether evident that Christ's censures are aimed at that exceptional and one-sided development which Pharisaism accorded to the principle of formal legality, which in its practical application inevitably led to falsehood and hypocrisy. But that the Gospel does not thereupon subject the core and general principles of Pharisaism to unconditional censure but readily acknowledges, on the contrary, its positive content is easy to be convinced of simply by recalling the first words of Christ's strongest sermon against them: "The scribes and the Pharisees sit on Moses' seat, all therefore whatsoever they bid you to observe, observe and do, but do not do their works, for they speak but do not."[171]

In this manner, the Gospel, by admonishing the Pharisees, first and foremost for not realizing their teaching *in deed*, justifies by the same token the *principle* of Pharisaism, which consists precisely in insisting on the *deeds of the Law*. Christ does not say that "deeds are not needed" but, on the contrary, that "deeds are needed, but you do not do them." How much should these reprimands be fortified if one were to direct and apply them to contemporary Christian society? Christ demanded that the righteousness of his disciples should exceed the righteousness of the scribes and the Pharisees. But for us even the latter constitutes a seemingly unachievable ideal. At least the Pharisees did not in principle allow for a separation between religion and life, between law and actual existence. On the contrary, their constant efforts were directed at making all human works be the fulfillment of the law of God. That is what they taught to observe, and about this, Christ said: observe and do. But we, since then, have managed to construe a principle from the contradiction between the demands of religion and the conditions of communal life, between God's commandments and all of our reality. This is why Pharisaism, which became consolidated in Talmudism, was not, and could not, to this day, be superseded by historical Christianity.

After the Essenes were swallowed up by the new religion and the Sadducees, who had lived in dependence on the Temple and its sacrifices, vanished with the Temple's destruction and the termination of its sacrifices, the Pharisees survived as the sole representatives of the whole of Jewry, and the collection of their teaching, the Talmud, became the religio-national codex of all Jews. It is noteworthy that following the Babylonian captivity, the first task of the Jews was the redaction of the Bible, and that, following the final Roman destruction, they, as soon as they recollected themselves, immediately and zealously dedicated themselves to the assembly and redaction of the Talmud. The national woes that beset the Jews impelled them to hold more firmly to their religious law and to study it more deeply, for they discerned that the real cause of their tragedy lay in the insufficient knowledge and fulfillment of this law. And if in Ezra's time that religious law consisted only of Moses's Torah, then in the days of the Roman destruction, as conceptions and relationships became more complex, the religio-ethical structures of Jewish private and social life demanded a supreme integration of exegetical interpretations and additional commentaries made by ancient scholars and sages (the *Amoraim* and the *Tannaim*), that is, the Talmud. And thus, following closely upon the insurrection of Bar Kokhba and the final destruction of Jerusalem, Rabbi Yehuda ha-Kadosh began to assemble and set to writing the main part of the Talmud: the Mishnah.[172] And at that time, when on the stage of world history, the bitter struggle between paganism and Christianity was replaced by the still more intense and bitter struggle within Christianity itself (the great heresies of the fourth and fifth centuries), and the church's external triumph intensified her internal discord, at that time Jewry, outwardly dispersed but inwardly concentrated, having hidden itself in the dark corners of Palestine and Mesopotamia, forged for itself its characteristically fitting arms for self-defense: two huge compendia of the remotest casuistic interpretations and legendary additions, the Jerusalem and the Babylonian Gemara,[173] which it added to the Mishnah, and thereby brought to a close Jewry's mighty fence, the so-called Talmud.

The Talmud secured Jewry's religio-national isolation for many centuries. Was this isolation necessary, and were the Jews right to separate themselves from the whole world by the wall of Talmudic law? Before answering this question in principle, we would like to give our readers, who are not at all acquainted with the Talmud, some concrete impression of the ethical spirit of this literary monument. Here, to begin with, are some Talmudic quotations and parables:

> A pagan who studies the Law of God (the Torah) is equal to the High Priest.[174] Whoever is born unlawfully, should he be learned, is more esteemed than an ignorant High Priest.[175]

> A pagan once came to Shammai and said, "Teach me, but only on the condition that you teach me the whole Torah while standing on one leg." Shammai hit him with the yardstick which he held in his hand and pushed him outside. The pagan then went to Hillel who fulfilled the demand by saying, "Do not do to others that which you would not have done to you. This is the essence of the whole law, the rest are details. Now go and study."[176]

> Let no one say, "I am going to occupy myself with the study of the Law so that people would call me wise, I am going to study the Mishnah so as to be called a rabbi and be head of a school." Do not

regard learning as a crown for beautifying[177] yourself, nor as an ax for gaining a living by it.[178]

The goal of wisdom are good deeds and rectification of life . . . and for anyone who does not do good deeds from love of goodness it would have been better if they had not been created.[179]

Another saying:

Let a man only occupy himself with the Torah and with good deeds, even if he should not do this for their own sake, for in time he will do this for their own sake.[180]

Everything is predetermined by the Eternal, but, nevertheless, the actions of men are free. The world is governed by grace, but the will of man is known by the abundance of his good deeds.[181]

No man can bruise his own finger, unless this be predetermined by God.[182]

The world to come is not like this world. There people neither eat nor drink nor give themselves over to any kind of sensual pleasures. There is no envy there and no hatred or strife, but the righteous rejoice with crowns upon their heads in the reflection of the deity.[183]

He who fulfills at least one duty, acquires for himself an advocate, and he who commits at least one sin, summons an accuser against himself.[184]

Do God's will as if it were your own so that He would make your will His. Sacrifice your will to His, that He may sacrifice the will of others to yours.[185]

He who has bread in a basket and troubles about food for the morrow, belongs to those who have little faith.[186]

A man should thank God for evil as much as for good.[187]

A man's words should always be few before God.[188]

He who shows concern for one's neighbor in prayer but does not act on it is a sinner.[189]

Who is wise? He who learns from everyone. Who is a hero? He who conquers his passions. Who is wealthy? He who is satisfied with his own possessions. Who is revered? He who reveres his own neighbors.[190]

An evil inclination is first like a traveler, then like a guest, and finally like a master.[191]

To a haughty person, God says: We cannot both dwell in the world.[192]

He who humbles himself, God will exalt him, and he who exalts himself, God will humble him. From him who searches for lordship, from him lordship flees, and he who declines from lordship, to him lordship comes unexpectedly. [193]

He who raises a hand to strike another man, even if he did not strike him, is deemed a lawless man.[194]

He who publicly shames anyone, is like unto one who has shed blood.[195]

It is better to belong to the persecuted than to persecutors.[196]

A similar saying states:

Those who are insulted but do not insult, hear themselves reviled without answering, those who forbear with love, and those who suffer with joy, to them applies the word: "The beloved of God will be like the sun which rises in its glory."[197]

He who forgives an insult against his own person, will have his sin forgiven by God.[198]

Be gentle and yielding like a reed, and not unbending and haughty like a cedar.[199]

Let your yes be a real yes, and your no be a real no.[200]

One must not deceive even a Gentile.[201]

Slanderous speeches are sins that cry out to heaven.[202]

Hypocrites will not see God.[203]

One must greet all people cheerfully.[204]

The virtue of almsgiving is equal in importance to all the other virtues combined.[205]

Amity is even higher than almsgiving.[206]

He who neglects the duty of almsgiving to the poor is like an idolater.[207]

As long as the Temple stood, the sacrificial altar atoned for the sins of the people, but now that the sacrificial altar is no more, a table set with a meal for the poor replaces the altar and redeems sins.[208]

He whose wife dies deserves pity like one in whose days the Temple was destroyed.[209]

If someone tells you, "I searched but have not found," believe him not, and if he says, "I have found, but did not search," also believe him not, but if he says, "I have searched and I found," believe him.[210]

He who is able to calculate the course of the heavenly luminaries but does it not, to him the scripture applies: "the works of God they do not regard, and the works of His hands they do not see."[211]

Rabbi Simeon ben Levi used to say, "The door is open to him who wants to be dishonest. In other words, opportunities will always present themselves for such people. However, assistance will also be given to him who wishes to be pure. " The school of Rabbi Ishmael explains this condition by means of the following parable. "There once lived a vendor of tar and balm. When someone would come to buy tar, the vendor would say, 'My merchandise is before you, weigh it and take it.' But when someone would come to buy balm, the vendor would say, 'Stand back, I will weigh some out for you myself, so that I too would smell nice.'"[212]

Rabbi Isaac used to say that while everyone is equal before the face of death, every righteous person is given a special habitation as befits his honor. This is explained by a proverb. When a king enters a town together with his servants, they all enter through one and the same gate, but when they settle down there for the night, each is given a separate lodging as befits his honor.[213]

Rabbi Eliezer used to say, "Repent one day before you die." His disciples asked him, "Does a man really know on what day he is going to die?" "This means," replied the rabbi, "that he must put things right precisely today, for he can die tomorrow. Thus, he will spend his whole life in repentance, according to the saying: 'Let your clothes be always white and let there be no lack of oil for your head.'"[214] To this teaching, Rabbi Yohanan (ben Zakkai) added the following parable. "A certain king invited his servants to a feast without appointing a time. The wise among them put on their best garments and waited near the palace, expecting everything there to be ready. The fools went on with their own affairs expecting the royal feast to require long preparation. Suddenly the king called his invitees. The wise came before him in clean and expensive garments, but the fools ran in dirty clothing. Then the king said, 'Let those who arrived in clean garments sit and eat. As for those who arrived in dirty ware, let them stand and watch.'"[215]

When Moses ascended the mountain of God, the archangels asked God, "What does he who is born of woman seek among us?"[216] "He has come," answered God, "to receive the Torah." "Are you really," they continued, "going to give this treasure, kept secret from the beginning of the world's creation, for nine hundred and seventy-four generations, to a human being? What is man that you are mindful of him, and the son of man that you care for him? How majestic is your name, O Lord, in all the earth, and your splendor which covers the heavens."[217] "Answer them," God told Moses. "I fear," he replied, "lest they burn me with the breath of their mouths." "Then hold on tight to the foundation of the Throne of my Glory and answer them." Then Moses began, saying, "Lord of the Universe, what is written in your Law which you wish to give me? Does it not begin thus: 'I am the Lord your God who brought you out of the land of Egypt, but you angels, did you perchance live in Egypt or work for the Pharaoh? Why then would you need such a law?' Further on it states, 'Let not foreign gods be your gods,'[218] and have you perchance lived among idolaters?[219] And again it states, 'Remember the sabbath day,' but do you perchance work, that you should need rest? And again it states, 'Do not bear false witness,' but is there perchance litigation amongst you? And again it states, 'Honor your father and your mother,' but do you perchance have parents? And again it states, 'Do not kill and do not commit adultery and do not steal. And are there perchance such deeds among you?'"[220] And God approved of Moses and the archangels came to love him.

The last parable supplies us with the leading thought for evaluating the whole Talmud. The Law is given for man[221] and not for angels. In other words, the Law cannot presuppose unconditional perfection in its practitioners, for in that case the Law itself would be unnecessary. The Talmud does not repudiate perfection as a goal, as a moral ideal. But it is precisely to save this ideal from remaining a vain dream that care must be given to the paths by which it may be realized, and these paths pass over the imperfection and sinfulness of human nature. Prior to accomplishing the absolute ideal, a man must habituate himself to limiting his own will, by nature directed not so much toward absolute moral perfection as to the satisfaction of his egoism. Law is the limitation of will, and thus the Talmud and the rabbis task themselves, in everything and everywhere, to limit man's self-will by the injunctions of divine law, making sure to not leave any matters of private or social life to personal arbitrary jurisdiction. In the Torah, they tallied up 248 injunctions and 365 prohibitions and then multiplied the sum total, the 613 laws, indefinitely by applying them to every possible individual circumstance. But that this multiplicity of laws does not constitute an independent goal for the Talmudists is already evident from the Talmudic indication that the number of commandments given at Sinai was later reduced by David to 11, by Isaiah to 6 and even to 2, by Micah to 3, and finally by Habbakuk to only 1 statute: that the righteous man should live by his faithfulness (*tsaddiq be'emunato yihyeh*; Habbakuk 2:4).[222] Comparing this injunction with Hillel's above-cited response to the pagan, it may be observed that there is no contradiction *in principle* between the legalism of the Talmudic and the New Testament morality founded upon faith and altruism. The principal debate between Christianity and Jewry pertains not to the moral but to the religio-metaphysical sphere, to the question of Christ's god-human significance and his atoning sacrifice.[223] It is true that in addition to this, one must acknowledge also that, in practice, the Talmudists and the people they guided would often forget or neglect the lofty ideals and moral perspectives of their Haggadoth and wholly immerse themselves in the study and application of formal Talmudic injunctions (the Halakha), in consequence to which, in Judaism, the principle of law or of formal truth was given decisively more weight than the principles of mercy (*hesed*) and inner truth (*emet*). Admitting fully this one-sidedness of Jewish development, we dare not condemn it unconditionally in view of the contrary and even more harmful extreme represented by the Christian world. If Talmudic Judaism is deemed excessive for its attempts to relate every detail of social and private life to religious law, then it is to be noted that our pseudo-Christian world not only brought into practice but also elevated in principle the idea of a complete separation between religious truth and real life, between religion and politics, between ideal norms which turn among us into empty words and actual relationships which we persistently strive to secure in their manifest abnormality. Against this godless principle, against this immoral division, Talmudic Judaism, with all of its strength, arises, and herein lies its justification.

For the Talmudists, who take their firm stand, in this regard, upon the ground of Moses's Torah, religion is the law of human life. *Ushmartem et huqotay ota haadam wahay bahem ani Yhwh* (Keep my statutes and my ordinances, for the man who will do them, will also live by them, I am the Lord; Lev. 8:5).[224] This instruction has been manifestly justified in Jewish national life. Only by the keeping of these statutes and ordinances, first given in the Torah and then hedged around in the Talmud, only through the keeping of these statutes does Jewry still survive as a nation, unique in the world as a nation by its longevity.[225] The best proof of Jewry's national vitality is furnished by antisemitism. For the bitterness of this movement in all cases witnesses to Jewry's strength. "Don't push a drunkard; he will fall himself," says the Talmudic proverb.[226] By adding force to their blows, the antisemites demonstrate the conviction that Jewry stands firmly on its own feet.

Logic, historical experience, and the word of God all teach us that the most important condition of *lasting power is truth*, that is, faithfulness to oneself and the absence of inner contradiction and division. Every kingdom divided against itself will not stand.[227] Struggle is an invariably necessary moment of life, but indeed only a particular moment, which enters into the makeup of a living whole. Jewry is stronger than the contemporary Christian world, because its inner struggle, which undoubtedly exists, exists nevertheless as a subordinate phenomenon which does not negate the essential unity of the whole. In the Christian world, on the other hand, this unity has lost all its reality and has become an abstract idea powerless to withstand the strife between its separate parts. True, the difference here derives partly from the fact that Jewry represents just one nation while the Christian world embraces a mass of national elements. But what then of the strength of that Christian *universalism* which people usually set up as a contrast to the narrow ethnic egoism of the Jews? If the New Testament religion is powerless to withstand the segregating action of ethnic groups, then the Jews are right to persist with their Old Testament religion, which proclaims its national character directly and openly. Thanks to this, they are delivered from that inner contradiction afflicting the majority of Christians who confess a religion that transcends ethnicity but is simultaneously swallowed up in purely national interests, passions, and prejudices. It is remarkable, by the way, that Jews are commonly accused simultaneously of narrow nationalism and cosmopolitanism. The point is that the most nationalist Jewish idea carries a famous universal significance, already proclaimed to the biblical Abraham: "and all the families of the earth will bless themselves through you."[228] And if the Jews do not wish to recognize in Christianity the realization of Israel's universal mission, then conscience prohibits us from claiming that it has been realized among us. We too believe that the realization of the universal idea is still in the future. And in this future fulfillment of Christianity, the Jews, according to the words of St. Paul, will play a unique and leading role. And it would be odd, in this respect, to place Jewry — from which, as from the most Mosaic religion, issued both Christianity and Islam — on par with this or that *distinct* ethnicity. One can juxtapose Jewry only with humanity as a whole, to which it relates as trunk to branches (not, understandably, from an ethnographic, but simply from a spiritual-cultural perspective).

Spanning the whole of human history, from its very beginning right up to our own day (which cannot be said of any other nation), Jewry assumes a virtually axial representative role in world history.[229]

And because Jewry plays such a central role in human history, all the positive as well as the negative forces of human nature express themselves in this people with special clarity. For this reason, the accusations that Jews are guilty of every possible vice may be grounded upon actual facts taken from Jewish history. But when, on the basis of these particularities, people wish to condemn all Jewry as a whole, one can only wonder at the brazenness of the accusers. When the national parties of various countries accuse the Jews of being insufficiently patriotic, then it is indeed impossible to understand how the Jews, remaining Jews, that is, a distinct people, can reconcile within themselves the contending patriotisms of all those other nations among which they also live. Real Jewish patriotism can only mean love of Jewry, and in this, it seems, they have no deficiencies. And as for condemning [them] for being too cosmopolitan, this is simply laughable given that such charges are directed against the only nation which, from time immemorial, and through the bitterest of trials, preserved its national uniqueness—and preserved it to such a level that those very people who reproach this nation for cosmopolitanism are frequently forced to join this reproach to its contrary and, as already noted, accuse the cosmopolitans of narrow nationalist segregation? And this last reproach too is just as strange as the first. For where has there been a people more receptive and open to foreign influences than the Jewish, which, having learned the spiritual essence of their own ethnicity, have never set store by its external natural features? For they even exchanged, and not just on one occasion, their language: on returning from Babylon, they spoke Chaldean; in Alexandria, they began to speak Greek; in Baghdad and Cordova, in Arabic; and now and everywhere they speak in a semi-German jargon, and, moreover, they have always and everywhere taken their personal names and familial nicknames from foreign and infidel peoples.

The conservatives of various countries and confessions unanimously charge the Jews with strong liberal sympathies and even deem them to be the principal progenitors and proponents of modern liberalism in Europe. If this is the case, it remains only to lament that the Jews have as yet so poorly fulfilled their task in our country where truly liberal principles and customs are especially wanting, for both the "sons of Israel" and the "people of the land." It is to be remarked, however, that the Jews derive their ideas of freedom and social justice, and with some basis, from naught else but Moses's Torah. And given such honorable antiquity, Jewish progressive ideas may be just as rightly regarded as being conservative or retrograde. Thus, any segment of civilized humanity can find sympathetic elements in Jewry which, in the meantime, transcends all their irreconcilable contradictions by subordinating them to its religio-national unity.

Given the plain bankruptcy of the common principal condemnations of Jewry and their mutually contradictory and self-undermining character, antisemites have been forced to choose another, more private and concrete basis for their assaults. And thus they renew those ancient complaints that the Jewish religious law, as contained in the Talmud, enjoins the chosen people to hate all infidels, especially Christians, and to harm them whenever possible. In truth, though, there would be nothing remarkable if Jewish religious books really did contain such injunctions. Do we need to recall here everything that the Jews have suffered at the hands of Christian peoples during the Middle Ages when persecutions against them reached such a pitch of rage that even so stern a proponent of militant Catholicism and so decisive an opponent of Judaism as Pope Innocent III published, in defense of the Jews, a special bull, *Constitutio Pro Judaeis*,[230] in which he, by the way, forbade Christians, under threat of excommunication, to destroy Jewish cemeteries and exhume buried bodies in order to extort *money*? It seems to us that all accusations of Jews of greed and exploitation of Christians pale before such witness. But let us leave these long-past affairs. Let us recall something closer in time and place. Many of our readers will probably find it interesting, although hardly comforting, to discover that less than one hundred fifty years ago, in 1738, in Petersburg, the Jew Leib Boruchov and the naval captain-lieutenant Voznitsyn were burned at the stake because the former converted the latter by means of dialogue to Jewry?[231]

In addition to the irresponsible antipathies and prejudices directed against the Jews, laws still exist in some, at least Christian, countries, which anathematize the Jewish religion and set an impenetrable wall between the Jews and the rest of the population as if they were carriers of the plague.

In view of this, it would be entirely appropriate to discover that Jewish juridical codices contained injunctions of a corresponding nature about Christians. But do the Jews actually possess such injunctions? Thanks to the new antisemitic movement, this question has been more or less resolved. The point is that as long as the Jews themselves, or their Christian defenders, have been affirming that the Talmud contains no injunction enjoining hatred of or causing harm to Christians, one could have dismissed such assurances as biased. But now even among the antisemites themselves, there are people who, possessing more or less scholarly means to handle such a problem, make every effort *per fas et nefas* to locate in the Talmud, as well as in other legal-religious Jewish books, that which they need, that is, laws enjoining Jews to hate and express enmity for Christians. And if, in the final end, the result of all these searches and attempts can be reduced almost to nil, then every nonbiased and impartial person will be convinced that on this basis, at least, the cause of the antisemites has been lost.

About fifteen years ago in Austria and Germany, there began, and has still not ended, an embittered literary and also in part a legal battle over the Talmud. The main trigger points for this battle were two antisemitic compositions, *Der Talmudjude* by Professor Rohling and *Der Judenspiegel* by Dr. Justus (a pseudonym).[232] Around these two books there sprouted up a whole polemical literature for and against Judaism, and, in part, for and against the Talmud.[233] Especially interesting to us is the composition of Justus, *Der Judenspiegel*. Its author, seeming to have practical familiarity with Talmudic literature, has attempted to extract from it a whole series of positive injunctions, incumbent, as he attests, also on contemporary Jews, and enjoining hatred and enmity toward Christians. Of such "laws" he has collected a whole hundred. True, their originality was decisively repudiated not only by Jews but also by Christian scholars, including, by the way, the well-known Hebraist and theologian Delitzsch. But as Justus also possessed learned defenders, the nonspecialist readers could find themselves in the relatively difficult position of not knowing whom to believe. Unfortunately for the antisemites, one of Justus's most serious and meticulous defenders, Dr. Ecker, in spite of his manifest enmity for the Jews, and in spite of all his bias for the author of the *Judenspiegel*,[234] turned out to be incapable of hiding the factual truth in this matter. He checked all of Justus's references and reprinted all of his "hundred" laws in his book *Der Judenspiegel im Lichte der Wahrheit*,[235] providing for each one the corresponding original text with the exact German translation. By this means, whatever a critic states from his own personal point of view does not in the least impede an impartial reader from forming a correct judgment on every point. And so, first of all, it turns out that Justus did not at all take his laws ready made from the Jewish juridical codex (*Shulchan Aruch*)[236] but composed each law from various excerpts, taken at times from various compositions of unequal worth and authority. In Justus's work, these excerpts were predominantly joined in a totally artificial manner, texts being mixed up with commentaries and general obligatory injunctions with private rabbinic opinions, and all of this was transmitted approximately, in his own words—a bad move when the matter involves *laws*. But most remarkable is that the more powerful expressions of hatred against Christians are simply inserted by Justus himself without any explanation or citation. Of the many examples we can adduce one: Under no. 23 in the *Judenspiegel*, we can read the following law: "Only those who bear a human name can be admitted as witnesses, whereas an Akum (a Christian) or a Jew who converts to Christianity, who is even worse than one who is born a Christian, *these in no case can be treated as human beings*, on which account, their legal witness holds no value." Here is a "law" which could have been very valuable for antisemites if only it were not false. In actual fact, the two texts of the Jewish codex which Justus cites, only state the following: (1) "A pagan (*goy*) and a slave are unfit to bear witness"; (2) "False informers (*ha-mosrim*), the godless (lit., "epicureans"—*ha-apikorosim*), and those who renounce the faith are worse than Gentiles and are unfit to bear witness." If, even against the direct testimony of many rabbis, one were to accept that the term "pagan" denotes a Christian, then, at any rate, the cited texts say nothing about such not being people. We are ready to grant that the centuries-long inhuman treatment of Jews by Christian peoples has managed to eclipse, in the eyes of the latter, the human dignity of their persecutors, and to squeeze out of Israel's heart fraternal feelings for the new Edom. But the issue here concerns not feelings but positive law. For we know, for example, that a hundred years ago, Orthodox cossacks, while warring with the final remnants of Rzecz Pospolita,[237] hanged on the same scaffold, wherever they could, a Jew, a Polish Ksentz (priest), and a dog, with the following inscription: "A Yid, a Pole, and a hound, by one faith bound."[238] But who, though, would dare to insert this formulation without any references to citations from the compendium of laws of the Russian Empire or from the canonical ordinances of the Orthodox Church? But this is precisely how the fabricators of pseudo-Talmudic laws behave.

Moving on to the content of Dr. Justus's one hundred laws, we discover among them a whole series of ordinances which prohibit Jews from participation in any way, direct or indirect, in the liturgies of Gentiles, which, it stands to reason, predominantly denotes Christians, given references to the following: carrying water for baptism, selling candles for use in church, selling icons or holy Christian books, greeting or giving presents to Christians on their feast days, and so on (pp. 58 ff.). In this manner, Jews are even blamed for not entering, even while remaining Jews, into religious relations with Christians! But would Christians admit such relations? In any case, before imposing such demands upon the Jews, it would be meet to await the restoration of religious solidarity between Christian denominations. Recently, the author of these lines received from a Protestant missionary several issues of an American missionary journal, which, by the way, observed that the main obstacle to the conversion of contemporary Russians and Bulgarians to Christianity consists in the fact that these peoples already consider themselves Christian.[239] On the other hand, one Orthodox spiritual orator, speaking ex cathedra was accustomed to draw a contrast between the Russian *Cross* and the Latin *Krzyż* as if they were two hostile principles. Given such conditions, every reproach of ours regarding religio-national segregation, every demand for broader religious tolerance, receives from the Jews a ready-made answer: "Physician, heal thyself,"[240] and also, "Hypocrite, take out first the log from your own eye and then you will see how better to remove the speck from your brother's eye."[241]

It is difficult to believe that the *Judenspiegel* reconstructs, by the way, as an accusatory document against the Jews, even those laws which enjoin the utmost caution upon them in dealing with Christians, lest they suffer death or some other vital harm on their account. It would be odd to even begin to demonstrate that such laws, formulated in the sixteenth century, possessed too many foundations and reasons. And in light of this, *who* stands to be blamed and shamed by these laws?

This is a relatively sad topic, but there are also some amusing passages in the *Judenspiegel*. To their number, doubtlessly, belongs law no. 76, which forbids Jews from sending their children to various Christian schools. How regrettable it is that our Ministry of National

Enlightenment didn't know anything about this attestation of Dr. Justus regarding a law which still remains obligatory, since this would have freed them from the labor of determining the normal percentage of Jews in Russian schools.

In conclusion, if one set aside from the accusatory document before us all that is forged, untrue, and discrepant, there would then remain seven or eight laws which antisemites could have, with some claim to verisimilitude, use of for their ends. Laws of this sort permit, for example, a Jew to not return a found article lost by a Gentile, or to exploit Gentile mistakes in accounting, or, finally, to exact interest on loans to people of other faiths (which is forbidden in dealing with Jews).

It would be somewhat remarkable if a Jewish codex deriving from the sixteenth century mandated equality between Jews and Christians, when the most enlightened Christian countries came to recognize this equality only a few decades ago, and while Jews still do not possess civil equality in that country which most of them inhabit.

The Talmudic law which allows one to exact interest only on loans to Gentiles is taken directly from Moses' Torah. But from what religious source do our pseudo-Christian states borrow the injunctions which permit usury for all without differentiation? In any case, is it not odd to demand that the Jews should treat us better than we treat them or even each other?

Nevertheless it is necessary to observe that the noted injunctions contain a negative character and express only a juridical limit to immoral action rather than any positive moral obligation. The Talmud only permits and in no way prescribes or justifies the seizure of things lost by Gentiles. And if the inventor of the one hundred laws sometimes transforms permission into prescription, then this is only one of his deceits, condemnable even by a favorably disposed critic (see, e.g., no. 36). In actual fact, laws of this type express only the extreme juridically prescribed *minimum* of moral acts. But, in preserving only a juridical demand for the minimal, these injunctions do not exclude the moral demand for the greater. On the contrary, the Talmud itself gives to this moral demand a positive foundation via three well-known principles of which Jewish ethics can be proud: the principles of the Sanctification of the Name (of God), *kiddush ha-Shem*; the Profanation of the Name, *hillul ha-Shem*; and the Ways of Peace, *darkhei shalom*. To do good deeds so that the true faith might be glorified by them, to do more than is formally prescribed by the law, to do good neither from fear nor for one's own honor but for the glory of the God of Israel — this is the meaning of the *Sanctification of the Name*. The Jerusalem Talmud relates that the disciples of Rabbi Simon ben Shetach once bought him a donkey from one Saratzin (a pagan), and found upon this donkey's saddle a priceless pearl. "Does the seller know of this?," asked the rabbi. "No," replied the disciples. "Then go quickly and return this treasure to him." When they had done this, the Saratzin exclaimed, "Praised be the God of the Jews!," and this exclamation of the Gentile, it is observed on this occasion (in the Talmud), was for Rabbi Simon more valuable than all the treasures of the world.[242] "Once our elders," related Rabbi Hanina, "bought from some passing Roman soldiers a bag of wheat and found therein a wallet with gold. They quickly caught up with the Roman soldiers and returned the found item to them, and those exclaimed, 'Praised be the God of the Jews!'"[243] Rabbi Samuel ben Sosarti went to Rome and found there a priceless decoration which had been lost by the empress, and about which it was publicly promulgated that whoever would find and return it before thirty days would receive a great reward, but that whoever would return it after thirty days would be executed. Rabbi Samuel returned this decoration on the thirty-first day. The empress asked him in surprise, "Did you not hear the proclamation?" "I heard it," answered Rabbi Samuel, "but I brought the item not out of a desire for reward and not out of the fear of execution, but simply out of fear of God." Then the empress exclaimed, "Praised be the God of the Jews!"[244]

But if the positive principle of *kiddush ha-Shem* is an ideal demand realized only by the righteous, then its negative corresponding principle, *hillul ha-Shem*, enjoins unconditional demands on every Jew. On the strength of this principle, if a well-known act permitted by the law turns out in certain circumstances to be inappropriate so as to bring forth slander upon Israel and upon its God, then such a deed, regardless of its abstract legality, becomes the greatest sin and a crime. The relative breadth of the application of this principle seemingly depends not on the Jews but on those peoples amidst whom they live. Thus, in Christian society, where money lending and all similar professions were considered an unconditionally base and dishonorable matter, the Jews, on the strength of the principle of the *Profanation of the Name* were obligated to restrain themselves from such professions.

Finally, the third principle, the *Ways of Peace*, demands that well-known, legally unnecessary actions, such as giving alms to Gentiles, bestowing funeral honors on their deceased, and so on, were fulfilled by Jews for the preservation and establishment of peaceful and friendly relations with all, on account of the *Ways of Peace* (*mipney darkhei shalom*). For according to the Talmud, *peace* comes third after *truth* and *justice* as a pillar upon which the universe stands, and friendship is the greatest of virtues.

And so the Talmud does not contain any of those bad laws which the antisemites would like to discover in it. Several distinct injunctions, which contemporary ethics, purified to a well-known degree from nationalism, may regard as unjust, lose all their practical force thanks to the principles of *kiddush ha-Shem, hillul ha-Shem,* and *mipney darkhei shalom.* And so the antisemites are constrained to return to the common principal charge against the Talmud. Being the fusion of the religio-national tradition, which assumes in large measure a strictly juridical character, the Talmud is that which secures Jewry in its segregation. It is the firmament which guards and separates the Jews from the rest of humanity, in other words, and before all else from the Christian world, with which history has bound them in the tightest manner. Against this firmament of Jewry, the Christian world has now, for fifteen centuries, been directing its material and spiritual weaponry. This weaponry has become very noticeably blunt, but the enemy firmament abides as always. We are firmly convinced that Jewish obstinacy alone does not account for its strength. Talmudic Judaism contains within itself a practical, *religio-national law of life*. It is impossible to set *such a law* in opposition to abstract ideas about universally human civilization. These subjects are completely heterogeneous and can therefore neither exclude nor replace each other. The Jewish tradition in no way rejects ideas arising from the modern Enlightenment. The Talmud in no way prevents the Jews from utilizing all the blessings of contemporary civilization or even from participating actively in the creation of these blessings. The exceptional segregating force of Talmudic Judaism is directed not outwardly *but inwardly*. It follows that in order to overcome this segregating force, one can only do so from *within*. The Talmud contains within itself *the religio-national law of life* for Jewry. If you do not like the fact that this law contains a religious character, then by all means attack religion directly. For it is self-evident that if Jewry as a whole were to lose its religious convictions, then there would not be any need even to speak of the Talmud. But if you yourselves stand upon religious ground, and if Talmudic Judaism repels you only by its national exclusivism and primitivism, then you ought to set up in opposition to this religio-*national* law of life (by deeds as well as by words) an alternate, religio-*universal* law of life. In the meanwhile, the representatives of Orthodox Christianity can demonstrate against Orthodox Judaism only by proclaiming abstract theological truths (accompanied in the best and rarest of cases with pious wishes and hopes). But such proclamations, religious and conscientious Jews can more or less answer as follows:

> In your theological discussions about the truth of Christianity, you forget two things: the nature of religion and the peculiarity of the Jewish character. You forget that Christianity *as a religion* must be *a system of life* and not a system of solely theological thoughts, and that consequently, it must be judged not solely by reference to theoretical, but, and principally, by reference to practical principles. In addition, you forget that Jews are distinguished from Greeks, Hindus, and Germans precisely by not according any value to contemplative truth *taken by itself* but only when it is applied *to life*, when it exerts a beneficent influence or brings real profit.[245] We Jews judge a tree neither by the greatness of its trunk, nor by the picturesque quality of its branches, nor by the form of its foliage, nor by the beauty of its flowers, but by the taste and the nutritional value of its fruit. Thus reasons not just Jerusalem but Galilee as well; and your own Teacher also held to the same view, and your Gospel records the pronouncement that every tree is known by its fruit.[246] Therefore, let us speak not about

the foliage of Christian theology but about the fruits of Christian life. I do not want to insist that these fruits have always been bitter for us Jews. Perhaps this bitterness derives neither from Christianity itself nor even from the meanness of Christians. Perhaps Israel itself is insufficiently firm in the commandments of its God, and He continues until now to test His people as he formerly tested it by means of Egypt, Assyria, Greece, and Edom. But what have the Christian peoples themselves derived from Christianity for living their life? I am not speaking of saints and righteous people; they exist in Christianity and outside of it, as a rare exception, but Christianity does not, indeed, pursue the impossible goal of correcting all people *one by one*, it does not limit itself by the Gospel of personal morality, it assumes the form of a collective whole, and emerges as a church. The church exists not only to fashion a saint, or to fashion saints *one by one*, but in order to arrange a *godly* social life, so that social justice[247] and personal righteousness[248] could mutually support and nurture each other. You Christians affirm that your religion is the highest and final stage of divine revelation, that it introduced into the world new living principles which Judaism did not know. If that is so, then these new principles should have renewed and re-created the entire life of Christian humanity; they should have continued to introduce the highest justice into all social, civil, and international relationships of the Christian world. We want a visible demonstration of Christian *social* successes. It is often noted that the preaching of the Gospel destroyed the main ulcer of the ancient world—slavery. It is remarkable, however, that one and a half thousand years before the appearance of Christianity, Mosaic legislation espoused considerably greater social and actual measures against slavery (namely, by the keeping of sabbatical and jubilee years) than the softening palliatives which we meet in ecclesial canons. It is indubitable that the moral *idea* of Christianity undermines slavery, but the issue here consists not in ideas but in deeds, and in the realm of deeds, slavery persisted in this or that form throughout the entire prevalence of the Christian idea and was decisively extinguished only in the eighteenth and nineteenth centuries, in other words, precisely in the epoch of religious decline and predominant unbelief. Exactly the same point must be made about the humanization of criminal justice, about the abolition of torture, and so on. The accomplishments in social morality which Christian peoples achieved in the past two centuries are not directly linked with Christianity. And in any case, these improvements in social morality are too superficial and hardly alter the general picture of your social life which is decisively alien to the Christian ideal. Our Jewish people has seen *how* Gentiles have lived, and it sees now how Christians live, and it does not find any real difference between those and these. The living foundations there and here are one and the same.[249] Both there and here, social life is founded not upon general moral solidarity but upon mutual opposition and the mechanical leveling of private forces and interests; both there and here, the strong persecute the weak and struggle with each other. Has Christianity subordinated the economic structure of society to some moral law? Has it introduced an intelligent wholeness and justice into the division of labor? Is not contemporary economic exploitation the violence of old, and is not contemporary free competition not the old war for *booty*? You pray to the God of truth and of love, but you serve the God of power and success, that same golden calf by which you reproach us (the injustice of this reproach is unmasked by your own Christian literature; in it, the typical servant of the golden calf is not the Jew Shylock but the Miserly Knight).[250] If the Christian society which we inhabit did not elevate money above all, then we too would have no cause to busy ourselves with monetary affairs. Monetary *Yiddishness* (*zhidovstvo*) is the product of your civilization: when we were independent, we were renowned on account of religion, not money, on account of the Temple, and not the stock market. That which is good in our nature comes from our father Abraham. That which is good in our condition comes from our legislator Moses, but all that is base in our nature and in our condition is the fruit of our accommodation to that society in whose midst we lived and live: formerly the pagan society and, later and especially, Christian society. Disregarding, however, this willing or unwilling "accommodation to the milieu" which has perverted our original type, we nevertheless preserve the main characteristics which elevate us, as over the pagans, so over Christians, namely, an unwavering attachment to our religious law, intimate mutual solidarity, and cordial family customs. To assimilate with contemporary Christian society would entail for Jewry the loss of its own moral foundations with no reciprocal gain.

Do not tell us that the debased structure and wretched life of Christian society does not vitiate the inward advantages of the Christian religion, and that religious truth possesses its own special sphere. This we know, and our Great Sanhedrin, already gave our religious life, in ancient times, three foundations: Study (of the Torah), worship, and deeds of loving-kindness.[251] But in *distinguishing* these three foundations, we consider it impermissible and impious *to separate* them from each other, to separate theory from practice, and worship from philanthropic love. In this separation there is falsehood. Therefore, even if we were to acknowledge that your Christian teaching is true and your worship right, still, seeing that your life and your works are not governed by the law of love and justice,[252] divine and human, we deem your religion powerless and do not wish to join it.

Even if we, Jews, could *grasp* the essence of Christianity, we would not, on any account, wish to *embrace*[253] your attitude to religion as to some abstract truth. In our view, truth cannot be abstract, and cannot be separated from practical life. We are a people of the Law, and for us truth itself is not so much an intellectual idea as a *law of life*. For you, on the contrary, truth exists on its own, as does practical life. Not only does your living reality not realize your religious ideal (something that cannot even be demanded), but you are not in the least embarrassed by the fact that the very *law* of your life, for example, in the sphere of politics or of social economy, directly contradicts your religious principles. Among you, people of the most diverse views concur that religious moral demands should have no role in politics or social economy, that here all should be decided not by love of one's fellow man and supreme justice but only by the self-loving interest of this or that ethnicity, or of this or that social class. Thus it is, and thus it must be according to you. Your religious ideal is the expression of supreme sanctity, but the law of your life is and remains the law of sin and of injustice. You are convinced that the ideal cannot be made practical and the practical cannot be made the ideal. But we, Jews, however low we might fall, to such a principled repudiation of true life and living truth, to such a legalized differentiation and contradiction between idea and deed, to the eternal powerlessness of justice, to eternal injustice, we do not assent.

The choice is clear: either your religion is really unrealizable, implying that it is simply an empty or an artificial fantasy, or it is realizable, implying that you, owing to your bad will, do not realize it. In that case, prior to calling others to join you, repent and correct yourselves. Learn to fulfill your own New Testament as we fulfill our Old Testament, and then we will come and join you. But now even if we wanted to come to you, we could not, since we do not know to whom, among you, we should go. Your kingdom has been divided against itself, and there is no unanimity between you. Show us that one and universal Christianity which would remove from us the fetters of ethnic exclusiveness.

This or some similar speech could be delivered to us by any religious Jew. And none of our objections against his conclusions would hold any convincing force as long as the practical conclusion of his speech remains incontrovertible.[254] It really is the case that we cannot consider the unification of Jewry with the Christian world as long as this same world is divided within itself. We cannot expect the Jews to sacrifice for our sake their ethnic exclusiveness while national enmity prevails over universal unity among us. We have no right to demand that religious Jews should abandon their hopes for the *future* kingdom of the Messiah while we cannot give them the Messiah's actual kingdom. We cannot, finally, convince the Jews to believe in Christianity while we ourselves believe in it so poorly. Those among us who think that Christianity will never attain unity in itself, and never acquire power over our life, admit thereby the powerlessness of their religion, and remain, before the Jews, without an answer.

Preserved, thanks to the Talmud and via its religio-national segregation, Jewry has not yet lost the meaning of its existence. It remains standing as a living admonition to the Christian world. It does not debate with us about abstract truths but turns to us with demands for justice and faithfulness: either to repudiate Christianity or to commit ourselves decisively to its realization in life. Our misfortune lies not in the excessive agency of the Talmud but in the insufficient agency of the Gospel. On us ourselves and not on the Jews depends the wished-for resolution of the Jewish question. We cannot force the Jews to repudiate the laws of the Talmud, but to follow evangelical precepts when dealing with Jewry itself is always within our power. The choice is clear: either the Jews are not our enemies, in which case the Jewish question simply does not exist, or they are our enemies, in which case we must deal with them in the spirit of love and peace. This is the only Christian resolution of the Jewish question.

CHAPTER 4

"The Jews(,) Their Religious and Moral Teachings(.) The Study of S. Y. Diminsky" (1891)

The author excuses (on p. 185) the shortcomings of his essay by citing "hasty labor conducted exclusively under the commission and moral pressure (?) of the chairman of the Minsk commission on the Jewish question."[255] Mr. Diminsky's booklet,[256] it turns out, wasn't even intended for publication; it comprises notes, hurriedly presented to the named commission. To compose the notes, as we also here learn, the author only had one and a half months. Under such circumstances, to write something significant, or relatively well grounded, about such a complicated and difficult subject would require expert knowledge of Jewry in general and of the Talmud in particular. This is precisely how the anonymous publishers of Mr. Diminsky's notes represent him, having published them posthumously (the author died several years ago) with a eulogistic preface. It only remains to inspect how the booklet itself corroborates this testimony of the interested parties who have chosen to conceal their names.

On page 59 we read, "I do not know exactly how much the Talmud itself explores the issue of interest rates among Jews themselves: I only remember that according to the determination of the Talmud such (?) a loan may be given with interest only by Talmud-Chakhams, that is, by learned Jews, in which case the interest may be represented under the robe[257] [sic] of a gift." In addition to the poor grammatical form of this declaration, one may note the oddity of its content: why, indeed, had the author not taken greater care to acquaint himself with the details of his subject matter? A little farther on we find an answer to this question, an answer, moreover, of a general character. On pages 105 and 106 we read the following: "The foregoing quotations from the ethical rulings regulating the dealings of Jews with adherents of other faiths and foreigners, characterizing the methodology which Talmudic teachers adopt in dealing with the sources of Old Testament revelation, I managed to extract from an apocryphal Jewish volume titled *Omer Ha Shikhah*[258] published in one of our native printing houses in the year 5621 from the creation of the world according to Jewish chronology, that is, in A.D. 1860 or 1861. I have not had the opportunity to collate all these quotations from official editions of the Talmud at this present time, not owning a personal copy of the Talmud and encountering obstacles to my attempts to corroborate my list of excerpts (?) against copies of the Talmud in Jewish possession." From this curious admission, it follows that Mr. Diminsky did not at all consult the Talmud while collating his notes: he didn't have his own copy, and experienced difficulties consulting others. Consequently, we were not especially surprised by the following additional admissions of this *expert:* "In the interpretations of this cited rule, known as *Be'er ha Gola*, attributed to the first-class authority on Judaism, the seventeenth-century rabbi Moses Rivkes of Vilna,[259] edited by himself in Amsterdam (*Of Certain Medieval Accusations*, p. 67; *The Talmudists' Worldview*, vols. 2 and 3, p. 81),[260] there are citations of Maimonides, of one Mardochai who is unknown to me, and likewise of the Talmudic tractate *Baba Bathra* (149.1) where, *as I suppose,*[261] the rules I presented regarding the treatment of proselytes are developed in more detail" (pp. 150–51). Thus, when the issue at hand concerns the Talmud, our author can only make presuppositions about the content of this or that passage in the famous Talmudic tractate, of whose existence he learned from some very recent work. By the way, such a loose attitude to sources is not, in his work, limited to the Talmud. A few sentences later we read (pp. 151–52), "Here one may note as remarkable the fact that the authoritative Jewish commentary on the last two points, known under the heading of *Siftei* [sic] *Kohen*, and belonging to the seventeenth-century rabbi Shabbetai Kohen,[262] consists only of quotations with many abbreviations *regarding authoritative Jewish works unknown to me but known to competent people,*[263] and, by the way, upon the volume of the renowned Rabbi Asher ben Yechiel, or the "Rosh," one of the greatest Jewish authorities of the thirteenth century (*Of Certain Medieval Accusations,* p. 102; *The Talmudists' Worldview,* vol. 1, p. 255). And so, not only the Talmud but also other authoritative Jewish works turn out to be completely unknown to Mr. Diminsky. His assurance, however, that these works are known to competent people is a consoling fact, even though it does not require any special confirmation. It is good, however, that our author so decisively excludes himself from the list of competent persons. With this self-evaluation everyone must agree. It is also impossible to object to his declaration on page 186, "I have done only what I could have done under the present circumstances." If *present circumstances* denotes, first of all, Mr. Diminsky's complete unfamiliarity with Jewish books in general, and with the Talmud in particular, and second, the resoluteness to present indiscriminate interpretations under the semblance of expertise in subjects he knows nothing about, then, undoubtedly, our author has done only that which he could have done, or to put it better, he could only do what he did. But the words which follow this declaration can in no wise be justified from the point of view of truth or even of plain common sense. "Adducing formal documents," writes Mr. Diminsky, "in order to describe Jewish[264] religious and moral teaching, I tried to speak in the language of these documents, but owing to the idiosyncrasy of Hebrew speech and to the complete novelty of the subject matter for the uninitiated, I was obliged *at times* to represent *some* documents in a *somewhat*[265] paraphrased and a diffused external aspect to make it comprehensible to such readers as may meet the subject matter I present for the first time" (p. 186). What is the meaning of "Adducing formal documents," and trying to speak in its language? When a document written in a foreign language is adduced, all efforts must first aim at transcribing it infallibly and then supplementing it (for the "uninitiated" reader) with an exact and, if possible, literal translation. Moreover, if one were to bear in mind such ultra-uninitiated readers as would not be able to understand the document, neither in a foreign nor in their own language, then nothing would

hinder the addition, for *such* readers, of special explanations and clarifications. But our author *always* (and not just sometimes, as he assures)
confines himself only to this third, additional problem. He never adduces any "formal documents," that is, any texts taken from Jewish
books, either in the original or in a Russian translation. He only trans-
mits in his own words (in indirect speech) various, seemingly Jewish,
regulations, statutes, and opinions and then sometimes puts into parentheses the titles of Jewish books, including by the way, Talmudic
tractates. These Jewish titles, as is apparent even from his own indications, he found in some most recently published and commonly accessible works regarding the Jewish question, predominantly in Russian,
such as, for example, the famous book of Professor Khvol'son regarding the medieval accusations against the Jews,[266] or the popular collection of articles, *The Talmudists' Worldview.*[267]

That there is *not a single* excerpt or quotation from any Jewish
book whatsoever—of this every reader, even an "uninitiated" one, may
easily be assured by personal witness, and if the author himself and his
publishers were to affirm the contrary, then, besides indifference to
patent truth, one could explain this only by positing that they do not
understand the difference between a quotation from a book and a reference to a book. The difference, however, is quite significant. One
could refer to whatever one wishes. Mr. Diminsky, by the way, also
refers to the Talmud, but as to quoting from it, he has not so much as
quoted a single line and, at any rate, could not, by his own admission,
for that sole reason that the Talmud, like a treasure, escaped his grasp:
his own copy he didn't have, and the copies of others, for some mysterious reasons, he wasn't able to use.

The Jewish titles taken from the most recent Russian works and
set in parentheses, by which the author has adorned his own conceptions, all these *Baba Kama, Sanhedrin, Abodah Zarah,* and so on, remain empty sounds, foreign to him and his readers alike. To accept this
collection of "awful words" as serious citations, or as "formal documents," to use Diminsky's expressions, one requires such a high level
of uninitiation as one finds only among an entirely special sort of
reader. It was probably on such highly uninitiated readers that the
publishers of this booklet counted, declaring on the jacket that the
total run, printed entirely on vellum paper, was 550 copies.

In order to perceive the power of Mr. Diminsky's "formal documents," let us just take one of his references to the unknown-to-him Talmud, namely, the reference regarding the most foundational and vital point. "The highest stage of knowledge, and consequently of piety," writes Diminsky on page 42, "is understood to be (i.e., among Jews)[268] the ability to prove the legality of an illegal action." And as proof of this weighty thesis we find inserted in parentheses: *The Babylonian Talmud*, Tractate *Sanhedrin* 17.2. These numbers signify the folio (leaf) and page of the Talmudic tractate *Sanhedrin* (about the Sanhedrin)—namely, the second page, or the verso of folio 17. Finding the stated place, we ascertain that it contains nothing pertaining to Mr. Diminsky's thesis.[269] But, perhaps, the author of that most recent work from which our "expert" extracted this citation counted the pages of each folio not from right to left, as the Jewish system requires, but from left to right? Indeed, on the first page of this folio there is a phrase, whose meaning writers of a well-known sort, with customary impudence and shamelessness, can twist to yield the stated sense.[270] The issue concerns the qualities which members of the Sanhedrin should possess. According to Rabbi Yohanan, one should even be tall and good-looking. The more commonly recognized requirements are wisdom, linguistic knowledge (so as not to be deceived by translators), and, according to Rashi, familiarity with Egyptian charms and tricks, so as not to have the wool pulled over one's eyes. Also adduced, by the way, is the view of the great teacher Yehuda in the following words: *amar rabbi Yehuda amar rab ein moshivin besanhedri(n)*[271] *ele mi sheyodea l'maher et hasherets.* In Russian this means: "Rabbi Yehuda said, the teacher said, do not give a seat in the Sanhedrin to one who does not know how to purify the *sherets*."[272] The word *sherets* means "a swarming thing" in the broad sense, embracing all reptiles, creatures that creep and swarm—snakes, frogs, lobsters, worms, and so on. All such animals were regarded by Jews as unclean and rendered unclean whatever object they touched. In view of the practical inconvenience of the various complicated purifications, it was permitted from ancient times to ease and limit the general principle, and conditions were recognized in which the unclean character of the *sherets* was removed, and Rabbi Yehuda opts for the widest application of these alleviating measures, demanding that, without fail, every member of the Sanhedrin should know them. Had this teacher opted for the opposite principle, then the honorable Diminsky would not have failed to represent him as a model of a merciless, all life-suppressing Jewish legalism. It is clear at any rate that the discussion pertains to ritual purity. As to the transformation of unlawful activities into lawful ones, there isn't even a mention.

"It is very possible," writes Mr. Diminsky, "that many would consider me as having overstepped due boundaries in regard to general, personally held views and deductions: in all such and similar cases I ask that such people take into consideration only the formal documents presented by me, setting aside my own views and generalizations and replacing them with their own" (pp. 186–87). Not a single formal document, not a single Jewish text either in the original or in translation, has been presented to us by Mr. Diminsky. His own conceptions and generalizations, in accord with his personal and completely legitimate request, must not be given any attention. Is there, however, any factual material in this booklet? In a different place, the author addresses this point somewhat hermetically and enigmatically: "On the literature dealing with the question of Jewish[273] religious and moral teaching, on the most varied premises and diametrically opposite inferences on this subject, I propose to speak subsequently, in accord with my preconceived plan, on the basis of the materials which I will find" (pp. 109, 110). A trifle like the Talmud is not included in these materials. They do, however, include the newspaper *Novoe vremya* [New Times], which our author very readily cites on statistical issues, and even more so on issues pertaining to religious and moral teaching. Moreover, Mr. Diminsky possesses even such factual material as remains completely unknown with regard to its sources. Such, by the way, is his verbose and bizarre tale about one baptized Jewish archimandrite who, it seems, "when asked about which Christian name he would adopt at holy baptism, answered that he wished to be called 'Bursar,' obviously," explains Mr. Diminsky, "because the responsibility of the monastic bursar interested him at this time, because he was elevated to the holy order of the archimandrite not for his piety but for his smarts and agility—first in his duties as a private servant, then in his duties as an economist, and because, as is no secret for those who know this archimandrite, when it comes to Orthodox priestly functions, he pronounces the exclamations with the greatest of difficulties and knows how to read only the Gospel texts pertaining to solemn feast days" (pp. 194–95). Behold the import of irrational jealousy: Mr. Diminsky aimed his denunciatory gossip at the Jews, but his shot went in a completely different direction!

From everything set out above, I suppose, it is sufficiently clear that Diminsky's note, published by unknown persons, lacking any single Jewish text, even in translation, and revealing the author's complete unfamiliarity with Jewish literature in general and the Talmud in particular, can merit attention only as an example of the cultural level of that audience which would receive this talentless and ignorant pamphlet as an important and authoritative study.

CHAPTER 5

"When Lived the Hebrew Prophets?" Review of Ernest Havet's *La modernité des prophètes* (1896)

———

The author of this booklet, who died in 1889, possessed a certain popularity in France, thanks to his work *Le Christianisme et ses origines*.[274] The present booklet is published separately and posthumously. I say *booklet*, and not book, because the seemingly significant scope of this composition turns out to be an outwardly deceptive typographical contrivance. In reality, it only reproduces (without alterations or additions) a journal article, originally issued in two installments of *Revue des Deux Mondes*, only sixty pages in total. Given this scope, Havet's treatise argues the following position: all the authors of the prophetic books in the Hebrew Bible, that is, the so-called *n'bijim*[275] *acheronim* (*prophetae posteriores*), from Isaiah to Malachi, lived *after* the Maccabean wars of liberation. . . .

In order to defend this conclusion, one requires several special qualities and conditions, which are brilliantly united in Havet. The first of these he directly identifies himself, namely, his ignorance of the Hebrew language, entailing that he could read the Old Testament only in translation (p. 6). In addition, he declares that he researched the question of the date of the prophets *for a whole year*, while delivering a public course on the subject ("Je viens de donner à l'étude de cette question une année entière pendant laquelle j'en ai fait le sujet d'un cours public"; p. 8). If the measure of this single year also contained a public course, that is, the communication of the *results* of research, then the time devoted to the research itself must now have been not a whole year but only a few months. For this reason, putting ignorance of Hebrew to the side, the attitude of this biblical "critic" to his subject is distinguished by a rare light-mindedness, as well as a striking naïveté, with which he himself underscores the radically superficial and hurried character of his studies. With his other qualities, which he himself acknowledges, we will become acquainted, in following his argumentation. . . .

III

. . . Quite wonderful are the last three verses of the chapter 19 [of Isaiah], "In that day a road will be opened from Egypt to Assyria, and Egypt and Assyria will serve (God). In that day Israel will be the third with Egypt and Assyria, a blessing to the whole earth, by which the Eternal Sabaoth will bless it, saying, 'Blessed is My people Egypt and the work of my hands Assyria and My inheritance Israel.'"[276] Havet feels no shyness in referring this passage to the struggle of the Seleucids with the Ptolemies, when Jerusalem passed several times from the hands of one into the hands of the other. But what do these military-political relations have in common with what the prophet speaks of: the spiritual union of Egypt, Assyria, and Israel in the service of the one God who blesses all three of them? . . . (p. 528). . . .

VII

In Havet's case, the misuse of higher criticism has reached a point of absurdity and become a laughable caricature. The ridiculous and the laughable have not been lacking, of course, on the other side. . .[277] Today, both extremes can be considered as buried. The real birthplace of higher criticism, Germany, increasingly repudiates hypercritical arbitrariness, while from the other side, England, the bastion of traditional exegesis in this field, follows the direction of general scholarship, even without skirting some enthusiasms which, in any case, are preferable to the previous stagnancy.

The fossilized rarities of a blind literalism are encountered today only on the pages and in the circles of those who consciously eschew scholarship, but alongside this, such enfants terribles of the opposite inclination as Havet are constrained to complain bitterly about the complete contempt accorded to their theory by scholars among whom "the only ones who have spared it are those who have said nothing of it" (*ceux-là seulement l'ont ménagée qui n'en ont rein dit*; p. 7).

Truth to tell, here too, as is usually the case, the contrary extremes of traditional and higher-critical approaches are simply the fruit of one and the same culture—of scholastic abstraction—they are begotten by the one and same spirit, or to put it better, by the one and same absence of spirit, by the same *indifference* to essence, to the inner meaning of the Bible and of the prophetic writings in particular.

But with indifference and inattentiveness to this essential content, to that which inspired the biblical writers, to that on account of which they acted and wrote, the very question of the time and circumstances of their activity loses its vital interest and is thereby deprived of the principal foundation for its correct resolution. For only the understanding of that *meaning* of Jewish history, which expressed itself in the Bible, gives us the firm point of support for a true judgment about the time and the historical frames in which the bearers of this meaning lived and acted. This, of course, should not eliminate interest in and the necessity of special philological and historical research, but these also necessitate an understanding of the essence of the matter, as the originating point and guiding thread of intellectual work.

Here, I do not at all have in mind some kind of metaphysical orientation or a priori conclusions about history: I approach the matter simply and elementarily. There exists an indubitable fact: a small, pulverized Hebrew nation survived in ancient times, and survived—with profit for itself, by internal development and growth—such historical catastrophes as destroyed, in the end, incomparably stronger and more integrated and cultured national bodies. This means that the Jewish people survived this not by means of material strength but by spiritual strength. This spiritual strength was indubitably connected with a national religion, since absent such, there were no other *significant* expressions of the ethnic spirit among the Jews. But this is still not what explains the matter. All other peoples also had a national religion, and, at first glance, it is difficult to find the essential difference between the original religion of the sons of Israel and the religion of the sons of Moab, Ammon, and Edom. But those perished, while Israel emerged indomitable. That means that in the religion of the Jews there was something greater than its visible national form; there was some kind of inner excellence thanks to which the spirit of the people was strengthened and became capable of surviving the destruction of its political body. This superiority, distinguishing the national religion of the Jews from all others, and expressing itself especially among the prophets, was not the abstract idea of monotheism but a keen consciousness and sense of the fact that that special God, who is the national providence of Israel and the personal providence of every Israelite, is, *first of all*, a universal God, Who holds *all* in His *power*, and, *second*, not a God of power only, but also a God of *truth*, truth not abstractly conceivable but really acting and realizing itself. From this union of power and truth it follows that all that happens must end to the glory of this God, and that for those who are loyal to Him, physical misfortunes are only trials, the means and tools of spiritual perfection and well-being. And from this there arises the *third* distinctive element of this higher religious consciousness: faith in a golden age *in the future*, in historical progress, in the meaning of history, in the final reign of righteousness.[278]

This higher consciousness is in truth *prophetic* since it presages the future and by this very presaging gives people moral strengths to draw near to and realize this ideal future. Only such a prophetic consciousness could have saved the Jewish people in extreme calamities, unendurable to other peoples. All external foundations of their existence were taken away from them. By what then, in actuality, was Jewry preserved as a single national spiritual society during the Babylonian captivity? They had neither their own country, nor government, nor common cult, nor even their own language. All was lost, all that the various other peoples had and by which these peoples did not manage to survive. Israel was saved by that which it alone had: by a spiritual union with the living God of Righteousness (*pravda*). Now one can ask: *When* did this inner strength arise in the Jewish people? When did the first bearers and proclaimers of this supreme consciousness live? Is it not clear that it was *before* those external catastrophes, to survive which this spiritual strength, this higher consciousness, was necessary? By the natural movement of history, those ideal principles which take control of collective wholes arise first in individually elected persons. If during the Babylonian captivity and after it, the whole Jewish community, at least in its leading circles, had to appropriate for its salvation a higher religious consciousness, then it is clear that the elect individuals had to attain this consciousness and proclaim it *prior to* the national disaster. They turned out to be prophets in three senses: (1) they *presaged* the kingdom of righteousness, ideally determining their own religious consciousness by means of it; (2) they admonished and judged the real condition of their people as being in contradiction to this ideal and *foretold* the national disasters as necessary consequences of this contradiction; (3) by their very appearance and activity, they *foreshadowed* the way out of this contradiction in the people's nearest future, indeed by their very recognition of this higher consciousness and by subordination to it.

And thus, upon such inner foundations, we must accept that the main Hebrew prophets lived in part *before* the Babylonian captivity and in part at its beginning, which is in complete accord both with ancient tradition and with the opinion of the most serious scholars of our present time.

The Bible as a whole and the writings of the prophets in particular are in essence the most ancient but not antiquated, still, to the present time *prophetic* expression of the highest and purest spiritual power acting in humanity. To treat this supreme memorial of world history and lose sight of its natural content or internal meaning, to see in it simply the reflection of external historical circumstances, is to not approach the subject as it is in itself, to treat it so means to act unjustly, falsely, *unscholarly*. On the other hand, to look upon the testimonies of the historical activity of the living God as upon a petrified and untouchable holy of holies is to show a dead faith and to sin against the Holy Spirit, who speaks through the prophets. Real scholarship demands *understanding* in the Bible that which really is in it essentially, namely, a prophetic spirit; and true religiosity demands the *reception* of this spirit, as an eternally living power which not only determined the fates of the Jewish people in the past, but upon which must depend the prospects of our own personal future.

CHAPTER 6

"The Kabbalah," from the *Encyclopedic Dictionary* (1896)

The mystical teaching and the mystical practice in Judaism, preserved originally by oral tradition, which is the actual meaning of the Hebrew word (*reception*, objectively: *tradition*).[279] Opinions regarding the antiquity of the Kabbalah diverge by more than three thousand years—from the epoch of Abraham to the thirteenth century A.D. The view that the Kabbalah may be of prebiblical antiquity has no historical character, while the contrary extreme view (regarding the Kabbalah's late medieval origins) is founded upon misunderstandings: the principal witnesses of Kabbalistic literature in their present form did in fact appear during the Middle Ages, but one cannot identify them with the actual contents of the Kabbalah, that is, with that sphere of traditional mystical ideas which were preserved in secret from the uninitiated, partly in the oral tradition of the teachers, partly in fragmentary writings which have not reached us. Clear traces of Kabbalistic conceptions and terms in the New Testament, and even more direct references to the Kabbalah in the most ancient parts of the Talmud, pertaining to the first centuries of our era, witness to the existence of Jewish theosophy, at least close to the time of the birth of Christ. In the Mishnah one may read the following declaration: "One is not to discourse on the *works of creation* (of the world) in the presence of two, nor on the *works of the chariot* (of God) in the presence of one, unless he has his own mind for this."[280] Here in the italicized words are indicated the two subdivisions of the theoretical Kabbalah (see *infra*). This declaration is already linked in the (more ancient) Jerusalem *Gemara* with a long dialectical story explaining the dangers of careless dealing with the secret theosophical teaching which thereby is here presupposed as something already settled. One may affirm with sufficient confidence that the Kabbalah arose not before the Babylonian captivity and not later than the latest Hasmoneans. As the collision of Jewish religious thought with Greek philosophy resulted in the original speculations of Philo, so the earlier mutual interaction of that same thought with Babylonian-Persian magic and theosophy begat the Kabbalah. This does not exclude subsequent Greek, Greco-Jewish, Greco-Egyptian, and Christian influences on the development of the Kabbalah, but such remain secondary. The foundation was firmly set in Babylon and Persia.

The Kabbalah is generally divided into the *theoretical* (*Kabbalah Iyunit*) and the *applied* (*Kabbalah ma'asit*). The theoretical Kabbalah consists again of two main parts or "works": *of cosmogony: ma'asê bereshit*, literally, *works* (of, about that which is in) *the beginning*, and *theosophy: ma'asê merkaba*, literally, *works of the chariot* or *riding out of God*. By the way, the cosmological and the theosophical speculations of the Kabbalah cross over from one to the other and are not subjected to separate exposition. The main literary witnesses to the theoretical Kabbala are the *Sepher Yetsira* (Book of Creation) and the *Zohar* (Splendor). The first is attributed to father Abraham but in reality pertains to the beginning of the Middle Ages, for in the ninth century commentaries were already written about it as about an ancient authority; apparently it was composed in the sixth or seventh century. The *Zohar* is attributed by the Kabbalists to the disciple of the famous teacher R. Akiba: Rabbi Simeon ben Yochai (second century), but since this dark writing contains clear references to the Muslims and even a hint about the death of Pope Nicholas III (1280), it may with complete probability be referred to a time close to 1300, and one may assume that its author was the Spanish rabbi Moses de Leon. Both books are printed for the first time in Mantua in 1558–62. In addition to the foundational role played in the formation of the theoretical system of the Kabbalah by these texts, special significance must be accorded to the following: the *Sepher ha Bahir*, the composition of

R. Isaac the Blind (thirteenth century), the *Pardes Rimonim* of R. Moses Kordovero, and finally the writings of R. Isaac Luria, nicknamed Leo (Ari). The latter two lived in the sixteenth century and completed the inner development of Jewish Kabbalism. From the fifteenth century there also appear Kabbalists among Christian writers: in Italy, Pico de Mirandola; in Germany, Reichlin ("De arte cabbalistica" and "De Verbo mirifico") and Paracelsus; in France, Wilhelm Postel (sixteenth century); in England, Robert Fludd, or de Fluctibus, and Henry More (sixteenth–seventeenth century). On the other hand, the interaction between Christianity and Judaism on the basis of the Kabbalah begat the messianic movement of Sabbatai Zvi (seventeenth century), Frank and the Frankists (eighteenth century), and finally Hasidism, with its *tsadiks*, which still flowers in southwestern Russia and Galicia.

The theoretical teaching of the Kabbalah derives from the idea of the sacred, unspoken deity, which, being higher than any determination or limitation, can be called only *ein soph*, that is, nothing or the Endless. In order to make room within itself for finite being, *ein soph* must limit itself. From here comes the "mystery of the drawing-back" (*sod tsimtsum*), the name given in the Kabbalah to these self-limitations or self-determinations of the absolute, granting in himself a place for the worlds. These self-limitations do not alter the unspoken in him himself but do give him the possibility of manifestation, that is, to also be for another. The primordial foundation or condition of this "other," according to the figurative conceptions of the Kabbalists is an empty space (in the first moment: only a point), arising within the absolute on account of his self-limitation or "drawing back." Thanks to this emptiness, the limitless light of the *ein soph* receives the possibility of "the descent of the ray," or emanation (since there is a *where* to which to emanate). This light is not tangible but is intellectually apprehensible, and its first rays are the foundational forms or categories of being; these are the 32 "ways of wisdom," namely, 10 numbers and spheres (*sephiroth*) and 22 letters of the Hebrew alphabet (3 foundational, 7 dual, 12 simple) to each of which there corresponds a special divine name. Just as it is possible to enumerate whatever one wishes by means of 10 numbers, so 22 letters are sufficient to write all possible books, and thus the unspoken divinity opens all its limitlessness via the medium of 32 ways. To the extent that it is possible to understand, the difference between the divine names corresponding to the *sephiroth* and the letters in this revelation consists in the former being the expression of the essence of the divine in the "other" or *objective* emanation (the direct rays of the divine light), while the letter names are conditioned by this emanation and are the subjective divine self-determinations (reflected rays).

The following are the names of the 10 *sephiroth:* (1) Crown (Keter); (2) Wisdom (Chokhmah); (3) Understanding (Binah); (4) Mercy and Magnanimity (Chesed or Gedulah); (5) Strength or Judgment (Geburah or Din, similarly Pahad); (6) Beauty or Splendor (Tipheret); (7) Victory (Netzach); (8) Glory or Greatness (Hod); (9) Foundation (Yesod); (10) Kingdom (Malkuth). Conceived as parts of a single whole, the *sephiroth* constitute the form of a perfect being: the primordial man (Adam-Kadmon). To strengthen the image, Kabbalists point to the correspondence between the separate *sephiroth* and the external parts of the human body: Keter, the scull; Chokhmah and Bina, the two eyes; Chesed and Din, the two hands; Tipheret, the chest, Netzach and Hod, the ribs, Yesod and Malkuth, the two legs. Such a representation complicates the introduction of sexual relations into the "tree of the *sephiroth.*" In general, in the realm of divine emanations, the Kabbalists distinguished divinity itself, as something that manifests itself, from its manifestation or "dwelling" in the other, which they called *Shekhinah* (tabernacle) and represented as the feminine side of God. The Shekhinah sometimes is identified with the last Sephirah: Malkuth, over against which, as a female principle, all the others, as male principles, are set, in which process the analogy with the human body is lost. Even more complex is the representation of the relationship in the book *Zohar.* Here Adam-Kadmon, as represented by the *sephiroth,* accommodates within himself three or even four faces. The Sephirah Mercy or Magnanimity with the three right or male *sephiroth* form the Long Face (Arik Anpin), or the Father (Aba). The Sephirah opposite to this, Firmness or Judgment along with the three left or female *sephiroth* form the Short Face (Zeir-Anpin) or Mother (Umah). The Sephirah Beauty or Splendor which proceeds from their union is called the "Pillar of the Middle" (Amuda Deemtsoita) and is represented sometimes as a new face or as a son; the remaining first highest Sephirah, the Crown, is sometimes related to the Father and sometimes is taken as a special face: the Eternal God as such, or the "Ancient of Days" (Atik-Yomin).

The *sephiroth* are essentially the general foundational forms of all being. The concrete universe, being dependent upon these forms, represents different stages of the distancing of the divine light from its primordial source. In the immediate proximity and complete oneness of the divine exists the World of Emanations (Atsiluth). Greater or lesser differentiation from the divine is represented by the farthest three worlds, which, according to the unique method of the Kabbalists, are derived by the following manner: in the beginning of the Book of Genesis (chs. 1 and 2) God's relationship to the world is expressed by three verbs: *create* (bara), *form* (yetser), and *make* (asah); from this stem three different worlds: the world of "creation" (*briya*), that is, the realm of creative ideas and of the pure spirits that live by them, then the world of "formation" (*yetsirah*), the realm of the souls and living creatures, and finally the world of "making" (*asiyah*), the sphere of material phenomena, our visible physical world. These worlds are not divided between themselves in an external way but are included in each other, like concentric spheres. The lower worlds realize that which is more ideally contained in the higher, while the beings and objects of the higher worlds, receiving from the first source divine influences, transmit them to the lower, serving in this way as channels, or "vessels" (*kelim*), of grace. Man simultaneously belongs to all the worlds: by the body and an affective *passionate soul* (*nephesh*), he relates to the lower phenomenal world; by the willing and *active* principle of his soul (*ruach*), he bears kinship to the world of creative powers; by his highest ideal spirit (*neshama*), he dwells in the world of intellectually apprehended beings; finally there is in him a still higher principle, which in the most intimate and profound way binds him with divinity: absolute unity (*yehida*), elevating him to a stage of immediate direct (nonartificial) emanations (*atsiluth*) of the eternal light. Nevertheless, belonging to all the worlds, man is naturally rooted in the lower material world which is united through him to divinity. The beings that naturally inhabit the higher worlds are the Angels. Kabbalistic angelology, borrowed chiefly from the Persians, comprises formal classifications; remarkable only is the idea of the solar angel, *Metatron* (seemingly a Hellenized form of Mithra), the highest mediator between God and the universe, sometimes identified with the archangel Michael and sometimes with the Messiah.

Our material world is still not the lowest step in the emanation of divine light; in that extreme realm, where this light is completely lost in total darkness, there forms the so-called *husks* of being or the *shells* (*Kelippot*); these are the impure spirits or demons, just as numerous as the angels and souls, for every kernel has a husk. This impure husk does not have its own being; it can vanish, but it cannot become pure. Human souls, on the contrary, are summoned to purification and perfection. The principal means for this is reincarnation, which is of two types: "revolution" (*gilgul*) and "intercalation" (also "impregnation") (*'ibbur*).[281] The first consists in gradual transmigration through all the spheres of being in ever new bodies unto perfect purification. *'Ibbur* means a special unification between a soul that has lived and a human being, of seven or even fourteen years of age, providentially aiming at the good of the former or latter or both. A helpful means for the elevation of the soul is the *applied* Kabbalah. It is bound to the *theoretical* by their mutually shared recognition of the mystical meaning of the letters and of the biblical names. By treating the Bible as an encoded text and applying different codes (attaching numerical meaning to letters, transposing letters in this or that determined order, etc.), it is possible to take one word and transform it into a completely different one and to reveal wondrous things (the main methods are called *gematria*, *notarikon, temura*). In this way, the Kabbalists guess the concealed and predict the future. The other part of the applied Kabbalah is magic; through the expedient implementation of the divine names various wonders are wrought (see Tsadiks, Chasidism). Compare Knorr de Rosenroth, "Cabbala denudata" (1677–84, here also is a Latin translation of the Zohar); Molitor, "Die Tradition oder Philosophie der Geschichte" (anonymous, incomplete; rich material and important references); Franck, "La Kabbale" (new ed. 1891); Jellinek, "Beitrage zur Geschichte der K." (1851); Myer, "Qabbalah" (Phila., 1888).

Foreword to "Kabbalah: The Mystical Philosophy of the Jews," by David Gintsburg (1896)

The proposed work, as far as I am aware, is the first independent composition on the Kabbalah in Russian.[282] The author, a learned Hebraist and Arabist, has managed to fit into a small volume the most abundant material, taken from primary sources. Having been written at my invitation for the *Encyclopedic Dictionary* of Brockhaus and Efron but acknowledged to be too specialized and insufficiently popular for the majority of readers of the general encyclopedia, this article finds its own proper place in a special section of a philosophical journal.[283]

Kabbalistic theosophy is not a system of a single thinker, or of a separate school, but is an entire, distinctive conception of the world, formed in the course of many centuries. Although this gigantic tree is several thousand years old, it has until the most recent time been yielding living, albeit not always healthy, offshoots. Its roots are concealed in the dark depths of the Jewish and Jewish-Chaldean religious thought, while the branches that are visible to historical inspection are intertwined with Gnostic and Neoplatonic conceptions. But to focus solely on these superficial branches and to see in the Kabbalah only a variation on Neoplatonism would be a mistake of the same magnitude as the supposition, on the basis of late revisions of Kabbalistic books in the thirteenth and fourteenth centuries, that the Kabbalistic teaching contained in these books is itself of medieval origin.

In actual fact, the Kabbalah is a product neither of medieval nor of Alexandrian thought. The indelible stamp of its ancient Hebrew origin and existential distinction from Neoplatonic thought we see in the special original realism and integral monism of this unique worldview. Characteristic for all Greek philosophy, wholly preserved in Neoplatonism in the antithesis between the world of intellectually comprehensible essences, the realm of the true, original being, and the world of material phenomena, this dualistic antithesis is completely absent in the Kabbalah: for it the material world is only the last radical stage in the realization and incarnation of the truly existent. And all four worlds recognized by Kabbalah (the world of radiance,[284] the world of creation, the world of formation, and the world of action) are only four main stages of the realization of the one and same absolute content. While in Neoplatonism the gradual transition from the transcendent One or Good through the world of minds and ideas to the world of souls and bodies is understood only from a negative point of view, as a descent, a darkening, a fall, the Kabbalah sees here also a positive side: completion, the incarnation of truth to the end, the realization of the fullness of being. And in the highest worlds nothing is conceived as abstract but all is represented in its concrete form, possessing a corresponding image in a lower world and connected to it ideally and really. In all the worlds, in addition to the unity of content, there is also affirmed the unity of common form, and this unified, all-encompassing form is the *human* form. To man on earth there corresponds a man in heaven, and all foundational human elements and relationships are harmoniously realized at various stages of creation, at which, as via Jacob's ladder, heavenly powers ascend and descend. This conception of man as the absolute and universal form is completely alien to Greek philosophy but is an original biblical truth, transmitted to the Christian world by the apostle Paul.

The real-mystical link between the all-existing, like the incarnation of the sole absolute content, this is the original point, or the foundation principle of the Kabbalah; the conscious and systematic anthropomorphism is its summit. The mysticism of numbers, letters, and names inters here as a subordinate element, inseparable from the governing anthropomorphic ideas.

The proposed learned article on the Kabbalah, having a predominantly historical and historico-literary character, conveys the metaphysics of the Kabbalists only in its principle features. For readers who are not Orientalists, wishing to become more closely acquainted with the details of this metaphysics, in addition to the works cited by the author, could benefit from two of the following: *Knorr de Rosenroth*, Cabbala denudata, 2 large volumes in 4, where is found, by the way, in a Latin translation, the book Zohar and the book of Isaac Luria, *De revolutionaibus animarum*, and Molitor, *Die Tradition oder Philosophie der Geschichte*, the incomplete multivolume work with comprehensive extracts from the Kabbalists and with profound exposition of Kabbalistic principles.

In addition to the Christian Kabbalists named in Baron Gintsburg's article, it behooves us to mention as well the English Robert Fludd (de Fluctibus), the French Wilhelm Postel, and the German Henryk Kunrat. To these should also be added the famous Swedenborg. Even though he, it seems, was not familiar with the writings of the Kabbalists, still his system in its very foundational and interesting points is in total correspondence with their teaching, which would hardly be possible if the Kabbalah was only an aberration of Jewish minds.

For Russian readers, completely unfamiliar with postbiblical Jewry, I have glossed the author's text with several explanatory comments, demarcated by my initials.

Vladimir Solovyov

CHAPTER 8

Obituary of Joseph Davidovich Rabinovich
†5 May 1899

———

Like the Jews of the first century who received Christ and dedicated themselves to creating Christianity, Joseph Rabinovich was a man nurtured on scripture, the tradition of the fathers, and secret wisdom — then oral, now written and even printed (the Kabbalah) — who came to the religious conviction that the Galilean rabbi, once executed in Jerusalem on being accused by the Judean priests and judged by the Roman procurator Pontius, was the anointed king of Israel, promised by the prophets, wondrously born and resurrected from the dead in his own transfigured body.[285] Believing in this, Joseph Rabinovich was baptized but did not surrender his Jewish patriotism. His patriotism now simply bestowed on him a new obligation: to preach to his Jewish brothers faith in the true Messiah as the sole way to salvation, not for people taken singly, but for the whole Israelite people, together with all the other peoples.

I knew Rabinovich, and had no doubts regarding not just his complete sincerity but also the fact that his soul was of that same quality as were the souls of the apostles of the first century. But his situation, alas!, was completely different. Externally, it was, of course, easier, since today's preachers must fear neither the lion's teeth nor the lictor's axes.[286] But inwardly it was graver and more tragic. The beasts of the circus and the iron of the Roman warrior could not separate a believing soul from the Christian God, as do now the historical heaps of falsehood and evil in the Christian world itself. And of course, those who feel these heaps most are the Jews. The spirit, truth, blows where it will; elect individuals, distinct groups of select religiously attuned people can spiritually break though these historical barriers. But by what right (if we ourselves do not set the example) shall we demand this from all Jews, or at least from their majority, or at least from some relatively significant minority? It is clear that Jewry sees in the Christian world only what those who call themselves Christians make visible by their deeds, and it would be too fantastic to expect the Jews to turn to Christianity, en masse and with sincere religious conviction, as to a religion of love, to the noise of pogroms against the Jews and "Christian" cries: "Death to the Yids, beat the Yids!"

While it is no wonder that Rabinovich's preaching had no extensive success, it nevertheless had a certain success in managing, without adhering to any existing Christian confessions, to found (in Kishinev) the community of the Israel of the New Covenant along with a temple and a steady divine service in ancient Hebrew. Having received baptism in Berlin from a spiritual member of one independent American sect, and not wishing to join either Orthodoxy or Lutheranism, Joseph Davidovich was not able to legalize his religious position for a long time. Nevertheless, in the end, he managed to attain at least a factual recognition of Christian status for himself and the community he founded. It has now lasted for about twenty years. Joseph Davidovich began his religious activity at the beginning of the 1880s at an advanced age. I met him in 1885, as a man who was already aging, although full of spiritual fervor and movement. Several conversations with him left within me an unalterable impression. The basic originality of his viewpoint consisted in his emergence right out of the Jewish Christianity of the first century: "I continue to preach the Messiah to the Jews," he said, "right from that spot where the first martyr Stephen stopped, a member of the most ancient Christian community in Jerusalem." Without doubt, the religio-national work of Rabinovich will remain a living seed and herald of a future Hebrew-Christian unity. But the further growth of this work *now*, under current conditions, is, in my view, impossible, as I said to the preacher himself. His mistake consisted in directly demanding that Jews who do not yet believe in the truth of Christianity should deal with the Christian world as if they were already true Christians. He demanded them to immediately forgive and forget all the evil borne in the Christian world by them. He, a Jewish patriot, wholeheartedly forgave his Romano-Germanic and Greco-Slavic brothers for this evil. He demanded the same from all Jews, forgetting that his own Christian all-forgiveness was preceded by his inner communion with Christ in faith, which verily remains psychologically and morally impossible for the majority of Jews given the continuing undue treatment of them by the Christian world.

But if Joseph Rabinovich was mistaken in his practical estimation of the historical situation, this cannot alter our high estimation of him personally. A man's true worth is determined by the direction and the measure of the effort exerted by his will. Such were his moral acts, and by such is the deceased justified. "Blessed indeed," says the spirit, "he will have rest from his labors, and his deeds will follow him."[287]

CHAPTER 9

Letters to Faivel Meir Bentsilovich Getz[288]

———

I.

1881

Honorable Mr. Getz,

I am returning to you your books with gratitude. I now intend to diligently busy myself with my article on Judaism.[289] A propos: I was told that the paper *Russkij evrej* [Russian Jew] printed a part of my lecture and promised a whole series of articles proposed by me. There is no harm done here, but it is untrue, whereby, if you have any links with this paper, it would be good to stop such false news.

By the way, despite such transactions, I have recently become convinced that among the active Russian intelligentsia, the most honest element is, nevertheless, the Jewish one.

I am leaving Petersburg, it seems, sooner than I expected. I don't know when and where we'll meet, but in any case, I cherish the most pleasant memory of our evening at your home.

I beg you to convey my heartfelt respects to that evening's companions.

Yours respectfully,
Vlad. Solovyov

2.

1883

Most Amiable Mr. Getz!

Today, unfortunately, I am not able to be with you. By the way, do not think that I am being lazy. I am reading both the Bible and the grammar. I hope, this *Saturday*, you will find that I have made some progress.

And so, until Saturday.

Thank you for the book.

Be well.

Vlad. Solovyov

3.

1886[290]

I came for you, so as to ride on together to Strakhov.[291] On Thursday, I am departing for Revel[292] for one week, and will then return and we will study again.

Vlad. Solovyov

4.

1885

Dear Faivel Bentsilovich, I am sending you in any case the Power of Attorney regarding the return of the manuscript of my "Talmud" from the editor of the *European Herald*,[293] in case it will not be printed. Make inquiries there *at the end of June*, not earlier. Today I am sending you an Arabic Bible, there was no Syriac one in Moscow, I'll send one from Vienna. I am departing either on Sunday or Tuesday. Write to me, please, at the following address: Austro-Hungary, via Vienne. Agram. A M-r le Président de L'Académie des Sciences M-r F. Račky pour M-r W. Solovieff.

The letters arrive better if addressed in French than in German.

I secreted in some deep recess the address of *ha-Melits*[294] and will not, I dare say, find it. Therefore, please, send it to me in Agram. I will need to correspond with you about several other matters.

Be well, and if you see Sacchetti, convey to him my heartfelt respects. Before departing, having a lot to do, I did not manage to visit him.

Cordially and faithfully yours,
Vlad. Solovyov

5.

1886

Dear Faivel Bentsilovich!

I have not responded to you for such a long time, because I have not had anything good to relate. First of all, instead of May, I managed to get abroad only at the end of June, because on the day of my scheduled departure, my servant stole from me 500 rubles, set aside for the trip, and I needed to spend some effort to replace them. Second, I received a letter from Stasyulevich,[295] that the "Talmud" cannot be published, since it is subject to prerequisite theological censorship which will probably forbid it. The third mishap, considerably less important but nevertheless depressing to me, is that on the eighth day of my stay in Vienna, I, despite all my efforts (personally and by commission) could not find anywhere a Syriac Bible.

In order to write to you at least something pleasant, I will relate that on the Austrian border I had the occasion to become convinced about the reality of the Jewish principle of *hillul ha-Shem*. Namely, one old Jewish man, changing my Russian money for Austrian through the window of the carriage, when the train suddenly started, and he did not return to me several guldens, ran to the next train stop and brought the remaining money, saying that he did not wish me to reproach a Jew for deceit.

I am continuing little by little my Hebrew reading—I am concluding Kings. Be well.

Thank you for the kind invitation. I hope to make use of it.

> Cordially and faithfully,
> Vlad. Solovyov

P.S. I just finished this little letter when your second letter arrived. I will answer it over these days.

6.

1886

Dear Faivel Bentsilovich!

Your second letter saddened me greatly, not by the news about my manuscript (which, actually, was not news for me, as I wrote to you), but by the news of new pogroms. I was reading *Moskovskie vedomosti*[296] in Zagreb, but it contained only a telegram about one pogrom without any explanation of the causes. What shall we do about this misfortune? Let the devout Jews fervently pray to God that He should place Russia's fates into the hands of religious and at the same time prudent and courageous people, who would desire to, know how to, and dare to do good for both people.

As to my article (which you admire more than I do myself), then there is here one new complication: while sending the copy to Stasyulevich, I could not entrust the original to my brother who departed to the Crimea. Other members of my family are in the Caucusus, and, similarly, all my Moscow friends have left for the summer. To resend the manuscript to you I then did not have the sense in the midst of those troubles and cares about which I wrote to you in the last letter. So it is that these pages remain lying somewhere either in my table or in a briefcase. Therefore, if it is necessary, in your opinion, to publish the article in Russia, then send the copy you have to the editor of *Russkaya mysl'*[297] (if I am not mistaken, Leontiev St., the house of Mamontov) and request [them] to either publish it quickly or immediately return the manuscript to you.

I am living at present in a beautiful mountainous place, Rohitsch Sauerbrunn (in Styria),[298] but I am still to be contacted at the previous address: Agram, Ac. des sc. prés. Dr. F. Rački pour le dr. V. Sol. Be well and do not lose heart. If you see Sacchetti,[299] give him [my] respect.

With sincere admiration,
Vlad. Solovyov

7.

1886

Why haven't you written to me, dear Faivel Bentsilovich; how and in what way were you ill? I hope that now your recovery is progressing and that you will soon send me a detailed letter. Please do not worry about my article: we have done what we could, and if it should appear, it will appear, and if not, then not. My life here may be described in two words: *oro et laboro*, but in order that you should not form too good an opinion about me, I will add a third, *bibo*, Croatian wine, which in a wondrous manner has delivered me from hemorrhoids and other ailments.

I am publishing the beginning of my composition and am reworking the continuation. To Russia I think [I'll return in] October. For this reason, unfortunately, our reciprocal wish to spend some time together in Lesnoy will not be realized.

I continue to read and reread the Hebrew Bible and take a look now and then at the grammar. Russian papers, which I read here, write nothing about Jewish affairs. Relate everything you know. Be well and do not forget your sincerely bound friend,

Vladimir Solovyov

8.

1886

My dear Faivel Bentsilovich!

Having returned to Zagreb after a three-week absence, I was pleased to find and read your letter. Regarding the publication of my

"Talmud" in *Russkaya mysl'* I knew nothing. Please, do not insult me by proposing that I would wish to seek some benefit from the German edition of this article. The reward is the laborer's, and all that you will have accomplished from my article, completely belongs to you. I bequeath to you the total and unconditional right to translate not just this essay but also everything I will ever write regarding Jewry.

In two weeks I will be returning to Russia and toward the middle or end of October I hope to embrace you, my amiable friend.

I have fewer and fewer friends in Petersburg. Last year two close companions died, and now Butlerov,[300] while the wife of my older brother (who is divorced from him but with whom I keep fraternal relations) is now moving to Moscow.

Please stay alive and well for the sake of your friends and your people, which requires good Israelites.[301]

And so, until we see each other soon. I send you my last poem in purely lyrical style.[302]

> Cordially yours,
> Vlad. Solovyov

9.

December 1886

I have not written to you, my amiable friend Faivel Bentsilovich, because I kept awaiting your answer to my last letter from Zagreb. It seems that you wrote to me but your letter disappeared.

Your present reports about the successes of my article abroad partly gladden me and partly disturb me. You, probably, know that I am now enduring a direct persecution. Every composition of mine, not only a new one, but also a reprint of an old one, is *unconditionally* forbidden. The Ober-Procurator of the Synod P(obedonosts)ev[303] told one of my friends that *every* activity of mine is harmful to Russia and Orthodoxy and, consequently, cannot be tolerated. And in order to justify this decision, various fables are invented and disseminated about me. Today I have become a Jesuit, while tomorrow, perhaps, I'll be circumcised; at present I serve the pope and Bishop Strossmayer,[304] while tomorrow I will probably serve the Alliance Israélite and the Rothschilds. Our state, church, and literary swindlers are so shameless and the public so stupid, that anything can be expected. I, of course, do not lose heart and keep to my motto: "Whom God will sustain, the swine won't retain."[305] But nevertheless it behooves one to be as cautious as possible. Therefore, I would not wish my article to be published abroad without certain clarifications and additions which we will need to discuss when we meet. I am considering coming to Petersburg in the middle of the winter, and perhaps even sooner. In any case, Jewry and the Talmud are such eternal subjects that one or two months, sooner or later, are of little significance in this issue.

Fare well, I remember you often. Give my respects to Sacchetti, if he still remembers me.

Cordially yours,
Vlad. Solovyov

10.

1886

Amiable friend!

I have pleasant news. Drop by on Saturday, at 8:00 P.M. I cannot ride to Tsarskoe Selo[306] this Sunday. We will postpone.

Your Vlad. Solovyov

By the way, if there is a train that leaves one hour earlier, then I, perhaps, will go. I need to be in Petersburg around 5:00. We'll decide on Saturday.

11.

1887

Be not angry with me, dear Faivel Bentsilovich, that I have not replied to you for so long. I am now enduring a very difficult time: *yahad alay yit'lahashu kol-son'ay, alay yah'shebu raa li: d'bar b'liyal yatsuq bo vaasher shayakab lo-yosiph laqum: gam ish sh'lomi asher-batachti bo okel lah'mi'igdil alay akeb.*[307] Nevertheless, all this does not hinder me from working. The first volume of *The History of Theocracy* should soon be published. I continue my Hebrew reading. In addition to the Torah and the historical Books, I have read all the prophets and have begun the Psalms. Now, praise be to God, I can partially fulfill the duty of religious courtesy by also adding to my daily prayers such Hebrew phrases as *Pne elay v'hanneni ki yahid v'ani ani, tsarot l'baby irhibu mimtsukotay ots'ieni.*[308]

I hope that for my good intentions God will be tolerant of my poor Hebrew pronunciation.

Sacchetti has written to me about the well-known matter, and I have already answered him from Kiev, but I have not yet received any direct news.

It seems that I will not manage to get to Petersburg this year. I regret very much that it will yet be a long while, perhaps, before we can see each other.

Convey my heartfelt respects to the Sacchettis, husband and wife.

It is now 5:30 in the morning and time to go to sleep.

Fare well.

Cordially and faithfully yours,
Vlad. Solovyov

I 2 .

April 11, 1887, Moscow

Dear Faivel Bentsilovich!

I am less guilty than you, perhaps, think, in my long silence. Upon my return from Trinity[309] to Moscow, I was ill three times and am now writing to you with difficulty on account of an inflamed eye.

I thank you heartily for the issues of the German and English journals and also thank you and L. A. Sacchetti for the telegram. In a few days I will be going to the countryside for an indefinite period. Here is my address: Moscow-Kursk Railway, Station Korennaya Pustyn',[310]

The honorable[311] Afanasii Afanasievich Shenshin[312] (village Vorobi-
evka), for V.S.S.

Two weeks ago I delivered here for the benefit of poor students a
public lecture, which brought these students nearly 2,000 rubles, and
to Moscow's Slavophile public's much displeasure.[313] Even though I
was delivering it weakly on account of my illness, I am satisfied that I
managed to say what I wanted, and also that my opponents were unable to pit anything against my thought except their displeasure—a
sign that the future does not belong to them. It seems that, fortunately
for me, there was nothing in the papers about this lecture, which would
subject me to fresh censorship, which, apparently, is beginning to
soften.

The first volume of my *Theocracy* is published and will be issued
in May. Let me know in writing whether to send it to you at your current Petersburg address or at your summer residence. Fare well. My
heartfelt respects to Sacchetti mit Gemahlin.

Faithfully yours in spirit,
Vlad. Solovyov

P.S. About the French translation I will write to you from the
countryside.

13.

August 8, 1887
Moscow-Kursk Railway
Station *Korennaya Pustyn'*,
at Af. Af. Shenshin's

My amiable friend!

All this summer I am suffering with nearly continuous neuralgia,
usually accompanied with insomnia. On top of that, there is much
hurried work and official urgent correspondence.

These are the reasons for my long silence. But I frequently remember you and was preparing finally to write to you, when I received
your last letter.

Of the copies of my book which were already sent to Russia a long time ago, several have reached their destination, others — not. Your copy, it seems, belongs to the list of the latter.

The cause of this distinction remains a riddle to me, as does much that transpires among us. I have not a single copy here with me, but I will have at the end of September in Moscow. From there I will send [one] to you without fail. According to the news I receive from Petersburg, the matter of my book's prohibition is settled.[314]

The Ministry of National Enlightenment in general and its antisemitic circular especially is one of the factors contributing to my nervous pains.[315] The question: what is to be done against these stupid and criminal politics? Within the narrow confines of my resources I imagine the following.

1) One of my friends (known to you) intends and hopes to acquire *Moskovskie vedomosti*.[316] He turned to me with a standing request for cooperation, and I promise this to him provided that he should not hinder me from writing in defense of Jewry. I think that he will agree, especially since *Moskovskie vedomosti* has not been infected by Judeophobia under Katkov.

2) I am preparing for publication a work in French, a work pertaining to the principal political problems, or as I call them, the *obligations* of Russia.[317] The bestowal of full civil rights upon Russian Jews is one of these obligations, and I will attempt to promote it in the most convincing manner.

If you should find some practical step which I could take in favor of this matter, then, knowing my feelings for your people, you may be assured that I will be grateful to you for every such instruction.

Fare well,

Cordially yours,
Vlad. Solovyov

14.

1887

Amiable Friend!
Your letter lay for about a week in Kursk, where it was delivered as registered, since the railway station that is closer to us does not re-

ceive registered mail. For this reason I am not to blame for the delay in my reply.

To my friendship and heartfelt sympathy, dear Faivel Bentsilovich, you may appeal every day, but as for as my influence with the authorities, I am afraid that it will turn out to be too meager even for this sole request of yours.

I am sending you two letters: to Theoktistov[318] and Maikov.[319] I hope that they are both in Petersburg. Countess Volkonskaya[320] has gone to the countryside and abroad, where her son is dying from consumption. I think that appealing to her now will be fruitless.

Of course it is not necessary for me to assure you that, even in spite of my personal relations with you, I will sincerely rejoice over the prospect of a Jewish paper with such a good editorial board and such leanings as I sympathize with. I hope that your effort will succeed. Do you not have any other way of appealing to Katkov? He is all-powerful in the matters of the press and, it seems, does not harbor prejudices against Jews. I, unfortunately, severed relations with him and so cannot appeal to him with a petition.

The first volume of my *Theocracy* was issued last month but for some reason has not been received in Russia. It is almost completely filled with Jewry. I hope that your copy will not be confiscated. Do not reproach me for mistakes in transcribing Hebrew words. This is the fault of the typography which dealt badly with Russian words as well.

Fare well, amiable friend. When shall we see each other? "I see but toil and sorrow, the restless sea of the future."[321]

Convey my friendly respects to Sacchetti, if he is in Petersburg.

All yours,

Vlad. Solovyov

15.

1887

Amiable Friend!

Registered letters are received here from the city (Kursk), and conveyed here (only) once every ten days. The last time I received two letters from you, both, seemingly, written before your receipt of my letter with the enclosed reference letters to Theoktistov and Maikov. In one of your letters you announce that you have abandoned your venture. Since this letter is undated (and I did not look in advance at the postmark and do not know to which envelope which letter belongs), I remain in ignorance: have you turned down the venture or not? Please inform me of this, and if you have abandoned the project, then let me know whether you delivered my letters as addressed, and about everything consequent.

My book, as I already wrote to you, already came out at the end of April, but it seems that the list of addresses (including yours) which I sent to the publisher vanished in the mail, even though it was sent by registered post. What is to be done with this state of affairs?

In waiting for news from you, I remain yours in true admiration and gratitude,

Vlad. Solovyov

16.

1887

Amiable friend!

I hurry to answer you, that I will be pleased to fulfill your wish— to write for *Novosti* [the News] an article on the Jewish question. I have nothing against *Novosti*. I don't have links with any other paper. What I wrote to you about *Moskovskie vedomosti* apparently will not transpire. It seems that the paper will remain under the previous editorship, that is, under the colleagues of Katkov, who imitate him only in what's bad.

Most probably, they will, when the occasion arises, join the Judeophobes. I have already begun to write under the title "The Sins of Russia."

These sins in my view are (1) Jewry's condition, (2) the russification of Poland, (3) the absence of religious freedom. To speak in print about the Jewish question in connection with these other untruths of ours I find in all respects more fitting.

And so, if you vouch that *Novosti* will not fear to print my article, and undertake to pass it on to the editor, then please write to me quickly when you are moving to Petersburg and whether your address there remains as before: Sr. Podyach. 16, 27—and then in a week or ten days you will receive my manuscript.

You see that my quill is always ready for the defense of Israel in distress, but what you write about my "friends" is fantastic. One of those named by you, may, in conversation, declare humane views but will probably not write or print a single word in support of the Jews, while the other (I do not want to say who exactly) was almost seriously arguing that all the Jews should be subjected to a well-known operation which once and for all will deprive them of the ability to multiply! Here then is your collective declaration in support of the Jews. But you are correct in this, that if anyone, even myself, should decisively and with the full signature of his name demonstrate against antisemitism, then this can summon others also and so in the end will establish some counterweight to these savageries. At present I can only offer my own work.

And so, write quickly to me, where should I send the manuscript to you.

> Cordially and faithfully yours,
> Vlad. Solovyov

I am still ill. I remain here until the 20th of September.

17.

[The envelope bears the date
October 5, 1887, Moscow]

Amiable friend!

Since until now the proofs of my article in Moscow have not been received, then I conclude that even this innocent venture on my part has turned out to be censurable, for which reason I leave the following articles in their draft form. If my conjecture is mistaken, then I ask you to inform me so that I would know what to do.

I am cordially grateful to you for your friendly invitation to stop over at your place in Petersburg. I will fulfill your amiable wish without fail, if only I will happen to find myself in Petersburg this winter, which is still unknown and does not totally depend upon me: I am still ill and have lost so much weight that my clothes, being found too wide, had to be altered. I am now writing to you half-dead from fatigue after two sleepless nights. For this reason, do forgive me for the brevity of this letter and believe in the unchangeable friendship

of one who truly admires you,
Vlad. Solovyov

18.

November 10, 1887
Moscow, Prechistenka St.,
the house of Likhutin[322]

Amiable Faivel Bentsilovich!

I am very sorry and indignant that you must still trouble yourself with foreign words because Jewry is denied its rights. But as you have now probably become convinced, my indignation must remain concealed in the depth of my heart, since even Mr. Notovich[323] finds his printed proclamation discomfiting. I have still not managed to obtain a sufficient number of [contraband] copies of my forbidden book so as to send them, as I promised, to Sacchetti and for the Jewish Literary Society. I send my deep respects to Sacchetti and thank him for his kind postscript to one of your letters.

Renan's[324] new book is known to me, but I am far from sharing your friend's views. First of all, this "History of Israel" is not historical, and, if one may express oneself so, not Israelite. Is it possible to write about Saul and David in such a feuilletonistic style, as if about Battenberg and Coburg?[325] I similarly do not understand how a true Jew can sympathize with a historian for whom Abraham and Moses are myths and David a lucky rascal. The Jews, impelled by enmity to Christianity to embrace the Renans and the Strausses,[326] remind me of those Japanese who, in order to mete out effective vengeance to an enemy, slice up their stomach.[327]

But have you read the first volume of Ranke's *Weltgeschichte*?[328] This is how a real scholar spoke about Israel, biblically!

Fare well, my amiable friend and do not lose heart too much; I firmly hope that we together will yet see better times.

Cordially yours,
Vlad. Solovyov

19.

January 18, 1888
Moscow. Prechistenka.
h(ome) of Likhutin

Dear Faivel Bentsilovich!

Having returned to Moscow (which I left for a whole month to save myself from festive inactivity), I found your telegram. I cordially thank you and L. A. Sacchetti. In February I will be going to Petersburg for several days, but, unfortunately, cannot take advantage of your amiable invitation to stay with you, since my new relative, the academic Bezobrazov[329] (his son has married one of my sisters), insists that I should invariably stay with him at the Academy of Sciences, and I must give preference to age and kinship over friendship.

I have not spent this time without purpose: I have finished the French book and am preparing the second volume of *Theocracy* for publication; on top of that, my article "Russia and Europe" should appear in the February issue of *Vestnik Evropy*.[330]

I have returned the proofs, and, it seems, there are no foreseeable obstacles from the censors. Stasyulevich[331] is very pleased and writes that "this is not only a good article but also a good deed." If this first [article] should pass successfully, then a second, more comprehensive article should follow.

Write, my amiable friend, how you are and what you are doing in Petersburg.

Convey my heartfelt greeting to Liberius Antonovich and his wife.

Wholly your Vlad. Solovyov

20.

February 23, 1888
Moscow. Prechistenka,
h. Likhutin.

Dear Faivel Bentsilovich,

I left for two weeks to stay at Trinity aiming at absolute solitude, wherefore not even a letter was sent to me there.

On my return to Moscow I found your two letters, and that same night your telegram arrived. I rejoice greatly about your intention and desire with my whole heart to help you, but, of course, I can accomplish very little.

If you still retain the reference letters which I wrote to you last summer, then one of these letters (to Theoktistov) you may now use. As far as Maikov is concerned, then he even formerly did not wholly accept me, and now (following the publication of my article in *Vestnik Evropy*), he must be completely angered. Moreover, he is a radical Judeophobe. Therefore, it's better to not approach him with my letter.

As far as Countess V(olkonskaya), do you not know that her husband is no longer in favor, since he has been blamed for all the failures of the new university statutes; and in consequence of the disfavor, husband and wife no longer hold any influence in governmental spheres. Nevertheless I, by your wishes, will write to her and speak (to her), upon arrival in Petersburg. I am preparing to go on March 8, and then abroad.

I look forward to seeing you soon, my amiable friend.

I send my respects to our mutual friends.

Cordially and faithfully,
Your Vlad. Solovyov

[Editor's Note: The following is the letter of Solyovov to Apollon Nikolaevich Maikov concerning Getz, mentioned in the previous

letter and letter #15 and included in Getz's collection of Solovyov's letters.]

Kind Sir,[332]
Deeply honorable Apollon Nikolaevich!

Mr. Getz, the bearer of this letter, is seeking permission to publish a journal for Jews.

I know Mr. Getz long and well, as my teacher of Hebrew, as a writer, and as a human being, and can witness in the most decisive manner to his education, remarkable talents, and wonderful moral qualities. He holds in theory and in life to a conservative, strictly religious inclination but is a complete stranger to any kind of fanaticism and honestly desires closer relations between Jewry and Christianity in the sphere of higher theological interests. To this end he has been already successfully laboring for several years as a journalist in Russia and abroad, and several brochures which he has published depict him as a man with a serious intellectual vocation. I think that among Russian Jews there is no other figure more capable of assuming, successfully and beneficially, the publication of a Jewish journal. I do not doubt that all who know Mr. Getz will corroborate my opinion and therefore hope that you will not decline to support with your weighty word Mr. Getz's petition for permission to publish.

With deepest respect,
Cordially and faithfully yours,
Vladimir Solovyov

2 1.

3, Rue St. Roch,
Hôtel de la Couronne
July 16–28, 1888, Paris

My amiable friend!
Your letter cheered me up, despite the mishap with the journal. I see that you do not lose heart and this is the important thing. I do not

know whether I'll have time to prepare something substantial for your volume of collected essays. September is close and I have yet to put finishing touches on my French book. I have published in advance a foreword to it in a separate brochure and, it seems, did well: there were articles in many papers and several publishers are offering their services.

In about two weeks I am departing from here, but not directly to Russia.

I am receiving ambiguous rumors about gossip in Russian papers purporting that I have converted to Catholicism, etc. In reality I am now even further from such a step than before.

I hope that these rumors will not prove harmful to my return.

I wrote to V. P. Bezobrazov and have thanked him for you and Frug.[333]

Fare well and do not forget your true admirer,

Vlad. Solovyov

2 2 .

[Editor's Note: This letter is written on the blank side of a telegram, the other side of which has the address: To F. B. Getz, Mogilevskaya, h. № 19.]

1889

Amiable friend!

Tomorrow, on Saturday, Terty Ivanovich Filippov[334] requests you to visit him *to make your first acquaintance* between 11 a.m. and 12 p.m. As this will not be a business visit, you can make it on Saturday. At 3:00 p.m. I will try to be at your place for our reading.

Philippov lives on the corner of Nevsky and Pushkinskaya, h. № 75 (on the Nevsky, the last entry before Pushkinskaya, if you are heading from the Admiralty).

Until we meet.

Cordially and faithfully yours,
Vlad. Solovyov

23.

In May 1890

My amiable friend,

Your messenger found me preparing to go to Muromtsev.[335] For the cards I thank you. Several of those on your list I will see myself. Others (e.g., Kluchevsky) are not even mentionable.[336] This is the historian of *Novoe vremya*. If you wish to receive immediately a dozen new signatures, then come to collect them on Sunday morning, for on Saturday I am counting on a great harvest.[337] By the way, I will be happy to see you also on Friday (tomorrow).

Cordially yours,
Vlad. Solovyov

[Editor's Note: Following letter #23 is a version of Solovyov's Protest letter, included below. Getz's filing of this version with the letter may witness to its date.]

The Text of the Protest against Antisemitism in the Press
Composed by V. S. Solovyov in May 1890

The movement against Jewry, propagated by the Russian press, represents an unprecedented violation of the most fundamental demands of justice and love of humanity. We consider it necessary to remind Russian society of these elementary demands. Forgetting them is the sole cause of the so-called Jewish question, while their simple and sincere recognition is the sole path to its resolution.

1) In all races there are worthless and malicious people, but there are not and cannot be a worthless and malicious race, since this would abolish personal responsibility, wherefore every hostile declaration or action, aimed against Jewry as a whole and against the Jews, as such, demonstrates either an irrational enthusiasm for blind national egoism or a personal selfishness and can in no wise be justified.

2) It is unjust to impose upon Jewry responsibility for those phenomena in its life which were evoked by millennia-long persecutions

of the Jews in Europe and by those abnormal conditions in which this people was placed. If during the course of many centuries the Jews were forcefully constrained to engage solely in monetary affairs, being debarred from all other kinds of employment, then the disagreeable consequences of this exclusive channeling of Jewish energies can in no way be eliminated by further constraints which only perpetuate the previous abnormal order.

3) Affiliation to the Semitic race and to the law of Moses presents nothing intrinsically blameworthy, and provides insufficient grounds for giving Jews a special civic status in comparison to Russian subjects belonging to other races and creeds. Since Russian Jews, belonging to their well-known social class, bear the same obligations as all the other representatives of the same social class, then in justice they should also hold the same rights in common.

The recognition and application of these elementary truths are important and necessary first of all for us ourselves. The exacerbated excitation of racial and religious enmity, so contrary to the spirit of Christianity, corrupts society at its root and can lead to moral dehumanization, especially given the already presently noted decline of humanitarian ideas and the weakening of the juridical principle in our life.

This is why even mere concern for national self-preservation should move us decisively to condemn the antisemitic movement not only as immoral in its essence, but as a radical danger to Russia's future.

Vl. Solovyov

24.

March 21 [1891]

Amiable friend, I arrived in Moscow with a rather heavy flu and for the first few days could hardly manage to rework the foreword, which nevertheless turned out fine, judging from the responses of all who read it (not excluding several antisemites who were beside themselves but acknowledged that the letter is well composed).

In Moscow I found the letter written long ago by Chicherin, permitting me to use publicly his declaration on the Jewish question, which he has sent in a new and even better edition; I used it immediately. It is no trouble that Chicherin's letter will appear in two places in your book; you should just read it.

I have long ago received and returned the proofs of the foreword, but have no news about the appearance of the book. If it is not late, then I suggest the following heading: F. G. "A Word to the Accused, with unpublished letters of Count L. N. Tolstoy, B. N. Chicherin, V. S. Solovyov, and V. G. Korolenko."[338] Tomorrow or after-tomorrow I depart for Petersburg and am bringing all three articles to Notovich.

I am very glad, my dear friend, that you are satisfied with your fate and hope to spend some time with you near Vilnius, if even for a short time.

Fare well and do not doubt the honest and unchangeable affection of

Your old friend,
Vlad. Solovyov

2 5.

March 5, 1891

My dear friend, you wish me to express myself once more on the Jewish question on account of your book.[339] I do so eagerly not only for your sake but also for mine: for the purification of my conscience touching our preachers of antisemitism. For as is stated by the prophet Ezekiel: "If you do not warn the wicked that he should turn from his (wicked) way and live . . . his blood I will require at your hand. But if you warn him and he does not turn from his wickedness, or from his wicked way, he shall die in his iniquity; but you will have saved your life."[340]

Ten years have already passed since the "father of lies"[341] stirred up in our society an antisemitic movement. During this time, I was obliged several times to highlight (first from the academic chair, then in the theological and secular press) the indubitable truth that the Jewish question is first of all a Christian question: the question as to how much Christian communities in all their relationships—by the way, and in their relationships with Jews—are capable of being directed in practice by the principles of evangelical teaching, which they confess verbally. I am not going to repeat here my reflections which can have no meaning for antisemites: whoever preaches an indiscriminate enmity against a whole people, shows thereby that the Christian point of view has lost for him its binding force. There is, however, the commonly binding basis of common sense and simple factual truth, and there also exist for antisemite-nationalists still more intelligible and impressive authorities than the Gospel.

"Absolutely nothing occurred in the Jewish world," wrote M. N. Katkov in April 1882.[342] "What existed a hundred years ago, fifty years ago, twenty years ago, one year ago, the same persists today. But now someone has whistled and shouted, 'Beat the Jews,' and all of a sudden, without any warning, there arose the Jewish question and everyone, each in his own way, went for the Jews.

"Everyone has something to say from the theoretical or practical point of view against the Jews, but a question may be instigated not only about the Jews in Russia, but about everything in the world. There is however, a difference between the question which matures, stage by stage, approaching its resolution, and the sudden instigation of a question, God knows whence and God knows why. But the power of every political intrigue lies indeed in the fact that it suddenly instigates questions among people which they haven't even thought about. It is impossible to gather all the Jews into one neck so as to chop off all their heads at one blow; it is likewise impossible to expel them all beyond our western border unless one identifies it with the flowing Dnieper; it is likewise impossible to relocate entirely these four million people[343] to Eastern lands; it is likewise difficult to send them all to Palestine or America. However many intelligent things we might suggest, we would still remain with Jews; of this the slightest serious view of the matter leaves no doubt. Whence now, especially now, comes the instigation which cannot lead to anything good? . . . Are we not becoming, in a blind passion, the executors of a criminal conspiracy?"

"The Jews are reproached," the famous publicist continues, "the Jews are reproached for exploiting the people and sucking them dry via taverns.[344] There is no doubt that the peculiarity of their situation, which was historically formed in places under Polish rule, turned the Jews predominantly into exploiters. The Polish economy kept the masses of its peoples enslaved like chattel. Between the Polish gentry [*pany*] and the people, the *yid* stood as the sole industrialist. He constituted that which is everywhere called the middle class. The *yids* were allowed to lease everything: the people, the lands, and the villein churches. They were treated like dogs, but in the meantime everything depended upon them. The isolation of the Jews established solidarity between them, but one should not infer that the masses of the Jewish population in the western region prosper and live in luxury at the expense of the people they exploit. No, for if more or less well-to-do and wealthy industrialists really emerge from their midst, their masses remain in poverty, about which people, who have seen Jewish life in the western region, speak with horror. These wretches eat each other.

"On the other hand, when speaking of taverns, is the Jew an evil here? Isn't the tavern as ruinous for the people in those places where there stands, in their midst, behind the counter, an Orthodox publican? In the western region the tavern business is run by Jews, but is it really better in Russia's other regions?"

"In the tavern *yid*," Katkov said even earlier, "we suddenly and for some reason perceived the culprit of Russia's ruin and of the calamitous condition of her peasantry. Isn't this a lie? Are the tavern *yids*, who turn the people into drunkards and who ravage and ruin the peasantry, a ubiquitous phenomenon in Russia? Neither in the provinces of Moscow, or Tula, or Ryazan', etc., is there a single tavern *yid*. Tavern *yids* are found only in the Trans-Dnieper. But inquire among people who really know where the populace is most drunk and where the peasant is predominantly ruined, and in which provinces this occurs, whether in the Kovenskaya, or in the Vilenskaya, or in the Volynskaya, or in the Podol'skaya, or in the Kievskaya,[345] or in those places among us where Jews are not permitted and where the tavern is run by an Orthodox publican or by a kulak? Drunkenness in the western region is not more but actually much less developed than in the rest of

Russia, and peasants there live not worse but better. A terrible, destructive poverty really reigns in the western region, but this poverty affects not the peasants but the Jews."

Our antisemites cannot treat the words of Katkov as they would, for example, treat my own discourses: one is not going to get around the corypheus of Russian "national politics" by clichés about liberalism, doctrinaire attitudes, idealism, and so on.

When Katkov so decisively affirmed that peasant welfare within the boundary of the Jewish Pale of Settlement is generally higher than outside of it, it is only important here to know whether he is speaking the truth or not. If Katkov's factual affirmation is false, then our antisemites have all the means to refute it.

The Pale of Settlement (every cloud has a silver lining!)[346] makes possible an exact statistical comparative study: comparing in different socioeconomic relations the province of long-standing and constant Jewish habitation with those places where they are not permitted, and taking into account all the secondarily significant conditions, it is possible with sufficiently scientific strictness to determine what exactly it is that Jews bring to the surrounding population, what are the effects of their activity upon the life of the people. Jews have been occupied with statistics rather diligently of late; there exist, for example, bulky volumes, published by the central statistical committee of the Ministry of Internal Affairs. In these volumes it is possible to find whatever one pleases except "the one thing needed,"[347] except the comparative statistical parallel between the western region and the native provinces. Such a study, omitted from the view of this semiofficial publication, constitutes, it would seem, a direct challenge to our antisemites, but they carefully avoid every serious experiment of comparative statistics, of the only means to take their sermon out of the realm of whistling and shouting and give it a solid factual basis. Do they really not feel in the depths of their soul that a scientific study would expose their falsehood and that Katkov knew what he was talking about? This circumstance should be pondered by those antisemites who are still capable of pondering. For such, another witness would also be beneficial: not the opinion of the publicist, who is excited by the course of events, by the impressions of the minute, but rather the considered and final conviction of a man who knows the matter from all angles, who has labored much and well in various professions, and in addition to all that, of a man who is considerably independent both in character and by position, who stands close to the life of the people and far from artificial agitations and intrigues—of a man who is interested only in the truth.

"I am convinced," Boris Nikolaevich Chicherin[348] writes to me, 'that there is no people in the world to whom humanity owes such gratitude as to the Jews. It is sufficient to say that from their midst emerged Christianity which created a revolution in global history. Whatever opinion we might have regarding religious questions, there is no doubt that the book which serves as the daily spiritual nourishment of many many millions of people belongs to the highest flower of humanity, the Bible—which is of Jewish origin. From the Greeks we received a secular education, but the Greeks vanished, while the Jews, despite unprecedented persecutions, and being scattered over all the earth, preserved inviolable their ethnicity and faith. This is the token of a great vocation. I also think that the government is obliged to defend and patronize all subjects whom providence has placed under its arm. . . . Speaking practically and by personal experience, having governed two estates during the course of twenty years, one in the Tambov province, where there is not a single Jew, and another in the Poltavskaya, where there are plenty, I see that in the latter the peasants are more moneyed and well-to-do, and moreover the conditions are better . . . In general I see with great sorrow that many of my compatriots do not face this question from the perspective of Christian love of neighbor, but from the purely pagan and even barbarian perspective. The antisemitic movement constitutes the shame of our time. Much would I give to wash this stain off of my native land."

Even at the end of his letter, B. N. Chicherin acknowledges our antisemitism to be an incurable illness. I completely agree with this and, not having any pretensions to heal anyone from the "fear of the Jews,"[349] only wish to propose a simple prophylactic medicine for those people for whom this heavy disease has not taken complete possession, but who are only more or less predisposed to it.

The easiest way to convince oneself of the falsehood of antisemitism is to read our antisemitic newspapers consistently and attentively.

Take for example *Grazhdanin*.[350] Just a few years ago we would encounter in it delightful articles and polemical observations in defense
of Jewry. Apparently, the pious and patriotic publicist finds that patriotism and piety do not compel one to torment Russian Jews but, on
the contrary, obligate one to defend them as subjects of that same government, as sons of that same native land, and as guardians of an ancient revelation. What then has transpired in the last few years? Why
has the conservative journalist, who initially, like Katkov, condemned
the gutter whistling and shouting of "Beat the Yids!" all of a sudden begun to whistle and shout more loudly and shamelessly than
anyone else?

Indeed, even in *Novoe vremya* one will not encounter such disgraceful outbursts as those with which the pious organ of Prince Meshhersky edifies its readers, announcing, for example, that Jews are not
people but filthy insects or harmful bacteria, subject to extermination.
One cannot condemn a change of view if such has respectable foundations. One might allow a man who is ripe in years to change his views
about a well-known subject or, in consequence to a new, better-
founded investigation of it, or in consequence to some sort of substantial change in the subject itself. But in Jewry, as substantial a change as
the transformation of people into bacteria, during these past few years,
manifestly, has not occurred; and on the other hand, the editor of
Grazhdanin, in spite of all his courage, would hardly dare to affirm
that he has dedicated these past few years to a serious study of Jewry
and of the Jewish question. Where is there here a respectable basis for
a change of view? We do not count ourselves as having the right to
imitate the bad example of our "patriots" and accuse whomever of dishonest prayer, having no direct evidence for such. We condemn the
named organ of defense only—and manifestly and without doubt—for
the uttermost light-mindedness and frivolity, thanks to which, in matters of such great importance, it conducts itself not by principles and
not by inquiry, but only by fickle whim and superficial impressions.

But if *Grazhdanin* represents such a splendid example of the frivolity and inanity of our pious Judeophobes, then we have plentiful
positive material for refuting antisemitism itself in the other antisemitic newspaper, which remains invariable in this respect. One is

amazed, in reading *Novoe vremya* attentively, by the sharp contrast between the vacuous spate of Judeophobic words (where fictitious or meaningless single cases substitute for factual foundations, and the coarsest sophisms and indiscriminate abuse replace logical argumentation) and between the diametrically opposite character of content-rich, factual exactitude and cogency in all those numerous communications, arriving from every corner of Russia, from which it clearly follows that in the present troubles in the life of the people, the Jews are just as little to blame as the Chinese. On the one hand, we see how the antisemitism of the honorable (!) newspaper and of its readers is nurtured by news items like the one that reports that in some city some Jew pushed some female official, or that one general's murderer is a Jew (although in reality he is not a Jew at all); or by such considerations and deductions as that although there are comparatively less murderers among the Jews than among Christians, then there are at least more thieves, meaning that Jews are especially dangerous for society (so that by this logic it's better to be knifed than robbed); or, finally, by such "psychological" discussions as note that the Jews have highly developed willpower, energy, mind, familial ties,[351] and so on, while the Russian people only have holiness, and therefore in the name of their holiness and to safeguard it from Jewish energy our holy people must in this or that way exterminate the Jews. But on the other side, in close proximity to all this disgraceful nonsense, we read in the same newspaper, for example, an impressive review of Sazonov's book,[352] which supplies documentary proof how in the Pskov region, where there are no Jews, the local Russian kulaks ultimately ruined the people, seized the land and livestock, so that the peasant population of entire *uyezds*[353] was forced either to go into Kabbalah-slavery,[354] or to become beggars; and similarly also about the diametrically opposite, southwestern region of Russia (where there are also no Jews) we read circumstantial excerpts from the newspaper *Nedelya* [the Week] (also seemingly an antisemitic organ) which relates, naming names and places, how "grubby landlords," that is, several dozen[355] *muzhiks* (including two or three German colonists but not a single Jew), have grown rich by buying up the majority of the estates and, pressing upon peasants, embittered them to such a degree that the latter burned one of those "landlords" alive along with his farmstead—a degree of malice which the organizers of pogroms against the Jews could never and nowhere induce in a wild crowd.[356] Such and similar news, one may find *Novoe vremya* reporting more or less about every place in Russia that is inaccessible to Jews. Who then harbors malice, and from whom should Russia be saved? And who will save! If the readers of the *Grazhdanin* could think that the role of savior belongs by right to the gentry, then *Novoe vremya* systematically destroys this illusion. The honored newspaper portrays the bankruptcy of our privileged layer so brightly that all its antisemitic outbursts pale in comparison.

In one of the latest issues, for example, on the front page and under the strident heading "Jews at the Gates," we find an article about Rothschild's accession to dominion over our oil. The article gives no factual proof that this dominion is pernicious but provides us instead with an exposition of an unknown author's assumptions about Rothschild's future deeds, how he will eventually begin to sell kerosene by surcharging by a penny, or two or three per pound, thereby multiplying his billions, giving him supremacy over the world, and allowing him to "take away the conscience" of Russian society. "But a society without a conscience," the author pathetically exclaims, "is such not a terrible specter of the future?" In order to evaluate the worth of these pompous trivialities and discover the extent to which Rothschild is guilty of taking away our society's conscience, it behooves the readers of *Novoe vremya* to simply turn the page and direct their attention to an article about the new proposed line of credit for landowners. Here, among other things, we read the following:

> Supporting and doing their utmost on behalf of the railroads, on behalf of their concessionaire-competitors and builders, how many people, and with what renowned names to boot, calculated to net and really did net the profits not worrying in the least about how, from whom, and what sort of money they took. . . . Supporting and doing their utmost on behalf of the *zemstvo*-guarantees for very many of these roads, how many glorious names of even local owners openly and consciously betrayed and sold out the interests of people they represented, only because, behind the gen-

eral tumult and commotion, they managed to net such profits as covered their earlier losses as local landowners. Supporting and making efforts to establish Land Banks[357] among us, "so urgently indispensable for satisfying the just needs of the straitened land-owners and agriculturalists," how many glorious names received the opportunity to net the profits and really did net them, attaining the establishment and ratification, in effect, of predatory dens of thieves, and not at all of banks with lines of credit, which would have been somewhat prudent and somehow possible. . . .

"Such a desperate thirst for more and more money, is a thirst that no proprieties can contain, it is an unbridled thirst!" And further on, on the basis of prior experience, the writer of *Novoe vremya* paints the following picture of the future credit-lending establishments to aid the landowners:

And so it begins again: favored representatives, competent and knowledgeable people, elected as supervisors . . . and the portions, the portions! . . . General tumult and chaos, in which nothing can be discerned, nothing heard, except for some separate words and phrases, no one knows to whom: "What kind of a count are you? You are a thief!" . . . "Tested zeal and trustworthiness" . . . "You have stolen . . . You promised to share but took everything for yourself!" . . . "Selfless service to the fatherland" . . . "You lie, I always said you can't be trusted!" . . . "Thief, Help!" (*Novoe vremya*, No. 5371).

If all this resembles reality, then one may ask in what way Rothschild or whoever could take away the conscience of people who are evidently deprived of it? In any case, one should acknowledge that our antisemites exterminate each other a lot more successfully than Jews.

I completely understand and share your pity for the present personal sufferings of your coreligionists, but I am sure, dear friend, that you do not attach to this feeling any fear for the future fate of your people. You also know its history. Is it really possible even for a moment to imagine that after all these glories and wonders, after so many triumphs of the spirit and endured sufferings, after all these astonishing forty centuries in the life of Israel, that he should fear some antisemites! Were this malicious and filthy campaign to provoke within me any fear, then of course it would not be for the Jews but for Russia. But I confess that I don't feel such fear either. Infatuation for imaginary "social opinion" is a rather transient phenomenon, and in the final end we have a government which stands above all passions and all intrigues; and the Russian people itself, is not an enemy unto itself; it knows enough to not kick against the goads[358] and to not argue with divine destinies. And it is not for nothing that providence has settled the greatest and strongest portion of Jewry in our native land.

Vladimir Solovyov
Moscow, March 5, 1891

26.

[March 28, 1891]
St. Petersburg. Hotel Europe[359]

Amiable friend!

Your book is finally published, but it will be read, probably, only by ministers, and even to acquire *these* readers you will have to take measures, namely, sending a petition to convey the books to a committee of ministers (signing it *only* as a candidate [of a doctoral program] in Oriental languages).

If you recall, I was far from sharing your and N-ch's[360] confidence about a successful outcome. I hope, however, that you will not lose heart as quickly as you sensed yourself to be happy on a new place. "But where is happiness?" justly asks my friend Fet:

Not here, in wretched quarters
But there it is, like smoke

There, there by nebulous road
Into eternity we'll fly[361]

I nearly flew away into eternity, having wounded myself in the head (in my temple) with the sharp end of a hanging lamp. On account of this I have spent several unnecessary days in Moscow. Now I think the danger is passed.

Cordially and faithfully yours
Vlad. Solovyov

27.

May 1, 1891
St. P., Hotel Europe

Amiable friend
Faivel Bentsilovich!
How are you?
I am in cares and straits. These include important matters about which it is at present uncomfortable to write. The fate of our book is still undecided. But the expectation of a good outcome is still a possibility. I have renewed acquaintance with E. M. Th,[362] by his wishes, and he has already visited me twice. I think that such an unusual kindness from his side signifies something.

I remain here, probably, until June and will be very happy to receive news from you.

After that, I hope, we shall meet in Vilnius.

Cordially and faithfully yours,
Vlad. Solovyov

28.

[Editor's Note: Excerpt from V. S. Solovyov's letter to F. G. Getz (June 1891)]

For lack of time I did not inform you earlier about two news items which may interest you.

1) About a month ago I decisively declined the offer of active involvement in a soon to be constituted central committee for the organization of Jewish emigration.[363] 2) I wrote for the *Severnyj vestnik*[364] a review of Diminsky's pamphlet. N. I B.[365] strongly approved this review (in composing which I took some of his suggestions) and found it from beginning to end a matter for the censors, whereby I hope that it will appear on August 1. As to your proposal to produce a detailed denial in the form of a separate booklet, I cannot assist you with it since that person to whom you aspire to turn is already abroad, and I do not know where exactly. Moreover, if this person wished twice annually to burn a certain amount of its money, then it can do that immediately in its own chimney, without exacerbating with superfluous cares the Ministry of Internal Affairs.[366] In any case my intercession here would be out of place.

I have just received your last letter and it gladdened me greatly. My hope that you understand your moral duty is realized. Now I too, from my side, not only recognize the ethical obligation but also feel the psychological possibility of reconciling with you. I hope that after this trial our friendship will be completely unshakable. In any case I can now sign without hypocrisy,

Your sincere admirer,
Vlad. Solovyov

P. S. The author of the ill-starred feuilleton, Evgeny Andreevich Solovyov, has sent me an amiable letter expressing every willingness. I then, under the influence of spite, responded too sharply about his writing, which is not devoid of talent but is only mediocre. Therefore, I ask you to not distribute my response. There is no need to make an unnecessary enemy, and such a casual one at that.[367]

29.

July 21, 1891
Petersburg

By the Blue Bridge. Voznesensky Prospect, h. № 16, apartment of Kuz'min Karavayev[368]

In one of your letters you offered to send me 50 rubles which you consider to be your duty. I judge the duty to be on my side rather than on yours, but since I presently find myself reduced to complete extremity (of which I most decisively ask you to not write to anyone in St. Petersburg: I am already in debt and obligated to everyone), then, if the money you speak of is available, I ask you to send it to me, as a loan, directly to the address of my present landlord, Vladimir Kuz'min-Karavayev.

You wrote to me about the editorial board at the *Encyclopedic Dictionary*. If your generous disposition to me was shared by the rest of humanity, then I, of course, would not only edit the *Encyclopedic Dictionary* but would also rule the Holy Roman Empire. S. A. Vengerov[369] told me that there can be no discussion of me being the editor in chief, while an editorship of one of the departments is a possibility, but nothing definite can yet be said. From N. I. Bakst,[370] who is especially kind to me and wished to speak in my favor, I have not yet had any reply. The designated editor in chief, K. K. Arseniev, has gone abroad.

Even though you wrote nothing to me [about it], I heard that you are unhappy with me regarding the question of emigration. You know that I consider full equality of rights to be the sole just resolution. This is what I declare to everyone. But since justice may be realized only tomorrow, counting days by God's accounting, that is, in a thousand years, then this does not eliminate the necessity of at least a temporary palliative lightening for the especially suffering section of Jewry. For you yourself, if you remember, almost moved to England.

This matter has already resulted in several good outcomes, which I will describe when we meet. For I still hope at least at the end of the summer to visit you.

Cordially and faithfully yours,
Vlad. Solovyov

30.

August 22, 1891, s. Dedovo

I doubted the awful typhus
I doubted it and was proved right
That awful typhus was a *mythos*

And my good Faivel's well and bright
But with the Talmud I was right
Yet dared not fight his gist
My dear "Rav"'s reading was too light[1]
Now mine is in a twist.

Your remark, dear friend, is completely right, and I myself sensed that R. Yehuda is citing here another authoritative rabbi and is speaking his words, as is usual in the Talmud (which I could sniff only faintly, but, having a relatively long literary nose, enough to feel its style); yes and "Rav," as an abbreviation of one's name, is not unknown to me.[371] But what is to be done? Now we have an incident. I beg you to not write about this to N. I. whom I would not like to upset by such a trifle. If it were possible to publish my articles and observations regarding Jewry in a corrected and supplemented form, then I will correct this mistake, for pointing out which in any case I thank you.

I thank you also for the brochures. I am sending you my two books with the young officer Kuz'min-Karavayev (the brother of my landlord). He is leaving to serve in Vilnius. I commend him to your amiable attention.

I have finally left Petersburg. I have now stopped en route in a village with the aunt of my younger brother. After that I will spend several days in Moscow, then in the Kaluzhskaya province, then in Kiev, and on the return journey to Petersburg (where the *Encyclopedic Dictionary* is calling me). I will drop by, perhaps, in Vilnius. I seriously desire this, even though I probably cannot promise it.

Fare well.

Cordially and faithfully yours,
Vlad. Solovyov

[1]Not you, but the one from Petersburg.

3 1.

[August 1892]

Much-honored friend!

I received your letter of the 19th only today, the 30th, and am replying quickly via C. A. Vengerov, since you did not write your full address, and I do not count on the intelligence and kindness of the post. Your letter reached me so late because I have not been at my dacha lately, and the servant girl was ill and could not arrange to have the letter forwarded to Moscow.

I rejoice with my whole soul, dear friend, in your good news about yourself and your spouse, to whom, please, convey my heartfelt greeting and the best of wishes. A sincere thanks to both of you for your good sympathies for me, rather poorly deserved. Arrival to Vilnius is for me a *pium desiderium* whose fulfillment is not in my will.

As for the translation of the *Critique of Abstract Principles*, I have decided on a second edition but only with the most unavoidable alterations. I do not know whether this book will deserve a German translation. Over these days I will take advice from various people and will send you my decisive answer. Once more I thank you and my sincere respects to your spouse.

Sincerely and loyally your
Vlad. Solovyov

It is always better to write to Moscow, Prechistenka, Likhutin's house.

St. Petersburg, Voznesensky Prosp. (by the Blue Bridge), h. 16, apt. 3, or Vestnik Evropy Press, Galernaya, 20.

32.

September 12, 1892
Moscow, Prechistenka,
Likhutin's house

Thank you, my dear friend, Faivel Bentsilovich, for the steadfastness of your friendly consideration. The second edition of *Critique of Abstract Principles* is ready for printing, and I will be sending you the pages of the proofs. Unfortunately, I was not able to carry out as radical a revision as I would have liked, but nevertheless the book is significantly corrected and can in this form appear before the German public. I will deal with the details in sending the first page of the proofs. I am now hurrying to inform you quickly about this decision of mine and I enclose several words to your amiable spouse.

Fare well, amiable friend.

Cordially and faithfully yours,
Vlad. Solovyov

33.

[1894]

Dear friend
Faivel Bentsilovich!

Thank you for the wonderful wine mehare Iehudah, with which I entertained, by the way, two priests—one Orthodox and another Catholic: they rank it with reverence, thinking, probably, that it was received from missionaries, even though I distinctly read out to them, "Kosher l'Pesach," but they must have completely forgotten their Hebrew.

L. S. Poliakov[372] visited me; yesterday I repaid him the visit and made acquaintance with his family, which I rather liked, just as I do him. Today I will be having dinner at their place.

As for the German translation of my article, I presume that it in itself is not so significant for publication abroad. The thing to do would be to publish a collection of Russian voices on the Jewish question, taking advantage of the two perished manuscripts of our friends: F.G. and N.B.[373] It would be possible to include this article there also. After I think about this more and speak with N. Bakst in Petersburg, I will write something conclusive to you.

After mailing this letter, I will drive off to obtain two booklets of my poetry for you and your spouse, to whom I ask you to convey my heartfelt greeting.

With unchangeable admiration,
Vlad. Solovyov

34.

February 21, 1895

Dear Friend
Faivel Bentsilovich!

How are you faring? Well, I hope. I am also not grumbling at God, except on those occasions, by the way, when it becomes necessary to get entangled in other people's private matters. In these cases, I go not so much by the Gospel as by Kant (following the interpretation of Schiller): I help my neighbors *with a profound loathing.*[374] By the way, I must now do something for one poor Jew, who seems to me to be an idealist and a fanatic, but whom the old professor N. N. declared to be a cheat, and, not confining himself to expressing this view theoretically, crossed over into practice and pushed him away from himself, with [the result of inflicting upon him] certain bodily injuries. The victim of the honored Hebraist's short fuse is named Chaim Naumovich De-Glin. He is the author of the Jewish composition *Sepher Miqdosh Aaron,* and he now wants to publish the same work in Russian, for which he wishes to receive a subsidy from the Ministry of National Enlightenment. Since you are friendly with Ivan Davydovich,[375] then would you not write him something on behalf of this unfortunate man? No positive proof of his dishonesty was provided by N.N. since the tangible argumentation in the sphere of De-Glin's spine and neck attests not so much to him being a cheat as to the stern character of N.N. I am assured that you will do all you can and all that is necessary in this matter.

About myself I will relate two principal things. (1) I have settled in Finland on the lake of Saima, from where I arrive in Petersburg with improved health and with a preserved wallet. (2) Instead of the second edition of *Critique of Abstract Principles,* I am publishing three more mature and thorough books: first of all *Moral Philosophy,* then *Instruction about Understanding and Metaphysics,* and finally *Aesthetics.* The first is already in print and must come out, if there is no delay, at the beginning of May; when I will receive clean copies, I will send them to you. *Aesthetics* is almost ready for printing, and I plan to complete Gnosiology and Metaphysics (which are half finished) this summer. But at the present moment I am writing a little article for a Jewish collection of essays against the insolent Hase,[376] who insists that *all* prophets wrote after the Maccabees.

Fare well; I send heartfelt respects to your wife and do not lose the hope of seeing you.

> Cordially and faithfully yours,
> Vlad. Solovyov

I am going to the funeral of N. S. Leskov, one of Jewry's friends.[377]

35.

1896

Amiable friend
Faivel Bentsilovich!

I am zealously recommending to you my good acquaintance Anatolii Yakovlevich Speshnev,[378] who is coming to live with you in Vilnius to serve in a military-juridical department. You, as an old Vilniusian, could be very beneficial for the newly arrived, and if you have not changed your good disposition toward me, then do this first for me, and then, when you become acquainted, Anatolii Yakovlevich, probably, will himself gain your sympathies. I too am preparing to head to your countries, to Kaunas and to Vilnius, but the publication of my big book, which is approaching its end, is delaying me in Petersburg. I did not send you the proof for various motives, which are too long to write about. Now you will soon read it in a clean form. I am sending you via A. Y. Speshnev a book about Muhammad, and a new edition of poetry for your spouse, to whom I am zealously sending respects.

> Cordially and faithfully yours,
> Vlad. Solovyov

N.B. Do not think that it is I who furnished the portrait of Muhammad for my book, it was the villain Pavlenkov[379] who let me down.

36.

[Editor's Note: The following is a short autobiography written by V. S. Solovyov in May 1887 and included in Getz's collection of Solovyov's letters.]

Vlad. Serg. Solovyov was born in 1853 in Moscow, the son of the Russian historian Sergey Solovyov. He was educated in one of the Moscow gymnasia and then studied the natural sciences in Moscow University. Passing the examination for candidacy to the Faculty of History and Philology (in the same university), he entered as an auditor the Moscow Theological Academy. In one year he passed the examination for the Master of Philosophy in the University of St. Petersburg and publicly defended his thesis "A Critique of Western Philosophy" in 1874, directed against positivism. Elected as a reader (*dozent*) for the vacant chair of philosophy in Moscow University, he there gave lectures on the history of ancient and modern philosophy and logic. He spent one year abroad in England, France, Italy, and Egypt. Having left the chair in Moscow University as a result of not wishing to participate in the party battles among the professors, he was appointed a member of a learned committee attached to the Ministry for National Enlightenment. In 1878 he read in St. Petersburg a course of public lectures on the philosophy of religion. In 1880 he published his work *A Critique of Abstract Principles* and defended it as a dissertation for the degree of Doctor of Philosophy in the University of St. Petersburg, where later (in 1880–82) he read lectures as an unestablished university lecturer (*privat-dozent*) on metaphysics and the philosophy of history.

At the same time he gave lectures on the history of ancient philosophy at higher education women's courses. Soon after that he left his service in the ministry and then his professorial activities as well and focused his studies upon religious questions, chiefly the question of the unification of the churches and the reconciliation of Christianity with Judaism.

Besides two mentioned dissertations and many minor articles, he published (1) "Twelve Lectures on Godmanhood"; (2) "The Philosophical Principles of Integral Knowledge"; (3) "The Religious foundations of Life"; (4) "The National Question in Russia"; (5) "Jewry and the Christian Question"; (6) "The Dogmatic Development of the Church."

At present he has prepared for publication a comprehensive work, "The History and Future of Theocracy," in three volumes, from which the first comprises *the philosophy of biblical history,* the second *the philosophy of church history,* and the third *the challenges of theocracy.*

CHAPTER 10

"The Sins of Russia" (1887)

———

[Editor's Note: This essay is also letter #37 in Getz's collection of letters.]

So long as your national and unacknowledged sins remain upon you, you will never wage a decisive victory, you will never restore your good name.[380]

Yuri Krizhanich[381]

In his book *Russia and Europe* the late N. Y. Danilevsky,[382] analyzing our history and progressiveness in his characteristic way, acknowledges that Russia is stricken by heavy illness. This illness, he states, completely impedes the realization of the great destinies of the Russian people and can end, despite all of Russia's visible state prowess, after draining the original spring of the ethnic spirit, by depriving the historical life of the Russian people of its inner creative energies, *consequently rendering useless and redundant its very existence*, for all that is deprived of inner substance constitutes mere historical junk (*Russia and Europe*, 2nd ed., p. 316). That Russia ails with an oppressive and dangerous illness is evident, but it is also evident now for everyone that the honorable Slavophile was decisively mistaken in his diagnosis when he determined this illness to consist in the impoverishment and weakening of the national spirit in Russian society. Had he not made a mistake in his diagnosis, then the remedy he went on to suggest should have taken effect. Let us not forget that Danilevsky wrote at the end of the *sixties*. "Impoverishment of spirit," he said, "can be healed only by raising and rousing the spirit which would rouse all the layers of Russian society and bring them into living interrelationships.

" . . . For liberation from spiritual captivity and slavery a tight bond is required between all the captive and enslaved brothers, struggle is necessary which, stripping away all the masks, would make all enemies face each other. . . . Only the hard knocks of life can accomplish this, only the harsh experiences of history. These healing events, from which saving lessons must be extracted, already arise on the historical horizon and are called '*the Eastern question*'" (317). Danilevsky, as all Slavophiles, has turned out to be a partial prophet. The Eastern question has really arisen and has begotten instructional events, but the meaning of these lessons turns out to be not at all the one assumed by the author of *Russia and Europe*.

"The Eastern question," states the same writer, "is not to be numbered among those subject to the decisions of diplomacy. History submits events like a flow of finely ground rubbish to the bureaucratic production lines of diplomacy, but her great universal decisions, which become the law of the life of nations for entire ages, she proclaims alone without any mediators, surrounded by thunder and lightning, like Sabaoth from the height of Sinai" (318). In seven or eight years after these words were written, the last Eastern war broke out. Of thunder and lightning there was enough in the Balkans, but our Sinai suddenly turned out to be in Berlin, and history, contrary to Danilevsky, desired not to resolve our destinies by herself but found a mediator in the person of Count Bismarck. And in the meanwhile, what Danilevsky wished and prophesied transpired before our eyes. For in 1876, from the beginning of the Serbian War, we had a "raising and rousing of spirit," for every layer of Russian society was roused and brought into living interrelationship; there was a heated patriotic surge, there was a tight bond between enslaved brothers and an open struggle with enemies. But what "saving lessons" did the "harsh experiences of history" give us?

That resolution of the Eastern question to which our triumphant war led has now been revealed in the partition of Turkey among the

European powers. England received Cyprus and Egypt; France, Tunis; Austria, in addition to Bosnia and Herzegovina, acquired dominance over the whole Balkan peninsula, while Serbia, Rumania, and both Bulgarias can now be considered de facto as Austria's vassal states. Such a manifest and, given the circumstances, irreparable wrecking of our Eastern politics is too great and weighty a phenomenon for anyone to shrug off by scapegoating it all on imaginary or real mistakes in our diplomacy, or on the imaginary or real absence of skilled politicians from our midst. For it is neither some incomprehensible *fatum* nor some meaningless chance event that Russia lacks sufficient political energies precisely at such a significant historical moment as when they are all the more necessary. From the dawn of time it has neither been nor heard that a great people could not accomplish its historical appointment or defend its living interests for lack of suitable people. There has never been such an occurrence in history that the cause should hang on people. When the French king Charles VII lacked dependable counselors and generals, there came instead a peasant girl from Domrémy; the Moscow Boyars weakened in the Time of the Troubles,[383] they were rescued by a butcher from the southern outskirts;[384] in 1812 we had no Suvorov,[385] we managed with Kutuzov.[386] But could we, in 1878, blame the insufficiency of suitable statesmen in national politics when our government and society possessed people of such orientation and such capability as Skobelev,[387] Ignatiev,[388] Aksakov,[389] Katkov?[390] But when even with capable people a nation turns out to be incapable, when her military victories are followed by the internal decline of energies and a great historical cause falls from its hands, only two suppositions are possible: either this people has completed the circle of its historical activity and has entered into the epoch of decline and fall or it has, in some way, been unfaithful to its true vocation and faces, in the immediate challenges which it sets for itself, some internal contradiction, some kind of falsehood. There are two possibilities then: either this people has lived out its life or it is bearing a punishment for certain historical sins. To judge Russia an outlived nation is groundless; this manifestly contradicts all probabilities and analogies. And so it remains to posit the second cause for our failures and ailments.

More recently, again as at Sevastopol,[391] as at Plevna[392] and at the Congress of Berlin, we hear idle and noxious speeches about Russia's extraordinary might, about how all she has to do is speak and all will be done in our way, that the whole world is waiting with trepidation what Russia will say and do. Were Russia to demonstrate its might in deeds, there would be no need to speak much about it, but if she cannot demonstrate it for some reason, such speeches are false and dangerous.

By the way, if many among us see patriotism in national boasting, such is their business. It behooves us to speak not about Russia's might and interests but about her sins and duties.

When the bankruptcy of serfdom-ridden, military- and bureaucracy-driven Russia was so clearly revealed at Sevastopol, the national conscience, personified in the deceased sovereign, immediately understood the root cause of our troubles, and Russia was cleansed of serfdom. This first *moral* success was reflected also in our external dealings. While Nicholas's militarism brought Russia only losses, the epoch of civil reforms broadened the borders of Russia's domain.[393] And all went well, while we were subduing the Circassians and the Turkmen[394] or restraining the enraged Turks. But as soon as we were presented with the concrete challenge to educate the peoples we liberated for a new independent life, Russia all of a sudden became confused, dropped its trophies, fought with her pupils, and was left with nothing. If Sevastopol was a just punishment for serfdom, for what was the Berlin Congress with its present consequences a punishment?

How can we resolve the Eastern question when we cannot with a clean conscience raise our banner bearing the inscription: "National, civil, and religious independence and free development for all the peoples of the Christian East"? No military exploits on behalf of these peoples can conceal our own sins; on the contrary, these exploits only more clearly expose the deep inner contradiction in which we stand. We are not speaking about political conditions, in the narrow meaning of this word. The existing foundations of the state system in Russia we accept as an *unchangeable* fact. That's not the point. But with every political system, be it a republic, a monarchy, or an autocracy, the government can and must satisfy, within limits, those demands of national, civil, and religious freedom which our official and officious patriots laid claim to and lay claim to before Turkey and Austria. This is a matter not of political reasoning but of public and state *conscience.* A great nation cannot live tranquilly and flourish while infringing *moral* demands. And as long as false political reasoning will preserve in Russia a system of forced russification at the frontiers, as long as, on the other hand, millions of Russian citizens will be forcibly separated from all other people and subjected to a new form of serfdom, as long as the system of criminal punishment will tower over religious convictions and the system of compulsory censorship over religious thought, so long will Russia, in all her dealings, remain morally bound, spiritually paralyzed, and incapable of seeing anything but failure.

Vlad. Solovyov

Here you have then, amiable friend, the first introductory article for *Novosti.* After tomorrow I will send you a letter and perhaps the second article.

N.B. Please send the proofs without fail to the following address: Ostozhenka, *State* (Shtatnyj) Lane, Averkiev's house, E. B. Mikhail Sergievich Solovyov.

CHAPTER 11

Correspondence with Tolstoy

———————

I.

[End of February 1890]

Dear and deeply respected Lev Nikolaevich,[395]

We approach you with an important matter. There are rumors here, of whose truth we are assured, about new regulations for Jews in Russia.[396] By means of these regulations, the Jews are deprived of almost every means of existence, even in the so-called Pale of Settlement.

At the present time each and every one of us who disagrees with this harassment and finds the Jews to be the same sort of people as all others, is declared to be either a traitor, a madman, or someone in the pay of *yids*. All this, of course, is not to be feared. What would be most desirable is for you to raise your voice against this outrage. "If you do not warn the wicked man about his wickedness, I will require his soul at you hand."[397] In what form this denunciation is to be made entirely depends upon you. It would be best if you would come out on your own, and speak in your own name. If this is, for some reason, impossible for you, then it would be possible to write collectively.[398]

Would you be so kind as to inform one of us your thoughts on this matter.

We will be waiting anxiously for your reply.

With heartfelt loyalty,
                Vladimir Solovyov, Emile Dillon[399]
We can receive your answer via Vladimir Grigor'ievich Chertokov.[400]

To h(is) r(adiance) Count Lev Nikolaevich Tolstoy.
W(ithout) a(nswer).[401]

2.

[Editor's Note: Part of this letter is published in F. B. Getz's *The Floor to the Accused* (1891), p. III.]

L. N. Tolstoy's Answer

[March 15, 1890]

I am very grateful, Vladimir Sergeevich and Mr. Dillon, that you are proposing and presenting me with an opportunity to take part in a good work.

With all my soul I am pleased to take part in this work and know ahead of time that if you, Vladimir Sergeevich, would express that which you think about this subject, then you will express my thoughts and feelings also, because the foundation of our disgust with the measures of repression of the Jewish nationality is one and the same: the consciousness of a fraternal tie with all peoples and especially with the Jews, in whose midst the Christ was born and who have so greatly suffered and continue to suffer from the pagan ignorance of so-called Christians.

It is natural for you to write, because you know what precisely threatens the Jews and what people say about this. I cannot enjoin myself to write on an assigned theme, and lack the impulse.[402]

May God help you in this good work.

                                        L. Tolstoy

3.

[January 29, 1891]

Deeply honored Lev Nikolaevich,

My friend[403] who visited you this spring is publishing now (in Russia) a book[404] on that same subject. He wanted very much to fortify and decorate it with your letters. If you have anything against this, then kindly write directly to him (he has given you his address), since I am leaving for Moscow, while he is in a hurry with his book. It is well constructed and can be beneficial.

I was expecting to be in Moscow much earlier and to also drive out to your place at Yasnaya Polyana, but various matters have delayed me.

Be well. I send my heartfelt regards to all yours.

Sincerely and loyally, your
Vladimir Solovyov

If you have nothing against the publication of your letters, then do not belabor yourself with writing: my friend will take silence as agreement.

4.

[January 26 or 27, 1892]

Dear Lev Nikolaevich,

A sad misunderstanding has occurred. Your declaration,[405] that you did not send any letters to the English newspapers, was understood to mean that the contents of those published letters are *forged*, whereby a heavy accusation has fallen in this alleged forgery upon the translator, my friend, Mr. Dillon. I have no doubt that the "letters" in the form in which they have appeared in *Moskovskie vedomosti* are not an exact reproduction of a series of your well-known articles. But Mr. Dillon should not be blamed for this. If the translation is not exact, then, of course, between an inexact translation and the original there must be an entire chasm. But to accuse him of forgery—him, a family man, unprovided for, and threatened with the deprivation of his appointment and permission to serve in England—would mean to completely deprive him of his means of subsistence. For God's sake, correct this mistake. I have no doubt that you will yourself wish to do this. But I am writing to you, as to a man who knows well Mr. Dillon and his present desperate situation. Resolve this matter in England in such a way that the responsibility for the unacceptable and inaccurate promulgation of your views (in Russia) would shift from Mr. Dillon upon those who are really to blame, that is, *Moskovskie vedomosti*. It is not for me to advise you how best to act. I am sure that you will receive this letter as proof of my sincere sympathy not only for Mr. Dillon but also for you yourself.

> Cordially and faithfully, your
> Vlad. Solovyov

5.

Petersburg, July 5, 1894

Dear Lev Nikolaevich![406]
After we parted, I was very ill—bleeding so much that I frightened the doctor, who prescribed for me a multitude of medicines; but as I bought them only out of politeness and abstained from using them, I recovered in my own time. This illness, and several other circumstances, delayed until now two things I promised to do: (1) set out the principal point on which we disagree and (2) [compile] a systematic Reader of your religious-moral writings. At present I am taking advantage of Mr. Krauskopf's trip to you, so as to assure you that both of these intentions of mine have not been set aside.[407] The first, requiring only three or four days of complete freedom and concentration, I hope to fulfill this month, while the second, more outwardly complicated, will demand, certainly, more free time. I am thinking of giving the Reader the following title: "A Criticism of Pseudo-Christianity, from the Writings of Lev Tolstoy." As far as materials are concerned,

I am currently missing only one of your latest works, "Christianity and Patriotism." Could you arrange it to be sent to me (by registered post) to the following address: St. Petersburg, Editor of *Vestnik Evropy*, Galernaya [Str.] 20, to so and so.

An acquaintance who just arrived from Paris informs me that your book (independently of its principal contents) came in very handy in giving the coup de grâce to the Franco-Russian deceit.

Be well, dear Lev Nikolaevich. Au revoir, I trust, but where and when I do not know, for in all probability, regardless of the cholera, I remain here for an indeterminate period.

Heartfelt regards to the countess and all yours,

Sincerely and faithfully yours,

Vlad. Solovyov

6.

July 28–August 2, 1894, St. Petersburg

Dear Lev Nikolaevich!

Since my last letter, sent via Mr. Krauskopf, I was seriously ill twice and no longer wish to delay the important conversation which I owe you.

The entirety of our disagreement can be concentrated in one concrete point, the resurrection of Christ.

I think that in your personal worldview (assuming I correctly understand your latest writings) there is nothing that would hinder the recognition of the truth of the resurrection, and that in fact there is something that necessitates recognizing it. To begin with, I'll say something about the idea of the resurrection in general and then about the resurrection of Christ.

(1) You admit that our world experiences a progressive development of its species, moving from the lowest forms and stages of being to the highest and more perfect. (2) You acknowledge the interaction between inner, spiritual life and the highest, physical, and (3) on the basis of this interaction you acknowledge that the perfection of spiri-

tual creatures finds expression when its own spiritual life subordinates its own physical life and subdues it.[408]

These three points, I think, lead inevitably to the truth of the resurrection. The point is that spiritual power in relation to material existence is not a permanent but a growing quantity. In the animal world it is generally found only in a concealed, potential state; in the human, it is liberated and becomes manifest. But this liberation is accomplished initially only ideally in the form of rational consciousness: I distinguish myself from my animal nature; I acknowledge my inner independence from it and superiority before it. But can this *consciousness* become a *deed*? It not only can, but partially does. As in the animal world we find certain rudiments and glimpses of intelligent life, so in humanity there indubitably exist rudiments of that highest perfect condition in which the spirit really, factually subdues material life. It struggles with the dark aspirations of material nature and subjugates them to itself (and doesn't just distinguish itself from them). The degree of inner spiritual perfection determines the greater or lesser *fullness*[409] of this victory. The utter triumph of the hostile material principle is death, that is, the liberation of the chaotic life of material parts by the destruction of their rational, purposeful bond. Death is the manifest victory of meaninglessness over meaning, of chaos over the cosmos. This is especially clear in living creatures of the highest order. The death of a human being is the destruction of a perfect organism, of the purposeful form and instrument of the highest intelligent life. This victory of the lower over the higher, this disarmament of the spiritual principle demonstrates, evidently, the insufficiency of its power. But this power *grows*. For a human being immortality is that which reason is for an animal. The meaning of the animal kingdom is a rational animal, that is, a human being. The meaning of humanity is the *immortal*, that is, the Christ. As the animal world aspires to the rational, so humanity aspires to immortality. If the battle with chaos and death is the essence of the world process, in which the light, spiritual side, even if slowly and in stages, nonetheless *overcomes*, then the resurrection, that is, the actual and final victory of a living creature over death, is the unavoidable moment of this progress, which in principle concludes in this. All remaining progress, strictly speaking, has only the character of extension; it consists in the universal assimilation of this individual victory or in the dissemination of its consequences upon the whole of humanity and upon the whole world.

If a miracle denotes a fact, contradicting the general way of things and on that score impossible, then the resurrection is a direct contrary to a miracle: it is a fact, unconditionally inevitable in the general way of things. But if a miracle denotes a fact, original in its occurrence, unprecedented, then the resurrection of the "firstborn from the dead"[410] is, of course, a miracle, completely the same as the emergence of the first organic cell in the inorganic world, or as the emergence of an animal amid primordial vegetation, or of the first man amid orangutans. Natural history does not doubt these miracles, so the history of humanity should not doubt the miracle of the resurrection.

It stands to reason, from the point of view of mechanical materialism that all this is *nul et non avenu* [null and void]. But I would be rather surprised to hear some kind of principled objection from your point of view. I am sure that the idea of the resurrection and of "the firstborn from the dead" is as natural for you as it is for me. But, it may be asked, has it been realized in that historical person whose resurrection is told in the Gospels? These are the grounds on which I affirm my conviction in the reality of the resurrection of this person, Jesus Christ, as of the "firstborn from the dead."

I. The victory over death is an inevitable natural consequence of an inner spiritual perfection; that person in whom the spiritual principle assumed power decisively and completely over all lower cannot be conquered by death. Spiritual power, having attained the *fullness* of its perfection, inevitably spills over, so to speak, the rim of subjective-psychic life, captures also the bodily life, transfigures it, and then conclusively spiritualizes and inseparably binds it to itself. But it is precisely the image of the full spiritual perfection that I find in the Christ of the Gospel. To deem this image imagined I cannot for a multitude of reasons, to adduce which there is no need, since you also do not consider the Christ of the Gospels a myth. If this spiritually perfect human being really existed, then he by the same token was the firstborn from the dead and there is no reason to wait for another.[411]

II. Allow me to explain the second foundation for my faith by means of a comparison from another realm. When the astronomer Le

Verrier[412] by means of famous calculations became convinced that behind the orbit of Uranus there must exist another planet, and then saw
it in the telescope exactly how his calculations predicted, there was
little rational cause for him to think that the planet he saw was not the
one that he found by calculation and that it was not real and that the
real one might still, perhaps, be revealed later. Similarly, when grounding ourselves on the general sense of the world historical process, and
its sequential stages, we find that after the manifestation of the spiritual
principle in the ideal form, on the one hand, in Greek philosophy and
art and, on the other, in the aesthetic-religious ideals of the Hebrew
prophets (in the conception of the Kingdom of God), the furthest,
highest moment of this revelation must have presented the appearance
of that same spiritual principle, *personal* and *real*, incarnate in a living
person, which, not only through ideas and artistic images, but by *deed*,
had to show the power and triumph of the spirit over the hostile dull
principle along with its extreme expression—death. That is, it must
have actually resurrected its material body into a spiritual one. And
when alongside this we find among the testifying eyewitnesses il-
literate Jews[E], lacking any conception of the world process, of its stages
and moments, a description of just such a man, personally and really
incarnating in himself [the] spiritual principle, and who, to boot, relate
with amazement, as an unexpected and incredible event, that this man
rose from the dead, that is, present purely empirically, as a sequence of
facts, that which for us bears an inner logical connection, then seeing
this coincidence, we decisively have no right to accuse these witnesses
of inventing a fact whose complete meaning was unclear to them. This
is almost as if we were to propose that the workers who built the telescope for the Paris observatory, while knowing nothing of Le Verrier's
calculations, nonetheless intentionally construed for him to see in this
telescope the phantom of a nonexistent Neptune.

   III. The third foundation of my faith in the resurrection of Christ
I will mention only in two words, since it is all too well known, which
does not lessen its power. The point is that without the fact of the resurrection, the unusual enthusiasm of the apostolic community would
have lacked sufficient foundation, and in general the entire original history of Christianity would appear as a series of impossibilities. It's as
if there is need to acknowledge (as some have done) that Christian

history lacked the first century and that it began right with the second or the third.

I personally, ever since acknowledging that the history of the world and of humanity is meaningful, have not the slightest doubt of Christ's resurrection, and all objections against this truth, by their weakness, only confirm my faith. The only original and serious objection I know belongs to you. In one recent conversation with me, you said that if one were to acknowledge the resurrection and consequently the special supernatural meaning of Christ, then Christians would be constrained to depend more for their salvation upon the mysterious power of this supernatural being than upon their personal moral work. But such an abuse of the truth in the final end serves only as a rebuke of the abusers. Since in fact Christ, albeit resurrected, can do nothing definitively for us without us, so for honest and conscientious Christians there can here be no danger of quietism. This could be admitted, if the resurrected Christ were to have for them a visible reality, but in actual conditions, when the actual, personal connection with him can be only spiritual, which presupposes personal moral human work, then only hypocrites or wretches could invoke grace in *detriment* to moral duties. Moreover the God-man is not the all-consuming absolute of Eastern mystics and union with him cannot be one-sidedly passive. He is "the firstborn from the dead," the pointer of the way, the leader and the banner for active life, combat, and perfection, and not for immersion in Nirvana.

In any case, whatever the practical consequences of Christ's resurrection might be, the question of its truth is not decided by them.

I would be interested to know, in the highest degree, what you would say about this substantially. If you do not have the desire or the time to write, I'll wait until we see each other. Be well, I cordially bow to all yours.

Sincerely and faithfully yours,
Vlad. Solovyov

Here is the address in any case: St. Petersburg, by the Blue Bridge, Voznesensky prosp[ect], No. 16, Apt. 3 (barracks, apartment of the military investigator Kuz'min-Karavaev).

7.

August 7, 1894

Dear Vladimir Sergeevich, I now opened your letter so as to answer it and was shocked on seeing that more than a month has transpired. Thank you for your kind intentions. I gladly await their realization.[413] Dr. Krauskopf turned out to be a man of very un-Christian spirit, which does no harm, nevertheless, to the great sensibility of his plan, and so I, however ineffective my sympathy might be, sympathize with him. As for the un-Christian spirit, I discerned it in the brochure he gave me on the theme "An Eye for an Eye" and nonresistance.[414] He states there that "an eye for an eye" is right, while turning the cheek is wrong, and that when it comes to being struck on the cheek and having one's cloak taken, one should neither turn the other cheek nor yield the shirt but show a fist and a whip. This appears to me to be rather odious, even though it is time to accustom oneself to odious measures of this sort among the punishments that surround us.

I read your article "The End of the Debate" and happened upon the responding article by Tikhomorov. Excuse me for giving unsolicited advice, but, liking and respecting you, I cannot refrain from advising you to once and for all renounce polemics. How much strength you would conserve! And you have much upon which to direct it. The harvest is plentiful.

I shake your hand in friendship,

L. Tolstoy

CHAPTER 1 2

The Protest Letter, London *Times*
(December 10, 1890)

[Editor's Note: Excerpt from the article "The Jews in Russia," from an Occasional Correspondent (E. J. Dillon).]

In view of the approaching protest meeting in London to protest against the persecution of Russian Jews,[415] I beg leave to lay before your readers some official and unpublished correspondence on the subject, such as now often passes between the different Russian authorities, and which has already been referred to in the course of the discussion as to whether any new oppressive laws have really been enacted or not. . . .

. . . The following is the protest intended to be made by a large number of literary Russians of Moscow and the provinces, headed by Count Leon Tolstoi, which has already been referred to in the *Times*. Its tone and arguments are so dispassionate and just that it might be echoed as a resolution at the coming meeting in the Guildhall, London. This is not a petition against Russian antisemitism, as telegram agency despatches have erroneously termed it. Every one who knows Russia is aware that Russians have no right whatever to make a collective petition, as that would immediately fall under the category of revolutionary action against constituted authority. This expression of opinion by some 60 or more Russians connected with art and literature is only a protest for the purpose of proving to the small set of narrow-minded journalists who disgrace their country by exciting the passions and prejudices of their half-benighted countrymen that many of their colleagues and fellow-workers are altogether opposed to this iniquitous and unchristian agitation. Unfortunately there is an official side to the matter. The Russian Government, which sets the horrible example with its inquisitorial restrictions on the Jews, not unnaturally sees in this protest an indirect condemnation of its own policy, as well as a reproof to the subservient scribes who have elected to assist in popularizing the evil principle adopted by their rulers. A peremptory prohibition has therefore been launched against the further progress of the protest, and this prohibition is signed by the very same literary gentleman, M. Feoktistoff, now head of the Censor Committee, who put his name to a precisely similar protest some years ago. Consequently I have been requested to ask you to kindly publish the text of this protest, without, of course, giving the names of those who have offered their signatures. To do so would at once place them in the category of revolutionists. The name of one only can be proclaimed with impunity — that of Count Tolstoi. The autocratic Government, which banishes even grand dukes for their social delinquencies, would think twice before sending to Siberia the world-renowned Christian philosopher, whose work is operating with more force against intolerance and arbitrary injustice than all the Nihilism and Socialistic propaganda put together. It may seem strange to English readers that such simple truths as those contained in the document below have to be addressed to a society calling itself civilized and European, but it will not surprise those who know anything of the moral and social confusion and disorder which now pervade all channels of Russian life. The protest runs as follows: —

The movement against the Jews, spread and fostered by the Russian Press, after the fashion of Germany, represents an unprecedented violation of the most fundamental principles of justice and humanity. We consider it necessary to remind the Russian public of these elementary principles, the candid acceptance of which is the only solution of the so-called Jewish question. The existence, in fact, of such a question is simply the result of these principles having been forgotten. As worthless and pernicious individuals exist among all races without necessarily contaminating and involving the entire race, which, if such were the case, would abolish the individual moral responsibility of its members, every appearance of hostility or action against the Jews as a body, or merely because they are Jews, represents an absurd infatuation of blind national egoism, or of narrow self-interest which cannot for a moment be justified.

It is unjust to hold the Jews responsible for failings induced by a thousand years of persecution and the abnormal conditions in which they have been compelled to live. If for centuries they have been forcibly obliged to engage in money business because debarred from all other occupations, the disagreeable effects of such an exclusive turn given to Jewish energy cannot be removed by further persecution, which only tends to perpetuate the evil.

Membership of the Semitic race and the practice of the laws of Moses, implying nothing wrong or blameable *per se*, cannot afford the slightest ground for special enactments and restrictions applicable exclusively to the Jews, and comparing unfavourably with those in force for Russian subjects of other races and creeds. As the Russian Jews bear the burdens and fulfil the obligations imposed by the State equally with all other members of the particular class to which they may belong, they ought in justice to have the same rights as those enjoyed by their Russian compeers.

The recognition and application of these elementary truths are important and necessary for our own welfare as well as for the good of the Jews. This intense excitation of racial and religious hatred, so opposed to the spirit of Christianity and so destructive of all feelings of justice and humanity, tends to corrupt society at the very core, and may lead to complete moral isolation. It appears all the more serious in view of the noticeable decline of humanitarian ideas and enfeeblement of the juridical principle in our present condition of society. The mere feeling, therefore, of national self-preservation demands that this anti-Semitic movement should be emphatically condemned, not only as immoral in itself, but as extremely dangerous for the future of Russia.[416]

CHAPTER 13

Solovyov's Protest Letter in the Memoirs of Korolenko (1909)

———

V. G. Korolenko
The "Declaration" of V. S. Solovyov[41/]

In October 1890 I received from the deceased Vladimir Sergeevich Solovyov (from Moscow) a letter, in which, among other things, was said:

"I am sending to you the attached declaration by literary persons and scholars with the request that you should sign it, I consider it redundant to expatiate on how much this signature is necessary. I consider it redundant to expatiate on how much the signature of the most talented of our newest artistic writers is necessary for giving full-weight to this declaration. As to the fact that you sympathize with its contents, this is attested, by the way, by your beautiful 'Pavlovo Sketches,' in which you so truthfully illustrated by a living example all the falsity of antisemitism. Departing during these days to Petersburg, I humbly ask you to sign and send the declaration to me there at the following address: The European Inn on the Mikhailovskaya Street. With all respect and at your service, Vladimir Solovyov."

The declaration itself, mentioned in this letter, was composed by Solovyov, bearing some signatures and then again corrected in various places by Solovyov's hand, read as follows:

> In view of the systematic and constantly growing attacks and insults, to which Jewry is subjected in the Russian press, we, who have signed below, consider it necessary to declare:

> 1) Recognizing, that the demands of justice and love of humanity are equally applicable to all people, we cannot allow that the affiliation to the Jewish race or to the Mosaic law should constitute in itself something blameworthy (which, of course, does not predetermine the issue of the desirability of attracting Jews to Christianity by purely spiritual means) and that, with regard to the Jews, no force should be given to that common principle of fairness by which the Jews, bearing the same obligations as do other peoples, should also bear the same rights.

> 2) Even if it were true, that the harsh, millennia-long persecutions of Jewry and those abnormal conditions in which it was placed, should have engendered the well-known disagreeable phenomena of Jewish life, then this cannot serve as the basis for the continuation of such persecutions and perpetuation of such an abnormal situation, but, on the contrary, should waken us to a greater tolerance to Jews and to take care about the healing of those sores which were inflicted by our ancestors.

> 3) The intensified arousal of national and religious enmity, so repellent to the spirit of true Christianity, suppressing the sense of fairness and humanity, corrupts society at its root and can bring it to a moral dehumanization, especially given the already presently noted decline of humanitarian sentiments and the weakening of the juridical principle in our life.

> On the basis of all this we decisively condemn the antisemitic movement in the press, come to us from Germany, as immoral in its essence, and as a radical danger to Russia's future.

At that time, when this declaration came to me, it was already signed by the following persons: L. N. Tolstoy, Prof. Gerie, Prof. Vinogradov, Prof. Timiryazev, Prof. Yanzhul, Prof. A. N. Veselovsky, V. A. Gol'tsev, Bezobrazov, Prof. F. Fortunatov, S. Fortunatov, V. S. Solovyov, Prof. Vsev. Miller, Prof. A. I. Chuprov, N. N. Milyukov, Sizov, Gambarov, Shhepkin, G. A. Dzhanshiev, P. P. Minilov, S. A. Muromtsev, Prof. Stoletov, Professor Count Komarovsky, Prof. Grot.

I eagerly adjoined my signature and thanked Solovyov for remembering me in this matter. Some redactional details prompted me to make some comments, but I did not think nuances should dissuade me from the deed. That is how, apparently, V. S. Solovyov regarded the matter. With respect to one correction, made by his hand (the German origin of Russian antisemitism), he informed me that he inserted this in response to the demand of several signatories, considering this insertion unnecessary but not wishing to draw out the matter with redactional arguments.[418]

My signature was far from the last. Solovyov very heatedly, passionately even, approached this literary undertaking, trying to unite under the declaration distinguished names in literature and science independently of their various different viewpoints on other questions. Those who should have first of all responded to his short formula were people for whom religious and national tolerance constitute an organic part of the common order of convictions. But to persons with whom he closely shared the other side of his very complex intellectual constitution, he appealed with arguments based on purely Christian morality, in which there was much strength and winsome charm. In *his* Christianity he did not go for compromise. For him, Christianity was a fount of absolute morality. From this font he drew also a formula on the Jewish question, distinguished by an unusual lightness and simplicity. He said: "If the Jews are our enemies, then deal with them according to the Gospel: love your enemies. If they are not enemies [and he verily thought that they were not enemies], then there is no need to persecute them." Many of Solovyov's dogmatic views are swathed in thick, often almost impenetrable metaphysical mists. But when he would descend from these misty heights, so as to apply these or those foundational formulas of Christianity to passing life, he was magnificent on account of his precise clarity of thought and for his skill in finding for it a simple and condensed formula. Such was his argumentation on the Jewish question. Listening to it, people, who would profess to possess a true Christian faith, had to either agree with his conclusion or to acknowledge that Christianity is only an abstract doctrine, inapplicable to broad phenomena of contemporary life, which must yield before anti-Christian invocations to hatred and vengeance. But this, from the point of view of a man of sincere faith, is blasphemy. In this manner, to the formula of a pure liberalism on a given question, Solovyov especially was able to involve a wide circle of people, far, perhaps, from being liberal in the exact meaning of this word, but sensitive to the logic of a sincere faith, which could be heard in Solovyov's liberal formulation.

In January 1891 I received from him another letter on that same subject. Among other things it said: "One of my friends is publishing a book on the Jewish question and he was asking me to inquire of you whether you would permit him to publish your letter, which you sent me with your signature under the literary declaration well known to you. . . . The fate of the latter is probably known to you." At the end of the letter it was related that our declaration was not published in Russia but abroad . . .

"The fate" of the declaration was then unknown to me, and only upon arriving at Petersburg did I discover what had transpired. And what had transpired was that, while Solovyov was busy gathering signatures, rumors about his plan became widespread in literary circles. They reached, by the way, the famous publicist of the reactionary camp, Mr. Ilovajsky,[419] who immediately sounded the alarm about it. The alarm was picked up in full measure by the antisemitic and reactionary press. Unfortunately, I am unable at present to adduce here the best pearls of this one-sided polemic, even though this could have been amusing. Nevertheless, its chief characteristic consisted in the fact that these gentlemen did not come down upon the view expressed but upon the very intention to express it. In the tone of Marat in *The Friend of the People* or Hébert in *Père Duchesne*,[420] the Ilovajskys proclaimed the fatherland to be in danger and cried to the consuls, without even naming concretely any names, but only drawing in indeterminate sinister ways the approaching "sedition."

The loud chirring had its usual effect. A circular of the Chief Directorate followed and the declaration which Solovyov conceived did not appear at that time in Russia.

Like true "sedition," it was published abroad (simultaneously in Paris and Vienna). For Europeans, it stands to reason, the declaration by Russian writers of axioms recognized by the cultured world could have been significant only as a curious illustration of the conventions of Russian censorship. But for us even now there is something instructive in this little episode. Exerting such heroic efforts so as to stifle Solovyov's attempt at its conception, the antisemitism of that time, as it were, granted to its enemies a degree of fear and respect. It was recognized that the very fact of a categorical declaration of the leading ranks of Russian writers can deliver a palpable blow to antisemitism, supported by the government.

Now, these are *tempi passati*.[421] It is true, the mainstream Russian press *said*, perhaps, everything that needed to be said about this question. But antisemitism also *did* almost everything that should not have been done, throwing to the side all regard for "highest principles" and for Christian, and all other morality.

1909.

CHAPTER 14

Letter to Konstantin Konstantinovich Arseniev

———————

24.

September 30, 1894[422]
Imatra. Raucha (pension Al'ma)[423]

Here you have [the article on] Kampanelli,[424] most honorable
Konstantin Konstantinovich, and as for [the article on] the Kabbalah,
then I sent it on to Margolin[425] in two parts: on the 27th of September
from Vyborg[426] and on the 28th from Imatra. I had to write it myself,
since Gintsburg's article, sound and substantial in itself, is written only
for scholars, and not for the public, and the Kabbalistic doctrine is presupposed rather than set forth; there are uncensored things with regard
to the Bible, etc. I will try to accommodate it in a philosophical
journal—there, in a special section is its rightful place. I will write to
the Gintsburgs, both son and father, and perhaps you will meet the
latter on a green field.[427] In that case, I ask you especially to convey my
congratulations for his son's article but at the same time to attest that
the editorial board makes brevity and popularity an invariable condition for articles, and that to abridge the article (in my view), in light of
its substantiality, would be a pity, whereby it would be much better to
publish it entirely in another place.

To show you how well Bar. Gintsburg's article satisfies the demands of popularity, I have copied and am sending you two of its

pages. As I said, the author himself does not set forth the theoretical teaching of the Kabbalah but, to have the reader understand this teaching's contents and style, invokes in an almost literal translation the beginning of the book Tsohor.[428]

Here it is (on a special page).

Is it not true that this passage, besides being itself indigestible, could easily give occasion to all kinds of mockery and fault-finding by *Novoe vremya* and K.

But please, support me in the eyes of the elder baron: You know, that I like him very much. In the meantime, I am thriving here. I am thinking of coming to Petersburg on the 17th. [Please convey] my heartfelt respects to Eugenia Ivanovna and Mary.

Cordially yours,
Vlad. Solovyov

CHAPTER 15

Letters to Baron David Goratsievich Gintsburg

I.

1896

Most honorable Baron, I fear that my letter, sent more than a month ago, has not reached you, and therefore I am briefly repeating its contents, this time sending it *registered*. Your article on the Kabbalah is extremely interesting and substantive, and I hope that you will accept [my]mediation in having it published in the Moscow philosophical journal: *Voprosy filosofii i psikhologii* (Questions in Philosophy and Psychology). It is slightly too long for the dictionary, or rather not popular enough. People who have *a little* familiarity with the Kabbalah, at least as much as I have, are negligibly few among us, and those who know nothing about the Kabbalah will find your article incomprehensible. It is a purely scholarly article, and in the dictionary as a whole such articles are permitted only in those specialized fields which can be understood on their own without difficulty (e.g., history, geography, zoology, etc.), or in fields which are studied by a large number of people (e.g., mathematics, mechanics, etc.). But as regards Jewish mysticism, not only does Russian society lack specialists, but dilettantes even, such as myself, for example, who are capable of understanding and appreciating another's scholarly labor, are found in single digits. To abridge your article or adapt it to the demand of persons who are completely unfamiliar with the subject would be a pity, for, to repeat my sincere opinion, your article is superb in its kind. Its rightful place is in a specific section of a philosophical journal where, I hope, you will delegate me to deliver it, after you supplement it with those comments about which you wrote to me, and also, perhaps, with others, since there is no reason for haste in dealing with a philosophical journal. If you have a different version of the article, then, after giving it its final shape, do please try to forward it to your father. If not, do inform me through him still, and I will send you the copy in my possession. I hope that you will not resent me for this *contretemps* and will not deprive our philosophical literature of your valuable contribution.

With sincere respect,
Vladimir Solovyov

2.

[undated, marked "Hôtel d'Angleterre" on the blank side]

I am hurrying to inform you, dear baron, that A. D. Obolensky has notified me that he can make our acquaintances either today (Friday) at the ministry until 12 o'clock, or tomorrow (Saturday) at his apartment (Bol'shaya Morskaya, 53) at 11 o'clock.

Until we meet tomorrow.

Faithfully yours,
Vladim. Solovyov

CHAPTER 16

Letters to Nikolai Yakovlevich Grot

30.

1896

My dear friend Nikolai Yakovlevich,[429]

I am sending to you a very substantial and learned article on Kabbalistic philosophy. Its author, Baron David Gintsburg (the son of the famous banker), is one of the favorite students of the academic Baron Rozen, who vouches for him as a solid Orientalist who knows about these things. I think that this article is very desirable for the special section "Questions"—as far as I remember, you still have nothing about Jewish philosophy.

Please inform me quickly about your decision on this matter. Regarding the Russian language of the article, if you have no time, I undertake to iron it out in the proofs. You will oblige me greatly with a speedy publication of this article, and towards the beginning of March I will send you my own.

I am busy up to my neck.

If you see Trubetskoi, then thank him for me for the Greek letter and say that I'll answer at the first leisure moment.

My heartfelt respects to yours, I kiss Levon and all.

Your Vladimir Solovyov

31.

1896

I beg you, dear friend Nikolai Yakovlevich, to send this immediately to the printer and to send me, as soon as possible, *two copies* of the first proofs. I must do this so as not to delay the publication of the volume.

Until we see each other soon.

Your Vlad. Solovyov

N.B. Without fail, place "The Kabbalah" in the May volume, otherwise do not count on my cooperation. Ultimatum.

CHAPTER 17

Letters to *Moskovskie vedomosti*
(October 1891)

———————

I.

October 22, 1891, № 291

A Letter to the Editor

Having read in № 291 of *Moskovkie vedomosti* the articles by Mr. Yu Nikolaev[430] and Afanasiev,[431] dedicated to my lecture to the Psychological Society, I deem it necessary to declare that in these articles my thoughts are conveyed completely inaccurately, of which one may become assured when the designated lecture will appear in print.

Vladimir Solovyov

2.

October 26, 1891, № 296

A Letter to the Editor

In addition to my brief declaration (in № 292 of *Moskovskie vedomosti*) I request you to publish the following:

1. The words "swindling and deceit" (and not "swindlers and de-ceivers"), invoked by me in closed debates after the lecture, did not have and, in the course of the discussion, could not have had any ref-erence to Christian or whatever other type of hermits and ascetics, but referred exclusively to those poor laypeople who hypocritically es-pouse the ideal of personal holiness and piety so as to free themselves by means of this pretext from any kind of work for the common good.

2. I never said and could not have said that Christianity only pro-duced the Inquisition.

3. My lecture contained neither "total" nor fragmentary "mockery over the Christian Church."

4. The Church in essence (from its divine and grace-filled aspect) was not at all the subject of my reflections, which were limited only by the historical vicissitudes[432] of Christian humanity.

5. I made no "ironical censure of the first Christians"; I said, on the contrary, that they, like the apostles after Pentecost, were really re-born through the Holy Spirit, having, according to the words of the Acts of the Apostles, one heart and soul.[433]

6. As there was in my lecture no attack on the Christian Church, so in the debates after the lecture there was no defense of her.

7. If my lecture, read with many abridgements, will be printed, then only in its full form, with the more detailed factual argumenta-tion, but without the tiniest alteration of thoughts and views.

To these seven points, relating to the accusations, made by Mssrs. Nikolaev and Afanasiev, I can also add an answer to three ques-tions, proposed to me by V. A. Gringmut[434] (in № 293 of *Moskovskie vedomosti*).

8. According to the teaching of the H(oly) Church, the operation of Christ's grace is not confined solely to the Church's sacraments, but has diverse forms. Consequently, my comparison between an unbe-lieving priest and an unbelieving historical figure possesses the follow-ing sense: as the grace of one form (the ecclesial-sacramental) has its strength in the unbelieving minister of the sacrament, so the grace of the other form (the moral-practical) can have its strength in the unbe-lieving public figure. In both cases the grace does not operate through faith: in the former, it operates according to the apostolic vocation of

the priestly minister for the spiritual welfare of people; and in the latter, according to the historical vocation of the public figure for the practical welfare of the same people. By the way, my argument can be expressed more directly and strongly, by taking for example not the sacrament of the Holy Sacrifice [Eucharist], but the sacrament of baptism. Indeed, if a simple layman, or even a pagan, could by necessity administer the sacrament of holy baptism, then *all the more so* could he serve Christ in the completion of His historical work. For the discussion was precisely about what *transpires by necessity* and not about ideal norms.

9. V. A. Gringmut's second question is based on a misunderstanding, or even on two misunderstandings. First of all, from the fact that I contrast real Christians and nominal or pretended Christians, it in no wise follows that there exist, according to me, only these two categories. On the contrary, I even recalled that between these extreme bounds, there exist a multitude of shades of more or less profound and more or less superficial Christianity. Second, it is self-evident that for a moral evaluation of Christian ministry, what is important is not so much the extent but also the quality of the ministry. I am in complete agreement with V. A. Gringmut that to act in the spirit of true Christianity is possible, in its sphere, also for women who are not occupied in various broad, common problems. I criticized not women, who carry out their private business, but public people, who have excused themselves from common and governmental labor on the pretext of an individual-transcendental stewing of the brain.

10. The third question of V. A. Gringmut is tied up with a false historical premise. Following the Reformation, religious persecutions and executions did not only gain strength in the Catholic Church but also appeared in communities that had separated from her (the burning of Michael Servetus[435] by Calvin, the bloody persecutions of the "Papists" in England under Elizabeth, etc.). Furthermore, I am unclear as to the sense in which V. A. Gringmut counsels me to follow the example of Luther, and, if this be irony, what is its force? For Luther, as is well known, separated from his Roman Catholic Church and provoked a schism within it. I cannot do likewise with regard to Roman Catholicism since I do not belong to it. As for following Luther's ex-

ample in the present circumstances, i.e., to separate from our Greco-Russian Church and to provoke a schism within it, this, of course, V. A. Gringmut will not counsel me to do from his point of view. As for my point of view, it is necessary to struggle not against this or that confession or church but solely against the anti-Christian spirit, wherever and however it may be expressed.

Vladimir Solovyov

3.

October 30, 1891, № 300

№ 296 of *Moskovskie vedomosti* adds new untrue accounts of the lecture of October 19 to those previously printed. In the footnote to the leading article it states: "The First Christians is a name given to the Christians of the first three centuries, whom Mr. Solovyov accused of one-sided egoism." Although by First Christians I have always called and will call the Christians of the original apostolic churches of Jerusalem and Antioch, the point lies not in this but in that the Christians of the following epoch also, the epoch of the martyrs and apologists, I never accused of one-sided egoism. This is what is said of them in my lecture: "The possibility of martyrdom was always and everywhere hanging over Christians and bestowed a cleansing, tragic character to their life. The important advantage of those centuries over the following was that Christians could be and were persecuted, but in no circumstance could they be persecutors. In general, to belong to a new religion was much more dangerous than profitable, and therefore it was normally sought out by the best of people, people of sincere conviction and inspiration. The life of that Church, even if it was not permeated *completely* by the spirit of Christ, then at any rate, the highest, religio-moral motifs abounded in her. *There was* in the midst of the pagan world a true Christian society, far from perfect, but nonetheless governed by life's best principle."

In that leading article the public is represented as having rewarded me with applause for daring words, about, by the way, Metropolitan

Filaret's[436] role in freeing the serfs. But neither about Metropolitan Filaret nor about any other Russian hierarch did I say a word in my lecture, and in the closed debates there was no public applause.

In the fueilleton signed by Yu. Nikolaev (the same issue of *Moskovskie vedomosti*) one point merits attention, appearing curious to the author himself. The persons who were in the closed assembly after the lecture will remember that in the debate with one member-contestant on the question of religious persecutions I gave two historical indications: first, I indicated that well-known fact, that the beginning of the *inquisition as an institution* was established by the Emperor Theodosius in Constantinople; and second, as a bright example of religious persecutions in the Byzantine Empire, I remembered the massacres of the Paulicians (the heretical dualists in Asia Minor) under Empress Theodora. These two facts, separated from each other by more than five centuries and, seemingly, equally unknown to my opponent, became conflated in his recollections, and an incompetent consultation with a textbook transformed it into a third fact, about which there could have been no discussion, since it is completely irrelevant. The ensuing muddle, of course, could make no sense to the reader who was not present at the closed quarters of the Psychological Society. Theodosius, who founded the Inquisition, and Theodora, who massacred the Paulicians, appear under the pen of Mr. Yu. Nikolaev in the form of Theodosia, massacring the . . . *Salonicans*! There follows an excerpted textbook story about this beating, so as to prove (as if someone could have doubted this) that it had no relationship whatsoever to religious persecution. But why then did Mr. Yu. Nikolaev not cite from another textbook the story about the battle on the plains of Catalonia or the Battle of Borodino? For here there were also beatings which also had no relationship to the Inquisition. And why still, on the other hand, did he not inform himself about the facts which I cited, regarding the beating of the Paulicians by Theodora and about the institutionalizing of the Inquisition by Theodosius the Great?

Apparently, he requires further directives which I am ready and pleased to supply for him. The massive executions of the Paulicians (with an inquisitorial process, and also without any process) were conducted in the year 848, and are related by Byzantine writers, the Continuer of Theophanes[437] and others, the number of the executed is variously determined, not less than ten thousand and not more than one hundred thousand. In every decent textbook of Church or Byzantine history this fact is set forth more or less amply.[438]

As far as the legislative institution of the Inquisition in Byzantium is concerned, then I will not encumber my opponent with citations of Byzantine legal codes. The editors of *Moskovskie vedomosti* probably have a Brockhaus or a Meyer. In the latter (Meyers Conversationslexicon, 4. Aufl., VIII. B., S. 970), in the article "Inquisition," Mr. Yu. Nikolaev can read the following brief but on first inspection sufficient note: "Already under the Emperor Theodosius the Great and Justinian, there were appointed special judges (*Gerichtspersonen*) for discovering people who did not belong to the Orthodox faith, e.g., the Manichees, whereupon the discovered persons were normally subjected to ecclesial but also to civil punishments." If, being dissatisfied with this, Mr. Yu. Nikolaev would turn to the legislative acts, then he will see that these punishments against the heretics or even against such schismatics as the Donatists extended to capital punishment.

In the same issue of *Moskovskie vedomosti*, V. A. Gringmut cites against me an Epistle of Greek Patriarchs, affirming that holy baptism can be performed only by the *Orthodox* and, furthermore, *by those who understand the importance of the sacrament*. Such a citation is in no wise convincing. When the discussion deals with the original teaching of the Church, then one needs to cite evidence that has universal, infallible authority, and not the opinion of a late hierarch lacking such authority. The declaration of the Greek patriarchs, besides disagreeing with Nicene and Carthaginian statutes, directly contradicts the most ancient and commonly known practice of our Russian Church. G. Gringmut, apparently, knows the examples of the Protestants or of Catholics who have joined our Church without being baptized again. It follows that their former baptism, even if performed by *non-Orthodox*, is recognized as real. As for the baptism of dying infants by simpletons or women, then, apparently, there is no possibility in such circumstances to determine the extent to which a midwife (perhaps a Jew or a complete unbeliever) understands the importance of the sacrament. In this way, V. A. Gringmut's citation proves too much and therefore does not prove anything.

But here V. A. Gringmut asks: "Could Vl. S. Solovyov seriously think that the whole matter turns on a *rite* and not on the agent of this rite?" This question I can only answer by another: Of what, finally, am I accused? Of insulting all that is holy, or of reverencing a rite? Of blasphemous rationalism or of blind ritualism? Of liberalism or papism? Of attacking historical Christianity or of defending Catholicism?

I do not know how my opponents will harmonize such accusations. I propose that the real cause of these attacks is my understanding of Christianity as the living spirit of Christ, all-encompassing and by nothing constrained.

Vladimir Solovyov

CHAPTER 18

Six Poems

Six Old Testament and Jewish-themed poems follow. For all but the last poem, the Russian original is accompanied by both a free English translation and an English translation that attempts to preserve the meter and rhyme; the latter is the version cited in Part II of the volume. The final poem is accompanied by a single English translation. The Russian original and free English translation have been reproduced side by side where space permitted. In several instances, the free translation is reproduced from Boris Jakim, *The Religious Poetry of Vladimir Solovyov* (Kettering, OH: Angelico Press, 2014), with the author's permission.

В стране морозных вьюг . . . [In the Land of Frosty Blizzards . . . (1882)]

В стране морозных вьюг, среди седых туманов
    Явилась ты на свет,
И, бедное дитя, меж двух враждебных станов
    Тебе приюта нет.

Но не смутят тебя воинственные клики,
    Звон лат и стук мечей,
В раздумье ты стоишь и слушаешь великий
    Завет минувших дней:

Как древле Вышний Бог избраннику еврею
    Открыться обещал,
И Бога своего, молитвой пламенея,
    Пророк в пустыне ждал.

Вот грохот под землей и гул прошел далёко,
    И меркнет солнца свет,
И дрогнула земля, и страх объял пророка,
    Но в страхе Бога нет.

И следом шумный вихрь и бурное дыханье,
    И рокот в вышине,
И с ним великий огнь, как молнии сверканье,—
    Но Бога нет в огне.

И смолкло всё, укрощено смятенье,
    Пророк недаром ждал:
Вот веет тонкий хлад и в тайном дуновенье
    Он Бога угадал.

In the Land of Frosty Blizzards . . . (1882)

In the land of frosty blizzards, amidst grey fogs[439]
    You, a female child, were born unto this earth.
And twixt two warring camps, for you, poor infant,
    there was no shelter.

But you would not be smitten by hostile cries,
    Neither by din of arms, nor by clang of swords,
In contemplation you stand and listen to the mighty
    Testament of days gone past.

As in ancient times God Most High to his chosen Jew[E]
    Swore [lit., "promised"] to reveal Himself,
So the prophet, aflame with prayer,
    Awaited his God in the desert.

A roar and a rumble pass far under the earth
    And the sun's light fades
The earth shakes, and fear grips the Prophet
    But in the fear there is not God.

Then the loud whirlwind and wild tempest followed
    And thunder high above,
And with it a great flame, like lightning's blazing,
    But in the fire there is no God.

And all grew still, bewilderment arrested,
    The Prophet waited not in vain,
A gentle breeze arrives and in its secret breathing
    He discerned God.

Rhymed Translation

In the land of frosty blizzards, 'midst winters wild,
    You came, girl, to this earth.
And twixt two warring camps, abandoned child,
    You had no sheltered berth.

But hostile cries would not confound you
    Nor din of arms, nor swords,
In thought you stand and hear the mighty
    Old Testamental words

As God Most High to Hebrews chosen
    Himself swore to reveal
This God, with ardent prayers spoken
    The prophet sought with zeal.

The depths then roared, the ground rumbled
    And the sun's light did fade
The earth rocked deep, but Prophet, humbled,
    Saw no God while afraid.

Then tempest came and whirlwind weather
    And thunder in the sky,
And mighty flame with lightning blazing—
    Yet no God did he spy.

Then all grew still, the storms had ended
    The Prophet, not in vain,
Discerned a voice of quiet stillness
    In which God spoke again.

На Т. И. Филиппова
[To T. I. Filippov
(October 1886)]

To T. I. Filippov
(October 1886)

Ведь был же ты, о Тертий, в Палестине,
И море Мертвое ты зрел, о епитроп,
Но над судьбами древней мерзостыни
Не размышлял твой многохитрый лоб.

И поддержать содомскую идею
Стремишься ты на берегах Невы . . .
Беги, безумец, прочь! Беги, беги скорее,
Не обращай преступной головы.

Огнем и жупелом внезапно опаленный,
Уже к теням в шеол содомский князь летит,
Тебя ж, о епитроп, боюсь, что не в соленый,
А в пресный столб суд божий превратит.

For you, o Tertius, did visit Palestine, [440]
And as a bishop you beheld the Dead Sea
But over the fates of foul human deserts
Your cunning mind did not ponder.

And now to uphold the Sodomite idea
you hasten upon the shores of the Neva,
Run and begone, o madman, run, more quickly
And turn not back your criminal old head,

And in an instant singed by fire and brimstone,
the Prince of Sodom flies to Sheol's shades,
I fear God's judgement, o bishop, will turn you
not into a salty but an insipid pillar.

Rhymed Translation

When Palestine my Tertius you did visit,
And even the Dead Sea construed to find,
The doom which rained down on the illicit,
foul ancient towns piqued not your devious mind.

And now you wish the Sodomite idea,
To buttress on our Neva's shores instead,
Run and begone, o madman, run more quickly.
And turn not back your criminal old head,

By fire and brimstone singed all-round and thickly,
To Sheol's shades you, Prince of Sodom, fled.
In God's sight, Bishop, fear I, not a salty,
But an insipid pillar you'll form, dead.

Эммануэль
[Immanu-el (March 11, 1892)]

Immanuel (March 11, 1892)

Во тьму веков та ночь уж отступила,
Когда, устав от злобы и тревог,
Земля в объятьях неба опочила
И в тишине родился с-нами-Бог.

Into the darkness of the ages had the night[441]
Receded when, worn out with evil and care,
The earth found rest in heaven's arms
And God-with-us born in the stillness.

И многое уж невозможно ныне:
Цари на небо больше не глядят,
И пастыри не слушают в пустыне,
Как ангелы про Бога говорят.

There is much that is now not possible:
No longer do kings look up at the sky
And shepherds do not listen in the desert
To the angels speaking about God.

Но вечное, что в эту ночь открылось,
Несокрушимо временем оно,
И Слово вновь в душе твоей родилось,
Рожденное под яслями давно.

But the eternal that had been revealed that night
Is that which cannot be destroyed by time,
And, born long ago in the manger, the Word
Has once again been born within your soul.

Да! С нами Бог,—не там, в шатре лазурном,
Не за пределами бесчисленных миров,
Не в злом огне, и не в дыханье бурном,
И не в уснувшей памяти веков.

Yes! God is with us—but not there in the azure
Cave, nor beyond the numberless worlds.
Not in the evil fire, not in agitated breathing,
Not in the dormant memory of the ages.

Он здесь, теперь,—средь суеты случайной,
В потоке мутном жизненных тревог
Владеешь ты всерадостною тайной:
Бессильно зло; мы вечны; с нами Бог!

He is *here and now.* — Amidst our random
    vanities,
Within the confused stream of life's anxieties
You possess a secret wholly joyous:
Evil is powerless. We are eternal. God is with us!

Rhymed Translation

In depths of time that night is now nested,
On which, fatigued from anger and much fuss,
The earth, embraced in love by heaven, rested,
And gave birth in the quiet to God-with-us.

And much indeed impossible is now.
Our kings no longer look up at the sky.
And shepherds do not listen in the desert,
How angels about God to humans cry.

But the eternal, which this night did open,
Time has no power to vanquish and consume,
And in your soul the new-born Word is spoken,
That was begotten in the manger's gloom.

Yes! God is with us,—not in tents enchanting,
Not in the sky's immeasurable deeps,
Not in the evil fire, nor in wild panting,
And not in memory of yore that sleeps.

He's now here,—in vanities accidental,
In the chaotic streams of daily strife
You hold the joyous mystery fundamental:
God is with us, ends evil, revives life.

Я был велик
[I Was Once Great (1892)]

I Was Once Great (1892)[442]

Я был велик. Толпа земная
Кишела где-то там в пыли,
Один я наверху стоял,
Был с Богом неба и земли.

I was magnificent. The earthly crowd
Swarmed somewhere down below me in the dust.
I alone stood there up above,
In company of the God of heaven and earth.

И где же горные вершины?
Где лучезарный свет и гром?
Лежу я здесь, на дне долины,
В томленье скорбном и немом.

But where are the mountain peaks?
Where are the radiance and the thunder?
I lie here, on the valley floor,
In mute and saddened languidness.

О, как любовь все изменила.
Я жду, во прахе недвижим,
Чтоб чья-то ножка раздавила
Меня с величием моим.

O, how everything's been changed by love.
I wait, remaining motionless in the dust,
I wait for someone's little foot
To crush me with my grandeur.

Rhymed Translation

I was once great, the earthly crowd,
Swarmed somewhere under in the dust,
Alone I stood, on Sinai, proud,
I spoke with God, the high and just.

But where now are the peaks of mountains?
Where now the radiant lightning's boom?
I lie in the ravine, here, mourning
In silent loneliness and gloom.

Oh how has love changed all around
I wait, unmoving, in the dust,
For some light foot to crush to ground,
Me with my proud ego's crust.

В землю обетованную
[To the Promised Land (January 1886)]

Посв<ящается> А. П. Саломону

"Покинь скорей родимые пределы,
И весь твой род, и дом отцов твоих,
И как стрелку его покорны стрелы —
Покорен будь глаголам уст моих.
Иди вперед, о прежнем не тоскуя,
Иди вперед, все прошлое забыв,
И все иди,— доколь не укажу я,
Куда ведет любви моей призыв".

Он с ложа встал и в трепетном смущенье
Не мог решить, то истина иль сон . . .
Вдруг над главой промчалось дуновенье
Нездешнее — и снова слышит он:

"От родных многоводных Халдейских
      равнин,
От нагорных лугов Арамейской земли,
От Харрана, где дожил до поздних седин,
И от Ура, где юные годы текли,—

      Не на год лишь один,
      Не на много годин,
      А на вечные годы уйди".

И он собрал дружину кочевую,
И по пути воскреснувших лучей
Пустился в даль туманно-голубую
На мощный зов таинственных речей:

"Веет прямо в лицо теплый ветер морской,
Против ветра иди ты вперед,
А когда небосклон далеко пред тобой
Вод великих всю ширь развернет,—

Ты налево тогда свороти
И вперед поспешай,
По прямому пути,
На пути отдыхай,

И к полудню на солнце гляди,—
В стороне ж будет град или весь,
      Мимо ты проходи,
      И иди, все иди,

Пока сам не скажу тебе: здесь!

      Я навеки с тобой;
      Мой завет сохрани:
      Чистым сердцем и крепкой душой

Будь мне верен в ненастье и в ясные дни;
      Ты ходи предо мной
      И назад не гляди,
      А что ждет впереди —
      То откроется верой одной.
      Се, я клялся собой,
      Обещал я, любя,

Что воздвигну всемирный мой дом из тебя,
Что прославят тебя все земные края,
Что из рода потомков твоих
Выйдет мир и спасенье народов земных".

Into the Promised Land
(January 1886)[443]

Dedicated to A. P. Salomon

"Abandon all at once your native land,
Your whole race, and your fathers' home,
And, as the archer's arrows are obedient
To the archer, so be obedient to my words.
Go forward without yearning for the past,
Go forward having forgotten it entirely.
Go forward — till I indicate to you
Just hither leads the summons of my love."

He rose from where he lay and, in tremulous
    perplexity,
Could not decide if this was truth or dream;
And all at once an unearthly breath came rushing
Above his head, and he could hear these words:

"From native Chaldean plains of many waters,
From mountain meadows of the Aramaic land,
From Harran, where you've lived till hoary age,
And from Ur, where your youthful years were
    passed —
Not just for one year,
Nor yet for many years,
But for all of eternity depart."

And so he gathered up a group of men.
And following the path of resurrected rays,
He set out into the distance, misty-blue,
Answering the mighty call of the mysterious
    speeches:

"The warm sea air blows straight into one's face.
Forward against the wind go forth.
And when the heavenly dome far off before you
Unfurls a vast expanse of the great waters,
Turn to the left and hasten forward
On a straight path. Rest on that path,
And toward midday look at the sun —
A city or a village will appear to one side,
But you must pass it by, and keep on going,
Keep on going, until I tell you this: Here!
I am with you forever.
Guard this my testament:
with a pure heart
And firm of soul be faithful to me.
In fair or in foul weather.
Walk on before me and do not look back.
And whatever lies ahead
Will be revealed to you by faith alone.
All this I swore. Loving. I promised
That I'd erect my universal house out of you,
That all the earthly lands would glorify you,
That out of the seed of your descendants,
Peace and salvation for all earth's peoples would
    come."

Rhymed Translation

Dedicated to A. P. Salomon

"Forsake with haste your native borders,
And all your race, and father's home.
And as the arrow heeds the archer,
My mouth's words heed as you roam.
Go forth, for former things not caring
Go forth, what's past, do not recall
Until I tell you keep on going,
To reach the place of my love's call."

He left his couch, confused and shaking
Unable to decide, was it truth or dream . . .
When suddenly he feels above a flutter
An alien gust—from which he hears *the theme*:

"From your native Mesopotamian plain
From Aram's grassy hillsides and earth,
From Haran, where grey hairs your own head
    did arraign,
And from Ur, where flowed quickly the years
    of your birth,

    Not just only one year,
    Not just numerous ages,
    But forever I bid thee to fare."

So gathering again his band of nomads
Directed by rising sun's new light
He hastened for the misty-blue horizons
Sustained by the call's mysterious might

"Warm and salty the sea breeze will buffet
    your face,
'gainst this wind, without stopping, go.
And when heaven's horizon recedes beyond
    trace,
And the waters stretch broadly below,

See that leftwards you turn
And proceed at a run,
The straight way do not spurn,
And seek rest from the sun,

And at noon when you feel the sun burn—,
Then a village you'll see or a city,
    Walk on then, pass it by,
    And go on, don't sojourn,

Until I myself say, It's here, see!

    I'm forever with you,
    For my covenant yearn,
    Pure in heart and of firm spirit be!

Remain faithful to me in mishap and fine days,

    Walk before me,
    Look not to past ways,
    What ahead awaits always
    By faith you will see.
    For I swear verily,
    And I promised in love,

That from you, I will raise up my home for
    the world,
That the ends of the earth will in fame your
    name hold,
That the seed of your race to each nation,
Will bring peace and their longed-for salvation."

Неопалимая купина
[The Burning Bush
(September 4/October 1891)]

Я раб греха: во гневе яром
    Я египтянина убил,
Но, устрашен своим ударом,
    За братьев я не отомстил.

И, трепеща неправой брани,
    Бежал не ведая куда,
И вот в пустынном Мидиане
    Коснею долгие года.

В трудах бесславных, в сонной лени
    Как сын пустыни я живу
И к Мидианке на колени
    Склоняю праздную главу.

И реже все и все туманней
    Встают еще перед умом
Картины молодости ранней
    В моем отечестве чужом.

И смутно видятся чертоги,
    Где солнца жрец меня учил,
И размалеванные боги,
    И голубой златистый Нил.

И слышу глухо стоны братий,
    Насмешки злобных палачей,
И шепот сдавленных проклятий,
    И крики брошенных детей . . .

Я раб греха. Но силой новой
    Вчера весь дух во мне взыграл,
А предо мною куст терновый
    В огне горел и не сгорал.

И слышал я: "Народ Мой ныне
    Как терн для вражеских очей,
Но не сгореть его святыне:
    Я клялся Вечностью Моей.

Трепещут боги Мицраима,
    Как туча, слава их пройдет,
И Купиной Неопалимой
    Израиль в мире расцветет".

The Burning Bush
(September 4/October 1891)[444]

I am sin's slave, in burning choler
  One Pharaoh's taskmaster I slew
But then quite frightened by my power,
  I failed my kin to avenge *as due.*

So trembling then from unjust anger,
  I speedily ran not knowing where.
Now within Midian's desert border,
  I live stagnating many a year.

For sleepy, slothful, ho-hum fees,
  Away my desert life I throw.
And on my Midianitess' knees
  My proud head I lowly bow.

And ever rarer, e'er more blurry
  Before my mind's eye still stand
The scenes of my youth's early *worry*
  As stranger in a strange land.

In mist its temples I descry
  The Sun-Priest's lessons *and his smile,*
The painted gods *of earth and sky,*
  The *flowing* blue and golden Nile.

Then mutely hear I my kin moan,
  And their oppressors' callous taunting,
The *drowned* cries of children thrown,
  The whispered curses, stifled, *haunting.*

I am sin's slave, but with fresh vigor
  Yesterday my spirit bloomed
A thorn-bush saw I in the desert
  Burning in fire but not consumed

And heard I from it "Now My people
  Is like the thorn-bush to foe's eyes.
To keep unquenched what's in it holy,
  I vow eternally *as my prize.*

Mitzraim's gods are doomed to tremble
  For like the clouds their fame will fade.
But Israel's glory, like this thorn-bush,
  Will flower and give the nations *shade."*

Appendix: The Protest Letter of Henry Edward Cardinal Manning, London *Times* (December 10, 1890)

———

Dear Sir John Simon, — To you and to your son, in 1882, I owe the knowledge which impelled me to take part in the meeting at the Mansion-house in behalf of the Jews then suffering cruel oppression in Russia; and to you and to your son, again, I owe now the ample and certain information which made me promise that I would move the second resolution at the meeting of the 10th inst. at Guildhall. To you, therefore, I must first write to say that I have now no words to express my deep regret that I am unable to keep that promise. For two months I have been kept to the house by a bad cold caught in September, and I'm afraid of its return at the beginning of winter. Sorely against my will, I am, therefore, unable to take part in the meeting of the 10th inst. For this reason I am compelled to say in writing what I would I could have said in words.

The second resolution seems to be well and wisely drawn. It assumes that the Czar of All the Russias has no share by will, or by knowledge, in the cruel acts of his distant provincial governors. The oppression of proconsuls has always been a stain in the history of great Empires. The personal and domestic virtues of the Czar are, indeed, a sure pledge that he is incapable of harshness to the least of his subjects; and the illustrious lady who shares his throne, like her Royal sister, to whom all Englishmen are chivalrously devoted, is a supreme guarantee of the Imperial justice and clemency. We therefore humbly petition his Imperial Majesty to order an inquiry to be made into the sufferings of the Jewish race, and the laws that affect them, both within the pale where they are compelled to reside, and wheresoever they may be found within the dominions of Russia.

I can hear some of our politicians asking with heat, why we assume to ourselves the freedom of intruding upon the domestic legislation of a friendly State, and even of a great Empire? In answer, I say at once, because we refuse to accept the modern theory of non-intervention, which had its first expression in the question, "Am I my brother's keeper?" We willingly acknowledge that intervention, even such as we exercise at the Guildhall, demands a justifying cause; and we contend that such a cause exists.

It exists manifestly in the fact that what afflicts the Jewish race in Russia afflicts the Jewish race in England, and in every civilized State. The people of Israel in their dispersion are like the nerves of sensation in which we are enveloped; wounded in one spot they suffer in all.

Six millions of men in Russia are so hemmed in and hedged about by penal laws as to residence, and food, and education, and property, and trade, and military service, and domiciliary visits, and police inspection, as to justify the words that "no Jew can earn a livelihood," and that "they are watched as criminals." The narratives before us may be highly coloured, they may be overcharged; but all deductions made, they show both a violent and a refined injustice, which is perpetually as "iron entering the soul."

And, further, when the cry of such a multitude of sufferings is wafted through the commonwealth of Europe, it is surely a part of the comity of nations that we should, with all due respect, make known what we have heard, in the confidence that if things be so, the first to seek out and to treat such evils would be the supreme authority of the realm from whence these wailing voices come.

We show no disrespect in believing that what reaches our ears may not have reached the ears of those who are most highly exalted. Knowledge travels more readily on lower levels, and often does not ascend to the highest regions; the highest are, as a rule, the last to know the excesses and malpractices of their local authorities. We therefore, with all due reverence, petition the Imperial Ruler of all the Russias to take account of all the governors of the Jewish pale; and even this we should not venture to do if the sufferings alleged were not of such a kind and of such an extent as to violate the great and primary laws of human society. On this broad and solid base of natural law the jurisprudence of European civilization rests. The public moral sense of all nations is created and sustained by participation in this universal common law; when this is anywhere broken, or wounded, it is not only sympathy but civilization that has the privilege of respectful remonstrance.

I am well aware of the counter-allegations, not only of the anti-Semitic press, but of guarded and responsible adversaries; nevertheless, it is certain that races are as they are treated. How can citizens, who are denied the rights of naturalization, be patriotic? How can men, who are only allowed to breathe the air, but not to own the soil under their feet, to eat only a food that is doubly taxed, to be slain in war but never to command—how shall such a homeless and cast-exiled race live of the life of the people among whom they are despised, or love the land which disowns them?

It would seem to me that if such were the sufferings of any nation, even in Central Africa, we should be not only justified, but called on, to intervene. How much more, then, in behalf of the race who, in their past and their present and their future, demand of us an exceptional reverence; a race for the sake or history of nearly four thousand years; a present without a parallel dispersed in all lands, with an imperishable personal identity, isolated and changeless, greatly afflicted, without home or fatherland; visibly reserved for a future of signal mercy.

Into this I will not enter further than to say that any man who does not believe their future must be a careless reader, not only of the old Jewish Scriptures, but even of our own. It is not our duty to add to their afflictions, nor to look on unmoved, and to keep the garments when others stone them.

If we know the mind of our Master who prayed for them in His last hour, we owe to them both the justice of the old law and the charity of the new.

Believe me always yours faithfully,
Henry Edward, Cardinal Archbishop

1. This work was first published as "Evrejstvo i khristianskij vopros" in the journal *Pravoslavnoe obozrenie*, in the issues of August (755–72) and September (76–114) 1884. As explained in note 11, the content represents a series of lectures Solovyov delivered in 1882 (for details, see Pt. II, ch. 7). The present translation is from *SSVSS*[10] 4:120–67. On the significance of the title and its translation, see Pt. I, ch. 2. Also note the citation in Pt. II, ch. 2, of El'tsova's reminiscence, "Regarding the Jewish question [Solovyov] used to say that before all else this is a Christian question, a question about the extent to which Christian societies, in their dealings, including with the Jews, 'are actually capable of being governed by the evangelical principles that they orally confess.'"

With regard to the point made by the epigraph, it may be noted that in his essay "When Lived the Hebrew Prophets?" (1896) (*SSVSS*[9] 2:528; see ch. 5 below), Solovyov also celebrates these last three verses of Isaiah 19, emphasizing that the prophet's principal concern is neither politics nor military matters but "the spiritual union of Egypt, Assyria and Israel in the service of one God, who blesses all three of them."

2. See John 13:34: "A new commandment I give unto you, That ye love one another; as I have loved you"; and John 15:12: "This is my commandment, That ye love one another, as I have loved you."

3. See Matt. 5:17: "Think not that I am come to destroy the law, or the prophets: I am not come to destroy, but to fulfill." See also Gal. 2:18, 21; 2 Thess. 1:11.

4. See Rom. 1:20.

5. The pogroms were commonly rationalized by leaders of the state, church, and national(ist) press as fit collective vengeance against Jewish domination of Russians. Thus see Pt. I, ch. 4, §8 and esp. §8.6, on how in 1881 *Novoe vremya* decided that in deliberating whether "to beat or not to beat" the Jews, "to beat" was the right policy for the regime; Pt. I, ch. 4, §8.7, on the tsar's authorizing Ignatiev to appoint commissions to discover the sources of Jewish exploitation and domination (assuming these phenomena as given); and Pt. I, ch. 4, §8.8, on the use of Brafman's *Book of the Kahal* by members of the Gotovtsev commissions.

6. Zech. 8:23: "Thus says the LORD of hosts: In those days ten men from the nations of every tongue shall take hold of the robe of a Jew, saying,

'Let us go with you, for we have heard that God is with you.'" On the child-Israel and the ten animals-nations, see Isa. 11:6 and 11:7.

7. The point anticipates the thesis of Solovyov's lecture of October 1891, "The Fall of the Medieval Worldview" (see Pt. II, ch. 14) and the defense of that lecture in the letters to *Moskovskie vedomosti* translated in Pt. III, ch. 17.

8. Religious indifferentism, denoting any theory denying that man has a duty to worship God by believing and practicing the one true religion, was condemned in Roman Catholic doctrine by Pope Gregory XVI in the Encyclical *Mirari vos* (Aug. 15, 1832); see, e.g., pars. 13 and 14. The challenge it posed to contemporary Christian European apologetics is registered by De Lamennais's *Essai sur l'indifférence en matière de religion* (1859), Newman's "The Difficulties of Latitudinarianism" (1891) and *Apologia pro vita sua* (1891), esp. ch. 5.

9. "Jealousy" and "zeal" are alternative connotations of the Hebrew *qina'* and the Greek *zēlos*, cognates of which are employed by St. Paul in representing the Jews as a party provoked to jealousy by the Gentile reception of the Gospel in Rom. 10:19; 11:11. As Solovyov quotes St. Paul's prophecy at the end of this paragraph, he is evidently seeking to develop his idea that the zeal of religious fanaticism may constitute a positive irrational element by alluding to Paul's teaching that such zeal/jealousy between the Jews and Gentiles may play a providential role. Solovyov may also be suggesting that the present situation is the reverse of the one St. Paul envisioned, since now it is Gentile Christendom, rather than Jewry, that suffers this *jealous zeal* or *zealous jealousy*, prompted perhaps by a primitive, irrational (Cainite) inability to tolerate Israel's claims to be God's elect.

10. Solovyov: "Justice demands one to observe that during the Middle Ages, in general, the highest representatives of the Church, especially the Roman popes, treated the Jews relatively philanthropically, while several popes even patronized them directly, for which they suffered heavy censure from their contemporaries."

11. Solovyov: "In 1882, in a lecture on the historical significance of Judaism, presented at the University of Petersburg and in upper-level courses for women."

12. Solovyov: "It was printed in this year's May–June issue of *Pravos(lavnoe) obozr(enie)* [Orthodox Observer]." Thus Nikanor's article appeared in the same journal and year as the original of the present article. For further discussion of Archbishop Nikanor and the significance of this citation for understanding Solovyov's rhetorical strategy, see Pt. II, ch. 8.

13. Solovyov's term *sud'ba* may be translated as "destiny," "lot," "fortune," or "fate." Scriptural precedent allows one to distinguish *destiny* and *lot* by correlating the former with what is providentially willed for Adam

from the beginning, "in the garden," and the latter with what Adam's children inherit in the "field of exile" (see Levi Khamor, *The Revelation of the Son of Man* [Petersham: St. Bede's, 1989], 8–18). Halfway between these connotations is that of temporal *allotted heritage*. The connotations thus range from (a) the high, divinely willed, and appointed *destiny* to the allotted *fortune / heritage* to the lowly, accidental *fortune* or *lot*. Context may help decide which of these connotations should be used to render Solovyov's usages of *sud'ba*. In the present passage, the first fact pertaining to Israel's original designation as the matrix of the incarnation suggests a high calling or *destiny*, while the second fact, pertaining to its nonrecognition of Christ, defining its present, suggests that what its present experiences is a *lot*. The question then is whether Solovyov's understanding of Israel's future *sud'ba* should be rendered by either of these. To speak of "fortune" or "lot" alone would be to leave this future to chance and fail to reckon with St. Paul's teaching, authoritative for Solovyov (see ch. 3 of this work), that providence preserves and intends to activate Israel's special gifts, heritage, and calling in the future (Rom. 9:4; 11:12, 11:15). This high calling is better captured by the terms "destinies" than by such terms as "lots" or "allotted heritages." The reason Solovyov offers a plural rather than a singular term here probably turns on his envisioning this destiny not as a onetime event but as a recurrent vocation.

14. *Bogochelovechestvo* is rendered here in this traditional manner so that it may resonate with the use of the term by Origen and Hegel as explained in Pt. I, ch. 2.

15. Solovyov here defines present-day Judaism negatively vis-à-vis the Christian proclamation of Jesus as Judaism's Messiah. This definition may offend Jews and contemporary Christian proponents of Christian-Jewish dialogue. Current Catholic reflections on the status of Judaism shift toward attempting to understand Judaism in its own terms by defining it positively in terms of its faithfulness to YHWH via his unrevoked covenants and messianic promises.

16. Cf. Rom. 8:23; 11:16; 1 Cor. 15:20, 23; Jam. 1:18; Rev. 14:4.

17. See Balaam's words in Num. 23:19: "God is not man, that he should lie, or a son of man, that he should repent. Has he said, and will he not do it? Or has he spoken, and will he not fulfill it?" Cf. also 1 Sam. 15:29.

18. Cf. John 10:35.

19. Rom. 11:26.

20. Matt. 27:25.

21. Eph. 1:7; Heb. 9:12. This interpretation of the words of the crowd before Pilate at Matt. 27:25 is infrequent but not unknown among New Testament scholars. See Desmond Sullivan, "New Insights into Matthew 27:24–25," *New Blackfriars* 73.863 (Sept. 1992): 453–57.

22. Luke 23:34.

23. John 20:28.

24. 1 Cor. 15:10.

25. The corollary of Solovyov's observation here is that Israel is a *theotokos*, the title traditionally and dogmatically ascribed to Mary at the Third Ecumenical Council at Ephesus in 431. A Christian objection to the attribution of this title to Israel would imply that Mary, as *theotokos*, neither represents nor fulfills any Israelite vocation to this effect. The objection would, in effect, drive a wedge between Mary as a person and her affiliation with the people of Israel. Since the Gospel portrays Mary using Old Testament threads, one may see in this portrayal the intention to present her, in her most glorious state, as the embodiment and representative of the prophetic daughter Zion, who plays the essential positive "helpmate" role in God's providential and salvific design for mankind (see Joseph Cardinal Ratzinger, *Daughter Zion: Meditations on the Church's Marian Belief* [San Francisco: Ignatius Press, 1983], passim). Solovyov does not develop this point further, but it may be implicit in the eschatological role he attributes to the Jews and to the "Woman Adorned with the Sun" in Solovyov's "Tale of the Antichrist."

26. Solovyov reinserted this section of the essay in his larger work on biblical history, *The Future and the Meaning of Theocracy*, bk. 3: "National Theocracy and the Law of Moses," ch. 6 (392–400).

27. Lit., *"zhidovskim materializmom."* Solovyov is using the pejorative term (*zhid = yid*) for rhetorical purposes to contend with the antisemitism of the right-wing audiences he is seeking to address on the pages of the journal that first published this essay.

28. For more details, see ch. 2 of "The Great Debate."

29. See Solovyov's two articles on the Kabbalah in chs. 6 and 7 below; Burmistrov, "Vladimir Solovyov i Kabbala"; Kornblatt, "Solov'ev's Androgynous Sophia" and "Russian Religious Thought."

30. *Sushij* is the Russian equivalent of the "Who Am" at Exod. 3:14 (cf. RST ad loc.; LXX reads *ho ôn*). Solovyov is therefore thinking here of the divine name (cf. RST Hos. 12:5; John 8:25). In the RST, the term has wider usage, as it is frequently employed to describe the God *"who is* in heaven," e.g., in the Lord's Prayer and parallel passages (Matt. 6:9; 16:17; Luke 11:2; John 1:18; 3:13; Rom. 9:5).

31. Cf. Solovyov's poem on Abraham, "V zemlyu obetovannuyu" (To the Promised Land), written in January 1986.

32. Note the divergence of the biblical text lying before Solovyov from the usual normative versions which read, "By faith, Moses, when he was grown up/become great," rather than "By his faith become great, Moses. . . . "

33. Solovyov's invocation of the concept of kinship to explain the covenant and his observation that the Israelite idea of a divine-human covenant is unique in the history of world religions anticipate the challenging articulation of both propositions in modern biblical studies by Scott Hahn, *Kinship by Covenant: A Canonical Approach to the Fulfillment of God's Saving Promises* (New Haven, CT: Yale University Press, 2009).

34. A key Russian term meaning "a heroic act, deed of renown, or exploit." "Exploit" would be an acceptable rendering, but the reader may prefer to see the key term preserved.

35. Cf. Exod. 33:11; 2 Chron. 20:7; James 2:23; 4:4.

36. Cf. Heb. 11:1: "Now faith is the substance of things hoped for, the evidence [lit., "verification, certainty, conviction" — *elenchos*] of things not seen."

37. John 20:29.

38. While the argument criticizes materialism and empiricism, it does not target those forms of empirical cognition that are required by the scientific method and that demand intellectual discipline and the virtues of honesty and humility before empirically deducible facts. In the late 1890s, Solovyov began to extol the virtues of empiricism more explicitly. The tenor of the present argument implies that empirical cognition is simply to be understood as the taking of external appearances for reality and is not to be confused with a methodology presupposing modern philosophies of science.

39. See Solovyov's review of "When Lived the Hebrew Prophets?," ch. 5 below.

40. This is the hymn "'Addîr Iû!" recited toward the conclusion of the Passover seder. Solovyov cites it following the Latin translation of Johannes Buxtorff (1564–1629), professor of Hebrew at Basel, author of more than fifty works, and owner of a great library on the Hebrew Bible, rabbinic writings, and Yiddish literature that found its way into the Basel Public Library at the beginning of the eighteenth century. His book *Juden-schül* (Jews' School), originally published in Latin as the *Synagoga Judaica* in 1604, and reedited many times, became a standard reference work on Jewish life, institutions, and beliefs. The work is heavily seasoned with Christian anti-Jewish comments, the antisemitic status of which is discussed in the introduction to the English translation of the *Synagoga Judaica* by Alan D. Corré at https://pantherfile .uwm.edu/corre/www/buxdorf/. The latter's translation of the "'Addîr Hû!" in ch. 13 diverges very slightly from Solovyov's.

41. The feminine gender of the Russian word and concept for nature, *priroda* (and likewise of matter, *materia*), is important here as elsewhere in Solovyov's thought since it relates to his Sophiology.

42. The Russian root for "sanctify" also carries the connotation "illuminate."

43. See previous note and n. 64 below.

44. This is the point at which the parallel with book 3.6 of *History and Meaning of Theocracy* ends. Book 7 of that work continues to develop the theme of the roles of sin and sacrifice in maintaining covenantal union with God. Note S. Solovyov's explanation that Solovyov anticipated later criticism of the idealism and romanticism underpinning part 3 by seeking to remove it from circulation.

45. In Judaic studies, character virtues may be called "soul traits."

46. Solovyov offers a reading differing from the M.T., LXX, and Church Slavonic, all of which lack this "to them." The RSV here reads: "By myself I have sworn, from my mouth has gone forth in righteousness a word that shall not return: 'To me every knee shall bow, every tongue shall swear.'"

47. "Tongues" here is supported neither by the M.T. nor by the LXX but only by Church Slavonic.

48. Matt. 5:5.

49. One could argue that Solovyov's conceptions of Hebraic ideas of Godmanhood and of the "goals" of Hebraic prophetic eschatology are too vaguely sketched here to accord with any Jewish self-understanding and eschatology. Christian theologians could also question whether, for lack of discussion of Christian sacramental theology, Solovyov's conception of the cross as the "means" to attaining the Christian goal is also accurate. Perhaps in recognition of the limitations of his present reflections, Solovyov will discuss this issue further in his "Talmud" (see ch. 3 below). Solovyov's fundamental point underscores the New Testament announcement that Christ brings what the Hebrew prophets announce. In this he clearly anticipates the chief tenets of Vatican II's *Nostra Aetate* and subsequent magisterial teaching regarding the messianic *hope* that unites Christians and Jews. Given the revolutionary theological and pastoral import of *Nostra Aetate,* the theological and pastoral import of Solovyov's point, underscoring the unity and theological kinship of Christians and Jews, cannot be underestimated.

50. It is significant that Solovyov here uses the word *dogovor,* "treaty, pact, agreement," rather than *zavet,* "covenant." At issue is whether this reduction of the concept of covenant to that of treaty reflects his own understanding of what a covenant is or his judgment on the limitations of those Jews who understood it so legally.

51. Note how Solovyov ignores the tradition of Jewish martyrdom expressed in books such as 1–4 Maccabees, in which the early Christian theology of martyrdom was rooted, and how he fails to draw a distinction between

what the Jews ought to have done as an occupied nation and what Christians did as private citizens of the Roman Empire. Although an inveterate opponent of capital punishment throughout his life, Solovyov never espoused pacifism but always advocated the principle of just war as evidenced in the anti-Tolstoyan polemic of book 1 of *Three Conversations,* which also does not advocate martyrdom as a course of action for Christian kingdoms.

52. "Earth" is feminine in Russian, and the poetic and theological implications of Solovyov's reflection would be impoverished by neutering her in translation. The same applies to "life" in the next paragraph.

53. The feminine relative pronouns referring to the earth and life are retained to help readers recognize resonances and interrelationships with Solovyov's reflections on Christianity's historical vocation and with his Sophiological ideas.

54. The acceptance of the cross becomes here, for Solovyov, the proof of a substantial and divinizing moral operation. The concept complements Solovyov's earlier explanation that Israel's covenantal theology presupposes the existence of moral kinship between God and man. For Solovyov, therefore, the moral is the spiritual, and goodness is godness. There is thus an implicit ontology in his covenantal theology, soteriology, and ethics that should be recognized when critiquing him for inadequate treatment of ontological issues when comparing and contrasting the goals of Christian and Jewish eschatology.

55. The Russian term here is *soblazn,* "temptation," but is here translated via its biblical connotation given that it is the equivalent of the New Testament Greek term *skandalon,* "stumbling stone" or "[rock of] offense."

56. See n. 25 above on Israel as the "god-bearer," or *theotokos.* It would be interesting to know if Solovyov connected this thought about "best elements that prepared the . . . matter for the incarnation" with Mary given his earlier emphasis that Christ was "by his flesh and human soul, the purest Jew." The NT portrays Mary as the fulfillment of prophecy regarding the attainment of the best element of Judaism: "Daughter Zion" (see Ratzinger, *Daughter Zion*). Solovyov's position depends on the extent to which he, in keeping with the role he accords to Mary in *Russia and the Universal Church,* as well as in book 3 of his *Three Conversations* and the late poem "The Sign" (see ch. 18 below), develops his earlier interests in Sophiology by identifying the eschatological woman of Rev. 12:1 with the Virgin Mary. See David Matual, "Mary and Ecumenism in the Eschatology of Vladimir Solovyov," *Diakonia* 29.3 (1996): 175–88.

57. The conception of the meaning of Godmanhood is developed in the *Meaning and Future of Theocracy* (1885–87), e.g., Book 5.4: "Man taken by

himself is not yet the goal of creation or the crown of divine work. He receives this significance only inasmuch as a real union between God and creation transpires in him or through him. This union, i.e., God's communication, to every other, of the fullness of absolute life, constitutes the true goal of creation. To attain this goal, real union between divinity and creation, the latter must first of all possess a *natural kinship* with the divine, it must in its own substance contain some real basis for absolute being, drawing it [creation] toward God and attracting divine activity toward itself, for unless the things to be united possessed a substantial link, it would be impossible to accomplish a *fully real* union between them" (*SSVSS*⁹ 4:531).

58. Cf. Rom. 8:22 as well as Isa. 11:6, 65:25. Solovyov's emphasis on humanity mediating salvation to the rest of creation also invokes the interplay of his interests in Sophia, ecology, and animal welfare. Solovyov was a vegetarian throughout his adult life, grounding this vegetarianism on the inference that the postdeluvian economy of the Noahic covenant, which permitted the eating of meat (and capital punishment), represented a compromise with divine intentions for creation and was therefore no longer "very good" in God's eyes. It is this biblical exegesis that also strengthens his opposition to capital punishment. In his later days, Solovyov perceived the presence of Sophia in nature, forests, and lakes and understood her as the divine idea behind and animating creation, as that ideal which creation is called, through human agency, to realize.

59. This shows that Solovyov, having located in postbiblical Jewish Kabbalistic tradition, a (nonproscribed) foundation for tolerating the idea of divine incarnation, considered but found wanting the thesis that Jews reject Christianity because of this doctrine.

60. Cf. Isa. 11:10, 12; 62:10; Ezek. 27:7.

61. "Fortunes" here is chosen to convey the multiplicity of senses, including "destiny" and "allotted heritages" (see note 14 above), that the word *sud'by* plays in this chapter. Solovyov's shift to the theme of Jewry's and Christianity's common social task anticipates a similar shift in contemporary documents pertaining to Jewish-Christian dialogue. See, e.g., Delegates of the Bishops Committee on Ecumenical and Interreligious Affairs of the United States Conference of Catholic Bishops (BCEIA) and the National Council of Synagogues (NCS), "Reflections on Covenant and Mission," *Origins* 32.15 (Sept. 5, 2002).

62. Solovyov's full meaning is unpacked in *The History and the Future of Theocracy* (1885–87). Here he is combining foundational biblical protology, which commands man to "subdue the earth" (Gen. 1.26), with classical prophetic eschatology, which envisions the attainment of that call via the restora-

tion of international harmony and the harmony between humanity and nature (cf. the superscription taken from Isaiah at the beginning of the work and other prophetic passages cited above), overcoming the temporary compromises of the Noahic covenant.

63. Rom. 11:1, 2, 5.

64. In Russian, a priest is a *svyashhennik*, either a "hallowed / consecrated" one or a "hallower / consecrator," a *sacerdos*.

65. The Russian plays on *napravlyat'* (to aim, direct, indicate), *upravlyat'* (to steer, navigate, govern; from *kubernesis*, the art of steering), and *ispravlyat'* (to rectify, redirect, repair, reform).

66. A fundamental rabbinic principle; see, e.g., *m. Aboth* (*Pirqe Avot, The Ethics of the Fathers*), 1:1.

67. See Solovyov's article on monothelitism in the Brockhaus-Efron *Encyclopedic Dictionary* (reprinted in *SSVSS*[10] 10:424–25). He also cites St. Gregory of Nazianzus's pacific address to the monothelites in treating of the ecclesial status of Jewish Christians in his 1885 article on the Israel of the New Covenant (see below).

68. For more detailed treatment of Solovyov's understanding of Islam, see "The Great Debate and Christian Politics" (1883); portions pertaining to the heirs of Ishmael in book 2, "The Primordial Destinies of Humanity and the Theocracy of the Patriarchs," in *The History and Future of Theocracy* (1885–87), and his *Muhammad, His Life and Religious Teaching* (1896).

69. For a more detailed discussion see Solovyov's "The Meaning of Protestantism" in ch. 6 of "The Great Debate and Christian Politics."

70. The original is the plural of *podvig*.

71. Isa. 36:6: "Behold, you are relying on Egypt, that broken reed of a staff, which will pierce the hand of any man who leans on it. Such is Pharaoh king of Egypt to all who rely on him."

72. Solovyov's footnote: "The book of the famous Strauss, *Der alte und der neue Glaube*, may serve as a sufficiently instructive confirmation of this statement." Solovyov is referring to David Friedrich Strauss's *Der alte und der neue Glaube: Ein Bekenntniss als Antwort*, which first appeared in 1872.

73. As evidenced by "The Tale of the Antichrist," the "Drama of Plato's Life," and the poem "Panmongolism," his growing realization that Russia would capitulate to secularism and betray the theocratic idea finally drove him and his last writings into an apocalyptic mood.

74. Conversations with Jonathan Sutton and Ewert van der Zweerde in the mid-1990s informed me that it is difficult for political historians to find the first instances of terms and concepts relating to the idea of civil society in nineteenth-century Russian literature. This paragraph clearly furnishes one such instance.

75. Solovyov's footnote: "We are familiar with a number of beautiful exceptions: those rare people who have self-sacrificially consecrated their life to the nation's welfare. Their noble activity will not remain fruitless, but it will not change the general situation."

76. Gen. 2:18.

77. The underlying Russian term is *druzhnomu*.

78. The underlying Russian term, *druzhinnomu*, carries the sense of teamwork.

79. Solovyov is punning on the words of the Polish anthem "Jeszcze Polska nie zginela" (Poland Has Not Yet Perished), also called "Dabrowski's Mazurka" or "The Song of the Polish Legions in Italy," which was written in July 1797 and became a national hymn in 1831 and the state anthem in 1926.

80. Compare Solovyov's position with that of Milton Anastos, *Constantinople and Rome*, Variorum Collected Studies (Aldershot: Ashgate, 2001), www.myriobiblos.gr/texts/english/milton1_index.html.

81. *Ne pozvolyam* (Russian) or *nie pozwolimy* (Polish) would have been the motion by which any member of the Polish feudal nobility (*szlachta*) in the Polish Parliament (Sejm) would exercise the notorious *liberum Veto*, issued in 1652, to block legislation and therefore, in the long run, weaken Poland's parliamentary system.

82. The term for the privileged class in Poland from the late Middle Ages up to the eighteenth century and to a lesser extent the nineteenth. In contradistinction to all other European nobility, all members of the *szlachta* elected the king (making Poland a res publica, or *Rzeczpospolita*), and no important legal, military, or economic change could be made by the king without their representative permission in Parliament.

83. Having been abolished in 1865 as a kingdom, Poland regained its independence in 1918, the second republic lasting from 1921 to 1939.

84. In "The Great Debate and Christian Politics," Solovyov lamented that Christianity, defined via its Godmanhood as a divine instrument for reconciling the contemplative, God-orientated Eastern culture with the pragmatic and human-oriented Western culture, was eventually split by the very East-West tensions or schism that it was designed to heal.

85. S. L. Frank's anthology of Solovyov's writings excluded this entire section, deeming it naive and "historically outdated." Removing it, however, fails to explain the relevance to the entire work of the prophecy of Isaiah 19:24 cited epigraphically at its start (see next note). One may observe, nonetheless, that Solovyov's understanding of Poland's vocation bears a striking similarity to John Paul II's formulation of the same on June 3, 1979, at the cathedral in Gniezno: "Does not Christ want, does not the Holy Spirit demand, that the

Pope, himself a Pole, the Pope, himself a Slav, here and now should bring out into the open the spiritual unity of Christian Europe" (for citation, see Peggy Noonan, *John Paul the Great: Remembering a Spiritual Father* [New York: Viking, 2005], 28; see also her article "We Want God," *Wall Street Journal,* Apr. 7, 2005, http://online.wsj.com/article/SB122479408458463941.html). Secular misinterpretations of the significance of this speech are critiqued in George Weigel, *Witness to Hope: The Biography of John Paul II* (New York: HarperCollins, 2005), 304–17 nn. 40–45). It is interesting to note how the impetus given by this Polish pope to East-West Christian and Jewish-Christian reconciliation fulfills Solovyov's vision of Poland's vocation.

86. See Isa. 19:24, the epigraph to this essay: "In that day Israel will be the third with Egypt and Assyria, a blessing in the midst of the earth." In the context of the argument, it may be inferred that Solovyov understood Egypt and Assyria in this text as archetypes for Eastern and Western cultures, or priestly and royal authorities, among which Israel must continually play a significant, prophetic role. However "historically outdated" part 3 of this work is, it expresses a commitment to a theocratic vision that played a central role in Solovyov's life and work at this period and is thus crucial to the vision informing this tract.

87. The Russian term here is *Narodnosti.* See the discussion of this term in Pt. I, ch. 2.

88. In Jewish idiom, this would be a *Beit ha-Midrash* or *Beit Midrash,* lit., "House/Hall of (Scripture) Study."

89. For more information on Joseph ben David Rabinovich (1837–99), see Pt. II, chs. 6 and 10.

90. See John 1:47. The Gk. *alēthōs* preceding *israēlitēs* is an adverb to be translated as "truly" or "indeed" but is easily mistranslated as an adjective.

91. See Nathaniel's words to Jesus at John 1:49. In the context of John 1, Solovyov's reference to "coming to Christ and seeing" echoes Jesus's invitation at John 1:39 to John the Baptist's disciples to "come and see" where he was staying. If Solovyov is also echoing Caesar's *veni, vidi, vici,* the last term, *vici,* would correspond to the acknowledgment of Christ's reign.

92. It may thus be inferred from this and from the explanation that the sermon cited below was enclosed with a letter (see text marked by note 97 below), that Solovyov met and corresponded with Rabinovich.

93. After the pogroms of 1881, Rabinovich became convinced that the Jewish problem would only be resolved by returning to a homeland. Arriving in Jerusalem in 1882, he began reading the New Testament to obtain descriptions of historic locations. Doing so, he recognized Jesus as "our brother" and as Messiah and became convinced that this recognition was prerequisite to Jewish welfare.

94. Rabinovich, returning to Kishinev in 1885 from Berlin, having been baptized there on March 24 by the Protestant Prof. C. Mead, but using a Hebrew formula he himself composed, meant to ensure that baptism would signify entry into Christianity but not into any of its Protestant denominations (see Wilkinson, *The Life of John Wilkinson,* 207–21; and Kai Kjaer-Hansen, "Rabinowitz and Lichtenstein," *Concordia Theological Quarterly* [1992]: 187–93). Subsequently, he established the first modern messianic Jewish congregation, The First Synogogue/Assembly of the Israelites of the New Covenant. It sought to preserve Jewish identity by maintaining Jewish feasts and orders of service while integrating the New Testament into the Hebrew scriptures but avoiding doctrinal and denominational controversies.

95. Solovyov's footnote: "I have been naturally bound to adjust the jargon of the literal translation of the Hebrew original by reference to Russian idiom."

96. The correct citation is Deut. 17:14–20.

97. Exod. 19:5.

98. Rom. 9:4; 11:15.

99. Lam. 2:13.

100. The M.T., LXX, RST, and Luther Unrevdierte (1545) versions of this well-known text all read: "I (am the) Lord, your healer." The Slavonic text reads: "For I am your Lord God, your healer." But the phrase and the title are so popular in Judaism that the replacement of "Lord" by "God" doubtfully reflects dependence on any actual text. If it comes from Rabinovich himself, it must be motivated by the pious Jewish practice of avoiding the divine name.

101. Isa. 10:33. Lit., "God Sabaoth"; the biblical expression is "Lord of Hosts" or "Lord Sabaoth." On the avoidance of the divine name, see note 101 above.

102. Isa. 11:1.

103. M.T., LXX, Slav., and RST versions of Isa. 11:1, 2, all read "stump" or "root" where Rabinovich or Solovyov offers "hewn tree."

104. 1 Sam. 16:11.

105. Cf. Luke 2:32; Acts 28:20; Rom. 5:2; Col. 1:27; Tit. 2:13.

106. Isa. 11:6.

107. 1 Kings 16:11–13 LXX, Vulg., Slav. = 1 Sam. 16:11–13 M.T.

108. 1 Sam. 17:8.

109. This is the title of the popular Jewish song "David Melech Yisrael Chai veKayyam," originating from the Talmud (*b.Rosh Hashanah* 25a), which records it as part of an instruction from Rabbi Yehudah the Prince, the second-century editor of the Mishnah, to the sages of Galilee to proclaim the new

month and, by adding this phrase, to affirm their allegiance to David's kingdom.

110. This is the M.T. and RST but not the LXX or Slavonic version of Gen. 49:10.

111. This is the M.T. and RST version of Isa. 45:15.

112. 1 Sam. 17:26; M.T., LXX, Slav., and RST all refer to the "uncircumcised Philistine." The version as cited lacks the word "Philistine."

113. 1 Sam. 17:33.

114. 1 Sam. 17:26. Instead of "claw" in the cases of the lion and the bear in this verse, the M.T., LXX, and Slav. read "hand"; the RST lacks "hand" or "claw."

115. 1 Sam. 17:37.

116. The text cites the Slavonic version of Ps. 118:22 and Matt. 21:42; Mark 12:10; Luke 20:17; Acts 4:11; 1 Pet. 2:4, 7.

117. 1 Sam. 17:25.

118. The correct reference is John 17:3. The error may be attributable to Rabinovich or Solovyov or the texts used by either.

119. Phil. 2:7, cited according to the Slavonic and not the RST version.

120. Deut. 17:16–20.

121. M.T., LXX, and RST version of Isa. 11:4.

122. RSV version.

123. The Divine Name is spelled out in Russian. This demonstrates that the previous replacements of the Divine Name by God are not necessarily motivated by reverence for the Divine Name but for some other reason.

124. Isa. 9:6.

125. "May He make peace upon us and upon all Israel," is the concluding benediction of the Kaddish.

126. Isa. 11:6, cited according to the M.T. and LXX but, owing to the use of the cognate of the Latin *pardus* (leopard), neither according to the RST nor the Slavonic version, suggesting perhaps a free translation.

127. 1 John 4:2, cited according to the Slavonic text.

128. Solovyov's footnote: "Joseph Rabinovich composed two confessions of faith: the long version with 25 articles and the short one with 7. We present the latter, only supplementing it at one point from the longer."

129. Cf. Rom. 10:19; 11:14; 11:25, citing Deut. 23:21.

130. Cf. Col. 1:20; Eph. 2:16; Rom. 5:11; 11:15; 2 Cor. 5:18–20.

131. Cf. Isa. 11:9; Hab. 2:14.

132. Cf. 2 Kings 19:15; Ps. 33:14; 99:1; Isa. 37:16. In biblical imagery, heaven is God's throne and earth his footstool (Isa. 66:1; Acts. 7:49).

133. "Faith alone" betrays a Lutheran reading of Rom. 3:28 (cf. the "allein durch den Glauben" in Luther's German Bible [1545], ad loc.). The

grounds for this "alone" are explored in commentaries and Catholic-Protestant polemics about the tension between Gal. 2:16 (3:11, 24), Rom. 3:28 (5:1; 10:4); and James 2:24. The reading "alone" hints at Rabinovich's moorings in Protestant Christianity and anticipates his eventual affirmation of this allegiance.

134. Cf. the Nicene Creed.

135. Rom. 3:30.

136. Cf. Gal. 3:28; Rom. 10:12.

137. Regarding the problem of monotheletism, condemned at the Sixth Ecumenical Council of Constantinople in 680, Solovyov's favorite church father, St. Maximus the Confessor (580–662), who presided at the Council, taught that Christ had two natural wills (*duo thelemata*), the divine and the human, but one opinion / thinking / object / willed will (*mia gnome*). See Henry Palmer Chapman, "Monothelitism and Monothelites, in *The Catholic Encyclopedia,* ed. Charles G. Herbermann, 1913:10, www.newadvent.org/cathen/10502a.htm.

138. Gregory the Theologian (Nazianzus), archbishop of Constantinople, delivered renowned orations to convert Arians and Macedonians or Pneumatomachi, followers of Macedonius, patriarch of Constantinople, who denied the divinity of the Holy Spirit. The heresy was condemned formally at the Ecumenical Council of Constantinople in 381 (see www.ccel.org/ccel/schaff/npnf207.iii.html).

139. Solovyov's footnote: "The Works of St. Gregory the Theologian. M. 1884. Part 4, pp. 12–13." In translating the passage, I correlated Solovyov's rendering with the translation of St. Gregory the Theologian, "Oration XLI. On Pentecost," pars. 7–8, by Browne and Swallow in *Christian Classics Ethereal Library,* www.ccel.org/ccel/schaff/npnf207.iii.xxiv.html.

140. Eph. 4:13; cf. 1:23.

141. Ps. 121:4.

142. John 7:38.

143. Eph. 2:2.

144. John 8:44.

145. Rom. 11:33.

146. This letter expresses ideas remarkably similar to those with which Solovyov's work "Jewry and the Christian Question" commences and which inform its contents. This suggests either that Solovyov received these ideas from Rabinovich or that he counseled Rabinovich to base the letter on these ideas.

147. Rom. 11:15.

148. The article was first published in the August 1886 edition of *Russkaya mysl'* (Russian Thought), and reprinted in *SSVSS*[9] 6:1–29.

The Karaites were a Jewish sect, prominent in the Middle Ages, that rejected rabbinic claims for the authority of their Oral Torah (and thus of the Talmud) and called for a return to the basics of Judaism through submission to the literal interpretation of Mosaic Law and the Hebrew scriptures (=*Mikra/Miqra*), from whence the community took its name, Karaites or Qaraites (proclaimers/readers [of Scripture], or people of the Scriptures). Rabbinic tradition traces their foundations to the Jewish Babylonian scholar Anan ben David (ca. 715–95). Remarkable similarities between Karaite and Qumran doctrine are often attributed to the influence of a Dead Sea Scroll discovery in the ninth century A.D., as reported by Patriarch Timotheus (see Simon Syszman, "A Propos du Karaisme et les Textes de la Mer Morte," *Vetus Testamentum* 2 [1952]: 343–48), although such late origins are disputed by the sect itself (see www.karaite-judaism.com).

149. These are sectarians related to the Moravians, Hussites, and Bohemians (cf. Henry Rimius, Henry, *A candid narrative of the rise and progress of the Herrnhuters* . . . [London: William Bradford, at the Sign of the Bible, in Second-Street, 1753]).

150. Alternatively spelled Molokane (Milk Drinkers), these are the sectarians belonging to the so-called spiritual Christians who flourished in the second half of the eighteenth century and early nineteenth century in Russia. They were founded either by Semyon Uklein, who abandoned Orthodoxy after marrying the daughter of Pobirochin, leader of the Dukhobors, or stemmed back further, along with the Dukhobors, to the iconoclasts. Their name is associated with their insistence on consuming milk and other prohibited foods during Lent and fast days to register their repudiation of the Orthodox Church and other ecclesiastical and civil practices, e.g., all external religious ceremonies, the principle of civil authority, oath taking. While denying the full divinity and humanity of Jesus Christ, they recognized no other teacher of the faith but him and laid stress on the Bible and the priesthood of all believers (see A. Schipman, "Raskolniks," in *The Catholic Encyclopedia*, vol. 12, www.newadvent.org/cathen/12648b.htm.

151. The *Kormchaya* (Book/Chart/Map of the Helmsman/Pilot/Navigator), either the equivalent of the ancient Greek Orthodox *Nomokanon* or the *Pedalion*, was the *Corpus Juris* of the Orthodox Church. It consisted of the *Nomocanon* and supplements of canonical collections of conciliar and patristic decisions and commentaries attributed to Photius and Theodore Balsamon and was published and reedited in 1650 and 1653 (it is cataloged in the Hollis Library under Russkaya pravoslavnaya tserkov' [author], *Kniga kormchaya* . . . 1653).

152. This principle defines the impetus behind the Reformed movement in Judaism in the 1840s.

153. Note the silver and golden rules of Judaism (*b.Shabbath* 31a) and Christianity (Matt. 19:19; 22:39; Mark 12:31, 33; Luke 10:27; Rom. 13:8–10; Gal. 5:14; James 2:8) as grounded on Lev. 19:18, 34, and the expression of the identical idea in the opening paragraph of Solovyov's "Jewry and the Christian Question."

154. Solovyov's invocation of his triadic theocratic principle harmonizes well here with the rabbinic conception of the "three crowns": of kingship, priesthood, and Torah; cf. *b.Yoma* 72b; Stuart Cohen, *The Three Crowns: Structures of Communal Politics in Rabbinic Jewry* (Cambridge: Cambridge University Press, 1990). The "cessation of prophecy" is a well-known construct of intertestamental Judaism.

155. For a detailed corroboration of this thesis, see Martin Goodman, *The Ruling Class of Judea: The Origins of the Jewish Revolt against Rome,* AD *66–77* (Cambridge: Cambridge University Press, 1987).

156. Matt. 22:16; Mark 3:6; 12:13. Cf. Mark 8:15.

157. Cf. the *'piqwrws* (derived from Epicurus and linked to *pqr* 'to be free of restraint') in *b.Sanhedrin* 38b, 90a, 99b, 100a; and *b.Beitzah* 22b; *Nedarim* 23a, 49b. See www.jewishencyclopedia.com/view.jsp?artid=1640& letter=A.

158. This was, in Greek mythology, the sacred image kept in Athena's temple at Troy, lending the city inviolability. In legend it was reported as being stolen by Odysseus and Diomedes (*The Little Iliad,* in Evelyn-White, *Hesiod, the Homeric Hymns and Homerica,* 1982; see also Ovid, *Metamorphoses* 13.340, 380) and brought to Rome by Aeneas (Pausanias, *Description of Greece* 2.23.5).

159. *m. Aboth.* 1.1.

160. Prior to the 1947 discovery of the Dead Sea Scrolls at Qumran, the basis for affiliating the Essenes with a community living below Engedi on the western coast of the Dead Sea came from Josephus, Philo, and Pliny. Solovyov's philosophical and theological observations on their significance are interesting vis-à-vis what was said of them in historical-deductive scholarship in his day and contemporary scholarship that has developed those views (cf., e.g., Emile Schürer's *The Jewish People in the Time of Jesus Christ (175* B.C.–A.D. *135),* trans. T. A. Burkitt et al.; rev. and ed. Geza Vermes and Fergus Millar [Edinburgh: T & T Clark, 1886]; Geza Vermes, *The Complete Dead Sea Scrolls in English: Complete Edition* [New York: Allen Lane/Penguin Press, 1997]). Solovyov's presumption that there were no more than three main parties or "philosophies" in Second Temple Judaism clearly derives from Josephus (*Ant.*

18.1.1–2; War 2.118–68), who classifies the Zealots as a late offshoot from the Pharisees (*Ant.* 18.1.6). Assuming that the community at Qumran was both Essene and harbored apocalyptic texts known elsewhere, such as 1 Enoch and Jubilees, it is interesting to note how Solovyov's use of "Essene" verges on what many contemporary scholars would also call "apocalyptic." Consequently, aspects of Solovyov's attempt to correlate apocalyptic philosophy with the formation of a concrete sect or party anticipates contemporary scholarly studies that followed Paul D. Hanson, *The Dawn of Apocalyptic* (Philadelphia, PA: Fortress Press, 1975); and Robert P. Carroll, *When Prophecy Failed: Cognitive Dissonance in the Prophetic Tradition of the Old Testament* (New York: Seabury Press, 1979).

161. Matt. 11:12.

162. This principle is evident in Solovyov's exposition of the petition for daily bread in seeking the kingdom in his commentary on the Lord's Prayer in *The Spiritual Foundations of Life* (1882–84). The principle itself is broadly disseminated in Aristotle's *Nichomachean Ethics*. Nietzsche echoed it at the time: "we premature births of an as yet unproven future need for a new goal also a new means. . . . " *The Gay Science*, §382 (1887), in Ansell-Pearson and Large, *The Nietzsche Reader*, 382.

163. Solovyov's footnote: "The Haggadah is the name of everything in the Talmud which does not relate directly to the Law but assumes a religious, educational, pedagogical, and poetic form."

164. Matt. 28:18.

165. Matt. 10:16.

166. Matt. 5:17.

167. Matt. 7:15–27; Luke 6:43–49.

168. Matt. 22:29.

169. The underlying Russian term is *podvig*.

170. John 11:50.

171. Matt. 23:2, 3.

172. Solovyov's footnote: "The Mishnah denotes repetition (the repetition of the Law), and consists of tractates, arranged into six orders, comprehensively dealing with all Jewish religious concerns and with all the mundane affairs with which they are inextricably bound."

173. Solovyov's footnote: "Gemara denotes completion or fulfillment."

174. All the following citations are to the tractates of the Babylonian Talmud unless otherwise stated. This citation comes from *Sanhedrin* 59a (cf. *Baba Kama* 38a; *Abodah Zarah* 3a, 26a). The passage is part of the rebuttal, in this case by Rabbi Meir, to Rabbi Yohanan's dictum, notorious in antisemitic polemics, that "a non-Jew who studies the Torah is worthy of death." The

broader context is as follows: "R. Yohanan said, 'A non-Jew who studies the Torah is worthy of death, as the verse states (Deut. 33:4), "Moses commanded us the Torah as an inheritance"—implying that it is for us but not for them [non-Jews]' . . . R. Meir said, 'How do we know that a non-Jew who studies the Torah is like a High Priest? From the verse which states (Lev. 18:5), " . . . that a man shall carry out these laws by which he shall live." The verse does not refer to Jews but to the generic "Man"—thereby teaching that even a non-Jew who studies Torah is like a High Priest.'" See ADL, "On the Use of the Talmud in Anti-Semitic Polemics," 9, 10.

175. *m.Horayoth* 13.

176. *Shabbath* 31a.

177. The Hebrew term in question means "to magnify," and the cognate noun denotes a garland used for glorifying people.

178. *m.Aboth* 4.7. See also *Nedarim* 62a.

179. *Berakoth* 17a. What Solovyov renders as "Rectification of life" is simply "repentance" in Hebrew.

180. *Pesachim* 50b. The actual text reads, "A man should always occupy himself with Torah and good deeds, even if not for their own sake, for out of [doing good] with an ulterior motive there comes [doing good] for its own sake."

181. *m.Aboth* 3.19. The actual text reads, "Rabbi Akiba said: All is foreseen, but freedom of choice is given. The world is judged in goodness, yet all is proportioned to one's work."

182. *Hullin* 7b.

183. *Berakoth* 17a. "Divine Splendour" = *Shekinah* in Hebrew.

184. *m.Aboth* 4.17; "duty" = "precept" in Hebrew.

185. *m.Aboth* 2.4. For "Sacrifice," the Hebrew reads "set aside/annul."

186. *Sota* 48b. Cf. Matt. 6:25–31, 34.

187. *Berakoth* 54a. The injunction is grounded on Deut. 6:5, the commandment to love the Lord with all one's heart, soul, and might. The word for "might" (*me'od*) resembles the words "to thank" (*modeh*) and "situation" (*midah*).

188. *Berakoth* 61a.

189. *Berakoth* 12b.

190. *m.Aboth* 4.1.

191. *Midrash Genesis Rabbah* 22.6. Cf. *Sukka* 52b; and Solomon Schechter, *Some Aspects of Rabbinic Theology* (New York: Macmillan, 1909), 248–49.

192. *Sota* 5a.

193. *Erubin* 13b. Cf. Matt. 23:12; Luke 14:11; James 4:6.

194. *Sanhedrin* 58b.

195. *Baba Metzia* 58b.

196. *Baba Kamma* 93a; *Megillah* 8.5.

197. *Shabbath* 88b and *Gittin* 36b, citing Judges 5:31. Instead of "beloved of God," the Hebrew reads "those who love him." The "him" assumes the form of an objective genitive noun suffix on the active participle "those who love," but the construction resembles the form of a plural noun with a possessive genitive suffix and hence may be read as "his lovers." See Gesenius, *Hebrew Grammar,* par. 116. I.

198. Cf. *Yoma* 23a; *Rosh Hashanah* 17a; *Shabbath* 151b; *Megillah* 28a on Lev. 19:8.

199. *Ta'anit* 20a–b.

200. *Baba Bathra* 49b. Cf. Matt. 5:34–37.

201. *Hullin* 94a. "Gentile" here translates *'obed kokhabim,* "worshipper of stars," i.e., idolator. The blanket condemnation of cheating anyone, including Gentiles, offsets the accusation, based on *Sanhedrin* 57a or *Baba Kamma* 113b, that Jews are not obligated to correct a Gentile's accidental business mistakes.

202. This teaching may have been adapted from *Arachin* 15b: "Reish Lakish said, 'One who slanders makes his sins reach unto heaven, as it is said, "They have set their mouths against the heavens, and their tongue walketh through the earth"'" (Ps. 73:9), or from *Midrash Rabbah on Ecclesiastes* 9:14: "There is a man who sins against earth but not against heaven, [and another who sins] against Heaven but not against earth. He, however, who utters slanders sins against both, as it is said, 'They have set their mouth against the heavens, and their tongue walketh through the earth.'"

203. *Sanhedrin* 103a, citing Job 13:16: "A hypocrite shall not come before God."

204. Either *m.Aboth* 1.15: "Receive all men with a cheerful countenance"; or *m.Aboth* 3.16: "Receive every man with good cheer."

205. *Baba Bathra* 9a: "Almsgiving (*tzedakah*) is equivalent to all the other religious precepts combined."

206. *Sukka* 49b; "*Gemiluth Hasidim* (acts of loving-kindness beyond the letter of the law) is greater than charity (lit. = "*tsedakah*" = "righteousness" = idiom for "almsgiving" given to fulfill Torah requirements), for it is said, 'Sow to yourselves according to your *tsedakah,* but reap according to your *hesed* (loving-kindness)'" (Hos. 10:12).

207. *Ketuboth* 68a: "if a person averts his eyes to avoid giving charity, it is as if he committed idolatry."

208. *Berakoth* 55a.

209. *Sanhedrin* 22a: "He whose first wife has died, [is grieved as much] as if the destruction of the Temple had taken place in his days, as it is written . . ." (Ezek. 24:16–18).

210. *Megillah* 6b.

211. *Shabbath* 75a, citing Ps. 28:5.

212. *Yoma* 38b–39a: "Resh Lakish said, if one comes to defile himself, the door is open (lit., "he has an opening"). But if he comes to purify himself, he is helped by heaven (see Prov. 3:34). The school of Rabbi Ishmael taught, if a shopkeeper sells naphtha and balm, when a customer wants to measure the naphtha, the shopkeeper says, 'measure it on your own,' but when a customer wants to measure balm, the shopkeeper says, 'let us measure it together, so that we both may become perfumed.'" *Shabbath* 104a also attributes the saying to Resh Lakish and not to Rabbi Simeon ben Levi. That Solovyov attributes the saying to Simeon ben Levi instead suggests, as may be suspected from the terminological divergences highlighted throughout these notes, that he is not citing or reading the Talmud directly but rather an anthology of rabbinic ethical maxims.

213. *Shabbath* 152a. This source lacks the phrase "while everyone is equal before the face of death," and is part of an exposition of Eccles. 12:5, citing the verse and reading: "'because man goes to his long home.' R. Isaac observed: This teaches that every righteous person is given a habitation . . . " This strongly implies that Solovyov is citing an anthology and not reading the text directly.

214. Eccles. 9:8.

215. *Shabbath* 153a. "We learnt elsewhere, R. Eliezer said: 'Repent one day before your death.' His disciples asked him, 'Does then one know on what day he will die?' 'Then all the more reason that he repent to-day,' he replied, 'lest he die to-morrow, and thus his whole life is spent in repentance. And Solomon too said in his wisdom, Let thy garments be always white; and let not thy head lack ointment.' R. Johanan b. Zakkai said: 'This may be compared to a king who summoned his servants to a banquet without appointing a time. The wise ones adorned themselves and sat at the door of the palace. ["For,"] said they, "is anything lacking in a royal palace?" The fools went about their work, saying, "can there be a banquet without preparations?" Suddenly the king desired [the presence of] his servants: the wise entered adorned, while the fools entered soiled. The king rejoiced at the wise but was angry with the fools. "Those who adorned themselves for the banquet," ordered he, "let them sit, eat and drink. But those who did not adorn themselves for the banquet, let them stand and watch."'" The divergences between this passage and Solovyov's citation again suggest the use of an intermediate source.

216. *Shabbath* 88b, 89a: R. Joshua b. Levi also said: "When Moses ascended on high, the ministering angels spake before the Holy One, blessed be He, 'Sovereign of the Universe! What business has one born of woman amongst us?' 'He has come to receive the Torah,' answered He to them. Said they to Him, 'That secret treasure, which has been hidden by Thee for nine hundred and seventy-four generations before the world was created. Thou desirest to give to flesh and blood! What is man, that thou art mindful of him, And the son of man, that thou visitest him? O Lord our God, How excellent is thy name in all the earth! Who hast set thy glory [the Torah] upon the Heavens!' 'Return them an answer,' bade the Holy One, blessed be He, to Moses. 'Sovereign of the Universe' replied he, 'I fear lest they consume me with the breath of their mouths.' 'Hold on to the Throne of Glory,' said He to him, 'and return them an answer,' as it is said, 'He maketh him to hold on to the face of his throne, And spreadeth his cloud over him,' whereon R. Nahman observed: 'This teaches that the Almighty spread the lustre of His Shekhinah and cast it as a protection over him.' He [then] spake before Him: 'Sovereign of the Universe! The Torah which Thou givest me, what is written therein? I am the Lord thy God, which brought thee out of the Land of Egypt.' Said he to them [the angels], 'Did ye go down to Egypt; were ye enslaved to Pharaoh: why then should the Torah be yours? Again, what is written therein? Thou shalt have none other gods: do ye dwell among peoples that engage in idol worship? Again what is written therein? Remember the Sabbath day, to keep it holy: do ye then perform work that ye need to rest? Again what is written therein? Thou shalt not take [the name . . . . in vain]: is there any business dealings among you? Again what is written therein, Honour thy father and thy mother; have ye fathers and mothers? Again what is written therein? Thou shall not murder. Thou shalt not commit adultery. Thou shall not steal; is there jealousy among you; is the Evil Tempter among you?' Straightway they conceded [right] to the Holy One, blessed be He, for it is said, 'O Lord, our Lord, How excellent is thy name,' etc., whereas 'Who has set thy glory upon the heavens' is not written. Immediately each one was moved to love him [Moses] and transmitted something to him, for it is said, 'Thou hast ascended on high, thou hast taken spoils [the Torah]; Thou hast received gifts on account of man: as a recompense for their calling thee man thou didst receive gifts.' The Angel of Death too confided his secret to him, for it is said, 'and he put on the incense, and made atonement for the people'; and it is said, 'and he stood between the dead and the living,' etc. Had he not told it to him, whence had he known it?" As with the preceding quote, the divergences between this passage and Solovyov's citation suggest the use of an intermediate source.

217. Ps. 8:1, 4.

218. I know of no version that grounds this reduplication of "gods" in the citation of Exod. 20:3 or Deut. 5:7.

219. Ginzberg's translation at this point reads: "Are there perchance idolaters among ye, that ye are in need of the Torah?" (*Legends*, 3:113). That the source of Solovyov's variant is not the Talmud again suggests that the text has been adapted by an intermediate source.

220. That Solovyov follows neither the biblical order of the commandments (honoring parents should precede murder, and the latter should precede bearing false witnesses) nor the imaginative details of the Haggadah at this point bespeaks a very free summary of the text and implies that the adaptation of the text derives not from Solovyov but from his source.

221. Cf. Mark 2:27.

222. *Makkoth* 23b–24a. Solovyov's transliteration here does not necessitate access to *Makkoth*. The text is frequently cited, and he did not need it to cite Habakkuk 2:4. Nevertheless, the citation of the Hebrew of Habakkuk 2:4 witnesses to his study of Hebrew with Rabbi F. Getz from 1879 on.

223. This is a vital sentence that clarifies and develops Solovyov's understanding of the essential root differences between Judaism and Christianity beyond what he wrote in "Jewry and the Christian Question." F. Getz commented: "This affirmation is upheld by learned specialists, Christian as well as Jews." Getz made the affirmation on the basis of his essay on Jewish-Christian relations in his *Slovo podsudimomu* (*The Floor to the Accused*), 5.

224. The transliteration should read: "ushemartem et-huqqotay *we et mishpatay asher ya'aseh* otam haadam wahay bahem ani Yhwh" (and you shall keep my statues *and my ordinances which* the man *who does them* will live by them, I am the Lord). Furthermore, the citation should read "Lev. 18:5" rather than "8:5." As Solovyov's knowledge of Hebrew would not have permitted him to make such errors, and as they are not mentioned in Solovyov's reflections in his correspondence with Getz about the errata in the text, they must come from the printer.

225. The reason for Solovyov's dismissal of the claims to this status by various Oriental nations and cultures would be interesting to clarify. His subsequent concerted reflection on these cultures, e.g., in "China and Europe" (1890; *SSVSS*[9] 6:84–134) takes stock of the objection: "The first fact (characterizing the Chinese ideal) is the historically unexampled strength and firmness of the Chinese national governmental body. During the time that other nations, living aloof like China, had either long before lost their independence, becoming an easy prey to foreigners, like India, or disappeared completely even in an ethnographical sense, like the ancient Mexicans or the Peruvians, China not only preserved without any loss, in the course of three or four thou-

sand years, its national and political originality but also extended its influence to neighboring tribes. . . . The admirers of China justly point to its longevity, as an important advantage, and they are right also in the fact that this advantage is not accidental but is really deserved by the Chinese. Having set as a foundation to their national life the commandment, *honor thy father*, they rightly received the promised reward: *that it may go well with thee, and that your days may be prolonged, upon the earth*. Honoring the dead above all, the Chinese became the most tenacious of life" (6:126–27). The citation in italics is from Deut. 5:16. See also n. 229 below.

226. *Shabbath* 32a. The text reads: "Leave the drunkard alone, he will fall of himself."

227. Matt. 12:25–26; Mark 3:24; Luke 11:17.

228. The Russian term for "families" here is literally "tribes," pointing to a Russian version of Gen. 28:14 rather than Gen. 18:18; 22:18; 26:4.

229. The continuation of the citation from "China and Europe" in n. 225 above contributes to an understanding of Solovyov's thought on Judaism's unique *historical* status: "But alongside this, there remains another equally indubitable fact, namely, that Chinese culture, with all its firmness and material richness, ended up being spiritually fruitless and useless to the rest of humanity. It is good for the Chinese themselves, but it yielded neither any great idea for the world nor any single eternal and unconditionally valuable creation in any field. . . . The single exception is Lao-Tse. But while one may wonder at the brave and original turn of his thought, one should not forget that everything essential in this thought had already been said with no less courage but with greater clarity and fullness by the Indian mystics, by the authors of the Upanishadas and the Baghavadgita. . . . But we need not criticize from a Christian and a European standpoint the limitations of Chinese life and thought and the impossibility for the human spirit to be completely satisfied by those boundaries of temperance and prudence which express the Chinese ideal. The bankruptcy of these limitations is criticized by the Chinese themselves, who strain whole masses to escape, at least in their individual existence, from the boundaries of the rational-moral order and harmony of Chinese life. Some do so physically, stupefying themselves with opium, which grants them a fantastically limitless life instead of that temperate reality to which they are doomed in the sober condition. Others turn to more spiritual means, which are offered to them by the servants of two mystical religions: Taoism and Buddhism—which are foreign to the Chinese proper, i.e., the Confucian ideal" (*SSVSS*[9] 6:127–28). Cf. Solovyov's 1896 review of E. Havet (1891), Pt. III, ch. 5.

230. Solovyov's footnote: "Innocent III, *Opera ed. Migne*, vol. I, col. 865." The bull *Constitutio pro Judaeis* issued by Innocent III in 1199 was first

issued in 1120 by Pope Callixtus II (1119–24) and reissued by successive popes until the fifteenth century. The bull reiterated the church's official position, established by Pope Gregory I (598), objecting to persecutions of Jews and synagogues and forced baptisms.

231. Solovyov's footnote: "See the *Complete Coll. of Laws*, No. 7612." The reference is to an earlier edition of the *Polnoe sobranie zakonov Rossijskoj imperii. . . s 1649 po 12 dekabrya 1825 goda.* The event referred to concerns Rabbi Baruch ben Leib, also known as Rabbi Leib b. Baruch or Baruch Leibov, and Alexander Voznitsyn who were burned on July 15, 1738.

232. Solovyov refers to the affair of Dr. August Rohling, a Prague academic who, on being charged with perjury by Rabbi Joseph Samuel Bloch for his *Talmudjude*, countersued the latter for libel. To wage his case, he employed Robert Pattai, M.P., and an apostate Jew named Ahron Briman, alias Dr. Justus, to write the *Judenspiegel*, a commentary on 100 alleged passages in the Jewish code, *Schulchan Aruch*, pertaining to Talmudic ordinances against Christianity, and asserting that the whole Talmud consists of such passages. Briman ended up in prison following a trial in 1883 for racist incitation by the district attorney of Münster where an antisemitic paper cited passages from his book. Rohling was persuaded to withdraw his complaint when he became persuaded that Christian scholars, especially Franz Delitzsch, testified that he could not win the case. Some sources pertaining to the works Solovyov cites at this point (see next note) are D. Löwy, *Der Talmudjude von Rohling in der schwurgerichtsverhandlung vom 28. oktober 1882* (Wien: D. Löwy, 1882); K. (Karpel) Lippe, *Der Talmudjude vor dem katholisch-protestantisch- orthodoxen Dreirichterkollegium Rohling-Stocker-Pobedonoscew* (Pressburg, 1884); K. Lippe, *Die Gesetzsammlung des Jedenspiegels zusammengestellt und gefälscht von Aron Briman, Justus [pseud.] Beleuchtet und berichtigt von K. Lippe.* (Jassy, Rumania: Buch & Steindruckerei H. Goldner, 1885); Adolf Lewin, *Der Judenspiegel des Dr. Justus, ins Licht der Wahrheit gerückt* (Magdeburg: Druck von D. L. Wolff; zu beziehen durch die Expedition der "Israelitischen Wochenschrift," 1884).

233. Solovyov's footnote: "We will only mention those compositions which we had occasion to read: Dr. V. Hoffmann, *Der Schulchan Aruch*, 1885; Dr. Joseph Kopp, *Zur Sudenfrage*, 2. Aufl., 1886; Der Jakob Ecker, *Der Judenspiegel im Lichte der Wahrheit*, 2 Aufl., 1884; Franz Delitzsch, *Rohling's Talmudjude*, 7 Aufl. 1881; idem, *Zweite Streitschrift in Sachen des Antisemitismus;* idem., *Neueste Traumgesiche etc.*, 1883; idem, *Schachmatt den Blutlügnern etc.*, 2 Abdr. 1883. Dr. M. Joël, *Meine Gutachten über den Talmud der Hebräer*, 1883. Of these eight authors (including Rohling and Justus), *three* are antisemites, *two* are Jews, and *three* are Christians."

234. Solovyov's footnote: "The bias is so strong that it even led to the voicing of the suspicion that Dr. Ecker only lent his name to the Apologia, which was written by Justus himself. This suspicion seems to us to have little factual basis."

235. See Ecker, *Der Judenspiegel*, 3rd ed., 1921.

236. Solovyov's footnote: "*Shulchan-Aruch*, i.e., a set table, composed by Rabbi Joseph Caro in the sixteenth century in Palestine and then revised for European Jews by Moses Isserles. This book pertains to the Talmud in approximately the same way as our *Kniga Pravil* [Book of Rules] relates to the ancient *Kormchaya*." On the *Kormchaya*, see n. 153 above.

237. Solovyov's footnote: "The title, deriving from the Latin *res publica*, of the Polish-Lithuanian kingdom of the Middle Ages."

238. Solovyov's footnote: "This fact is related in S. Solovyov's *The History of Poland's Decline*." Solovyov here cites his father, the historian Sergei Mikhailovich Solovyov. The work was well known, having been already translated into German in 1865.

239. Solovyov's footnote: "If the matter concerned the poor implementation of Christian commandments in national life, this reproach would have been just, even though it could, more or less, be applied to all religious confessions. But the honorable missionary deems us pagan not because of that but simply because we belong to the Orthodox Church."

240. Luke 4:23.

241. Matt. 7:5; Luke 6:42.

242. Jerusalem Talmud, *Baba Metzia* 2.5, 8c. Also see the midrash *Debarim Rabbah* 3.3: "Once, Rabbi Shimon ben Shetach bought a donkey from an Arab. His students went and found a precious stone hanging around [the donkey's] neck. Rabbi said to him (Prov. 10:22): 'It is the blessing of G-d that enriches.' R. Shimon ben Shetach said to him, 'I bought a donkey. I did not buy a precious stone.' He went and returned it to the Arab and the Arab said, 'Blessed is the G-d of Shimon ben Shetach.'"

243. Jerusalem Talmud, *Baba Metzia* 2.5, 7a.

244. Jerusalem Talmud, *Baba Metzia* 11.

245. Solovyov's and editor's footnote: "Regarding the unique aspects of the Jewish *Weltanschauung*, see our article 'Jewry and the Christian Question' (inserted in vol. 4 of the Complete Works. [G. R.])."

246. Matt. 12:33; Luke 6:44.

247. The underlying word is *pravda*.

248. The underlying word is *pravednost'*.

249. An echo of Solovyov's work *The Spiritual Foundations of Life*.

250. The phrase directly echoes Alexander Pushkin's poetic drama *Skupoj rytsar'* (The Miserly/Covetous Knight).

251. *m.Aboth*, 1.2.

252. The underlying word is *pravda*.

253. Solovyov's words for "grasp" (understand) and "embrace" (accept / receive) are *ponyat'* and *prinyat'*, respectively.

254. The proposition echoes the basic principle of Solovyov's "Jewry and the Christian Question."

255. The present article, translated from the text reprinted in *SSVSS*⁹ 6:340–46, is a review of the work by Stepan Iakovlevich Diminsky, *Evrei, ikh verouchenie i nravouchenie*, published in St. Petersburg in 1891 on the basis of a master's thesis written at the Kiev Theological Seminary titled "A Study of the Talmud," 1868, published in Kiev in 1869 and reprinted in 1893 (218 pp.), without the punctuation errors in the title sarcastically highlighted by Solovyov.

256. Solovyov uses the term *knizhka* (booklet) rather than *kniga* (book). He uses the same term in reviewing E. Havet's work (ch. 5 in this part), explaining as follows: "I say *booklet*, and not book, because what seems to be the significant scope of this composition turns out to be a deceptive outward appearance, created only by typographical contrivance. In reality, this is only a reproduction (without changes and additions) of a journal article" (*SSVSS*⁹ 6:523).

257. The word in question should be "role." The translation attempts to convey the orthographic error highlighted by Solovyov in the passage that reads *rod* (genre, species) instead of the presumed word *rol'* (role).

258. A work by R. Isaiah b. Judah Loeb Berlin (1725–99), also known as Isaiah Pick after his father-in-law, Wolf Pick, of Breslau. His claim to fame rests on his extensive literary activities devoted to glosses and textual notes on Talmudic literature. The *Omer ha-Shikhah* (Forgotten Sheaf), one of these, contains Talmudic halakhot not mentioned by the codifiers (of the Talmud). It was first published as an addendum in his *Kashot Meyushav* and printed separately in 1866 in Johannisberg, Germany.

259. Moses b. Naphtali Hirsch Rivkes (1695–1771/72) was one of the spiritual leaders of the Lithuanian Jewish community. Having escaped the Chmel'nitsky massacre of 1648 and survived the Polish-Russian War, he settled in Amsterdam, where he wrote a commentary on the *Shulchan Arukh* and the work *Be'er ha-Golah* (The Well/Explanation of the Exile), after a term in the Mishnah (*Erubin* 10.14). The *Shulchan Arukh* (Set Table) is a repository of Jewish law, written originally by Rabbi Yosef Karo, containing the opinions only of the great Sephardic sages, the *Rishonim*. The *Mapah* (Table-Cover) of Rabbi Moses Isserles (the "RAMA") supplemented it with the opinions of the great Ashkenazic *Rishonim*.

260. For references, see n. 267 below.

261. Solovyov's footnote: "*Italics mine.*"

262. Rabbi Shabbetai Kohen (1621–62), known by acronym as the "Shakh" after writing his major halakhic commentary, *Siftei Kohen* (The Lips of a Priest, taken from Mal. 2:7). Born in Vilna, he fled to Moravia during the Chmel'nitsky massacres in 1648–56. His commentary covers the sections "*Yoreh Deah*" and "*Choshen Mishpat*," in the *Shulchan Aruch*, dealing with the Laws of *kashrut* as well as with monetary and business affairs. It is not clear why Solovyov glosses *Siftei* with a "(*sic*)." He either thinks this is a mistake for *Sifrei* ("books of") or wishes to correct the reader who might think so. Given that the previous instance of *sic* ("robe," instead of "role" above) marked a palpable mistake and that authors typically use "*sic*" to highlight errors in a source on which they are commenting, it is probable that this time Solovyov himself mistakes the word.

263. Solovyov's footnote: "*Italics mine.*"

264. The Russian original here is *evrejskij*. As it is a citation, it is rendered "Jewish" rather than Jewish[E].

265. Solovyov's footnote: "*Italics mine.*"

266. The work is that of Daniil Abramovich / Avraamovich Khvol'son (1819–1911), *O nekotorykh srednevekovykh obvineniyakh protiv evreev: Istoricheskoe issledovanie po istochnikam* (On various medieval accusations against the Jews: a historical source study), St. Petersburg, 1880. Khvol'son was a well-known Orientalist and paleographer. In academic circles, he was remembered for a polemical dispute with his onetime student Abraham Harkavy regarding the Karaite manuscripts from the collection of Abraham Firkovich (1786–1874), a Karaite leader and scholar. His significance for Jewish-Christian relations in Russia lies in his status as a Jewish convert, early membership in the Society for the Promotion of Jewish Enlightenment (see Pt. I, ch. 4, §5.4) and effectiveness in refuting the blood libel charge on two important occasions in Russian history, once in 1854 and again in 1879, as explained in Pt. I, ch. 4, §§4.5, 7.1.

267. This is the collection of articles by Samuel Joseph Fünn (1818–90), Chayim Leib Katsenelenbogen (1814–76), and Lev Osipovich Levanda (1835–88), *Mirovozzrenie talmudistov*, published in St. Petersburg in 1874–76.

268. This being a citation, "Jew" is the translation of *evrej*.

269. Solovyov's footnote: "For the 'uninitiated' reader we will note that the numbering of the folios of Talmudic tractates remains invariable in all editions."

270. Solovyov's footnote: "A few years ago I was obliged to familiarize myself well with the tricks used by the tendentious denouncers of the Talmud. See my article on this subject in the August edition of *Russkaya mysl'*, 1886."

271. Solovyov's footnote: "Addition mine."

272. *Sanhedrin* 17a: "Rab Judah said in Rab's name: None is to be given a seat on the Sanhedrin unless he is able to prove the cleanness of a reptile from biblical texts. Rab said: 'I shall put forward an argument to prove its cleanness.'" "Rab" here is not an abbreviation for a rabbi or a "teacher" but the title of Abba Arika, a Babylonian rabbi of the third century, a disciple of Rabbi Judah the Prince, who established the principles of analyzing the Mishnah that led to the compilation of the Babylonian Talmud. On this error, not caught by N. I. Bakst, while proofreading the article for publication, see Solovyov's letters to Getz, #28, #29.

273. This being a citation, "Jew" is the translation of *evrej*.

274. The translation is based on the version of the review reprinted in *SSVSS*[9] 6:521–42. Only the first and the last two pages of this review are translated here, since the rest principally deals, like *The History and the Future of Theocracy*, with biblical matters and requires a broader and separate treatment.

275. This is Solovyov's spelling. The transliteration of the "aleph" with a "j" may be a typographical error.

276. This passage is translated in this volume because the quotation from Isa. 19:23–25 serves as the epigraph to "Jewry and the Christian Question."

277. The ellipsis is Solovyov's.

278. The underlying word is *pravda*.

279. Solovyov's knowledge of the Kabbalah is documented by Kornblatt, "Russian Religious Thought" and "Solov'ev's Androgynous Sophia"; and Burmistrov, "Vladimir Solovyov i Kabbala." Essential information, including a description of his early notebooks from 1875 pertaining to his studies in the British Museum, remained unknown until the publication of Sergei M. Solovyov's biography in 1977. The present article was originally published as an entry on the Kabbalah in the *Encyclopedic Dictionary*, 26 (1894): 782–84, and reprinted in *SSVSS*[9] 9:111–16. Solovyov developed it from his introduction to David Gintsburg's article on the Kabbalah (see the following text).

280. m. *Hagiga 2.1*: "The [subject of] forbidden relations (incest) may not be expounded in the presence of three nor the work of creation in the presence of two nor [the work of] the chariot in the presence of one, unless he is a sage and understands of his own knowledge."

281. Solovyov's footnote: "Kabbalistic tradition also speaks of a third type of reincarnation: the *dybbuk* which involves possession by a disembodied spirit, demonic or human."

282. Solovyov wrote this article as a foreword to the article by David Gintsburg, "Kabbala, misticheskaya filosofiya evreev" (Kabbalah: Mystical

Philosophy of the Jews), *Voprosy filosofii i psikhologii* 22 (1896): 277–300. Solovyov's foreword is reprinted in *SSVSS*[12] 12:332–34.

283. Solovyov's footnote: "In my generally accessible abridgement *Kabbalah* (in the named *Dictionary*) I have obtained from the amiable author the permission to utilize by the way some data and citations from his article, which I could not cite while it was not published. I hurry to fulfill this obligation."

284. In mystical philosophical literature, *Atsiluth* is traditionally rendered "Emanation."

285. The obituary is translated from the reprint in *SSVSS*[9] 8:441–44.

286. As the escorts of magistrates who held power (*imperium*) in ancient Rome, the *lictors* carried *fasces*, bundles of rods surrounding an ax. The rods and axes were used to lash and execute people, respectively.

287. Rev. 14:13. Solovyov has adjusted the verse to give a singular form to the plural in the original final clause: "**they will rest** from **their** labors and **their** deeds will follow **them**."

288. These letters were collected and published by E. L. Radlov in *Letters*, 2:142–91 (see bibliography, *Letters of Vladimir Solovyov*). The footnotes in the margins are usually the editor's, presumably Radlov's, but are occasionally signed "F.G.," indicating glosses by Getz. All such footnotes will be in quotations below. For a bibliography of Getz's works on Solovyov and scholarly articles about him, see Pt. II, ch. 6, Conclusion. The formatting of the letters below seeks to simulate as much as possible the formatting of the original by Radlov

289. Solovyov calls Iudejstvo (Judaism) the subject of the famous article and work that was eventually titled "Evrejstvo [rendered by me as Jewry] and the Christian Question."

290. This is the date in the manuscript.

291. Nikolai Nikolaevich Strakhov (1828–96) was a literary critic, Neo-Slavophile, nationalist-idealist philosopher, and editor of the Slavophile journals *Vremya* (Time), *Epocha* (Epoch), *Zarya* (Dawn). See Linda Gerstein, *Nicolai Strakhov, Philosopher, Man of Letters, and Social Critic,* Russian Research Center Studies 65 (Cambridge, MA: Harvard University Press, 1971). His significance in the context of Solovyov's Jewish writings is multifold, as explained in Part II above, e.g., as the chief exponent of the time of Danielevsky's nationalism and target as such for Solovyov's polemical label as a "Western/mechanistic Buddhist/passive pacifist" (see Pt. II, ch. 1).

292. Revel = Tallinn, the capital of Estonia.

293. *Vestnik Evropy,* a monthly journal dedicated predominantly to historical and political commentary by leading academics with a liberal tendency.

It was edited from 1866 to 1908 by the well-known historian, liberal activist, and publicist/journalist Mikhail Matveyevich Stasyulevich (1826–1911).

294. The first newspaper written in ancient Hebrew in Russia, founded in Odessa by Alexander Cedarbaum in 1860 and transferred to St. Petersburg in the mid-1870s. Joseph D. Rabinovich contributed regularly to the paper, espousing the ideas of the Jewish Enlightenment (Haskalah). See Pt. I, ch. 4, §6.1.

295. For the identity of M. M. Stasyulevich, see n. 293 above.

296. *Moskovkiya (Moskovskie) vedomosti* was Russia's largest newspaper, published daily since 1859 and edited by Mikhail Katkov in 1850–55 and 1863–87 and by S. A. Petrovsky between 1887 and 1896. Mikhail Nikifirovich Katkov (1818–87) was a leading architect, along with K. P. Pobedonostsev, R. A. Fadeev, D. A. Tolstoy, and others, of a reform in Russian conservative ideology based on liberal political ideals and national ideology. In addition to editing *Moskovskie vedomosti*, he founded and edited from 1861 the literary and political monthly journal *Russkij vestnik* (Russian Herald), which published the best known works of Turgenev, Tolstoy, and Dostoevsky. Dostoevsky criticized his position in "Polemika protiv M. N. Katkova," *Polnoe sobranie sochinenij.* T.19. L., 1985. See also the Third Norton Edition of *Crime and Punishment.* Klier notes that while he was suspicious of the influence of the *kahal* and objected to Jewish privilege, he consistently opposed Judeophobic positions, e.g., by resisting the linking of the assassination of the tsar to Jewish revolutionaries (see Pt. I, ch. 4, §§6.4, 8.2, 8.4). Such judgments in current scholarship will find noteworthy Solovyov's testimony to Katkov's ultimate influence on Russian-Jewish relations.

297. *Russkaya mysl'*, the most widely read monthly literary-political journal in Russia (reaching a circulation of 14,000), was published in Moscow from 1880 to 1918 and abroad until 1927. It was founded and chaired until 1905 by the publisher and translator Vukol Mikhailovich Lavrov and espoused the principles of constitutional democracy. The chief editor from 1880 to 1885 was Sergei Andreevich Yuriev (1821–88), under whom it bore a Slavophile character distinguished by a mystical devotion to the freedom of speech and conscience. After Yuriev's death it was edited by Viktor Aleksandrovich Gol'tsev (1850–1906), under whom it took on a decidedly progressive line. The journal received two official warnings, one in 1883, the second in 1893 (a third warning was fatal to a journal). See http://ru.wikipedia.org/wiki/Russkaya_Mysl'_zhurnal.

298. One of three spas in the province of Styria celebrated for waters favorable for diseases of the digestive organs (of which Solovyov probably died).

299. Liberio Antonovich Sacchetti (1852–1916) was the son of the solo flutist Antonio Sacchetti, professor of history, musical theory, and the phi-

losophy of aesthetics. In 1886 he became associate professor of music at the St. Petersburg Conservatory.

300. Alexander Mikhailovich Butlerov (1828–86), well-known professor of chemistry in Kazan' and St. Petersburg, who died in France in 1886.

301. Cf. Jesus's description of Nathanael as "a true Israelite in whom there is no guile," in John 1:47.

302. Getz identified this as the poem "Wordless thoughts and nameless feelings." Sergei Solovyov notes that Fet considered it one of Solovyov's best (S. Solovyov, *Zhizn'*, 231).

303. Constantine Petrovich Pobedonostsev (1827–1907), jurist, statesman, adviser to three tsars, and Ober-Procurator (director-general) of the Orthodox synod from 1880 to 1905. According to Dubnov's conspiracy theory, the pogroms were the direct result of his reactionary program of Russification and response to the assassination of Alexander II. This view has been rejected by Rogger, who nonetheless calls him the most articulate antisemite in the government until his retirement in 1905. See Pt. I, ch. 4, §7.7, 9, 9.3.

304. Joseph George Strossmayer, bishop of Bosnia and Sirmium and archbishop of Djakovo in Yugoslavia, patronized Solovyov's ecumenical efforts to move Orthodoxy to recognize the bishop of Rome and so unite the Slavs with the West.

305. Lit., "God will not betray, the swine won't eat": a Russian proverb whose literary instances have been variously translated in English, e.g., "Touch wood; it's sure to come good"; "That never ends ill which begins in God's name"; "Whom the Good Lord a hand lends, no one in the way stands." See http://cab.al.ru/eproverb/027.html.

306. The summer residence of the imperial family and visiting nobility, located sixteen miles from St. Petersburg.

307. Getz identified this as the Hebrew of Ps. 41:8–10: "All who hate me whisper together about me; they imagine the worst for me. They say, 'A deadly thing has fastened upon him; he will not rise again from where he lies.' Even my bosom friend in whom I trusted, who ate of my bread, has lifted his heel against me."

308. Getz identified this as the Hebrew of Ps. 25:16–17: "Turn thou to me, and be gracious to me; for I am lonely and afflicted. Relieve the troubles of my heart, and bring me out of my distresses." The work read as *v'ani* should have been read as *v'oni*.

309. This is the Holy Trinity Lavra, the immense Orthodox monastery founded by St. Sergei of Radonezh in 1337, in dedication to the Holy Trinity, in the Sergiyev Posad Moscow district; see www.stsl.ru/. Solovyov retired there for three weeks to cope with his romantic and political troubles, his deteriorating health, and ensuant vocational crises (see Mochulsky, *Vladimir*

Solovyov, ch. 11; S. Solovyov mentions Solovyov's exhaustion at this time, *Zhizn'*, 250–51.

310. The Root Hermitage, a famous monastery situated, according to tradition, on the site of a miraculous spring marking the appearance of the Kursk Root Icon of the Holy Virgin in 1295; see www.kurskroot.com/korennaya _hermitage_home.html. Solovyov wrote to his mother of devotionally carrying this icon in company with Fet's Christian wife, Maria Petrovna (S. Solovyov, *Zhizn'*, 243).

311. The text gives the abbreviation for "Ego Vysokorodie" (lit., "his high/noble birth") the honorific title for persons of the fifth class (brigadiers and state counselors) in the Table of Ranks inaugurated by Peter the Great in 1721.

312. This is the address of the renowned poet Afanisy Afanasievich Fet (Shenshin) (1820–92), a great friend and maternal relation of Solovyov. S. Solovyov describes their relationship in some detail (S. Solovyov, *Zhizn'*, 243–44). As Fet was conservative and pantheist, their friendship cooled as Solovyov swung leftward at the start of the 1890s but was still warm at this time. During this stay, Solovyov entertained Fet by reciting Catullus to him by heart and the two were translating eighty lines of Virgil's *Aeneid* a day. They translated book 6 together, and Solovyov translated books 7–10 and the Fourth Eclogue on his own (*Letters*, 4:106; S. Solovyov, *Zhizn'*, 244).

313. Solovyov writes of this also to his poet friend Fet (*Letters*, 3:115; S. Solovyov, *Zhizn'*, 241).

314. Solovyov is referring to the first volume of his *Theocracy*. See the letter of June 20 / July 2, 1887, to Fr. P. Pierling, a Russian Jesuit and expert in Russian-Vatican relations. Cf. *Letters*, 3:148; and S. Solovyov, *Zhizn'*, 246–47.

315. This is a reference to the tsar's order on Dec. 5, 1886, to the minister of education, Ivan Delianov, to limit Jewish access to education. Delianov drew up the *Numerus Clausus* (quotas), which were passed in July 1887. See Pt. I, ch. 4, §9.5.

316. Mikhail Katkov retired from the editorship of *Moskovskia vedomosti* in 1887. The succeeding editor from 1887 to 1896 was S. A. Petrovsky. Solovyov is probably referring to his friend, the poet, philosopher, and publicist Dmitry Nikolaevich Tsertelev (1852–1911) who was considered but rejected for the post in 1896. See www.hrono.info/organ/rossiya/mos_ved.html, Dec. 16, 2009.

317. *La Russie et l'Église universelle* was Solovyov's principal 1887 summer project, according to S. Solovyov, *Zhizn'*, 244.

318. Evgeny Mikhailovich Theoktistov (or Feoktistov), head of the State Ministry for the Affairs of the Press. In his correspondence, Solovyov ob-

serves that in spite of the friendly letters he received from Theoktistov, the state censors have stopped the publication of his article "The Sins of Russia" at the same time that ecclesial censors put pressure on his *Theocracy* (*Letters*, 2:187–91; S. Solovyov, *Zhizn'*, 237).

319. Apolon Nikolaevich Maikov (1821–97), a realist Slavophile poet, renowned for glorifying Russia's beauty, for "The Lay of Prince Igor's Campaign" and other poems, including "The Wanderer." Dostoevsky shared with him on Dec. 11, 1868, his idea for Prince Myshkin of *The Idiot*, and Vasily Perov and Ivan Kramskoy drew well-known portraits of him in 1872 and 1883.

320. Princess Elizaveta Grigorievna Volkonskaya (1838–97), an active proponent of Catholicism, author of two polemical books, who converted to Catholicism in 1887 and maintained a correspondence with Strossmayer and the Jesuits. Her home was the center of the Catholic movement in Russia. She befriended Solovyov in 1880 and exerted on him, according to Mochulsky, a strong Catholic influence (Mochulsky, *Vladimir Solovyov*, ch. 11).

321. A citation from Pushkin's "Elegy" of 1930. It reads somewhat like this: "The snuffed out mirth of my mad years / weighs gloomily upon me like a hangover / But then as wine - the sorrow of past days / the older in my soul it is, the stronger / My path is sad - I see but toil and sorrow / the stormy sea of my tomorrow. // But oh, my friends, I do not wish to die / I wish to live, to think and ache / I know that pleasures come / in sorrows, cares and heartache / I'll drink of harmony again / and pour out tears on my vision / And then perhaps my sad decline / will be lit up by love's bright smile" (trans. mine). The word translated as "sad" (in "my path is sad" above), *unyl*, "cast down, despondent," is the root of the word *unyvat'*, which Solovyov has used on several occasions in corresponding with Getz, the last time saying that he is not growing despondent on account of Pobedonostsev but is cheering himself up with the motto: "Whom God sustains, swine won't retain," or perhaps "Whom God assumes, swine won't consume."

322. Prechistaya (Pure) Street in the central administrative district of Moscow was named in connection with the miracle-working icon of Our Lady of Smolensk, which was housed in the Novodevichy monastery to which the street led from the Kremlin. The house of Likhutin is No. 39 and was, according to Solovyov's letter to his sister Nadya in 1886, one of his two favorite places on earth (S. Solovyov, *Zhizn'*, 225). It was later the residence of the artist M. A. Vrybel' and the composer N. A. Rimsky-Korsakov; see http://ru.wikipedia.org/wiki/Улица_Пречистенка.

323. Osip Konstantinovich Notovich (1849–1914) the Jewish journalist and playwright who converted to Russian Orthodoxy and edited the liberal newspaper *Novosti*. For more detail, see Part II, ch. 11 and n. 166.

324. Ernest Renan (1823–92), French philosopher and author of the influential *Vie de Jésus* (*Life of Jesus*), which sought to treat Jesus's life and the Bible with the same scientific methodology as was to be accorded any historical subject.

325. The reference is to the princes of the ruling house of the Battenberg family (anglicized as Mountbatten in Britain) and of the ruling house of Saxe-Coburg and Gotha (the Windsors in Britain), perhaps specifically to Alexander Joseph of Battenberg, who lost his throne in Bulgaria in 1886 and was replaced by Prince Ferdinand Maximilian Karl Leopold Maria of Saxe-Coburg and Gotha in 1887.

326. David Friedrich Strauss (1808–74), German theologian and author of *Das Leben Jesu* (*The Life of Jesus*), the pioneer work that grounded the modern (liberal) scholarly quest for the historical Jesus.

327. A reference to *kanshi*, a specialized form of seppuku, a feudal Japanese practice whereby a lord's servant protests the lord's decision by ritual suicide.

328. Leopold Von Ranke (1795–1886), the German historian considered, by his insistence on primary sources, emphasis on narrative history, avoidance of (Hegelian) philosophical summations and unifying theories, to be one of the founders of modern source-based history, along with the likes of Heinrich Schliemann (1822–90) and Christian Matthias Theodor Mommsen (1817–1903).

329. Vladimir Pavlovich Bezobrazov (1828–89), economist and publicist and father of Pavel Vladimirovich Bezobrazov, Byzantine historian and promoter of women's and animal rights (1859–1918) who married Solovyov's sister Maria Sergeyevna.

330. *Vestnik Evropy* (European Herald); see n. 294 above.

331. See n. 293 above.

332. The letter to Apolon Nikolaevich Maikov (1821–97) was written in 1887. As noted by Radlov, it was mentioned in letters #15 and #20 to F. B. Getz.

333. Simeon Grigorievich (Shimon Shmuel) Frug (1860–1916), a popular Russian Jewish poet and publicist who wrote in Russian, Yiddish, and Hebrew. From the 1880s, he played an active role in Palestinophile (proto-Zionist) movements, consoling and supporting Jews with national songs and ballads. By 1887 he had published two well-reviewed books of poetry, richly nurtured by biblical and prophetic motifs, and was contributing energetically to leading progressive Russian and Jewish papers. In spite of this he had pariah status in Petersburg, from which he was banned in 1891 and finally allowed to live in 1892. His funeral in Odessa was attended by 100,000 people (www .eleven.co.il/article/14375).

334. Terty Ivanovich Filipov (1825–89), Russian government activist, senator (from 1883), and acting secret counselor (from April 1889) and State Controller (chancellor) of the Russian Empire (from July 26, 1889), also famous as a conservative-nationalist publicist and Orthodox theologian specializing in questions of ecclesial division, as well as a collector of sung Russian folklore who was wont to assist troubled composers and musicians. On Solovyov's letters to him of July 30, 1889, and Sept. 27, 1890, see Pt. I, ch. 10, end.

335. On S. A. Muromtsev, see Pt. II, ch. 12.

336. Vasily Osipovich Klyuchevsky (1841–1911), a historian and member of St. Petersburg's Academy of Sciences. On Solovyov's father's death in 1879, Klyuchevsky replaced him, having also studied under him at the University of Moscow from 1879, serving as the dean of the Faculty of History and Philology and rector of the university in 1887–89, during which time he also lectured at the Moscow Theological Seminary and in upper-level women's courses. Espousing enlightened autocracy and Russia's imperial greatness, he was entrusted in 1893 to teach Russian history to Alexander III's son Gregory (see www.hrono.ru/biograf/klyuchev.html). This also explains why Solovyov discounts him as a possible signatory.

337. In his recollections of the proceedings, Getz wrote, "The signatures, which are here spoken of, refer to the collective signatures under the *protest* against antisemitism in the press, in which Vl. S. S. took lively interest. With this aim, Vl. S. appealed first of all to Count L. N. Tolstoy with the proposal to compose the text of the designated protest and received from him the answer given below, an excerpt from which, with the permission of Count L. N., he gave me to include in my book, *The Floor to the Accused.*" Getz then cites the entire second paragraph of Tolstoy's letter of March 15, 1890, translated below, ch. 11, as letter #2.

338. Lev Nikolaevich Tolstoy (1828–1910) was one of the world's greatest novelists and most influential educational, social, and political reformists whose literal interpretation of the Sermon on the Mount turned him in later life into a fervent anarchist and pacifist. On his relationship with Solovyov, see Pt. I, chs. 4, 11, 15.

Boris Nikolaevich Chicherin (1828–1904) was a large-scale estate owner from the Tambov province and by profession a jurist, Hegelian philosopher, economist, historian, and honorary member of the Petersburg Academy of Sciences. He firmly defended the principle of authority and was a critic of revolutionary ideology, which endeared him to conservatives in the reign of Alexander II, but also actively campaigned for the expansion of civil rights to all social classes, which endeared him to liberals. In effect, he was a Westernizing classical-liberal moderate who criticized Russian serfdom as well as socialism and Marxist Communism. For a recent translation of his essays, see

Boris Nikolaevich Chicherin, *Liberty, Equality, and the Market: Essays*, ed. and trans. G. M. Hamburg (New Haven, CT: Yale University Press, 1998).

Vladimir Galaktionovich Korolenko (1853–1921) started out as a militant populist, for which he was arrested and exiled from Moscow in 1876, which prompted him to make writing his career. He was exiled to Siberia for three years for refusing to sign an oath of allegiance to Alexander III in 1881. On his return he served as a correspondent for *Russkie vedomosti* (Russian News), was eventually made an honorary member of the Petersburg Academy of Sciences, a post he resigned in 1902, following which he continued to criticize social injustices until his death in 1921.

339. This is Solovyov's foreword to Getz's 1891 book on the Jewish question, referred to repeatedly in Solovyov's correspondence with Getz. All manuscripts of the book were confiscated by the St. Petersburg Censorship Committee. The copy that Getz saved was reprinted along with several unpublished letters by Tolstoy and Korolenko under the title, *Slovo podsudimomu*, 1891. A copy of the book was also reprinted in 1906 as *Evrejskij vopros—khristianskij vopros: Sobraniye statej* (The Jewish Question—A Christian Question [A Collection of Articles]), in St. Petersburg, Moscow, Warsaw, and Kiev. For some reason, many of the surviving editions lack Chicherin's article.

340. Ezek. 3:18–19. In his *Ob otnoshenii* . . . , 6–7, after describing Solovyov's unparalleled humanitarian efforts to relieve the plight of the Jews, Getz identifies this clause concerning the duties of personal conscience as revealing the key to understanding the sources of Solovyov's exceptional attitude to Jews.

341. Getz glossed this paragraph with the following explanation: "A reference to the court pastor ('father') Shtekmer, the leader and inspirer of German antisemites." However, no such person as Shtekmer existed. Getz is undoubtedly thinking of Adolf Stoecker (1835–1909), Bismarck's court pastor and preacher, author of at least twenty titles (see Hollis catalog), who founded the Christian Socialist Workingmen's Union and stirred up a bitter and scandalous conflict with the Jews in 1880–81, thereby turning antisemitism into a national issue and becoming, in the process, the principal formulator of modern antisemitism and therefore, in Solovyov's terms, "its father." As explained in Parts I and II, however, Solovyov is referring to Ignatiev. See Pt. I, ch. 4, §8.5 and n. 155, and Pt. II, ch. 13, n. 180.

342. According to the recollection of Solovyov's childhood and family friend, K. M. El'tsova ("Dreams of/from Elsewhere: Toward the Twenty-Fifth Anniversary of the Death of V. S. Solovyov," in Averin and Bazanova, *Kniga O Vladimire Solovyove*, 142). Katkov's article referred to here is to be found

in the *Moskovskiya* (*Moskovkie*) *vedomosti* (Moscow News). As on other occasions, I employ "Jew" and "Jewish" for instances of *evrey* where Solovyov is offering a citation. See Pt. I, ch. 2.

343. F. Getz's footnote: "The Jewish population in Russia 25 years ago, as now, was not 4 but 5 1/4 million. The growth of the Jewish population over this time, estimated to be 1 1/4 million people, emigrated from Russia, chiefly to America."

344. The point that Judaism wholly represents the enterprising middle class in Poland closely parallels the argument developed by Solovyov in part 3 of his "Jewry and the Christian Question." Comparisons between Solovyov's and Katkov's observations on this score may help to clarify what in Solovyov is and is not original, but the correspondence here simply demonstrates that it was a basic given, an indisputable fact, in such discussions. Solovyov's rhetorical allusion to it thus illustrates his skillful appeal to "plain common sense" and "factual truth" in debate.

345. The order of these provinces follows the text given in *Evrejskij vopros—khristianskij vopros: Sobranie statej* (St. Peterburg: Pravda, 1906), 25, and is different from the order in Radlov's edition of the letters, which is "the Kovenskaya . . . Vilenskaya . . . Kievskaya . . . Volynskaya . . . Podol'skaya," illustrating that slightly different versions of the foreword survived.

346. The proverb Solovyov employs is *"net huda bez dobra!"* = "there is no bad without good."

347. Cf. Luke 10:42; Mark 10:21 // Luke 18:22.

348. On Chicherin, see n. 338 to letter #24 above.

349. The underlying term is *zhidoboyazn'*; cf. Esther 8:17; John 7:13, 19:38, 20:19.

350. "The Citizen," a newspaper edited by Count Meshhersky, which circulated between 1872 and 1914.

351. The translation of *Nachalo* aims to preserve its senses of "principle" and "origin" (whereby Jews are being attributed either strong family principles or a strong sense of kinship).

352. Sergei Dmitrievich Sazonov (1861–1927), a landowning noble, brother-in-law of Stolypin, and diplomat from 1883. In 1910 he was promoted by Nicholas II to become Russia's minister of external affairs (1910–16), in which capacity he played a leading role in the July crisis that brought on World War I. After the Bolshevik Revolution in November 1917, he represented the anti-Bolshevik groups in Paris. His memoirs, *Vospominaniya*, published in Paris in 1928, are now available in English translation as *Fateful Years, 1909–1916: The Reminiscences of Serge Sazonov* (New York: Kraus Reprint Co., 1971).

353. Technical term for administrative units in imperial Russia.

354. "Debt slavery." It is unclear whether the word bears any etymological relationship to the Kabbalah (e.g., as "slavery to kabbalists"?).

355. Lit., "ten."

356. This statement and those that conclude this paragraph and letter imply that the pogroms of the previous decade did not reach the pitch of violence and burning that one usually associates with them. My reading of the works cited in Pt. I, ch. 4, allow that pogroms that involved burning postdate the 1900s. This could explain the sense of hope that informs the conclusion of Solovyov's letter (and Getz's own reflections on the matter). For further clarification, see Cathy A. Frierson, *All Russia Is Burning! A Cultural History of Fire and Arson in Late Imperial Russia* (Seattle: University of Washington Press, 2002).

357. Russia's Ministry of Finance stabilized its currency by establishing the State Bank in 1866 and enabled enterprising farmers to acquire more land by founding the Peasant Land Bank in 1882. The Ministry of Internal Affairs countered this policy by helping the nobility forestall foreclosures of their mortgages by establishing the Nobles' Land Bank in 1885.

358. RST Acts 26:14.

359. Hotel de l'Europe opened on 1875 and evolved by self-reinvention into the Grand Hotel Europe. See www.grandhoteleurope.com/web/stpeters burg/grand_hotel_europe_introduction.jsp.

360. Most likely a reference to O. K. Notovich; see n. 323 above.

361. Radlov's note: "See Fet's 'Lyrical poems': St. Petersburg, 1894, vol. I, p. 269, 'May night.' Fet's third line reads: 'After him, after him, by a misty road . . .'"

362. This is Evgeny Mikhailovich Theoktistov; see letter #15 to Getz and n. 318.

363. This must be the Central Committee of the Jewish Colonization Association, founded and incorporated in London by Baron De Hirsch in Sept. 1891, whose purpose, as defined by its charter, was to assist and promote Jewish emigration from any parts of Europe or Asia, especially those where they were subjected to economic, political, or other disabilities, to any other, non-European parts of the world (cf. www.jewishencyclopedia.com/view .jsp?artid=271&letter=J). Getz supported the OPE's official opposition to resolving the Jewish question in Russia by emigration, in which an increasing number of Jews were showing interest. See Pt. I, ch. 4, §8.9–11; §1–2, 11; and Pt. II, ch. 13.

364. The *Northern Herald*, a monthly literary journal founded in 1885 by Anna M. Evrejnova to promote literary-scholarly and social-political com-

mentary. The support of contributors such as Tolstoy, Korolenko, and Chekhov evidence its liberal populist leanings. In 1890 Evrejnova sold the journal to a group of shareholders who in turn entrusted it to the editorship of the young literary critic and philosopher A. L. Volynsky, who used it to promote idealist philosophy, aesthetics, and symbolism. The journal was frequently subjected to the pressures of tsarist censorship.

365. "N. I B." (the "I" is missing a period), being known to Solovyov and Getz and a source of advice to Solovyov about the article is not necessarily a person associated with the journal but rather an independent Jewish figure knowledgeable in rabbinics. As observed in Pt. II, ch. 14, he evidently failed to catch the error implicit in Solovyov's translating the title "Rab" as "teacher" in Solovyov's article on Diminsky (in the citation of the Babylonian Talmud tractate *Sanhedrin* 17a). The subsequent letters identify N.I.B. as Nikolai Bakst. See Pt. II, ch. 13; Pt. I, ch. 4, §§8.11, 9.4.

366. F. Getz's footnote: "This is a hint regarding my confiscated and burned book 'The Floor to the Accused' which this person published."

367. F. Getz's footnote: "I do not remember whether it was in May or June 1901 that there appeared in *Novosti* the feuilleton signed "S" which praised one composition by Vl. S. Solovyov. One provincial man of letters, with close ties to Petersburg's literary circles, allowed himself in one society, in my presence, to stipulate that the named feuilleton belongs to Vl. Solovyov himself. I deemed it my duty, naturally, without naming this mentioned man of letters, to inform Vl. Solovyov of the need to prompt the editors of *Novosti* to do something on their side to remove the aforementioned misunderstanding, which it did do in № 124. Having received this № of *Novosti*, I induced the aforementioned man of letters to confess before that society about his (false) stipulation that the named feuilleton belongs to Vl. Solovyov, of which I in turn informed V. S. Solovyov."

In his letter of Aug. 9, 1891, to his friend N. Ya. Grot, editor of *Voprosy filosofii i psikhologii*, Solovyov writes the following: "Have my articles for 'Novosti' about the philosophical journal reached you? Notovich abridged the second at the end, in consequence of which my praise of your 'Introduction' turned out mysterious. After that, he played out yet another turn with me, in consequence to which I have decided to finish with him completely: he gave out as mine an article of one of my namesakes, in which that other twice praised me. It's tedious to describe the details: I'll relate them when we meet." Consequently, it would seem that the misunderstanding to which Getz refers took place not in 1901 but in 1891.

368. Vladimir Dmitrievich Kuz'min Karavayev (1859–1927), jurist, social and political activist, and frequent contributor to the journals: *Pravo, Vestnik*

Evropy, Severnyj kurier, and *Rus'*, as well as the editor in 1911–16 of the *Encyclopedic Dictionary,* edited by Brockhaus and Efron, involving eminent scholars from St. Petersburg and Leipzig. It was issued in 1890–1907 in two editions: 41 + 2 small volumes, and 82 + 4 large volumes.

369. Semyon Afanas'evich Vengerov (1855–1920), literary critic, literary historian, and bibliographer. His mother was the German Jewish writer Paulina Julievna Vengerova (Epstein). Having completed a law degree, he devoted himself to historical-literary and bibliographical activities from the 1890s, including work on Brockhaus and Efron's new *Encyclopedic Dictionary.*

370. F. Getz's footnote: "N. I. Bakst: a famous physiologist who died in 1904." On the identity of Nikolai Ignatievich Bakst, born Noah Isaacson Bakst (1843–1904), see Pt. I, ch. 4, §9.4; and Pt. II, ch. 13. As letter #30 highlights, N.I.B. was a rabbi in St. Petersburg. The fact that N.I.B. failed to correct Solovyov's translation of "Rab" as "rabbi" suggests that N.I.B.'s knowledge of rabbinics was rudimentary. The present letter (#29), by highlighting that Solovyov has not yet heard from Bakst about his chances of a high appointment on the editorial board of the *Encyclopedic Dictionary,* suggests that Bakst was either a board member or close to it.

371. As n. 19 (n. 272 above) of the translation of Solovyov's review of Diminsky's pamphlet explains, the issue here relates to Solovyov's translation of the passage in the Babylonian Talmud tractate *Sanhedrin* 17a, which reads: "Rab Judah said in Rab's name: none is to be given a seat on the Sanhedrin unless he is able to prove the cleanness of a reptile from biblical texts. Rab said: 'I shall put forward an argument to prove its cleanness. . . . '" Solovyov translated the word "Rab" here as "teacher," whereas it is the common designation ("the Master") of Rabbi Arika, a Babylonian third-century disciple of Rabbi Judah the Prince, who established the principles of analyzing the Mishnah. The error would be a source of embarrassment for N.I.B., who proofread the article for Solovyov. Letters #28 and §30 identify him as N. I. Bakst, who had some rabbinical training, hence the double pun in the poem both on his being a rabbi and on Solovyov's misuse of the term "Rab."

372. Lazar Solomonovich Poliakov (1842–1914), Russian banker, Jewish social activist and philanthropist, assumed father of the ballerina Anna Pavlova and brother of Samuel Solomonovich Poliakov, the railroad magnate, cofounder of the OPE with Evzel Gintsburg, and, after the Gintsburg dynasts, the second most important Jewish intercessor of the age. See Pt. I, ch. 4, §5.2; §8.11.

373. As noted, the work of F. Getz that was destroyed with hardly any copies remaining was *Slovo podsudimomu* (The Floor to the Accused). I thank Fr. Yakov Krotov for drawing my attention to the fact that the title, literally,

"A Word to the Accused," refers to the right in Russian courts to give the accused "the last word." Bakst's work in question, *Russkie lyudi o evreyakh* (Russian People on the Jews), published in St. Petersburg in 1891, was a collection of painstakingly obtained positive testimonies of Russian people from diverse sectors of society, published under the pseudonym N. Borisov and Ph. Nezhdanov. It too was destroyed by the censors with but a few copies remaining. (http://dic.academic.ru/dic.nsf/enc_biography/7502/Бакст [Dec. 23, 2009]. One well-preserved copy was auctioned in Russia in Nov. 2009 (see p. 81, Lot #143, at www.auction-imperia.ru/books-180_255-4small.pdf.

374. Friedrich Schiller satirized Kant's *Categorical Imperative* with the following epigram in his *Philosophical Letters:* "I love to serve my friends, and do it still / With pleasure; so it seems I'm doing ill." // "Yes, you must hate them, then your duty's clear ; You do with loathing what was once so dear." See Henry W. Nevinson and Eric S. Robertson, eds., *The Life of Friedrich Schiller* (London: Walter Scott, 1889), 52.

375. F. Getz's note: "Count I. D. Delianov—a former Minister of National Enlightenment." This is the same Delianov who under tsarist order prepared the *Numerus Clausus* of 1887!

376. A typographical error for "Have(t)," which Solovyov writes as "Ave." For a portion of his review of Havet, see below.

377. Nikolai Semyonovich Leskov (1831–March 5, 1895), Russian storyteller, novelist, and journalist. Tolstoy declared him to have been the writer who captured the nature of Russian identity best. The date of Leskov's death, March 5, indicates that at least the postscript was not added and the letter not sent until a few days after that date. On the significance of his 1883 work, *Jews in Russia* (www.vehi.net/asion/leskov.html), see Pt. II, ch. 16.

378. Anatoly Yakovlevich Speshnev (1863–1908), a military officer who distinguished himself in his military duty and became both a military tribunal judge and a major general in 1908.

379. Florenty Fedorovich Pavlenkov (1839–1900), a well-known publisher.

380. Lit., "fame."

381. Yuri Krizhanich (1617–93) was a Croatian polymath dedicated to Slavic unity. For details of his biography, see Pt. II, ch. 10.

382. Nikolai Yakovlevich Danilevsky (1822–85) was a leading exponent of Pan-Slavism, the advocacy of the political unification of Slavic people, as espoused in his classic *Russia and Europe*, called by Dostoevsky "the coffee-table book of every Russian"; see Pt. I, ch. 4, §7.4.

383. The technical term for the critical period of anarchy in Russian history, 1604–13.

384. A reference to Kuz'ma Minin, butcher and merchant from Nizhny Novgorod who became a national hero for defending the country against invading Polish armies on Nov. 1, 1612.

385. Count Alexander Vasielivich Suvorov of Rymnik, prince in Italy (1729–1800), was the fourth and last generalissimus of the Russian Empire who never lost a battle and is famed for his manual, *The Science of Victory*.

386. Count Mikhail Illarionovich Kutuzov (1745–1813) the Russian field marshal who defeated Napoleon's army during France's invasion of Russia in 1812.

387. Mikhail Skobelev (1843–82) was a general famous for his conquests in Central Asia and his heroism during the Russo-Turkish War of 1877–78, described as the world's "ablest single commander" between 1870 and 1914 by the British field marshal Bernard Montgomery.

388. Count Nikolai Pavlovich Ignatiev (1832–1908), statesman and diplomat. On his impact on Russian-Jewish relations in 1881–82 as minister of the interior, see Pt. I, ch. 4, §8.5; 9. The context here presupposes knowledge of his military career and especially the fact that after securing Outer Manchuria from China at the Convention of Peking (1860), he worked to liberate the Bulgarians and Christian nationalities from the Ottomans via the Russo-Turkish War, which, going badly, led to his losing favor with Alexander II and his treaty with the Ottomans being revised at the Treaty of Berlin (1878) signed on behalf of Russia by his rival, Count Pyotr Shuvalov.

389. Konstantin Sergeyevich Aksakov (1817–60; son of the writer Sergei Aksakov and brother of the journalist Ivan Aksakov), critic, writer, leading Slavophile, and the most influential intellectual Judeophobe of the period (see Pt. I, ch. 4, §6.9).

390. On Aksakov's and Katkov's approaches to the Eastern question and the Russo-Turkish War, see Pt. I, ch. 4, §7.5.

391. A reference to the Siege of Sevastopol (1854–55) by the British, French, Sardinian, and Turkish troops during the Crimean War and to Russia's destruction, at its retreat, of the city and fleet to prevent them from falling into enemy hands.

392. A reference to the Siege of Plevna (1877–78) during which Russians and Rumanians suffered unacceptable losses at the hands of the defending Turks and so were delayed from advancing into Bulgaria.

393. Nicholas I died on March 2, 1855; the Crimean War, known in Russia as "the Eastern War," lasted from March 1854 to February 1856. The Epoch of Reforms began with Alexander II (b. Apr. 29, 1818; crowned tsar Mar. 3, 1855; d. Mar. 13, 1881), also known as Alexander the Liberator for the Emancipation of the Serfs in 1861 and other reforms. See Pt. I, ch. 4, §5.

394. Circassians (from the Turkish *Cherkess*) are the Caucasian peoples of the northwestern Caucasus; Turkmen are the Turkic peoples speaking the Turkmen language in the Central Asian states of Turkmenistan and Afghanistan, northern Iraq, and Iran.

395. Radlov published two of Solovyov's letters to Tolstoy, those of July 5, 1894, and July 28–August 2, 1894, in *Letters*, 3:37 and 3:38–42, respectively. The remaining, "unpublished," correspondence of L. Tolstoy and V. S. Solovyov was later published by V. Popov in *Literaturnoye nasledstvo* (Literary Heritage) 37–38 (1939): 268–76, and reprinted as an addendum in the Brussels (1970) edition of *SSVSS* as *Pis'ma i prilozhenie*, 4:253–64. The latter correspondence includes six letters of Solovyov to Tolstoy, dated May 3, 1875, Feb., 1890, Jan. 29, 1891, Jan. 26 or 27, 1892, Dec. 1892–Mar. 1893, Oct.–Nov. 1, 1894, and three of Tolstoy to Solovyov, dated Mar. 15, 1890, Aug. 7, 1894, and Nov. 9–15, 1894. Popov took the letter of Jan. 26 or 27 from Dillon's *Count Tolstoy*. The letters relevant to Solovyov's and Tolstoy's correspondence on the Jewish question are translated here, omitting thereby the letters of May 3, 1875, Dec. 1892–Mar. 1893, Oct.–Nov. 1, 1894, and Nov. 9–15, 1894. The letters are arranged chronologically and renumbered to facilitate cross reference in this volume.

396. Popov notes the passage of the following regulations at that time: (1) the land legislation of 1890 depriving the Jews of participation in all land organizations; and (2) on March 28, 1891, the prohibition against Jewish artisans settling in Moscow and its provinces and relocation of those who already lived there to the Pale of Settlement. This repressive legislation received retroactive force and was extended to Jews already living in Moscow on the basis of rights granted them long ago. The "Forty Clauses" rumor that prompted Solovyov and Dillon's letter concerned the establishment of a special commission to limit Jewish civil rights by Sen. Vyacheslav Kontantinovich von Plehve (1846–1904), director of tsarist Russia's police (from 1881), member of the Governing Senate (from 1884), and assistant minister of the interior (from 1885). See Pt. I, ch. 4, §9.6.

397. Solovyov frequently appeals to this principle from the prophet Ezekiel (3:18; 33:8) but seemingly improvises on its Slavonic version from memory, as evidenced by the correspondence of his citation to the bold portions of either of those passages:

> Ezekiel 3:18: "**If I** say to the wicked, '**You shall surely die,**' and **you give** him **no warning,** nor speak **to** warn **the wicked from his wicked way,** in order to save his life, that wicked man shall die in his iniquity; but **his blood I will require at your hand.**"

Ezekiel 33:8: "**If** I say to the wicked, O wicked man, you shall surely die, and **you do** not speak to **warn the wicked to turn from his** way, that wicked man shall die in his **iniquity, but his blood I will require at your hand.**"

398. Popov explains that the Protest was written by Solovyov and signed by Tolstoy and that its fate was described by the unpublished letter of F. B. Getz to Tolstoy of Nov. 15, 1890: "Your noble initiative attained brilliant success. The most leading Russian scholars and literary activists followed your encouraging example. More than 50 signatures were already collected by V. S. Solovyov, and he could have collected at least as many more signatures but for the false denunciations by the antisemitic press that the protest was directed against the government, which elicited a powerful circular by the Ministry of Internal Affairs from the 8th of this month prohibiting the publication of any sort of collective declaration pertaining to the Jews, under threat of the most severe punishment. This prohibition at once demolished all the hope and trust that was set on the protest." In its time, the protest was printed unsigned only by the London *Times*, on Dec. 10, 1890.

399. Popov notes that Emile (Mikhailovich) J. Dillon (1854–1933) was an English journalist and correspondent for the *Daily Telegraph* (1887–1914) who lived for a long time in Russia and wrote prolifically on Russia and Russian literature, under the pseudonym Lanin, serving also as a translator for Tolstoy, whom he met in 1890. For more details, see Pt. II, ch. 10.

400. According to Popov, this postscript was added by Dillon.

401. According to Popov, this is written in Tolstoy's hand.

402. Popov notes that Tolstoy wrote to F. B. Getz on May 22, 1890: "I regret the persecutions which the Jews suffer, considering them not only unjust and cruel but mad. But this subject does not command me exclusively or predominantly over and above other feelings and thoughts. There are many matters which worry me more than this one and for this reason I cannot write about this matter something that would touch people."

403. F. B. Getz.

404. Popov notes this is the brochure *The Floor to the Accused* and that it was to include the unpublished letters of Tolstoy, Chicherin, and Korolenko, with a foreword by Solovyov, as well as Tolstoy's letters to Getz and one to Solovyov. The brochure was confiscated.

405. The letter was published in English in 1934 in Emile J. Dillon, *Count Leo Tolstoy: A New Portrait* (London: Hutchinson & Co., 1934), 202. The Russian version provided by Popov is translated by him from the English and the end of the letter from a photocopy. The letter was brought personally by Dillon, who arrived at Begichevka (Tolstoy's headquarters in the Rayevsky

property in the province of Ryazan') on Jan. 28, 1892. Tolstoy corroborated that Dillon translated his original letters on famine. The complications of this issue are described in ch. 14, "The Newspaper War between Tolstoy and Dillon," in *Count Leo Tolstoy.*

406. The letter, reprinted in *Letters*, 3:37, was first published under the title "Iz pis'ma Vladimira Sergeevicha Solovyova k grafu L'vu Nikolaevichu Tolstomu" (From the Letter of Vladimir Sergeevich Solovyov to Count Lev Nikolaevich Tolstoy), in *Voprosy filosofii i psikhologii* 79 (1905): 241–46.

407. In editing Tolstoy's and Solovyov's correspondence, Popov explains, in commenting on the letter of Aug. 7, 1894, that Joseph Krauskopf (1858–1923) was a rabbi who came to Russia in 1894 to investigate the condition of Jewish colonies. Taking advantage of a recommendation by the U.S. diplomat in St. Petersburg, A. Waite, he visited Tolstoy in Yasnaya Polyana. He later founded in America an agricultural school, considering Tolstoy his ideological inspiration. See http://americanjewisharchives.org/collections /ms0183/.

408. As "subdue" echoes Gen 1:28, the term it translates, *ovladevaet*, is also cognate with the root of the term occurring in the Russian Synodal version (*vladychestvujte*) of Gen. 1:28 but especially of the Slavonic text (*ôbladajte*) and is therefore probably an allusion to it.

409. In light of the emphasis and repetitive uses of this term, it is probably an allusion to the "fullness" *Pleroma* of Eph. 1:10, 23; 3:19; 4:13; Col. 2:9, 10; and John 1:16.

410. See Col. 1:18, Rev. 1:5.

411. An allusion to Matt. 11:14 and Luke 7:22.

412. The French mathematician Urbain Le Verrier (1811–77) famously explained the discrepancies in the orbit of Uranus by means of mathematical calculations that allowed him to predict the existence and position of Neptune.

413. Popov notes that Solovyov proposed editing religious-moral writings by Tolstoy into a collection under the title "A Criticism of Pseudo-Christianity, from the Compositions of Leo Tolstoy."

414. A reference to Krauskopf's brochure "'Eye for an Eye' or 'Turning the Other Cheek.'" On p. 4 of the brochure there is a paragraph explaining that the teaching to "not resist evil" is not of Jewish origin and is essentially imprudent.

415. This is the Guildhall meeting of Dec. 10, 1890 (reported on p. 9 of the same issue of the *Times*), whose requisition, on behalf of London's citizens, signed by 83 persons, and headed by the archbishop of Canterbury and Cardinal Manning, petitioned the tsar to grant the Jews of Russia political and social equality with the rest of his subjects. The tsar refused to officially receive

the communication, and it was returned through the foreign office. See www
.jewishencyclopedia.com/view.jsp?artid=158&letter=M; and Pt. I, ch. 4, §9.6,
above).

416. There follows a letter from Henry Edward Cardinal Manning.

417. First appearing in *Russkie vedomosti* 20 (1909), the present text follows the version included in vol. 9 of Korolenko's *Collected Works* (1914):
257–60. It was written in 1903 as a response to the pogrom against the Jews in
Kishenev under the title, "From the Correspondence with V. S. Solovyov," and
sent to *Russkie vedomosti* but was not approved by the censors. This version
was accessed at http://vehi.net/soloviev/korolenko.html; alternatively see
http://ruslit.traumlibrary.net/book/korolenko-ss05-03/korolenko-ss05-03
.html#work002003.

418. Solovyov answered Korolenko in January 1891 (as quoted in Part
II): "That letter of yours truly gladdened me and it would be very beneficial
to publish it. It produced the best impression upon all to whom I read it. By
the way, the observation which you disliked regarding the German origin of
antisemitism was inserted by me according to the demand of one of the signatories, and I am in complete agreement with you that it is redundant. It would
seem that it has been omitted in the English and the German translations
which have been published in London and Vienna." N. V. Korolenko and
A. L. Krivinskaya comment as follows on Solovyov's answer: "The friend of
V. S. Solovyov, about whom the letter speaks, is the learned Jew at the academic district of Vilna, who teaches Jewish history, the writer Faivel Meir
Bentselevich [*sic*] Getz. Solovyov took Hebrew lessons from him. In 1891
Getz published a book on the Jewish question, *The Floor to the Accused*, with
a foreword and unpublished letters by V. S. Solovyov, L. N. Tolstoy, P. N. Chi-
gerin [*sic*] and V. G. Korolenko. This book was confiscated by the Censor
Committee" (*Letters*, 2:17–18).

419. P. D. Ilovajsky (1832–1920), historian, publicist, and author of history textbooks. His activities prompted the Ministry of the Affairs of the Press
to issue a special circular to prohibit the publication of the collective protest
composed by Solovyov.

420. The newspapers of the agents of the French Revolution, J. P. Marat,
L'Ami du people (1789–93), and J. R. Hébert, *Père Duchesne* (1791–94), were
distinguished by the sharpness of tone, intransigence, and demand for universal execution of the "enemies of the people."

421. "Passed times" (Italian).

422. This letter, #24, to Arseniev, editor of the *Encyclopedic Dictionary*,
is translated from *Letters*, 2:91. For commentary on Arseniev, see Pt. II, ch. 17.

423. A guesthouse in Imatra, Finland, by Lake Saimaa and the Vuoksi
River, 130 miles northwest of St. Petersburg.

424. Tommaso Campanella, baptized Giovanni Domenico (1568–1639), Italian philosopher and writer, one of the earliest representatives of utopian socialism.

425. Moisei Markovich Margolin (b. 1862), the secretary, from 1891, of the editorial board of the *Encyclopedic Dictionary* and later editor of the Jewish journals *Voskhod* (Dawn) and *Evrejskaya zhizn'* (Jewish Life); see www .rulex.ru/01130199.htm (Feb. 4, 2010).

426. A town near the head of the Bay of Vyborg 80 miles northwest of St. Petersburg.

427. Probably a reference to an upcoming game of croquet (I thank Yakov Krotov for the suggestion).

428. The Book of Zohar. Burmistrov wonders why Solovyov, knowing Hebrew, would have rendered the word with this spelling.

429. Nikolai Yakovlevich Grot (1852–99), editor of the journal *Voprosy filosofii i psikhologii* (Questions of Philosophy and Psychology) and good friend of Solovyov; see Pt. II, chs. 14, 16..

430. The identification of the issues of *Moskovskie vedomosti* in which this and the subsequent two letters were published is supplied by Radlov, editor of Solovyov's letters, in *Letters*, 3:196, 197, 200 (Letter #4, 204–8, is omitted here). Yuri Nikolaev(ich Govorukha-Otrok) (1850–96) was a participant in left-wing revolutionary movements of the 1870s who shifted to the right in the 1880s and was invited in 1889 by the editors of *Moskovskie vedomosti* to serve as the paper's literary reviewer. He accused Solovyov of using the expression "swindlers and deceivers" to describe Christian ascetics in *Moskovskie vedomosti*, nos. 291 and 293, respectively.

431. I cannot find biographical details on the right-wing journalist "M. Afanasiev" who represented Solovyov as providing a "total mockery over the holy and Orthodox Church" and pouring "audacious ridicule over the whole of the Christian Church," in *Moskovskie vedomosti*, nos. 291 and 293, respectively.

432. Lit., "fortunes" or "fates"; see n. 61 above.

433. Acts 4:32.

434. Vladimir Andreevich Gringmut (1851–1907) was the radical right-wing political activist and one of the principal founders of the Black Hundreds. Born into a German Silesian Lutheran family that came to teach in Moscow in the 1840s, he was, from 1871 an active participant in the conservative press, contributing to Katkov's newspaper *Moskovksie vedomosti* and the journal *Russkij vestnik* and to Count Meshhersky's *Grazhdanin* and *Russkoe obozrenie*. He became the editor of *Moskovskie vedomosti* in 1896 and remained in that post until his death. From 1874 he taught Greek in the Katkov Lyceum, founded by Mikhail N. Katkov and Pavel M. Leontiev, and served as

its director in 1894–96. In 1876 he received Russian citizenship and in 1878 converted to Orthodoxy. In time, he founded the Russian Monarchical Party, which constituted one of the groupings of the Black Hundreds, reactionary antirevolutionary and antisemitic groups constituted in Russia during the Revolution of 1905–7. The name derives from the old Russian term for a military-administrative unit of a populated suburban district. According to the recollections of Solovyov's lecture to the Psychological Society by Ya. Kolubovsky (see Mochulsky, *Vladimir Solovyov*, ch.12), Gringmut, as secretary of *Moskovskie vedomosti*, was one of those who objected to Solovyov's lecture, took part in the closed debate that followed, and initiated, that same night, an incessant, two-month-long polemical attack on Solovyov by *Moskovskie vedomosti*.

435. Michael Servetus (1511–53), a Spanish theologian, physician, and humanist who participated in the Reformation but contested the Trinity and infant baptism, for which he was branded a blasphemer deserving of death by Calvin and burned by the Protestant Geneva Governing Council.

436. Filaret (Drozdov), metropolitan of Moscow (1782–1867), was the most influential figure in the Russian Church of the mid-nineteenth century. He was a preacher at Troitse-Sergieva Lavra in 1806 and a professor at the Alexander Nevsky Lavra in St. Petersburg in 1810. He was greatly moved by Russia's victory over Napoleon in 1812, took monastic vows in 1817, and, following successive episcopal appointments between 1819 and 1826, became metropolitan of Moscow in 1826. In this post he helped to modernize the church by repressing Old Believers, promoting a Russian translation of the Bible, and influencing Alexander II's proclamation on the liberation of the serfs.

437. Solovyov's footnote: "Theophanes Continuatus, the anonymous continuer of the chronicle of St. Theophanes the Confessor (760–818), Byzantine monk, chronicler, confessor."

438. Solovyov's footnote: "I surmise that the probable prompt for Mr. Yu. Nikolaev's replacement of the heretical Paulicians by the heresy-free citizens of Salonika derived from St. Ambrose of Milan's protest against the massacre of the Salonicans, since I did mention this great prelate in my lecture. But I mention him not in connection with the Salonicans (about which I had no cause to speak either in the lecture, or in the debates), but on account of his joint principled protest with St. Martin of Tours against the execution of heretics (when the leaders of the *Priscillian* heresy were executed in Trier by the Usurper-Emperor Maximus.)"

439. For the original, see S. Solovyov, *Vladimir Solovyov: Stikhotvoreniya*, 75–76. The first and last stanzas of the poem are cited and com-

mented on by S. Solovyov in *Zhizn'*, 207, 213. Cf. Jakim's rendering in his *Religious Poetry of Vladimir Solovyov*, 21–22. Cf. French and Italian translations at www.biblisem.net/meditat/solovaup.htm; and www.superzeko.net/poetry/PoesieDiVladimirSergeevicSoloviev.pdf, 21/52.

440. For the original, see *Letters*, 4:28; and Vladimir Solovyov, *Stikhotvoreniya i shutochnye p'esy*, ed. Z. G. Mints (Leningrad: Sovetskij pisatel', 1974), 145. The first stanza is cited and commented on by S. Solovyov in *Zhizn'*, 266.

441. The poem is undated. For the original, see S. Solovyov, *Vladimir Solovyov: Stikhotvoreniya*, 135. The free translation is taken from Jakim, *The Religious Poetry of Vladimir Solovyov*, 45.

442. The poem was written between Jan. 31 and Feb. 3, 1892. For the original, see *Letters*, 4:159; and V. Solovyov, *Stikhotvoreniya i shutochnye p'esy*, ed. Z. G. Mints, 87. Sergei Solovyov cites and comments on it in *Zhizn'*, 282. The free translation is taken from Jakim, *The Religious Poetry of Vladimir Solovyov*, 43.

443. For the original, see S. Solovyov, *Vladimir Solovyov: Stikhotvoreniya*, 85–86. The free translation is taken from Yakim, *The Religious Poetry of Vladimir Solovyov*, 28–30, including "Into" rather than "To" in the title. Sergei Solovyov comments on the poem, citing one stanza, in *Zhizn'*, 224.

Aleksandr Petrovich Salomon (Solomon) (1855–1908) was a graduate and later director of the Alexandrov Lyceum, a participant in the Russo-Turkish War, secretary of the Prison Council of the Ministry of Internal Affairs, director of the chief Prison Bureau, and an Arabist. He became acquainted with V. Solovyov in 1877, and his relationship with Solovyov was described in some detail by Ukhtomsky to Lukianov, especially in their conversation of May 30, 1920. Salomon reprimanded Solovyov for his March speech encouraging the tsar to forgive his father's assassins but supported him morally nonetheless; Solovyov once assumed Salomon to have Jewish roots and confessed that he would give anything to have some Jewish blood. See S. M. Lukianov, "Zapis' besed s. E. E. Ukhtomskim," "Iz razgovora 30-go maya 1920 g.," in *Materialy k biografii*, www.rodon.org/svs/_mkbvssiasml.htm. See also www.runivers.ru/new_htmlreader/?book=5600&chapter=83883._

444. For the original, see S. Solovyov, *Vladimir Solovyov: Stikhotvoreniya*, 100–101; and his commentary on it in *Zhizn'*, 282. Only the rhymed translation is presented here on the presumed strength of its accuracy. Words added to the text are italicized. The phrase "Stranger in a strange land" explains "in my strange/alien fatherland" as an allusion to Exod. 2:22, where Moses recalls his life in Egypt as that of "a stranger in a strange land." The last *shade* alludes to Isa. 4:6.

BIBLIOGRAPHY

COLLECTED WORKS OF VLADIMIR SOLOVYOV

Four editions of the *Collected Works of Vladimir Sergeevich Solovyov* [= *SSVSS*] have appeared. The last seeks to be a critical edition in 20 volumes.

Radlov, Ernest L., ed. *Sobranie sochinenij Vladimira Sergeevicha Solovyova.* 9 vols. [= *SSVSS*[9]]. St. Petersburg: Obshhestvennaya pol'za, 1901–7.

Radlov, Ernest L., and Sergei M. Solovyov (the younger), eds. *Sobranie sochinenij Vladimira Sergeevicha Solovyova.* 10 vols. [= *SSVSS*[10]]. St. Petersburg: Prosveshhenie, 1911–14.

Sobranie sochinenij Vladimira Sergeevicha Solovyova. 12 vols. [= *SSVSS*[12]]. Brussels: Zhizn' s Bogom, 1966–70. [Based on the preceding volume.]

Solovyov, V. S. *Polnoe sobranie sochinenij i pisem v dvadtsati tomakh* [= *SSVSS*[20]]. Edited by Aleksandr A. Nosov, Aleksei P. Kozyrev, and Nikolai V. Kotrelyov. Moscow: Nauka, 2000– . (As of this writing, vols. 1–4, 1873–82, have been completed.)

Collections of Solovyov's works are available online at the HathiTrust Digital Library, http://babel.hathitrust.org/cgi/ls?a=srchls&anyall1=all&q1=Solov yov+Vladimir&field1=author&op2=AND&anyall2=all&q2=Sobrani%CC %84e+sochineni%CC%84i%CC%86&field2=title&op3=AND&yop= after&facet_lang=language%3ARussian&facet_lang=&facet_format=; and at the library of Yakov Krotov, http://krotov.info/library/18_s/solovyov/00solov .html.

LETTERS OF VLADIMIR SOLOVYOV

Radlov, Ernest L., ed. *Pis'ma Vladimira Sergeevicha Solovyova.* Vols. 1–3. St. Petersburg: Obschchestvennaja Pol'za, 1908–11; Vol. 4. St. Petersburg:

Vremya, 1923. Unless otherwise stated, all citations of Solovyov's letters are from the reprint of all four volumes published in Brussels by Zhizn' s Bogom, Foyer Oriental Chrétien, 1970.

POETRY OF VLADIMIR SOLOVYOV

Solovyov, Sergei M., ed. *Vladimir Solovyov: Stikhotvoreniya.* 7th ed. Moscow: Russkij knizhnik, 1921. http://catalog.hathitrust.org/Record/006758647; http://babel.hathitrust.org/cgi/pt?id=inu.30000005019819;view=1up; seq=8.

Solovyov, Vladimir. *Stikhotvoreniya i shutochnye p'esy.* Edited by Z. G. Mints. Leningrad: Sovetskij Pisatel', 1974.

Solovyov's poetry is also published in *SSVSS*[12]: 12.

TWO-VOLUME ANTHOLOGIES OF SOLOVYOV'S WORKS

Kotrelyov, Nikolai Vsevolodovich, and Evegeny Borisovich Rashkovsky, eds. *V. S. Solovyov: Sochineniya v dvukh tomakh.* Moscow: Filosofskaya publitsistika, 1989.

Losev, Aleksei F., and Arsenii V. Gulyga, eds. *Vladimir Solovyov: Sochineniya v dvukh tomakh.* Moscow, 1988.

PHILOSOPHICAL DICTIONARY ENTRIES BY SOLOVYOV

Solovyov, Vladimir. *Filosofskij slovar' Vladimira Solovyova.* Rostov-na-Donu: "Feniks," 1997. www.rodon.org/svs/sdebie.htm.

SELECT WORKS BY SOLOVYOV CITED FROM THEIR ORIGINAL CONTEXTS

"Chteniya o bogochelovechestve" (Lectures on Godmanhood), *Pravoslavnoe obozrenie* (Orthodox Survey) Mar. 1878 (pt. 1:472–84; Apr. 1878 (pt. 2:714–26); May–June 1878 (pt. 3:308–30); July 1878 (pt. 4:477–79); Sept. 1878 (pts. 5 and 6: 108–13); Oct. 1879 (pts. 7 and 8:223–51), Nov. 1880 (pt. 9:441–56); Feb. 1881 (pt. 10:317–38); Sept. 1881 (pts. 11 and 12:12–32). (Reprinted collectively as *Chteniya o bogochelovechestve,* edited by

Mikhail Katkov. Moscow: Universitetskaya tipografiya, 1881. Also reprinted in *SSVSS*[9] 3:1–168.)

"Iz pis'ma Vladimira Sergeevicha Solovyova k grafu L'vu Nikolaevichu Tolstomu" (From the letter of Vladimir Sergeevich Solovyov to Count Lev Nikolaevich Tolstoy), *Voprosy filosofii i psikhologii* 79 (1905): 241–46.

On Helena Blavatsky:

> "Review of Madame Helena Blavatsky's Book *The Key to Theosophy.*" *Russian Review* (1890): 881–86. Reprinted in *SSVSS*[12] 6:291–92.

> "E. P. Blavatskaya." In Semyon Afanas'evich Vengerov, *Kritiko-biograficheskij slovar' russkikh pisatelej i uchenykh*, 36:316–18. St. Petersburg: I. Efron, 1892.

WORKS BY SOLOVYOV PUBLISHED OUTSIDE HIS COLLECTED WORKS IN FRENCH

L'Idée russe. Paris: Librairie Académique Didier-Perrin, 1888.

La Russie et l'Église universelle. Edited by Albert Savine. Paris: Nouvelle Librairie parisienne, 1889, 1906; Paris: Delamain Boutelleau, 1922. http://babel.hathitrust.org/cgi/pt?idnjp.32101068979747;view=1up; seq=15.

"Saint Vladimir et L'Etat Chrétien." *L'Univers*, Aug. 4, 11, 19, 1888. Russian translation by G. A. Rachinsky, "Vladimir Svyatoj i khristianskoye gosudarstvo," *SSVSS*[12] 11:119–38.

SEPARATE RUSSIAN EDITIONS AND COLLECTIONS OF SOLOVYOV'S WORKS ON JUDAISM

"Ob antisemiticheskom dvizhenii v pechati: neizdannaya stat'ya Vl. S. Solovyova." *Budushhnost'*, 35 (1901): 684–85.

Evrejskij vopros — khristianskij vopros: Sobranie statej (The Jewish Question — a Christian Question: A Collection of Essays). St. Petersburg: Pravda, 12, 1906.

Evrejstvo i khristianskij vopros (Jewry and the Christian Question). Kniga dlya vsekh, 59. Berlin: Mysl', 1921.

Ob otnoshenii Vl. Solovyova k evrejskomu voprosu: Talmud i novejshaya polemicheskaya literatura o nyom; Evrei — ikh verouchenie i nravouchenie; Ob otnoshenii Vl. Solovyova k evrejskomu voprosu. Edited by Faivel Getz. Berlin: Zarya, 1925.

O Evrejskom narode: Stat'i, pis'ma. Vl. Solovyov. Jerusalem: M. Wainstein, 1987.

Stat'i o evrejstve: Problemy iudeo-khristianskogo dialoga. Edited by Archbishop John of San Francisco. Jerusalem: Maslina, 1979.

SOLOVYOV'S WORKS IN TRANSLATION

Anonymous, trans. "Vladimir Solovyov's Letter to L. Tolstoy on the Resurrection of Christ." *Sobornost* 1 (March 1935): 8–12 (= *Letters*, 3:38–42).

Attwater, Donald, trans. *God, Man and the Church: The Spiritual Foundations of Life.* Cambridge: James Clarke, 1974 (= *Dukhovnye osnovy zhizni* [1882–84], *SSVSS* 3).

Bakshy, Alexander, trans. *War, Progress, and the End of History (including a Short Story about the Antichrist): Three Conversations.* London: University of London Press, 1915; revised and edited by Thomas R. Beyer. Hudson, NY: Lindisfarne Press, 1990.

Duddington, Natalie A., trans. *The Justification of the Good: An Essay on Moral Philosophy.* Revised and edited by Boris Jakim. Grand Rapids, MI: Wm. B. Eerdmans, [1918] 2005) (= *Opravdanie dobra: Nravstvennaya filosofiya* [1897, rev. 1899], *SSVSS* 8).

Frank, Simeon L., ed., and Natalie A. Duddington, trans. *A Solovyov Anthology.* New York: Charles Scribners' Sons, 1950.

Gill, Richard, trans. *Plato.* London: S. Nott, 1935.

d'Herbigny, Michel, trans. *Les fondements spirituels de la vie.* 2nd ed. Tournais: Casterman, 1948.

Jakim, Boris, trans. and ed. *The Crisis of Western Philosophy: Against the Positivists.* Hudson, NY: Lindisfarne, 1996.

Jakim, Boris, Sergius Bulgakov, and Laury Magnus, trans. and eds. *The Religious Poetry of Vladimir Solovyov.* Kettering, OH: Semantron, 2014.

Kline, George L., and Boris Jakim, trans. *The Concept of God: Essays on Spinoza.* Carlisle, PA: Variable Press, 1999 (= "Ponyatie o Boge v zashhitu filosofii Spinozy" [1897], *SSVSS* 9:1–25).

Marshall, Jane, trans. *The Meaning of Love.* Revised and edited by Thomas R. Beyer Jr. Edinburgh: Floris Books, [1945] 1985.

Meerson, Michael Aksionov. "The Retrieval of Neoplatonism in Solov'ëv's Trinitarian Synthesis." In van den Bercken, de Courten, and van der Zweere, *Vladimir Solov'ëv: Reconciler and Polemicist,* 233–50.

Nollan, Valeria Z., trans. *The Philosophical Principles of Integral Knowledge.* Grand Rapids, MI: Wm. B. Eerdmans, 2008 (= *Filosofskie nachala tsel'nogo znaniya* [1877], *SSVSS* 1).

Reese, Herbert, trans. *Russia and the Universal Church*. London: Centenary Press, 1945.

Ryland, Ray, ed. *The Russian Church and the Papacy*. Foreword by Christoph Cardinal Schönborn. El Cajon, CA: Catholic Answers, 2002.

Tavernier, Eugène. *Trois entretien sur la guerre, la morale et la religion*. Paris: Plon, 1916.

Wozniuk, Vladimir, trans. and ed. *The Heart of Reality: Essays on Beauty, Love, and Ethics by V. S. Soloviev*. Notre Dame, IN: University of Notre Dame Press, 2003.

Wozniuk, Vladimir, ed. *Freedom, Faith, and Dogma: Essays by V. S. Soloviev on Christianity and Judaism*. Albany: State University of New York Press, 2008.

Zouboff, Peter, trans. and ed. *Lectures on Divine Humanity*. Revised and edited by Boris Jakim. Hudson, NY: Lindisfarne, 1995.

MISCELLANEOUS BIOGRAPHICAL MATERIALS PERTAINING TO SOLOVYOV

Photograph of Solovyov's tombstone (reading, "Solovyov, Vladimir Sergeiivich, 1853–1900, publitsist filosof"). www.openmoscow.ru/kladbnovo devichy/27big.html.

ELECTRONIC BIOGRAPHICAL AND OTHER REFERENCE TOOLS

The Catholic Encyclopedia: An International Work of Reference on the Constitution, Doctrine, Discipline, and the History of the Catholic Church. Edited by Charles G. Herbermann et al. 16 vols. New York: Encyclopedia Press, 1913–14. http://en.wikisource.org/wiki/Catholic_Encyclopedia_%281913%29.

Elektronnaya evrejskaya èntsiklopediya (The Jewish Encyclopedia in Russian on the Web. Based on *The Shorter Jewish Encyclopedia*. Jerusalem: Hebrew University, 1976–2005). www.jewishvirtuallibrary.org/jsource; www.eleven.co.il/.

Èntsiklopedicheskij slovar' (Brokhaus i Efron). 3 CD-ROMs. Edited by Nauchnoe izdatel'stvo "Bol'shaya rossijskaya èntsiklopediya," Moscow. http://ru.wikisource.org/wiki/ÈSBE = http://ru.wikisource.org/wiki/Èntsiklopedicheskij_slovar'_Brokgauza_i_Efrona.

Evrejskaya èntsiklopediya (Jewish Encyclopedia). 16 vols. St. Petersburg: Ob-shhestvo dlya Nauchnykh Evrejskikh Izdanij i Izdatel'stvo Brokgauz-Efron (Society for Academic Jewish Publications and the Publishing House of Brockhaus and Efron), 1906–13. http://ru.wikisource.org/wiki/Evrejskaya_èntsiklopediya_Brokgauza_i_Efrona.

Groberg, Kristi. "Vladimir Sergeevich Solov'ev: A Bibliography." Compiled on behalf of the Transnational Vladimir Solovyov Society in *Modern Greek Studies Yearbook* 14–15 (1998). www.asociacion-soloviev.es/Archivos/Soloviev/ArchivosSolovievBibliografia.htm.

Jacob Rader Marcus Center of the American Jewish Archives. http://american jewisharchives.org/ and www.jewishvirtuallibrary.org/jsource/.

The Jewish Encyclopedia. Edited by Isidore Singer et al. New York: Funk and Wagnalls. 12 vols. 1901–6. www.jewishencyclopedia.com/.

Khronos: vsemirnaya istoriya v internete. Biograficheskij spravochnik. http://hrono.ru/biograf/index.php.

Kratkaya evrejskaya èntsiklopediya (The Shorter Jewish Encyclopedia). Edited by Yitzhak Oren (Nadel), Michael Zand, Naftali Prat, and Ari Avner et al. 11 vols. Jerusalem: Obshhestvo po issledovaniyu evrejskikh ob-shchin (Society for Study of Jewish Communities), 1976–2005. www.eleven.co.il/.

Polnoe sobranie zakonov Rossijskoj imperii: poveleniem Gosudarya Imperatora Nikolaya Pavlovicha sostavlennoe sobranie pervoe s 1649 po 12 dekabrya 1825 goda. 33 vols. St. Petersburg: Tip. II Otdeleniya Sobstvennoj Ego Imperatorskago Velichestva Kantselyarij, 1830–1916. www.nlr.ru/e-res/law_r/search.php and www.webcitation.org/65EGhxSRe.

Polovtsev, A. A., ed. *Russkij biograficheskij slovar'* (Russian Biographical Dictionary). 1896–1918 (consisting of the *Encyclopedic Dictionary* [Brockhaus and Efron] and *Novyj èntsiklopedicheskij slovar'* [New Encyclopedic Dictionary]). www.rulex.ru/.

Russkaya Literatura i Fol'klor: Fundamental'naya elektronnaya biblioteka. http://feb-web.ru/.

Zaikin, S. P. *Trudy o Vl. Solovyove* (Works about Vl. Solovyov). (Covering the period 1874–2001). www.rednet.ru/~zaikin/sol/about.htm.

Websites of Places Referred to in the Work

Korennaya (Kursk Root) Hermitage of the Birthplace of the Holy Theotokos. www.kurskroot.com/monastic_life.html.

Svyato-Troitskaya Sergieva Lavra. www.stsl.ru/.

Ulitsa Prechistenka (Prechistenka Street in Moscow). https://ru.wikipedia.
org/wiki/Ulitsa_Prechistenka.

Secondary Literature

Aelen, Peter, OI. "Ideya bogochelovechestva v filosofii Vladimira Solovyova."
In Borisova and Kozyreva, *Solovyovskij sbornik*, 272–306.

Aksakov, Ivan Sergeyevich. "Eshhyo o vozzvanii 'Vsemirnogo Izrail'skogo
Soyuza'" (More on the Manifesto of the Universal Israelite Alliance).
Rus' (Dec. 15/27, 1883): 57.

——. "Evrejskaya internatsionalka i bor'ba s Evrejstvom v Evrope" (The
Jewish International and the War with Jewry in Europe). *Rus'* 21 (Nov. 1
[o.s.]/13 [n.s.], 1883): 20–26.

——. "Polskij vopros i zapadno-russkoe delo; evrejskij vopros, 1860–1886."
In *Sochineniya, 1860–1886*, 3:722–27. Moscow: M. G. Volchaninov,
1886–87.

——. "Razbor tsirkulyarnogo vozzvaniya 'Evrejskogo Vsemirnogo Soyuza'"
(Analysis of the Manifesto of the International Jewish Alliance). *Rus'* 23
(Dec. 1/13, 1883): 2–12.

Aleksandrov, Shmuel. *Miktebei Mehqar u-Biqoret* (Letters of Research and
Criticism). Vol. 1. Vilna: ha-Almanah veha-ahim Rom, 1907.

Allen, Paul Marshall. *Vladimir Soloviev, Russian Mystic*. Blauvelt, NY: Steiner-
books, 1978.

Anastos, Milton V. *Constantinople and Rome*. Variorum Collected Studies.
Aldershot: Ashgate, 2001. www.myriobiblos.gr/texts/english/milton1
_index.html.

Anonymous. "Nam pishut." *Russkij evrej* 8 (Feb. 18, 1882): 301.

——. "[Obituary of] Nikanor, Arkhiepiskop Khersonskij i Odesskij"
(Nikanor, Archbishop of Kherson and Odessa). *Novoe vremya* 5327
(Dec. 28, 1890/Jan. 9, 1891): 1.

——. "Otgoloski pechati." *Nedel'naya khronika voskhoda* 6 (Feb. 5, 1895):
133–35.

——. "Pamyat'i Vl. S. Solovyova." *Voskhod* 69 (Sept. 3, 1900): 6–7.

——. "Peterburgskaya letopis." *Nedel'naya khronika voskhoda* 8 (Feb. 19,
1882): 184.

——. [Akim Volynsky (= A. Flekser)]. "Peterburgskaya letopis'." *Nedel'naya
khronika voskhoda* 9 (Feb. 26, 1882): 212–13.

——. "V. S. Solovyov." *Voskhod* 60 (Aug. 3, 1900): 18–19.

Anti-Defamation League (ADL). "The Talmud in Anti-Semitic Polemics."
Feb. 2003. www.adl.org/presrele/asus_12/the_talmud.pdf.

Aronson, Michael. *Troubled Waters: The Origins of the 1881 Anti-Jewish Pogroms in Russia.* Pittsburgh, PA: University of Pittsburgh Press, 1990.

Averin, Boris Valentinovich, and Dar'ya Bazanova, eds. *Kniga o Vladimire Solovyove.* Moscow: Sovetskij Pisatel', 1991.

Babintsev, Valentin Pavlovich. "Evrejskij vopros v sotsial'no-filosofskoj mysli rossijskoj imperii (XIX–nachala XX v.)." PhD diss., University of Belgorod, 1999.

Bakst, Nikolai Ignat'evich (b. Noah Isaacson). "Pamyati Vladimira Sergeevicha Solovyova" (In Commemoration of Vladimir Sereevich Solovyov). Speech delivered Nov. 12, 1900, before the Society for the Dissemination of Education among the Jews. *Voskhod* 11 (1900): 84–93.

———. *"Pamyati Moiseya Mendel'sona k stoletiyu so dnya ego smerti* (In Commemoration of the Centenary of the Death of Moses Mendelsohn). St. Petersburg, 1886.

———. [N. Borisov and Ph. Nezhdanov, pseud.]. *Russkie lyudi o evreyakh* (Russian People on the Jews). St. Petersburg: A. M. Wolff, 1891. http://dic.academic.ru/dic.nsf/enc_biography/7502/Бакст.

von Balthasar, Hans Urs. "Soloviev." In *The Glory of the Lord,* translated by Andrew Louth et al. 3:279–352. Edinburgh: T & T Clark, 1986.

Bar-Yosef, Hamutal. "The Jewish Reception of Vladimir Solov'ëv." In van den Bercken, de Courten, and van der Zweerde, *Vladimir Solov'ëv,* 363–92.

Baron, Salo W. *The Russian Jew under the Tsars and Soviets.* New York: Macmillan, 1964.

Belkin, Dmitrij. "'Evrejskij vopros' kak 'khristianskij vopros': K interpretatsii odnoj formuly V. S. Solovyova." In Borisova and Kozyreva, eds., *Solovyovskij sbornik,* 466–74.

———. *"Gäste, die bleiben": Vladimir Solov'ev, die Juden und die Deutschen* ("Guests Who Stay": Vladimir Solov'ev, the Jews, and the Germans). Hamburg: EVA Europäische Verlagsanstalt, 2008.

———. "Die Rezeption V. S. Solov'evs in Deutschland." PhD diss., Tübingen, 2000. http://d-nb.info/963186256/34.

Berdyaev, Nicholas. *Christianity and Anti-Semitism.* New York: Philosophical Library, 1954.

Berger, David, ed. *The Legacy of Jewish Migration: 1881 and Its Impact.* New York: Brooklyn College Press, 1983.

Berlin, Israel. "Talmud." In *Evrejskaya èntsiklopediya,* edited by A. Harkavi, D. Gintsburg, Yu. Gessen, S. Dubnov, I. Markon, and N. Pereferkovich et al., 14:721–23. St. Petersburg: Obshhestvo dlya nauchnykh evrejskikh izdanij, izdatel'stvo Brokhaus-Efron, 1906–12. www.runivers.ru/lib/book7069/.

Berlin, Pavel A. "Russkie mysliteli i evrei: Vl. Solovyov, S. Bulgakov, P. Struve, V. Rozanov" (Russian Thinkers and the Jews: V. Solovyov . . .). *Novyj zhurnal* 70 (1962): 223–35.

Berlin, R. Isaiah b. Judah Loeb. *Kashot Meyushav*. Koenigsburg: Hayyim Arye, 1860.

Berline, Paul A. "Russian Religious Philosophers and the Jews (Soloviev, Berdyaev, Bulgakov, Struve, Rozanov, and Fedotov)." *Jewish Social Studies* 9.4 (1947): 271–318.

Betankur, Byakster. "Brafman, Yakov Aleksandrovich." In *Russkij biograficheskij slovar'*, edited by A. A. Polovtsev, 3:336–37. St. Petersburg: Tip. Glavnogo Upr. Udelov, 1908.

Bey, Major Osman [Frederick Millingen]. *Die Eroberung der Welt durch die Juden* (The Conquest of the World by the Jews). Basel: Krüsi, 1873; 7th ed., Wiesbaden: Bechtold, 1875. 1878 English translation by F. W. Mathias, available at https://archive.org/details/ConquestOfTheWorldBy TheJews and www.scribd.com/doc/25983863/Bey-Osman-the-Conquest -of-the-World-by-the-Jews-Trans-1878-by-F-W-Mathias-Zionism -Jewish-Lob.

Bezobrazova, Maria, S. "Vospominaniya o brate Vladimire Solovyove (Recollections about [My] Brother Vladimir Solovyov) (1908). In Averin and Bazanova, *Kniga o Vladimire Solovyove*, 77–112.

Bialik, Hayyim Nahman. *Collected Poems, 1899–1934: Critical Edition* (in Hebrew). Edited by Dan Miron et al. Tel-Aviv: Dvir, 1990.

Biel, Anna. "Nikolai Nekrasov's Representation of the Decembrist Wives." *Australian Slavonic and East Europrean Studies* 25 (2011): 39–59. http:// miskinhill.com.au/journals/asees/25:1-2/nekrasovs-decembrist-wives .pdf.

Biffi, Giacomo Cardinal. "L'Ammonimento profetico di Vladimir S. Soloviev" (Meditation preached on Feb. 27, 2007). *Il Foglio*, Mar. 15, 2007. http:// holyqueen.altervista.org/teol_att_anticristo_solovev.htm.

——. "Antichrist Is an Ecumenist, Vatican Preacher Warns" (Mar. 11, 2007). www.cardinalrating.com/cardinal_13_article_5353.htm.

——. "Soloviev and Our Time." *Inside the Vatican* (June–July 2000): 24–25. www.christendom-awake.org/pages/soloviev/biffi.html.

Billington, James H. *Mikhailovsky and Russian Populism.* Oxford: Oxford University Press, 1958.

Blavatsky, Helena Petrovna. "Answer to a Russian Philosopher" (Response to V. Solovyov's review of her *Key to Theosophy*). In de Zirkof, *H. P. Blavatsky,* 12:334–49.

Boehme, Jacob. *Mysterium Magnum*. Translated by John Sparrow. London: John M. Watkins, 1924.

Bojkov, Viktor Fedorovich. *Tajna Izrailya: "Evrejskij vopros" v Russkoj religioznyj mysli kontsa XIX—pervoj poloviny XX v.v.* St. Petersburg: Sofia, 1993. http://imwerden.de/pdf/tajna_izrailja_rus_mysl_19-20_veka.pdf.

Bojkov, Viktor Fedorovich, et al., eds. *Vladimir Solovyov: Pro et Contra: Lichnost' i tvorchestvo Vladimira Solovyova v otsenke russkikh myslitelej i issledovatelej: Antologiya.* St. Petersburg: Russkij khristianskij gymanitarnyj institut, 2000.

Bojkov, Viktor Fedorovich, and Yuri Yur'evich Bulychev et al., eds. *Vladimir Solovyov: Pro et Contra: Lichnost' i tvorchestvo Vladimira Solovyova v otsenke russkikh myslitelej i issledovatelej: Antologiya.* Vol. 2. St. Petersburg: Russkij khristianskij gymanitarnyj institut, 2002.

Borisov, N., and Ph. Nezhdanov [Nikolai Ignatievich Bakst]. *Russkie lyudi o evreyakh* (Russian People on the Jews). St. Petersburg: A. M. Wolff, 1891.

Borisova, Yevgeniya V., and Anna P. Kozyreva, eds. *Solovyovskij sbornik: Materialy mezhdunarodnoj konferentsii "V. S. Solovyov i ego filosofskoe nasledie"* (A Solovyovian Collection: Materials for the International Conference "V. S. Solovyov and His Philosophical Legacy"), *28–30 August 2000.* Moscow: Fenomenologiya-Germeevtika, 2001.

Borzova, Elena Petrovna, and A. I. Novikov. "Mariya Bezobrazova—pervaya zhenshhina-filosof 'serebryanogo veka.'" In *O blagorodstve i preimushhestve zhenskogo pola: iz istorii zhenskogo voprosa v Rossii* (Sbornik nauchnykh trudov), edited by R. Sh. Ganelin, 153–58. St. Petersburg: Peterburgskaya gos. akademiya kul'tury, Nevsky institut yazyka i kul'tury, Zhenskaya gumanitarnaya kollegiya, 1997.

Bourdeaux, Michael, ed. *The Politics of Religion in Russia and the New States of Eurasia.* Armonk, NY: M. E. Sharpe, 1995.

Brafman, Yakov. *Kniga Kagala: Materialy dlya izucheniya evrejskogo byta. Sobral i perevyol Iakov Brafman.* 1st ed. Vilna: Pechatnya. Vilenskogo Gubernskogo Pravleniya, 1869. *Kniga Kagala.* 2nd ed., 2 vols. St. Petersburg, 1875. *Kniga Kagala: Vsemirnyj evrejskij vopros.* 3rd ed., 2 vols. Edited by Alexander Brafman. St. Petersburg: Tip. S. Dobrodeeva, 1882.

Brent, Jonathan, and Vladimir Naumov. *Stalin's Last Crime: The Plot against the Jewish Doctors, 1948–1953.* New York: HarperCollins, 2003.

Briman, Aron Israel [Dr. Justus, pseud.]. *Judenspiegel; oder, 100 [i.e. Hundert] neuenthüllte, heutzutage noch geltende, den Verkehr der Juden mit den Christen betreffende Gesetze der Juden; mit einer die Entstehung und Weiterentwicklung der jüdischen Gesetze darstellenden, höchst interessanten Einleitung.* Paderborn: Bonifacius [J. W. Schröder], 1883.

Brovkovich, Nikanor (bishop of Kherson and Odessa). "Pouchenie." *Strannik* (Oct. 1890): 235–40.

——. *Pozitivnaya filosofiya i sverkhchuvstvennoe bytie (kritika na kritiku chistogo razyma Kanta)*. St. Petersburg: Tip. F. Eleonskogo i Ko, 1888.

——. *Vospominaniya Archiepiskopa Nikanora*. Moscow: Synodal Typography, 1908.

Browne, Charles Gordon, and James Edwards Swallow, eds. *Christian Classics Ethereal Library*. www.ccel.org.

Burmistrov, Konstantin Yur'evich. "Vladimir Solovyov i Kabbala: K postanovke problemy" (Vladimir Solovyov and the Kabbalah: Towards a Formulation of the Problem). *Issledovaniya po istorii Russkoj mysli* (1998): 7–104.

Buxtorff, Johannes. *Juden-schül*. Published in Latin as *Synagoga Judaica* (Full title: *Synagoga judaica; hoc est, Schola judæorum in qua nativitas, institutio, religio, vita, mors, sepulturaq; ipsorum e libris eorundem; a M. Johanne Buxdorfia . . . graphice descripta est. Addita est mox per eundem judæi, cum Christiano disputatio de Messia nostro-æutraque Germanica nunc Latinè reddita sunt opera & studio M. Hermanni Germbergii. Accessit Ludouici Carreti Epistola, de conuersione eius ad Christum, per eundem ex Hebræo Latinè conuersa*). New York: G. Olms, 1989 (lst ed. 1604, 3rd ed. 1622, 4th ed. 1680). English translation by Alan D. Corré available at www.uwm.edu/People/corre/buxdorf/index.html.

Bychkov, Sergei Sergeevich. *Khronika neraskrytogo ubijstva* (A Chronicle of an Unsolved Murder). Moscow: Russkoe reklamnoe izdatel'stvo, 1996. www.alexandrmen.ru/books/bychkov/bych01.html.

Byrnes, Robert Francis. *Pobedonostsev, His Life and Thought*. Bloomington: Indiana University Press, 1968.

Carlson, Maria. "Gnostic Elements in the Cosmology of Vladimir Soloviev." In Kornblatt, *Russian Religious Thought*, 49–67. http://american-buddha .com/lit.soloviev.gnosticelements.htm.

Carroll, Robert P. *When Prophecy Failed: Cognitive Dissonance in the Prophetic Tradition of the Old Testament*. New York: Seabury Press, 1979.

Ch., I. [full name unknown]. "Gets, Fajvel' Meer Bentselovich." In *Evrejskaya èntsiklopediya* (Jewish Encyclopedia), 6:467. St. Petersburg: Obshhestvo dlya nauchnykh Evrejskikh izdanij i izdatel'stvo Brokgauz-Efron (Society for Academic Jewish Publications and the Publishing House of Brockhaus and Efron), 1910.

Chapman, Henry Palmer. "Monothelitism and Monothelites." In *The Catholic Encyclopedia*, edited by Charles G. Herbermann, 10. 1913. www .newadvent.org/cathen/10502a.htm.

Chicherin, Boris Nikolaevich. *Liberty, Equality, and the Market: Essays*. Edited and translated by G. M. Hamburg. New Haven, CT: Yale University Press, 1998.

Cioran, Samuel. *Vladimir Solov'ev and the Knighthood of the Divine Sophia.* Waterloo, ON: Wilfrid Laurier University Press, 1977.

Cohen, Rabbi David [Rav ha-Nazir]. *Rabbi David Cohen Memorial Book, Nazir Ehav* (The Nazirite among His Brethren). 3 vols. Jerusalem: Nezer David Assoc., 1977.

Cohen, Stuart. *The Three Crowns: Structures of Communal Politics in Rabbinic Jewry.* Cambridge: Cambridge University Press, 1990.

Cohn, Norman. *Warrant for Genocide: The Myth of the Jewish-World-Conspiracy and the Protocols of the Elders of Zion.* New York, Harper & Row, 1967.

Cohn-Sherbok, Dan. *Messianic Judaism.* New York: Continuum International, 2000.

Copleston, Frederick Charles, SJ. *Russian Religious Philosophy: Selected Aspects.* Notre Dame, IN: University of Notre Dame Press, 1988.

de Courten, Manon. *History, Sophia and the Russian Nation: A Reassessment of Solov'ëv's View of History and His Social Commitment.* Bern: Peter Lang, 2004.

——. "Two Narratives on History in Vladimir Solov'ëv: The Polish Question." In Borisova and Kozyreva, *Solovyovskij sbornik,* 475–502.

Dahm, Helmut. *Vladimir Solovyev and Max Scheler: Attempt at a Comparative Interpretation.* Translated by Kathleen Wright. Dordrecht: D. Reidel, 1975.

Daniel, Wallace L. "Father Aleksandr Men and the Struggle to Recover Russia's Heritage." *Demokratizatsiya* 17.1 (2009): 73–92. www.alexandrmen .ru/english/demokratizatsia/Father_Aleksandr_Men_and_the_Struggle _to_Recover_Russia.html.

Davies, Norman. *Europe: A History.* Oxford: Oxford University Press, 1996.

Delegates of the Bishops Committee on Ecumenical and Interreligious Affairs of the United States Conference of Catholic Bishops (BCEIA) and the National Council of Synagogues (NCS). "Reflections on Covenant and Mission." *Origins* 32.13 (Sept. 5, 2002).

Dell Acta, A. "Realizm V. S. Solovyova" (The Realism of V. S. Solovyov). In Borisova and Kozyreva, *Solovyovskij sbornik,* 272–94.

Dillon, Emile J. *Count Leo Tolstoy: A New Portrait.* London: Hutchinson & Co., 1934.

Diminsky, Stepan Iakovlevich. *Evrei(,) ikh verouchenie i nravouchenie(.) Issledovanie S. Ia. Diminskago.* St. Petersburg: I. N. Skorokhodova, 1891.

——. "Issledovanie o Talmude" (A Study of the Talmud). Master's thesis, Kiev Theological Seminary, Aug. 1868. Republished as *Issledovanie o Talmude.* Kiev: Tip. Kievopecherskoj Lavry, [1869] 1893.

Dostoevsky, Anna. *Dostoyevsky: Reminiscences.* Translated by Beatrice Still-man. New York: Liveright, 1977.

Dostoevsky, Fyodor Mikhailovich. *The Brothers Karamazov.* Translated by Richard Pevear and Larissa Volokhonsky. New York: Farrar, Straus and Giroux, 2002.

———. *Crime and Punishment: The Coulson Translation, Backgrounds and Sources, Essays in Criticism.* 3rd ed. Translated by George Gibian. New York: W. W. Norton, 1989.

———. "I. Evrejskij vopros," "II. Pro I contra," "III. Status in statu. Sorok vekov bytiya," "IV. No da zdrastvuyet bratstvo!" In *Polnoe sobranie so-chinenij 1888 goda.* Vol. 11. *Dnevnik pisatelya za 1877 god,* 81–85, 85–89, 90–95, 95–98. 3rd ed. St. Petersburg: Tip. Brat. Panteleevykh, 1888. http://imwerden.de/pdf/dostoevsky_pss_1888_dnevnik_1877.pdf.

———. "Polemika protiv M. N. Katkova." In *Polnoe sobranie sochinenij v 30 tomakh (33 knigakh).* Vol. 19. Leningrad: Nauka, 1985.

———. *Sobranie Sochinenij v 15 Tomakh.* Vol. 15. *Pis'ma. 1834–1881.* Lenin-grad: Nauka, 1991.

Dubnov, Simon Markovich. *History of the Jews: From the Congress of Vienna to the Emergence of Hitler.* Translated by Moshe Spiegel. 2 vols. New York: A. S. Barnes, 1973.

———. *History of the Jews in Russia and Poland, From the Earliest Times until the Present Day.* (Vol. 1: *From the Beginning until the Death of Alexan-der I* [1825]; Vol. 2: *From the Death of Alexander I until the Death of Al-exander III* [1825–94].) Translated by I. Friedlaender. Philadelphia, PA: Jewish Publication Society of America, 1916. Reprinted by KTAV, 1975.

———. *Kniga zhizni.* Riga: Jaunatnes Gramata, 1934–35.

———. *Vsemirnaya istoriya evrejskogo naroda ot drevnejshikh vremen do nas-tojasshego.* 10 vols. Riga: Dzive un Kultura, 1936–39.

Dubnov, Simon Markovich, and Gregory Ya. Krasnyi-Admoni, eds. *Materialy dlya istorii anti-evrejskikh pogromov v Rossii.* 2 vols. Petrograd: Gosu-darstvennoe Izdatel'stvo, 1919–23.

Dubnova-Erlich, Sofiya. *Khleb i Matsa: Vospominaniya, stikhi raznykh let.* St. Petersburg: Maksima, 1994.

Dudakov, Savely Yur'evich. *Ètyudy lyubvi i nenavisti.* Moscow: Rossijskij gosudarstvennyj universitet, 2003. http://lib.rus.ec/b/136492/read.

———. *Paradoksy i prichudy filosemitizma i antisemitizma v Rossii.* Moscow: Rossijskij gosudarstvennyj gumanitarnyj universitet, 2000. http://book.e-reading-lib.org/book.php?book=94034.

———. "Vladimir Solovyov i Sergei Nilus." In *Russian Literature and His-tory: In Honour of Professor I. Serman,* edited by Wolf Moskovich et al.,

163–69. Jerusalem: Hebrew University of Jerusalem, Department of Russian and Slavic Studies, 1989.

Dunlop, John B. "The Russian Orthodox Church as an 'Empire-Saving' Institution." In Bourdeaux, *The Politics of Religion in Russia and the New States of Eurasia*, 32–36.

Dupuy, Bernard. "Les juifs, l'histoire et la fin des temps selon Vladimir Soloviev." *ISTINA* 37 (1992): 253–83. Reprinted in *Œcuménisme et eschatologie selon Soloviev*, edited by Société Vladimir Soloviev. Paris: F.-X. De Guibert, 1994. 108–41.

Ecker, Jakob. *Der Judenspiegel im Lichte der Wahrheit; eine wissenschaftliche Untersuchung.* 3rd ed. Paderborn: Druck und Verlag der Bonifacius-Druckerei, 1921.

Ellis, Jane. *The Russian Orthodox Church: A Contemporary History.* London: Croom Helm, 1986.

El'tsova, K. M. "Sny nezdeshnie: K 25-let'iyu konchiny V. S. Solovyova (1926)." In Averin and Bazanova, *Kniga o Vladimire Solovyove*, 112–55.

Ettinger, Shmuel. "Ha-reka ha-idiologi le-hofa'ata shel ha-sifrut ha-antishemit he-hadashah be-Rusia" (The Ideological Background of the Appearance of Modern Antisemitic Literature in Russia). *Zion* 35.1–4 (1970): 194–95.

Evtuhov, Catherine. Review of D. Belkin, *"Gäste, die bleiben"* (2008), and J. D. Kornblatt, *Divine Sophia* (2009). *Kritika: Explorations in Russian and Eurasian History* 11.1 (Winter 2010): 193–200.

Fackenheim, Emil. "Demythologizing and Remythologizing in Jewish Experience: Reflections Inspired by Hegel's Philosophy." In *Myth and Philosophy*, edited by George F. McLean, OMI, 16–27. Proceedings of the American Catholic Philosophical Association, vol. 45. Washington, DC: Catholic University of America, 1971.

———. *Jewish Philosophers and Jewish Philosophy.* Bloomington: Indiana University Press, 1996.

Faresov, Anatoly I. "Umstvennye perelomy v deyatel'nosti N. S. Leskova" (Intellectual Fractures in the Oeuvre of N. S. Leskov). *Istoricheskij vestnik* 3 (1916): 785–99.

Feuerbach, Ludwig. *Das Wesen des Christenthums.* Leipzig: Otto Wigand, 1841; 2nd ed. 1843; 3rd ed. 1849.

Flekser, A. A. [Chaim L.; Akim Lvovich Volynsky, pseud.]. "Istoricheskaya rol' evrejstva: Lektsiya prof. Vl. Solovyova." *Rassvet* 9 (Feb. 26, 1882): 335–37.

Florovsky, Georges. *Ways of Russian Theology.* Edited by Richard S. Haugh, translated by Robert L. Nichols. 2 vols. Belmont, MA: Nordland, 1979, 1987. www.holytrinitymission.org/books/english/way_russian _theology_florovsky.htm.

Flusser, David. "Vladimir Soloviev und unsere Lage." *Freiburger Rundbrief* 21 (1969): 8–11.

Fomin, Sergei Vladimirovich, ed. *Rossiya pered vtorym prishestviyem* (Russia before the Second Coming). Moscow: Rodnik, 1994.

Frank, Semyon L. *A Solovyov Anthology.* Translated by Natalie Duddington. London: SCM Press, 1950. Reprinted with a new preface by Giacomo Biffi and an introduction by Hans Urs von Balthasar. London: Saint Austin Press, 2001.

Frankel, Jonathan. "The Crisis of 1881–1882 as a Turning Point in Modern Jewish History." In *The Legacy of Jewish Migration: 1881 and Its Impact,* edited by David Berger, 9–22. Social Science Monographs. New York: Brooklyn College Press, 1983.

——. *Prophecy and Politics.* Cambridge: Cambridge University Press, 1981.

Frierson, Cathy A. *All Russia Is Burning! A Cultural History of Fire and Arson in Late Imperial Russia.* Seattle: University of Washington Press, 2002.

Fünn, Samuel Joseph, Kh. L. Katsenelenbogen, and Lev Osipovich Levanda, trans. and eds. *Mirovozzrenie talmudistov: Svod religiozno-nravstvennykh pouchenij (v vyderzhkakh iz glavnejshikh knig ravvinskoj pis'mennosti).* St. Petersburg: Eduard Gonne, 1874–76. Reprinted Moscow: Nauchno-Izdatelskii tsentr "Ladomir," 1994.

Gaidenko, Piama Pavlovna. *Vladimir Solovyov i filosofiya serebrenogo veka.* Moscow: Progress-Traditsiya, 2001.

Gallaher, Brandon. "The Christological Focus of Vladimir Solov'ev's Sophiology." *Modern Theology* 25.4 (2009): 617–46.

——. "Graced Creatureliness: Ontological Tension in the Uncreated/Created Distinction in the Sophiologies of Solov'ev, Bulgakov and Milbank." *Logos: A Journal of Eastern Christian Studies* 47.1–2 (2006): 163–90.

Gaut, Greg, "Can a Christian Be a Nationalist? Vladimir Solov'ev's Critique of Nationalism." *Slavic Review* (Spring 1998): 77–94.

Gerstein, Linda. *Nicolai Strakhov, Philosopher, Man of Letters and Social Critic.* Russian Research Center Studies 65. Cambridge, MA: Harvard University Press, 1971.

Gessen, Iulii, I. *Istoriya evrejskogo naroda v Rossii* (History of the Jewish People of Russia). 2 vols. Leningrad: n.p., 1925, 1927.

Getz, Faivel. "Nekotorye vospominanija ob otnoshenii V. S. Solovyova k evreyam." *Voskhod* 63 (Aug. 13, 1900): 30–35; 79 (Sept. 7, 1900): 18–25. Reprinted in *Budushnost'* 63 (1960): 30–35.

——. "Ob otnoshenii Vl. S. Solovyova k evrejskomu voprosu" (Vladimir Solovyov's Attitude to the Jewish Question). *Voprosy filosofii i psikholo-*

gii 56 (Jan.–Feb. 1901): 159–98. Reprinted with introduction in Faivel Getz, *Ob otnoshenii Vl. S. Solovyoa k evrejskomu voprosu.* Moscow: I. N. Kushnerev, 1901; 2nd ed. 1902, 1–44; and in Bojkov and Bulychev, *Vladimir Solovyov: Pro et Contra,* 2:695–725.

——. *Slovo podsudimomu. S pis'mami L. N. Tolstogo, B. N. Chicherina, Vladimira Sergeevicha Solovyova i V. G. Korolenko.* St. Petersburg: Tip. Gaz. Izvestiya, 1891.

Gilbert, Martin. *The Routledge Atlas of Russian History.* 3rd ed. London: Routledge, 2002.

Gintsburg, David. "Kabbala, misticheskaya filosofiya evreev" (Kabbalah: Mystical Philosophy of the Jews). *Voprosy filosofii i psikhologii* 22 (1896): 277–300.

Ginzberg, Louis. *The Legends of the Jews.* 6 vols. Philadelphia: Jewish Publication Society, 1909–28. Vols. 1–4 available at http://philologos.org/__eb-lotj/.

Glants, Musya. *Where Is My Home? The Art and Life of the Russian-Jewish Sculptor Mark Antokolsky, 1843–1902.* Plymouth, MA: Lexington Books, 2010.

Glazov, Gregory. "Vladimir Solovyov and the Idea of the Papacy." *Communio* 24.1 (1997): 128–42.

Glazov, Yuri. *The Russian Mind since Stalin's Death.* Dordrecht: D. Reidel, 1985.

——. *Tesnye vrata, vozrozhdenie russkoj intelligentsii.* London: Overseas Publications Interchange, 1973.

——. *V krayu otsov: Khronika nedavnego proshlogo.* Moscow: Istina i Zhizn', 1998.

Glouberman, Emanuel. "Fyodor Dostoyevsky, Vladimir Soloviev, Vasilii Rozanov, and Lev Shestov on Jewish and Old Testament Themes." PhD diss., University of Michigan, 1974.

Gollerbakh, Erikh Fedorovich. *Vstrechi i vpechatleniya.* St. Petersburg: Inapress, 1998.

Goodman, Martin. *The Ruling Class of Judea: The Origins of the Jewish Revolt against Rome AD 66–70.* Cambridge: Cambridge University Press, 1987.

Gorky, Maxim. "N. S. Leskov." In *N. S. Leskov: Izbrannye sochineniya v 3 tomakh* (Selected Works in 3 Volumes), edited by Aleksandr Amfiteatrov. St. Petersburg: I Grzhebin, 1923.

Gougenot des Mousseaux, Henri-Roger. *Le juif, le judaïsme et la judaïsation des peuples chrétiens.* Paris: H. Plon, 1869.

Greenberg, Louis. *The Jews in Russia: The Struggle for Emancipation.* 2 vols. in 1. New Haven, CT: Yale University Press, 1965.

Gregory XVI, Pope. *Mirari vos* (On Liberalism and Religious Indifferentism; Encyclical Promulgated Aug. 15, 1832). www.ewtn.com/library/encyc/g16mirar.htm.

Groberg, Kristi. "Vladimir Sergeevich Solov'ev: A Bibliography." *Modern Greek Studies Yearbook* 14–15 (1998–99): 299–398.

Grossman, Leonid Petrovich. "Dostoevskii i pravitel'stvennye krugi 1870-kh godov." *Literaturnoe nasledstvo* 15 (1934): 83–162.

Gruzenberg, Semyon [Shlomo]. "Solovyov, Vladimir Sergeevich." In Brokgauz-Efron, *Evrejskaya èntsiklopediya* 14 (1912): 445–447.

Ha-Am, Ahad. "'Al-Shtei ha-Se'ipim'" (Between Two Opinions). In *Kol Kitvei Ahad Ha-am* (Collected Works of Ahad Ha-am). Tel-Aviv: Devir, 1947.

Hagemeister, Michael. "Pavel Florenskij und der Ritualmordvorwurft." In *Appendix 2: Materialien zu Pavel Florenskij* [Anhang zu Pawel Florenski, Werke in zehn Lieferungen], edited by Michael Hagemeistrer and Torsten Metelka, 59–74. Berlin u. Zepernick: Kontext, 2001.

———. "The Protocols of the Elders of Zion: Between History and Fiction." *New German Critique* 35.1 (2008): 83–95.

———. "Vladimir Solov'ëv and Sergej Nilus: Apocalypticism and Judeophobia." *Eastern Christian Studies* (2000): 287–96.

Hahn, Scott. *Kinship by Covenant: A Canonical Approach to the Fulfillment of God's Saving Promises.* New Haven, CT: Yale University Press, 2009.

Halevi-Levin, Shemaryahu. "Me-Olam Ha-sifrut: Ha-Leumiut me-ha-hashkafa hamussarit" (From the World of Literature: Nationality from the Moral Point of View). *Ha-Melitz* 32 (Feb. 7, 1895): 5–6.

Halpérin, Jean. "Vladimir Soloviev Listens to Israel: The Christian Question." *Immanuel* 26–27 (1994): 198–210.

Hamant, Yves. *Alexandre Men: Un témoin pour la Russie de ce temps.* Paris: Editions mame, 1993.

Hanson, Paul D. *The Dawn of Apocalyptic.* Philadelphia, PA: Fortress Press, 1975.

Hegel, Georg Wilhelm Friedrich. *Vorlesungen über die Philosophie der Geschichte,* and *Vorlesungen über der Religion.* In *Werke,* edited by Eva Moldenhauer and Karl Markus Michel, vols. 11 and 12. Frankfurt am Main: Suhrkamp, 1969–71. English translations = *The Philosophy of History.* Translated by J. Sibree. New York: Dover, 1956. *Lectures on the Philosophy of Religion.* Translated by Peter C. Hodgson et al. Berkeley: University of California Press, 1998.

d'Herbigny, Michel. *Un Newman russe: Vladimir Soloviev (1853–1900).* 3rd ed. Paris: G. Beauchesne, 1911. English translation = *Vladimir Soloviev: A Russian Newman (1853–1900).* Translated by Anna Maud Buchanan, edited by Fr. Thomas J. Gerrard. London: R. & T. Washbourne, 1918.

Hesiod. *Hesiod: The Homeric Hymns and Homerica.* Translated by Hugh Gerard Evelyn-White. Cambridge, MA: Harvard University Press, 1982.

Hessen, Sergius. "Der Kampf der Utopie und der Autonomie des Guten in der Weltanschauung Dostoewskis und W. Solowjows." *Die Padagogische Hochschule* 5 (Oct. 1929).

Horowitz, Brian. *Jewish Philanthropy and Enlightenment in Late-Tsarist Russia.* Seattle: University of Washington Press, 2009.

Iseroff, Ami. "Pogrom." *Zionism and Israel–Encyclopedic Dictionary.* Apr. 6, 2009. www.zionism-israel.com/dic/pogrom.htm.

Jelavich, Barbara. *Russia and the Formation of the Romanian National State, 1821–1878.* Cambridge: Cambridge University Press. 2004.

John Paul II. *Encyclical Letter* Fides et ratio *of the Supreme Pontiff John Paul II to the Bishops of the Catholic Church on the Relationship between Faith and Reason.* Vatican: Libreria Editrice Vaticana, 1998.

———. "Homily of His Holiness John Paul II: Victory Square, Warsaw, 2 June 1979." www.vatican.va/holy_father/john_paul_ii/homilies/1979/documents/hf_jp-ii_hom_19790602_polonia-varsavia_en.html.

Kantor, D-r A. "Vladimir Sergeevich Solovyov" (in Hebrew). *Ha-Dor* 2 (1901): 9–12; 4 (1902): 7–9.

Kantrowitz, David. *Judaic Classics.* Brooklyn, NY: Institute for Computers in Jewish Life, Davka Corp., and Judaica Press, 1991–2003. CDRom. Version 3.0.6.

Katz, Benzion. *Zikhronot: Hamishim shanah ba-historyah shel Yehude Rusyah* (Memoirs: Fifty Years in the History of Russian Jews). Tel Aviv: N. Tverski, 1963.

Kaufman, Abram Evegen'evich. *Druz'ya i vragi evreev.* St. Petersburg: Pravda, 1907.

Kautsch, Wilhelm, *Hebrew Grammar.* Edited and enlarged by E. Kautzsch. Oxford: Clarendon Press, 1988.

Kel'ner, Viktor Efimovich, and D. A. Elyashevich. *Literatura o evreyakh na russkom yazyke 1890–1947: Bibliograficheskij ukazatel'.* St. Petersburg, Akademicheskij Proekt, 1995.

Khamor, Levi. *The Revelation of the Son of Man.* Petersham: St. Bede's, 1989.

Khomiakov, Aleksei Stepanovich. *Zapiski o vsemirnoj istorii* (Notes on Universal History). In *Polnoe sobranie sochinenij.* Vols. 5–8. Moscow: Universitetskaya tipografiya, 1904–6.

Khoruzhy, Sergei S. "Nasledie Vladimira Solovyova sto let spustya" (The Legacy of Vladimir Solovyov a Hundred Years Later). In Borisova and Kozyreva, *Solovyovskij sbornik,* 1–29.

Khvol'son, Daniil Abramovich/Avraamovich. *O nekotorykh srednevekovykh obvineniyakh protiv evreev: Istoricheskoe issledovanie po istochnikam.* St. Petersburg: Tsederbaum and Goldblum, 1880.

Kireev, Aleksandr Alekseevich "Iz perepiski Vladimira Solovyova s A. A. Kireevym" (From the Correspondence of Vladimir Solovyov with A. A. Kireev). *Russkaya mysl'* (Russian Thought) 7–8 (1917): 137–38.

Kjaer-Hansen, Kai. *Josef Rabinowitsch og den messianske bevægelse: Jødekristendommens Herzl.* Århus Forlaget: Okay-Bog, 1988. English translation = *Joseph Rabinowitz and the Messianic Movement: The Herzl of Jewish Christianity.* Translated by Birger Petterson. Grand Rapids, MI: Wm. B. Eerdmans, 1995.

———. "Rabinowitz and Lichtenstein." *Concordia Theological Quarterly* (1992): 187–93.

Klier, John Doyle. "The Ambiguous Legal Status of Russian Jewry in the Reign of Catherine II." *Slavic Review* 35.3 (1976): 504–17.

———. "Evrejskij vopros v slavyanofil'skoj presse 1862–1886 gg." *Vestnik evrejskogo universiteta v Moskve* 1.17 (1998): 41–60.

———. *Imperial Russia's Jewish Question, 1855–1881.* Cambridge: Cambridge University Press, 1995.

———. "No Prize for History (Review of Solzhenitsyn's *Dvesti Let Vmeste*)." *History Today* 52.11 (Nov. 1, 2002): 60–61.

———. *Russia Gathers Her Jews: The Origins of the "Jewish Question" in Russia, 1772–1825.* DeKalb: Northern Illinois University Press, 1986.

———. *Russians, Jews, and the Pogroms of 1881–1882.* Cambridge: Cambridge University Press, 2011.

Klimenko, M. "Vladimir Solovyov o meste Rosii v mire." In Borisova and Kozyreva, *Solovyovskij sbornik,* 426–33.

Kline, George L. "Hegel and Solovyov." In *Hegel and the History of Philosophy,* edited by Joseph J. O'Malley et al., 159–70. The Hague: Martinus Nijhoff, 1974.

———. "Russian Religious Thought." In *Nineteenth-Century Religious Thought in the West,* edited by Ninian Smart et al., 2:208–17. 3 vols. Cambridge: Cambridge University Press, 1985.

Kolubovksy, Yakov Nikolaevich. "Iz literaturnykh vospominanij." *Istoricheskij vestnik* 4 (April 1914): 134–149.

Kook, Rabbi Abraham Isaac ha-Cohen. *Iggrot H.R.A.I.H.* (The Letters of Rabbi Kook). 3 vols. Jerusalem: Mosad Harav Kook, 1985.

Kopelwitz, Ezra, and Ari Engelberg. "A Framework for Strategic Thinking about Jewish Peoplehood." Nadav Fund, Tel Aviv, 2007. www.nadavfund.org.il/Peoplehood_Position_Paper.pdf.

Kornblatt, Judith Deutsch. *Doubly Chosen: Jewish Identity, the Soviet Intelligentsia, and the Russian Orthodox Church.* Madison: University of Wisconsin Press, 2004.

———. "Is Father Alexander Men' a Saint? The Jews, the Intelligentsia, and the Russian Orthodox Church." *Toronto Slavic Quarterly* 47 (Winter 2014). www.utoronto.ca/tsq/12/kornblatt12.shtml.

———. "Russian Religious Thought and the Jewish Kabbala." In *The Occult in Russian and Soviet Culture,* ed. Bernice Glatzer Rosenthal, 75–95. Ithaca, NY: Cornell University Press, 1997.

———. "Solov'ev's Androgynous Sophia and the Jewish Kabbalah." *Slavic Review* 50.3 (1991): 487–96.

———. "Visions of Icons and Reading Rooms in the Poetry and Prose of Vladimir Solov'ev." In *Aesthetics as a Religious Factor in Eastern and Western Christianity,* edited by Wil van den Bercken and Jonathan Sutton, 125–41. Eastern Christian Studies 6. Leuven: Peeters, 2005.

———. "Vladimir Solov'ev on Spiritual Nationhood, Russia and the Jews." *Russian Review* 56.2 (1997): 159–77.

Kornblatt, Judith Deutsch, and Richard F. Gustafson, eds. *Russian Religious Thought.* Madison: University of Wisconsin Press, 1996.

Kornblatt, Judith Deutsch, Boris Jakim, and Laury Magnus, trans. and eds. *Divine Sophia: The Wisdom Writings of Vladimir Solovyov.* Ithaca, NY: Cornell University Press, 2009.

Kornblatt, Judith Deutsch, and Gary Rosenshield. "Vladimir Solovyov: Confronting Dostoyevsky on the Jewish and Christian Questions." *Journal of the American Academy of Religion* 68 (2000): 69–98.

Korolenko, Vladimir Galaktionovich. "'Deklaratsiya' V. S. Solovyova: k istorii evrejskogo voprosa v russkoj pechati." Written in 1903 in response to a pogrom in Kishinev and sent to but not published in *Russkie vedomosti* 20 (1909); published in his *Polnoe sobranie sochinenij,* 9:257–60. St. Petersburg: A. F. Marks, 1914; and *Rasskazy* 3 (1903–15), http://ruslit.traum library.net/book/korolenko-ss05-03/korolenko-ss05-03.html#work 002003\ and http://vehi.net/soloviev/korolenko.html.

———. *Vospominaniia.* Paris: Knigoizdatel'stvo E. Siial'skoy, 1927.

Kostalevsky, Marina. *Dostoevsky and Soloviev: The Art of Integral Vision.* New Haven, CT: Yale University Press, 1997.

Krahmalnikova, Zoya, ed. *Russkaya ideya i Evrei: Rokovoj spor: Khristianstvo, antisemitizm, natsionalizm.* Moscow: Nauka, 1994.

Krauskopf, Joseph. "'Eye for an Eye' or 'Turning the Other Cheek.'" In *The Stage as a Pulpit: A Sunday Lecture before the Reform Congregation Keneseth Israel.* Ser. VII, no. 29. Philadelphia: S. W. Goodman, 1894.

Krotov, Yakov. "75-ya godovshhina so dnya rozhdeniya svjashhennika Aleksandra Men'ya" (On the 75th Anniversary of Fr. Aleksandr Men's Birthday). Radio Svoboda, Jan. 23, 2010. www.svoboda.org/content/transcript /1980645.html.

———. "Who Killed Fr. Men'?" http://krotov.info/yakov/varia/engl/engl_01 .htm.

Lamennais, Félicité Robert de. *Essai sur l'indifférence en matière de religion.* Paris: Imprimerie de Baudoin Freres, 1859.

Landau, Adolph [Aharon]. "Otgoloski pechati." *Nedel'naya khronika voskhoda* 36 (Sept. 7, 1886): 955–60; 47 (Sept. 9, 1886): 980–84; 38 (Sept. 21, 1886): 1005.

Leskov, Andrei. *Zhizn' Nikolaya Leskova po ego lichnym, semejnym i nesemejnym zapisyam i pamyatyam v dvukh tomakh* (The Life of Nikolai Leskov According to His Personal, Familial, and Extra-Familial Writings and Recollections in Two Volumes). Moscow: Khudozhestvennaya literatura, 1984.

Leskov, Nikolai. *Evrei v rossii: Neskol'ko zamechanij po evrejskomu voprosu* (1883). Edited by Valery G. Kadzhaya. Moscow: Mosty Kultury, 2003.

Lewin, Adolf. *Der Judenspiegel des Dr. Justus, ins Licht der Wahrheit gerückt.* Magdeburg: Druck von D. L. Wolff, 1884.

Lippe, K. [Karpel]. *Die Gesetzsammlung des Jedenspiegels zusammengestellt und gefälscht von Aron Briman, Justus [pseud.] Beleuchtet und berichtigt von K. Lippe.* Jassy, Rumania: Buch & Steindruckerei H. Goldner, 1885.

———. *Der Talmudjude vor dem katholisch-protestantisch-orthodoxen Dreirichterkollegium Rohling-Stocker-Pobedonoscew.* Pressburg: n.p., 1884.

Loeb, Isidore. "Pis'mo v redaktsiyu Tsentral'nogo Komiteta Izrailskogo Vsemirnogo Soyuza" (Letter to the Editor from the Central Committee of the Universal Israelite Alliance). *Rus'* 24 (Dec. 15/27, 1883): 56–57.

Losev, Aleksei Fedorovich. *Vladimir Solov'ev i ego vremya.* Moscow: Molodaya Gvardiya, 2000.

Lossky, Nikolai Onufrievich. *Istoriya russkoy filosofii.* Moscow: Vysshaya shkola, 1991. English translation = *History of Russian Philosophy.* New York: International Universities Press, 1951.

———. "V zashhitu Vl. Solovyova." *Novyj zhurnal* 33 (1953).

Löwy, David. *Der Talmudjude von Rohling in der schwurgerichtsverhandlung vom 28. Oktober 1882.* Vienna: D. Löwy, 1882.

Lukashevich, Stephen. *Ivan Aksakov, 1832–1886: A Study in Russian Thought and Politics.* Cambridge, MA: Harvard University Press, 1965.

Lukianov, Sergei Mikhailovich. *Materialy k biografii Vl. S. Solovyova iz arkhiva S. M. Lukianova* [composed 1914–22]. Edited with introduction and annotations by A. N. Shakhanov. Rossijskij Arkhiv, Istoriya Otechestva v svidetel'stvakh i dokumentakh XVIII–XX vv., Al'manakh. Moscow: Studiya TRITÆ, 1992. http://az.lib.ru/s/solowxew_wladimir_sergeewich/text_0150.shtml. Also available at www.rodon.org/sva/_mkbvssiasml .htm.

——. *O Vladimire Solovyove v ego molodye gody: Materialy k biografii.* Edited by A. A. Nosov. Vols. 1–3, Petrograd, 1916–21; vol. 4, Moscow, 1990.

——. "Pamyati Vl. S. Solovyova: Stikhotvorenie." *Vestnik Evropy* 8 (1901): 513–14.

——. "Poeziya Vl. S. Solovyova." *Vestnik Evropy* 3 (1901): 128–61.

——. *Yunosheskij roman Vl. S. Solovyova v dvojnom osveshhenii.* Peterburg: Senatskaya tipografiya, 1914.

——. "Zametki o teoreticheskoj filosofii Vl. S. Solovyova." *Zhurnal ministerstva narodnogo prosveshheniya* 1 (1909): 1–66.

Lvov, Leonid. "Fascist and Antisemitic Activity Poisons Interethnic Relations in St. Petersburg." Report, May 27, 1998. *News from UCSJ* (Union of Councils for Soviet Jews). www.fsumonitor.com/stories/052798mws .shtml.

Lyass, Fedor. "O Statie Gennadiya Kostyrchenko, 'Deportatsiya-Mistifikatsiya,' opublikovannoj v zhurnale, 'Lechaim.'" *Zametki po evrejskoj istorii* 22 (Nov. 2002). http://berkovich-zametki.com/Nomer22/ Lyass1.htm.

Marx, Karl. "Zur Judenfrage." *Deutsch-Französisch Jahrbücher* 1 (Feb. 1844): 182–214.

Matual, David. "Mary and Ecumenism in the Eschatology of Vladimir Solovyov." *Diakonia* 29.3 (1996): 175–88.

McCabe, Herbert. *God Matters.* London: G. Chapman, 1987.

Meerson, Michael Aksionov. "The Life and Work of Father Alexandr Men'." In *Seeking God: The Recovery of Religious Identity in Orthodox Russia, Ukraine, and Georgia,* edited by Stephen K. Batalden, 13–28. DeKalb: Northern Illinois University Press, 1993.

——. "The Retrieval of Neoplatonism in Solov'ëv's Trinitarian Synthesis." In van den Bercken, de Courten, and van der Zweerde, *Vladimir Solov'ëv,* 233–50.

——. *The Trinity of Love in Modern Russian Theology: The Love Paradigm and the Retrieval of Medieval Love Mysticism in Modern Russian Trinitarian Thought (from Solovyov to Bulgakov).* Quincy, IL: Franciscan Press, 1998.

Men', Alexander. "Vladimir Sergeevich Solovyov" (1989). In *Mirovaya dukhovnaya kultura, Khristianstvo, Tserkov': lektsii i besedy,* edited by Anastasiya Andreeva et al., 425–26. 2nd ed. Moscow: Fond imeni Aleksandra Menya, 1997. www.alexandrmen.ru/books/mdc/mdc4_02.html.

Men', Pavel. "Aleksandra Men'ya ubili spetssluzhby, schitaet ego brat" (The Security Services Killed Aleksandr Men', According to His Brother). Interview, Newsru, Feb.17, 2014. www.newsru.com/religy/17feb2014/ pavel_menj.html.

Merezhkovsky, Dmitry. "Zemlya vo rtu" (Earth in the Mouth). In *Bol'naya Rossiya*. St. Petersburg: Obshhestvennaya pol'za, 1910. www.e-reading .ws/chapter.php/97223/40/Merezhkovskiii_-_Bol%27naya_Rossiya .html.

Michelis, Cesare G. de. *Il Manoscritto inesistente: i "Protocolli dei savi di Sion"—un apocrifo del XX secolo.* Venice: Marsilio, 1998.

Midrash Rabbah. *The Soncino Midrash Rabbah.* Brooklyn, NY: Judaica Press, 1983.

Milbank, John. "Sophiology and Theurgy: The New Theological Horizon." In *An Encounter between Eastern Orthodoxy and Radical Orthodoxy: Transfiguring the World through the Word,* edited by Adrian Pabst and Christoph Schneider. Aldershot: Ashgate, 2009.

Mochulsky, Konstantin. *Vladimir Solovyov: Zhizn' i uchenie.* 2nd ed. Paris: YMCA Press, 1951.

Monter, Barbara Heldt. *Koz'ma Prutkov: The Art of Parody.* Paris: Mouton, 1972.

Moss, Walter G. *Russia in the Age of Alexander II, Tolstoy and Dostoyevsky.* London: Anthem Press, 2002.

———. "Vladimir Soloviev and the Jews in Russia." *Russian Review* 29.2 (1970): 181–91.

———. "Vladimir Soloviev and the Russophiles." Ph.D. diss., Georgetown University, 1968.

Motroshilova, Nelli V. "Die philosophischen Grundbegriffe Vladimir Solov'ëvs und die Lehre des Spinoza." *Studia Spinozana* 11 (1995): 319–41.

Müller, Ernst. "Solowjeffs Gedanken über Judentum." *Der Jude* 1 (1916–17): 815–22.

Müller, Ludolf. *Solovjev und der Protestantismus. Mit einem Anhang: Vladimir Solovjev und das Judentum.* Freiburg: Herder, 1951.

Murphy, Francesca Aran. *The Comedy of Revelation: Paradise Lost and Regained in Biblical Narrative.* Edinburgh: T & T Clark, 2001.

Nathans, Benjamin. *Beyond the Pale: The Jewish Encounter with Late Imperial Russia.* Berkeley: University of California Press, 2002.

Nevinson, Henry W., and Eric S. Robertson, eds. *The Life of Friedrich Schiller.* London: Walter Scott, 1889.

Newman, John Henry Cardinal. *Apologia pro vita sua.* London: Longmans, Green, 1891.

———. "The Difficulties of Latitudinarianism." In *Tracts for the Times* 5.85 (1891). Reprinted in *Discussions and Arguments on Various Subjects.* London: Longmans, Green, 1891. www.newmanreader.org/Works/ arguments/index.html.

Nichols, Aidan. "Solovyov and the Papacy: A Catholic Evaluation." *Communio* 24.1 (1997): 143–59.

Nietzsche, Friedrich Wilhelm. *The Nietzsche Reader.* Edited by Keith Ansell Pearson and Duncan Large. Oxford: Blackwell, 2006.

Nikitin, Victor N. *Evrei zemledel'tsy: Istoricheskoe, zakonodatel'noe, administrativnoe i bytovoe polozhenie kolonij so vremeni ikh voznikoveniya do nashikh dnej. 1807–1887.* St. Petersburg: Tip. Gaz. "Novosti," 1887.

Nilus, Sergei, ed. "Protocols of the Elders of Zion." 2nd ed. Published as an appendix in Sergei Nilus, *Velikoe v malom i antikhrist, kak blizkaya politicheskaya vozmozhnost': Zapiski pravoslavnogo* (The Great in the Small and the Antichrist as an Imminent Political Possibility: Notes of an Orthodox Believer). Tsarskoe Selo: Tip. Tsarskoselskago komiteta Krasnago Kresta, 1905. 4th ed. Reprinted in *"Bliz est', pri dverech": O tom, chemu ne zhelayut verit' i chto tak blizko* ("He/It is Near, Even at the Doors": Concerning That Which People Wish Not to Believe and Which Is So Near). Sergiev Posad: Holy Trinity Monastery, 1917. (The lst ed., a variant of the above, was edited by Pavel Krushevan under the headline "Programa zavoevaniya mira evreyami" [The Jewish Program to Conquer the World] in nine issues of his newspaper *Znamya* in 1903.)

Noonan, Peggy. *John Paul the Great: Remembering a Spiritual Father.* New York: Viking, 2005.

———. "We Want God" (On John Paul II's sermon on June 3, 1979, at the cathedral in Gniezno). *Wall Street Journal,* Apr. 7, 2005. http://online.wsj .com/article/SB122479408458463941.html.

Obolensky, Aleksei D. "Dve vstrechi s L. N. Tolstym." In Lev Nikolaevich Tolstoy, *Pamyatniki tvorchestva i zhizni,* edited by Vyacheslav Izmail Sreznevsky. 4 vols. St. Petersburg: Ogni, 1917–23.

Opalski, Magdalena. *Poles and Jews: A Failed Brotherhood.* Hanover, NH: University Press of New England, 1992.

Ovid. *Metamorphoses, English and Latin.* Translated by Frank Justus Miller. Cambridge, MA: Harvard University Press, 1977–84.

Patrashnikov, A. "Vladimir Solovyov o Evreyakh." *Golos zarubezh'ya* 3 (1976).

Paul VI. "Declaration on the Relation of the Church to Non-Christian Religions *Nostra Aetate* Proclaimed by His Holiness Pope Paul VI on October 28, 1965." Holy See. www.vatican.va/archive/hist_councils/ii_ vatican_council/documents/vat-ii_decl_19651028_nostra_aetate_en.html.

Pausanias. *Description of Greece.* Translated by W. H. S. Jones and H. A. Omerod. 3 vols. Cambridge, MA: Harvard University Press, 1931–55.

Pereltsvaig, Asya. "Birobidzhan: Frustrated Dreams of a Jewish Homeland." Apr. 27, 2012. http://geocurrents.info/place/russia-ukraine-and -caucasus/siberia/birobidzhan-frustrated-dreams-of-a-jewish-homeland.

Phillips, Melanie. "An Illiberal and Ignorant Judgment." *Spectator,* Dec. 16, 2009. http://images.spectator.co.uk/melaniephillips/5641976/an-illiberal -and-ignorant-judgment.thtml.

Pieper, Joseph. *The Silence of St. Thomas: Three Essays.* Translated by Daniel O'Connor. London: Faber and Faber, 1957.

Pipes, Richard. "Catherine II and the Jews: The Origins of the Pale of Settlement." *Soviet Jewish Affairs* 5 (1975): 3–20.

———. "Russian Conservatism in the Second Half of the Nineteenth Century." *Slavic Review* 30.1 (1971): 120–28.

———. "Solzhenitsyn and the Jews, Revisited." *New Republic* (Nov. 2002): 26–28.

Pobedonostsev, Konstantin Petrovich. *Konstantin P. Pobedonostsev i ego korrespondenty: Pisma i zapiski.* Foreword by M. P. Pokrovsky. 2 vols. Moscow: Gosizdat, 1923.

———. *Pis'ma Pobedonostseva k Alexandru III.* Foreword by M. P. Pokrovsky. 2 vols. Moscow: Novaya Moskva, Tsenterarkhiv, 1926.

Podskalsky, G. P. *Wladimir Solovjov und die Juden.* Zurich: Judaica, 1954.

Popov, Pavel Sergeevich, ed. "Perepiska L. Tolstogo s V. S. Solovyovym" (L. Tolstoy's Correspondence with V. S. Solovyov). In *L. N. Tolstoy. II,* edited by Vladimir V. Zhdanov. Literaturnoe nasledstvo (Literary Heritage), vols. 37–38. Moscow: Akademiya Nauk, 1939.

Posnov, Mikhail Emmanuilovich. "Mitropolit Antony, kak pravoslavnyj bogoslov-dogmatist." *Tserkovnye vedomosti (Archiereevskogo sinoda)* 11–12 (1930): 7; 13–14 (1930): 8; 17–18 (1930): 8–10.

Pospielovsky, Dimitry V. "The Russian Orthodox Church in the Postcommunist CIS." In Bourdeaux, *The Politics of Religion in Russia and the New States of Eurasia,* 56–62.

Prat, Naftali [unsigned]. "Solovyov, Vladimir Sergeevich." In *Kratkaya evrejskaya èntsiklopediya,* 8:418–21. Jerusalem: Obshhestvo po issledovaniyu evrejskikh obshchin (Society for Study of Jewish Communities), 1996.

Pravoslavnaya Beseda [Internet Portal]. "O sozhzhenii knig v Ekaterinburge" (On the Burning of Books in Ekaterinburg," Apr. 6, 1999. http:// pravbeseda.ru/archive/arc2/1196.html.

[Q.]. "Lektsiya prof. V.S. Solovyova." *Russkij evrej* 9 (1882): 344.

Rashin, Alexander. *Why Didn't Stalin Murder All the Jews? The 50th Anniversary of the Doctor's Plot and Stalin's Death.* New York: Liberty, 2003.

Ratzinger, Joseph Cardinal, *Daughter Zion: Meditations on the Church's Marian Belief.* San Francisco: Ignatius Press, 1983.

Renan, Ernest. *Vie de Jésus.* 5th ed. Paris: Michel Lévy Frères, 1863. http://nrs .harvard.edu/urn-3:HUL.FIG:002578189.

Riasanovsky, Nicholas V. *Russia and the West in the Teaching of the Slavophiles: A Study in Romantic Ideology.* Cambridge, MA: Harvard University Press, 1952.

Rimius, Henry. *A candid narrative of the rise and progress of the Herrnhuters, commonly call'd Moravians, or Unitas Fratrum; [microform]: with a short account of their doctrines, drawn from their own writings. To which are added, observations on their politics in general, and particularly on their conduct whilst in the county of Budingen, in the circle of the Upper-Rhine, in Germany by Henry Rimius, Aulic Counsellor to His late Majesty the King of Prussia, and author of the memoirs of the House of Brunswick.* London: William Bradford, at the Sign of the Bible, in Second-Street, 1753.

Roberts, Elizabeth, and Ann Shukman. *Christianity for the Twenty-First Century: The Life and Work of Alexander Men.* London: SCM, 1996.

Rogger, Hans. "Government, Jews, Peasants and Land in Post-Emancipation Russia." *Cahiers du Monde Russe et sovietique* 17.2–3 (1976): 5–21, 171–211.

———. *Jewish Policies and Right-Wing Politics in Imperial Russia.* Berkeley: University of California Press, 1986.

———. "Russian Ministers and the Jewish Question, 1881–1917." In *California Slavic Studies,* edited by Nicholas V. Riasanovksy, Gleb Struve, and Thomas Eekman, 8:15–76. Berkeley: University of California Press, 1975.

Rohling, August. *Der Talmudjude: Zur Beherzigung für Juden und Christen aller Stände.* Münster: Adolph Russell, 1877. https://archive.org/details/ Rohling-August-Der-Talmudjude.

Rosenthal, Bernice Glatzer, and Martha Bohachevsky-Chomiak. *A Revolution of the Spirit: Crisis of Value in Russia, 1890–1924.* New York: Fordham University Press, 1990.

Russian Orthodox Church (Russkaya pravoslavnaya tserkov'). *Kniga pravil svyatykh apostol, svyatykh soborov vselenskikh i pomestnykh, i svyatykh otets* (The Book of Rules of the Holy Apostles, the Holy Ecumenical and Local Councils and of the Holy Fathers). Moscow: Synodal'naya tipografiya, 1893.

———. *Kormchaya, napechatannaya s originala patriarkha Iosifa* (The Book of the Helmsman, printed from the original by Patriarch Joseph). Moscow: Zhurnal "Tserkov'," [1650] 1912.

Salomoni, Antonella. "State-Sponsored Anti-Semitism in Postwar USSR: Studies and Research Perspectives." *Quest: Issues in Contemporary Jewish History* 1 (Apr. 2010). www.quest-cdecjournal.it/focus.php?id=212.

Saltykov-Shhedrin, Mikhail E. "Iyul'skoe Veyanie." *Otechestvennye zapiski* (Homeland Notes) 8 (1882): 248–58.

Saprykin, Yuri, ed., and Irina Ineshina, prod. "Sovety Stareishin: Vyacheslav Ivanov, uchenyj, 82 goda" (The Councils of Elders: Vyacheslav Ivanov, Scholar, 82 Years). *Afisha*, Feb. 6, 2012. http://daily.afisha.ru/archive/gorod/archive/wise-advices-ivanov/.

Sazonov, Serge. *Fateful Years, 1909–1916: The Reminiscences of Serge Sazonov.* New York: Kraus Reprint Co., [1928] 1971.

Schäfer, Peter. *The Jewish Jesus: How Judaism and Christianity Shaped Each Other.* Princeton, NJ: Princeton University Press, 2012.

Schaff, Philip, et al., eds. *(A Select Library of the) Nicene and Post-Nicene Fathers of the Christian Church.* 1st ser. 14 vols. Grand Rapids, MI: William B. Eerdmans, 1956.

Schaff, Philip, and Henry Wace, eds. *(A Select Library of the) Nicene and Post-Nicene Fathers.* 2nd ser. 14 vols. Grand Rapids, MI: William B. Eerdmans, 1952–57.

Schechter, Solomon. *Some Aspects of Rabbinic Theology.* New York: Macmillan, 1909.

Schelling, Friedrich Wilhelm Joseph. *The Grounding of Positive Philosophy: The Berlin Lectures.* Translated and edited by Bruce Matthews. Albany: State University of New York Press, 2007.

———. *Philosophische Einleitung in die philosophie der Mythologie, Sämmtliche Werke [SW].* Edited by K. F. A. Von Schelling. Augsburg: J. G. Goota'scher Verlag, 1856–61.

Schipman, A. "Raskolniks." In *The Catholic Encyclopedia,* vol. 12. www.newadvent.org/cathen/12648b.htm.

Schmidt, Anna. "Iz rukopisei: S pis'mami k nei Vl. Solovyova." *Russkie Zapiski* 9 (1916): 324–27.

Schürer, Emile. *The History of the Jewish People in the Age of Jesus Christ (175 B.C.–A.D.135).* Translated by T. A. Burkitt et al.; revised and edited by Geza Vermes and Fergus Millar. Edinburgh: T & T Clark, 1973–87.

Schuster, Oleg. "Kak Nikolai Leskov o evreyakh pisal." *Secret* (June 6, 2011). www.jewish.ru/history/press/2011/12/prn_news994302543.php.

Schwarz, Dov. "Dmuto ve-kavei ishiuto shel mistikan yehudi bedoreinu" (On the Personality and Character of a Jewish Mystic in Our Generation). *Tarbiz* 51 (1992): 139–42.

———. "Ha-rav ha-nazir al ma'amad ha'isha" (The Rabbi Hermit on Woman's Status). *Telalei Orot* 5 (1984): 185–96.

Sergeev, Mikhail. *Sophiology in Russian Orthodoxy: Solov'ev, Bulgakov, Loskii and Berdyaev.* Lewiston, NY: Edwin Mellen Press, 2006.

Shestov, Lev. "Umozrenie i apokalipsis." In Bojkov and Bulychev, *Vladimir Solov'ëv: Pro et Contra,* 2:467–530.

Shlonsky, Avraham [signed Eshel, pseud.]. "Al Ha-Ahava (A Translation of a Long Paragraph from Solovyov's *Znachenie Lyubvi* [*The Meaning of Love*])." *Ketuvim* 19 (Dec. 31, 1926): 3.

Sigrist, Seraphim Joseph. "Assasination [*sic*] of Father Men." *Christian History Institute* (Sept. 2007). www.alexandermen.com/Assasinatioin_of_Father_Men.

Sliozberg, Henri Borisovich. *Baron G. O. Gintsburg: Ego zhizn' i deyatel'nost': k stoletiyu so dnya ego rozhdeniya* (Baron H. O. Ginzburg: His Life and Work: On the Centenary of His Birth). Paris: Komitet po chestvovaniyu pamyati Barona G. O. Gintburga, 1933.

Slutski, Yehuda. *Ha-Itonut ha-Yehudit-Russit bame'ah ha-tsha'esreh* (Russian Jewish Journalism in the Nineteenth Century). Jerusalem: Bialik Institute, 1970.

Smith, Oliver. "The Sophianic Task in the Work of Vladimir Solov'ëv." *Journal of Eastern Christian Studies* 59.3–4 (2007): 167–83.

———. "Vladimir Solov'ev and the Spiritualization of Matter." PhD diss., University College London, 2009. Published as *Vladimir Solov'ev and the Spiritualization of Matter.* Studies in Russian and Slavic Literatures, Cultures, and History. Boston: Academic Studies Press, 2011.

Solovyov, Sergei Mikhailovich (the elder). *Istoriya Rossii s drevnejshikh vremyon* (The History of Russia from Earliest Times). 3rd ed. 29 vols. St. Petersburg: Izd. Tovarishhestva "Obshhestvennaya pol'za," 1851–79. For English translations online, see www.ai-press.com/Soloviev.html.

———. "Nablyudenie nad istoricheskoj zhizn'yu narodov." *Vestnik Evropy* (1868–76). http://dugward.ru/library/solovyev_s_m/solovyev_s_m_nabludeniya_nad_istorich.html.

Solovyov, Sergei Mikhailovich (the younger). *Zhizn' i tvorcheskaya evolyutsiya Vladimira Solovyova* (written 1922–23); Brussels: Zhizn' s Bogom, 1977; edition used here edited by I. G. Vishnevetsky (Moscow: Respublika, 1997). English translation = *Vladimir Solovyov: His Life and Creative Evolution.* Translated by Aleksey Gibson. 2 vols. Fairfax, VA: Eastern Christian Publications, 2000.

Solovyov, Vsevolod Sergeyevich [front cover erroneously lists first name as Vladimir]. *A Modern Priestess of Isis.* Edited and translated by Walter Leaf. Cambridge: Cambridge University Press, 2011.

Solowjoff, Sergei Mikhailovich (the elder). *Geschichte des Falles von Polen (nach russischen Quellen).* Translated by Julius Spörer. Gotha: Verlag von E. F. Thienemann, 1865.

Solzhenitsyn, Aleksandr I. *Dvesti let vmeste* (Two Hundred Years Together), *1795–1995*. Moscow: Russkij put', 2001.

Sonina, Elena Sergeevna. "Vzlety i padeniya peterburgskogo isdatelya: O. K. Notovich i gazeta 'Novosti'" (The Rise and Fall of an Editor in St. Petersburg: O. K. Notovitch and the Paper 'News'). *Izvestiya (Ural'skogo gosudarstvennogo universiteta)* 4.68 (2009): 85–94. http://proceedings .usu.ru/?base=mag/0068%2803_$04-2009%29&xsln=showArticle.xslt &id=a13&doc=./content.jsp.

Sorkin, David. "Montefiore and the Politics of Emancipation (Review of Abigail Greene, *Moses Montefiore: Jewish Liberator, Imperial Hero* [HUP, 2010])." *Jewish Review of Books* 2 (2010). www.jewishreviewofbooks .com/publications/detail/montefiore-and-the-politics-of-emancipation.

Speransky, Valentin. "Vladimir Solovyov o evrejskom voprose." *Rassvet* 5 (1929): 12–14.

Springer, Arnold. "Gavriil Derzhavin's Jewish Reform Project of 1800." *Canadian-American Slavic Studies* 10.1 (1976): 1–24.

Stanislawski, Michael. *Tsar Nicholas I and the Jews: The Transformation of Jewish Society in Russia, 1825–1855*. Philadelphia, PA: Jewish Publication Society, 1983.

Stanislawski, Mikhail. "A Capsule History of East European Jewish Scholarship." In *The Oxford Handbook of Jewish Studies*, edited by Martin Goodman, Jeremy Cohen, and David Sorkin. Oxford: Oxford University Press, 2002.

Steinman, Eliezer. "A Tribute to Solovyov on the 25th Anniversary of His Death." *Ketuvim* 19 (Dec. 31, 1926): 3.

Stoyanov, T. [K. E. Istomin]. "Obrazovannye evrei v svoikh otnosheniyakh k khristianstvu." *Vera i razum* 2 (1886).

———. "Sovremennaya apologiya Talmuda i talmudistov." *Vera i razum* 2 (1888–89); 1 (1890).

Strauss, David Friedrich. *Der alte und der neue Glaube: ein Bekenntniss als Antwort*. Leipzig: S. Hirzel, 1872.

———. *Das leben Jesu, kritisch bearbeitet*. Tübingen: C. F. Osiander, 1835–36. http://nrs.harvard.edu/urn-3:HUL.FIG:002254155.

Strémooukhoff, Dimitry. *Vladimir Soloviev and His Messianic Work*. Translated by Elizabeth Meyendorff. Belmont, MA: Nordland, 1980.

Sullivan, Desmond. "New Insights into Matthew 27:24–25." *New Blackfriars* 73.863 (Sept. 1992): 453–57.

Sutton, Jonathan. "Religion, Civil Society, and the Nation: Reflections on the Russian Case." In *Nation, Religion, Civil Society: Modernization in Context*, Studies in Intercultural Philosophy 12, edited by Wout Cornelissen,

Gerrit Steunebrink, and Evert van der Zweerde. Amsterdam: Rodopi, 2004.

———. *The Religious Philosophy of Vladimir Solovyov: Towards a Reassessment.* Basingstoke: Macmillan, 1988.

———. "Vladimir Solov'ëv as Reconciler and Polemicist." In van den Bercken, de Courten, and van der Zweerde, *Vladimir Solov'ëv*, 1–12.

Syrkin, Nahman. "V. Solovyov ve-yihusso lisheelat ha-Yehyudim" (Solovyov's Attitude to the Jewish Question). *Sefer-ha-Shana* 3 (1902): 70–77.

Syszman, Simon. "A Propos du Karaisme et les Textes de la Mer Morte." *Vetus Testamentum* 2 (1952): 343–48. www.karaite-judaism.com.

Talmud. *The Soncino Talmud.* Brooklyn, NY: Judaica Press, 1973.

Tavernier, Eugène. Introduction to *Trois entretien sur la guerre, la morale et la religion.* Translated by Eugène Tavernier. Paris: Plon, 1916.

Taylor, Jackson. "Review of B. N. Chicherin's *Liberty, Equality, and the Market: Essays* (New Haven: Yale University Press, 1998)." *H-Russia* (June 1999). www.h-net.org/reviews/showrev.php?id=3187.

Tobin, Thomas H. "Logos." In *Anchor Bible Dictionary,* edited by David Noel Friedman et al., 4:348–56. New Haven, CT: Yale University Press, 1992.

———. "The Prologue of John and Hellenistic Jewish Speculation." *Catholic Biblical Quarterly* 52 (1990): 252–69.

Tolstoy, Lev Nikolaevich. *Pamyatniki tvorchestva i zhizni.* 4 vols. St. Petersburg: Ogni, 1917–23.

Tolstoy, Lev Nikolaevich, and Nikolai N. Strakhov. *Polnoe sobranie perepiski.* Edited by L. D. Gromova, T. G. Nikiforova, and A. A. Donskov. 2 vols. Moscow: Ottava, 2003. http://feb-web.ru/feb/tolstoy/default.asp?/feb/tolstoy/texts/selectpe/ts6/ts6-7.html.

Tolstoy, Lev Nikolaevich, and Sofia Andreevna Tolstaya (with Nikolai N. Strakhov). *Perepiska L. N. Tolstogo s N. N. Strakhovym.* Edited by V. V. Zhdanov. Literaturnoe nasledstvo. Vols. 35–38. Moscow: Akademiya nauk (Institut russkoj literatury [Pushkinskij dom]), 1939. http://feb-web.ru/feb/litnas/default.asp?/feb/litnas/texts/l35-38.html.

———. *Tolstovskij Muzej.* 2 vols. Edited by Tolstovskij Muzej (Obshhestvo). St. Petersburg: Izd. Obshhestva Tolstovkago Muzeya, 1911–14.

Trotsky, I. *Kniga o russkom evrejstve: Ot 1860-kh godov do revolyutsii 1917g.* Jerusalem: Gesharim, 2002. http://old.ort.spb.ru/history/ort_statis.htm.

Trotsky, Leon. *My Life: An Attempt at an Autobiography.* New York: Charles Scribner's Sons, 1930. www.marxists.org/archive/trotsky/works/1930-lif/ch08.htm.

Trubetskoy, Evegeny N. *Mirosozertsanie Vl. S. Solovyova* (Vl. Solovyov's Worldview). 2 vols. Moscow: Izdanie avtora, 1913.

Trubetskoy, Sergei N. "Smert' V. S. Solovyova 31 Iyul'ya 1900 g." *Vestnik Evropy* 9 (1900). Reprinted in Averin and Bazanova, *Kniga o Vladimire Solovyove*, 294.

Tsinberg, Israel. *Istoriya evreiskoj pechati v Rossii v svyazi s obshhestvennymi techeniyami.* Petrograd: Tip. i Fleitmana, 1915.

Valliere, Paul. *Modern Russian Theology: Bukharev, Soloviev, Bulgakov: Orthodox Theology in a New Key.* Grand Rapids, MI: Wm. B. Eerdmans, 2000.

———. "Solov'ëv and Schelling's Philosophy of Revelation." In van den Bercken, de Courten, and van der Zweerde, *Vladimir Solov'ëv*, 119–29.

———. "Sophiology as the Dialogue of Orthodoxy with Modern Civilization." In *Russian Religious Thought*, edited by Judith Deutsch Kornblatt and Richard F. Gustafson, 176–91. Madison: University of Wisconsin Press, 1996.

Van den Bercken, Wil, Manon de Courten, and Evert van der Zweerde, eds. *Vladimir Solov'ëv: Reconciler and Polemicist. Selected Papers of the International Solov'ëv Conference Held in Nijmegen, September 1998.* Leuven: Peeters, 2000.

Van der Zweerde, Evert. "Vladimir Solov'ëv and the Russian-Christian Jewish Question." *Journal of Eastern Christian Studies* 55.3–4 (2003): 211–44.

Velichko, Vasily L'vovich. *Vladimir Solovyov: Zhizn' i tvoreniya.* St. Petersburg: Knizhnyj magazin A. F. Tsinzerlinga, 1904.

Vermes, Geza. *The Complete Dead Sea Scrolls in English: Complete Edition.* New York: Allen Lane/Penguin Press, 1997.

Volkonskaya, Elisaveta Grigor'evna, knyaginya. *O tserkvi: Istoricheskij ocherk.* Berlin: B. Behrs Verlag, 1888.

Voplato, Chiara. "Empowering the 'Jewish Threat': *The Protocols of the Elders of Zion.*" *Journal of US-China Public Adminstration* 6.1 [no. 44] (2009): 23–36.

Walicki, Andrzej. *The Slavophile Controversy: History of a Conservative Utopia in Nineteenth-Century Russian Thought.* Translated by Hilda Andrews-Rusiecka. Notre Dame, IN: University of Notre Dame Press, 1975.

Ware, Timothy, K. *The Orthodox Church.* London: Penguin, 1993.

Weigel, George. "John Paul II and the Crisis of Humanism." *First Things* 98 (1999): 31–36. www.orthodoxytoday.org/articles/WeigelJohnPaulII.php.

———. "Pope John Paul II and the Dynamics of History: The 2000 Templeton Lecture on Religion and World Affairs." *Watch on the West: A Newsletter of the Foreign Policy Research Institute's Center for the Study of America and the West* 1.6 (2000). www.fpri.org/ww/0106.200004.weigel.pope history.html.

———. *Witness to Hope: The Biography of John Paul II.* New York: Harper-Collins, 2005.

Weinberg, Robert. "Visualizing Pogroms in Russian History." *Jewish History* 12.2 (1998): 71–92.

Wenzler, Ludwig. *Die Freiheit und das Böse nach Vladimir Soloviev.* Freiburg and Munich: Alber, 1978.

Wilkinson, Samuel H. *The Life of John Wilkinson: The Jewish Missionary.* London: Morgan & Scott, 1908.

Wojtyla, Karol (John Paul II). *Love and Responsibility.* San Francisco: Ignatius Press, 1993.

Wozniuk, Vladimir. "Appendix A: The Jews in Russia." In Wozniuk, *Politics, Law, and Morality,* 291–92.

———. "Vladimir S. Soloviev and the Politics of Human Rights." *Journal of Church and State* 41.1 (1999): 33–50.

———, ed. *Politics, Law, and Morality: Essays by V. S. Soloviev.* New Haven, CT: Yale University Press, 2000.

Yampolsky, Peter Abramovich. "Slovo, proiznesennoe Kievskim ravvinom D-rom P. A. Yampolskim v molitvennom dome L. I. Brodskogo v subbotu 14. Okt. 1900 g. posle zaupokojnogo bogosluzheniya po pokojnom russkom myslitele-filosofe Vladimire Solovyove" (A word Uttered by a Kievan rabbi, P. A. Yamolski, in the Home of L. I. Brodsky on Saturday, 14 Oct. 1900, Following the Funeral Service for the Deceased Russian Philosopher-Thinker Vladimir Solovyov). Kiev: S. Iofe i G. Znatopol'skij, 1900. 16 pp.

Zdenek, V. David. "The Formation of the Religious and Social System of Vladimir Soloviev." PhD diss., Harvard University, 1960.

Zenit News Agency. "Retreatants Hear of Guises of the Antichrist: Preacher (Cardinal Giacomo Biffi) Draws on Work of V. S. Solovyov." Feb. 28, 2007. www.zenit.org/en/articles/retreatants-hear-of-guises-of-the-anti christ.

Zernov, Nicholas. *Three Russian Prophets: Khomiakov, Dostoevsky, Soloviev.* Gulf Breeze, FL: Academic International Press, 1973.

Zionist Aid Fund in London. *Die Juden-pogrome in Russland.* 2 vols. Cologne: Herausgegeben in Auftrage des Zionistischen Hilfsfonds in London, 1910.

de Zirkof, Boris. *H. P. Blavatsky: Collected Writings.* Wheaton, IL: Theosophical Press, 1980. 12:334–49. www.theosophyonline.com/ler.php ?id=223#.URAWF_JO-So.

GENERAL INDEX

The index uses the following abbreviations:

AIU — Alliance Israélite Universelle
D — Dostoevsky, Fyodor
ED — *Encyclopedic Dictionary*
FMW — "The Fall of the Medieval Worldview"
Lectures — *Lectures on Godmanhood*
Mv — *Moskovskie vedomosti*
OPE — Society for the Promotion of Jewish Enlightenment
P — Pobedonostsev, Konstantin
Protocols — *Protocols of the Elders of Zion*
S — Solovyov, Vladimir Sergeevich
SFL — *The Spiritual Foundations of Life*
T — Tolstoy, Leo N. (count)
"Tale" — "The Tale of the Antichrist"
TSMD — "Third Speech in Memory of Dostoevsky"
Vfp — *Voprosy filosofii i psikhologii*

BIBLICAL, CHRISTIAN MAGISTERIAL, AND RABBINIC INDEX

An asterisk (*) signifies allusions and citations not marked in the endnotes. The abbreviation "V" after a biblical citation refers to a unique Vulgate reading.

BOOKS OF THE BIBLE

CHRISTIAN CREEDS AND PATRISTIC AND MAGISTERIAL SOURCES

Rabbinic Literature
Josephus

Rabbinic Hymns

Mishnah

Jerusalem Talmud

Midrash Rabbah

GREGORY YURI GLAZOV is professor of biblical studies at Immaculate Conception Seminary School of Theology. He is the author of *The Bridling of the Tongue and the Opening of the Mouth in Biblical Prophecy.*

CPSIA information can be obtained
at www.ICGtesting.com
Printed in the USA
LVOW12*2148270816

501714LV00003BC/7/P